The Act of Teaching

Sixth Edition

DONALD R. CRUICKSHANK

The Ohio State University

DEBORAH BAINER JENKINS

University of West Georgia

KIM K. METCALF

University of West Georgia

McGraw Hill

Connect
Learn
Succeed™

THE ACT OF TEACHING, SIXTH EDITION

Published by McGraw-Hill, a business unit of The McGraw-Hill Companies, Inc., 1221 Avenue of the Americas, New York, NY 10020. Copyright © 2012 by The McGraw-Hill Companies, Inc. All rights reserved. Previous editions © 2009, 2006, and 2003. No part of this publication may be reproduced or distributed in any form or by any means, or stored in a database or retrieval system, without the prior written consent of The McGraw-Hill Companies, Inc., including, but not limited to, in any network or other electronic storage or transmission, or broadcast for distance learning.

Some ancillaries, including electronic and print components, may not be available to customers outside the United States.

✪ This book is printed on recycled, acid-free paper containing 10% postconsumer waste.

Printed in the United States of America.

2 3 4 5 6 7 8 9 0 QDB/QDB 1 0 9 8 7 6 5 4 3 2

ISBN 978-0-07-809791-1
MHID 0-07-809791-6

Vice President & Editor-in-Chief: *Michael Ryan*
Vice President EDP/Central Publishing Services: *Kimberly Meriwether David*
Publisher: *Michael Sugarman*
Senior Sponsoring Editor: *Allison McNamara*
Executive Marketing Manager: *Pamela S. Cooper*
Editorial Coordinator: *Marley Magaziner*
Project Manager: *Robin A. Reed*
Design Coordinator: *Margarite Reynolds*
Cover Designer: *Mary-Presley Adams*
Cover Images: © *image100 Ltd (upper);* © *Creatas/PunchStock (lower)*
Buyer: *Susan K. Culbertson*
Media Project Manager: *Sridevi Palani*
Compositor: *Laserwords Private Limited*
Typeface: *10/12 New Baskerville*
Printer: *Quad/Graphics*

All credits appearing at the end of the book are considered to be an extension of the copyright page.

Library of Congress Cataloging-in-Publication Data

Cruickshank, Donald R.
  The act of teaching / Donald R. Cruickshank, Deborah Bainer Jenkins, Kim K. Metcalf.—6th ed.
    p. cm.
  ISBN 978-0-07-809791-1
  1. Teaching. 2. Lesson planning. I. Jenkins, Deborah Bainer. II. Metcalf, Kim K. III. Title.
  LB1025.3.C78 2011
  371.102—dc22

                                                    2010052729

www.mhhe.com

About the Authors

Donald R. Cruickshank

Donald R. Cruickshank received degrees from the State University College at Buffalo, New York, and the University of Rochester. After stints as a teacher and principal in the Rochester schools, he began a college teaching and administrative career that took him to SUNY Brockport, the University of Tennessee, Wheelock College, and The Ohio State University. Professor Cruickshank has been the recipient of Fulbright-Hayes senior scholar awards to Australia and Brazil and served in the Thai Ministry of Education and the United Nations' Bangkok office. Additionally, he worked for the Asian Development Bank in Indonesia and Manila. He has taught and lectured in Australia, Brazil, Canada, England, Scotland, Thailand, and Wales as well as throughout the United States and Puerto Rico. He has authored numerous articles and encyclopedia entries, and this is his ninth book. He is best known for his pioneering efforts in developing teaching simulations and reflective teaching and his research on teacher problems and teacher clarity. His graduate students have won seven outstanding dissertation awards and have fashioned accomplished careers in teaching, scholarship, service, and administration.

Deborah Bainer Jenkins

Deborah Bainer Jenkins is a professor at the University of West Georgia. She received her B.S. in biology from Geneva College, her M.S. in environmental education, and her Ph.D. in teacher education from The Ohio State University. She taught middle school and high school science in the United States and in Asia and was formerly a faculty member at Biola University and at The Ohio State University. Currently, her teaching and scholarship focus on teacher preparation and supervision. Dr. Jenkins has worked extensively with school-based partnership programs aimed at enhancing instruction. She has authored numerous articles and book chapters on her research on teachers' professional development, partnerships, and supervision. She was awarded the distinguished teaching and scholarship awards from The Ohio State University and has received community service awards for her work with teachers.

Kim K. Metcalf

Kim K. Metcalf is Dean of the College of Education at the University of West Georgia. Dr. Metcalf was awarded his M.A. and Ph.D. in teacher education and educational research and evaluation from The Ohio State University. He was professor of education and director of the Indiana Center for Evaluation at Indiana University Bloomington, and he has served as both a classroom teacher and as director of assessment for Monroe County Community Schools. He has worked with education agencies and schools throughout the United States and Europe to conduct large-scale evaluations of educational programs and policies. Among these projects have been examinations of statewide class size initiatives, nationwide and local comprehensive school reform efforts, international programs for civic education, and longitudinal studies of voucher programs in Ohio. His work has been recognized by a number of organizations including the Association of Teacher Educators, the American Evaluation Association, and the Association for Psychological Type.

Contents in Brief

Contents in Detail

CHAPTER 8

Four More Instructional Alternatives: Cooperative Learning, Discovery Learning, Constructivism, and Direct Instruction

Preface

What Teachers Should Know and Be Able To Do

The decision about what content to include in this book derives from several sources: work done at Educational Testing Service (ETS) to determine what a competent *beginning* teacher should know and be able to do; work done by the National Board for Professional Teaching Standards to determine what a competent *experienced* teacher should know and be able to do; the advice of persons engaged in the preparation of beginning teachers; and our personal experiences as teacher educators and scholars.

What is a competent beginning teacher? Here we looked at both the recommendations made by ETS researcher Reynolds (1992)[1] and the ETS Praxis III standards.[2]

Reynolds reviewed the research literature on learning to teach and on the act of teaching itself. She concludes that on entering their first classroom, novices must have a thorough knowledge of what they will teach, a desire to find out about their students and their school, a solid grasp of instructional methodology, and a firm intention to reflect on their teaching actions and the behavior of their students. Soon thereafter, they should be able to plan and teach lessons that help students relate new learning to prior understanding and experience, develop rapport with students, arrange the physical and social conditions of the classroom in ways conducive to learning, assess student learning using a variety of measurement tools and then adapt instruction accordingly, and show improvement in their ability to reflect on teaching.

The Praxis III™ standards, or criteria set up for beginning teachers, require novices to become familiar with students' background, knowledge, and experience; articulate clear and appropriate learning goals; understand the connections among the content to be learned, content learned previously, and future content; be able to select teaching methods, activities, and materials appropriate to lesson goals and students; be able to create or select proper evaluation strategies; create a class climate that promotes fairness; establish and maintain rapport with students; communicate challenging learning expectations; establish and maintain consistent standards of student behavior; ensure a safe environment conducive to learning; make instructional goals and procedures clear; make content clear to students; encourage students to extend their thinking; monitor student understanding and provide corrective feedback; use time effectively; reflect on how well instructional goals have been met; demonstrate a sense of efficacy; build relationships with others; and communicate with parents and caregivers.

What is a competent experienced teacher? The **National Board for Professional Teaching Standards (NBPTS)**[3] was established to set "high and rigorous" standards for experienced teachers. In order to do so, committees were set up composed mostly of distinguished teachers and complemented by experts in child development, teacher education, and subject matter specialists. Subsequently, standards have been developed for early childhood, middle childhood, early adolescent, and adolescent and young adult teachers. For example, the standards for teachers of middle childhood (7 to 12 year olds) expect teachers to know and/or be able to do the following: understand their students' abilities, interests, and aspirations; make sound decisions about what is important for students to learn; establish a caring, inclusive, stimulating, and safe community of learners; help learners respect differences; develop and use a rich, varied collection of learning materials; help learners integrate knowledge across subject fields and understand how what they study relates to the world around them; know and be able to use a range of generic instructional alternatives so that students are provided with multiple paths to learn; understand the strengths and weaknesses of different assessment methods; create positive relationships with caregivers; regularly reflect on the quality and effectiveness of their practice; and work to improve schools and to advance education knowledge and practice.

[1]Reynolds, A. (1992, Spring). What is a competent beginning teacher? *Review of Educational Research, 629*(1), 1–35.
[2]Educational Testing Service (2007). *The Praxis Series: Professional Assessments of Beginning Teachers. Praxis III: The Classroom Performance Assessments Orientation Guide.* Princeton, NJ: Author.

[3]http://new.nbpts.org/standards/framework.pdf

Confirmation from teachers. When preservice and practicing teachers are asked what they believe to be the knowledge necessary for effective teaching they support the Reynolds, Praxis III, and NBPTS recommendations, asserting that teachers need pedagogical knowledge of how to teach; knowledge of children; content or subject matter knowledge; knowledge of classroom management and organization; and knowledge of self and others (Fives and Buehl, 2008).[4]

The Act of Teaching Is Special in That It Is:

Comprehensive. *Part One* introduces the reader to the *Context of Teaching*—why teachers teach as they do, challenges they face in a changing society, student diversity, how learning occurs, and how teachers can come to know their students and motivate them to learn.

Part Two brings readers to the *Act of Teaching* itself. Herein they consider how to plan instruction, how to use eight powerful instructional methods, and how to evaluate student learning.

Part Three explores the *Effective Teacher*—the personal qualities and skills that enable teachers to be both effective and reflective. Teaching skills vital to effective lesson delivery and follow-up and to managing the classroom are the focus.

The *Practice Teaching Manual* provides the opportunity to practice important teaching skills, reflective teaching, and problem solving. Students are encouraged to apply what they have learned about themselves as teachers, learner diversity, learning theory, motivation, planning, instructional methods, effective and reflective teaching, and problem solving.

Unique in Its Content. In addition to attending to the topics commonly found in learning to teach courses, chapters are devoted to additional topics such as:

- Factors that influence why we teach as we do (Chapter 1).
- Schools of thought that illustrate how different kinds of learning occur (Chapter 4).
- How teachers can find out more about their students and better motivate them to learn (Chapter 5).
- The need to utilize instructional variety (Chapters 7 and 8).
- Multiple methods for evaluating students' learning and using assessment information (Chapter 9).

[4]Fives, H. & Buehl, M. (2008). *What do teachers believe? Contemporary Educational Psychology, 33,* 134–176.

- Multiple definitions of good or *quality* teachers (Chapters 10 and 11).
- Personal qualities and skills that lead to effective teaching (Chapters 10 and 11).
- Strategies to organize and manage today's complex classroom settings (Chapter 12).
- Strategies for preventing discipline problems in today's diverse classrooms (Chapter 12).
- Challenges teachers face and how to resolve them (Chapter 13).

Unique in Its Features. The text contains many features competitor texts do not.

- *Emphasis throughout is on reflection,* utilizing "reflective questions" in page margins that ask readers to consider the personal meaning and application of what they are learning, "Issues and Problems for Discussion" at chapter endings that require readers to consider how they feel or what they believe about information that has been presented, "Theory into Practice Activities" at chapter endings that cause them to engage in introspective tasks, and Reflective Teaching exercises in the Practice Teaching Manual.
- *"Spotlight on Research"* boxes contain the latest findings on important topics such as class size, multicultural teaching, instructional objectives, instructional variation, effective teacher presentations, effective discussions, cooperative learning, discovery learning, and use of praise.
- *"Highlight"* boxes mostly contain suggestions for best practices such as how parents can help children succeed in school, how to recognize abused children, how to motivate at-risk learners, what makes a good individualized education program or IEP, how to recognize and promote use of multiple intelligences, how to teach to a variety of learner abilities, how to make a good explanation, how technology is used in the classroom, how to manage aggressive students, how to resolve differences with parents, and how to manage special needs students.
- *"Case"* boxes illustrate such things as an at-risk student, a mainstreamed student, a child with ADHD, individualization of instruction, cooperative learning, concept learning, and DISTAR.
- *"Lesson plan"* boxes illustrate each of the eight instructional alternatives contained in Chapters 7 and 8.
- *Cross reference of the book's content to the INTASC Standards-based Praxis II™ Exam topics* on inside cover.
- *Web links* of selected Internet sites that provide related and/or extended information.

Timely and Research-Based. Care has been taken to promote what is known about teaching and learning from credible research, rather than the authors' personal bias and commitments.

Instructor friendly. The Online Learning Center (www.mhhe.com/cruickshank6e) contains materials to assist instructors in planning their courses and evaluating their students. See the section on Online Supplements for more information.

New to the Sixth Edition

Two hallmarks of *The Act Of Teaching*. It provides both knowledge and know-how. *The Act of Teaching* continues to surpass all other texts by providing the most comprehensive, cutting-edge, and reliable professional information teachers need to know. Additionally, it gives them the latest planning, instructional, assessment, and classroom management know-how required to become highly effective in the classroom and community.

Engaging New Feature. Chapters now begin with a *Conversation Starter*. Each identifies a compelling underlying chapter issue, presents both sides, and encourages students to think and discuss it before reading the chapter. Here are a few of those issues.

- How important is it for us to know why we teach the way we do?
- What most influences student learning—home or school?
- Should teachers be responsible for meeting the needs of every student?
- How do kids learn best?
- How important is it to understand and motivate students?
- How important is it to plan instruction?
- What are the best ways to teach?
- What are some causes of and solutions to classroom problems?

After reading the chapter it is useful to ask students if—and in what ways—their opinions on these issues have changed.

ADDITIONS OR SUBSTANTIAL REVISIONS TO CHAPTER CONTENT

Chapter 1. How the way we prefer to learn affects the way we teach. How other teachers and supervisors affect how we teach.

Chapter 2. Family, community, and school influences on children and school learning. Children living in poverty. Helping and teaching abused and neglected children. Working with children at risk of school failure. Resilient children. Overscheduled children. Disengaged children. Helping and teaching Generation M children. Using the "whole child" approach.

Chapter 3. Helping and teaching culturally different children. Helping and teaching boys as compared with girls. Helping and teaching learners with different learning styles or preferences.
  New Spotlight on Research: *Avoiding Special Education*

Chapter 4. Humanistic school of thought revisited.

Chapter 5. Intrinsic vs. extrinsic rewards.
  New Highlight: *Paying for Performance?*

Chapter 6. The value of specific objectives. Subject matter resources on the Internet revisited.
  New Highlight: *How Chinese Teachers Plan*

Chapter 7. Contracts with students. The Project Method revisited.
  New Spotlight on Research: *Homework: Questions and Answers*
  New Spotlight on Research: *What Kinds of Learning Choices Do Teachers Give Students?*
  New Highlight: *How Teachers Are Using Blogs, Wikis, and Podcasts*

Chapter 8. Direct Instruction revisited.

Chapter 9. Improving data-sharing via professional learning communities. Using ongoing formative assessment to aid benchmarking. Utilizing standards-based report cards.

Chapter 10–11. Substituting prevalent scholarship and research terminology.

Chapter 12. How to create and maintain a positive classroom climate. How to use more preventative techniques and less punishment. Managing a classroom of diverse learners.

Chapter 13. Updates only.

Chapter 14. Reflection as a process utilizing three levels of thinking.

Practice Teaching Manual. Six new Reflective Teaching Lessons.

Overall

- New "reflective questions" in page margins
- New Online Learning Center (OLC) websites
- New Key Terms
- More intuitive index
- Added and updated references
- New pictures

Online Supplements

An *Online Learning Center* is located at www.mhhe.com/cruickshank6e

FOR THE INSTRUCTOR

The instructor side of the Online Learning Center offers an *Instructor's Manual* containing rationales for each chapter, chapter objectives and outlines, additional learning activities, and additional resources. The *Test Bank* contains multiple-choice, definitional, and essay/short answer questions. Many features of the book provide the opportunity to engage students in meaningful learning. For a username and password to access the instructor materials, contact your McGraw-Hill sales representative.

FOR THE STUDENT

The student side of the Online Learning Center contains student study materials including case studies for Praxis™, video clips of classrooms in action, and links to related websites.

Acknowledgments

We are grateful to a number of people whose contributions made the fourth edition possible. They include scholars and researchers whose names appear in the book's author index, illustrator Kathy Grossert, cartoonists, those who have reviewed the text in its several editions (listed below) and developmental editors at McGraw-Hill as follows: Lane Akers, Beth Kaufman, Terry Wise, and Cara Harvey-Labell. Our thanks also to the many other McGraw-Hill people working behind the scenes.

Reviewers who helped in the development of this sixth edition include:

Annette Ayers, Surry Community College

Marjorie Checkoway, Madonna University

Alan W. Garrett, Eastern New Mexico University

Dr. Carol A. Scatena, Lewis University

Michael F. Shaughnessy, Eastern New Mexico University

James Russell Smith, Jr., North Carolina State University

Laura Stewart, Daytona State College

Others reviewed previous editions of the book and offered comments and suggestions that were most helpful. Following is a partial list of our resource persons: Kay Alderman, University of Akron; Leo Anglin, Berry College; Leigh Chiarelot, Bowling Green State University; Gerald R. Dotson, Front Range Community College; Kathleen A. Gosnell, Duquesne University; Denise M. Grant, Kennesaw State University; Gail P. Gregg, Florida International University; Mary Lynn Hamilton, University of Kansas; Barbara J. Havis, Southern Illinois University; C. Michelle Hooper, Stephen F. Austin State University; Gae Johnson, Northern Arizona University; Karla Lynn Kelsay, The Florida State University; Catharine C. Knight, University of Akron; Philip McKnight, University of Kansas; Robert McNaughton, Cleveland State University; Robert McNergney, University of Virginia; Janice Nath, University of Houston; Jeanette Nunnelley, Indiana University Southeast; Lem Londos Railsback, Texas A&M University; Sherry Rulfs, Stephen F. Austin State University; Diane Sopko, The University of Memphis; Melba Spooner, University of North Carolina; Gary Stuck, University of North Carolina; Barbara Tea, Wright State University; Marie Tuttle, Brigham Young University; Patrick Walton, The University College of the Cariboo; Jian Wang, The University of Nevada at Las Vegas; and Kinnard White, University of North Carolina.

How to Use This Text Well

Please take time to become acquainted with this book. The following should be helpful:

1. Turn to the **Contents in Brief** on page vii. Note that the text contains several parts. **Part One, The Backdrop of Teaching,** permits you to better know yourself and to find out what is known about diversity and human learning. **Part Two, The Act of Teaching,** focuses on functions competent teachers must perform: instructional planning, instruction, and assessment. **Part Three, The Effective Teacher,** looks at the personal attributes and professional abilities that competent teachers need, including classroom management skills. Finally, the **Practice Teaching Manual,** contains activities intended to increase selected classroom skills, your ability to reflect and learn from your teaching experiences, and your ability to be a better classroom problem solver. The text also contains a **glossary** and **indexes** (both subject and author).

2. Turn to the next page, **Contents in Detail.** Now you can see precisely what content is found in each chapter and in the Practice Teaching Manual.

3. Select and turn to any of the first several chapters to see how one is set up.

Note that in the side margins there are questions we refer to as **reflective questions.** These questions are intended to prompt you to consider your personal experiences and knowledge. There are no "correct" answers to them. You and your peers should find them provocative, and they should generate considerable class discussion of that section of the chapter.

Also in the margins are recommended websites you can link through www.mhhe .com/cruickshank6e.

Next, note the figures, tables, cases, "Spotlight on Research" and "Highlight" sections. They serve to reinforce, summarize, or add new information. Occasionally you will see a cartoon that we think illustrates something text related.

At the end of each chapter is a **Chapter Summary** followed by **Key Terms, Issues and Problems for Discussion, Theory into Action Activities** and **References.**

Issues and Problems for Discussion contains questions for class debate or classroom problems that classroom teachers supplied. You will find many of these issues and problems challenging and thought-provoking.

Theory into Action Activities are critical and will help you to put what you have just learned into practice. Many of these activities will result in artifacts that can be put into your professional portfolio.

We suggest that before reading each chapter you go through it, reviewing all these elements, *but this time read the reflective questions, the chapter summary, issues and problems, and theory into action activities.* Doing these things will prepare you for the material ahead.

Getting Started

Before embarking on a career in teaching, there are at least two things we should think about. *First,* why do we want to teach? Do we have sufficient, compelling reasons? To help us think about why we want to teach, the exercise "Why teach?" is included below.

A second thing we need to think about is the value of our professional education program. Some argue that all we need to know is subject matter—what we will teach. However, nearly every practicing teacher argues that knowledge of subject matter is necessary but not sufficient to being a good teacher. To see what one teacher-leader has to say about this consider the essay below "Why we must learn how to teach."

HOW SHOULD TEACHERS BE PREPARED?

Traditional teacher preparation assumes that to teach well, instructors must know their subject matter *and* how to teach it. It also assumes they must have knowledge about students and how they learn, know how to manage a classroom, and have extended, supervised teaching experience. As a consequence, preparing to become a teacher requires considerable professional study and is a lengthy process.

However, many persons believe that traditional teacher preparation is not essential. What is requisite is the desire to teach and knowledge of subject matter; so nontraditional teacher education programs bypass some or most of traditional preparation in order to get students who know their subject matter into classrooms more quickly. They claim that teacher preparation is unnecessarily long and expensive and that it excludes qualified persons from teaching. ***How do you think teachers should be prepared?***

WHY TEACH?

Congratulations! You are in the process of becoming a VIP in the lives of children, their parents, and caregivers.

At this point, it might be insightful to consider the reasons people chose to teach and which of them hold meaning for you. It might also be fun to share your reasons with one another. Finally, it might be beneficial to put your reasons in writing and put that essay in your teaching portfolio.

Here are a dozen. Maybe you can think of others.

WHY I WANT TO TEACH

- I will teach because I want to make a contribution to society.
- I will teach because it is an honorable profession.
- I will teach because I want to help others succeed.
- I will teach because I enjoy working with children.
- I will teach because I enjoy being a student and learning.
- I will teach because I enjoy a subject(s) and want others to also.
- I will teach because it is challenging.
- I will teach because I have found the act of teaching pleasurable.

- I will teach because I can exercise individuality and creativity.
- I will teach to make use of my abilities.
- I will teach to be around people.
- I will teach because teaching provides a secure, satisfying lifestyle.

WHY WE NEED TO KNOW MORE THAN THE SUBJECT MATTER WE WILL TEACH

In order to be a good teacher, we need to know our subject matter and a lot more. Below is a statement made by a teacher-leader that makes this clear.

WHY WE MUST LEARN *HOW* TO TEACH

Leila Christenbury, president of the National Council of Teachers of English, recounts why learning to teach is so important. When she entered teaching, she had solid preparation in her subject field with both a bachelor's and master's degree in English but no professional preparation. She notes:

> I knew all about literature and literary theory; . . . I know literary history . . . But that simply wasn't enough. What didn't I know? I knew nothing about how people learn, especially people unlike myself, who were not motivated . . . I was not prepared to teach anyone who wasn't pretty much like me. I didn't know how to run a class discussion or how to set up a small group. I had never created a test of any kind or considered how to grade and evaluate. Until I began teaching, I thought these things just happen. In short, I didn't know pedagogy. I was a good student who was expected to make an automatic transfer to being an effective teacher. And that didn't happen for many years . . . The study of pedagogy is indispensable to teacher success . . . The act of teaching, the consideration of teaching—and thus the consideration of learning—is utterly at center stage. . . . What we learn in pedagogy is that teaching is a complex enterprise requiring an instructor's knowledge, perception of student needs, and real willingness to adjust and adopt . . . to the only thing that ultimately matters: student learning . . . Clearly, the schoolchildren of America deserve knowledgeable teachers who are experts in their fields, who know what they are teaching. America's schoolchildren also deserve knowledgeable teachers who know how to teach, how to reach each and every one of them, how to make learning effective, individual, and long lasting. (Christenbury, 2002)

Christenbury, L. (2002, June 18). Op-ed piece distributed to newspapers around the country.

COURSESMART eTEXTBOOKS

This text is available as an eTextbook from CourseSmart, a new way for faculty to find and review eTextbooks. It's also a great option for students who are interested in accessing their course materials digitally and saving money. CourseSmart offers thousands of the most commonly adopted textbooks across hundreds of courses from a wide variety of higher education publishers. It is the only place for faculty to review and compare the full text of a textbook online, providing immediate access without the environmental impact of requesting a print exam copy. At CourseSmart, students can save up to 50% on the cost of a print book, reduce their impact on the environment, and gain access to powerful web tools for learning including full text search, notes and highlighting, and email tools for sharing notes between classmates. For further details contact your sales representative or go to www.coursesmart.com.

MCGRAW-HILL CREATE

www.mcgrawhillcreate.com

Craft your teaching resources to match the way you teach! With McGraw-Hill Create you can easily rearrange chapters, combine material from other content sources, and quickly upload content you have written, like your course syllabus or teaching notes. Find the content you need in Create by searching through thousands of leading McGraw-Hill textbooks. Arrange your book to fit your teaching style. Create even allows you to personalize your book's appearance by selecting the cover and adding your name, school, and course information. Order a Create book and you'll receive a complimentary print review copy in 3–5 business days or a complimentary electronic review copy (eComp) via email in about one hour. Go to www.mcgrawhillcreate.com today and register. Experience how McGraw-Hill Create empowers you to teach *your* students *your* way.

The Backdrop of Teaching
PART ONE

The five Backdrop of Teaching chapters will help you better know and understand yourself, your students, and the way you and they learn. In Chapter 1, Factors That Influence How We Teach, you will learn how your personal characteristics, previous experiences in schools, and the setting you will work in influence how you will teach. In Chapter 2, Teaching in a Changing Society, you will find out how societal changes are affecting America's population, families, children and youth, and schools. Chapter 3, Teaching Diverse Students, will help you understand many of the important ways students differ from one another. Chapter 4, Three Schools of Thought about Learning and Teaching, will enable you to understand several prominent theories about the way humans learn and about the values and uses these theories have for teachers. Finally, Chapter 5, Getting to Know Your Students and Motivating Them to Learn, will tell you how to find out about your students and encourage them to learn.

Factors That Influence How We Teach

Conversation Starters

How important is it for us to know why we teach the way we do?

Many believe that teachers would be wiser and more effective if they understood *why* they behave as they do in the classroom. For example, teachers need to understand how their gender, personality, beliefs, and past experiences affect how they teach.

    Others believe that all teachers need to know is the subject matter, how to present it, and how to control the class. They see little need for teachers to have a lot of self-understanding.

What do you think? How important is it for us to understand why we teach the way we do?

Would you believe you have been a student for over 15,000 hours? During that time, you have observed all kinds of teachers. Have you ever wondered how they became the way they are? Have you questioned why they teach the way they do? Have you thought about what kind of teacher you will be? In this chapter we will consider three sets of factors that have influenced your teachers and likely will affect your teaching as well (see **Figure 1.1**).

One set consists of your *personal characteristics,* such as gender, age, experience, personality, beliefs and your preferred way of learning. A second set consists of your *experience and preparation in education.* This set includes how you have been taught, how you prefer to teach, your knowledge of subject matter, and your teaching or pedagogical preparation. A final set of factors affecting teaching derives from the *context,* or setting, in which you teach. Context is determined by the kinds of pupils you have, class personality and size, availability of instructional equipment and material, time available for instruction, the nature of your lesson, and the dominant or prevailing views about the best way to teach.

Personal Characteristics

To a large extent, your personal characteristics dictate what you will be like as a teacher. These characteristics, mentioned in the previous paragraph and illustrated in **Figure 1.2**, include gender, age, experience, personality, and beliefs.

HOW GENDER INFLUENCES OUR TEACHING

In today's world we hear a lot about gender and **gender differences,** so we thought you would be interested in knowing how male and female teachers differ.

Studies seem to indicate male teachers, on average, appear to be more dominant and authoritarian. Relatedly, their classrooms are more organized and teacher-controlled (Dunkin, 1987; Weiner, 1995). Males also are more likely to use more aggressive discipline toward boys (Rodriguez, 2002). They also refer fewer of their learners with behavioral problems for special education help which may be good or bad: good if the students do not require it, bad if they do (McIntyre, 1988).

The same studies report female teachers more often maintain "warmer" classrooms and are more tolerant of misbehavior (more special education referrals to the contrary). Furthermore, in classrooms with female teachers, students are more likely to initiate a question or statement, give more incorrect answers, and take risks by guessing answers. Female teachers also seem to praise more frequently and are more likely to provide the correct answer when students can't or don't.

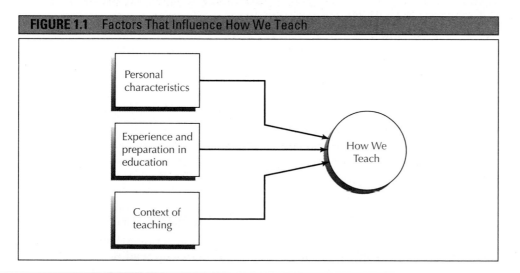

FIGURE 1.1 Factors That Influence How We Teach

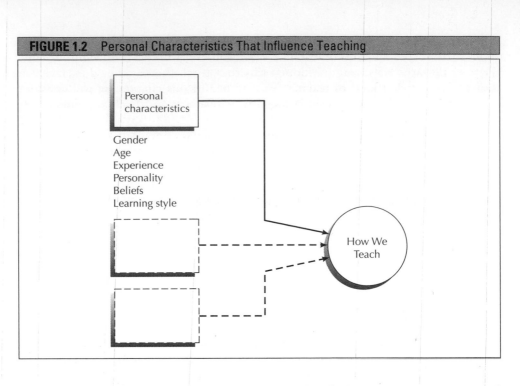

FIGURE 1.2 Personal Characteristics That Influence Teaching

Personal characteristics

Gender
Age
Experience
Personality
Beliefs
Learning style

How We Teach

Dunkin concludes that, on balance, female teachers' classrooms are warmer and more nurturing, while male teachers' classrooms are better organized and more task oriented. Coulter (1987) reports similarly on gender differences. He finds that female student teachers are more "tender-minded and pupil supportive and less authoritative than males." Moreover, he notes that these gender differences are more prominent among secondary than elementary student teachers (p. 591).

Relatedly, female teachers of younger children consider boys more active, loud, and aggressive and consider them less teachable and more difficult to work with. On the other hand, they describe girls as quiet, talkative, and sensitive (Hyun & Tyler, 1999). In another study it was found that female teachers of younger children who are anxious about math believe boys are better in that subject (Wortel, 1996).

Both male and female teachers pay more attention to boys, perceive boys demonstrate more initiative and a greater capacity for independent learning, are more likely to chastise and criticize them, and hold boys to higher intellectual standards. They both hold lower expectations for girls and are more likely to reward them for good behavior and tidiness (Duffy, Warren, & Walsh, 2001; Weiner, 1995).

Do male or female teachers rate their male or female students more highly? On average, ratings are the same except that white male teachers perceive white female students as less able (Ehrenberg, Goldhaber, & Brewer, 1995).

Most teachers today probably believe that boys and girls should be treated equitably. However, are teachers' beliefs about gender equity and how they treat boys and girls consistent? In one study elementary teachers were interviewed to obtain their views about gender equity and then observed during teaching to see if the teachers' actions were consistent with their words. Although the teachers spoke of gender-equitable intentions (treating boys and girls the same), to varying degrees their actions belied their words (Garrahy, 2003).

Do students learn more from male or female teachers? Studies provide mixed results. Some research supports that gender matters: having a teacher of the same sex helps students learn (Dee, 2006).

Others report that neither teacher gender, race, nor ethnicity seem to affect how much students learn (Ehrenberg, Goldhaber, & Brewer, 1995). Regardless of whether the teachers or students are male-female, black-white-Hispanic, students learn about the same amount in math, science, history, and reading.

1.1 Have your teachers shown any of the gender-related behaviors reported in research?

1.2 How do you think gender may influence your teaching?

Are male or female teachers better motivators? In general, girls are more academically motivated than boys regardless of who teaches them (Marsh, Martin, & Cheng, 2008).

How do males and females differ in their views toward their teacher preparation? Female secondary education majors are more optimistic that their preparation will make them better teachers, more likely to use student-friendly instruction, more likely to accept responsibility for teaching exceptional students, and more likely to have realistic expectations regarding teaching. They are less confident in themselves as teachers which may account for their more realistic expectations (Kalaian & Freeman, 1994).

HOW AGE AND EXPERIENCE INFLUENCE OUR TEACHING

Several studies focus on how our age and years of **teaching experience** influence our teaching and students' perceptions of us.

They suggest that

- teachers with fewer than three years experience are less effective (Rice, 2003; Rivkin, Hanushek, & Kain, 2005).
- younger and less experienced public school teachers have higher levels of satisfaction than older and more experienced teachers (Perie & Baker, 1997).
- beginning teachers have a tendency to accept innovations and change more easily, although ready acceptance may simply be a signal that newer teachers are less discriminating—everything looks good until you try it (Barnes, 1987).
- beginning teachers are more controlling and authoritarian, probably as the result of several factors. First, teacher educators, mentor teachers, and school principals often counsel novice teachers to be strict—"don't smile until Winter break." Second, novice teachers may well be a bit in awe in their first classroom and don't want to lose control (Fuller & Bown, 1975).
- younger, less experienced teachers are more concerned with personal and social dimensions of teaching than with academics. They tend to work hard to develop a unique teaching identity and pay more attention to student interests than to involving them in instruction and monitoring their achievement (Artiles, Mostert, & Tankersley, 1994; Housner & Griffey, 1985; Szpiczka, 1990).
- many confident beginning student teachers lose a measure of self-assurance when they confront classroom life. This is to be expected when novice idealism meets reality (Coulter, 1987; Cruickshank, 1990).
- experienced teachers are better able to attend to everything going on in the classroom and use what they observe to adjust their teaching (Ainley & Luntley, 2004).
- experienced teachers connect new material to be learned to what learners already know, encourage more open discussion, and are more flexible (O'Connor, Fish, & Yasik, 2004).

 1.3 How have age or experience seemed to affect your teachers?

 1.4 What differences have you seen between novice and experienced teachers?

HOW TECHNOLOGICAL KNOW-HOW AFFECTS OUR TEACHING

If you were born after 1978 you are a "Millennial" and are seen as being quite different from earlier generations labeled Traditionalists (born before 1945), Baby Boomers (born between 1946 and 1964), and even Gen Xers (1965–1977). One significant characteristic of most Millennials is a high level of comfort with technology. After all, you probably were raised on such things as e-mail, text messaging, weblogs, wikis, Facebook, and YouTube. Technology probably is part of your DNA. Therefore, it is likely that you will rely more on technology to provide instruction and will be able to help teachers lacking in your level of experience to do so. Moreover, you probably will expect to provide and receive information electronically and so will your students. This text makes a humble effort to make you aware of

Internet sites that contain information useful to teachers. (See Online Learning Center or OLC website icons in some page margins.) Most certainly, you will be able to expand your knowledge of teaching using electronic sources and teach your future students to use and even create electronic resources.

HOW PERSONALITY AFFECTS OUR TEACHING

We use the term *personality* to mean the totality of character and behavioral traits peculiar to an individual. No two persons are alike in this respect, not even identical twins. Naturally, what we are like, our personality, affects everything we do, including our teaching and our satisfaction with it.

Certain personality traits are related to our satisfaction with teaching and, subsequently, to how we feel and behave in the classroom. Conscientiousness, extraversion, and the relative absence of abnormal behaviors such as anxiety or fears seem to be good traits to have (Judge, Heller, & Mount, 2002).

Suppose that you are a conscientious, extraverted, emotionally stable, warm person, enthusiastic, persevering, and curious. You have broad interests and value originality. How might each of these characteristics and behavioral traits influence your teaching behavior and your relationships with learners (see Spotlight 1.1)? How might the absence of these things play out in a classroom?

Our personality needs may be particularly influential when it comes to deciding how we will teach a particular lesson or lessons. For example, if we feel the need to dominate, we may choose ways of teaching that put us front and center, such as presenting or lecturing. If affiliation is our goal, then we may be prone to use discussions.

Several research findings relate to **teacher personality.** Coulter (1987) reports that education majors place more value on and have a stronger commitment to people and personal relationships than noneducation students do. Morrison and McIntyre (1973) report similarly that teachers are more people-oriented than persons in most other occupational groups. Both the Coulter and the Morrison and McIntyre studies note that teachers correspondingly place less value than others on economic success. As human service professionals, teachers seem to be more interested in establishing and maintaining helping relationships than in their level of income (Powell, 1992).

Coulter also found that education students, when compared with experienced teachers, are more liberal, idealistic, and supportive of K–12 students. As with self-confidence, however, these personal dispositions diminish for some students as they engage in field experiences such as student teaching. Once again, the shock of actual classroom experience probably accounts for this attitudinal change. Although disconcerting, reality shock probably occurs in every profession—a fact we should keep in mind.

Pigge and Marso (1987) find several things related to the attitudes of prospective teachers. They note that elementary education majors and students who make an early commitment to become teachers seem to share generally positive attitudes toward teaching. On the downside, Pigge and Marso find that education majors are anxious about such things as finding teaching satisfying, convincing pupils to follow directions, preparing lessons, and being able to control a class. Other concerns are that they will lack sufficient instructional materials and be unable to meet the needs of different pupils, a problem we will discuss in the next chapter.

HOW OUR BELIEFS AFFECT OUR TEACHING

What teachers *generally* believe probably influences what they promote in the classroom and how they behave. Here are some general beliefs held by teachers. Compared with similarly educated other Americans, teachers are a little less supportive of free speech, express more conservative views on homosexuality, are more liberal regarding school prayer, are more likely to believe the world is more good than evil, are about the same

"Mirror, mirror, on the wall, who's the most sensitive, open, student-centered, and innovative teacher of all?"

1.5 Are you surprised, encouraged, or disappointed by the findings regarding personality characteristics of teachers?

1.6 How do you think your personality may affect your teaching? What positive traits do you have? What negative traits must you overcome?

Students age 11–15 were given a list of teacher characteristics that might have a positive effect on their attitudes toward learning. Following are the top teacher characteristics the students deemed "very important" and the percentage of students who thought so (Zamorski & Haydn, 2002).

> Interacts 'normally' (63%)
> Friendly (63.0%)

Enthusiastic (54.3%)
Sense of humor (52.2%)
Lets pupils talk as they work (50.0%)
Praises and encourages (45.7%)
Courteous (45.4%)
Relaxed (45.3%)
Strict (34.8%)

Similarly, preservice teachers were given a list of 20 supposedly positive teacher

characteristics and were asked to rank order them. Highest ranked by female preservice teachers are: enthusiasm, respect for students, high expectations, humorous, and provision of extra help. Highest ranked by males are: enthusiasm, knowledge of subject, respect for students, humorous, entertaining, and easy to talk with (Mowrer-Reynolds, 2008).

with regard to trusting others, and are about the same with regard to how they feel about whether the government should help others (Slater, 2008). Surprised?

What teachers *specifically* believe about students, schools, and teaching is even more likely to play out in the classroom. Here are some specific beliefs held by teachers. Among other things, teachers tend to believe the following: higher-ability students are easier to teach and manage; students of similar ability should be grouped together for instruction (homogeneous grouping); different curricula should be provided for good and weak students (Block & Hazelip, 1995); attractive children are more capable and sociable; girls' behavior is preferable to boys', majority students can do better than minority students (Biehler & Snowman, 2008); math is a male subject (Li, 1999); it is better to employ student-directed as opposed to teacher-directed learning and to teach students *how* to learn than it is to teach them specific information or skills; it is not important that students spell correctly at all times; it is not always important that students provide a correct answer; when giving final grades it is more important to grade according to a student's overall performance than it is to reward them for achievement on any single, class-wide test or standard; students should be able to write and speak standard English; parents are a real asset to children's learning; social promotion (passing a child because of age rather than achievement) is not good; and teachers should have sufficient authority to maintain classroom order (Barnes, 2002). Teachers in poorer communities believe their school climate is less positive and stimulating and that their students are of lesser ability (Solomon, 1996). Teachers generally believe that children with a low socioeconomic status have less promising futures (Auwarter & Aruguete, 2008).

What if these beliefs are not well founded but merely misconceptions or biases? Or what if they are true yet unhelpful? What might be the unfortunate outcomes?

Whether or not their beliefs are true, teachers mostly tend to act on them (Fang, 1996). For example, teachers who believe and expect students can learn teach more content and insist on higher student achievement. Similarly, teachers who believe all students can learn provide more sufficient and clear explanations and instructions, link what is to be learned with what kids already know, ask more challenging questions, and provide more and better feedback (Rubie-Davies, 2007). Teachers who accept responsibility for student achievement have kids who learn more in reading (LoGerfo, 2006). Teachers who believe that students learn best when they are actively engaged in such things as projects, problem solving, and reflective thought (such as writing essays) are much more likely to have them use the Internet (Ravitz, Becker, & Wong, 1998).

1.7 What beliefs about students, teaching, and learning do you hold that may have either a positive or negative influence on your teaching?

Unfortunately, beliefs are resistant to change even when attempts are made to clear up misconceptions or counter negative beliefs that may, in fact, hold true (Nettle, 1998; Tynjala et al., 2001). See Highlight 1.1.

Finally, what we believe about ourselves professionally—such as how capable we are—influences our classroom performance. (See Spotlight 1.2 on page 10)

HOW THE WAY WE PREFER TO LEARN—OUR LEARNING STYLE—AFFECTS OUR TEACHING

1.8 Can you describe a teacher who taught in a way compatible with your learning style?

Each of us has preferred ways of learning. For example, some like to learn through listening while others prefer to learn by doing. Understandably, teachers teach in a fashion similar to the way in which they learn (Gordon, Dembo, & Hocevar, 2007). The danger is that it is easy to presume our students prefer to learn in the same ways we do.

In order to avoid this potential pitfall there are a few things we can do. First, assume students may have learning styles different from ours. Second, find out what their styles are. (See "Learning Styles Differences" in Chapter 3.) Third, learn to teach in a variety of ways. (See Chapters 7 and 8.)

1.9 How do you *not* wish to be taught?

Related research: If you are an elementary education major you probably like to learn in groups, enjoy creative ways of learning such as **role playing**, enjoy **divergent or open-ended thinking**, like to **synthesize**, like classes that are well-organized, and do not like individual oral presentations. You also are likely to believe it is important to help students become independent and self-regulating. (See Spotlight 1.3 on page 11, Skipper, 1985; Sloan, Daane, & Giesen, 2004). Teachers do not necessarily teach according to the way they prefer to learn. They usually identify individual student's learning styles and actively seek out the best ways to connect with them (Haar, Hall, Schoepp, & Smith, 2002).

Experience and Preparation in Education

A second set of factors influencing how you will teach are your educational experiences. Those experiences include the way you were taught, your knowledge in your chosen teaching or academic field, and the kind and amount of teaching preparation you are receiving (see Figure 1.3 also on page 11).

HOW THE WAY WE WERE TAUGHT AFFECTS OUR TEACHING

If it is true that "you teach as you were taught," then your teaching will model the teaching of your mentors, most of whom you encountered in K–12 schools. A number of investigators have observed K–12 teachers, and they have identified two dominant styles of teaching: direct and indirect. **Direct teaching,** also referred to as *expository teaching,* occurs when teachers dominate by presenting information to students, giving students directions, and using criticism. Direct teaching is associated with a teacher-centered or teacher-controlled classroom in which the teacher decides what, when, and how to teach. Teachers with a direct style tend to (1) set definite academic goals, (2) use structured, sequential learning materials, (3) prescribe what students will do and how they will do it, (4) monitor and check student progress toward the goals and provide them with corrective feedback, and (5) allow sufficient time to learn the prescribed materials. Although direct teaching may sound cold and impersonal, it need not be. You may recall teachers who were direct but also creative, stimulating, and humorous.

1.10 Have you mostly been exposed to direct or indirect teaching? Which style do you prefer, and why?

You have also witnessed **indirect teaching,** used by teachers who prefer to draw things out of their students. For example, these teachers may provide students with an experience or a block of information and then help them develop their own conclusions from it (see Case 8.2 and Lesson Plan 8.3). A teacher with a direct

HIGHLIGHT 1.1
Don't Let Your Beliefs Get In Your Way!

When you entered teacher preparation you brought along many beliefs about a whole lot of things including students and how to teach them. These beliefs are quite robust and resistant to change. Beliefs act as a filter. When new information is consistent with our beliefs we tend to accept it. When new information is not compatible with what we believe we tend to reject or at least not remember it (Kane, Sandretto, & Heath, 2002).

Here is an example of how your beliefs can influence your teaching:

Teachers who believe or expect students are not as able to learn, give them less time to answer questions, do not help them to answer questions, provide less praise and are more prone to criticism, seat such learners farther away, give them less demanding work, and are less friendly toward them (Good & Brophy, 2002). Conversely, "teachers with high expectations of their students teach them more and teach it more warmly . . . [and they] tend to give [them] greater opportunities for responding and [better] feedback" (Rosenthal, 2003).

Consequently, carefully examine your ideas about learning, teaching, and schooling. So far as you can, clarify what you believe and then try to determine whether that belief is true or merely a personal bias. Never get caught thinking, "Don't confuse me with the facts."

style might present information about the worldwide refugee problem, encourage students to discuss the information, and then evaluate the solutions currently used. On the other hand, a teacher with an indirect style might ask students to find out about the worldwide refugee problem and to present additional suggestions regarding its resolution. Teachers with an indirect style seem to be aware of and to make the most of student diversity; they also tend to be more democratic and flexible (Dunkin & Biddle, 1982, pp. 97–98). Teachers with an indirect style (1) set general rather than specific goals, (2) use more, and more varied, learning materials, (3) may set a task to be accomplished but permit students to decide how to do it, (4) serve as facilitators or mentors when students need help, and (5) provide sufficient time to accomplish the task and to consider its merit.

You will learn more about direct and indirect teaching in Chapter 4, Three Schools of Thought about Learning and Teaching, and in Tanner (2001).

The way you will be inclined to teach depends in part on the teaching styles to which you have been exposed. Yes, experience teaches.

HOW OUR KNOWLEDGE OF SUBJECT MATTER AFFECTS OUR TEACHING

It seems reasonable that we need extensive knowledge of the subjects we will teach. However, having substantial **subject or content knowledge** alone does not ensure good teaching or student learning. If it did, teachers with the most advanced knowledge in their fields would have students who learn the most. Contrary to that expectation, studies of teacher subject or content knowledge have failed to find a consistent relationship. Yes, all of us have had teachers who knew their subject well but didn't or couldn't help us learn it. Can you recall some?

However, Grossman (1995) suggests that teacher content knowledge affects both what and how we teach. For example, when deciding what to teach, we are more likely to give greater coverage to areas in which we are more knowledgeable and to skip or downplay areas about which we know less. (Many states require so many hours of instruction in certain subjects partly to ensure that they actually get taught.) Additionally, if we are content-secure teachers, we are more likely to ask students more critical and challenging questions.

We presume that knowledge of our subject has other benefits too. It may enable us to create more interest in and enthusiasm for what we teach, show students how knowledge in the subject is developed (for example, what scientists do and how they do it), show the relationship of that subject to others (for example, the relationship

1.11 To what extent are you master of the subjects you will teach? How can you increase your mastery?

Do you believe you can teach well? Another factor affecting our teaching is the extent to which we *believe* we are capable instructors—that we can organize and execute teaching well. This characteristic is called *teacher sense of efficacy.* Other things being equal, having a higher sense of efficacy permits us to approach and manage a task better than someone who has less self-assurance. Consider two teachers with equal teaching potential but differing levels of efficacy. The one with more self-assurance likely will perform more effectively. Similarly, consider two basketball players both with equal free throw shooting skill. The one with greater confidence is more likely to make a better percentage of free throws in an actual game. So, if you have more self-assurance about your teaching skill you probably will perform better in the classroom. However, self-assurance cannot substitute for lack of teaching ability. Just because we believe we are good does not make us so. Self-assurance lets us demonstrate only our true potential. Lack of it makes us appear less able.

Teachers who have a greater sense of efficacy in their ability to teach when compared with teachers who have lesser self-assurance have been found to be better planned and organized, more likely to be interested in and focussed on their students, trusting, open, and satisfied with teaching. Moreover, there is a substantial link between teachers who are self-assured and student learning (Goddard, Hoy, & Hoy, 2004).

Relatedly, a school faculty's overall sense of efficacy matters. "The research . . . suggests that a strong sense of *collective efficacy* enhances teachers' sense of efficacy and vice versa" (Goddard et al., p. 10). Thus, if you are in a school where the collective sense of efficacy is high, your self-efficacy will prosper. It appears that one way collective teacher efficacy is increased is when teachers are given power to influence important school decisions.

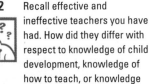

"They meet in there. Some kind of support group."

1.12 Recall effective and ineffective teachers you have had. How did they differ with respect to knowledge of child development, knowledge of how to teach, or knowledge of how we learn?

of mathematics to science), use both direct and indirect teaching, and function as a resource for learners. Additionally, knowledgeable teachers are less dependent upon textbooks and more aware of other learning resources.

HOW OUR TEACHING PREPARATION INFLUENCES OUR TEACHING

Another contributor to the way you will teach is the quality of the teaching or **pedagogical** preparation you are receiving. Professional education for teaching includes study of both the parent disciplines of education—such as psychology, philosophy, and sociology—and their offspring, the applied fields of educational psychology and sociology, child and adolescent development, and pedagogy (the way we plan and deliver instruction and evaluate learning). The extent and quality of the professional preparation you receive will influence both the quality and the style of your teaching. A number of studies indicate that having knowledge of how to teach has beneficial impact on such things as our classroom teaching performance, ratings we get from our supervisors and students, and, in some instances, student learning (Darling-Hammond, Gatlin, & Holtzman, 2005; Rice, 2003). The more knowledge and skill you have in planning and delivering instruction and evaluating learning, the better your students should learn. Persons without sufficient pedagogical or teaching knowledge are forced to teach by instinct and are doomed to trial-and-error approaches. As noted earlier, Kagan (1992) finds that novice teachers, with little knowledge of pupils and teaching, "tend to grow increasingly authoritarian and custodial. Obsessed with classroom control, they may also begin to plan instruction designed not to promote learning, but to discourage children's misbehavior" (p. 145).

Although knowledge of and skill in teaching are critical to success, you also need positive attitudes toward teaching, schools, and students, attitudes that university and K–12 school personnel need to foster and reinforce (Cole & Knowles, 1993).

Student teachers and graduates of various colleges of education are often distinguishable as a result of the teacher preparation they have received. It is not

Self-regulated learners are self-motivated, self-directed, and persist at their learning tasks. They find a good place to study; set goals; seek, plan, and organize information; keep track of what they are learning; rehearse/practice what is to be learned; seek necessary assistance; and reward themselves. This is how they prefer to learn. The good news is self-regulated learners learn more. The bad news: most preservice and in-service teachers are not self-regulated. If you are fortunate enough to be a self-regulated learner then you also are more likely to teach your students to be so and they, in turn, will learn more.

Bonus: Teachers who are more self-regulated in how they learn and teach also have more self-regulated classrooms wherein kids are taught and expected to be personally responsible for their behavior. Looks like a win-win situation.

Source: Gordon, Dembo, & Hocevar (2007).

uncommon for public and private schools to favor student teachers or graduates from a particular university because they feel these persons are better prepared and that they will have a more positive, immediate impact on students.

Context

The final set of factors influencing you as a teacher encompasses the context of your workplace. Several ingredients will affect your workplace and, consequently, the way you will teach: (1) the number and kinds of learners you have, (2) **class and classroom size,** (3) the availability of instructional materials and equipment, (4) time, (5) the nature of the lessons you must teach, and (6) national educational imperatives (see Figure 1.4).

HOW STUDENT DIFFERENCES AFFECT OUR TEACHING

In Chapters 2 and 3 you will be reminded that student variability is a fact of life in all schools and classrooms. You as a teacher must recognize that diversity—whether economic, cultural, gender, motivational, or other—and take it into account.

FIGURE 1.3 Educational Experiences That Influence Teaching

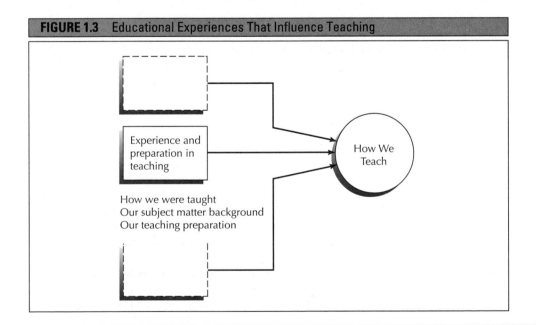

Experience and preparation in teaching

How we were taught
Our subject matter background
Our teaching preparation

How We Teach

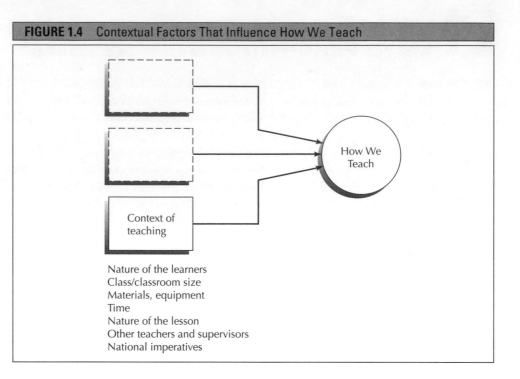

FIGURE 1.4 Contextual Factors That Influence How We Teach

How We Teach

Context of teaching

Nature of the learners
Class/classroom size
Materials, equipment
Time
Nature of the lesson
Other teachers and supervisors
National imperatives

Since you will have little, if any, control over the nature of the pupils placed in your care, you are well-advised to discover who they are and accept them as they are. Unhappily, newer teachers are more likely to have difficulty recognizing and responding to student variability. They are more apt to see or to want to see the class as an entity, a whole—to view it as more homogeneous than it actually is. To novice teachers the class seems to have a single face rather than many faces (Cruickshank & Callahan, 1983). However, as you study child development and gain teaching experience, you are more likely to see, accept, and provide for differences among learners.

Case 1.1, written by a first-year teacher, demonstrates that many teachers do accept students as they are and can learn from them.

HOW CLASS AND CLASSROOM SIZE AFFECT OUR TEACHING

Imagine yourself teaching a large number of students, perhaps 40 or more, as is normal in many classrooms throughout the world. Class size, to some extent, dictates how you will teach. In such a crowded, complex environment it is more likely, all things being equal, that you may choose to teach the class as a whole and that you may use direct or expository teaching. Conversely, having fewer learners and teaching in a less complex environment would seem to permit more teacher–student interaction. Smaller classes, therefore, would more likely be characterized by individual and small-group instruction. However, studies of instruction in smaller classes only partially support such expectations. On one hand, they indicate that differing class sizes do not lead to significant differences *in the way* teachers teach. They do reveal that teachers in smaller classes spend less time on discipline and more time teaching and working with individuals and small groups (Holloway, 2002). Relatedly, students in smaller classes in elementary grades are more engaged in learning and less disruptive, possibly because their teachers get to know them more intimately and develop a greater tolerance for their behavior (Finn et al., 2003). Make sense?

Class size also seems to have a bearing on how well students learn and behave. Generally, research on class size supports smaller classes (Bracey, 1999; Rivkin, Hanushek, & Kain, 2005). Glass (1987) notes that "the relationship of class size to

1.13 What do you suppose it would be like to teach children of lower as opposed to higher socioeconomic status (SES); girls as opposed to boys; a child with a hearing impairment; a child with learning disabilities; Desmond from Case 1.1 on the next page?

Dear Desmond,

Now that you are a young adult out in the world, you may not remember your first-grade teacher, but I remember you. I remember your blonde hair, big brown eyes, and freckles just as clearly as if you were standing here now. You were so tall, and I can still see you looking down the row of heads in front of you after I'd sent you to the back of the line for something you swore you hadn't done. I remember your smiles, your tears, your fists, your heavy boots, and your angry, unhappy words.

You probably didn't know that I was a first-year teacher and that I had never experienced anyone like you before. Maybe you did know. I didn't know that working with you that year would become one of the most memorable experiences of my career. I didn't know that there were so many of you, at least one every year.

Do you remember greeting us each morning by throwing your books on the floor after finally making your way to your desk? Do you remember the range of responses that drew from me? Every day was a new challenge. I'd go home at night, often in tears, and plan my strategy for the next morning's book slam. One day, I'd be stern and take away some privilege, and then the next day I'd try ignoring you. The day after that you might have been praised for not slamming the books as loudly as before. I'm sure it was

great fun for you to try and guess what was coming next. However, I was determined to keep trying and, admittedly, I spent a lot more time trying to figure you out than I did making bulletin boards that year.

Maybe some of the other events of the year are starting to come back to you now. There were so many, and I know that I learned much, much more from them than you did. The one experience that stands out above all the rest was the day you shut yourself in the locker and you couldn't get out.

The class was coming in from recess in their usual noisy way. I remember watching the other classes walking in fairly quiet, straight lines and thinking how we really *should* work on this line stuff some. As most of the class sat down, we heard four muffled, high-pitched shrieks coming from the hall. The shrieks quickly turned into screams and by then I realized what had happened. I tried to get your locker open, but part of your coat was jammed in the door and I couldn't get the door to budge. I yelled for the custodian to please help me and possibly remove the door. I noticed his sense of urgency subsided when he heard it was you in the locker. Remember how mad he was when you started the "How High Can You Shoot?" contest in the boys' restroom? Then, after a few long moments, you were out. When the door

finally opened, you ran out and came straight for me and I hugged you easily. I felt you shaking, and for the first time I saw you as a child and not as the reason I was having doubts about my being a teacher.

So every year as I deal with others like you, I remember the locker. I remember learning that no matter how tough we act, we are *all* afraid of something. I also learned that this awareness of fear doesn't give me the right to hold it over your head but, rather, to keep your actions in perspective. I have since tried harder to find out why children do what they do instead of just dealing with their behavior afterward.

I hope you were lucky enough to have some teachers along the way that had learned these things before you came along. Thank you for teaching me.

Source: Kathy Tatham, Searforce Elementary School, Johnstown, Ohio

---

INVESTIGATING AND SOLVING THE CASE

1. What personal factors probably affected the way the teacher thought about and reacted to Desmond?
2. If Desmond were your student, what personal factors do you think would influence your behavior toward him?

---

pupil achievement is remarkably strong. Large reductions in class size [by a third to a half] promise learning benefits of a magnitude commonly believed not to be within the power of teachers to achieve" (p. 544).

Specifically, the longer younger children are enrolled in smaller classes (fewer than 20 kids), the more successful they will be (Spotlight 1.4). Furthermore, the gains that younger students in small classes make are carried over when they move into upper grades (Biddle & Berliner, 2003).

Class size also affects the *behavior* of learners. Students in large classes are less likely to pay attention and to engage in off-task behavior (Blatchford et al., 2003).

 1.14 How has class size affected teaching and learning in your experience? Has it impacted your learning?

A study conducted in Tennessee (Project Star) found substantial advantages for K–3 children in smaller classes (13 to 17 students). Specifically, on average, they performed better on all tests of academic achievement. A follow-up study was done to see whether the benefit of having been in smaller classes carried over into later grades. Findings include that, on average, students who attended small K–3 classes for only one year performed no better in grades 4, 6, or 8 than students who had attended larger classes; students who attended for two years performed a bit better; and students who were in small classes for three years showed important carryover effects in the later grades (Finn, Gerber, Achilles, & Boyd-Zaharias, 2001).

California accepted that class size affects student learning and reduced primary classes from an average of 30 to 20 students. Evaluations confirm that students enrolled in those smaller classes perform slightly better than students in larger ones. Additionally, teachers say they spend more time teaching and less time disciplining (Strecher et al., 2001). Interestingly, high student achievers benefit the most (Konstantopoulos, 2008).

In summary, we know that class size affects the way teachers teach and the behavior of students. We also know that small classes contribute to improved student learning. What we need to know is, what do teachers in small classes do that results in greater learner achievement?

A number of Internet sites focus on class size. See the Educator's Reference Desk website.

Web Link
Class Size

The physical size of your classroom also has an impact on your teaching. The availability of space in a room permits use of many more instructional options than does a crowded environment. A larger room also provides everyone more private space. However, it should be said that expert professionals find ways to be effective despite any restrictions imposed by class or classroom size.

HOW OTHER TEACHERS AND SUPERVISORS AFFECT OUR TEACHING

Other teachers and supervisors affect how we teach. On average, the more credible people are, the more influential they are. Thus, if people are perceived to be expert and trustworthy, we tend to believe them and follow their lead, maybe even mimic them. We might not only do as they say, but do as they do.

Peers and supervisors may also be influential in structured ways that promote interaction and collaboration. Structured ways that teachers collaborate and influence each other include classroom and special education teachers working together to meet the needs of learners with disabilities, and teachers teaming to improve planning and instruction. Thoughtful, reflective professional interactions are the means. Improved student learning is the goal.

A side effect of teacher collaboration may be improvement in a school's ability to foster student achievement (Goddard, Goddard, & Tschannen-Moran, 2007).

HOW AVAILABILITY OF MATERIAL AND EQUIPMENT AFFECT OUR TEACHING

1.15 What educational resources will you need to be the best you can be?

Teachers are limited when there are insufficient resources. A well-stocked "larder," in your case the classroom, provides greater potential for instruction. A visit to so-called developing countries reveals that teachers without adequate educational materials, even textbooks, are severely limited in how or what they can teach. For example, Masai children of eastern Africa are mostly taught by educated tribesmen who have few if any resources to draw upon. In such countries and in poorer areas in America, students share desks and books and have little paper and no audiovisual equipment. Compare this to any American classrooms where nearly every educational resource is available—multiple textbooks, reference materials, television, and computers. Thus, teachers in a poorer school often lecture out of necessity. By contrast, teachers in a wealthy school may choose to lecture but can employ other instructional alternatives.

HOW AVAILABLE TIME AFFECTS OUR TEACHING

There are limits to the amount of instructional time available to teachers. Therefore, time, or lack of it, has a real impact on how you will teach. If you have more time, you can employ more indirect learning strategies such as experimentation and discussion. When time is short, you may have to be more direct, telling learners what they need to know through lecture, since that is a reasonably efficient way of presenting large amounts of information in a short amount of time. Of course, the burden often is placed on the learner to process, understand, and remember it.

You must never forget that *how* you use instructional time is extremely important. An hour of instruction can be either beneficial or wasteful. If, in that hour, you can keep your students involved and engaged, they will learn (Cotton, 2001). Chapters 4, 10, and 13 provide an important perspective on time considerations.

1.16 How will you maximize the amount of time available for instruction?

HOW THE NATURE OF LESSON OBJECTIVES AFFECTS OUR TEACHING

In Chapter 6, Planning Instruction, you will learn that there are three kinds of learning outcomes: cognitive, psychomotor, and affective. Here is an example of each:

1. *Students know that 6 sevens are 42.* This is a cognitive objective that primarily requires the use of mental processes.
2. *Students can hold and manipulate a paint brush to create a particular brushstroke.* This is a psychomotor objective that primarily requires physical dexterity.
3. *Students enjoy listening to orchestral music.* This objective requires the learner to "feel" something. It is sensoral and affective.

The nature of **objectives** will influence the way you teach. Each kind of objective probably requires you to teach somewhat differently? For example, suppose your objective is to help students *understand* why 6 sevens are 42. If so, you will need to use some kind of discovery or constructive experience. When you teach students how to hold and use a paint brush, demonstration seems appropriate. If you want students to enjoy orchestral music, you might rely more on listening and valuing experiences. Chapters 7 and 8 describe different ways of teaching.

1.17 Do your instructors seem to vary their teaching according to the learning objectives they have in mind?

HOW NATIONAL IMPERATIVES AFFECT OUR TEACHING

Here are two examples of how national priorities influence our teaching:

The desire to be first worldwide in educational achievement has resulted in federal legislation to "leave no child behind." That goal translates into making sure that all children are especially competent in reading and mathematics. In order to achieve this goal, students are regularly tested, and their teachers and schools are held accountable for the test scores. Schools serving less educationally advantaged learners are less likely to meet the educational standards. Consequently, teachers in those schools are under great pressure to raise test scores. To do so, teachers frequently "teach to the test," that is, they teach what learners must know on exams. The result is that teachers more likely use **direct teaching** described on page 8 and **direct instruction** described in Chapter 8.

The desire to promote use of technology has resulted in the placement of computers in classrooms with attendant pressure on teachers to use them and to teach students their usage. Consequently, you will be expected to utilize computer-based instruction which implies greater emphasis on **independent study** and **individualized instruction** described in Chapter 7.

1.18 How do you feel about the various national imperatives such as "No Child Left Behind"?

1.19 How might "teaching to the test" affect your teaching?

What Factors May Be Affecting Specific Teacher Practices?

Below are some of the findings of a study that looked at how teachers teach (U.S. Department of Education, 1999). Why do you think teachers do these things? Which of the aforementioned "Factors that influence how we teach" may be causing each teaching practice?

- Nearly all teachers use both whole-class instruction and individualized personalized instruction.
- 86 percent use small group instruction which is used more by teachers in lower grades.
- 63 percent give presentations.
- About two-thirds have learners complete practice exercises or worksheets in class.
- Two-thirds assign practice exercises as homework.
- Most use print materials quite often (textbooks, supplementary reading materials, workbooks, and worksheets).
- Two-thirds ask students to explain how what they are learning is related to the real world.
- Elementary teachers are more likely to have learners engage in explanations in an effort to see if they really understand.
- Teachers of low-ability students more often use newer recommended instructional alternatives in class while teachers of high-ability students were more likely to incorporate them into homework.
- Teachers in schools serving larger proportions of low-income students are more likely to use discussion and hands-on learning.
- Teachers in schools serving larger proportions of low-income students are more likely to have students do routine exercises in school and as homework.
- Less experienced teachers are more likely to use newer recommended instructional practices.
- Teachers with masters degrees are more likely to have students do group projects, engage in discussion, use supplementary materials, use calculators, and engage them in applying what they are learning.

1.20 In which of these practices will you or will you not engage?

Some Final Thoughts

Try Activities 1.1 and 1.2

Yes, the context in which you will work, your prior experiences in education, and your personal characteristics will influence your teaching. To the extent that you understand this, your insight into yourself and your teaching will grow. You will become more aware of who you are as a person and as a teacher and why you teach the way you do. As a consequence, your wisdom will grow, enabling you to address penetrating questions about yourself: How might my personal characteristics affect my teaching for better or worse? How might my prior experiences in education help or hinder me and my learners? How can I make the very most of my teaching situation? If you can answer these questions, you are well on your way toward becoming a reflective practitioner. Your teaching will be guided by insight rather than history, tradition, or compulsion. To learn what student teachers believe influences their teaching, see Spotlight 1.5.

How do our experiences prior to entering a teacher education program influence how we think about teaching and how we teach? Powell (1992) conducted a study to find some answers. Forty-two education undergraduates participated in the study: 17 traditional students were entering teaching as their first profession while 25 nontraditional students had had other jobs before deciding they wanted to teach.

On the first day of the general methods course, each completed an autobiographical questionnaire and then created a "concept map" of teaching. This means they were asked to write down and group terms that came to mind when they thought about teaching; for example, terms such as *preparation, motivation, presentation,* and *knowledge.* During the second week, participants were videotaped as they taught brief lessons to each other. Afterward, the teachers were asked to talk about why they did certain things as they taught; for example, why did they ask particular questions of students? Thus, the teachers were asked to reflect on what they did and, more importantly, why they did it. Teachers were later interviewed to discuss their former work experience, to describe all prior nonclassroom teaching experiences, to further discuss their concept maps, and to explain the process used to plan the peer lesson. In this context, they were shown a part of their videotaped lesson and asked to recall what influenced them to do what they did.

The results of this study indicate that when we embark on a teaching career we will be influenced by the following:

- K–12 experiences and college experiences as a student; for example, the influence of prior teachers. Mark said that the way he presented his lesson was influenced by "teachers I had before."
- Teacher education; for example, Aaron said that he planned his lesson using ideas he gained in an earlier education course.
- Beliefs and a value system; for example, Jill believed that "There is more to teaching than the student in a chair. That student is a real person with real needs."
- Personal learning style; for example, Christy used posters in her lesson and explained that "I feel more interested when I see something."
- Beliefs about students; for example, Shelly said, "Students have things to contribute to a classroom" and "the teacher needs to trust the students."

Other factors that students noted as influences on their thinking about teaching and how they taught included personal needs, prior work, nonclassroom teaching they had done (such as in church work), relatives who were educators, experience as a parent, and knowledge of the subject being taught.

CHAPTER SUMMARY

- Your personal characteristics, experience in education, and the context in which you work influence how you teach.
- Personal characteristics that affect teaching include gender, age, experience, personality, and beliefs.
- Although men and women are not unlike in the way they teach, men's classrooms seem to be more task oriented, businesslike, and organized, while women's seem to be more nurturing and accepting.
- Many teachers appear to be at their best after a few years. Novice teachers seem more controlling and authoritarian. Experienced teachers are better able to attend to and take into account multiple concurrent classroom happenings and they are more likely to be flexible and open.
- Given your unique personality needs and dispositions, you will teach in particular ways, making your classroom different than any other. However, many teachers share common traits, such as a commitment to others, a desire to have good relationships, and certain anxieties related to teaching success.

SUPPLEMENTAL RESOURCES

Go to the text's Online Learning Center at www.mhhe .com/cruickshank6e to access the chapter's **study tools** including web links, practice for Praxis™ case studies, and video clips.

- Some of your beliefs about students and teaching may be ill-founded and result in negative behavior. Additionally and unfortunately, beliefs are resistant to change.
- Your past experiences in education affect your teaching. The way you were taught is very important since beginning teachers often model or imitate their former teachers. Most of your teachers probably used a direct style, so, for good or bad, you will probably tend to do so.
- Your personal learning preferences will likely cause you to presume that your students want to learn in the same way as you.
- As your knowledge of subject matter increases, so too should your confidence and competence in teaching and the likelihood that your students will learn and appreciate what you teach.
- Both the extent and quality of your professional preparation will affect your teaching. Professional knowledge and skill enable you to be wiser and more resourceful and less authoritarian and custodial.
- The context or setting in which you work will also affect your teaching. The ability to recognize and accept learner diversity and to adapt your teaching accordingly is becoming increasingly important.
- As class size increases, it becomes more difficult to deal with individual students and overall class variability. Likewise, the physical size of classrooms, the availability of materials and equipment, and the instructional time available all affect the richness of any learning environment.
- Different kinds of learning objectives call for different ways of teaching and, often, for different teaching environments.
- National interests influence how we teach. For example, because of demand that all students must pass certain tests, teachers are increasing their use of direct teaching. Additionally, because of demand that all students be computer literate, teachers place greater emphasis on independent study and individualized instruction to teach them.

KEY TERMS

Gender differences, 3
Teaching experience, 5
Teacher personality, 6
Teacher beliefs, 6
Teacher experience and preparation, 8

Teaching/learning styles, 8
Direct teaching, 8
Indirect teaching, 8
Subject or content knowledge, 9

Teacher preparation, 10
Class and classroom size effects, 11
Objectives, 15

ISSUES AND PROBLEMS FOR DISCUSSION

ISSUES Here are some issues for you to debate.

1. When you seek a teaching position, what do you think are the most important factors upon which you should be judged and why? Consider and perhaps rank order these factors among others: your gender, age, experience with youth, personality, beliefs, and preparation for teaching.
2. Considering the three major factors that influence how we teach (personal characteristics, experience and preparation in education, and context of teaching), which of them do you think is most influential and why?
3. If you were in charge of preparing teachers, what would you make sure they know and are able to do?

PROBLEMS The following problems have been shared with us by teachers. How might they be resolved?

1. Clearly, boys and girls should be treated equitably but I find myself being influenced by stereotypes about the one or the other. I know better but just can't seem to quit.

2. Some teachers in the school have what I would call lots of personality. In some cases it seems to make them better teachers. I am reserved and more businesslike but my students learn just as much or more. However, I know the students would like me to be more friendly and enthusiastic.

3. I want to believe that all kids can learn but I have been in the classroom long enough to see kids have different levels of ability and motivation. I want all of them to succeed but I feel like I am attempting mission impossible.

4. There are so many ways to teach but I find myself relying on only a couple. What is the matter with me?

5. My best friend teaches in a new suburban school. When I visited his classroom I knew that that is the kind of school I want to be in. At the same time, I know that most of the jobs will be in urban schools where the kids are less likely to bring many advantages to school and where the school and classrooms will not be so bright and sunny. I'm also concerned because I hear teaching materials can be in short supply and that teachers are expected to get every child to learn.

THEORY INTO ACTION: ACTIVITIES FOR PRACTICE AND YOUR PORTFOLIO

ACTIVITY 1.1: A Teaching Self-Portrait and Analysis Describe what you think you will be like as a teacher. As a teacher, I think I will be:

_____

_____

_____

Now describe how you believe some of the factors mentioned in this chapter or in other chapters may shape your teaching behavior.

ACTIVITY 1.2: Your Cooperating or Mentor Teacher's Self-Portrait If you are in a field experience, share your self-portrait with the cooperating or mentor teacher. Ask him or her to react. Perhaps your mentor would then be willing to talk about what he or she is like and the factors that seem to be influential in his or her teaching. Can you discover other factors that impact a teacher's classroom behavior?

REFERENCES

Ainley, J., & Luntley, M. (2004, June). *What teachers know: The knowledge bases of classroom practice.* Final report on AHRB project: Attention and the Knowledge Bases of Expertise. University of Warwick, UK.

Artiles, A. J., Mostert, M. P., & Tankersley, M. (1994). Assessing the link between teacher cognitions, teacher behaviors, and pupil responses to lessons. *Teaching and Teacher Education, 10*(5), 465–481.

Auwarter, A., & Aruguete, M. (2008, March–April). Effects of student gender and socioeconomic status on teacher perceptions. *Journal of Educational Research 101*(4), 243–244.

Barnes, C. (2002, September). What do teachers teach: Survey of America's fourth and eighth grade teachers. *Civic Report # 28,* University of Connecticut: Center for Survey Research and Analysis.

Barnes, J. (1987). Teaching experience. In M. J. Dunkin (Ed.), *International encyclopedia of teaching and teacher education* (pp. 608–612). Oxford: Pergamon Press.

Biddle, B., & Berliner, D. (2003). Small class size and its effects. In *Annual editions: Education 03/04* (pp. 167–175). Guilford, CT: McGraw-Hill/Dushkin.

Biehler, R., & Snowman, J. (2008). *Psychology applied to teaching.* Boston: Houghton Mifflin.

Blatchford, P., Edmonds, S., & Martin, C. (2003, March). Class size, pupil attentiveness and peer relations. *British Journal of Educational Psychology, 73*(1), 15–36.

Block, J., & Hazelip, K. (1995). Teacher beliefs and belief systems. In L. Anderson (Ed.), *International encyclopedia of teaching and teacher education* (pp. 25–28). Oxford: Pergamon Press.

Bracey, G. (1999, November). Reducing class size. *Phi Beta Kappan, 81*(3), 246–247.

Cole, A., & Knowles, J. (1993). Shattered images. *Teaching and Teacher Education, 9*(516), 457–471.

Cotton, K. (2001). *Educational time factors.* Portland, OR: NW Respond Education Laboratory School Improvement Research Semes #8.

Coulter, F. (1987). Affective characteristics of student teachers. In M. J. Dunkin (Ed.), *International encyclopedia of teaching and teacher education* (pp. 589–597). Oxford: Pergamon Press.

Cruickshank, D. (1990). *Research that informs teachers and teacher educators.* Bloomington, IN: Phi Delta Kappa.

Cruickshank, D., & Callahan, R. (1983). The other side of the desk: Stages and problems of teacher development. *The Elementary School Journal, 83*(3), 251–258.

Darling-Hammond, L., Gatlin, S., Holtzman, D. (2005). Does teacher preparation matter? *Education Policy Analysis Archives, 13*(42), 1–47.

Dee, T. (2006, Fall). The why chromosome. *Education Next, 6*(4). http://www.hoover.org/publications/ednext/3853842.html

Duffy, J., Warren, K., & Walsh, M. (2001). Classroom interactions. *Sex Roles, 45*(9/10), 579–593.

Dunkin, M. J. (1987). Teacher's sex. In M. J. Dunkin (Ed.), *International encyclopedia of teaching and teacher education* (pp. 606–608). Oxford: Pergamon Press.

Dunkin, M. J., & Biddle, B. J. (1982). *The study of teaching.* Washington, DC: University Press of America.

Ehrenberg, R., Goldhaber, D., & Brewer, D. (1995, April). Do teachers' race, gender, and ethnicity matter? Evidence from the National Educational Longitudinal Study. *Industrial and Labor Relations Review, 48*(3), 547–561.

Fang, L. (1996). A review of research on teacher beliefs & practices. *Educational Research, 38*(1), 47–65.

Finn, J., Gerber, S., Achilles, C., & Boyd-Zaharias, J. (2001, May). The enduring effects of small classes. *Teachers College Record, 103*(2), 145–183.

Finn, J., Pannozzo, G., & Achilles, C. (2003, Fall). The "why's" of class size. *Review of Educational Research, 73*(3), 321–368.

Fuller, F. F., & Bown, O. H. (1975). Becoming a teacher. In K. Ryan (Ed.), *Teacher education.* 74th Yearbook of the National Society for the Study of Education, Part II (pp. 25–52). Chicago: University of Chicago Press.

Garrahy, D. (2003). Speaking louder than words: Teachers' gender beliefs and practices in third grade classrooms. *Equity and Excellence in Education, 36*(1), 96.

Glass, G. V. (1987). Class size. In M. J. Dunkin (Ed.), *International encyclopedia of teaching and teacher education* (pp. 540–545). Oxford: Pergamon Press.

Goddard, R., Hoy, W., & Hoy, A. (2004, April). Collective efficacy beliefs. *Educational Researcher, 33*(3), 3–13.

Goddard, Y., Goddard, R., & Tschannen-Moran, M. (2007, April). A theoretical and empirical investigation of teacher collaboration in public elementary schools. *Teachers College Record, 109*(4), 877–896.

Good, T., & Brophy, J. (2007). *Looking in classrooms.* Ninth Edition. New York: Pearson.

Gordon, S., Dembo, M., & Hocevar, D. (2007, January). Do teachers' own learning behaviors influence their classroom goal orientation and control ideology? *Teaching and Teacher Education, 23*(1), 36–46.

Grossman, P. (1995). Teachers' knowledge. In L. Anderson (Ed.), *International encyclopedia of teaching and teacher education.* Second Edition (pp. 21–24). Tarrytown, NY: Elsevier Science.

Haar, J., Hall, G., Schoepp, P. & Smith, D. (2002. Jan/Feb) How teachers teach to students with different learning styles. *Clearing House, 75*(3), 42–45.

Holloway, J. (2002, February 2). Do smaller classes change instruction? *Educational Leadership, 59*(5), 91–92.

Housner, L., & Griffey, D. (1985). Teacher cognition. *Research Quarterly for Exercise and Sport, 56*, 45–53.

Hyun, E., & Tyler, M. (1999, April 19–23). *Examination of preschool teachers' biased perceptions on gender differences.* Paper presented at the Annual Conference of the American Educational Research Association. Montreal, Quebec.

Judge, T., Heller, D., & Mount, M. (2002). Five-factor model of personality and job satisfaction. *Journal of Applied Psychology, 87*(3), 530–541.

Kagan, D. M. (1992, Summer). Professional growth among preservice and beginning teachers. *Review of Educational Research, 62*(2), 129–169.

Kalaian, H., & Freeman, D. (1994). Gender differences in self-confidence and educational beliefs. *Teaching and Teacher Education, 10*(6), 647–658.

Kane, R., Sandretto, S., & Heath, C. (2002, Summer). Telling half the story: A critical review of research on the teaching of beliefs and practices. *Review of Educational Research, 72*(2), 177–228.

Konstantopoulos, S. (2008, March). Do small classes reduce the achievement gap? *Elementary School Journal, 108*(4), 275–291.

Li, Q. (1999). Teachers' beliefs and gender differences in mathematics. *Educational Research, 41*(1), 63–76.

LoGerfo, L. (2006, Summer). Climb every mountain. *Education Next,* no. 3. Access: www.hoover.org/publications/ednext

Marsh, H., Martin, A., & Cheng, J. (2008, February). A multilevel perspective on gender in classroom motivation. *Journal of Educational Psychology, 100*(1), 78–95.

McIntyre, L. (1988, June–July). Teacher gender: A predictor of special education referral. *Journal of Learning Disabilities, 21*(6), 382–83.

Morrison, A., & McIntyre, D. (1973). *Teachers and teaching.* Harmondsworth, Middlesex, England: Penguin Education.

Mowrer-Reynolds, E. (2008, March). Preservice educators perceptions of exemplary teachers. *College Student Journal, 42*(1), 214–24.

Nettle, E. (1998). Stability and change in the beliefs of student teachers during practice teaching. *Teaching and Teacher Education, 14*(2), 193–204.

O'Connor, E., Fish, M., & Yasik, A. (2004). Influence of teacher experience on the elementary classroom system. *Journal of Classroom Interaction, 39*(1), 10–16.

Passel, J. & Cohn, D. (2008). *U.S. Population Projects: 2005–2050.* Washington, DC: Pew Research Center.

Perie, M., & Baker, D. (1997). *Job satisfaction among America's teachers: Effects of workplace conditions, background characteristics, and teacher compensation.* Washington: National Center for Education Statistics.

Pigge, F., & Marso, R. (1987). Relationships between student characteristics and changes in attitudes, concerns, anxieties, and confidence about teaching during teacher preparation. *Journal of Educational Research, 81*(2), 109–115.

Powell, R. R. (1992, June). The influence of prior experiences on pedagogical constructs of traditional and nontraditional preservice teachers. *Teaching and Teacher Education, 8*(3), 225–238.

Ravitz, J., Becker, H., & Wong, Y. (1998). *Constructivist compatible beliefs and practices among U.S. teachers.* Irvine, CA: Center for Research on Information Technology and Organizations, University of California at Irvine.

Rice, J. (2003). *Teacher quality.* Washington, DC: Economic Policy Institute. 64 pp.

Rivkin, S., Hanushek, E., & Kain, J. (2005, March). Teachers, schools and academic achievement. *Econometrica, 73*(2), 417–458.

Rodriguez, N. (2002). Gender differences in disciplinary approaches. ERIC Document SP041019.

Rosenthal, R. (2003, October). Covert communication in laboratories, classrooms, and the truly real world. *Current Directions in Psychological Science, 12*(5), 151–154.

Rubie-Davies, C. (2007). Classroom Interactions: Exploring the practices of high and low-expectation teachers. *British Journal of Educational Psychology, 77,* 289–306.

Skipper, C. (1985, March 31–April 4). *Instructional methods and course goals preferred by preservice elementary and secondary teachers.* Paper presented at the annual meeting of the American Educational Research Association. Chicago, IL. (Eric Document Reproduction Center ED261031).

Slater, R. (2008, Winter). American teachers. *Education Next, 8*(11). http://www.hoover.org/publications/ednext/10823521.html

Sloan, T., Daane, C., & Giesen, J. (2004, September). Learning styles of elementary pre-service teachers. *College Student Journal, 38*(3), 494–500.

Solomon, D. (1996). Teacher beliefs and practices in schools serving communities that differ in socioeconomic level. *Journal of Experimental Education, 64*(4), 327–347.

Stretcher, B., Bohrnstedt, G., Kirst, M., McRobbie, J., & Williams, T. (2001, May). Class-size reduction in California. *Phi Delta Kappan, 82*(9), 670–674.

Szpiczka, N. A. (1990). Display of self. Unpublished doctoral dissertation, Syracuse University, Syracuse, NY.

Tanner, B., (2001). *Instructional strategies: How teachers teach matters.* Atlanta, GA: Southern Regional Education Board.

Tynjala, P., Helle, L., & Murtonen, M. (2001). Computer science and teacher students' beliefs. Paper presented at the 9th European Conference on Learning and Instruction: Fribourg, Switzerland.

U.S. Department of Education (1999). National Center for Education Statistics. *What happens in classrooms? Instructional practices in elementary and secondary schools, 1994–1995,* NCES 1999-348, by R. R. Henke, X. Chen, & G. Goldman. Project Officers, M. Rollefson and K. Gruber. Washington, DC.

Weiner, G. (1995). Gender and racial differences among students. In L. Anderson (Ed.), *International encyclopedia of teaching and teacher education.* Second Edition (pp. 319–323). Tarrytown, NY: Elsevier Science.

Wortel, E. (1996). *Teacher gender-role identity and gender attribution of student mathematical ability.* Unpublished doctoral dissertation, Pace University.

Zamorski, B., & Haydn, T. (2002). Classroom management and disaffection. *Pedagogy, Culture and Society, 64*(2), 257–278.

Teaching in a Changing Society

Conversation Starters

What probably most influences student learning—home or school?

Two explanations are offered to account for the difference between kids who do well and those who do poorly in school. The first is that the quality of schools they attend cause the difference. Kids who do well attend good schools. Among other things, a good school has highly qualified and effective teachers, an outstanding principal and staff, rich instructional resources, and an adequate facility. A good school also promotes high standards.

   A second explanation for the differences in academic achievement between higher and lower achieving students is that the higher achieving kids simply come from more advantaged homes and communities. Generally, kids raised in higher socio-economic status (SES) families do better in school and that is due more to the home advantages they enjoy than to the schools they attend. Yet some high SES students do poorly while some low SES students do well.

What do you think is the answer?

As teachers we must understand the dynamic, ever-changing context or setting in which schools exist and teaching takes place. This context includes population, family, and children. *Fact:* Population is growing and changing in its diversity. *Fact:* Different kinds of families are emerging. *Fact:* Children are more diverse and present greater challenges. As a result, schools and teachers are challenged to: acknowledge, celebrate, and capitalize on student diversity; appreciate and support a growing number of family styles; and ensure each student overcomes any disadvantage he or she may bring to school. To the extent you understand and take into account this context and the variables therein, you will be able to improve your students' chances for success and your personal joy in teaching.

Try Activity 2.1

2.1 How have schools you attended differed in terms of neighborhood, family, and student characteristics? How did those differences play out in classrooms?

America's Changing Population

America's **population** has surpassed 300 million and will reach 400 million by 2039, with Hispanic and Asian minorities leading the way. Thus there are and will be more students to teach, and they will be more culturally and racially diverse. Presently 45 percent of children under age 5 are minority. At the same time, the population is graying.

MINORITY POPULATION GROWTH

America is known as a place where immigrants of different cultures and races form an integrated society while maintaining their ethnicity. Each group of immigrants brings with it different fertility and mortality rates, which keep the racial and ethnic composition of the country in flux. At last count, the racial, ethnic composition is approximately as follows:

White	67%
Hispanic	14%
Black	13%
Asian, Pacific Islander, American Indian, Alaskan Native	5%

However, by 2050, it is expected the composition will be:

White	46%
Hispanic	30%
Black	15%
Asian/other	9%

During this time span what is expected to happen? First, the percentage of whites will decline. Second, Hispanics will outnumber African-Americans and account for nearly one-third of the population. Third, the percentage of Asian/others will increase dramatically. Overall, Hispanics and Asians will account for over half of the U.S. population growth every year for the next 50 years (U.S. Census 2008).

MINORITY POPULATION DISTRIBUTION

Over the next 25 years, minority concentrations are expected to increase in every section of the country. The greatest increases will be in the South, Southwest, and West. By 2025, minorities are expected to account for 50 percent or more of the populations of California, Hawaii, New Mexico, Texas, and the District of Columbia. Additionally, the minority population of New York, Maryland, New Jersey, Alaska, and Louisiana will exceed 40 percent (U.S. Census 2000).

OTHER NOTEWORTHY POPULATION CHANGES

Lower Percentage of Children: Higher Percentage of Senior Citizens The number of children continues to grow, but the percentage of children in the population is declining. Presently, children constitute about 26 percent of the total population. By 2025 that percentage is expected to dip to 24. However, just as minority populations are not distributed evenly, neither is the child population. Thus, some states and parts thereof will have a greater growth in the child population while others may experience decline.

The nation is also aging. Besides minorities, the other high-growth sector is people over age 55. This group, which includes the front edge of the baby boom generation, grew at a 40 percent rate from 1990 to 2000. Not only will the baby boom generation get older; its lifespan is expected to reach new highs.

Lots of population information is available online at the census website.

Web Link
Population Information

THE CHANGING PUPIL POPULATION

Changes in the nature of the general population and its distribution result in changes in the school population. For example:

- Sixty percent of students live in the South and West.
- More public students now attend schools in suburbs, towns, and rural areas than in urban areas.
- About 17 percent of public school students attend public "schools of choice," that is they attend schools outside their attendance area. About 2 percent attend charter schools and 3 percent magnet schools. Two percent more are home schooled.
- Over one-third of public school students are low-income with 16 percent below the poverty level.
- Almost 14 percent of public school children receive some special education. About three-fourths of them are educated in regular classrooms.
- Four of ten public school students are children of color. That number will rise to fifty-fifty by 2020.
- African-American and Latino students are much more likely to attend high-poverty schools.
- More than half of African-American and Latino students attend public schools in which at least three-quarters of students are of color.
- One of ten public school students is learning the English language. About one in five is a child of immigrants (Center on Educational Policy, 2006; Passel & Cohn, 2008).

Try Activities 2.2 and 2.3

2.2 How well do you think you are prepared to teach minority children?

2.3 How willing are you to teach in locales needing teachers the most?

CHALLENGES YOU MAY FACE THAT RESULT FROM POPULATION CHANGES AND OTHER FACTORS

Wherever you teach, you will be challenged to educate an increasingly racially, culturally, and linguistically diverse student population. If you teach in an urban public school, you are more likely to work with children of color, many of whom attend higher-poverty schools segregated by family income. Many such children will at first be alien to you unless you have experienced similar conditions. Since nearly one in five children attend "schools of choice," including home schools, you may be competing to hold onto your school's population. Additionally, you may need to court senior citizens, who are increasing in number and may be less able and interested in supporting education.

The Changing Family

From time immemorial, the family has been the fundamental unit responsible for the health, education, and general well-being of children; indeed, the family has been the central organizing principle of societies everywhere. In the United States, the structure and function of families have undergone profound changes in the last 30 years. Let's look at some of them.

FAMILY TRENDS

Since family is important in the lives of youths, let's consider what is happening with families today. On average they are smaller because women are bearing fewer children, and consequently children have fewer siblings. Second, parents tend to be older because more marriages occur later in life.

Third, family styles are changing. For example, there are fewer traditional families consisting of a working father, homemaker mother, and children, and there are more single-parent families. Some diversity in family styles is attributable to both parents working (thus no stay-at-home parent), but most is due to the approximately 50 percent divorce rate. As a result of divorce, the proportion of children living with two parents has declined to the point that over one-fourth of American families are now headed by a single parent. Two-fifths of white and three-fifths of African-American children will experience a second divorce. The high divorce rate means that 30–40 percent of all marriages are remarriages, which often create blended families ("his, hers, and theirs"). Two-parent families do seem to be staging a modest comeback and perhaps more notably, the proportion of poor kids living with a single mother declined (Dionne, 2001). Other family styles, including single-adoptive (a single person having or adopting one or more children), are growing in number. Another growing phenomenon is grandparents raising grandchildren. For comprehensive information on the family, visit the OLC web link.

Spotlight on Research 2.1 makes clear some of the advantages of growing up in a home with two happily married parents.

Hacker (1982) and Popenoe (1993) attribute a changing attitude toward the traditional family to our unwillingness to accept its obligations and constraints. Signs supporting this contention include our reluctance to remain in a less-than-ideal marriage and to invest time, money, and energy in family life. However, others maintain that the movement toward alternative family styles merely shows our acceptance of varying lifestyles (Suransky, 1997) and the shift of women into the paid labor market (Fraser, 1989).

Web Link
Family Trends in U.S.

2.4 How do you think the changes in families are affecting children and teachers?

"Kim, this is Eddie. He only has one set of parents!"

- How do children in households with one biological parent differ from children in households with two? On average, children with two continuously happily married parents are less likely to experience cognitive, emotional, and social problems even in adulthood. (For example, children in such households are half as likely to develop serious psychiatric illnesses

and addictions.) Children in stepfamilies tend not to have better outcomes, on average, than children in single-parent homes.

- What accounts for the differences between such children? Children in stable, two-parent families generally have a higher standard of living, receive more effective parenting, experience more cooperative co-parenting, are emotionally closer

to both parents (especially fathers), and are subject to less stress.

- What are the implications? It seems important to increase the number of children growing up with two happily, continuously married parents. Additionally, the well-being of children living in other family structures must be improved.

Sources: Amato (2005); Weitloft et al. (2003).

2.5 What kind of family do you think is best?

Web Link

Family Trends in Canada
Child Trends Data Bank

Ultimately, the question is how well does each family type fulfill the traditional family functions of nurturance, caring, and intimacy; cultural transmission; and economic support? Some conclude that the transformed American family is largely unprepared to meet the challenges of raising a child and therefore calls upon government health care institutions, schools, and voluntary organizations to help (Coontz, 2000; Fraser, 1989; Hamburg, 1992). Others, feel that every kind of family has strengths that can be fostered and weaknesses that can be avoided. Canadian readers can learn about family trends in Canada on the Family Trends in Canada website. All can benefit from the Child Trends Data Bank.

FAMILY, COMMUNITY, AND SCHOOL INFLUENCES ON CHILDREN AND SCHOOLING

Several factors influence children and their school learning. They include family and home conditions, and community and school characteristics.

How Families and Home Conditions Influence Children and School Learning

> Long before schools begin their job . . . teaching and learning take place in the family. The quality of that home and family teaching makes a large difference in how much children know and how ready they are to learn when they get to school. Home and family experiences and conditions continue to influence learning, too, once children start school (Barton & Coley, 2007).

How Family Wealth and Social Status Influence Children and School Learning
Decades ago, the landmark "Coleman Study" revealed just how influential outside-of-school factors are (U.S. Dept. 1966). The major, consistently supported finding is that pupil academic achievement is most closely tied to family **socioeconomic status (SES)**—measured by parent and caregiver education, occupational status, and income (Surin, 2005, Rothstein 2004). SES simply overwhelms all other in- and out-of-school factors in its power to predict student success. Said another way, *on average*, parents and caregivers with better education, better jobs, and more wealth have kids who do better in school. Since *on average* applies, keep in mind that fewer but some academically talented students are found at all socioeconomic levels.

Just why do kids with a higher SES often do better? Several factors enter the equation. Partly their school success is a function of how much they are read to and talked to beginning at birth. For example, preschool children in families with a higher SES hear about 2,000 words each hour, a working class family's child hears 1,000, while a welfare child hears only 600. By age 3 children in professional families hear 30 million more words than do children on welfare (Hart & Risley, 2003). Also conversations with children in families with a higher SES include more questioning and explaining and greater provision of positive feedback to kids regarding what they do and how well they do it. Furthermore, parents with a higher SES are able to provide reading materials, computers, quiet places to study, and richer summer experiences (Bracey 1995, Jencks et al., 1972, US Dept.1966, Walberg & Fowler 1987).

A second influential factor is the teacher. Students with a higher SES have teachers who, in most cases, are better prepared, more experienced, have fewer absences, use more technology; and these students are more likely to attend safer schools. Often this is because experienced teachers use their seniority to obtain assignments in communities with a higher SES.

Finally, but just as important, children with a higher SES enjoy the benefits of more available and better health care.

Poverty: The Countervailing Factor   Poverty is the antithesis of wealth and, regrettably, although the U.S. is the wealthiest nation, it ranks highest among developed countries in childhood poverty. About 20 percent of children live below the federal poverty line. These children are twice as likely to repeat a grade, be suspended or expelled, drop out of school, and/or be in special education classes (Warren, 2008). They also are much more likely to live in a household headed by an unmarried mother and to have a parent among the 1 in 99 Americans in prison. Minority children are most likely to be poor. African-American children, on average, are three times more likely to live in poverty and to lag behind academically. Additionally, they are three times as likely to be in classes for slow learners.

How Family Attributes and Behaviors Influence Children and School Learning

Parental Characteristics   A number of parental characteristics are helpful to children. They seem to have greater school success when parents are more educated (especially mothers), and when they are more involved with their children at home and at school (Miles, 2003). Two additional parental characteristics associated with child school success are their attitude toward education and their academic expectations for their children. On average, parents who value education and expect their kids to learn at a higher level are rewarded. One survey finds that almost all students who earn mostly A's and B's report their parents encourage them academically while nearly half of children earning C's say their parents provide little encouragement (Metropolitan Life, 1998). Other parental characteristics that seem to serve children well include parental attention (the more of it the less likely they are to have early sex, smoke, or engage in substance abuse), and parental presence (especially before and after school and at dinner) (Resnick, 1997).

Parental Control and Child Rearing Practices   Parents are responsible for a number of things associated with student learning including getting students out of bed and off to school, establishing rules for electronic game playing and television watching, talking with them and reading to younger children (Barton 2003, Barton & Coley, 2007). Raspberry, speaking for the Black community, insists that parenting skills must be improved, especially for those who were not exposed to good parenting themselves and for teen-aged mothers. He argues that communities should have regular training sessions where parents learn tricks and good techniques–for example, how to get kids up and ready for school. Moreover, parents should learn how to engender in children attitudes and habits that make school learning possible such as patience and persistence, and love of reading and learning (Raspberry, 1993).

2.6   In what ways did your family influence your success in school?

Parent Relationship to Education and Involvement in Their Children's School   When parents are involved in the education of their children they have greater school success. Sources for information on parent involvement in schools are the National

Web Links

National Coalition for Parent
Involvement in Education

National Education
Association/Parents and
Community

Coalition on Family Involvement and the National Education Association. See the OLC web links in the page margin.

Teachers, regardless of age and experience, report that establishing and maintaining good relationships with significant adults in the child's life, such as parents and guardians, is a primary goal. You will learn more about this challenge in Chapter 13. Beginning teachers report their biggest challenge is communicating with and involving parents (Metropolitan Life, 2004–2005).

Two sets of factors determine whether parent involvement will happen. The first is *family related* and includes the parents' ethnicity, their prior school experiences, family structure, the family work schedule, and family circumstances. The second is *school related* and involves teacher attitudes toward families, and school and teacher expectations (Carlisle and others, 2006). Let's look at schoolrelated factors first.

Family Ethnicity   When the cultural background of families and teachers differ, parents may feel teachers do not understand or accept them as equals. Additionally, culturally different families may have different ideas regarding what is appropriate involvement in school matters: some may even feel it is meddling and disrespectful to teachers. Parents with limited English proficiency may be embarrassed or feel they won't be understood. Less educated parents may feel inferior and intimidated.

Parent/Guardian Past Educational Experiences   Parents who have enjoyed positive experiences as students and/or who hold positive attitudes toward school are more likely to become involved. Such parents often had better school success and attained higher levels of education. Conversely, parents with less good school experience and less education may be hesitant to get involved and/or doubt they have the ability to help their children succeed in school.

Family Structure   Families in which both parents are present in the home are more involved in their children's education. Biological mothers in two-biological-parent families are most likely to be highly involved in a child's education. Stepmothers are found to be least involved. For fathers, most involved are biological fathers in single-parent families. Least involved are stepfathers. This brings us to a finding underlining the importance of having a father involved in the home and school. "Children who grow-up with fathers do far better . . . in every way we can measure than children who do not. This holds true [regardless of race class and income]. The simple truth is that fathers are irreplaceable in shaping the character of their children" (Blankenhom in Alexander, 2005). Some sobering statistics include: children in fatherless homes account for 71 percent of dropouts, 85 percent of kids with behavior problems, 63 percent of teen suicides, 70 percent of juveniles in detention centers, 85 percent of youths in prison, 75 percent of those in chemical abuse treatment programs, 80 percent of rapists, and 90 percent of runaways and homeless. A detention center juvenile counselor in the Blankenhom study challenges, "If you find a gang member who comes from a complete nuclear family, I'd like to meet him. I don't think he exists" (ibid.). Cole reiterates, "Maturity does not come with age, but with the responsibility of one's actions. The lack of effective, functioning fathers is the root cause of America's social, economic, and spiritual crises" (ibid.). African-Americans increasingly are worried about fatherless homes. Raspberry (2005) believes the decline of marriage in lower-income Black communities is the main culprit. In those settings, a disproportionate percentage of less-well educated males are unemployed and incarcerated which makes them less marriage eligible. Unfortunately, they are likely to become absentee, uninvolved fathers.

Family Work Schedules and Social Networks   Understandably, demanding work schedules make school involvement difficult. This is especially true when both parents work or when a child is in a single-parent working family. Interestingly, the more social relationships a family has, the more likely parents are involved in their child's education.

Family Circumstances   With persons marrying later in life and women increasingly pursuing careers, more kids have relatively older, more harried caregivers with less time to give them or their schools. Increasingly parents also are caregivers to their own parents. A few families confront extraordinary difficulties. Beyond normal work, health, and welfare problems, they may be coping with family breakdown, substance abuse, inadequate knowledge of good child rearing practices, and caregiver stress.

Turning to *school related factors* that influence family involvement we have several.

Teacher Attitude toward Parent Involvement   Whether the teacher and school are pro-family involvement and whether they believe "it takes a village to raise a child" seem critical. Parents and guardians must be made to feel welcome and made to understand how influential they are. However, a few teachers are reluctant to have parents in their school and classroom, fearing they and/or their teaching may be misjudged. Some do not easily accept parent observations or opinions: some just don't want to hear them.

School and Teacher Expectations Regarding Parent Involvement   At work here are such things as whether the teacher, as a child, received parental assistance with homework, whether the teacher has witnessed positive parental involvement, whether other teachers value it and so forth. Ninety percent of teachers of young children agree that parent involvement is critical to having a good school (Jones, White, Aeby, & Benson, 1997).

School to Home Communication.   Some data seem to indicate that parents feel they do not get adequate or timely information about how they can be school-involved.

In Chapter 13 you will find that one of the five major challenges of teaching is "improving parent relationships and home conditions." Take a look.

How Home Conditions Influence Children and School Learning

Home as a Learning Resource   The home is a learning resource when it can make available a newspaper, books and magazines, a computer with Internet access, a quiet place to study, and when use of television and game playing is monitored. Obviously, availability of some of these tools is a result of family income.

Home as a Safe, Stable Haven   Violence in the home is extremely disruptive. Unfortunately, it permeates too many, particularly in communities with a low SES which also may be gang infested. Children in unstable, violent home situations are more likely to seek gang affiliation as a proxy for family and more likely to be referred to child protective services and placed in foster care.

Remaining in the same school seems to be good for most children. Students who frequently change schools are at greater risk for academic and social problems, including lower achievement, more behavioral problems, and fewer friends. However, these negative outcomes may be attributable to problems caused by other than just moving. Transient kids are more likely to be children of low income families, of migrant workers, or homeless. (Education Week, 2004; Rumberger, 2003)

Home as Environmentally Safe   Environmental hazards in the home can be a huge danger for children. For example, almost half a million children ages 1–5 have unsafe blood lead levels mostly resulting from living in housing containing deteriorated lead paint. Lead poisoning causes learning disabilities, behavioral problems, and at very high levels can cause seizures and coma.

2.7   To what extent and in what ways were your parents involved in school matters? How did that affect you?

2.8   What ideas do you have for increasing family involvement?

2.9   How have home conditions affected you or your friends in relationship to school learning?

How Communities and Schools Influence Children and School Learning

Quality of Communities   Community characteristics also are associated with a child's development and school achievement. Studies report that children living in disadvantaged communities are more likely to live in a single-parent home, less likely to complete school, more likely to affiliate with antisocial persons, and more likely to observe or be affected by violence (Holloway, 2004). Youth organizations help kids sort things out in life and improve their chances of happiness and success. Relatedly, mentoring programs provide great support for at-risk kids. Social services are of great value to those in need. Keep in mind that supportive communities exist even in poorer areas and that they can do much to overcome problems faced by children and families.

Quality of Schools and Teachers   Perhaps most influential in the community is the school. School factors that have been tied to student learning include teacher experience and regular attendance, how teachers are prepared, class size (see Chapter 1), academic rigor of the curriculum, and availability of appropriate technological instruction (Barton 2003). Several specific teacher skills and characteristics contribute to student learning (see Chapters 10 and 11). One particularly helpful teacher characteristic is called **academic optimism**, which refers to teachers who emphasize intellectual activity and student achievement, who trust in students and parents, and who believe that the faculty of a school can collectively make a difference (Hoy, Tarter, & Hoy, 2006).

Other Factors That Influence School Learning

Quality of Day Care: Supervision of Children   Six of ten children younger than 5 are cared for part of the day by someone other than their parents. Only one-quarter of them are fortunate enough to be in high-quality child care programs and will benefit in their language, mathematical, and social skills. They are less likely to repeat grades, drop-out, require special education services, or break laws. Even if good care is available, poor families likely cannot afford it.

Quality of Health Care and Other Health Issues   Children with physical or mental health issues certainly are more at risk of school failure. Besides missing more school, they may be unable to focus on learning or to make friends. Of course, poor children have less access to health services in general and high quality services in particular. Poor children are also less likely to have health insurance. Regardless of their SES and backgrounds, children who drink, smoke, or use drugs are at greater risk of having long-term physical and mental health problems. Moreover, use of some substances has a negative affect on school attendance and classroom attention.

Youth Employment   By age 16, around three-fourths of youth now have or have previously held jobs. Employment provides them with different kinds of skills and the opportunity to accept responsibilities. Jobs can also promote self-assurance and confidence. Of course, kids work for different reasons. The vast majority work for "spending money." However, in some households they must contribute to family income and/or provide money for college. Working more than half-time can interfere with school success.

THE RESULTANT ACHIEVEMENT GAP

On average, children who enjoy more favorable family and home conditions, communities, and schools have better school success. The difference between their achievement and the lower achievement of their less advantaged counterparts is called the **achievement gap.** Since children with a higher SES receive better and additional benefits before entering formal schooling, it is not surprising

Try Activity 2.4

2.10   How have community and school conditions affected the school success of you or your friends?

that they outperform children with a lower SES beginning in kindergarten (See Highlight 2.1).

In an effort to close this gap, a number of compensatory programs have been put into effect including free school breakfast and lunch, tutoring, after school enrichment programs, Saturday School, and reduced class sizes. An interesting aside is that kids with a lower SES keep better pace academically during the school year. However, probably due to sterile summer learning environments, they fall behind during those breaks (Bracey, 2002). Consequently, summer enrichment programs also are being tried. To learn more about programs intended to close the achievement gap go to the Institute for Urban and Minority Education website.

Web Link
Institute for Urban and Minority Education

Some speculate that part of the achievement gap may be the result of cultural differences. For example, on average Asian-American students excel when compared with others (See Spotlight on Research 2.2 on page 33). However, the gap also exists within ethnic groups; for example, within groups of African-American, Latino, white, or Asian-American students from similar upper middle-class families who attend the same schools. Naturally, parents of the underachieving kids are concerned and ask why? (See Spotlight on Research 2.3 on page 34.)

Since so many problems children face have social and economic roots, an increasing number of persons question whether merely changing schools—for example making them more demanding—is sufficient to close the achievement gap.

> If as a society we choose to preserve big social class differences, we must necessarily also accept substantial gaps between the achievement of lower-class and middle-class children. Closing those gaps requires not only better schools, although those are certainly needed, but also reform in the social and economic institutions that prepare children to learn . . . (Rothstein 2004).

Rothstein goes on to recommend substantial investments in the following: creating greater income equality, providing better and stable housing, increasing and improving early childhood education, providing quality dental and medical care for children and parents, improving social services, and providing better after-school and summer programs (Rothstein 2008).

How You Can Help Close the Achievement Gap

Bring Parents and Caregivers Aboard

- Respect parents and caregivers. Make sure they feel welcome and important. Listen to them. Invite them to become involved in school activities.
- Help parents and caregivers overcome any negative past experiences they may have had with teachers and schools.
- Value parents and caregivers. Have them contribute time or talent to your class.
- Establish positive, ongoing relationships with them—relationships of mutual respect and trust. (See Chapter 13, "Parent Relationships and Home Conditions.")
- Help direct parents and caregivers that require family services support in order to provide a better home environment.
- Help them understand the many ways they can contribute to their children's school success. (See Spotlight on Research 2.4 on page 34.)

Foster Student Social Development and Learning

- Build good relationships with your students by, among other things, noticing them, calling them by name, answering their questions, talking with them respectfully, and helping and supporting, rather than judging them (Payne 2008).
- Make sure all students are connected to and involved with their peers. (See Chapter 5, "Using Sociometry.")

At the beginning of the school year, education reporters Rossi and Ihejrika observed and talked to teachers in two Chicago kindergarten classes—one in a low-performing and the other in a high-performing school. They found these classes to be "worlds apart."

In the low-performing school class: Only one-third of the kids were present the first day and, of those, almost 25 percent arrived late, 19 percent had no preschool, 35 percent were born to teen mothers, 50 percent had mothers who were dropouts, none had mothers with a college education, less than half were from two-parent families, some held books upside down and looked through them from back to front, and generally they had trouble following directions.

In the high-performing school class: Less than 5 percent of kids were absent on day one and only 8 percent of those arrived late, 8 percent had no preschool, none were born to teen mothers, 23 percent of mothers dropped out of school and a like percent had mothers with college degrees, 84 percent were from two-parent families, and the majority were easily able to follow directions.

Additionally, low-performing school kids were much less able to write their first names clearly, suffered greater separation anxiety, had many fewer books in their homes, were read to less often at home, more often were picked up after school by other kids, and had fewer computers in the home.

Notably, 99 percent of the low-performing kids' families were low income, compared with 46 percent of the high-performing children.

Comment:

When presented with the above information, research economist W. Stephen Barnett made these comments: "The average poor child starts kindergarten 18 months behind the other kids. My guess is that one class never catches up with the other class and falls farther behind despite the best effort of the schools" (ibid.).

Source: Rossi & Ihejrika (2005).

- Encourage students to use more formal oral language that is expected in educational and workplace settings rather than using neighborhood or street style talk.
- Make sure all students know the "rules of school" which may differ from the rules of home. For example, it may be acceptable to argue at home but not at school.
- Monitor and keep track of each student's achievements in relationship to classroom and school standards.
- Utilize the best instructional alternatives for a given learning task (see Chapters 7 and 8). For example, use a discussion when a discussion is called for.
- Encourage them to use out-of-school time wisely in activities that foster development and learning. For example, tell them what television channels are really educational as opposed to being merely entertaining. Direct their out-of-school learning activities toward using these resources as well as libraries.
- Provide compensatory or make-up educational activities for those who need them due to absences, illnesses, and so forth.
- Make extra effort to help transient kids enjoy comfortable and successful adjustments to your classroom (Rumberger 2003).
- Be *academically optimistic* that your students can learn: emphasize intellectual activity and achievement, trust in your students and their families, and believe that the faculty in your school can make a difference in the lives of kids.
- Teach every child as if he or she were your own.

2.11 What else might be done to close the achievement gap? What have you seen other teachers do?

Given what we know, a formula for school success is: **parent effort + teacher effort = greater student learning.**

Additionally, be an advocate for children. Help policy makers understand the importance of a range of other factors that, in addition to teachers, affect student

Are Asian-American Kids Smarter, or What?

Asian-American students and families, particularly those of east Asian heritage, usually do well in school and in life. According to Breckenridge (2003), they

- comprise only 5 percent of the population, yet constitute 15 percent or more of the enrollment at the best universities.
- top all ethnic groups in their SATs.
- maintain the highest secondary school grade point averages and score the highest on state proficiency tests.
- hold a higher percentage of degrees.
- have the highest median income.

Explanations that have been offered to account for such outstanding school achievement include:

- Asian-American families see education as a springboard to success and its attainment as a way to avoid discrimination. (Eight in ten Asian-American families would sell their homes and give up their financial futures to support their children's education.)
- Education is a bedrock family value. It is ascendant to everything else, including dating, sports, and television. Parents often relieve children of chores to clear time for study. How well children do in school is seen as a reflection on the family. School failure is associated with shame.
- Parents are actively involved in the education of their children.

Both Chinese Americans and whites, on average, do better in school than minority African-Americans and Latinos. Pearce (2006) investigated these two groups seeking to discover behavior that minority kids could be taught or recommendations their families could follow that would increase the achievement of their children. His findings suggest most importantly that minority parents, rather than becoming directly involved in their child's educational experience, should adopt a parenting style that favors strict discipline regarding study and clearly articulate high academic expectations.

Read what Latino and Asian high school kids say are the reasons why they perform well or poorly (Becerra, 2008).

achievement, including high quality early childhood and preschool programs, after school and summer programs, and programs that develop parents' capacity to support their children's education; development of the child as a whole person having good physical health, character, social development, and non-academic skills; small class size in the early grades for disadvantaged children; health services for parents and children; and learning activities after school and during summers (A Bolder Approach to Education).

The Changing Nature of Childhood and Youth

Yes, America is changing, and so is the process of growing up in it. The following headlines portray a bleak picture of being raised in America today: "More Kids Live in Poverty," "Study of 8th Graders Finds 20% at High Risk of Failure," "Latchkey Kids More Likely to Smoke, Drink," "Students Studying TV More than Books," "Fifth Graders Organize Rebellion," "Rapes by Children Expected to Rise."

You may feel that such headlines are sensational and exaggerated. However, in most cases the news stories are based upon governmental and scientific reports. As you might suspect, the scenarios are worse for the poor and minorities, which are the most rapidly growing segments of a declining youth population. However, majority and more affluent youth, while less affected by these concerns, are more affected by others. Let's look briefly at some of the problems that affect childhood today.

CHILDREN LIVING IN POVERTY

The Incidence and Locale of Poverty Shockingly, in this comparatively wealthy country, one in five children lives below the poverty line. This condition is mostly the result of income disparity between rich and poor—the top 50 percent of Americans receive over 80 percent of the total income (U.S. Census Bureau, 2008). In addition,

SPOTLIGHT ON RESEARCH 2.3
Are Parents Responsible for the Racial Gap in Student Achievement?

The book, *Black American Students in an Affluent Suburb* (Ogbu & Davis, 2003) presents the results of a study done in Shaker Heights, Ohio, an upper middle-class, racially mixed suburb where it is found that many African-American students lag academically behind their white and Asian-American classmates even though they enjoy the same advantages of family education and stability.

Black parents reasonably ask, "What is going on?" Ogbu and Davis suggest *they* are part of the problem. The researchers found black parents generally do not involve themselves in school

and do not spend enough time supervising their children's education. Ogbu and Davis also blame students who admit they fail to put forth as much academic effort, don't listen in class, and don't study properly. Furthermore, the anthropologists argue that African-American kids should be encouraged to choose better role models than black athletes, entertainers, and rappers.

Columnists Clarence Page and Thomas Sowell read Ogbu's book. Sowell (2003) concurs with Ogbu that too many black students and their families have unhelpful, distracting priorities including

nonacademic activities such as sports and entertainment and that black children are unduly caught up in hanging out with friends in person or on the phone. Sowell cites another barrier from McWhorter's book *Losing the Race* (2001)—that affirmative action reduces the incentive for black students to do their best.

Page (2003) reflects, "By facing . . . realities openly and honestly, we [parents] can begin to encourage a self-image among black youths that will help them value their brains as much as their basketballs or the 'bling-bling' and 'ching-ching' of rappers."

when economic times are tough or tragedies like Hurricane Katrina occur, more children are impoverished (Nieves, 2008).

A disproportionate number of poor children are minorities. Hispanic children are twice as likely, and Black children three times more likely to be raised in low-income homes.

Typically, we believe poor children live in central cities and rural areas. However, there has been a steady shift of low-income families toward suburbia where now a slight majority live. These families often are referred to as the "working poor" (Berube, 2007).

Conditions of Childhood Poverty   Unless we have been raised in poverty we may have little understanding of what life is like for many of these children. They are more likely to be born outside marriage; be raised by teen-aged mothers; live in unstable, chaotic and violent households; live with one-parent; have a working mother; have medical and dental problems; engage in sexual activity at an early age; change schools more often; live in rental housing or are homeless; and become involved in drug abuse, violence and crime.

Furthermore, the homes of children living in poverty are more likely to be of lower quality located in deteriorating, less-safe communities; more crowded and noisy; and less likely to be well-heated or cooled. Parents or guardians are less likely to be responsive to their needs and less able to offer emotional support, less involved in their school or their learning, and less likely to read to them. At the same time, parents or guardians are more likely to be authoritarian and punitive. Meanwhile, the kids' peers are more likely to be aggressive. Poor children have fewer books to read, have less access to technology, and watch more television. Their nutrition and healthcare are problematical. In sum, many low-income kids are disproportionately exposed to many more adverse economic, psychological, social, and physical conditions (Evans 2004).

Homeless Children   About 1 in 50 children is homeless on any given night. These youngsters are referred to as the "new untouchables who grow-up in environments plagued by infectious illnesses such as whooping cough and tuberculosis, come to school so tired and hungry that they cannot concentrate, and carry the smell of destitution with them—the smell of sweat and filth and urine" (Kozol, 1990, p. 52).

SPOTLIGHT ON RESEARCH 2.4

How Parents Can Help Children Succeed in School and How Schools Can Help Parents

Here are some ways parents can help kids succeed in school.

- Ensure kids are in school each day and have a good attitude toward learning.
- Create a home environment conducive to learning.
- Make clear the importance of learning.
- Encourage reading.
- Find a suitable place for study.
- Have frequent discussions with children regarding schoolwork.
- Encourage children regarding their schoolwork and homework.

- Help with and monitor homework.
- Hold high expectations for educational success.
- Encourage children to think well of themselves.
- Maintain good relationships with children.
- Support and get involved in school parent involvement programs.

Relatedly schools can help parents:

- Parents need strong, ongoing support from schools and teachers. This support is especially necessary for low-income parents.

- Parents and their children seem to benefit when schools provide parents a wide range of programs designed to improve parental reading skills, reduce financial stress, and meet health and nutritional needs.
- Low-income children especially benefit when they are exposed to after-school, summer, or year-round schooling.

Sources: Marzano, 2003; Molner, 2002; Thorkildsen & Stein, 1998.

Case 2.1 provides an example of a child, Kayla, who is homeless. Increasingly, older homeless children are found in the streets (see Case 2.2 on page 37).

Happily, awareness of children living in poverty, and concern for them, are growing and resultant programs are growing. Among other things, they promote supplementary food, prenatal care, child immunization, and early education programs such as Head Start. Additionally, the number of agencies interested in helping economically disadvantaged families and children is increasing. They include the Children's Defense Fund, American Agenda, Committee for Economic Development, and the National Coalition for the Homeless.

Results of Childhood Poverty on Learning   As a consequence of numerous disadvantages, many children who live in poverty enter school with low knowledge and skill levels. For example, they are less likely to know colors, numbers, and letters; and their vocabularies may be restricted. Generally, they are less oriented toward school learning. As a direct consequence, poor children are more likely to be mislabeled early on as special education students.

The Education of the Poor   To make matters worse, schools and day care facilities available to poor children often are of lesser quality; they have fewer experienced and qualified teachers, higher teacher turnover, and more teacher absenteeism. Furthermore, few teachers want to teach children living in poverty. Only 6 percent of beginning teachers plan to teach in low-income schools (You and the System 1990). Chin and others (2004) note: "Poverty does not present schools with just a single problem; poverty multiplies its impact on the schools in a variety of ways—in the need for increased services for students, in the lack of resources from the surrounding communities that schools and teachers rely upon in educating, and in the daily challenges teachers face in working with students who may not have enough to eat" (p. 21).

A number of organizations are working to encourage more of the best and the brightest of college graduates to teach in poorer settings. Best known is Teach For America that is founded on premises that educational inequality exists along socioeconomic and racial lines, children growing up in low-income communities face extra challenges but their schools lack sufficient capacity to meet those extra

2.12   What experience do you have with children whose SES differs from yours? What further experience would help?

2.13   "How willing are you to teach children from poor families? What pluses and minuses would you bring to this task?

Kayla: A Homeless Child

Ten-year-old Kayla's mother was intent on keeping her in her elementary school even though, for two years, they had to survive living in an old Toyota van. During that period, fast food restaurants and truck stops provided places to do homework, restrooms, and showers.

Kayla's grades suffered, and she was unable to make friends for fear they would find out. For her, the embarrassment was overwhelming. "It's sort of like a secret thing because you don't want anybody to know about it. You sort of have to make up lies. . . . "

Unlike some homeless people, Kayla's mom was not homeless because of addictions; rather, she was a member of the working poor and held a part-time job at the YMCA (Ruiz, 2005).

(Kayla is one of 1.35 million children who experience homelessness in a given year. Such children are more likely to be delayed in their development, suspended from school, or placed in special education programs. They also encounter difficulties related to legal guardianship and receiving proper immunizations.)

INVESTIGATING AND SOLVING THE CASE

1. What difficulties do homeless children encounter?
2. What can teachers and schools do to help them overcome the difficulties?
3. What experience have you had with homeless people? What did you learn from it?

Web Link

Teach For America

2.14 What do you believe are the most important things teachers can do to help poor children?

needs, and that too many believe schools can't help economically disadvantaged kids and children of color. Teach For America addresses these concerns by identifying and then preparing high quality persons to teach in settings often shunned by others.

Helping and Teaching Low SES Youth Three things seem essential in order to help children living in poverty. First, early intervention by communities and schools is required that focuses on improving family and home conditions including nutrition, health care, and opportunity to learn. Second, children of the poor must be convinced that they are worthy, they matter, and they count. Moreover, efforts must be made to generate in them a sense of **efficacy** or control over their destiny. "Yes we can." Third, these children (as all children) must be taught as well as we know how and they must be expected to learn. Here are some teaching suggestions with good support (Ferguson 2002, Haberman 2004).

- Respect each child's background and family.
- Be open and understanding.
- Encourage all children to learn and expect them to learn.
- Provide engaging learning activities. Make learning interesting and worthwhile.
- Make sure that children understand what is being taught. Provide individual help.
- Teach specific knowledge and skills that will help kids do well on important tests.
- Teach thinking and problem-solving skills.
- Make clear that learning is a good thing in itself and not just something you do to get a job.
- Teach gently. Use and promote the use of kindness. Avoid being judgmental.
- Set and maintain high standards for behavior. Maintain a safe classroom environment conducive to learning.
- Teach appropriate behavior rather than using punishment if inappropriate behavior occurs.
- Try not to be easily shocked.

"Look at me here. I am 13 years old. I don't have a father. I don't have a home-like house, I am hungry, I don't know a mother's love, I sleep on the streets, under the bridge, in cellars and gardens, I get cold, I tried to sell newspapers and nobody bought them; I tried cleaning car windscreens and they told me to piss off; I tried selling knickknacks and almost nobody bought them. So that you take notice of my existence, I am knocking you over, assaulting you, and taking from you the only thing in life that you believe is important: your money. Who knows, maybe then you will remember that half a million children like me don't have a decent house to sleep a decent child's sleep . . ."

Source: de Oliveira (1991).

INVESTIGATING AND SOLVING THE CASE

1. What factors contribute to such helplessness?
2. What can teachers do for such children?

Debated Solutions to the Goal of Improving the Lot of Poor Kids An often debated issue is, How can disadvantaged children be "saved"—that is, helped to enjoy greater educational success? On one side are those who believe better schools, school leadership, and teachers are the most necessary ingredients. They lament that academic expectations for poor kids are too low, their principals and teachers underpaid and less qualified, their classes too large, their schools too undisciplined. To them, failing children are the direct result of failing schools. Thus numerous and diverse reforms have been and are being tried. They include trying to attract better school personnel, providing more staff training, reducing class size, increasing the amount of time children are in school, and even paying kids to come to school every day and do well. Sadly, little evidence exists that existing school reform strategies are able to close more than a fraction of the overall achievement gap separating disadvantaged children from their more advantaged peers living in wealthier communities. This is true despite the fact that schools with large numbers of poor children often spend more per pupil than schools serving middle-class kids (Traub, 2000).

On the other side of this issue are those who feel that improving the lot of poor children is beyond the resources schools have to offer. They propose solutions such as ameliorating the negative social and economic conditions in their lives outside school (Rothstein, 2004), providing better employment opportunities for their caregivers (Berliner, 2005), and improving their health and well-being (see Highlight 2.2).

Some attribute success in life mostly to luck and on-the-job competence which they equate with personality. Personality trumps job skill (Jencks et al., 2005).

For more facts on child poverty visit the National Center for Children in Poverty web site.

OLC Web Link
National Center for Children in Poverty

CHILDREN WITH INADEQUATE SUPERVISION

Many, many children are home alone. A majority do not have a parent in the home full time (Eberstadt, 2001). Contributing to this phenomenon are increases in the number of single-parent families with that parent working and increases in the number of households where both parents work. Thus, numerous parents and guardians must count on kids to care for themselves or they must seek child care help from relatives, friends, or day care providers.

One-third of school-agers are regularly left home alone. They are called **latchkey children** (see Spotlight on Research 2.5 on page 39). At times unsupervised children seek refuge in libraries. Seventy-six percent of librarians report significant numbers of unattended children ages 10–12. The frequency of self-care and

HIGHLIGHT 2.2

Breaking the Cycle of Poverty and Despair

The Nurse-Family Partnership is a promising program intended to break the cycle of poverty and despair into which so many kids are born and raised. The idea is simple. Train nurses to visit poor and at-risk mothers during pregnancy and through the first two years to teach them parenting skills, support them in their parenting, hold them accountable for good parenting behaviors, and monitor the infants' health and development.

Follow-up study of this strategy suggests that it can work: participation in the program improves prenatal health, reduces child abuse and injuries, improves school readiness, and reduces likelihood that mothers or children through age 15 will have criminal or behavioral problems.

To learn more, go to the Nurse-Family Partnership home page. To read a compelling account of the program in action written by a Pulitzer Prize–winning journalist, see Boo (2006).

---

day care is so great that today's children often are referred to as the "day-care generation." Some even go so far as to argue that children today experience near abandonment (Louv, 1990).

What are the effects of being unsupervised? A study of eighth graders raises concerns. Sixty-eight percent of these children cared for themselves at least some time after school. Compared with supervised peers, these children are *twice* as likely to be under stress, in conflict with the family, to indicate parents are gone too much, and to call themselves "risk-takers" and to take risks. Furthermore, they are angrier, skip school more, are more afraid when alone, and go to more parties (Dwyer et al., 1990). Children who begin self-care later (in middle school or beyond) are *three* times more likely to abuse substances (Weisman, 1990).

Of course, children with a parent or guardian at home are not necessarily adequately supervised. Furthermore, children differ in their need for supervision.

When is a child ready for self-care? Alston (cited in Spotlight on Research 2.5) suggests when, among other things, the child is self-confident, takes initiative, is able to follow directions, is a good problem solver, is able to assume responsibility, is outgoing, has good peer relationships, is calm when something unexpected occurs, and is able to resist pressure from others. Given this array of positive personality traits, one can see why many latchkey children are vulnerable.

What are the effects of being supervised by someone outside the home? There are few conclusive data about the effects of day care. However, babies or infants in day care seem to be at greater risk of developing insecure relationships with their mothers. And children cared for outside the home are at greater risk of sickness due to increased exposure to other children and adults (Wingert & Kantrowitz, 1990). Probably the quality of those providing the day care is critical.

ABUSED AND NEGLECTED CHILDREN

Child abuse is all too common. It is estimated over 2 million children are either **abused** or neglected *each year*. Abuse and neglect are defined in Public Law 93-247 as "physical or mental injury, sexual abuse, negligent treatment, or maltreatment of a child under 18 by a person who is responsible for the child's welfare under circumstances which indicate that the child's health or welfare is harmed or threatened thereby" (Child Abuse Prevention and Treatment Act of 1974). Generally, abuse and neglect are associated with single parents, larger families, and parents who were themselves abused as children; stress brought about by poverty, unemployment, marital problems, or isolation; low level of parental education; poor information concerning child rearing; and a violent environment (Kauffman, 2000).

2.15 How were you supervised as a child? How did that work for you?

2.16 As a child did you or others close to you ever experience abuse or neglect? If so, what effect did that have?

Fifteen million, or one-quarter, of children are regularly unsupervised while parents or guardians work or are away for other reasons.

- These latchkey children care for themselves an average of six hours a week.
- Self-care is more prevalent among middle than elementary school kids.
- Self-care *increases* with family income. (Poor families are less likely to leave children alone because they deem

their neighborhood unsafe and have no one to respond in case of emergencies.)

- Fifty-one percent do poorly in school.
- One-third of complaints to child welfare agencies involve latchkeys.
- Eighth graders left alone 11 or more hours a week are twice as likely to abuse drugs.
- Much teenage sex occurs in the afternoon in the homes of latchkey boys.

- Unsupervised kids are more likely to be depressed, smoke cigarettes and marijuana, and drink alcohol.
- Unsupervised youth are more likely to be crime victims.

Sources: Alston (2004); Ash (2009); Gardner (2007); Smith (2000).

All fifty states have laws requiring teachers to report all suspected cases. Indicators of physical and sexual abuse and neglect appear in **Highlight 2.3**. Much information on this topic is available at the Child Welfare Information Gateway and Child Abuse Prevention web links.

Web Link
Child Abuse Prevention

Helping and Teaching Abused or Neglected Children Do these things when you are interacting with children who disclose something that indicates abuse or neglect:

- Find a private place to talk. If you are uncomfortable discussing this subject, arrange for the student to talk with someone else he trusts.
- Be calm. Control your feelings and listen carefully to what the child is saying.
- Believe the child. The child may have tried to tell others who wouldn't listen and now is in special need of your trust.
- Make it clear that the child is not at fault. However, be careful not to make negative statements about possible perpetrators.
- Be supportive. Assure the child that she is doing the right thing by disclosing this information. Let the student tell you the story in whatever manner is most comfortable.
- Respect the child's privacy. Let him know that you won't tell other teachers or students about the abuse. However, explain that you are required to report the abuse to the proper authorities.
- Be truthful. These children need to learn to trust adults again. Explain as much as you know about what action will be taken and what is likely to happen. Assure the student of your support and assistance throughout the process, and follow through on the assurance.
- Make an immediate report. Notify the proper authorities for the sake of the child and to fulfill your legal responsibilities.
- Be a continuing advocate. The child will need support after a report has been made. Do your best to quell rumors and gossip. Provide a shoulder for the child to lean on. Listen to what she has to say. You may need to advocate that the child receives professional counseling. (Gootman, 1993; Wolverton, 1988)

HIGHLIGHT 2.3
Indicators That Children May Be Abused or Neglected

- Appear to be different from others in physical and emotional makeup.
- Parents describe them as different or bad.
- Child is afraid of parent(s).
- May have bruises, welts, sores, or other skin injuries that seem untreated.
- Receive inappropriate food, nutrition, and/or medication.
- Receive inadequate supervision.

- Child is chronically unclean.
- Exhibit extreme behavior (e.g., often cry/never cry or aggressive/passive).
- Child is wary of physical contact, especially with adults.
- Exhibit a sudden change in behavior.
- Have learning problem that can't be diagnosed.
- Are habitually truant/late to school, may have prolonged absences due to injury.

- Often tired and may fall asleep in the classroom.
- Often dressed inappropriately to cover scars and bruises on arms and legs.
- Isolated from persons outside the home.

For more information go to the Child Abuse Prevention Network website.

AT-RISK CHILDREN

If students in your classroom are affected by circumstances that can torment childhood they are at substantial risk of school failure and dropping out. Some of these circumstances, we already know, are poverty, lack of supervision, and abuse and neglect. Common characteristics of children **at-risk** include

- being raised in a low-income home.
- living in a single-parent home, with limited human and financial resources.
- being unsupervised for long periods of time.
- having parents with little education.
- having a disability.
- having poor language skills.
- having siblings who dropped out of school.
- frequently being tardy and having poor school attendance.
- engaging in "self-handicapping" behaviors such as goofing-off, procrastinating, or acting out.
- performing poorly in school.
- having repeated a grade.
- not valuing school nor expecting to graduate.
- moving often.

One or more of these factors affect almost half of our students (Kominski, Jamieson, & Martinez, 2001).

Case 2.3 describes a study of Aaron, a child at risk. What are some of the factors placing him at risk?

Minorities are more often affected by risk factors. For example, African-Americans are twice as likely as whites to come from low-income and single-parent families. Hispanics are much more likely than whites to have limited English proficiency (LEP) and to have parents who did not complete secondary school.

Werner and Smith (1994) traced 200 high-risk Hawaiian children into adulthood. These born-into-poverty children were exposed to three risk factors: health problems at birth, parents without secondary education, and family histories of alcoholism or mental illness. Werner and Smith found that about two-thirds of

Aaron: A Child at Risk

Aaron Allen is an 11-year-old boy in the sixth grade. He has a small and slender build for this grade level. He comes to school well groomed and usually well dressed.

Aaron lives with his mother in a low-income area. They live in a little three-room house and receive public assistance. Aaron is an only child, and his parents are divorced. Mrs. Allen is willing to talk about Aaron. She appears to care very much about him, but admits she is losing control over him. She took a babysitting job this last summer for extra money.

Mr. Allen is in prison and has been out of the home since Aaron was six years old. This means that Aaron has been without a male figure in the home. As a result, he became very close to a 24-year-old uncle. This uncle did not work; he lived with his mother and received whatever he wanted. Constantly in trouble, the uncle was a very bad influence on the boy. Aaron's uncle was killed in a bar shooting last year. The tragedy left Aaron with no male figure to relate to at all.

Aaron gets whatever he wants at home and goes wherever he pleases. He rides his bicycle most places, but if his destination is too far, he takes a bus. He associates with older children, and most of his close friends attend the junior high school, which is two blocks from the elementary school and one block from his house. Aaron is fairly well accepted by his peers. He has no juvenile record, but the police have talked to him and warned him for various actions. Mrs. Allen explains that he was caught stealing several times and was reported at the scene of a fire. When there is a problem, Mrs. Allen says she gets her son out of trouble, talks to him, and hopes he won't do it again. She explains that she threatens him, saying if he doesn't behave, "he will be taken away to a detention home in hopes that it will scare him and he will straighten up."

The information in Aaron's cumulative school folder states that he has an average IQ, but his performance is very much below the grade-level standards. He reads at a third-grade level. Aaron seems disinterested in school, with a definite "I don't care about school" attitude. He has stated many times that he does not like school and that he would not come if he did not have to. His record shows increasingly poor attendance. When he loses interest, he becomes a problem for his teachers. He continually disrupts the class and is often sent to the office. So far, this does not seem to have improved his behavior.

Recently Aaron's behavior has gotten worse. He could not care less about school or what happens to him. When his mother was contacted, she said she felt helpless and had more or less given up. For the past five to six weeks, the regular teacher has been ill, and the room has had six different substitutes. This has affected all the students in the room, but Aaron is in trouble more than usual because the substitutes will not tolerate any behavior problems. School, with the room in such turmoil, presents a real problem for Aaron.

For more information visit the Helping America's Youth web site.

Source: Barbara Dahmke, Grandview Heights Middle School, Columbus, Ohio.

INVESTIGATING AND SOLVING THE CASE

1. What factors described in this chapter seem to put Aaron at risk?
2. Create a plan that Aaron's teacher and school could follow that might have a positive impact on Aaron's academic learning and satisfaction.

these high-risk children had serious learning or behavioral problems by age 10, or delinquency records, mental health problems, or an unplanned pregnancy by their eighteenth birthday. However, they found delinquent children living with both parents were significantly less likely to become adult criminals. Relatedly, they discovered that those who recovered from mental health problems were twice as likely to have had two parents at home during their adolescent years. Although circumstances alter individual cases, it appears that family economic well-being and intactness are two factors having a considerable impact on K–12 student learning and social adjustment.

Fortunately, a number of at-risk children turn out all right. Werner and Smith report that one of every three such students in their study developed into competent, confident, caring adults by the time they were 18. Such children are termed resilient.

2.17 How do you think you might feel or behave when you discover a child may be "at risk"?

Web Link
Helping America's Youth

Working With Children At-risk of School Failure Children who do not keep up academically (or socially) mostly have been either retained in grade, given special education labels, put in homogenous classes with similarly challenged kids, and/or taught using such instructional alternatives as mastery learning and direct instruction described in Chapters 4 and 8 respectively. Although these placements and treatments have selective, positive outcomes, additional measures are urged including:

- having confidence in your ability to help them learn
- expecting that they can and will learn
- accepting them as they are and treating their backgrounds and experiences as assets rather than liabilities
- using better motivational techniques (see Chapter 5)
- assisting them in establishing reachable, specific goals and in charting their progress
- helping them reach those goals; making sure they see the link between their success and their effort
- developing their higher-order thinking skill (see Chapter 6)
- employing meaningful learning (see Chapter 4) and
- using a greater variety of instructional alternatives (see Chapters 7 and 8). (Alderman 2007, North Central Regional Educational Laboratory 1996)

Web Link
North Central Regional
Education Library

Much more on this topic can be found at the North Central Regional Educational Laboratory OLC Web Link.

CHILDREN WITH INCARCERATED PARENTS

> Every hand went up when a former prison warden visited a Baltimore elementary school classroom and asked, "How many of you know a family member who is in prison?" He got the same response when he asked the children if they had ever been inside prison for a visit (Rodricks, 2008). On any given day, more than 1.5 million children have a parent behind bars. In nine out of ten cases the child is Black. (Bouchet 2008)

Beginning in the Seventies, America began a "tough on crime" era that continues unabated today. As a consequence, presently one of every 99 Americans is behind bars and this country is referred to as the "incarceration nation." Furthermore, there are six times as many more adults on probation. Over half of those incarcerated and paroled have a child under 18 whose family may struggle, among other things, with poverty, domestic violence, and inadequate housing and education. Some of the children are particularly vulnerable to school performance problems, shame, stigmatization and maltreatment. As such, they are considered an at-risk group. A variety of programs are in place both at correctional settings and in communities that attempt to help. They include parent education, improving child contact with incarcerated parents and improving child visitation at prisons. Unfortunately, the larger problems these families and children face in the community and at school are not well-addressed (Phillips & Gleeson, 2007).

What are some visible effects of having parents in prison? Children whose fathers were in jail have a higher degree of depression symptoms and their teachers report they act out more (Wilbur et al., 2007). They are five to six times more likely to become incarcerated themselves (Oregon Department of Corrections, 2003). As teachers, we need to identify these kids and do whatever we can to help them succeed.

RESILIENT CHILDREN

Resilient children are those who overcome adverse circumstances in their lives and do better in school than one might expect (see "Matthew" Case 2.4).

Matthew Cardinale was a child at risk. Fortunately, he was a resilient one. Recently he graduated from Tulane University and will enroll at University of California–Irvine to pursue a master's degree in sociology.

Who would have thought? At fourteen years of age he lived in a homeless shelter until he was turned out. Then he slept in a field and lived behind a supermarket. During those high school years, he took three public buses in order to get to school.

On several occasions he thought about dropping out since the school was "not designed for people in crisis." He says, "A bus ticket and a more supportive principal would have helped."

How could such a child become an honor student and earn the rank of Eagle Scout? Fortunately, Matthew saw "learning as liberating and empowering." He says of himself, "[Fortunately], I had a stronger educational background [than certain homeless teens] so I had different ideas of what is possible."

Source: Vail (2003).

INVESTIGATING AND SOLVING THE CASE

1. What factors seem to explain Matthew's resiliency?
2. Create a plan that you might follow to help students become more resilient.

What are Resilient Children Like?   When these children are younger, their parents describe them as having been healthier, affectionate, and active. They had good physical and language skills and were able to help themselves. In their teens they have a greater feeling of efficacy or control over their lives, are goal and achievement oriented, and have good self-esteem. Their families tend to have fewer conflicts.

In school they are satisfied, attentive, and organized; they feel support from teachers and friends, are involved in activities, assume leadership, experience few conflicts with other students, and perceive their teachers as having high expectations for them. Resilient children also display feelings of efficacy, self-esteem, and motivation to achieve, and they spend time reading and doing homework. They seem to do better than their non-resilient counterparts when teachers teach the class as a whole and do most of the talking and directing. (That is not to mean this is a better way to teach them.)

What Interferes with Resiliency?   Teachers suggest that factors contributing to low resiliency include lack of parental involvement and low student motivation and self-esteem. Some teachers are aware that they also contribute by how they teach and behave toward such children.

What Can Be Done to Increase Resiliency?   In part, the answer lies in better teaching. At-risk students are more likely to become resilient when teachers provide explanations, encourage student thinking and responses, show students how to learn, encourage success, and are caring. Furthermore, we need to provide positive classrooms where there is good cohesion among the kids and loads of teacher support. Schools can help kids attain greater resiliency by forging alliances with the family, community organizations, and businesses. Resiliency also can be increased by improving factors in a child's life: reduce vulnerability and exposure to risks, reduce stress, improve self-efficacy and self-esteem, create new opportunities, and increase resources by mobilizing good sources of support (Waxman, Gray, Padron, 2003).

2.18   If you have known a resilient child, what may have accounted for his or her resiliency?

Children of Immigrants Seem Especially Resilient   Some kids who overcome great odds and succeed in school are Asian–Vietnamese, Laotian, and Chinese (Caplan, Choy, & Whitmore, 1991). Given that they often attend low SES schools how is this possible? The incongruity is attributed to **family culture**. Being Asian seems to be a better predictor of academic success than being rich, having an intact family, or any other factors. Why? Among other things, Asian families, typically do not accept low grades. Asian parents do not accept grades lower than A- while white parents will accept B- and African-American parents C- (Thernstrom & Thernstrom, 2003). Immigrants with a low SES but with strong cultural and family traditions and carrying the burden of limited English proficiency seem to engender in their children the attitude that success in education and life comes from hard work rather than luck or circumstances of birth. (See Spotlight 2.4.) This finding and the similar one reported in a previous section "Parental Characteristics" support each other. A prominent factor in a child's school success seems to be parental expectations.

HURRIED AND OVERSCHEDULED CHILDREN

Hurried Children   Child advocates feel that children should be allowed to be children, that they should not be **hurried** into school and faced with formal learning requirements at very young ages. Elkind (2001) and Postman (1994) are among those who decry the shortening and even disappearance of home-based childhood in favor of early schooling. Among the factors that contribute to rushing children through childhood are working parents, television, and growing materialism. Working parents simply have less time to spend with their offspring, and the time they do share is often marred by the stress and exhaustion of the adults' lives.

Of course, television has its good and bad aspects, and those who study child development continue to debate its impact on childhood behavior. However, it is well known that children, as well as adults, imitate what they see. And what they often see is distorted teenage and adult conduct that exaggerates violence, cruelty, and sexual behavior. It has been said that television reveals all adult secrets that young children formerly could not easily discover. As a consequence, young children, who naturally try to imitate adult behavior, may be led into recreating acts of violence and sexual intimacy. Fortunately, there are efforts (although not well supported) to offer more television programming options that match children's normal developmental needs and interests.

Materialism is the doctrine that comfort, pleasure, and wealth are the highest goals and values one can aspire to. Society is deluged by reminders of materialistic needs, including better jobs, vacations, houses, cars, and entertainment. Parents who buy into materialism are more likely to expect their children to be achievers in all things so they, too, will obtain "the good life." Such children can be constantly on the run, participating in a variety of activities that may be undertaken more as means to an end (achieving) than as ends in themselves (fun). Thus, to some extent, children are hurried because adults are, too. However, child advocates like Elkind (2001) warn that we are so overvaluing adulthood and undervaluing childhood that adult pressures are harming children (see **Highlight 2.4**).

Overscheduled Children   Some studies paint a different picture and conclude that over-scheduling children mostly is a myth (Mahoney, Harris, & Eccles, 2008). Kids say that they engage in organized activities for a number of reasons, not just because they are encouraged by parents. Furthermore, only 60 percent participate in out-of-school activity and less than one in ten of them can be considered over-scheduled. Those who do participate do so, on average, less than ten hours per week. Furthermore, participation in well-run organized activities produces

"That class ought to come with a warning: 'May cause drowsiness.'"

2.19   How was your childhood different from those of children you may teach?

Twenty years ago, I didn't see children in my therapy practice who resembled burnt-out, career-driven, Type A adults. I didn't see kids with chronic stress-related headaches, stomach aches, and free-floating anxiety. I do now. Lots of them! Little kids. Big kids. Kindergartners with stress headaches because they're not learning to read fast enough (even though developmentally they're doing just fine). Little girls who are afraid to tell their parents that they don't want to spend four hours a day practicing ice skating or gymnastics. Ninth graders who tell me they have to play competitive league basketball all summer or else their high school coach will think they're not serious about making next year's team. Parents of a fourth grader asking me if I think their daughter has the "right stuff" for an Ivy League college. FOURTH GRADE!!!

I was "allowed" to have a childhood. I played thousands of hours of sports, not supervised or controlled by adults. We worked out the "rules" of the games we played. We settled (most) arguments peacefully. We developed skills at our own pace. Everyone played. No one was denied playing time because they weren't "good."

My friends and I weren't pressured to be the best at everything, faster than everyone else. We hung out. We goofed around. We got in trouble. We got scared. We did our jobs. We were kids. . . .

So when you see your kid "doing nothing," whether she's sitting on the front steps, seeming to stare into space, or making a space colony under the dining room table, or rereading a comic book for the 100th time, let her be. She's just taking a little time out of her busy day to have a childhood.

Source: Kendrick (n.d.).

---

positive results such as skill building, the formation of friendships, higher self-esteem, higher rates of school completion, and improvement in some school subjects. However, over-participation (twenty hours a week or more or participation in five or more activities) can have negative effects.

Studies of at-risk children show that lack of participation in organized out-of-school activities can contribute to such things as poor academic performance, obesity, dropout, and crime.

DISENGAGED CHILDREN

In a study of high school students in California and Wisconsin, 40 percent say they are **disengaged** or off-task—bored and just going through the motions in school. Boredom can result from many things, including feelings of inadequacy (Reim, 1997). Signs of boredom in school include reading material unrelated to class, daydreaming, doing work for other classes, and talking with peers (Plucker & Omdal, 1997). Disengaged students report that friends influence school performance and drug use more substantially than parents' positive practices at home. However, researchers find that students who come from homes where parents are firm, loving, and respectful are more likely to be engaged in school learning.

Besides taking in the potentially negative influence of friends, disengaged students are often busy with nonacademic pursuits. Two-thirds of teens work: half more than 15 hours per week. When not working, teens spend 20–25 hours weekly with friends (or texting them) (Steinberg, Brown, & Dornbusch, 1996).

2.20 How would you motivate a disengaged student to learn?

Helping and Teaching Disengaged/Bored Students   To increase the feeling of belonging and to increase engagement these suggestions are offered.

- Involve students in lots of classroom interaction (teacher to student and student to student dialogue) and activities that keep them absorbed in the lesson.

- Use higher-order questions to stir student interest; for example, "Why do you suppose President Obama was elected?" (For information on good questioning see Chapter 11.)
- Involve students in figuring things out for themselves and problem solving through use of Discovery Learning and Constuctivist Learning (Chapter 8).
- Have students work together and help one another as in Cooperative Learning (Chapter 8).
- Discuss important aspects of the lesson.
- Relate the material to be learned to student interests and try to show the application of what is being learned.
- Allow students to be involved in at least some decisions that affect them (e.g. assignment deadlines). Provide options.
- Emphasize and reward understanding, enjoyment, and effort.
- Do not talk too much; but be enthusiastic about what you want them to learn.
- Help rather than shame kids having difficulty and make it clear that everyone makes mistakes.
- Explain, explain, explain and correct misunderstandings.
- Maintain a sense of humor. (Cero, Cauley, & Chafin, 2003; Turner et al., 2002.)

ALIENATED CHILDREN

2.21 Have you known an alienated child? How would you help such kids?

The human need for acceptance, belonging, and recognition is exceptionally strong. Thus, positive relationships with significant others in a child's life are necessary for them to succeed in school and social settings. High quality interpersonal relationships contribute to academic motivation, engagement, and achievement (Martin & Dowson, 2009 p. 351). Unfortunately, some children are unattached, disconnected, even alienated at home and/or in school. They do not feel close to parents, caregivers, teachers, or peers. Characteristics of these kids may include fear of intimacy, feelings of being unloved and unlovable, lack of trust (see "Trust" in Chapter 12) and perceptions of unworthiness. Some of these kids gravitate toward gangs where they *are* accepted. Some try to become invisible and may be subjected to bullying (see "Bullying" in Chapter 12). Others resort to acting out and, in the extreme, to violence as was the case at Columbine. (To find out more about "social rejection" see that entry in *Wikipedia*.) Consequently, you are urged to create the kind of inviting, trusting, caring classroom (see "Planning the Psychological Environment" in Chapter 12). Your classroom needs to be a community in which everyone cares for everyone. Sociometry is often used by teachers to help determine which kids are alienated. More about that in Chapter 5. To find out how to work toward "connecting" your students go to the School Connectedness and Meaningful Student Participation website on the OLC.

Try Activity 2.5

Web Link
School Connectedness and Meaningful Student Participation

GENERATION M KIDS

This generation of children easily can be called the *Media Generation* since they devote more than a quarter of each day to it in some form. Young people mostly, in order, watch TV, listen to music, CDs, tapes, and MP3s, use computers, go online, read magazines and books, play video games, watch videos and DVDs, play handheld video games, read newspapers, watch prerecorded TV, and go to movies. Furthermore, when they leave home, they take portable media with them.

Over a week, that is more than the equivalent of a full-time job. And this doesn't take into account that some kids are multitasking, that is, using more than one form of media at once. By comparison, they spend about two hours hanging out with parents, an hour and a half in physical activity, 50 minutes with homework, and one-half hour on chores.

We also know that:

- kids who spend the most time using media are also those whose lives are most filled with family, friends, sports, and so forth.
- older teens spend more time with music and the computer.
- boys spend twice as much time with video games; girls listen to music more.
- African-American kids spend far more time than whites watching TV, movies, and playing video games.
- over half say their families have no rules about TV watching.
- youngsters who are most avid users of computers and video games also spend more time watching TV.
- about one-quarter of kids use more than one form of media at the same time.
- Generation M feels mostly happy and adjusted. However, those who are least content or get lower grades spend more time with video games and less time reading.
- Access to and frequent use of the Internet is common across each major racial and socioeconomic group. However, lower SES kids are much less likely to have Internet access (Roberts, Foehr, & Rideout, 2005).

Helping and Teaching Generation M Children Suggestions for effectively working with Gen M kids include these from Abrams (n.d.) and Roberts, Foehr, & Rideout, 2005:

- Listen to and learn from them,
- Become familiar with digital media and sources they use such as My Space, Facebook, DIGG, Yahoo, You Witness News, and Second Life,
- Attend workshops and courses on media and learn multimedia production,
- Learn about and perhaps use Web 2.0 for communication and opinion sharing (such as blogs, wikis, podcasting, folksonomies, social networking),
- Encourage "interactivity," creativity, productivity,
- Try to make production tools such as cameras available, and
- Include media projects when planning units or work and lessons and use real world problems as suitable.

See "Using Technology in Teaching" in Chapter 7.

ARE TODAY'S CHILDREN LESS TEACHABLE?

Given the attention to economically disadvantaged, inadequately supervised, abused, neglected, at-risk, and hurried children, we might assume that today's kids are less teachable. But are they? Opinions certainly differ. Talk with teachers and you get mostly a "yes" response. Greene and Forster (2004) say "no." They define *teachability* as the personal advantages and disadvantages that kids bring to school and look at 16 factors believed to affect it. Those factors are organized into six categories as follows:

1. *Readiness for school:* preschool enrollment (a measure of preparation for school), parent education, and native language in the home.
2. *Economics:* the material well-being of children measured by family income.
3. *Community:* the presence of helpful or harmful social influences in children's lives.
4. *Health:* the physical and mental well-being of students.
5. *Race:* the racial composition of the student population.
6. *Family:* family structure that imposes educational challenges.

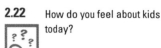

2.22 How do you feel about kids today?

Their "teachability study" looked to see if there were changes in these factors over a 30-year period. Findings include that preschool enrollment has grown and health and economic security have improved, offsetting broken homes and lack of English in the home. The conclusion is that, on average, students are somewhat more teachable now. That does not mean things are better, but rather they are no worse. The most teachable children are located in the Dakotas, Maine, New Hampshire, and Vermont. Hardest to teach kids are in Louisiana, Texas, Arizona, New Mexico, and the District of Columbia.

Some warn this study has methodological shortcomings and a political agenda as well—notably that it can be used to suggest today's students are not contributing to school or teacher failures. What do you think?

USING THE "WHOLE CHILD APPROACH" TO HELP KIDS LEARN

To meet the challenges of teaching in a changing society, several professional organizations, led by the Association for Supervision and Curriculum Development (ASCD), have embarked on a campaign to spread the word that each learner needs to be *healthy, safe, engaged in learning, supported by caring adults, and academically challenged*. Here is the framework adapted from http://www.wholechildeducation. org/about/.

Each student should enter school *healthy* and learn about and practice a healthy lifestyle For students to learn at high levels they must be healthy. Students who are sick, who come to school hungry, who can't breathe because of asthma, who have poor vision, who can't concentrate because of pervasive toothaches or depression, or who are excessively obese are unlikely to do well academically. To ensure that all students are healthy, ASCD recommends:

- A school health advisory council made up of students, family, community, and business members
- Routine screening for immunizations, vision, hearing, dental, and orthopedic concerns
- PE and health classes emphasizing lifetime healthy behaviors
- Healthy food choices at school

Each student should be provided an intellectually challenging environment that is physically and emotionally *safe* For students to learn at high levels they must feel safe and secure. Students who are fearful, bullied, distracted by fights and other disruptive behavior are unlikely to do well academically. To ensure that all students are safe, ASCD recommends:

- Students, school staff, and family members establish and maintain behavioral expectations, rules, and routines
- Families are welcomed by school staff as partners in their children's education

Each student should be actively *engaged* in learning and connected to the school and community For students to learn at high levels, they must be motivated to learn and be interested in their studies. Students who are bored by their classes, who don't feel motivated to achieve and who don't see the connection between what they're learning in school and their real-world goals are unlikely to do well academically. To ensure that all students are adequately engaged ASCD recommends:

- Students participate in a wide array of extracurricular activities
- Schools provide opportunities for community-based apprenticeships, internships, or projects
- Teachers use active learning strategies such as cooperative learning and project-based learning

**Each student should have access to personalized learning and be *supported* by quali-
fied, caring adults**   For students to learn at high levels, they must feel supported by
caring, qualified adults. Students who don't have access to adult role models, advi-
sors, mentors, counselors, or teachers who understand their social and emotional
development are unlikely to do well academically. To ensure that all students are
adequately supported, ASCD recommends:

2.23   How do you feel about the
"whole child approach"?

- Every student has an adult advisor or mentor
- Students have access to school counselors or other student support systems

**Each graduate should be *challenged* by a well-balanced curriculum and prepared for
further study, college, or employment**   For students to learn at high levels, they must
have access to a curriculum that challenges and inspires them. Students who spend
most of their day being lectured and drilled in reading and math only, and who
don't have access to courses in the arts, music, social studies, civics, and other
broadening courses, are less likely to do well in school and life.

To ensure that all students are academically challenged by a well-balanced curriculum, ASCD recommends:

- Schools provide a well-rounded curriculum for all students
- Students have access to rigorous programs in arts, foreign languages, and social
  studies
- Schools maintain flexible graduation requirements

ASCD has a *Facebook* site on the Whole Child approach *http://www.facebook.com/
pages/Whole-Child/20386944150*

2.24   How have your teachers
made your school
environment healthier, safer,
more engaging, supportive,
or challenging? What might
you do?

The Changing School

For the past several decades, America has been trying to cope with an ever-increasing
number of scientific, economic, and **educational challenges.** Several are depicted in
Figure 2.1.

Whatever the challenge or its source, Americans expect their public schools to
"fix whatever is broken." For the most part, America's schools have accepted these
challenges and, as a consequence, have transformed themselves in a number of
ways. Following is a brief description of selected challenges that our schools have
accepted and how they have changed to meet them.

FIGURE 2.1   External and Internal Challenges That Have Changed Schools

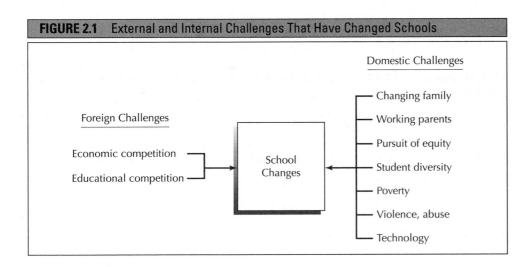

Challenge 1—To Foster Equity   The pursuit of equity is transforming both our society and its schools. You have matured during a period when the concept of equal treatment and opportunity has blossomed. You are probably already familiar with some of the ways this concept has affected education. For example, it has triggered the desegregation of schools and classrooms, the elimination of most same-sex schools, the inclusion of special-needs students in regular classrooms, the development of special programs for children with no or limited English proficiency, the fostering of multiethnic education, and so forth. This equity challenge pervades each and every day of a teacher's life. It requires that you be proactive and vigilant to ensure that all students have equal opportunity and receive equal treatment.

Challenge 2—To Achieve World-Class Academic Standards   America is having a more difficult time providing its citizenry with the level of living they have become used to. America's declining position within this fierce global economic competition has been attributed in part to improved education abroad and declining education at home. Analysts frequently cite comparative student test scores that seem to show that American students are not achieving at a world-class level. Schools are attempting to answer this challenge by introducing new, more rigorous curricula, by instituting the practices of our most effective schools into those with poor track records, and by utilizing more promising teaching practices. Further, you will find that students are taking many more tests in an effort to monitor their progress better.

Challenge 3—To Support Families   Throughout history, the family was expected to support the school. More recently, the school is being asked to support the family. Among other things, schools are asked to provide before- and after-school child care. Some schools begin their day before sunrise and conclude it after sunset. In addition, it is more difficult to communicate with working parents, and fewer are available as school volunteers than before. On average, children are less likely to receive the nurturing they need, so you must be prepared to listen to them and to help them in nonacademic ways.

Challenge 4—To Celebrate Diversity   Given the changing demography of America, you will find students are more diverse. Since a section on the diversity of students follows, at this point it is sufficient to say that schools are responding to this diversity not only by accepting it but also by promoting its value and richness.

2.25   How important are the five challenges schools face? Which of these challenges might be most difficult for you?

2.26   Some would argue that schools cannot be all things to all people, that they are changing too much in order to meet such challenges. How do you feel? What do you think the role of the school should be?

Challenge 5—To Utilize Technology   As society has become increasingly dependent on technology, schools are challenged to use that technology and to foster its use among students. Albeit slowly, schools have accepted the challenge. Some school districts conduct their own television broadcasts, teach broadcasting, and produce programs. Likewise, many schools have computer laboratories as well as computers in classrooms. Most schools, however, still grapple with the problem of how to help students become discriminating television consumers and sophisticated rather than merely game-playing computer users.

As a future teacher, you must keep abreast of these and other challenges facing schools today. Furthermore, you must work to respond appropriately to them. You can do so by getting behind school district and school building response efforts and, perhaps more importantly, by conducting your classrooms accordingly. More specifically, as you plan your curriculum and instruction, you must always be alert for opportunities to foster equity, celebrate diversity, provide for children's special needs, foster a high level of learning, utilize technology, and support your students' families and communities.

Some Final Thoughts

As teachers, we must know as much as possible about children collectively and about school-age children in particular if teaching is deserving of the label "helping profession." So many children are experiencing poverty that, on average, one of every five students is likely to be ill-nourished and in poor health, unprepared to learn, and, in some cases, homeless. Consequently, you must take your students' physical, mental, and emotional condition into account and, when necessary, be prepared to access child services supplied by the school district and community. Since poor children and their families are more poorly represented politically, teachers and schools must be visible, loud, and continuous in their support.

Unfortunately since some children have inadequate supervision, you must be prepared to have students who come to school ill, tardy, anxious, or lonely. Without unduly infringing upon family situations, you may need to keep track of children involved in self-care. Make sure they are not unnecessarily at risk due to their self-care arrangements and that they are knowledgeable about what to do in problem or emergency situations. Also, given the increased incidence of child abuse and neglect, you will need to watch for telltale signs and report suspected cases in accordance with school policy. Monitor the stressed-out children of high-pressure parents who want their children to hurry up and "make it" as well. Finally, try to find ways to engage the disengaged.

CHAPTER SUMMARY

- To be an effective teacher you need to be aware of and take into account the distinguishing characteristics of our changing society. Among those characteristics are a growing minority population; a lower percentage of children; an increasing variety of family styles; recognition that families influence school learning; and an awareness that too many children live in poverty, lack adequate supervision, and are neglected, abused, hurried, or disengaged from school and learning.

- America's minority population is fast growing. By 2025 it is expected that the percentage of whites will decline further, Hispanics will outnumber African-Americans and the percentage of Asian-Americans will close in on 10 percent. Over one-third of Americans will be nonwhite. Population changes create challenges for teachers who must educate a more ethnically and racially diverse student body, many of whom will have limited English proficiency.

- American families represent a variety of types including traditional, remarried, blended, and single-adoptive. Each presents different challenges to family members as they strive to meet family functions such as nurturance, caring, intimacy, cultural transmission, and economic support.

- America's families are also changing. Parents start families later in life, and families are smaller, less stable, and increasingly likely to be headed by one parent.

- A strong relationship exists among family background, income, educational level of parents, and achievement in school. Children from low-income, single-parent homes are more likely to be lower achievers and develop school problems. Children with multiple at-risk factors are most likely to have serious learning and/or behavioral problems. Additionally, if they live in single-parent homes, they are more likely to become involved in crime and less likely to recover from mental health problems.

- Certain family factors seem to positively influence student learning: parent attention, parent presence, high parental expectations, parent socioeconomic status, and parent involvement in school.

SUPPLEMENTAL RESOURCES
Go to the text's Online Learning Center at www.mhhe.com/cruickshank6e to access the chapter's **study tools** including web links, practice for Praxis™ case studies, and video clips.

- More children, particularly minority youth, are growing up in poverty; more lack parental supervision; more are reported abused and neglected; and more are being hurried to grow up.
- Among the challenges you will face are to foster equity in your classroom, provide children with a world-class education, support families, celebrate diversity, and utilize technology.

KEY TERMS

Population change, 23

Family trends, 25

Family influence, 26

Achievement gap, 30

Poor children, 35

Latchkey children, 37

Abused children, 38

At-risk children, 40

Resilient children, 42

Family culture, 44

Hurried children, 44

Disengaged children, 45

Educational challenges, 49

ISSUES AND PROBLEMS FOR DISCUSSION

ISSUES Here are some issues for you to debate.

1. To what extent do you think teachers can or should be knowledgeable about societal changes and their impact on children?
2. As a teacher which of these factors do you believe has the most critical impact on children and learning: society, family, wealth, schooling and teaching?
3. What kind of family do you think is best for children?
4. How can schools help families have a more positive impact on their children's education?
5. To what extent should schools and teachers assume any of the normal family functions such as nurturance, caring, or intimacy?
6. How can schools and teachers offset or overcome the effects of poverty, lack of home supervision, child neglect or abuse, low parental and child expectations toward education, gender stereotyping, crass materialism, or other negative factors?
7. How involved should teachers get when students are at risk?

PROBLEMS The following problems have been shared with us by teachers. How might they be resolved?

Problem 1: When school started today, one of the children came into the room in tears. She was so poorly dressed that she was just about frozen. She wore no gloves or boots and had a very thin scarf on her head. Her hands, ears, and feet were very cold. She came from a home without heat.

Problem 2: Today got off to a frustrating start. Many children had runny noses, red eyes, and seemed drowsy. Some children had no breakfast, since their parents are still out or are asleep when they leave home.

Problem 3: When the lesson began, many children were unable to provide a paper and pencil, since it was late in the month and their parents' welfare money had run out.

Problem 4: A student from a migrant family is having trouble with subtraction facts. The other students make fun of him. I think the student considers this a racial thing, and he has become resentful and defensive.

Problem 5: There are several non-English-speaking children in class. They are well-behaved but need an inordinate amount of individual attention that I don't have the time to provide.

Problem 6: One boy refuses to leave the room, fearful that boys from another school are waiting to kill him. He says the problem is the result of an incident that occurred over the weekend.

Problem 7: A boy came into the room in obvious pain with strips of cloth wrapped around his right hand. He says that his mother's boyfriend held his hand on a toaster.

Problem 8: One of the girls in gym class is very upset that she cannot participate in square dancing. Her parents do not condone any kind of dancing.

THEORY INTO ACTION: ACTIVITIES FOR PRACTICE AND YOUR PORTFOLIO

ACTIVITY 2.1: Implications of Population, Family Diversity, and Family Circumstances for Teaching As you read this chapter make a list of things you have learned and their implications for classroom practice. For example:

Major Learning	Possible Implication(s)
1. Our population is increasingly diverse ethnically and racially.	1. I will need to be effective working with whites, Blacks, Hispanics, and Asians, so I will need to know how to interact with children of diverse cultural backgrounds.

ACTIVITY 2.2: Teaching in an Ever-Changing Society Prepare a paragraph or so on the topic "What I think it will be like to teach in a context filled with population and family diversity."

ACTIVITY 2.3: Preparation for Teaching in an Ever-Changing Society Prepare a paragraph or so on the topic "What I need to know and be able to do to teach in a context filled with diversity and how I can gain that knowledge and skill."

ACTIVITY 2.4: Obtain Teachers' Views about Teaching in a Changing Society Talk with classroom teachers about teaching in an ever-changing society. Ask them the following:

- Have you noticed any changes in the population of the school neighborhood?
- Have you noticed changes in the families of students?
- If so, how do you think these things are affecting learners?
- How and how well is the school meeting the challenges resulting from changes in population and family?

ACTIVITY 2.5: Choose one category of children with some risk factor such as "abused and neglected" and prepare a plan for what you will do for interventions to help them.

REFERENCES

A profile of American 8th graders. (1990). Washington, DC: U.S. Government Printing Office.

Abrams, A. (n.d.). *Understanding Generation M.* Online http://www.arnieabrams.net/handouts/Gen_M_handout.pdf

Alderman, M. K. (2007). *Motivating for achievement.* New York: Routledge.

Alexander, M. (2005, July 17). *Fatherless in America.* Access: www.Townhall.com

Alston, F. (2004, February 25), *Latch key children: About our kids.* New York: New York University Child Study Center.

Amato, P. (2005, Fall). Impact of family formation change on the cognitive, social, and emotional well-being of the next generation. *The Future of Children, 15,* 2. Access: www.futureofchildren.org

Ash, K. (2009, October 14). More children alone after school. Education Week, 29(7), 4.

Barton, P. (2003). *Parsing the achievement gap.* Princeton, NJ: Educational Testing Services. Access: www.ets.org/research/pic/parsing.pdf

Barton, P., & Coley, R. (2007). *America's smallest school.* Princeton, NJ. Educational Testing Service.

Becerra, H. (2008, July 16). Why do Asian students generally get higher marks than Latinos? *Los Angeles Times online edition.*

Berliner, D. (2005, August 2). Our impoverished view of educational reform. Presidential invited speech. Montreal: American Educational Research Association Meeting.

Berube, A. (2007, February 13). *Geography of U.S. Poverty: Testimony before the Ways and Means Subcommittee on Income Security and Family Support.* Washington, DC.

Biddle, B. (1997, September). Foolishness, dangerous nonsense, and real correlates of state differences in achievement. *Phi Delta Kappan 79(1),* 9–13.

Bolder Approach to Education. Retrieved from www.BOLDAPPROACH.ORG

Boo, K. (2006, February 6). Swamp nurse. *New Yorker, 81(46),* 54–65.

Bouchet, S. (2008, January). *Children and families with incarcerated parents.* Baltimore, MD: Annie E. Casey Foundation.

Bracey, G. (1995, March). The myth of school failure. Paper presented at the Association for Supervision and Curriculum Development Conference. San Francisco, CA.

Bracey, G. (2002, March). What students do in the summer. *Phi Delta Kappan, 83(7),* 497–498.

Breckenridge, T. (2003, December 7). Are Asian kids smarter than everyone else? *Cleveland Plain Dealer,* p. A12.

Brown, B. F. (1980, April). A study of the school needs of children from one-parent families. *Phi Delta Kappan, 62(8),* 537–540.

Carlisle, E., Stanley, L., & Kemple, K., (2006). Opening doors: Understanding school and family influences on family involvement. *Early Childhood Education Journal, 33* (3), 155–62.

Caplan, N., Choy, M. H., & Whitmore, J. K. (1991). *Children of the boat people: A study of educational success.* Ann Arbor: University of Michigan Press.

Center on Educational Policy (2006). *A public education primer.* Washington, DC: CDC. Access: www.cep-dc.org/pubs/publiceducationprimer/PublicEducationPrimer.pdf

Cero, J., Cauley, K., & Chafin, C. (2003, Winter). Student perspectives on their high school experience. *Adolescence, 38(152),* 705–724.

Chin, E., Young, J., & Floyd, B. (2004, February 9). *Placing beginning teachers in hard-to-staff schools.* Papers presented at the American Association of Colleges of Teacher Education, Chicago, IL.

Coontz, S. (2000). *The way we never were.* New York: Basic Books.

Dahmke, B. (n.d.). Aaron, a child at risk. (unpublished).

Dionne, E. (2001, February 10). 2-parent families are in comeback. *Columbus Dispatch,* p. A10.

Dowd, F. S. (1990). *Latchkey children in the library and community: Issues,* strategies, and programs. Phoenix, AZ: Oryx Press.

Duiguid, L. (2005, December 28). Addressing 0 will improve school performance. *Kansas City Star,* p. 24.

Dwyer, K., Richardson, J., Donley, K., Hansen, W., Sussman, S., Bronnon, D., Dent, C., Johnson, C., Flay, B. (1990, September). Characteristics of eighth-grade students who initiate self-care in elementary and junior high school. *Pediatrics, 86(3),* 448–454.

Eberstadt M. (2001 June–July). Home alone America. *Hoover Institution Policy Review, 102,* 1–10.

Education Week. (2004, September 21). Student mobility. *Education Week: Research Center online* http://www.edweek.org/rc/issues/student-mobility/

Elkind, D. (2001). *The hurried child: Growing up too fast too soon.* Cambridge, MA: Perseus.

Evans, G. (2004). The environment of childhood poverty. *American Psychologist, 59(2),* 77–92.

Ferguson, R. (2002). *Addressing racial disparities in high-achieving suburban schools.* Naperville, IL: North Central Regional Education Laboratory.

Fraser, A. (1989, Spring). The changing American family. *In Context, 21,* 2–7.

Gardner, M. (2007, January 3). After school struggle to juggle school and work. *Christian Science Monitor.* Access: www.csmonitor.com

Gootman, M. (1993). Reaching and teaching abused children. *Childhood Education, 70.* 20–23.

Greene, J., & Forster, G. (2004, September). *The teachability index: Can disadvantaged students learn?* New York: Manhattan Institute.

Haberman, M. (2004, May). Can star teachers create learning communities? *Educational Leadership, 61(8),* 52–56.

Hacker, A. (1982). Farewell to the family? *New York Review of Books, 29,* 37–45.

Hamburg, D. A. (1992). *The family crucible and healthy child development.* New York: Carnegie Corporation.

Hart, B., & Risley, T. (1999). *Meaningful differences.* Baltimore: Paul Brookes.

Hart, B., & Risley, T. (2003, Spring). The early catastrophe. *American Educator, 27*(1), 4–9.

Hofferth, S. L., and associates (1998). *Healthy environments, healthy children.* Ann Arbor, MI: Institute of Social Research, University of Michigan.

Holloway, J. (2004). How the community influences achievement. *Education Leadership (61)* 8, 89–90.

Hoy, W., Tarter, C., & Hoy, A. (2006, Fall). Academic optimism of schools: A force for student achievement. *American Educational Research Journal, 43*(3), 425–46.

Jacobson, L. (1998, November 18). Study tracks how children spend their time. *Education Week, 18*(12), 8.

Jencks, C., Smith, M., Aclond, H., Bane, M., Cohen, D., Gintis, H., Heyns, B., & Michelson, S. (1972). *Inequality: A reassessment of the effect of family and schooling in America.* New York: Basic Books.

Jencks, C., Smith, M., Aclond, H., Bane, M., Cohen, D., Gintis, H, Heyns, B. & Michelson, S. Inequality: A reassessment of the effect of family and schooling in America. In Grusky, D. (2005) *Social Stratification* (pp. 498–504). Philadelphia: Westview Press.

Jones, I., White, C., Aeby, V., & Benson, B. (1997). Attitude of early childhood teachers toward family and community involvement. *Early Education and Development, 8*(2), 155–163.

Kauffman, J. M. (2000). *Characteristics of emotional and behavioral disorders in children and youth.* Englewood Cliffs, NJ: Prentice Hall.

Kendrick, C. (n.d.). The hurried child. *Family Education.* Access: www.familyeducation.com/article/0,1120,1-1233,00.html

Kominski, R., Jamieson, A. & Martinez, G. (2001). At-risk conditions of U.S. school-age children. U. S. Bureau of the Census: Washington, DC.

Kozol, J. (1990, Winter-Spring). The new untouchables. *Newsweek* Special Issue, 48–49, 52–53.

Louv, R. (1990). *Childhood's Future.* Boston: Houghton Mifflin.

Mahoney, J., Harris, A. & Eccles, J. (2008, February). The over-scheduling myth. *Research-to-Results: Child Trends Brief.* Publication #2008–12. Washington, DC: Child Trends.

Martin, A., & Dowson, M. (2009, Spring). Interpersonal relationships, motivation, engagement, and achievement. *Review of Educational Research, 79*(1), 327–365.

Marzano, R. (2003). *What works in schools.* Alexandria, VA: Association for Supervision and Curriculum Development.

Masten, A. S., Best, K. M., & Garmezy, N. (1991). Resilience and development: Contributions from the study of children who overcome adversity. *Development and Psychopathology, 2,* 425–444.

McWhorter, J. (2001). *Losing the race.* New York: Harper Collins.

Metropolitan Life. (1992). *Ready or not: Grade level preparedness: Teachers' views on current issues in education.* New York: Metropolitan Life Insurance Co.

Metropolitan Life. (1998). *Survey of the American teacher.* New York: Metropolitan Life Insurance Co.

Metropolitan Life. (2004–2005). *Survey of the American teacher.* New York: Metropolitan Life Insurance Co.

Miles, J. (2003). Family influences on educational achievement. Doctoral dissertation. Boston College, 2003 *Dissertation Abstracts International,* A 65/02.

Molner, A. (Ed.) (2002, January). *School reform proposals: The research evidence: Section Seven: Parent-family involvement.* Tempe, AZ: Arizona State University, Educational Policy Research Unit.

Nieves, E. (2008, December 21). In tough times, the ranks of homeless students are rising. *Boston Globe.* Boston.com.

North Central Regional Educational Laboratory (1996). *Critical issue: Providing effective schooling for students at risk.* Retrieved from http://www.ncrel.org/sdrs/areas/issues/students/atrisk/at600.htm

Ogbu, J., & Davis, A. (2003). *Black American students in an affluent suburb.* Mahwah, NJ: Erlbaum.

Olson, L. (2000, September 7). Children of change. *Education Week, 20*(4), 31–41.

Oregon Department of Corrections. (2003). *Children of Incarcerated Parents Project.* Eugene, OR: The Department. Retrieved from http://egov.oregon.gov/DOC/PUBAFF/docs/oam/2003_childrens_project.pdf

Page, C. (2003, August 5). *Black parents have too little positive effect on teenagers. Columbus Dispatch,* p. A11.

Passel, J. & Cohn, D. (2008). *U.S. Population Projections: 2005–2050.* Washington, DC: Pew Research Center.

Patrikakou, E., & Weissberg, R. (1999, February 3). The seven P's of school-family partnerships. *Education Week, 18*(21), 34, 36.

Payne, R. (2008, April). Nine powerful practices. *Educational Leadership, 65*(7), 48–52.

Pearce, R. (2006, Spring). Effects of cultural and social structural factors on the achievement of White and Chinese American students at school transition points. *American Educational Research Journal, 43*(1), 75–101.

Phillips, S, & Gleeson, J. (2007, July). *What we know now that we didn't know about the criminal justice system's involvement in families with whom child welfare agencies have contact.* Chicago: University of Chicago Center for Social Policy and Research, Retrieved from http:/www.uic.edu/jaddams/college/

Plucker, J., & Omdal, S. (1997, June 18). Beyond boredom. *Education Week, 16*(38), 32.

Popenoe, D. (1993). American family decline. *Journal of Marriage and Family, 55*(3), 27–42.

Postman, N. (1994). *The disappearance of childhood.* London: Vintage Books.

Raspberry, W. (1993, January 14). Parents must instill kids with will to learn. *Columbus Dispatch/Forum,* p. 13A.

Raspberry, W. (2005, July 25). Why Black families are failing. *Washington Post,* p. A19.

Reim, S. (1997, April). An underachieving epidemic. *Educational Leadership, 34*(7), 18–22.

Resnick, M. (1997, September 10). Protecting adolescents from harm. *Journal of the American Medical Association, 278*(10), 823–832.

Roberts, D., Foehr, U., & Rideout, V. (2005). *Generation M: Media in the Lives of 8–18 Year-olds.* Washington, DC: Kaiser Foundation.

CHAPTER 2
Teaching in a Changing Society

Rodicks, D. (2008, June 1). Teachers endure major tests. *Baltimore Sun*. Retrived from http:/www .Baltimoresun.com

Rossi, R., & Ihejrika, M. (2005, October 16). Two kindergarten classes worlds apart. *Chicago Sun Times*, p. 13.

Rothstein, R. (2004). *Class and schools: Using social, economic, and educational reform to close the black-white achievement gap*. Washington, DC: Economic Policy Institute.

Rothstein, R. (2008, April). Whose problem is poverty? *Educational Leadership*, 65(7), 48–52

Ruiz, K. T. (2005, May 21). The secret homeless. *Inland Valley Daily Bulletin*, p. 1.

Rumberger, R. (2003). Student mobility and academic achievement. *ERIC Digests online* http://www.ericdigests .org/2003–2/mobility.html

Smith, K. (2000). *Who's minding the kids? Child care arrangements: Fall 1995*. Washington, DC: U.S. Census Bureau.

Sowell, T. (2003, February 28). *Pair of books bluntly expose 2 nimesises of U.S. education. Columbus Dispatch*, p. A15.

Steinberg, L., Brown, B., & Dornbusch, S. (1996). *Beyond the classroom: Why social reform has failed and what parents need to do*. New York: Simon and Schuster.

Suransky, V. (1997). *The erosion of childhood*. Chicago: University of Chicago Press.

Surin, S. (2005, Fall). Socioeconomic status and academic achievement. *Review of Educational Research*, 75(3), 417–53.

Thernstrom, A., & Thernstrom, S. (2003). *No Excuses: Closing the Racial Gap in Learning*. New York: Simon & Schuster.

Thorkildsen, R., & Stein, M. (1998, December). Is parent involvement related to student achievement? Research Bulletin. *News, Notes and Quotes: Newsletter of Phi Delta Kappa International, 43*(2), 17–20.

Traub, J. (2000, January 30). Schools can't save the urban poor. *Columbus Dispatch*, p. B1–2.

Turner, J., Midgley, C., Meyer, D., Gheen, M., Anderman, E., & Kang, Y. (2002). The classroom environment and student reports of avoidance strategies in mathematics. *Journal of Educational Psychology, 94*(1), 88–106.

Urban Institute. (2002). *Primary child care arrangements of employed parents*. Washington, DC: The Institute.

U.S. Census 2008. Access: www.census .gov/main/www/cen 2008.html

U.S. Department of Health, Education and Welfare. (1966). *Equality of educational opportunity. Summary report*. (The Coleman Report). Washington, DC: U.S. Government Printing Office.

Vail, K. (2003, June). Where the Heart Is. *American School Board Journal, 190* (6), 1–8.

Walberg, H., & Fowler, W. (1987, October). Expenditure and size efficiency of public school districts. *Educational Researcher, 16*, 5–13.

Warren, J. (2008). *One in 100: Behind bars in America*. Washington, DC: Pew Charitable Trusts.

Waxman, H., Gray, J., & Padron, Y. (2003). *Review of research on educational resilience*. Santa Cruz: University of California at Santa Cruz Center for Research on Education, Diversity and Excellence.

Weisman, J. (1990, September 19). Latchkey 8th graders likely to possess emotional risk factors, study discloses. *Education Week, 10*(3), 6.

Weitloft, G., Hjern, A., Hagland, B., & Rosen, M. (2003, January). Mortality, severe morbidity and injury in children living with single parents in Sweden. *The Lancet, 361*(9354), 289–295.

Werner, E. E., & Smith, R. S. (1994). *Overcoming the odds: High-risk children from birth to adulthood*. Ithaca, NY: Cornell University Press.

Wilbur, M., Marani, J., Appugliese, M., Woods, R., Seigal, J., Cabral, H., & Frank, D. (2007, August 31). Socio-emotional effects of fathers' incarceration on low-income, urban, school-aged children. *Pediatrics, 120*(3), 678–685. Retrieved from http://pediatrics .aappublications.org

Winfield, L. F. (1991, November). Resilience, schooling and development in African-American youth: A conceptual framework. *Education & Urban Society, 24*, 3–14.

Wingert, P., & Kantrowitz, B. (1990, Winter–Spring). The day care generation. *Newsweek* Special Issue, 86–92.

Wolverton. (1988). *Teaching the abused*. Washington, DC: ERIC Digest ED293680/

You and the system. (1990, April). *Teacher Magazine*, 7(1). 10.

Teaching Diverse Students

Student Diversity
- Socioeconomic Differences
- Cultural Differences
- Gender Differences
- Sexual Preference Differences
- Developmental Differences
- Personality Differences
- Learning Style Differences
- Learning Aptitude Differences
- Interest Differences
- Implications for Teachers

Some Final Thoughts

Conversation Starters

To what extent should teachers be responsible for meeting the needs of diverse learners?

On one side of the question are those who feel that teaching is demanding enough without modifying it to meet the needs of every child who brings a different configuration of culture, gender, ability, interests, and challenges into the classroom. There is not enough time to cover what needs to be taught let alone modify it or how it is taught to meet the needs of every student. Furthermore, supporters of this position believe that real life is not so accommodating and that kids need to learn to adjust, to assimilate.

On the other hand are advocates who believe children need individualized and personalized attention so that they may reach their fullest potential. They believe it is even easier to cover and have students learn the required course content if instruction is differentiated to meet the needs of diverse students. Re-teaching would be unnecessary. Failure would be lessened. Those holding this position claim that, in the end, the additional teacher commitment bears fruit for both teachers and their students. They feel that providing for the needs of kids *now* will enhance their success in the real world.

What do you think?

In this chapter we look at another important challenge—understanding and providing for student diversity. Consequently, among other things, you will learn how your students differ socioeconomically, culturally, in terms of gender, developmentally, in learning style, and in ability. Having such knowledge and understanding will enable you to accommodate, and even celebrate, your students' differences.

Unfortunately first year teachers generally give low marks to their preparation to teach diverse kids. Interestingly, teachers working in high-needs schools report their preparation was more helpful. All report the need for good on-the-job help from other teachers (Rochkind, Ott, Immerwahr, Doble, & Johnson, 2008).

Student Diversity

When you look at our students, you see African-Americans, whites, Asians, Hispanics, Native Americans, and the list goes on. What does that say to us? It says our schools reflect our community. We live in a time of change, and it's important that we understand we must bring out the best in one another. Our purpose here today is to create a self-imposed safe and healthy climate in our schools. It doesn't matter where you come from. It doesn't matter the amount of money your parents may have. It doesn't matter what color you are. It doesn't matter your religion or your gender. Our purpose is to say that once you are here, you can expect to be treated with all the respect that any human being should receive. (Wake County, North Carolina Superintendent Bill McNeal addressing students attending a student diversity summit, September 2002.)

3.1 How do you feel about Mr. McNeal's message?

Student diversity is a fact of life in all our schools and classrooms. And students differ in more ways than we can count. To be effective, teachers must be aware of important ways students vary and consciously take that diversity into account when planning and instructing. We cannot successfully teach subject matter without teaching the child. Let's examine some kinds of diversity. (See Figure 3.1.)

FIGURE 3.1 Some Ways in Which Students Differ

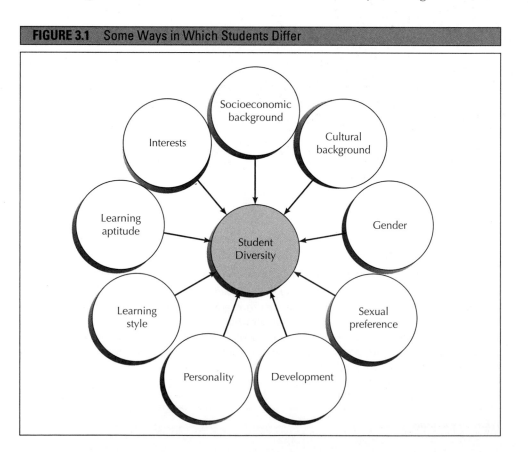

SOCIOECONOMIC DIFFERENCES

Children differ widely in terms of their social and economic status (SES) or well-being. SES typically is divided into three categories; high, middle and low. Since SES mainly is a function of family education, occupation, and income, by definition kids with a high SES have parents or caregivers with more schooling, higher status jobs, and deeper pockets.

Typically, children with a higher SES get higher grades and test scores. Mostly these result from specific advantages they enjoy—greater parental education (especially the mother's), high parental and teacher expectations for their academic success, the availability of educational materials and equipment including books and computers in the home and school, and summer enrichment opportunities. They also enjoy the benefit of being in schools with like-students and, as a result, usually are more challenged by their peers and teachers.

Children from middle and especially low SES share fewer advantages. Kids living in poverty, as mentioned in Chapter 2, face many obstacles to school success. Consequently, although they may have good learning ability it may go undiscovered, unchallenged, or thwarted unless they are internally motivated to succeed or they have parents, caregivers, or teachers who enable them.

Lots of teachers refer to kids with a high SES as "easy teaches" which means they are advantaged and motivated to learn. Teachers of poor children usually do not consider their pupils likewise. This presents a huge obstacle for students with a low SES whose teachers may not provide rich opportunities to learn or expect them to do so.

Suggestions for helping and teaching poor children are contained in Chapter 2. Understanding and teaching affluent children is a relatively unstudied topic (Luthar & Latendresse 2005).

CULTURAL DIFFERENCES

People who share things such as language, values, traditions, and ways of doing things are said to possess a common culture. When most people share that culture, it is called the majority or dominant culture. For example, there are dominant American and Canadian cultures. However, within majority cultures are numerous subcultures or groups of people who differ from the majority in language, values, traditions, and ways of doing things. Thus, within dominant American or Canadian cultures are minority subcultures such as Latino-American or French-Canadian. In order to be successful in our changing society, you need to be increasingly aware of the cultural variations among your students and especially the differences among and within subcultures. To illustrate, it is far too easy to generalize that all Hispanic kids are gregarious or that all African-American kids like and are good at sports (Gutierrez & Rogoff, 2003). All kids who may look alike or talk alike or act alike may not be alike in many other ways, even the ways they learn.

What can contribute to making a minority child disadvantaged? Being somewhat different from members of the majority culture, that is, being a so-called minority student, does not make a child disadvantaged. However, in cases where ethnicity and/or race are tied to low SES, minority students often do less well in school. This reflects the fact that, regardless of subculture, low SES families usually cannot or do not provide their children with the kinds of early stimulation and academic preparation more typically afforded by middle- and upper-class families. Headden (1997) provides an example. Hispanics have a drop-out rate close to 41 percent, but one-third of Hispanic children live in poverty and "start school at a substantial disadvantage: they rarely attend preschool, and their parents, often ill-educated or illiterate, don't read to them" (p. 64). Again, being disadvantaged is more a function of economics than of culture.

Low SES minority kids are better able to make it in school if they and their families so choose. However, this is a complicated matter. It seems they are more

3.2 What experience do you have with children whose *socioeconomic* or *cultural backgrounds* differ from yours? What further experience would help?

3.3 What socioeconomic or cultural differences have you perceived?

likely to succeed *if* the family voluntarily came to this country in order to improve its well-being and *when* they try to assimilate. Those who came to this country unwillingly or not necessarily to succeed and those who experience persistent discrimination are less likely to succeed or try to assimilate. These so-called "caste" minorities try to preserve their ethnic identify rather than be assimilated into the mainstream. Unfortunately, kids who identify themselves by ethnic categories such as Chicano or Latino have lower grades and high dropout rates (National Center for the Dissemination of Disability Research, 2003).

A major problem when minorities encounter schools is that school policy, curriculum, and instruction normally reflect the majority American culture, that may be at odds with values and behaviors children learn at home. For example, Hispanics and Native Americans are accustomed to group learning and mutual assistance, while schools are often organized around competitive, individual learning experience.

Osborne (1997) reports an oddity with regard to cultural differences in self-esteem. In general boys and girls who are white, Hispanic, or African-American identify very positively with academics in the eighth grade. However, as they move through secondary school, both their self-esteem and their identification with academics drop off. After analyzing data collected from nearly 25,000 students, Osborne found, unexplainably, that black students continue to hold the most positive view of themselves even though their grades and test scores fall increasingly below those of students in the other groups. He notes, in general, that African-Americans maintain the highest levels of self-esteem at all ages, but by twelfth grade, African-American boys, to a greater degree, detach their self-esteem from academics, and their self-esteem remains relatively high despite lesser school success. "They're removing school from their self-esteem equation as time goes on." Just why black males come to care less about academics than other groups is unclear. This underscores the importance of teachers tending to the academic needs of these youth.

Minority students, on average (with the exception of Asian Americans and perhaps Black students immigrating from Caribbean countries) do not do as well in school. These achievement differences appear at school entry. They widen in elementary school and then remain fixed in high school. Thus, raising minority achievement is a national priority. The question is, how? In general minority kids have fewer educational resources and less-qualified teachers, get poorer quality instruction, take fewer advanced placement and honors courses, and receive harsher discipline. However, the gaps still persist in integrated, largely middle-class and upper middle-class suburbs like Evanston, Illinois; Montclair, New Jersey; and Shaker Heights, Ohio. Others blame the achievement gap on family culture. James Harris, president of the Montclair NAACP, notes, "There is a level of under involvement of Black folks at every level of the education enterprise" (Johnston & Viadero, 2000). Kimberly Gibson feels it is the fault of low-income Black parents—being Black in itself is no excuse. Specifically, she is concerned that Black students learn that academic achievement is "uncool and acting white" (Gibson, 2000). A parent, Cheryl Johnson, feels part of the problem is that African-American kids are held to a lower academic standard (Viadero, 2000). Finally, many feel the achievement gap exists because minority and majority children fail to appreciate the worth of minorities and diversity.

Helping and Teaching Culturally Different Students   Here are examples of programs intended to help these students.

The Bilingual Education Act (1968, 1974) recognizes the need for limited English proficient (LEP) children to learn the dominant language. In doing so it builds upon the fact that younger children acquire language more easily. In the earliest grades instruction is conducted in the children's native language, e.g. Spanish, so that they can keep up with English-speaking peers. However, in the second or third grade they begin to be instructed in English. Suggestions about how to help and teach limited English proficiency kids follow.

- Get to know your LEP students.
- Avoid causing embarrassment by forcing them to speak. Allow plenty of time for students to prepare English responses.
- When they don't understand, reply "You don't understand. Okay . . ." and provide more clarity rather than correcting them.
- Use pictures and objects. Visuals help.
- Give them an outline of a presentation you are making to help them follow.
- Rather than having children listen, have them learn by doing things.
- Teach reading skills such as skimming, outlining, making predictions from headings, making vocabulary lists, writing responses and summarizing.

Keep in mind that children learn English more easily when their parents are more fluent in their native language and when that native language is closer to English. (Glencoe online—Aardvark's English Forum online; TESL Journal online)

Multicultural Education refers to efforts made to help students understand and appreciate their culture and the culture of others. Following are examples.

- *Teaching the culturally different.* These programs primarily try to help students "develop and maintain their own cultural identity" while also helping them develop competence in the dominant culture. Development of a positive self-concept is a central goal.
- *Human relations.* The intention in such programs is to help "students of different backgrounds learn to communicate more effectively with others while feeling good about themselves."
- *Single-group studies.* These are primarily programs directed toward a targeted ethnic group. They celebrate that group's identity and achievements. Thus children engage in African-American studies, Native-American studies, and Hispanic-American studies.
- *Multicultural programs.* In an effort to raise the consciousness of all students about various cultures and their contributions, multicultural programs have emerged. They cut across subcultures, focusing on ethnic minority music, arts, or literature, and the history of minorities in America. (Presented in Cushner, McClelland, & Safford, 2008.)

Suggestions about how to help and teach minority children are found in Spotlight on Research 3.1. Considerable information on how to teach culturally diverse learners is available online at the *Teaching Diverse Learners* website available at the OLC.

 **Web Link**
Teaching Diverse Learners

GENDER DIFFERENCES

Since most of us will teach both boys and girls, it is useful to know how and to what extent they are similar and how and to what extent they differ.

The Gender-Different and Gender-Similar Schools of Thought
Two opposing hypotheses exist about gender differences. The *gender-different* hypothesis holds that boys and girls, men and women are unlike in numerous ways. This theory has gained popular support from millions who have read bestselling books such as *Men Are from Mars, Women Are from Venus* and *You Just Don't Understand: Men and Women in Conversation.* Its counterpart, the *gender-similar* hypothesis, holds that the genders are much more alike than different.

Studies of successful teachers of minority children reveal that learners benefit most when teachers

- care for each child.
- get to know them both in and out of school.
- form relationships that permit them to understand the beliefs and values students bring from home.
- allow them to be who they are—to feel good about their heritage.
- accept and accommodate their differences.
- take into account their cultural and language differences when planning lessons.

- boost their self-esteem.
- increase expectations of what they may become.
- expect they can and will learn.
- give them successful learning experiences.
- explain the importance of accomplishing the task at hand.
- use a variety of instructional alternatives.
- use instructional alternatives that work well.
- determine how they learn best, and teach accordingly.
- keep them on task.
- accompany hard work with praise.
- check for understanding.

- openly discuss students' academic successes.
- provide them with books they can keep.
- get them to become increasingly independent as learners.
- help them understand the *school* behaviors and rules they need to exhibit and follow.
- involve parents and caregivers as well as older siblings.
- provide after school academic help.
- keep improving their teaching skills.

Sources: Burnette (1999); Hall & Kennedy (2006); Quindlen (2002).

First, let's look at the beliefs and findings of the gender-*similar* group. To do so, we rely on a synthesis of many major studies of gender differences by Hyde (2005). Hyde notes that researchers indeed report many differences between boys and girls, with some being more pronounced. She contends, however, that only a few of the differences are pronounced enough to be believable. Consequently, she reports that, on average, males and females are more alike than different in terms of most measures. She accepts only a few areas in which pronounced, therefore believable, differences exist.

- Males and females are most different in motor performance. For example, particularly after puberty, boys can throw objects farther and faster.
- Boys engage in sexual behavior significantly more and have a more positive attitude toward casual and uncommitted relationships.
- Boys are more physically aggressive.

Hyde also looked to see if there might be other pronounced differences between boys and girls that seem to occur only at a given developmental stage or age. In this case, she accepts and reports

- a small difference favoring girls in computation in elementary and middle school but no difference in high school.
- no gender differences at any age in complex problem solving.
- girls' self-esteem declines with adolescence, but so does boys'.
- with age, girls feel less confident than boys in computer use.

Hyde also accepts and reports that some gender differences may also occur only in certain situations or contexts. For example, she notes that

- when girls are anonymous, they can demonstrate just as much aggressive behavior as anonymous boys.
- boys are more likely to be helpful or heroic in more dangerous situations.

Let's turn to beliefs and findings of the gender-*different* group. Recall that they believe there are major differences between boys and girls and report these, among other, findings:

- Girls generally exhibit greater verbal aptitude and ability.
- Girls more frequently excel in language arts (spelling, writing, and reading).
- Boys excel more often in mathematical reasoning and *spatial relationships* (seeing the relationships between objects).
- Boys speak more in class because they have learned to use language more publicly in play. Girls speak less because they learn to use language more privately with friends and for sharing secrets (Slavin, 2008; Snowman & Biehler, 2008; Tannen, 1991). See also Highlight 3.1, which presents teacher perceptions of gender differences.

The major difference between the groups is that one may want to *believe* in gender difference and the other in gender similarity. As a result, the former may use more stringent standards for what constitutes pronounced gender differences, while the latter is more willing to accept a lower threshold. The truth may be somewhere in the middle.

What Contributes to Gender Differences?
An unanswered question is whether boy and girl differences are genetic or learned. If the latter, you might be influential (see Spotlight on Research 3.2 on page 65).

Hyde believes them to be the result of interaction of the two. Take aggression. Maybe boys' greater aggressiveness is genetic, the result of having more testosterone. However, the environment (family and community) may magnify the difference in aggression through expectations—boys should be more aggressive, girls less so. Moreover, boys' continued engagement in aggressive behavior probably affects their brains. More practice with aggression may make them more aggressive. Might this account for the aggressive off-field behavior of some athletes?

Are Gender Differences Healthy?
Although some amount of *gender role learning* is realistic and healthy—boys should be this way and girls that—efforts are being encouraged to avoid perpetuating the kind of **gender role** stereotyping that encourages boys to be aggressive and reluctant to show emotion and girls to be dependent and passive. Some hope that the genders display **psychological androgyny,** behavior that is more alike than different, and that this would result in better social adjustment.

Do Boys and Girls Do Better with Men or Women Teachers?
One study reports that 13-year-old kids who have a same-gender teacher have higher achievement, while those with an opposite-gender teacher do worse. Here are a couple of examples:

- Boys with a male teacher perform better in reading, girls worse.
- Girls with a female science or math teacher perform better, boys worse (Dee, 2005).

Do Teachers Respond Differently to Boys and Girls? Should They?
Teachers, as noted in Highlight 3.1, seem to notice and often report differences between boys and girls. They also react to them differently.

Some teachers give girls less attention and reinforcement and expect less of them (Levy, Den Brok, Wubbels, & Brekelmans, 2003). Boys receive more attention, disapproval, and blame, while girls tend to be punished more promptly for aggressive behavior such as calling out answers without first being acknowledged (Jones & Dindia, 2004; Slavin, 2008). Good and Brophy (1999) relate additional ways teachers respond differently to gender. Teachers give blander feedback to girls and more animated, detailed feedback to boys. They sometimes perform complex tasks for

3.4 Do you believe the genders are more alike or different?

3.5 How do you think heredity and environment have contributed to your sense of gender?

Testimony by Pat Reed

Since reading a recent cover article in *Time* magazine on gender differences in math and science performance, I have made some personal observations of my 8th grade math classes. Boys much more frequently raise their hands to answer question . . . with little worry or concern that their answer may be wrong. They speak their answers with great confidence. Many girls are unlikely to raise their hands at all, and when called on, often respond with the correct answer, but phrase it as a question: "Five thousand and twenty-two?" as if unsure that their answer is correct. . . . Interestingly, the math grades for my students show more girls with A's than boys. This I attribute to greater diligence and care, rare failure to turn in homework assignments, very few errors in work due to consistent checking and rechecking of homework, quizzes, and tests before submitting. . . . It was interesting (and somewhat disappointing) to review their scores on the high school entrance exams. For many of the boys, their best scores were in math, and their worst scores in language arts. The opposite was true for most girls. It wasn't that their math scores were poor, just that math was not their best score. I wonder if this phenomenon can be attributed to girls doing more reading than boys. I am also concerned that it is something we as teachers are doing or not doing in the classroom that is promoting boys in math more than girls. I've tried to be very conscious of it, and build up the confidence level of the girls by involving them in math competitions and so forth, but am not sure what effect this strategy will have.

Testimony by N.M.F.

In my experience, the major gender difference that I have noticed is the interest in different types of reading materials. I have found that most of the boys in my room are reading nonfiction during self-selected reading times. Most of the girls are reading fiction stories. Of course, there are some exceptions to the rule, and I encourage my students to read a variety of materials. It just seems that boys prefer nonfiction and girls prefer fiction.

Testimony by N. Meeker

I teach language arts and my experience has always been that girls perform better than boys in my classes. I sometimes think this is because boys tend to pay more attention to factual material and want the "right" answer. They are willing to answer grammar-related questions because the answers are either right or wrong. Literature is another story. Girls are more apt to see the bigger picture, able to apply what they have read to other situations. I think much of this can be attributed to boys and girls having very different interests. A large percentage of grading in my class is given for class participation. I am sure I would have a lot fewer boys participating in class discussions of literature if they could rely on tests to get them by.

Source: WikEd online.

girls but merely coach boys to task completion. They encourage girls in grooming and manners but boys in academic striving and accomplishment. Overall, teachers tend to interact more with boys than girls.

Classrooms with more girls seem to have a positive influence on learning (see Spotlight on Research 3.3). On the other hand, boys seem not as well suited to school (see Highlight 3.2 on page 66). To catch a glimpse of middle school boys, see Highlight 3.3 on page 67.

3.6 How do you think student gender will affect the way you teach?

Helping and Teaching Boys vs. Girls   A number of ideas exist regarding how best to teach boys. Included are:

- Boys learn more when teachers talk less.
- Boys learn more when teachers use lots of joking and humor.
- Boys learn more when teachers themselves are captivated by the great, universal themes that engage male minds and hearts, such as facing adversity and danger, embarking on great adventures, attaining strength and competence, fighting battles for good and for glory; testing yourself and becoming a hero.
- Boys learn more when teachers are neither awed nor enraged by boys' physicality and displays of anger, but respond in calm and measured ways.

SPOTLIGHT ON RESEARCH 3.2
How Dads Influence Daughters' Interest in Math

How about differing interest in math and science between boys and girls? Do you think that is genetic or learned? To find out how environment influences differing interests, hundreds of children and their parents were observed over a period of 13 years. Among the observations: (1) parents provide more math-supported home environments and activities for their sons; (2) they spend more time on math and science activities with their sons; (3) parents who provide more math and science environments in the home have more children with higher achievement and interest in those subjects. Especially telling is that girls' interest in math decreases as their *fathers'* gender stereotypes increase, whereas boys' interest increases. For example, girls whose fathers have strong gender stereotypes (e.g. "girls are not interested in and are not good at math") have less interest and do less well (Davis-Kean, 2007).

SPOTLIGHT ON RESEARCH 3.3
Girls Make a Difference

What is the academic impact of girls on boys? Hoxby (2002) reports that both elementary school boys and girls perform better in reading when the class has a larger share of girls. That may be attributable to the fact that an all-girls class would, on average, outperform an all-boys class in reading anyway (see text).

Boys and girls also perform better in math when they are in classes with larger numbers of girls. This finding is less explainable since boys usually excel in math. Hoxby suggests this anomaly may be due to any of the following: classes with more girls may have fewer disruptions, girls in a female dominated class might consider math a more female subject and become more enthusiastic about it, or girls' better skills in reading may be a factor even in math learning.

Hoxby's study raises interesting questions. Would the same result occur in other subjects or at other grade levels? In what subjects might a preponderance of boys have a positive impact on both genders?

- Boys learn more when the teacher does not humiliate them by forgetting that genuine vulnerability and lack of confidence lie underneath their cocky displays of toughness and bravado.
- Boys learn more in structured, authoritative educational environments, under clear teacher control that provide them with safety and security from the power plays and putdowns of other boys.
- Boys learn more when competition gets them excited, when they need to learn so they can do well for their team, when they get to be active, when they get breaks, when they are having fun, and when teachers make the point of the learning activity clear.
- Boys learn more when teachers praise and mentor them and when they believe that the teacher understands, likes, and respects boys (Kleinfeld, 2007).

See also Gurian and Stevens (2006).

Here are ideas for consideration when teaching girls.

- Tie what you are teaching to the real world. Girls are more likely to be interested in applying what is to be learned to real life situations.
- Use stories such as "story problems" in mathematics. Putting a problem or task into a story format makes it more understandable and easier to solve.
- Use stories in reading and literature that focus on experiences and relationships. Girls are interested in emotion and motivation.

All does not bode well for boys. On entering school they are developmentally two years behind and not genetically suited to sitting in school. Later, they are more likely to be in special ed classes, more likely to be diagnosed as AD/HD, less likely to be able to delay gratification, less likely to try to do their best in school, less likely to be proficient readers, less likely to value school and more likely to drop out, less likely to complete college, more likely to "boomerang" and live with parents, more likely to commit suicide, less likely to vote, and more likely to see their earnings eroding. Boys seem to be in a funk.

Not too many years ago girls were the worry. However, due to the women's movement and changing attitudes of teachers toward girls that have made the classroom more girl friendly, girls have soared. Additionally by way of their natures, Garbarino (2000) notes, "Girls are better able to deliver in terms of what modern society requires of people—paying attention, abiding by the rules, being verbally competent, and dealing with interpersonal relationships."

What to do? Suggestions include: educating parents and teachers to the problem, putting in place reading intervention programs, modifying instruction to make it more boy friendly, helping boys with social and emotional skills, changing the attitudes of boys toward academic learning and achievement, weaning them from TV and electronic game violence, getting more males to teach and serve as role models, and establishing advocacy groups for men. Some worry that righting boys problems could end up wronging girls. However, most agree that providing equal opportunities for boys and girls can be attained.

Sources: Boys' academic slide calls for accelerated attention (2003); Conlin (2003).

- Use role-playing that allows them to consider how they would feel in a certain situation (for example, if boys were picking on you?) (Sax, 2009).

Teaching for Gender Equality   Teachers want to create classrooms in which boys and girls have the same opportunities. Here are some benchmarks to ponder when you step into a classroom of your own.

1. Will you ensure that boys and girls have equal chances to participate?
2. Will you call on and talk with both equally?
3. Will you ask both the same kind and difficulty of questions?
4. Will you give boys and girls the same amount of time to answer questions?
5. Will you ensure that neither boys nor girls dominate learning?
6. Will you respond to boys' and girls' correctness or incorrectness in the same ways?
7. Will you ensure that both have equal opportunity to succeed in all things?
8. Will boys and girls be given equal access to technology?
9. Will you reward and discipline both to the same degree?

Your students may not previously have been in classrooms that promoted equal gender opportunity. In such cases, you may need to overcompensate until all of them feel they are treated much the same.

Some, despite Hyde's findings, feel boys and girls differ in a number of ways that must be taken into account when teaching them. Sax (2005) claims, for the most part, that boys' hearing is less sensitive to a female teacher's voice; girls are better able to interpret a teacher's facial expression; boys are more attuned to movement; girls are more aware of color and texture—boys of location, speed, and direction; girls and boys enjoy different interests; girls find things by using visual landmarks (it is near the coffee shop) while boys use direction and distance (it is north about one-half mile); girls are more able to write and talk about emotion; boys are more

When a New England writer visits a middle school to watch and listen to boys, this is what he reports.

- A boy's basic outfit is a T-shirt, pants, and sneaks. They only get haircuts when they have to.
- Plastic toys are out. Action videogames are in.
- Discovery, Science, and Military channels are in. So are sports programs and MTV. Nickelodeon is out, "It's young, not cool."
- News is out. "Only as a last resort."

- Instant messaging is in, although it is monotonous and boring.
- Saturday is the best day. "Just go out and play with friends. Kickball, capture the flag, manhunt. Ride bikes and scooters."
- Having lots of homework is a bad thing.
- Having a girlfriend can mean sitting at the girl's lunch table. Going out is just to say you do.
- Sleepovers are tough the next day.

- During a science lesson, boys want to know how bees fight.
- They have no interest in Princess Diana.
- They love "Yo Mama" jokes they find on Internet. "Yo mama is so fat she walked into a zoo and the elephant threw peanuts at her."
- Snacks are staples. Swapping lunch items is frequent.

Source: Miller (2005).

likely to take risks and to disobey; boys overestimate their ability while girls underestimate theirs; boys are more attracted to violence and conflict and more aggressive; friendships among boys revolve around a common interest while girls' friendships are spent talking, sharing secrets, and going places; boys are less likely to seek help with schoolwork and are less likely to study when they find the subject uninteresting; boys are more motivated to work when there is stress and time constraint while girls do not function well in such situations. Given such differences, Sax argues, they should be taught differently.

Single-Sex Classes? Since gender differences exist, why not separate classes for girls and boys? Such classrooms and schools existed in the past. Not surprisingly, the single-sex classroom movement again is raising its head (Weil, 2008). There are a handful of single-sex public schools and a small number of experimental programs where girls study math and science separately from boys. Where such switches have occurred the results have been mixed. For example, after a Seattle elementary school switched to single-sex classrooms, its reading scores tripled and discipline referrals plummeted. The Martin Luther King Jr. Middle School in Atlanta is experimenting with single-sex education. Teachers there say the new approach is working: behavior is improved, students are paying more attention, girls wear less revealing outfits. The kids say: you learn more without the distractions of [boys] and it is boring without the girls around. On the other hand, a 12-school effort in California was a disappointment (Donsky, 2003).

For more on gender differences go to the OLC link education.com and click on "Special Editions: Gender Differences" which addresses these topics: What's all the fuss about gender differences? Are boys' and girls' brains really so different? How are boys disadvantaged? Do boys and girls cope with stress and emotions differently? Do boys and girls experience the classroom differently? Should boys and girls be educated in separate classrooms? Are there differences in boys' and girls' experience of special needs?

 Web Link
Special Editions: Gender Differences

SEXUAL PREFERENCE DIFFERENCES

If you teach adolescents, you especially should be aware that some of those in your care may have concerns about sexual orientation. Therefore, according to the

American Academy of Pediatrics (1993), you should be able to provide factual, current, nonjudgmental information to them in a confidential manner.

Additionally, as we know, gay and lesbian adolescents may be stigmatized, isolated, or targets of hatred by others, even parents and caregivers. Peers may engage in cruel name-calling and even physical abuse. Parents and caregivers may be critical, harass, and even reject. Such treatment by significant others may lead to isolation, runaway behavior, homelessness, depression, and substance abuse. The difficulties homosexual youth face are reflected in their much higher tendency toward suicide. Accordingly, schools and teachers increasingly are searching for ways to deal with the sensitive question of homosexuality and to ensure that homosexual students enjoy a safe school environment.

Bickmore (1999) argues that it is important to discuss sexuality even with elementary students just as we might discuss other human differences and tolerance for them. She feels that homosexuality is readily visible to children through public images—television, film, newscasts—and cannot be easily overlooked since children are inherently interested in understanding their world. She also feels that the mini-society of elementary classrooms becomes more inclusive when all members respectfully interact with diverse individuals and unfamiliar ideas.

Clyde and Lobban (2000) provide an annotated bibliography that focuses on the issues of homosexuality in books for children most of which are for adolescents.

DEVELOPMENTAL DIFFERENCES

Students differ developmentally across and within age groups. In other words, 10-year-olds not only differ from 15-year-olds, they differ from each other. These psychosocial, cognitive, and moral differences are well documented in child development textbooks. Snowman and Biehler (2008) present selected theories of development and then draw implications for teaching. Each theory emphasizes that children must go through predictable developmental or growth stages, and effective instruction should aim at each student's appropriate developmental level.

Psychosocial Development Erikson (1993) suggests that our adult personal and social characteristics result from passing through certain life stages. During that journey, we resolve dichotomies and conflict between positive and negative traits—for example, between trust and mistrust, autonomy and shame, initiative and guilt, industry and inferiority, identity and role confusion, generativity and stagnation, and intimacy and isolation. A healthy personality results when we emerge with more positive than negative traits; that is, we are more trustful, more self-confident, more initiating, more productive, and clearer about our sexual and occupational roles.

It is suggested that we can facilitate development of more positive student personalities by

- allowing young preschool children more free play and guided experimentation, and by not shaming them.
- providing preschool children with activities that foster initiative and a sense of accomplishment, while not censuring them for their questions and actions.
- presenting elementary students with tasks that are within their capacities and then rewarding accomplishment, and encouraging self-competition and cooperation.
- assisting secondary students to consider who they are, accept their appearance, reflect on their sex roles, and explore and confirm occupational choice. (Snowman & Biehler, 2008.)

One trait that educators deem crucial to healthy personality is **self-esteem,** defined as our personal judgment of our worthiness or how favorably we regard ourselves. It was referred to in the earlier section on cultural differences. Unfortunately, although high self-esteem may be healthy, it does not by itself translate into better school academic performance (see Spotlight on Research 3.4). Thus, school programs geared to raise self-esteem do not necessarily improve student learning. Improvement in learning is more specifically related to *self-esteem as a learner,* and that seems only to result from actual improved academic performance. Said another way, if we want students to have confidence that they can succeed academically, we must ensure they are having successful academic experiences. There is no simple fix.

Evans (1999) feels that the recent emphasis on raising self-esteem has, in some cases, gone too far and is harmful. He questions certain practices that teachers and parents use to make students feel good about themselves or to avoid hurting their feelings including: excessive use of praise unrelated to accomplishment, failure to discipline, and not telling students when they are "selfish, mean, lazy or rude" or that their behavior is otherwise unacceptable. Evans notes that some teachers are now even unwilling to praise individual students for an accomplishment since that might make other students feel bad. As a consequence of shielding and even misleading children in this way, children lose the ability to feel shame on the one hand and true pride on the other.

3.7 What will be your approach toward balancing a child's self-esteem with reality?

Cognitive Development Piaget (1999) and his colleagues suggest that intellectual development has four stages: sensorimotor, preoperational, concrete operational, and formal operational. Furthermore, all youth proceed through all stages but at different rates. During the **sensorimotor stage** (birth to 2 years), the intellect develops primarily through using the senses and engaging in motor or physical activity. During the **preoperational, prelogical stage** (2 to 7 years), young learners develop knowledge from their personal experience, by exploring and manipulating real objects and by learning the three Rs and other basic knowledge and skills. In this stage, youngsters start to use symbols such as words and numerals to represent objects.

At the **concrete operational stage** (7 to 11 years), children become capable of logical thought. Among other things, they come to understand conservation (that matter is neither created nor destroyed, but merely changes shape or form). They also can arrange or classify objects into categories, and they can place objects in order according to characteristics such as size, length, or weight.

The **formal operational stage** (11 years and up) is achieved when children more regularly are able to deal in abstractions or perform activities mentally, or "in their heads." At this stage, students are capable of understanding more abstract mathematical concepts, such as ratio. They also now are able to use complex forms of language including proverbs, metaphors, sarcasm, and satire.

In order to utilize what is known about cognitive development, it is suggested that you as a teacher

- determine the stages of thinking of your students.
- plan learning experiences in terms of these stages.
- use lots of hands-on activities that allow children to manipulate objects.
- mix more advanced with less advanced thinkers so that children can think with and learn from each other.
- encourage students to share with others the mental processes they use for reaching concepts and conclusions. (Snowman & Biehler, 2008.)

Moral Development Piaget (1999) and Kohlberg (1981) have ideas about how **moral development** occurs. Piaget claims that children are capable of two types of moral reasoning: morality of constraint and morality of cooperation. Typical

SPOTLIGHT ON RESEARCH 3.4
Student Self-Esteem: What We Know about It

A long-held belief is that what we think of ourselves—our self-esteem (SE)—is related to our behavior generally and our achievement specifically. *Higher SE is better.* Consequently, SE-boosting programs have proliferated, and teachers, in particular, have been expected to make students feel better about themselves. Recently this seemingly logical belief and resultant practice have been the subject of much study. A review of the research was done by Baumaster, Campbell, Krueger, and Vohs (2005). Selected findings related to young people are:

- Raising student SE offers little academic achievement benefit.

- When children are asked to nominate their most liked and least liked classmates, the results showed little association between those rankings and nominees' SE. Said another way, students with high or low SE are not usually viewed by others as those students view themselves.
- Students with higher SE seem to have the ability to initiate new contacts and friendships.
- Students with higher SE are less inhibited in sexual activity and more prone to engage in sex.
- Little or no relationship is found between SE and use of alcohol.

- A declining level of academic motivation causes SE to drop and, in turn, seems to relate weakly to use of marijuana.
- Bullies report less anxiety and are more sure of themselves than other children.
- Happiness and SE seem to be closely linked.
- High SE seems to improve persistence in the face of failure.
- Low SE is a risk factor for certain eating disorders.

6-year-olds hold to **morality of constraint.** This means that they regard rules as sacred and unchangeable: Everyone should obey rules in the same way, with no exceptions. On the other hand, typical 12-year-olds hold to **morality of cooperation.** They have reached a point where they believe that rules are flexible and that there can be exceptions to them. Typical 6-year-olds, compared with 12-year-olds, are more adamant that punishment should follow rule breaking. Conversely, 12-year-olds like to take into account the circumstances causing the rule breaking. They are also concerned that misbehavior violates some mutual social agreement.

Kohlberg (1981), too, feels that children proceed through stages of moral reasoning. He originally identified three levels of moral reasoning development, each including two stages. In the earliest of Kohlberg's levels, children 9 or younger stay out of trouble only to avoid punishment or retribution. At the second level, youth 9 to 20 years stay out of trouble because they recognize that rules have been established in order to maintain security and order. At the highest level, reached only after age 20 and only by relatively few adults, people understand, accept, and adhere to the moral principles that undergird our social rules and conventions.

As teachers, we can encourage moral development by engaging students in the discussion of moral dilemmas and moral issues (for example, capital punishment). Additionally, involving our students in the development and maintenance of classroom rules provides an excellent opportunity for children to model the thinking required to make moral decisions that govern many people.

3.8 How will you take children's developmental differences into account?

PERSONALITY DIFFERENCES

Personality is defined as the totality of character and behavioral traits peculiar to an individual. Such traits are innumerable. The two selected for presentation here will play an important role in how well your future students achieve and behave. Know them well.

Temperamental Differences Every person has a different way of thinking, behaving, and reacting. This is called **temperament.** It is a joy to be the parent or teacher of children who have good or even temperaments. Ill-tempered children are another matter.

Temperament, though inborn, is shaped by other people and events in our lives. Temperament traits of children include the following:

- *Activity:* Is the child always moving and doing something, or does she have a more relaxed style?
- *Rhythmicity:* Is the child regular or haphazard in her habits?
- *Approach/withdrawal:* Does she "never meet a stranger" or tend to shy away from new people or things? (See Highlight 3.4.)
- *Adaptability:* Can the child easily adjust to changes in routines or plans, or does she resist them?
- *Intensity:* Does she react strongly to situations, either positive or negative, or does she react calmly and quietly?
- *Mood:* Does the child often express a negative outlook, or is she generally a positive person? Does her mood shift frequently, or is she eventempered?
- *Persistence and attention span:* Does the child give up as soon as a problem arises, or does she keep trying? Can she stick with an activity a long time, or does her mind tend to wander?
- *Distractibility:* Is the child easily distracted, or can she shut out distractions and stay with the current activity?
- *Sensory threshold:* Is she bothered by external stimuli such as loud noises, bright lights, and so forth, or does she tend to ignore them? Obviously, many of these traits affect everyday school behavior and success.

These traits combine into three basic temperament types.

- *Easy or flexible children* are generally calm, happy, regular in habits, adaptable, and not easily upset. Because of their easy style, time must be set aside to talk with them about their frustrations and hurts. They won't demand or ask for it.
- *Difficult, active, or feisty children* are often fussy, irregular in habits, fearful of new people and situations, easily upset by noise and commotion, high strung, and intense in their reactions. Providing areas for vigorous activity (with some freedom of choice) to work off stored-up energy and frustration allows these children to be more successful. Preparing these children for activity changes will help their transition from one thing to another.
- *Slow to warm up or cautious children* are relatively inactive and fussy and tend to withdraw or to react negatively in and to new situations. Their reactions, however, gradually become more positive with continuous exposure. Sticking to a routine and to your word, along with allowing ample time to establish relationships in new situations, is necessary to help their independence unfold.

The following suggestions may help when temperament is at issue.

- Be aware of student temperamental differences and respect the uniqueness of *each* child. Be aware of your own temperament and adjust your natural responses when they clash with a student's.

3.9 How does your temperament affect you as a student and person?

- Communicate and explain your decisions and motives and listen to the student's point of view. Collaborate to solve problems.
- Set limits on self-control. Respect opinions but remain firm on important limits.
- Be a good role model because children learn by imitation.

(This section is adapted from Oliver, 2002.)

Self-Discipline Differences   Self-discipline and self-denial vary widely among learners. They are most notable among better students, who are more willing to "stay

3.10 When, as a student, have you demonstrated self-discipline and self-denial?

CHAPTER 3
Teaching Diverse Students

Sara is a quiet child who loves to draw pictures in exquisite detail. But Sara's reserved manner troubles her . . . teacher. She worries that Sara focuses too much on the details in her drawings and projects and not enough on the other children around her.

Teachers like Sara's often assume that something is wrong with quiet ones. They may be considered handicapped, fearful, less intelligent, unsociable, or uncooperative. In reality, these students may be academically or otherwise talented, thoughtful, studious, and conscientious. In any case, in Western cultures they often are ignored, while in Eastern cultures and in Native-American circles quiet ones are thought of as polite, restrained, and reflective. When Native-American and Asian children find themselves in most classrooms, they may be viewed as slow or lacking in social skill.

Tips for teachers:

- Ask questions that are more open ended and reflective—that require deeper thinking (see Chapter 11, Using Questions).

- Praise quiet ones when they respond.

- Provide opportunity for quiet ones to work alongside outgoing kids.

- Encourage them to pursue their passions, which may be more contemplative, such as art or music.

Source: Weingarten (2005).

---

the learning course" by paying attention, completing assignments, and generally applying themselves. Unfortunately, academic self-discipline and denial may have short-term costs. Two examples: A child voluntarily delays play of electronic games until homework is completed; a child foregoes a social activity to study for an exam.

Some feel that lack of self-discipline is the major reason some American students fall short academically. They have trouble sacrificing immediate, short-term pleasure for distant, long-term gain. Examples are kids who drop out or high school graduates who chose work over further education because they want to earn money for the immediate pleasures of partying, a more expensive car, clothes, or electronic gadgets.

Studies show the importance of self-discipline. (See Highlight 3.5 and Spotlight on Research 3.5.)

3.11 What has been your experience trying to improve your own or another person's temperament or self-discipline?

There are no guaranteed ways to instill self-discipline or improved temperament. However, Chapter 4 presents learning theories that can be used toward these ends. Chapter 5 presents information on how to motivate learners. The following principles also have application.

LEARNING STYLE DIFFERENCES

No question, different students prefer to learn different subjects. Some prefer the humanities (art, music, history, literature, philosophy, language). Others like the social sciences (sociology, anthropology, psychology). And, of course, there are those who love science or mathematics. These likes probably influence what you expect to teach.

Not only do we differ in *what* we prefer to learn, we also differ in *how* we prefer to learn it. Some of us like to learn on our own, while others enjoy learning in the company of others. Some like information to be presented visually, while others like to hear it or talk about it. Still others prefer having hands-on experiences whereby they learn by doing. Differences in the way one prefers to learn are called **learning style preferences.**

Psychologists and others have developed little tests that can be taken to determine learning style preferences. Should you be interested in exploring your learning style, take one or more of the tests online (see Highlight 3.6 on page 74).

HIGHLIGHT 3.5
Why Able Kids Fail

Washington, D.C., area high school English teacher Patrick Welsh (2006) shares that too many able, born in America kids are just not willing to put in the time and effort to master their subjects. Apart from reaching this conclusion based upon personal experience, he cites a study in which kids were asked to identify the most important factors in their performance in math. The percentage of Japanese and Taiwanese students who answered "studying hard" was double that of American kids, who chose to blame teachers for their success or failures.

Welsh feels that busy, guilt-ridden parents subscribe to their children's theory and play the blame-the-teacher game. Teaching colleagues of Welsh add:

- Nowadays, it's the kids who have the power, and they scream and yell when they don't do the work and get lower grades.

- Parents whose capable children get Cs and Ds accuse us of destroying their future.

- Kids manipulate guidance counselors to help them avoid certain classes.

Welsh suggests the best lesson he can pass along to his upper- and middle-class students is to pay attention to their foreign-born classmates and get to work. "Education in American is still more a privilege than a right," he says.

SPOTLIGHT ON RESEARCH 3.5
When Grades Count, Self-Discipline Matters (and Girls Are Good at It)

A child's self-discipline is a better predictor of his future academic success than his IQ. Thus, improving self-discipline may be the key to building academic success.

Duckworth and Seligman (2005) studied 140 children (average age 13 years). In the autumn the children, their parents, and teachers provided information about the children's self-discipline. Were the children able to follow rules, avoid acting impulsively, and put off instant rewards for later gratification? Results showed that kids who displayed self-discipline had better grades, better spring exam scores, and better results in selection into a high school of choice.

A second study with 164 children (average age 13) followed a similar procedure but also involved the children's taking an IQ test in the autumn. Self-discipline again predicted later academic performance, as measured by their average grade for the year and their spring exam result. Moreover, the researchers found that the children's self-discipline scores accounted for twice as much of the variation in their later academic performance as their IQ.

A later study shows that elementary, middle, and high school girls earn higher grades than boys although they do not outperform boys on achievement or IQ scores. The authors suggest that girls' grade dominance is the result of their being more self-disciplined (Duckworth & Seligman, 2006).

The researchers conclude: "Underachievement among American youth is often blamed on inadequate teachers, boring textbooks, and large class sizes. We suggest another reason for students falling short of their intellectual potential: their failure to exercise self-discipline."

Now, let's look at four of the ways students differ in learning style: (1) their conceptual tempo, (2) whether they are field sensitive or field independent, (3) whether they are convergent or divergent thinkers, and (4) their perceptual modality preferences and strengths.

Conceptual Tempo We all know both impulsive and reflective people. These people differ in **conceptual tempo.** Impulsive people like to work fast, make decisions quickly, and may do things without serious forethought. Consequently, they often rush through their work in what seems to be a careless way, perhaps completing the task incorrectly because they neglect to read the directions or do not persist long enough to complete the task. Because they rush, impulsive students tend to perform more poorly in school tasks requiring analysis and attention to detail.

While impulsive students like to work quickly, reflective students are likely to take considerable time in their work and in making up their minds, usually because they consider several alternative responses before arriving at their answer. Rather than speed, they are concerned about accuracy and about ensuring that they have a good answer. Reflective learners sometimes receive poor evaluations because they are so meticulous. Although they may not finish a task, what they have completed may be nearly perfect. Reflective learners may not participate in class discussions or respond when called upon. Quite literally, they are still thinking about their answer!

Woolfolk (2007) makes clear that not everyone who works fast is impulsive. "Some people are simply very bright and quick to understand" (p. 150). Nor are slow workers necessarily reflective; they might be less bright or able to understand. She notes that some people are fast-accurate or slow-inaccurate thinkers.

As part of normal development, children become more reflective with age. However, the tendency to respond either impulsively or reflectively remains fairly stable. Children can become more reflective by learning to think before they respond or by talking themselves through each step of a complex task (Meichenbaum, 1999).

Field-Dependent versus Field-Independent Learners (Witkin et al., 1962, 1981) Students also differ along this continuum. On the one hand are students who view situations in their totality, seeing a whole pattern, or gestalt. They "see the forest" as opposed to seeing individual trees therein. Such children are called **field dependent** or *field sensitive*. Persons who have difficulty reading a diagram and putting together something requiring detailed assembly may be field dependent.

Field-dependent learners seem to share certain characteristics. They tend to be more gregarious or people oriented and cooperative. Second, they are better at learning material with social content such as social studies, social sciences, and literature. Third, they have difficulty noticing or picking out details and working with material presented to them in an unstructured way. For example, field-dependent learners may have difficulty with math word problems because they do not identify and distinguish between relevant and irrelevant information. Finally, these learners are more responsive to praise and other kinds of reinforcement and more adversely affected by criticism.

On the other hand are **field-independent** learners. They focus more easily on "the trees," or the details. Their characteristics include being more curious and self-reliant, and less conforming and obedient. Furthermore, they are more task oriented, and they work better with unstructured tasks such as problem solving. On the downside, perhaps, field-independent students have more difficulty learning social content and working with others. Compared with field-dependent or field-sensitive students, they need less praise and are less affected by criticism.

Some studies (Fritz, 1992) indicate that boys are generally more field-independent, which may result from different child-rearing patterns. Furthermore, some believe that field dependency is related to one's cultural heritage. For example Latino-American and African-American youth have been reported to be more field-dependent than majority Americans (Ramerez & Price-Williams, 1974). Although, over time, persons may become more or less field-dependent or -independent, each of us tends to remain one or the other and not to cross over.

Convergent/Divergent Thinking   A third difference in learning style is convergence/divergence. Persons who tend to think in independent, flexible, and imaginative ways are considered more creative. Such persons are sometimes called **divergent thinkers** because they have the ability to come up with different ideas for accomplishing a task or solving a problem. Persons predisposed to think in conventional, typical ways are termed **convergent thinkers.** They search for a single, logical answer. When asked what a pencil might be used for, convergent thinkers reply that a pencil is for writing. Divergent thinkers may add that a pencil can be used for punching holes in paper, rolling clay into sheets, or as a handle for a slingshot.

3.12   What is your learning personality? Are you impulsive or reflective, field dependent or independent, convergent or divergent?

Perceptual Modality Preferences/Strengths   This fourth learning style difference describes a learner's tendency to use different sensory modes to understand experiences and to learn. For example, some students prefer to learn visually, by seeing information. You may have heard a friend say, "I'm a visual person." Such persons learn most easily by reading material or seeing something demonstrated. Others are auditory learners who need to hear information in order to learn. Lectures with careful explanations or hearing a textbook on tape are effective ways for these students to learn. Kinesthetic, or tactile, learners need to be physically or even emotionally involved in order to learn. Students who need to count on their fingers to complete arithmetic computations or to manipulate objects or materials are often kinesthetic learners.

Dunn, Dunn, and Price (2001) believe we should determine the preferred learning styles of each of our students and adjust our teaching accordingly. Consequently, they have developed the Learning Style Inventory for this purpose. Kolb (2005) has developed another learning style inventory. You may find out what your learning style is at the Learning Style website.

Web Link
Learning Style

Although the notion of learning styles is attractive to many administrators and educators, research supporting curriculum or teaching changes based solely on some aspect of learning styles is murky at best (Pashler, McDaniel, Rohrer, Bjork, 2009). However, research on learning styles has contributed some key understandings that can guide us as teachers. These include recognizing that people are different; that learners will respond differently to a variety of instructional methods; and that we need to respect and honor individual differences among the students who make up our classes (Brandt, 1990).

Finally and importantly, as noted in Chapter 1, we must realize that our personal learning style and teaching style generally match. Consequently, we often assume that all of our students enjoy the same kinds of learning experiences we do. Wrong! To be effective, we will have to provide many different kinds of learning activities. In the classroom, variety truly is "the spice of life."

3.13   Are you a visual, kinesthetic, or auditory learner?

Helping and Teaching Learners with Different Learning Styles or Preferences   These suggestions might be useful when trying to meet the various learning styles of your students:

- For **auditory learners,** who learn best by listening and talking, provide lots of group activities and class discussion. Use audio and videotapes, storytelling, songs, memorization, and drill.
- For **visual learners,** who learn best by observing or seeing things, use flash cards, charts, pictures, posters, graphs, and PowerPoint presentations. Try to provide visuals of new concepts—for example, "a peninsula." When visuals aren't available, try to create a mental picture for these learners.
- For **kinesthetic learners,** who learn best through physical activity, provide hands-on activity, physical movement, and change. Use simulations, role-play, and competition. Let them learn by doing and practicing.
- For **tactile learners,** who learn best through touch, use board games, projects, and role play. Have them do things such as taking notes *while* listening.

LEARNING APTITUDE DIFFERENCES

We all differ in our aptitude or potential to learn and do different things. Some of us have high aptitude for language (speaking, reading, writing) or second language learning. Others have high potential in mathematics, music, or sport. Such aptitudes, like all human characteristics, are normally distributed in the population. This means that all persons have some potential to achieve, say, in music. However, only a few have high or low potential. Most will fall somewhere in the middle. Consider another example, sport. Most have average potential. Only a very few have enough to become professional athletes.

Of course, opportunity plays a big role in whether or not our aptitudes blossom. One could have a high aptitude for language, math, music, or sport but no opportunity to grow in those ways. There probably are potentially great musicians or athletes who are not aware of their rare aptitudes or have never had an opportunity to pursue them. You may be one.

As teachers, we need to be aware of the different kinds of strengths students have and be committed to helping each utilize his or her potential talents to the fullest. Think of yourself as a talent scout.

Eight Kinds of Aptitude   So what kinds of learning aptitudes are there? Four have just been mentioned (language/linguistic, mathematical, musical, sport/body kinesthetics). According to Gardner, there are at least eight (see Highlight 3.7). They are the body parts of Gardner's theory of **multiple intelligences.** Gardner has been the major advocate of broadening the definition of intelligence to include more than merely verbal and mathematical abilities (Gardner, 2006).

If you wish to take a multiple intelligence test, go to the Learning Disabilities Resource Community website.

Teaching to Multiple Intelligences   Since learners possess multiple intelligences in varying degree, teachers could try to teach in such a way that a given lesson appeals to as many of the intelligences as possible. Look at the lesson plans in Chapters 7 and 8. What intelligence(s) does each plan appeal to? How could each be revised to take more intelligences into account?

How Aptitudes Are Identified   One way to determine a student's aptitudes is through classroom observation. Teachers frequently do this, sometimes accurately, sometimes mistakenly. Over- or underestimating a child's potential can be very, very damaging.

Another way to determine aptitude is to test for it. You will note in the Chapter 5 appendix that the students were routinely given tests for mental and musical

"We studied genetics at school today. If you wanted a smart child, you should have adopted one."

Web Link
Learning Disabilities

3.14   What kinds of intelligence seem to serve you best and least?

3.15   Do you believe any of your aptitudes have been under- or overestimated?

- *Linguistic intelligence* is the capacity to use language, your native language and perhaps other languages, to express what's on your mind and to understand other people. Poets really specialize in linguistic intelligence, but any kind of writer, orator, speaker, lawyer, or a person for whom language is an important stock in trade highlights linguistic intelligence.

- People with a highly developed *logical-mathematical intelligence* understand the underlying principles of some kind of a causal system, the way a scientist, mathematician, or a logician does.

- *Spatial intelligence* refers to the ability to represent the spatial world internally in your mind— the way a sailor or airplane pilot navigates the large spatial world, or the way a chess player or sculptor represents a more circumscribed spatial world. Spatial intelligence can be used in the arts or in the sciences. If you are spatially intelligent and oriented toward the arts, you are more likely to become a painter or a sculptor or an architect than, say, a musician or a writer. Similarly, certain sciences like anatomy or topology emphasize spatial intelligence.

- *Bodily kinesthetic intelligence* is the capacity to use your whole body or parts of your body—your hand, your fingers, your arms—to solve a problem, make something, or put on some kind of a production. The most evident examples are people in athletics or the performing arts, particularly dance or acting.

- *Musical intelligence* is the capacity to think in music, to be able to hear patterns, recognize them, remember them, and perhaps manipulate them. People who have a strong musical intelligence don't just remember music easily—they can't get it out of their minds, it's so omnipresent. Now, some people will say, "Yes, music is important, but it's a talent, not an intelligence." And I say, "Fine, let's call it a talent." But, then we have to leave the word intelligent out of all discussions of human abilities. You know, Mozart was damned smart!

- *Interpersonal intelligence* (aka *emotional intelligence*) is understanding other people. It's an ability we all need, but is at a premium if you are a teacher, clinician, salesperson, or politician. Anybody who deals with other people has to be skilled in the interpersonal sphere.

- *Intrapersonal intelligence* refers to having an understanding of yourself, of knowing who you are, what you can do, what you want to do, how you react to things, which things to avoid, and which things to gravitate toward. We are drawn to people who have a good understanding of themselves because those people tend not to screw up. They tend to know what they can do. They tend to know what they can't do. And they tend to know where to go if they need help.

- *Naturalist intelligence* designates the human ability to discriminate among living things (plants, animals) as well as sensitivity to other features of the natural world (clouds, rock configurations). This ability was clearly of value in our evolutionary past as hunters, gatherers, and farmers; it continues to be central in such roles as botanist or chef. I also speculate that much of our consumer society exploits the naturalist intelligences, which can be mobilized in the discrimination among cars, sneakers, kinds of makeup, and the like. The kind of pattern recognition valued in certain of the sciences may also draw upon naturalist intelligence.

Source: Gardner (2006).

ability. However, tests have often been shown to under- or overestimate, too. Judging student potential for learning anything is a tricky business.

Children with Exceptional Abilities or Special Needs   In the preceding section, we learned there are many kinds of aptitude or intelligence. We also learned that we vary in how much of each kind we have. Take *mathematical intelligence*: a few of us have great math potential, most have average, and a few have very little.

Children with great potential in math, kinesthetics, and/or any other of the intelligences are referred to as gifted or talented. On the other hand, individuals with little potential in math or another intelligence are considered challenged, handicapped, or having special needs.

Gifted and Talented Learners and Underachievers   Kids who have high learning potential and use it are often called "easy teaches." They are achievers, and every teacher wants them in his or her classroom. Here are some of their characteristics:

- They usually already know and can do a lot.
- They learn and work quickly.
- They understand more completely than other students do.
- They often ask higher-level "why" and "how" questions: Why is the sky blue? How can we limit our dependence on gasoline?
- They have unusual interests or interests more similar to those of older children.
- They may prefer to work independently.

Unfortunately, many learners, including some gifted and talented ones, do not achieve their potential early on. Einstein was 4 years old before he could speak and 7 before he could read. When Thomas Edison was a boy, his teachers told him he was too stupid to learn anything. F. W. Woolworth got a job in a dry goods store when he was 21, but his employers would not let him wait on a customer because he "didn't have enough sense." A newspaper editor fired Walt Disney because he had "no good ideas." Caruso's music teacher told him, "You can't sing, you have no voice at all." Winston Churchill failed the sixth grade. And the list goes on.

3.16 Are you or anyone else you know gifted underachievers? To what do you attribute this?

The causes of this underachievement are many and include: lack of parental interest, support, and guidance; teacher failure to recognize the child's high potential or failure to challenge the child sufficiently; and the child's lack of interest or motivation and/or low self-esteem. Of course, these impediments to achievement exist for all kids, not just the gifted.

Gifted and talented kids are identified more often in schools serving higher socioeconomic populations. When gifted kids are identified in schools serving the poor, problems often exist, so that they are not properly encouraged and nurtured. (See Case 3.1.)

Helping and Teaching the Gifted and Talented   Here are some suggestions:

- Give them opportunity to interact with others of similar talent.
- Give them more complex, challenging tasks.
- Allow them to pursue individual interests, expand their time to read and explore.
- Have them pursue higher-order thinking (for example, rather than asking them when America was discovered, ask why it was discovered at that time).
- Encourage creativity in thinking and expression (for example, have them look for different ways to check the correctness of their arithmetic, have them prepare PowerPoint presentations to share learning).
- Move them through the curriculum at a quicker pace.
- Provide for their social and emotional needs.

Highlight 3.8 (on page 80) tells how one teacher provides for gifted kids.

For more on gifted education and how you can meet the needs of gifted students, go to the TeachersFirst.com website > classroom > resources and type in gifted children.

Web Links
Teachers First

Handicapped or Challenged Children   Children with less than average potential in math, reading, interpersonal, or other kinds of intelligence have more difficulty

CASE 3.1
Gifted but Forgotten

Seven years old, Devion lives in a ramshackle house opposite a pawnshop in a midsize city. He and an older brother sleep on bare mattresses in the front room because a raccoon gnawed through their bedroom ceiling.

Devion scored higher than 99 percent of children on an intelligence test and was the only African-American in his school to qualify for gifted services. In first grade he arranged cubes in intricate patterns and solved logic puzzles designed for older children.

However, this year his school district dropped its gifted program. Devion now daydreams in the back of the class and rarely raises his hand. His report card brims with unsatisfactory marks, he often doesn't turn in homework, and he has been suspended four times. His mother says he is bored and needs that "one-on-one attention."

Specialists say that when the intellectual needs of gifted kids aren't met, some exhibit behavior problems.

Source: Golden (2003).

INVESTIGATING AND SOLVING THE CASE

1. What are some factors that allow Devion to be considered gifted?
2. What could you do without a gifted program for kids like Devion?

---

performing well. They are harder to teach and require teachers with great understanding and patience. Keep in mind that some gifted children also underperform significantly or behave inappropriately.

Learners who lack such potential and learners with potential who do not live up to it are considered to have handicaps, disabilities, or disorders and are labeled as **children with special needs** or *challenged individuals*.

Depending upon their special needs, students are placed in categories in order to provide them with special education. Difference of opinion exists regarding the labels of special education categories and disabilities that fall within each. However, they include learning, developmental, communication, behavioral, and mental health disorders. Special education teachers recognize disorders and are taught how to help children manage or overcome them. Efforts are being made to reduce the number of special education kids (see Highlight 3.9).

Attention-deficit/hyperactivity disorder (AD/HD), communication disorders, and learning disabilities are three of the more common challenges special needs children face.

Attention-Deficit/Hyperactivity Disorder   Having AD/HD can make it hard for a person to sit still, control behavior, and pay attention. These difficulties usually begin before age 7 but may not be noticed until a child is older. As many as five out of every 100 children in school may have AD/HD, and boys are three times more likely to have it (see Case 3.2 on page 81). There are three main signs, or symptoms, of AD/HD: problems with paying attention, being very active (called hyperactivity), and acting before thinking (called impulsivity). AD/HD learners are of one of three types.

(1) *Inattentive type children* with AD/HD have problems paying attention. Inattentive type children often

- do not pay close attention to detail.
- can't stay focused on play or school work.
- don't follow through on instructions or finish school work or chores.
- can't seem to organize tasks and activities.

The whole class worked on the theme of "great lives" and read about the life of Nelson Mandela. The most able pupils were asked to analyze features of texts of different kinds (autobiography, biography, or historical account) in order to explore how each genre used language to achieve its effects. All members of the class were asked to write a short biography of a chosen person (real or fictitious), while the most able were asked to write a script for a 10- or 15-minute radio program that *evaluated* the person's achievements. The program was tape-recorded and presented to the class. The most able pupils were asked to: select suitable incidents for commentary and discussion, create dialogue for linking sequences, tape-record the program, and present the program to the class.

Source: Qualifications and Curriculum Authority online.

Due to lack of special education teachers, the cost, and the number of children being assigned to special education classrooms (particularly the "over-assignment" of poor and minority kids), school districts are looking for programs that may more accurately identify potential special needs children and provide earlier diagnosis and help.

For example, when he was six years old, Dylan had to be bribed to read. His mom feared that her only son would be headed for special education. Instead the school district intervened providing Dylan with daily reading and vocabulary tutoring. In some districts special education enrollment has dropped by half.

However, early mediation programs known as "response to intervention" (RTI) do not please everyone. Parents feel that, as a consequence, a child may be denied or delayed needed special education (Silverman 2008).

- get distracted easily.
- lose things such as toys, school work, and books.

(2) *Hyperactive-impulsive type children* are always on the go (hyperactive). However, as they get older, the level of activity may go down. These children also often act before thinking (impulsive). For example, they may run across the road without looking or climb to the top of very tall trees. They may be surprised to find themselves in a dangerous situation and may have no idea of how to get out of the predicament. Hyperactivity and impulsivity seem to go together. Such kids may:

- fidget and squirm.
- get out of their chairs when they're not supposed to.
- run around or climb constantly.
- have trouble playing quietly.
- talk too much.
- blurt out answers before questions have been completed.
- have trouble waiting their turn.

Dusty: A Child with AD/HD

Dusty Nash, an angelic-looking blond child of 7, awoke at 5:00 one recent morning in his Chicago home and proceeded to throw a fit. He wailed. He kicked. Every muscle in his body flew in furious motion. Finally, after 30 minutes, Dusty pulled himself together sufficiently to head downstairs for breakfast. While his mother bustled about the kitchen, the hyperkinetic child pulled a box of Kix cereal from the cupboard and sat on a chair.

But sitting still was not in the cards this morning. After grabbing some cereal with his hands, he began kicking the box, scattering little round corn puffs across the room. Next, he turned his attention to the TV set—or rather, the table supporting it. The table was covered with a checkerboard Con-Tact paper, and Dusty began peeling it off. Then he became intrigued with the spilled cereal and started stomping it to bits. At this point, his mother interceded. In a firm but calm voice, she told her son to get the dust pan and broom and clean up the mess. Dusty got out the dust pan but forgot the rest of the order. Within seconds he was dismantling the dust pan, piece by piece. His next project: grabbing three rolls of toilet paper from the bathroom and unraveling them around the house.

It was only 7:30, and his mother, who teaches a medical school course on death and dying, was already feeling half-dead from exhaustion. Dusty was to see his doctors that day at 4:00, and they had asked her not to give the boy the drug he usually takes to control his hyperactivity and attention problems. . . . It was going to be a very long day without it.

Source: Wallis (1994).

INVESTIGATING AND
RESOLVING THE CASE

1. What makes Dusty AD/HD?
2. How would you treat him in your classroom?

- interrupt others when they're talking.
- butt in on the games others are playing.

(3) *Combined type.* Children with the combined type of AD/HD have symptoms of both of the types described above. They have problems with paying attention, with hyperactivity, and with controlling their impulses.

AD/HD behaviors can cause a child to have real problems at home, at school, and with friends. As a result, many children with AD/HD will feel anxious, unsure of themselves, and depressed. These feelings are not symptoms of AD/HD. They come from having problems again and again at home and in school.

Helping and Teaching Children Who Have AD/HD   Keep in mind that from time to time, all children are inattentive, impulsive, and too active. Furthermore, some children with anxiety, depression, or neurological dysfunction may have similar symptoms. With children who have AD/HD, these behaviors are the rule, not the exception. Unfortunately, there is no magic bullet to cure AD/HD. However, the symptoms of AD/HD can be managed. It's important that the child's family and teachers:

- Learn more about AD/HD. Go to the OLC Website NIMH> "Health & Outreach> ADHD ADD"
- Create an educational program that fits the child's individual needs. Figure out what specific things are hard for the learner. For example, one student with AD/HD may have trouble starting a task, while another may have trouble ending one task and starting the next. Each student needs different help.
- Help the child manage his or her behavior. Post rules, schedules, and assignments. Clear rules and routines will help a student with AD/HD. Have set times for specific tasks. Call attention to changes in the schedule.

 Web Link
Health and Outreach AD/HD

- Show the student how to use an assignment book and a daily schedule. Also teach study skills and learning strategies, and reinforce these regularly.
- Help the student channel his or her physical activity (e.g., let the student do some work standing up or at the board). Provide regularly scheduled breaks.
- Let the learner take tests in a quiet area so as not to be distracted.
- Make sure directions are given step by step, and that the student is following the directions. Give directions both verbally and in writing. Many students with AD/HD also benefit from doing the steps as separate tasks.
- Let the student do work on a computer.
- Work together with the student's parents to create and implement an educational plan tailored to meet the student's needs. Regularly share information about how the student is doing at home and at school.
- Have high expectations for the student, but be willing to try new ways of doing things. Be patient. Maximize the student's chances for success.

Without special care, AD/HD children have an extremely high rate of school failure, substance abuse, and lawbreaking. Additionally, over time, they often have few friends, and their parents are blamed for their difficulties.

(Much of the above is adapted from The National Dissemination Center for Children with Disabilities website.)

 Web Link
National Dissemination Center for Children with Disabilities

Communication Disorders: Speech, Language, and Hearing   Communication is considered delayed when a learner is noticeably behind in speech acquisition or language skills. About 5 percent of all children have some communication disorder. They comprise over 20 percent of the total school special education population. Such disorders arise from many sources. Speech disorders occur when persons have difficulty producing speech sounds or have problems with the way their voice sounds. Common disorders include stuttering, trouble making certain sounds like *l* or *r*, and difficulties with voice pitch, volume, or quality. Speech, language, and hearing disorders can isolate afflicted children from peers. Working with communication disabled children requires help from therapists and special education personnel.

Helping and Teaching Communication Challenged Kids

 **Web Link**
Psychology Today

- Learn more about communication disorders. Go to the OLC Website, Psychology Today>Diagnosis Dictionary>Communication Disorders.
- Talk with specialists.
- Implement instructional procedures recommended by specialists.
- When working with children with language disorders: allow them to talk about things of interest, ask questions that require thought such as *how* and *why* and allow plenty of time for responding, encourage them to ask questions, and accept their language as it develops.
- When working with hearing-impaired children, try to ensure classroom acoustics are good, seat such children where they hear best, try to face them when teaching, and consider use of a teacher microphone and a receiver worn by children.

About Learning Disabilities   Learning disabled individuals have in common that there is a gap between their ability and their achievement (see **Case 3.3**). They demonstrate *unexpected underachievement*. A learning disability (LD) is a result of any disorder that makes it hard for an otherwise normal person to listen, think, speak, read, write, spell, or do mathematical calculations (Individuals with Disabilities Education Act). Estimates are that about 8 percent of the school-age population is LD. Moreover, 50 percent of all students receiving special education fall into this category. Learning disabilities vary from person to person: one may do better in

Learning Disabled Sara

When Sara was in the first grade, her teacher started teaching the students how to read. Sara's parents were really surprised when Sara had a lot of trouble. She was bright and eager so they thought that reading would come easily. It didn't. She couldn't match the letters to sounds or combine the letters to create words.

Sara's problems continued in second grade. She still wasn't reading, and she was having trouble with writing, too. The school asked Sara's mom for permission to evaluate Sara to find out what was causing her problems. Sara's mom gave permission for an evaluation.

The school conducted the evaluation and learned that Sara had a learning disability. She started getting special help right away.

Sara's still getting that special help. She works with a reading specialist and a resource room teacher every day. She's in the fourth grade now, and she's made real progress! She is working hard to bring her reading and writing up to grade level. With help from the school, she'll keep learning and doing well.

INVESTIGATING AND RESOLVING THE CASE

1. What might make reading difficult for Sara?
2. How will you work with learning disabled students?

---

certain subjects than in others. Sara, in the example above, has trouble with reading and writing. Others may have problems understanding math or understanding what people are saying. Remember children with LD are otherwise normal: they are not dumb or lazy. The causes of LD are many and not well understood. They can be attributed to heredity, parental abuse of substances (alcohol and drugs), poor prenatal care, premature birth, exposure to lead, diabetes or meningitis, malnutrition, and differences in brain structure. When students have LD, they may

- have difficulty learning new skills and remembering new information.
- have difficulty following directions.
- have trouble handling deadlines.
- find it hard to keep work organized and neat.
- have difficulty understanding rules of conversation.
- have difficulty taking turns.
- make inappropriate remarks.
- have difficulty changing from one subject or class to another.
- find it hard to play and get along with age mates.
- learn language late.
- have trouble learning the alphabet, rhyming words, or connecting letters to their sounds.
- mispronounce words.
- fail to speak in full sentences.
- have a limited vocabulary and be challenged to learn more.
- find it hard to read accurately—make many mistakes when reading aloud—repeat and pause often.
- have difficulty understanding what they read.
- have trouble remembering the sounds that letters make or hearing slight differences between words.
- be unable to retell stories.
- have trouble organizing what to say or not be able to think of a word needed for writing or conversation.

- have significant trouble with spelling.
- have messy handwriting or hold a pencil awkwardly.
- struggle to express ideas in writing.
- have trouble understanding jokes, comic strips, and sarcasm.
- have difficulty doing math.
- confuse math symbols and misread numbers.
- struggle to draw or copy.

Web Link
Learning Disability

Helping and Teaching LD Children   If a child has unexpected problems learning to read, write, listen, speak, or do math, then teachers must find out why. Overall, teachers who suspect a child has LD should

- learn more about LD. Go to the OLC website Psychology Today>Diagnosis Dictionary>Learning Disability.
- talk with specialists including special education teachers.
- review the child's school records (see Chapter 5 Cumulative Records).
- break learning tasks into smaller steps, and give directions verbally and in writing.
- give the student more time to finish work or take tests.
- let the student with reading problems use textbooks-on-tape (available through Recording for the Blind and Dyslexic).
- let the student with listening difficulties borrow notes from a classmate or use a tape recorder.
- let the student with writing difficulties use a computer with specialized software that spell checks, grammar checks, or recognizes speech.
- learn about the different testing modifications that can really help a student with LD show what he or she has learned.
- teach organizational skills, study skills, and learning strategies. These help all students but are particularly helpful to those with LD.
- work with the student's parents to create an educational plan tailored to meet the student's needs.
- establish a working relationship with the student's parents. Through regular communication, exchange information about the student's progress at school.

It is not easy to determine what causes LD nor is it easy to remedy. However, with appropriate guidance and instruction in decoding skills, foundational strategies for comprehension, and advanced strategies for making inferences from text reading, children can be helped dramatically.

(Much of the above is adapted from the National Dissemination Center for Children with Disabilities and the Division for Learning Disabilities of the Council for Exceptional Children websites.)

Web Links
Council for Children and
Exceptional Children

Since learning in the early years is crucial, providing stimulating learning environments for young children is critical. The National Institute of Health argues that, in addition to your need to stimulate children, you need to identify those who need special education. Unfortunately, most children who might benefit don't go into special education until about 9 years of age (Pipho, 1997).

Mainstreaming Children with Special Needs   Before the passage of federal laws, including the Individuals with Disabilities Education Act (IDEA), children with special needs were taught in separate special education classrooms by specially prepared teachers. Now, however, the goal is to teach them in regular classrooms as much as possible. This revolutionary turn is called **mainstreaming.** Its intention is to ensure that special needs children are educated in as normal, or least restrictive, environment (LRE) as possible. This means that if children can be successfully educated *with support* in the regular classroom for all or part of the day, then that is where they should be. Support can include tutoring by special education teachers, modification of lessons and ways of teaching (perhaps use of more hands-on activity), or providing additional time for test taking. IDEA also requires that regular classroom teachers receive preparation in order to work effectively with each type of special needs child in the classroom. Case 3.4 depicts a mainstreamed child.

Noble in intention, mainstreaming is not without its problems. School districts report these obstacles, among others: classes receiving special needs kids can become too large and complex; special needs students feel lost and intimidated and some feel they cannot keep up and blend in; regular students get distracted by the behavior of special students; and not enough teacher support is possible. As a result, at times mainstreamed students refuse to go to school (Gottlieb, 2006).

Moreover, teachers often feel overwhelmed when asked to meet the needs of children they are not well prepared to serve. One requirement is that for each student, they meet with others (perhaps parents, special education teachers, guidance personnel) to draw up an individualized education plan (IEP) that spells out in detail the accommodations that will be made so that the child will more likely succeed (see Highlight 3.10 on page 87). A video of how the IEP process works is located at the *Disability Scoop* website. Click on "The IEP and You." See the OLC web link in the margin for this and other on-line resources.

Special education teacher Simpson empathizes with regular teachers trying to meet the needs of special children.

> I have seen great teachers killing themselves trying to serve special education students in their classrooms. . . . They work as hard as a human being can work and they fail. . . . Why do they fail? Because they have too many kids [to teach]. Reduce class size to 15, give [them an assistant] and [they] will provide individualized education to every student. . . . There [is not enough time nor not enough adults] in a classroom to allow a general education teacher to spend the ten or fifteen minutes each period needed to help some students learn. . . . (Simpson, 2005)

INTEREST DIFFERENCES

Each child brings his or her interests and motivation to the classroom. One bit of advice you will be given in Chapter 5 is, "Try to meet the interests of learners."

Many believe that children perform or achieve differently mostly because they have different interests, motivation, or cultural background (Graham, cited in McPhail & Palincsar, 2006). If we take Graham's *interest* assertion seriously, one thing we should do is support children working within academic or vocational areas they enjoy. For example, if a child is drawn to music, science, or whatever, so be it. On the other hand, when a child finds himself in a situation where what is to be learned does not capture his imagination or arouse his curiosity, he may tune it out. "When a teacher asked the class at the end of an activity, 'What good is the compass going to be to us?' Tui whispered to himself, 'Nothing'" (Rosenshine 2006). Of course, to determine the true interests of students, you must get inside their minds—you must really come to know them. Chapter 5, Getting to Know Your Students and Motivating Them to Learn, will help. Interest lacking, you must be an enthusiastic person and a good motivator.

IMPLICATIONS FOR TEACHERS

Teachers are effective in large part because they care about children enough to accommodate their endless diversity. Wang (1998) tells us that "what works is

OLC Web Links
Websites on individualized education planning that contain sample IEPs:

IEPs online

Disability Scoop

Family Village School

Learning Disabilities Online

3.17 How well do you think you can handle the challenges of student diversity?

Candy: A Mainstreamed Child

Candy is a child with cerebral palsy who was placed in Louise DeFelice's English class. DeFelice worried about a number of things: she had no experience with handicapped youth, she was apprehensive about Candy's ability to speak, and she wasn't sure how her classmates would react to her.

Candy, on the other hand, was neither worried nor self-conscious. She wasn't seeking sympathy or any kind of special treatment.

Ms. DeFelice soon became concerned about whether Candy could handle an upcoming oral report and asked her if she would rather substitute another assignment. Candy insisted that she could do it. On the day of the reports, when Candy's turn came, DeFelice was apprehensive as the girl "lumbered to the front of the classroom." She reports:

> It began much as I feared. The students sat looking down at their desks or giving one another embarrassed sidelong glances as Candy stammered and stuttered her way through the first few minutes . . . After a few more minutes each of the students began to whisper to each other (page 640).

However, just as the teacher was about to say something, Vince, a class leader, turned to his peers and told them "to shut up and pay attention." Afterward, the other kids began to look straight at Candy and concentrate on what she was trying to say. Wonderfully, at the conclusion of Candy's report the class applauded and her eyes gleamed tearfully.

Candy's belief in herself followed by what Ms. DeFelice terms "classroom magic" forever justified her faith in teaching and students.

Source: DeFelice (1989).

INVESTIGATING AND SOLVING THE CASE

1. Which "Tips for Teachers" seem applicable for Candy?
2. Create a plan Ms. DeFelice could follow to help Candy.

---

adapting instruction to students' diverse backgrounds and needs, an approach that determines how each child learns . . . and then tailoring instruction to meet those needs" (p. 39). Less effective teachers often have a difficult time either noticing or attending to the variability of students in their classes. They want and tend to see the class more as a homogeneous group. While this makes instruction less complicated, if you are to advance from a novice to a more expert teacher, you must learn to teach children who are socioeconomically, culturally, and developmentally diverse and diverse in terms of gender, exceptionality, learning style, and learning ability. To summarize, our schools need teachers who will

Try Activity 3.1

Try Activity 3.2

- care about socially and economically disadvantaged youth and be willing to work with them.
- accept, appreciate, and promote culturally specific characteristics.
- assist LEP learners.
- improve minority student learning.
- promote the best attributes of both genders in all children.
- provide students with experiences that may help them develop positive personalities.
- take into account students' varying levels of cognitive development when teaching.

Try Activity 3.3

- encourage growth in moral development.

Try Activity 3.4

- show concern for and willingness to work with exceptional students.
- allow for students' learning, thinking, and cognitive styles and their multiple intelligences.
- help students gain a feeling of **efficacy** or control over their destinies.

HIGHLIGHT 3.10
A Good Individualized Education Plan

- Must be based upon a careful assessment of the learner.
- Must describe why the plan is necessary and contain objectives with a timetable for reaching each.
- Must be developed by a team of individuals that work directly with the learner such as teachers, tutors, social workers, and clinicians.

- Should define what should be taught and how, who will teach it, where it will be taught, when the program will begin, how long it will last, when it will be reviewed, how special education and related service will be provided, and how the learner will be educated in the "least restrictive" or most normal environment possible.

- Should be discussed and finalized at a meeting involving the regular classroom teacher, special education teacher, representative of the school district, and possibly the learner.
- To the extent possible, parents or caregivers should be involved.

Some Final Thoughts

This chapter describes some of the many faces of student diversity and challenges they present. To the extent you recognize that your learners are unique and take that uniqueness into account, you are more likely to increase their academic and social success. Consequently, you will be remembered by them as a teacher who made a difference in their lives. Hopefully, you had one or more teachers who took a personal interest in you, who cared about you as an individual. Pass it on!

CHAPTER SUMMARY

- To be an effective teacher you must know the many ways learners differ and take those differences into account.
- Children of the poor suffer many disadvantages, including family and housing instability, neighborhood crime and deterioration, poor or inadequate nutrition, and minimal or no health care.
- Schools serving the poor often lack resources to meet the many educational, psychological, and social needs of students.
- Minority children may also be disadvantaged because of such factors as English language deficiency and inability to adapt to majority cultural ways and expectations.
- Schools and society need to permit and encourage minority students to feel good about themselves and their cultures. However, minority children are more likely to succeed when the family comes to the United States to improve its well-being and when it tries to assimilate into the majority culture.
- With regard to gender differences, there is lack of agreement over whether boys and girls are more alike or different. Relatedly, there is lack of agreement about whether gender differences are genetic or learned. A final matter of dispute is whether gender differences are healthy. In any case, teachers need to create classrooms wherein boys and girls share equal opportunity to learn.
- Children reach certain developmental stages at different times and go through them at different rates. Thus, teachers need to accept differences in maturity and maturation.
- Diversity of student temperament means that some kids will have good or even temperaments while others may be ill tempered and more difficult.

SUPPLEMENTAL RESOURCES

Go to the text's Online Learning Center at www.mhhe.com/cruickshank6e to access the chapter's **study tool**s including web links, practice for Praxis™ case studies and video clips.

www.mhhe.com/cruickshank6e

CHAPTER 3
Teaching Diverse Students
87

- A desirable characteristic of students is self-discipline. Another is self-denial. These qualities may be more important to student academic success than teachers, learning materials, or class size.
- How a child prefers to learn—learning style—is important and needs serious consideration. Teachers who take learning style factors into account are more likely to help kids learn.
- There are many kinds of aptitude or potential for learning. Historically, we have thought only or mostly of IQ. Now we recognize student potential in several other realms, including language, mathematics, music, interpersonal activities, and sport. Recognition and acceptance of multiple kinds of intelligence permits many different kinds of learners to be successful and encourages teachers to strive for different kinds of learning outcomes.
- Exceptional children include the gifted and talented and challenged children with special needs. Among the challenges kids face are attention deficits, disorders in speech, language, or hearing, and learning disabilities. Whereas special needs students had been taught primarily in special education classrooms, they now are mainstreamed or taught in regular classrooms so that their education is as normal as possible.

KEY TERMS

Gender roles, 63

Psychological androgyny, 63

Self-esteem, 69

Sensorimotor stage, 69

Preoperational, prelogical stage, 69

Concrete operational stage, 69

Formal operational stage, 69

Moral development, 69

Morality of constraint, 70

Morality of cooperation, 70

Personality, 70

Temperament, 70

Learning style preferences, 72

Conceptual tempo, 73

Field dependent, 74

Field independent, 74

Divergent thinkers, 75

Convergent thinkers, 75

Multiple intelligences, 76

Children with special needs, 79

Mainstreaming, 84

Efficacy, 86

ISSUES AND PROBLEMS FOR DISCUSSION

ISSUES   Here are some issues for you to debate.

1. To what extent do you believe teachers can accommodate the many kinds of differences learners bring to the classroom?
2. What, in your mind, are the most important kinds of learner differences (Figure 3.1) that teachers should try to accommodate?
3. To what extent should learners be grouped according to their likenesses and differences? For example, what might be the advantages and disadvantages of grouping learners according to cultural background, gender, development, learning style, or learning ability?
4. How well prepared are you to work with diverse children? How can you increase your ability to do so?

PROBLEMS   The following are some related, verbatim, day-to-day problems teachers have shared with us. How might you resolve them?

Problem 1:   Artis tells you that you don't like him.

Problem 2: Tipp's mother feels he is developing a very negative self-esteem.

Problem 3: Every lesson you assign seems to result in some children finishing ahead of others and some not doing the assignments well.

Problem 4: The girls complain that you always call on the boys and give them special privileges.

Problem 5: James is very upset with his report card. He comments, "I try real hard, but all I get are bad marks. I give up!"

Problem 6: Kimberly's mother doesn't want her in the low reading group.

THEORY INTO ACTION: ACTIVITIES FOR PRACTICE AND YOUR PORTFOLIO

ACTIVITY 3.1: Personal Feelings about Teaching Diverse Students   Write a paragraph or so on the topic "What I think it will be like to teach diverse children." Compare your thoughts with others.

ACTIVITY 3.2: Five Student Types   Five types of children have been noted by Good & Power, 1976. How would you serve each?

1. *Successful.* These students are academically successful in school. They work hard and cause few problems. They like school and teachers.
2. *Social.* These students are more interested in the social aspects of school life than in the academic. They are popular and friendly. Their socializing can cause problems.
3. *Alienated.* These students may be openly hostile toward the school and teachers, or they may be passive and withdrawn.
4. *Dependent.* Such students are emotionally and/or academically insecure. They need approval and help.
5. *Phantom.* Such students are quiet, independent, and seldom seen or heard.

Names of students I have identified and how I would work with each:

1. Successful _____

2. Social _____

3. Alienated _____

4. Dependent _____

5. Phantom _____

ACTIVITY 3.3: Obtain Classroom Teachers' Views about Student Diversity   Talk with one or more classroom teachers about student diversity. Perhaps they would respond to questions such as:

- What differences do you see among children from different SES backgrounds?
- What differences do you see among children with different cultural backgrounds?
- What is the difference between teaching majority and minority students?
- What is the difference between teaching boys and girls?

- In what ways do your students differ developmentally (e.g., in terms of their personalities, self-esteem, thinking ability, sense of morality)?
- How do you work with special needs kids?
- How do your students differ in the way they like to learn? In their learning abilities?
- How do all these differences affect how you teach?

ACTIVITY 3.4: The Implications of Student Diversity for Teaching After reading this chapter, make a list of five to ten *major* things you have learned and their possible implications for classroom practice. For example:

Major Learning	Possible Implication
1. Students differ from one another in many ways.	1. To be effective as a teacher, I need to know how my students vary and how I can accommodate their differences. I certainly can't expect to teach them all successfully without using different approaches from student to student and from time to time.

REFERENCES

Aardvark's English Forum. Access: www.englishforum.com/00/

American Academy of Pediatrics. (1993, October). Homosexuality and adolescence: Policy statement. *Pediatrics, 92*(4), 631–634.

Baumeister, R., Campbell, Krueger, J., & Vohs, K. (2005, January). *Exploding the self-esteem myth.* Scientific American.com. Access: www.sciam.com/article .cfm?chanID=5a00b&colID= 1&articleID=000CB565-F330-11

Bickmore, K. (1999, April 19–23). *Why discuss sexuality in elementary school?* Paper presented at the Annual Meeting of the American Educational Research Association, Montreal (ERIC Document Reproduction Services ED 434 893).

Boys' academic slide calls for accelerated attention. (2003, December 22). *USA Today,* p. 17A.

Brandt, R. (1990). On learning styles: A conversation with Pat Guild. *Educational Leadership, 48*(2), 10–13.

Brophy, J. (1985). Interactions of male and female students with male and female teachers. In L. Wilkinson & C. Marrett (Eds.), *Gender differences in classroom interaction* (pp. 115–142). Orlando, FL: Academic Press.

Burnette, J. (1999). *Critical behaviors and strategies for teaching culturally diverse students.* (ERIC Clearinghouse on Disabilities and Gifted Education ED 435147).

Checkley, K. (1997, September). The first seven and the eighth. *Educational Leadership, 55*(1), 8–13.

Chin, E., Young, J., & Floyd, B. (2004). Placing beginning teachers in hard to staff schools. Paper presented at the annual meeting of the American Association of Colleges for Teacher Education. Chicago, IL.

Clyde, L. & Lobban, M. (2000). *Out of the closet and into the classroom: Homosexuality in books for young people.* Victoria, Australia (ERIC Document Reproduction Services ED 437 482).

Conlin, M. (2003, May 26). The new gender gap. *Business Week Online.*

Cushner, K., McClelland, A., & Safford, P. (2008). *Human diversity in education.* New York: McGraw-Hill.

Davis-Kean, P. (2007, May 31). How dads influence their daughters' interest in math. Paper presented at Educating a STEM Workforce conference. Ann Arbor: University of Michigan.

Dee, T. (2005). Teachers and the gender gaps in student achievement. NBER Working Paper No. 11660. Also *A teacher like me: Does race, ethnicity or gender matter?* Invited Presidential Session of the American Educational Research Association (2005, April).

DeFelice, L. (1989, April). The Bibbidibobbidiboo Factor in Teaching. *Phi Delta Kappan, 70*(8), 639–641.

Dembo, M. H. (2000). *Applying educational psychology in the classroom.* New York: Addison-Wesley Longman.

de Oliveira, F. J. (1991). *A Geração Insatisfeita.* Belo Horizonte, Brasilia: Edições Paulinas.

Donsky, P. (2003, August 21). King Middle School: Splitting-up boys and girls. *Atlanta Constitution,* p. 8.

Duckworth, A. L. & Seligman, M. (2005). Self-discipline outdoes IQ in predicting academic performance of adolescents. *Psychological Science, 16,* 939–944.

Duckworth, A. L. & Seligman, M. (2006, February). Self-discipline gives girls the edge. *Journal of Educational Psychology, 98*(1), 198–208.

Dunn, R., Dunn, K., & Price, G. (2001). *Learning style inventory.* Lawrence, KS: Price Systems.

Dusek, J. (1987). Sex roles and adjustment. In D. B. Carter (Ed.), *Current conceptions of sex roles and sex typing* (pp. 211–222). New York: Praeger.

Educational Testing Service. (1997). *ETS gender study: How females and males perform in educational settings.* Princeton, NJ: Educational Testing Service.

Elias, M., Zins, J., Weissberg, R., Fry, K., Greenberg, M., Haynes, N., Kessler, R., Schwab-Stone, M., & Shriver, T. (1997). *Promoting social and emotional learning.* Alexandria, VA: Association for Supervision and Curriculum Development.

Erikson, E. (1993). *Childhood and society.* Second Edition. New York: Norton.

Evans, D. (1999, October 20). The excesses of self-esteem. *Education Week, 19*(8), 47.

Fritz, R. L. (1992). *A study of gender differences in cognitive style and volition* (ERIC Document Reproduction Services ED 354 379).

Garbarino, J. (2000). *Lost boys: Why our sons turn violent and how we can save them.* New York: Anchor Books/Doubleday.

Gardner, H. (1988). Beyond the IQ: Education and human development. *Harvard Educational Review, 57,* 187–193.

Gardner, H. (1993). *Frames of mind: The theory of multiple intelligences.* New York: Basic Books.

Gardner, H. (1995). Reflections on multiple intelligences. *Phi Delta Kappan, 77*(30), 200–209.

Gardner, H. (2000). *Intelligence Reframed: Multiple Intelligences for the 21st Century.* New York: Basic Books.

Gardner, H. (2006). *Multiple intelligences.* New York: Basic Books.

Gardner, H. & Hatch, T. (1989). Multiple intelligences go to school. *Educational Researcher, 18*(8), 4–10.

Gibson, K. (2000, August 5). Poverty is no excuse for a poor education. *Columbus Dispatch,* p. A11.

Glencoe online. Access: www.glencoe.com/sec/teachingtoday/educationupclose.phtml/24

Golden, D. (2003, December 29). Brain drain: Initiative to leave no child behind leaves out gifted. *Wall Street Journal, 242*(126), pp. A1, A6.

Goleman, D. (2005). *Emotional intelligence.* New York: Bantam Books.

Good, T. & Brophy, J. (1999). *Contemporary educational psychology: A realistic approach.* New York: Longman.

Good, T. & Power, C. (1976). Designing successful classroom environments for different types of students. *Journal of Curriculum Studies, 8,* 1–16.

Gottlieb, R. (2006, February 5). A class struggle: City inclusion effort brings serious problems. *Hartford Courant,* p. 13.

Gurian, M. & Stevens, K. (2006, Winter). How boys learn. *Educational Horizons, 84*(2), 87–93.

Gutierrez, K. & Rogoff, B. (2003, June/July). Cultural ways of learning. *Education Researcher, 32*(5), 19–25.

Hall, D. & Kennedy, S. (2006). *Primary progress, secondary challenge.* Washington, DC: Education Trust

Headden, S. (1997, October 20). The Hispanic dropout mystery. *U.S. News & World Report, 123*(15), 64–65.

Hoxby, C. (2002, Summer). The power of peers. *Education Next, 2*(2), 56–63.

Hyde, J. (2005, September). The gender similarities hypothesis. *American Psychologist, 60*(6), 581–592.

Hyde, J. & Linn, M. (1988, April 5–8). Gender differences in verbal ability: A meta-analysis. Paper presented at the annual meeting of the American Educational Research Association. New Orleans, LA.

Internet TESL Journal. Access: http://iteslj.org/

Johnston, R. & Viadero, D. (2000, March 15). Unmet promise: Raising minority achievement. *Education Week, 19*(27), 1, 18–23.

Jones, S. & Dindia, L. (2004, Winter). Meta-analytic perspective on sex equity. *Review of Educational Research 74*(4), 443–471.

Kohlberg, L. (1981). *The philosophy of moral development.* New York: Harper and Row.

Kohn, A. (1994). The truth about self-esteem. *Phi Delta Kappan, 76*(4), 272–283.

Kolb, D. A. (2005). *The Learning Style Inventory Version 3.1.* Boston, MA: Hay Resources Direct.

Kleinfeld, J. (Winter 2007). Teacher gender. *Education Next, 7*(1), 6–7.

Levy, J., Den Brok, P., Wubbels, T., & Brekelmans, M. (2003). Students' perceptions of interpersonal aspects of the learning environment. *Learning Environments, 6,* 5–36.

Luthar, S & Latendresse, S. (2005, February). Children of the affluent. *Current Directions in Psychological Science, 14*(1), 49–53.

McNeal, B. (2002, September). Speech given at a student diversity summit. Wake County, NC.

McPhail, J. & Palincsar, A. (2006, July). Minds and more. *Teaching and Teacher Education, 22*(5), 538–546.

Meichenbaum, D. (1999). *Cognitive behavior modification: An integrative approach.* New York: Plenum.

Miller, G. (2005, June 26). Boys today: They're pretty much the same as they've always been. *Rhode Island News,* p. B3.

National Center for the Dissemination of Disability Research. (2003). Access: www.ncddr.org/du/products/dddreview/culturalother.html

Oliver, K. (2002). *Understanding your child's temperament.* Family Life Month Packet. Columbus, OH: Ohio State University, Family and Consumer Sciences.

Osborne, J. A. (1997, December). Race and academic disidentification. *Journal of Educational Psychology, 89*(4), 728–735.

Pashler, H., McDaniel, M., Rohrer, D. & Bjork, R. (2009, December). Learning styles: Concepts and evidence. *Psychological Science in the Public Interest, 9*(3), 105–119.

Piaget, J. (1999). *The moral judgment of the child.* New York: Free Press.

Pipho, C. (1997, September). Reshaping special education. *Phi Delta Kappan, 79*(1), 5–6.

Qualifications and Curriculum Authority online. Guidance on teaching the gifted and talented. Access: www.qca.org.uk/qca_2346.aspx

Quindlen, T. (2002, August). Reaching minority students: Strategies for closing the achievement gap. *Education Update, 44*(5), 1, 6–8.

Ramerez, M. & Price-Williams, D. (1974). Cognitive styles of children of three ethnic groups in the United States. *Journal of Cross-Cultural Psychology, 5*(2), 212–219.

Rochkind, J., Ott, A., Immerwahr, J. Doble, J, Johnson, J. (2008). *Lessons learned*. Washington, DC: Public Agenda online www.publicagenda .org/lessonslearned3/pdfs/lessons _learned_3.pdf

Rosenshine, B. (2006, July). Struggles of the low-scoring student. *Teaching and Teacher Education, 22*(5), 555–562.

Sax, L. (2005). *Why gender matters*. New York: Random House.

Sax, L. (2009). *What are some differences in how girls and boys learn?* Education.com online. http:// www.singlesexschools.org/research -learning.htm

Select Committee on Children, Youth and Families. (1989). *U.S. children and their families: Current conditions and recent trends, 1989*. Washington, DC: U.S. Government Printing Office.

Silverman, J. (2008, April 21). *Catching problems early, schools try to avoid special ed*. New York Times

Company online http://www .boston.com/news/education/k_12/ articles/2008/04/21/catching _problems_early_schools_try_to _avoid_special_ed?mode=PF

Simpson, S. (2005, October 31). Special education: The myth of the least restrictive environment. *Ed.Net Briefs*. Snoqulamie, WA: Simpson Communications, Box 325, 7829 Center Blvd. SE.

Slavin, R. (2008). *Educational psychology: Theory and practice*. Boston: Allyn & Bacon.

Snowman, J. & Biehler, R. (2008). *Psychology applied to teaching*. Boston: Houghton Mifflin.

Support4learning.org.ukhttp:// www.support4learning.org.uk/ education/learning_styles.cfm

Tannen, D. (1991, July 19). Teachers' classroom strategies should recognize that men and women use language differently. *Chronicle of Higher Education, 37*(40), B1, B3.

U.S. Census Bureau (2002). *Survey of income and program participation*. Washington, DC.

Viadero, D. (2000, March 22). Lags in minority achievement defy traditional explanations. *Education Week, 19*(28), 1, 18–22.

Vincent, A. & Ross, D. (2001, Summer). Learning style awareness.

Journal of Research on Technology in Education, 33(5), 24–26.

Wallis, C. (1994, July 18). Life in overdrive. *Time, 144*(3), 50.

Wang, M. (1998, June 24). Comprehensive school reform. *Education Week, 17*(41), 39, 52.

Weil, E. (2008, March 2). Teaching boys and girls separately. *New York Times Magazine*, 12–13. online http://www .nytimes.com/2008/03/02/ magazine/02sex3-t.html

Weingarten, T. (2005, April 26). When quiet kids get forgotten in class. *Christian Science Monitor*, p. 23.

Welsh, P. (2006, May 7). For once, blame the student. *U.S.A. Today*, p. 11A.

WikEd. Access: www.wik.ed.uiuc .edu/index.php/Gender _Differences

Witkin, H. [A.] & Goodenough, D. (1981). *Cognitive styles*. Madison, CT: International University Press.

Witkin, H. A., Dyke, R., Faterfon, H., Goodenough, D., & Korp, S. (1962). *Psychological differentiation: Studies of development*. New York: Wiley.

Woolfolk, A. (2007). *Educational psychology*. Boston: Allyn & Bacon.

You and the system. (1990, April). *Teacher Magazine, 7*(1), 10.

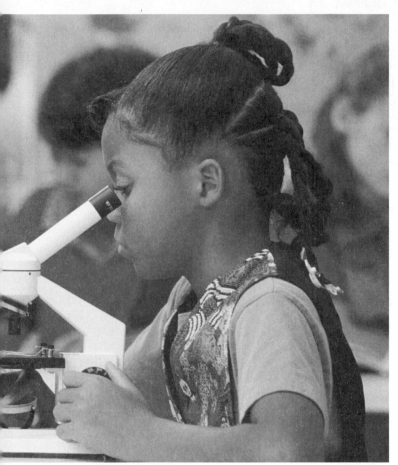

Conversation Starters

How do kids learn best?

There are several points of view about how children learn best. One is that kids learn best when teachers utilize what is known about learning—how new information is taken in, processed, stored, and retrieved. Teachers should understand the mental processes of learning and put to use what is known about such things as attention, memory, and the ways information can be made more understandable.

A second explanation suggests that learning improves when the classroom is more humane and when the school is made to fit the child, rather than the other way around. This school of thought about learning values children having good self-concepts and being secure, treating each other with respect, and providing for individual student needs.

The third explanation contends that learning is best accomplished when teachers know how to alter the learning environment to encourage learning. Among other things, teachers should present what is to be learned in smaller chunks, help learners associate what is to be learned with what they already know, provide more practice, and reward learners when they do correct things.

What do you think helps kids learn best?

Have you been in classrooms where a teacher was teaching, but not all students were learning? This could happen when you teach. If it does, ask yourself, "what should I be doing that I'm not doing?" Hopefully, when you ask that question, you will have answers. Many of the answers come from learning theory—what we know about learning. That's why the information about learning contained in this chapter is so important to your success. You simply cannot fail at teaching if you put it to use.

This chapter presents basic information from three, among other, schools of thought about how students learn. The schools are cognitive, humanistic, and behavioral (see Figure 4.1). Although the ideas from the three appear to be independent, you will see they share many beliefs.

4.1 What do you recall about how we learn from previous course work and experience?

The Cognitive School of Thought

The first school of thought we will examine has its roots in cognitive science, a field that studies how people think. Specifically, cognitive scientists try to fathom what goes on inside our heads when we are learning. They have contributed two important, wide-ranging ideas that help us understand how people learn and remember. They are information processing and meaningful learning.

Information processing refers to the study of how we mentally take in and store information and then retrieve it when needed. If we understand and use what we know about information processing, we should be able to help our students become better at taking in and remembering information. **Meaningful learning** involves the study of how new information can be most effectively organized, structured, and taught so that it might be used, for example in problem-solving situations. Let's look at these two somewhat different and sometimes overlapping ideas.

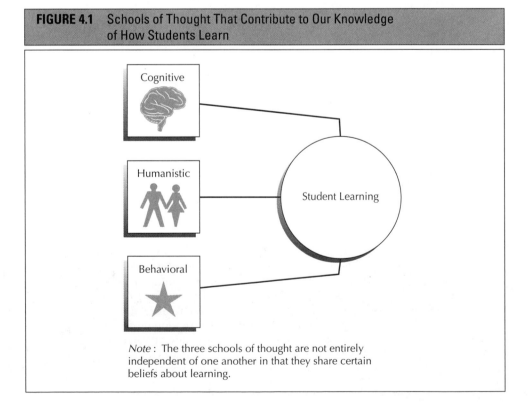

FIGURE 4.1 Schools of Thought That Contribute to Our Knowledge of How Students Learn

Cognitive

Humanistic

Student Learning

Behavioral

Note: The three schools of thought are not entirely independent of one another in that they share certain beliefs about learning.

INFORMATION PROCESSING

If you have taken a psychology course, you know that cognitive scientists—persons interested in information processing—study how we *attend to, recognize, transform, store, and retrieve information.* They develop models, such as the one shown in Figure 4.2, to illustrate how they believe information is processed. Essentially models such as this one suggest that although we encounter many stimuli (A), we pay attention to only some of them (B). Of the stimuli we notice, some will be discarded almost immediately, while the rest go into our short-term (C), or working, memory. **Short-term memory,** as the term suggests, is a storage system that holds only a limited amount and certain kinds of information for a few seconds. When these stimuli reach our short-term memory, the items we then use (think about) to any degree are transferred to our long-term, or permanent, memory and saved (D). As the name implies, long-term memory is where we keep information for a longer time. Information that we do not use to any degree, and that therefore does not reach **long-term memory,** is forgotten as if we had never been exposed to it in the first place. Much information to which we have been exposed is lost for lack of proper storage and use.

Computers also have short-term and long-term memory. To illustrate, if we search the Internet using the keyword "learning theory," we may find our three schools of thought about learning—cognitive, humanistic, and behavioral. If the computer is not told to "save" this knowledge before it is shut down, the information is lost since it existed only in its short-term memory. However, if the computer is told to save the information, perhaps placing it in a document or folder, then it is transferred into the hard drive or the computer's long-term memory.

As you might expect, cognitive scientists often try to answer questions that are very important to teachers, such as, What attracts and holds a learner's attention? How can more information be placed into short- and long-term memory? How should we organize and present information to make it more memorable? How can students best study or learn new information? Following are some major beliefs and findings of cognitivists that are related to such questions. These beliefs and findings should have direct bearing on the way you teach.

FIGURE 4.2 How Learners Gain or Lose Information

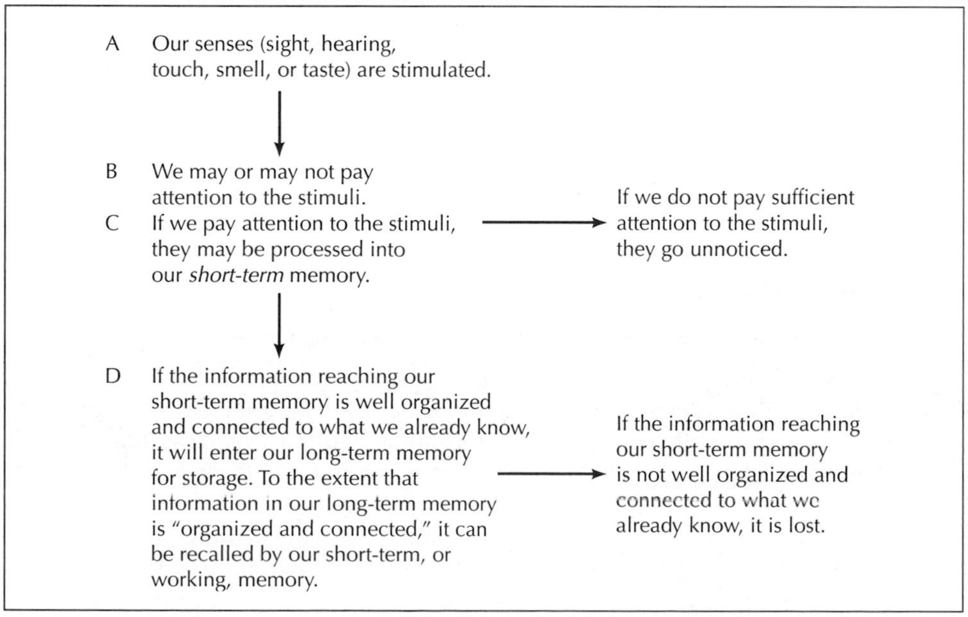

A   Our senses (sight, hearing, touch, smell, or taste) are stimulated.

B   We may or may not pay attention to the stimuli.

C   If we pay attention to the stimuli, they may be processed into our *short-term* memory.   →   If we do not pay sufficient attention to the stimuli, they go unnoticed.

D   If the information reaching our short-term memory is well organized and connected to what we already know, it will enter our long-term memory for storage. To the extent that information in our long-term memory is "organized and connected," it can be recalled by our short-term, or working, memory.   →   If the information reaching our short-term memory is not well organized and connected to what we already know, it is lost.

"First, you have to get their attention."

4.2 Can you describe instances when your teachers either followed or violated one of the principles for gaining attention?

4.3 What will you most keep in mind about getting and keeping student attention?

Beliefs about Attention   Getting students to "pay attention" to information is a very real, everyday teacher challenge. Cognitivists suggest teachers use the following guiding principles to gain and hold learners' **attention:**

- *Learning experiences should be as pleasant and satisfying as possible.* Students are more likely to attend to something (mathematics, music, sports) when they have had previous positive experiences with it. If learners' previous experiences with that stimulus has been unpleasant, the experiences you give them must be especially good.

- *Whenever possible, lessons should take into account the interests and needs of students.* Students are more likely to pay attention to lessons that focus on what they want to know or what they want to be able to do. A major task for you will be to encourage them to attend to things in which they may have little or no interest.

- *The attention of learners can be gained and held longer by making use of different sensory channels and change.* A student is more likely to attend to lessons that employ a variety of stimuli, that is, when shifts occur from listening to talking to doing, and so forth. Novelty also helps. Avoid monotony!

- *Learners can attend for only so long, and they differ in their ability to attend.* Younger children and those with dyslexia (a reading impairment) and attention deficiency disorders (described in Chapter 3) have shorter attention spans.

- *Since it is easier to maintain attention when learners are alert, schedule work that requires intense concentration during the morning and work that may be more intrinsically interesting and/or may require less concentration in the afternoon.* For this reason, elementary teachers try to schedule art, music, and physical education later in the day.

- *Call direct attention to information of importance.* Highlight key points or say, "This is important."

- *Distractions interfere with attention.* Find ways to eliminate the many interruptions to learning that students, other teachers, and administrators can cause. Be aware that you too can cause interruptions.

- *Learners can attend to only so much information at any one time.* Students should not be overwhelmed or they may become so confused that they attend to nothing.

To the extent that you can get learners to pay attention by applying these guidelines, the information and experiences they have will enter their short-term memories.

Beliefs about Short-Term Memory   The stimuli we attend to find their way into short-term memory, now often referred to as working memory. But, how do we get some of this information beyond short-term and into long-term memory? Cognitivists believe the following principles to be true.

- *Short-term memory capacity is severely limited.* Estimates are that adult learners can hold only about five to nine bits of new information at one time. Therefore, it is difficult to remember a meaningless series of numerals, such as a long-distance telephone number or a Social Security number. Young children's short-term memory is much more limited, usually three to five bits.

- *To overcome the limited capacity of our short-term memory, new information can be both* organized *and* connected *to what we already know;* for example, learners can be helped to combine, or "chunk," new information. Thus a 10-bit, long-distance telephone number is placed into three chunks, such as (614) 292–1280. Chunking a 9-bit-long Social Security number also aids short-term memory. Consequently, if it were important to remember the names of the first nine U.S. presidents, we might group them in threes: (Washington, Adams, Jefferson), (Madison, Monroe, Adams), (Jackson, Van Buren, Harrison). Short-term memory also is enhanced by using mnemonics, or systems to aid memory; for example, we more easily recall the names of the Great Lakes if we use the familiar word *HOMES* (*H*uron, *O*ntario, *M*ichigan, *E*rie, *S*uperior) to spur our recall.

- *Information can be remembered better by connecting it with what students already know.* Consider the following task. You are helping students learn multiplication facts. They know that six 6s are 36. You help them see that seven 6s is one 6 more.

- *To forestall forgetting new information, we must manipulate it or, as cognitive scientists say, engage in active "rehearsals" with it.* Such rehearsals can involve either practicing repeatedly or simply thinking about the information. When we engage in recurrent practice, we can move information to our long-term memory through sheer repetition or memorization. Many of us learned multiplication facts in this way, repeating $9 \times 7 = 63$ ad infinitum. Spaced rehearsal, however, seems preferable. Thus, repeating $9 \times 7 = 63$ every hour for five hours is better than repeating it five times in one minute. We might also think about the information, for example, questioning "How can we prove nine 7s are 63?"

4.4 Which knowledge about short-term memory has been most useful to you?

Beliefs about Long-Term Memory   As noted, information that learners process extensively, or use in a meaningful way, finds its way into long-term memory. Cognitivists believe the following to be true with regard to long-term memory:

- *The capacity of our long-term memory seems limitless.* We never run out of room to learn.

- *We are best able to retrieve information from our long-term memory if that information was related to something we knew at that time.*

- *We can call up, or recollect, related information from long-term memory when processing new information in short-term, working memory.* For example, as you receive new information about how people learn, you can compare it with information you have already learned. In this instance, as you go along, you are able to compare what you already know about short-term memory with what you are learning about long-term memory.

- *Reviewing information fixes it more firmly.* Think about how you have retained the multiplication facts (see Spotlight on Research 4.1).

- *Mnemonic or memory tricks can also be used to aid remembering.* Two are linking new information to visual cues and using the PQ4R method. Go to msn.Encarta and search "Four Memory Tricks," or "12 Memory Tricks."

"I knew the answers. I just couldn't retrieve them from my memory bank."

Web Link
Encarta

General Beliefs about the Memory Process   The general beliefs of cognitivists with regard to memory include the following:

- *Information in short-term memory is lost either when that memory is overloaded or with the passage of time.*

- *When information in short-term memory is lost, it cannot be recovered.* If we forget a telephone number, we must relearn it. In contrast, information in long-term memory can be retrieved and used when conditions are right.

- *Retrieval, or remembrance, of information in our long-term memory is enhanced if we connected the information to something we already knew at the time we originally learned the new information.* Additionally, retrieval is easier when the information is originally presented in an organized way and when that information is reviewed periodically.

4.5 Why do you forget?

MEANINGFUL LEARNING

While some cognitive scientists are interested in information processing (attention, short-term/working, and long-term memory), others are interested in how information can be made more meaningful so that it can be better understood and used. These scientists address "meaningful learning," and their work has led to the development of approaches to it that teachers use. The approaches (based upon

For a new skill (e.g., hitting a softball) to become automatic or for new knowledge (e.g., multiplication) to become long-lasting, practice beyond the point of mastery is required. Here is an example. Suppose you are teaching students how a bill becomes a law. They should periodically study these facts and regularly be tested on them. Even when they have mastered the facts, they should continue to study them since memory is prone to forgetting. The key here is to *overlearn* in order to offset forgetting. Without overlearning, most material is forgotten within 3 or 4 years. With overlearning, material can be recalled and used as long as 50 years after the last practice. Therefore if long-term learning is critical—teach, reteach and test, retest. Experts in a skill (e.g., musicians) or knowledge field (e.g., mathematicians) become so mostly because they work hard for extended periods of time. For example, best violinists indicate they practice more. Generally, individuals must practice intensively for at least 10 years before they make significant contributions in their field. Of course talent counts too but as Thomas Edison remarked, "Genius is one percent inspiration and ninety-nine percent perspiration." In some cases, the school curriculum will ensure that students practice something of long-term significance over years (e.g., arithmetic procedures such as multiplication and division). In other cases, you must decide what skills and knowledge are of most worth and engage your students in overlearning them.

Sources: Willingham (2004); Ross (2006); Gladwell (2008).

OLC Web Link
Institute of Educational Sciences

"I know my seven-digit phone number, my nine-digit zip code, my four-digit address, and my three-digit area code. There's just one thing I don't know. What's a digit?"

principles gleaned in part from the literature on information processing cited above or elsewhere) include how to

- prepare students for learning.
- present information logically and clearly.
- connect new information to what learners already know.
- vary the way information is presented or obtained.
- have learners review or rehearse information.
- have students process—think about and use—new information.
- provide students with assistance when needed.
- help students summarize what is learned.
- help students apply what is learned.

To the extent we use meaningful approaches, students will understand and be able to use knowledge.

An online practice guide *Organizing Instruction and Study to Improve Student Learning* (2007) is available at the OLC "Institute of Educational Sciences" site.

COGNITIVE APPROACHES TO TEACHING AND LEARNING

One way of teaching based on meaningful learning is called "expository teaching" or "reception learning." Most often we call it *presentation* whereby the teacher directs the learning activity (prepares students for learning, presents information logically and clearly, connects the information to be learned with what students already know, and uses variety in presenting new information). However, just as importantly, the teacher engages and supports learners (has learners review and think about the new information, provides learners with assistance, helps them summarize what they have learned and, when possible, has them consider how to apply it to life situations). Chapter 7 elaborates on presentation since it is a very common instructional alternative. Chapter 11 provides verification that effective teachers use meaningful approaches to learning. Take a look.

All eight instructional alternatives presented in Chapters 7–8 of the text are effective ways to teach since they are based wholly or in part on meaningful learning.

Here are other recommended ways of teaching that are expansions or elaboration of forms of meaningful learning. (See also **Spotlight on Research 4.2**.)

What Brain Research Seems to Suggest, or Does It?

Neuroscientists study how our brains develop and work. Some of them, cognitive neuroscientists or brain researchers, study how the brain helps us think and learn.

Some educators hold that brain research provides clear support for certain educational practices. Others argue that most of what we believe is mere speculation without scientific support (Dietrich & Kanso, 2010).

Here are some widely accepted findings and implications for teaching practice.

- Concrete, real life experiences make more lasting changes in the brain. You don't learn how to play a piano or swim by reading about it.
- Teach to both halves of the brain. The hemispheres of the brain must work together for us to engage even in a simple act.

- The more ways information is presented to the brain (visual, auditory, etc.), the richer the memory.
- The brain is programmed to pay attention to information that appeals to one or more of our emotions (e.g., curiosity, pride, happiness, or wonder).
- Retention of information is maximized using repetition or rehearsal, visualization, etc.

Here are some debatable findings and implications.

- Left Brain, Right Brain. Both brain scientists and psychologists repeatedly deny claims that there is much to the left-brain, right-brain argument that persons who are one or the other are more logical or creative, or better at reading, arithmetic or spatial reasoning.

- Brains as Sponges. Another claim is that there is a critical or sensitive learning period from 4 until 10 during which children learn faster, easier, and with more understanding. Bruer (2003–4) notes, "Despite what we read in the brain-based literature, neuroscience has not established that there is a sensitive period between the ages of 4 and 10 during which children learn more quickly, easily, and meaningfully."

As Fischer, Director of the Mind and Brain Education Program at Harvard warns, "You can't [automatically] go from neuroscience to the classroom, because we don't know enough neuroscience" (Straus, 2001). A neurologist concurs: "It would be against my medical training to claim that brain-based strategies for teaching are valid." (Willis, 2007.)

Authentic Learning   **Authentic learning** suggests knowledge is more meaningful and remembered longer when it can be related to, or results from, a child's real world or when children "learn by doing." So, rather than tell students what they should know, give them tasks requiring them to learn directly from their environment. For example, when students are learning about weather, they learn about and use the tools meteorologists have. When it is necessary to use the library, students learn library skills. When children are to learn numbers they see how numbers are a part of their environment—that there are many reasons they need to know arithmetic, and so forth. Such experiences also provide a sense of personal achievement and self-discovery. See Highlight 4.1 for an example of authentic learning. For another example, see the Online Learning Center link at USA Today.

Authentic learning is similar to the concept of *direct experience*. Both conclude that firsthand, personal experience is better than secondhand vicarious or abstract kinds. You learn by doing.

Student teaching is a good example of authentic learning/direct experience.

Scaffolding   The term **scaffolding** puts us in mind of painters and window washers who use scaffolds for support. Providing learners with support also makes sense. When learners need help or guidance, wise teachers provide better directions and better explanations (see Chapter 11), or provide additional learning resources. Some teachers are more able to provide help since they are sensitive to when kids are having trouble and have ideas about what to do about it. You will find that students are very good at helping each other. They often have a sense of what their peers may not understand and why. Peer helping or teaching

4.6 What authentic learning experiences have you had? What do you recall about them?

OLC Web Link
USA Today

4.7 Think of a time when you did not understand something. What kind of scaffolding did your teacher use to help you succeed?

When you learned that the nearby elementary school was being given money by the parent teacher organization to build a playground, you happened to mention it to your middle-school students. It somehow caught their attention, and two of the students, Leah and Tyler, eagerly wondered if they or the class could help design it. The principal of your school and the elementary school thought it would be a great idea to have children design children's play space.

Soon your class was enthusiastically making diagrams and deciding what kinds of equipment and space were necessary, the extent of fencing required, and so forth. Models were constructed. Students were faced with various problems: How do you draw to scale? How do you measure angles? How much pea gravel do we need? What are the safety requirements? Soon everyone was engaged in using arithmetic, geometry, measurement, and other subjects.

During the process, students also improved their social ability to work together and their ability to communicate their design ideas to the elementary school's students and interested adults.

Source: Bransford et al. (2002).

---

is a trademark of certain kinds of cooperative learning presented in Chapter 8 (see Case 8.1).

Reciprocal Teaching (ReT) **Reciprocal teaching** is an instructional activity during which a dialogue or interchange takes place between teacher and students regarding what is to be learned (Palincsar, 1986). The dialogue is characterized by higher-order thinking, as you will see below.

Usually ReT is thought about as a way to help kids comprehend or understand what they read. Before, during, and after reading, they are directed to employ at least four learning strategies:

- *Predicting:* Readers predict beforehand what the "story" will be about based on the title, illustrations, or graphics. ("What do you think ReT is?")
- *Questioning:* Readers make up questions they would like answered as they read. ("How does ReT work?")
- *Clarifying:* Readers clarify what they do not understand, getting help from further reading or other students. ("What does *reciprocal* mean?")
- *Summarizing:* In their own words, learners identify key ideas and bring them together to create a summary. ("Here are the key ideas about ReT and how they relate so that I can use it when teaching.")

Everyone thinks aloud about what they will read or have read using these four strategies and others. (See Highlight 4.2.)

Reciprocal teaching has other shades of meaning (Seymour & Osana, 2003). One is the gradual shifting of teaching responsibility to students. Suppose the instructional objective you have is to teach students how to summarize. As you teach summary making, you gradually shift teaching responsibilities to students. For example, you ask Julio or Kathleen to tell how they summarize and how that may differ from your preferred method. You stand aside and listen. You prompt reactions and comments from other students. At other times you might ask learners to go to the board and demonstrate and describe how to multiply fractions or diagram a sentence. Such instances are always accompanied by student interchanges (more thinking aloud, more clarification or other mental processing of the information to be learned).

(Notice how the teacher leads but shares teaching with student Claire. Notice how the learners interact, comment, and raise questions.)

Teacher, *reading from the text:* The pipe fish change their color and movements to blend with their surroundings. For example, pipe fish that live among green plants change their color to a shade of green to match the plants.

Claire, *child leading the discussion:* One question that I had about this paragraph is, What is special about the way that pipe fish look?

Keith, *clarifying:* Do you mean the way that they are green?

Andy, *elaborating:* It's not just that they're green—they're the same color as the plants around them, all around them.

Claire, *resuming her role as discussion leader:* Yes, that's it. My summary is, this part tells how the pipe fish looks and that it looks like what is around it. My prediction is that this is about its enemies and how it protects itself and who its enemies are.

Monty, *amplifying:* They also talked about how the pipe fish moves.

Keith, *summarizing:* It's always back and forth.

Teacher, *questioning:* What do we call it when something looks like and acts like something else? The way that the walking stick was yesterday. We clarified this word when we talked about the walking stick.

Angel, *predicting:* Mimic.

Teacher, *reinforcing:* That's right. We would say that the pipe fish mimics the . . . ?

Several students, *predicting:* Plants.

Source: Adapted from Palincsar & Brown (1989).

Some forms of cooperative learning, described in Chapter 8, seem to draw heavily from the concept of reciprocal teaching.

Problem Solving   Another approach to learning that cognitive scientists like is problem solving. **Problem solving** requires that a situation exists in which a goal is to be achieved and learners are asked to consider how they would attain the goal. There are different types of problems. Snowman and Biehler (2008) describe two. One type, often encountered when studying something exacting like math or science, is a *well-structured problem* that can be solved by applying a specific mathematical or scientific procedure. As a young student, you worked on well-structured mathematical problems that required the application of multiplication or division to obtain an answer: For example, "If you have 18 apples and wish to fill gift boxes with 6 apples each, how many boxes can you fill?" Another example: Each time as a teacher that you prepare a classroom lesson, you will be solving a well-structured problem since there is a goal you hope to achieve (writing the plan) and there are specific procedures to be followed (described in Chapter 6).

Then there are *ill-structured* or *unstructured problems.* Here, no specific procedure exists that can be followed or applied to obtain a finite solution such as those above (to place 18 apples, 6 to a box, 3 gift baskets would be needed). Furthermore, ill-structured problems address larger, more comples issues or real-life concerns such as: What should be served in a school lunch room? How can toxic wastes be disposed of? What is good art? *Problem-based learning* is recommended when ill-structured problems arise. This procedure suggests that learners: (1) be quizzed to find out what they already know about the problem, (2) decide what they need to learn and what available resources exist, (3) engage in learning, and (4) organize and present what has been found out (DeRoche, 2006). Problem-based learning is mostly associated with discovery learning (see Chapter 8).

To summarize, major beliefs about problem solving include the following:

4.8

Can you think of any "well-structured" problems in the subject matter you will be responsible for teaching?

4.9

What are some other "ill-structured" problems you have faced?

4.10 How prepared are you to teach problem solving?

4.11 What is your feeling about cognitive approaches to learning?

Try Activity 4.1 a or b

- A major goal of education is to help students learn to solve all types of problems, both subject-matter-related (well-structured) and people- or life-related (ill-structured).
- Some problem-solving strategies tend to be subject-area-specific, such as procedures for solving mathematical or scientific problems. For example, we apply the quadratic formula in order to solve a quadratic equation, or a procedure for solving "train problems" involving distance-rate-time calculations.
- Other problem-solving strategies are more useful when dealing with ill-structured problems. A general problem-solving strategy might include the following steps: (1) State the goal to be achieved, (2) identify the obstacles standing in the way, (3) project alternative ways to achieve the goal, (4) consider the consequences of each possible solution, (5) decide how to implement the best proposed solution and do so, and (6) evaluate your degree of satisfaction with the problem resolution. Chapter 14 will help you learn how to solve ill-structured challenges classroom teachers face.

The Humanistic School of Thought

A second school of thought offered to explain how we learn and, therefore, how we should teach comes from humanistic education and social psychology. Humanists maintain education should be based upon the needs and interests of learners. After all, needs and interests are what drive or motivate us. Moreover, they want education to be based upon the needs and interests of *individual* learners. Thus, education should be as personal as possible. Social psychologists want us to recognize the importance of social interactions and social influences on behavior including learning.

Said another way, the humanistic school urges that we teach according to the interests and needs of children and, furthermore, that we create healthy social and emotional classroom environments characterized by acceptance and respect. Doing these things enhances learning.

BELIEFS OF THE HUMANISTIC SCHOOL

This view of how we learn holds the following beliefs:

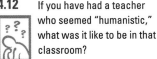

4.12 If you have had a teacher who seemed "humanistic," what was it like to be in that classroom?

- The school curriculum should provide for both the *needs* and *interests* of kids. Needs include personal safety and security, love, belonging, achievement (see Figure 12.4 and Maslow, 1998) and autonomy, competence, and healthy social relationships (Deci & Ryan 1990). For example, **affiliation** is a strong human need. Therefore the school should ensure that all children have the opportunity to have good relationships with their peers and the teacher (see Chapter 13). With regard to their interests, among other things, children are interested in their environment and should have the opportunity to learn in and from it.
- Learning should be individualized and personalized. It should be self, rather than teacher-directed. Kids should be given latitude to learn what they personally have interest in and how they wish to learn. The school should fit the child not the child fit the school (Neill, 1969).
- Learners should not only regulate what and how they learn but also be responsible for evaluating themselves and their progress (Schunk, 2008).
- Knowing *how* to learn is more important than the acquisition of specific knowledge (Gage & Berliner, 1998).
- Developing attitudes and values are as important as acquiring knowledge. Therefore teachers should make sure **affective or attitudinal learning objectives**

are pursued. For example, learners should learn how to "attend to, respond to, value, internalize, and act on information or knowledge." They must know *how to think about* and *what to do with* information. (See Instructional Objectives in Chapter 6.)

- Learners learn best in a psychologically safe environment where they are accepted and valued. Each child should be accepted as he is, not judged by what he should or could be (Rogers & Russell, 2002).

- Learners learn best when they have good feelings about themselves and others. They prosper when they have self-respect and a feeling of **efficacy** or control over what happens to them. (See Motivating Students to Learn in Chapter 5.)

- We would do well to try to place ourselves in the shoes of learners in order to see learning from their perspectives.

Major contributors to this school of thought include Carl Rogers, Abraham Maslow, Paulo Freire, Ivan Illich, John Holt, and Malcolm Knowles.

HUMANISTIC APPROACHES TO TEACHING AND LEARNING

Some examples of humanistic teaching and learning are presented in Chapters 7 (Individualized Instruction) and 8 (Cooperative Learning). The **project method** permits kids to pursue their personal learning interests. **Cooperative learning** promotes social and emotional growth where children share, accept and respect each other ("all for one, one for all"). Here are other examples.

Inviting School Success Inviting School Success was developed to get teachers to communicate to learners that they are "responsible, able, and valuable" people (Purkey & Novak, 1996, p. 3). To convey this, invitational learning calls upon teachers to (1) know learners' names, (2) have individual contact with each learner, (3) show learners they respect them, (4) be honest with learners and themselves, (5) not take a student's rejection personally, and (6) respect themselves as teachers. Creating an "inviting classroom" follows. (See "Planning the Psychological Environment" in Chapter 14.)

Values Clarification Values clarification refers to techniques by which learners (1) identify how they feel or what they believe about something, (2) value that feeling or belief and, (3) if valued, act on it (Simon, Howe, & Kerschenbaum, 1995). The intention is for learners to become aware of the values they hold, since those values influence their behavior. Then, they consider the legitimacy or goodness of what they value. For example, learners could be asked to what extent they believe in gun control. After stating their preference, they are encouraged to share and explain their position and why they hold it. Once they have examined their value in relationship to the values others hold, learners are better able to prize their value or to modify or reject it. Once the value is prized, learners are expected to go the next step and act on the value. For example, learners might be asked, "All right, if you believe that strongly about gun control, what can *you* do?"

Moral Education Moral education is akin to character education, values education, and citizenship education. These techniques are designed to help learners develop more responsible behavior both in and out of school. Teachers can do a number of things to enhance higher levels of students' morality and character, such as (1) serving as role models who are always respectful and caring of others and who intervene as necessary to get students to be respectful and caring, too, (2) creating a family or community atmosphere in the class so that all students feel worthwhile and care about one another, and (3) encouraging students to hold high academic and

4.13 How might you use some humanistic beliefs about learning?

4.14 Have you had experience with any of the humanistic approaches to education? Which ones?

behavioral standards in order to teach the value of work as a way to develop oneself and contribute to a community (Lickona 2004).

For an extensive overview of Moral Education go to the Office for Studies of Moral Development in Education at the University of Illinois, Chicago. For a "how to" book go to Nucci 2008.

Multiethnic Education   Multiethnic education refers to educational practices that encourage learners to revere their roots and culture—ideas, customs, skills, arts, and so forth—*and* to revere the culture and diversity of others. Proponents want learners to see the advantages of our pluralistic society. Related educational practices include helping learners become aware of the various contributions of ethnic and national groups to a nation's development and well-being, and encouraging learners to find out more about their own ethnic and cultural backgrounds. See Chapter 3, Cultural Differences.

Humanistic approaches seem to produce wonderful results. For example, they have been found to increase school attendance; decrease the dropout rate; and improve student attitudes, behaviors, and academic achievement (Ragozzino et al., 2003).

The Behavioral School of Thought

The third school of thought about learning, teaching, and education is behaviorism. **Behaviorists,** as the name implies, help us understand why we behave as we do. They are interested in finding out how external, environmental stimuli cause overt or observable learner behavior and how modifying a learner's environment can change behavior.

If you have studied psychology you probably learned something about contiguity, classical conditioning, operant conditioning, and social learning—concepts of prime interest to behaviorists.

CONTIGUITY

Contiguity refers to simple stimulus-response (S-R) pairings, associations, or connections, such as lightning and thunder, which occur closely together. When one thing, a stimulus, is regularly associated with another, a response, an S-R connection is established. Like the combination of lightning and thunder, the S-R connection usually occurs within a very brief time span, thus, the *contiguity* label. We can learn by simple S-R pairing such facts as Columbus landed in America in 1492 and $9 \times 7 = 63$. Many concepts and facts are learned through simple stimulus-response learning, for example:

Stimulus	Response
Einstein	Theory of Relativity
Sodium chloride	Salt
Van Gogh	Artist
Eiffel Tower	Paris
Gershwin	Composer

CLASSICAL CONDITIONING

Classical conditioning refers to learning that occurs when we already have an established connection (contiguity) between a primary or original stimulus and a response, and then we pair a new, secondary stimulus with the original stimulus long enough that it begins to evoke the original response even when the original stimulus is absent. Remember Pavlov's dogs? Pavlov, a Russian psychologist, found that his experimental dogs naturally salivated (responded) when his lab assistants fed them

4.15   What is your reaction to humanistic approaches to learning?

Try Activity 4.2 a or b

4.16   Think of a subject you avoid. Now think of why you may dislike it. What might be done to change your attitude?

4.17   What kinds of S-R responses might you want from your learners? How can the responses be associated with something desirable so that they occur?

meat powder (a stimulus). Later, he found that the mere presence of his lab assistants (new stimulus) caused the dogs to anticipate being fed and to salivate. Let's consider a school example. Students and teachers alike associate a bell (stimulus) with the ending of a class period. Teachers often assign homework at or near the close of class. Thus, the mere assignment of homework (new stimulus) will elicit many behaviors or responses associated with the ringing of the bell—packing book bags and so forth. For this reason, some teachers assign homework at the beginning of class.

OPERANT CONDITIONING

Operant conditioning refers to learning facilitated through **reinforcement.** A learner does something correctly or appropriately and, consequently, receives a reward. Operant conditioning presumes that if we do something we are rewarded for or which is rewarding in itself, we will do it again. Conversely, if we do something that is not rewarded or rewarding, we will be less likely to repeat the behavior. Operant conditioning is based upon a pleasure-pain view of human behavior. To illustrate, consider Jason, a learner who has turned in an essay on gun control. The teacher has dutifully analyzed the essay and responded to it as follows: "This assignment is complete and well written. You have found and used many references. You have presented the major points on both sides, and you have drawn your own thoughtful conclusions. Obviously, you enjoy studying issues and responding to them. May I place your paper on our bulletin board?" Assuming Jason finds the teacher's comments and the display of his paper rewarding, he likely will want to write another essay. Chapters 11 and 14 will discuss more about reinforcement.

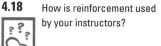 **4.18** How is reinforcement used by your instructors?

OBSERVATIONAL LEARNING

Observational learning's main tenet is that you can learn a lot by watching others. According to its chief theorist, Bandura (1986), for observational learning to be effective, learners must attend to someone's behavior, retain what they observed the "model" doing, imitate or reproduce the behavior they saw, and experience reinforcement or satisfaction as a consequence. We know learners are most likely to model persons who are somewhat like themselves and whom they perceive as competent, warm, or powerful. Thus, primary children frequently identify with parents or with television or movie characters, especially superheroes, and mimic what they do. A kindergarten teacher describes an example of social learning:

 4.19 To what extent do you believe you will model a former teacher(s)? In what ways?

> The resurgence of Batman: Raymond brought in a "cape" and all the children were anxious to wear it and run around the room in it. During free play, children were busy making Batman equipment. Story time and singing time were always interrupted by children who were busy describing Batman antics. The entire morning was Batman-oriented and the children could not be interested in much else.

If an elementary school has a Halloween parade, characters such as Scooby-Doo, Snow White, Spiderman, or Harry Potter readily appear. On the other hand, if middle and secondary students have the occasion to wear costumes, they would more likely dress and act like rock or rap personalities or athletes.

Such learning also occurs when we see something good or bad happen to another person. For example, if we were to see a friend praised for her schoolwork, we might try to imitate what she does so we can be praised, too. Conversely, we might avoid doing what another student does if her behavior is not well received.

If you hold to classical conditioning, operant conditioning, and observational learning, you will do the following:

"Of course I believe that a teacher should offer a positive role model; however . . ."

- *Make the classroom enjoyable intellectually, socially, and physically* so that learners feel safe and secure.
- *Be open and specific about what needs to be learned.* Use specific behavior objectives when writing lesson plans (see Chapter 6) and share those objectives with learners.

- *Be certain that learners have basic knowledge and skill* that will enable them to learn new material.
- *Show connection of new learning to previous learning.*
- *When new material is complex, introduce it gradually.* Organize new material into sequential, short, easily learned parts.
- *Associate what is to be learned with things learners like.* For example, associate poetry with rap. Conversely, don't associate what is to be learned with things learners don't like. For example don't use schoolwork as punishment.
- *Tell learners what is most important. Cue them.*
- *Recognize and praise improvement.* Don't expect students to learn at the same pace and in the same amounts.
- *Find out what is rewarding to each student* and use that to reinforce student learning. Some learners may be rewarded by receiving verbal public praise while others may find it embarrassing.
- *When a task is new or difficult, provide more regular reinforcement.* Once learners have mastered a new task, use only occasional reinforcement.
- *Reinforce the learning behavior you expect from students:* for example attending, engaging, trying, responding, improving, completing.
- *Encourage shy or insecure learners' responses.* Look for shy children who do not volunteer and give them opportunity. Caution students to respect responses of others that differ from their own, or even are incorrect.
- *Create situations whereby each student has the opportunity to succeed.*
- *Model behavior that you want learners to imitate.* For example, show enthusiasm for learning and respect for all.
- *Draw attention to students who demonstrate desirable behavior* or produce quality work but not to the point of causing them to be alienated from their peers.
- *Ask parents to reinforce desired behaviors at home*—to recognize enthusiasm for learning, effort, and growth.

4.20 What behavioristic beliefs do your teachers seem to use most and least?

You will notice many behaviorist beliefs described previously are similar to those held within the cognitive school of thought. The major differences are that behaviorists more often advocate that: new knowledge should be organized into shorter more easily learned parts, improvement should be recognized and praised, every child should have opportunities to succeed, *learning* behaviors should be reinforced (e.g., attending, trying, completing), mutual respect is essential (everyone counts and is important), and that learning is never associated with punishment. Behaviorists are more likely to use "carrots and sticks" to get kids to learn.

Since the dignity of learners is important to behaviorists, some of the above characteristics are like those held within the humanistic school.

BEHAVIORAL APPROACHES TO TEACHING

Certain instructional alternatives are more supportive of the beliefs of behaviorists. Of those, direct instruction (described in Chapter 8) comes closest. DI generally advocates presenting information in small steps, using many illustrations and examples for reinforcement, asking learners many questions in order to check for understanding and providing corrective feedback, providing lots of practice, ensuring learning by keeping students on task for as long as it takes, and so forth. Take a look at Lesson Plan 8.4.

Additional ways of teaching advocated by behaviorists:

Programmed Instruction (PI) PI involves organizing material to be learned or practiced into small parts called *frames* (see Highlight 4.3). Learners respond to a question or problem (stimulus) in each frame; if their response is correct, they receive

HIGHLIGHT 4.3

An Illustration of Programmed Instruction That Follows an Operant Conditioning Pattern

Fill in the blank in each frame (1 to 5) and then check the answer against the correct answer "hidden" at the right, proceeding downward on the page.

1. The third prominent school of thought about learning is _____.

2. This school of thought is interested in our _____ behavior.

3. When one stimulus is regularly associated with a response, a bond or _____ is formed.

4. When a second stimulus has been associated with the original stimulus, that second stimulus may evoke the same response. This is called _____ conditioning.

5. When we watch others and mimic their behavior, we call this _____ learning.

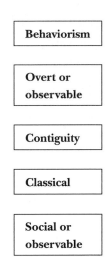

Behaviorism

Overt or observable

Contiguity

Classical

Social or observable

---

positive reinforcement and the next frame is presented. When learners respond incorrectly, they may be asked to repeat or be given more information to help them produce a correct response. Learners utilizing programmed instruction typically work at their own pace.

Computer-Assisted Instruction (CAI)   CAI refers to the use of computers to present programmed instruction or to otherwise assist learners with specific learning tasks. Many different kinds of CAI programs are available, and most require learners to engage in lots of drill and practice. Although most CAI programs follow an operant conditioning, stimuli-response-reinforcement pattern, CAI also can be used as a cognitivist approach; some CAI programs, like programmed instruction, teach new concepts, and others engage learners in creative tasks and problem solving. For example, some computer software programs encourage children to make up stories and to illustrate them.

Programmed instruction and CAI seem to be a little more effective than normal educational practices, probably because they make extensive use of practice and reinforcement.

Download and try out free educational software at these sites: Owl and Mouse Educational Software (click on Educational Software from Owl and Mouse).

 Web Link
Owl and Mouse Educational Software

Mastery Learning   Mastery learning is a third educational practice based upon behavioral theory. It, too, allows students to learn academic material at their own pace. In practice, all students in a class might be expected to reach a certain level of proficiency, for example, at least 80 percent correct answers on a geography test. Those who fail to reach that criterion level may receive additional time and corrective instruction until they obtain that score. The general intent is to give immediate, additional help to low or slow achievers so they stay even with higher or faster achievers. While low or slow achievers receive corrective instruction, high or fast achievers engage in enrichment work on the same or on a similar topic.

Advocates of mastery learning propose you (1) prepare a lesson with clear, specific objectives, (2) use learning material that allows students to accomplish those objectives, and (3) prepare not one, but two, tests. Following instruction, students take test 1. Those that meet some preestablished passing criterion, such as 80 percent, move on to supplementary enrichment activities, while those falling short receive corrective instruction based on a different instructional approach or using different instructional materials. After additional instruction, a second, similar test (test 2) is given to the lower achievers. When a large majority of all students (perhaps 80 percent) have passed either test 1 or test 2, the class moves on to new work. The cycle can be repeated until you, the teacher, feel that a large enough majority has reached mastery to permit going on.

Mastery learning seems most important when the material to be learned is critical or "high stakes" material, for example, the basic information or skills in any content field.

Precision Teaching (PT)   PT occurs when learners master a fact or skill (such as correctly spelling a word or applying an arithmetic algorithm such as division), and then *continue* practicing these skills until they achieve a high level of precision or fluency. "Practice makes perfect." Teachers using PT give daily one-minute practice exercises (e.g., multiplication facts) and chart how many items are correct. Learners also chart progress. Its tenets derive from principles of information processing (see the section on short-term memory).

Applied Behavioral Analysis (ABA)   ABA also is based upon behavioral beliefs and findings and is informed by principles of operant conditioning. It is used mostly in clinical settings (hospitals, prisons, schools) to modify the behavior of clients toward more normal or acceptable patterns. ABA follows a prescribed procedure. First the practitioner—for example, you the teacher—identify a student (client) and the student's behavior that is to be changed. You then determine how often the student presently performs the desired behavior—for example, completing homework. This is called the *baseline*. Next, you introduce an intervention. An intervention is usually some reinforcement the student receives every time she performs the desirable behavior. Use of reinforcement encourages your student to behave appropriately more often, that is, more than the client did at the outset or baseline.

Here is an illustration of ABA in a classroom. Jane produces very little when given a writing assignment, even one of her choice. In most cases, her text amounts to a few short sentences. Because she is fairly conversational, you decide you might encourage her to be more forthcoming by having her tell you what she would like to say. As she does, you prompt her to write down the ideas she is expressing. Each time Jane writes her ideas in a writing assignment, you praise her for any increase in the number and range of her ideas. When you evaluate her written work, you comment that, increasingly, Jane's compositions are more complete and interesting. You may even share one or more with the class.

Behavioral analysis always uses the principles of operant conditioning. A close cousin is behavior modification, which is also an attempt to change behavior but is a more general concept that includes use of hypnosis, drug therapy, and electroconvulsive shock treatment as well.

4.21   What do you think of the behavioral approach to learning?

Try Activity 4.3 a or b

Is There a Single Best Approach to Student Learning?

We have identified three views of learning that influence the approaches teachers take to instruction. Figure 4.3 brings them together for comparison. Each approach has been defined and its major beliefs and findings noted. Some have fostered the development and use of specific educational practices which are briefly described. Table 4.1 (on page 110) compares the three approaches.

A great deal of controversy exists as to which of the approaches to learning is superior (Viadero, 1996). If you ask your university instructors, you may be surprised

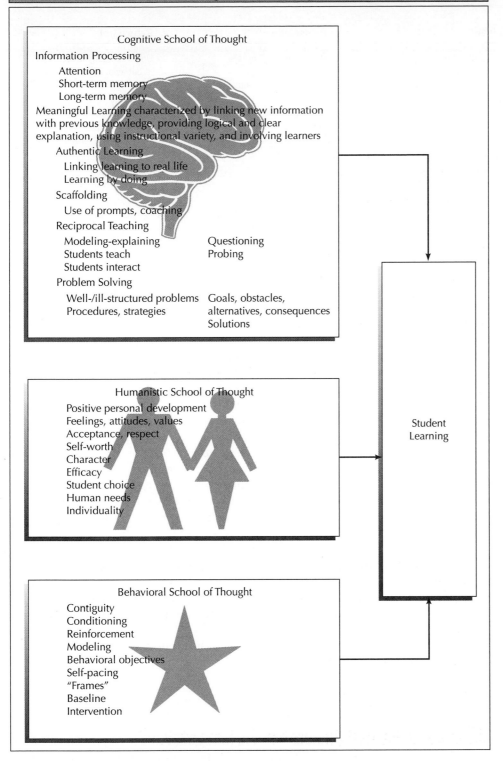

Cognitive School of Thought

Information Processing
  Attention
  Short-term memory
  Long-term memory
Meaningful Learning characterized by linking new information with previous knowledge, providing logical and clear explanation, using instructional variety, and involving learners
  Authentic Learning
    Linking learning to real life
    Learning by doing
  Scaffolding
    Use of prompts, coaching
  Reciprocal Teaching
    Modeling-explaining   Questioning
    Students teach   Probing
    Students interact
  Problem Solving
    Well-/ill-structured problems   Goals, obstacles,
    Procedures, strategies   alternatives, consequences
                                    Solutions

Humanistic School of Thought
Positive personal development
Feelings, attitudes, values
Acceptance, respect
Self-worth
Character
Efficacy
Student choice
Human needs
Individuality

Behavioral School of Thought
Contiguity
Conditioning
Reinforcement
Modeling
Behavioral objectives
Self-pacing
"Frames"
Baseline
Intervention

Student Learning

at the strength of their feelings. You may especially find that those who espouse cognitive or humanistic beliefs shun behaviorism, although the reverse is also true.

Teachers who work with exceptional individuals (see Chapter 3), especially those with learning and behavioral deficiencies, often find the behaviorist school of thought is most helpful. There certainly is strong research support for applying its beliefs and findings. For example, Walberg (1986) reports that 98 percent of

TABLE 4.1 A Comparison of Cognitive, Humanistic, and Behavioral Views

	Cognitive	Humanistic	Behavioral
Focus	Understanding how we acquire knowledge	Understanding how we develop feelings, attitudes, and values	Understanding how our behavior is modified by our environment
Topics/Themes	Information processing Meaningful learning	Basic needs Affect (emotions, feelings, attitudes, values, predispositions, morals)	Contiguity Classical conditioning Operant conditioning Observational learning
Special Concepts	Attention Short-, long-term memory Linking new and old information Clarity Instructional variety	Self-worth Efficacy	Reinforcement
Some Instructional Approaches that Support . . .	Expository teaching Authentic learning Scaffolding Reciprocal teaching Problem solving	Cooperative learning Inviting school success Values clarification Moral/character education Multiethnic education	Direct instruction Programmed and computer-assisted instruction Mastery learning Precision teaching Applied behavioral analysis

studies investigating the effects of behavioral learning on students have positive findings. At the same time, Walberg tells us good support also exists for cognitive and humanistic approaches to instruction (p. 97). What do students think is the best approach to learning? When several hundred 12- to 14-year-old students were asked, they reported 10 to 1 they preferred to learn in meaningful ways (Kinchin, 2004). That's a big margin.

Dembo (1994) reminds us there are differences of opinion about learning not only among but also within the various schools of thought. He also points out what you have probably already concluded by now, that most educators draw from all three schools of thought. The secret, Dembo informs us, is to have a knack for knowing when to use ideas from the various perspectives since each has strengths and weaknesses, depending on the purpose you may have in mind. Anderson, Reder, and Simon (1996) agree. Speaking to the same point, Snowman and Biehler (2008) note that advocates of discovery learning do not suggest that students discover every fact or principle or formula they need to know but rather that certain types of learning outcomes can best be achieved through personal discovery.

Brophy (2003) concludes "There are several qualitatively different kinds of learning, each with its own set of optional instructional settings, activities and techniques . . . these distinctions remind us that different types of learning require different [kinds of instruction]" (p. 201).

4.22 Which features of which schools of thought about learning attract you? why?

Some Final Thoughts

Helping your students learn is the "bottom line." However, as you can recall from your own school experiences and from the teacher-reported problems that follow, doing so is not always simple. Therefore, you need to learn all you can about learning and teaching and to recognize that the two are inextricably bound together. You can be an excellent teacher *only* when you understand what is known about each and can put that knowledge to work every single time you arrange a learning experience. If your students experience difficulty or failure, you must "go back to the books" and analyze what may be interfering with learning (see Highlight 4.4).

HIGHLIGHT 4.4
What to Do When Students Aren't Learning

The Harvard Tripod Project suggests that when kids aren't learning, we should do these things:

- Look at students' work and identify where the problems are.
- Talk with the kids and find out what it is that they don't understand and why.

- Alter instruction to help them succeed.

Were the students ready for the work? Did they have adequate background and preparation so that they could succeed? Was the work clearly presented? Were differences in learner ability and interests taken into account? Was additional help provided when necessary?

Source: Harvard Education Letter online (2006).

Never shrug your shoulders or give up on a single child. The knowledge needed to help each child learn is available; it is up to you to find and use it. Reflect on each incidence of failure to learn, and then regroup and try again and again. Remember, teachers are professionals with the opportunity, knowledge, and responsibility to make a difference.

Try Activity 4.4

CHAPTER SUMMARY

- Three major schools of thought on learning and teaching are the cognitive, humanistic, and behavioral perspectives.

- Cognitivists are interested in how knowledge is acquired. Their study centers around information processing and meaningful learning. Information processing looks at the phenomena of attention, short-term memory, long-term memory, remembering, and forgetting. Meaningful learning focuses on how learners can best learn to understand and use information. Educational practices promoted by cognitivists include reception learning, authentic learning, scaffolding, reciprocal teaching, and problem solving.

- Humanistic proponents believe in the importance of meeting the needs and interests of students through individualizing and personalizing instruction. As a consequence, they support that learning should be *more* student- and *less* teacher-directed and that students should take greater responsibility for their successes and failures. Equally important, humanistic learning advocates the necessity of having classrooms where kids feel physically, socially and emotionally secure. Educational practices that support humanistic learning include individualized instruction, the project method, some types of cooperative learning, inviting school success, values clarification, and moral education.

- Behaviorists are interested in how the environment can be changed or manipulated in order to change behavior in a desirable direction. They study contiguity, classical conditioning, operant conditioning, and social or observational learning as means to behavioral change. Educational practices that support the behaviorist school of thought include programmed instruction, computer-assisted instruction, mastery learning, precision teaching, and applied behavioral analysis.

- Most teaching draws from all three schools of thought according to the learning task at hand and the characteristics and needs of the students.

SUPPLEMENTAL RESOURCES

Go to the text's Online Learning Center at www.mhhe.com/ cruickshank6e to access the chapter's **study tools** including web links practice for Praxis™ case studies, and video clips.

KEY TERMS

ISSUES AND PROBLEMS FOR DISCUSSION

ISSUES   Here are some related issues for you to debate.

1. Which school of thought—cognitive, humanistic, or behavioral—seems best under what learning circumstances?
2. What seem to be the most critical findings about learning that you should know and apply?
3. How should teachers be held personally accountable for using what is known about learning?

PROBLEMS   Following are some verbatim daily learning-related problems that teachers have shared with us. How does each relate to what we know about learning? How might you resolve them?

Problem 1:   "Today, during a lesson on fractions, the class became rowdy. Since fractions seem especially difficult for them, they become frustrated. One of the girls blurted out, 'You can't make people learn who don't want to.'"

Problem 2:   "The incident that caused me the greatest concern today happened during a reading class while working with a group of eight third-grade children. These children are unable to read or write above a first-grade level at best. The frustrating part is that they don't know words they have gone over and over before."

Problem 3:   "Today I tried to teach the concepts of 'first, middle, and last' to the slow children in my kindergarten. Many approaches were used—three pictures placed on the chalkboard, three objects placed on the floor, three children standing behind each other in a line. Only a few got the concepts."

Problem 4:   "The thing that bothered me today was brought to mind by something another middle-school teacher said in the faculty lounge. She stated that nearly all her students can read and spell but do not understand what they are reading or the meaning of words they are spelling. During the next few days, I paid attention to the teacher's comment when working with my students. Yes, they can read and spell words, but half the time they have little or no understanding."

Problem 5:   "A mother came to the door before 9 o'clock dragging her seventh-grade son. She had to hit him just to get him into the room. The boy is a truant and just sits in class without participating in work or activities. This upsets me because I have tried sincerely and affectionately to get him involved."

Problem 6: "I am concerned with the poor quality of handwriting. Only about a half dozen students seem to be able to turn in readable work. Even though standards are set up for handwriting quality and handwriting is considered as part of the grade, it makes very little difference."

Problem 7: "Many of the students I teach have very low self-esteem. They don't think much of themselves and have little confidence in their ability to learn or do anything. Some are just waiting to drop out."

Problem 8: "Mary is such a shy girl who is very easily embarrassed. Consequently, she avoids performing publicly. That is very difficult in a foreign language class. Yet, she seems to enjoy learning and does all right in other ways."

THEORY INTO ACTION: ACTIVITIES FOR PRACTICE AND YOUR PORTFOLIO

ACTIVITY 4.1: Cognitive Approaches

a. How do teachers use the cognitive approach? If you are assigned to a classroom, observe your mentor teacher and describe how he or she uses any of the following cognitive approaches and related beliefs or findings: authentic learning, scaffolding, reciprocal teaching, problem solving.

b. Plan and teach The Clear Teacher or Magic Square Task in the Practice Teaching Manual (Part Four of this book) in the most meaningful way.

ACTIVITY 4.2: Humanistic Approaches

a. How do teachers use the humanistic approach? If you are assigned to a classroom, observe the mentor teacher and describe how he or she uses *any* of the following approaches to learning: individualized-personalized instruction, greater self-directed learning and self-evaluation, creating a classroom wherein kids feel secure physically, socially and emotionally.

b. Plan and teach the Block Diagram Task, The Good Teacher Task or the Redrification Task found in Unit 2 of the Practice Teaching Manual.

ACTIVITY 4.3: Behavioral Approaches

a. How do teachers use the behavioral approach? If you are working in a school, observe your mentor teacher and describe how he or she uses any of the following or other behavioral approaches and related beliefs and findings: programmed instruction, computer-assisted instruction, mastery learning, precision teaching, applied behavioral analysis.

b. Plan and teach The Chisanbop Task or Good Teacher Task contained in the Practice Teaching Manual according to principles from the behavioral school.

ACTIVITY 4.4: Which School of Learning Theory Most Appeals to You?   Are you mostly a cognitivist, humanist, or behaviorist, or are you about evenly some of each? Below are twenty-one statements related to learning. Although you may agree with most or even all of them, pick only seven by placing seven check marks on the corresponding blanks. Then go to the key that follows to find out which school of thought each statement you checked is most closely related to.

_____ 1. Students must make connections between new information and the information they already possess.

_____ 2. Anxious students should be given successful academic and social experiences.

_____ 3. Teachers should give greater attention to helping students learn more about themselves.

_____ 4. New information must be logically organized and presented to students.

_____ 5. Information presented to students should be associated with something they like or want.

_____ 6. Students' behavior is mostly the result of their feelings of confidence, self-worth, and personal dignity.

_____ 7. Students forget information unless they rehearse or think about it.

_____ 8. Students should be made aware of specifically what they must know and be able to do at the end of instruction.

_____ 9. Students should be encouraged to believe that they are academically and socially capable.

_____ 10. Students should interact with teachers and be encouraged to ask questions.

_____ 11. Reinforcement of appropriate student learning behavior is essential.

_____ 12. Students should be given a secure environment in which they are encouraged to make wise academic and social choices.

_____ 13. When students discover something on their own, they learn better.

_____ 14. Students need to see other students and/or the teacher demonstrating appropriate learning behavior.

_____ 15. Students should be accepted regardless of their school achievement, feelings, or other behavior.

_____ 16. Students need to learn how to learn.

_____ 17. Parents must reinforce their children's learning behavior.

_____ 18. Students should learn to respect themselves and others.

_____ 19. A most important goal of education is to help students become better problem solvers.

_____ 20. Material to be learned should be presented in small, sequential steps.

_____ 21. Students should be encouraged to pursue their own interests.

Key

Cognitively oriented statements are 1, 4, 7, 10, 13, 16, 19.

Behaviorally oriented statements are 2, 5, 8, 11, 14, 17, 20.

Humanistically oriented statements are 3, 6, 9, 12, 15, 18, 21.

REFERENCES

Anderson, R., Reder, L. & Simon, H. (1996). Situated learning and education. *Educational Researcher, 25*(4), 5–11.

Bandura, A. (1986). *Social foundations of thought and action: A social cognitive theory.* Englewood Cliffs, NJ: Prentice Hall.

Bransford, J., Brown, A., & Cooking, R. (2002). *How people learn.* Washington, DC: National Research Council, Bringing Real-World Problems to Classrooms, Box 9.1.

Brophy, J. (2003, June). An interview with Jere Brophy. *Educational Psychology Review, 15*(2), 195–204.

Bruer, J. (2003/2004). *In search of . . . brain-based education. Annual Editions: Educational Psychology.* Guilford, CT: McGraw-Hill/Dushkin.

Combs, A. W. (1965). *The professional education of teachers.* Boston: Allyn & Bacon.

Deci, E. & Ryan, R. (1990). A motivational approach to self. In R. Dienstbier (Ed.), *Nebraska symposium on motivation* (pp. 240–250). Lincoln: University of Nebraska Press.

Dembo, M. H. (1994). *Applying educational psychology in the classroom.* New York: Addison-Wesley Longman.

DeRoche, S. (2006, May). An adventure in problem-based learning. *Educational Leadership, 87*(9), 705–708.

Dietrich, A. & Kanso, R. (2010, September). A review of EEG, ERP, and neuroimaging studies. *Psychological Bulletin, 136*(5), 822–848.

Gage, N. & Berliner, D. (1998). *Educational Psychology.* Florence, KY: Cengage Learning.

Gladwell, M. (2008). *Outliers.* New York: Little, Brown and Company.

Guskey, T. (1996). *Implementing mastery learning.* Belmont, CA: Wadsworth.

Harvard Education Letter online (2006, November/January). An interview with Ronald Ferguson: Recent research on the achievement gap. Access: www.edletter.org/current/ferguson.shtml

Kinchin, I. (2004, Winter). Investigating students' beliefs about their preferred role as learners. *Educational Research, 46*(3), 1–12.

Leinhardt, G. (1992, April). What research on learning tells us about teaching. *Educational Leadership, 49*(7), 20–25.

Lickona, T. (2004). *Character matters.* New York: Simon & Schuster.

Maslow, A. H. (1998). *Toward a psychology of being,* Second Edition. New York: John Wiley.

Neill, A. S. (1969). *Summerhill: A radical approach to child rearing.* New York: Hart.

Nucci, L. (2008). *Nice is not enough.* Upper Saddle River, NJ: Prentice-Hall.

Nuthall, G. (1995). Heuristic models of teaching. In L. Anderson (Ed.), *International encyclopedia of teaching and teacher education* (pp. 122–127). Oxford, UK: Elsevier Science.

Palincsar, A. (1986). The role of dialogue in providing scaffolding instruction. *Educational Psychologist, 21,* 73–98.

Palincsar, A. & Brown, A. (1989). Classroom dialogues to promote self-regulated comprehension. In J. Brophy (Ed.), *Advances in research on teaching. Vol. 1: Teaching for meaningful understanding and self-regulated learning.* Greenwich, CT: JAI.

Purkey, W. W. & Novak, N. (1996). *Inviting school success.* Belmont, CA: Wadsworth.

Ragozzino, K., Resnik, H., Utne-O'Brien, M., & Weissberg, R. (2003, Summer). Promoting academic achievement through social and emotional learning. *Educational Horizons, 169,* 168–171.

Rogers, C. & Russell, D. (2002). *Carl Rogers.* Roseville, CA: Penmarin Books.

Ross, P. (2006, August). The expert mind. ScientificAmerican.com.

Schunk, D. (2008). *Learning Theories.* Upper Saddle River, NJ: Prentice-Hall.

Seymour, R. & Osana, H. (2003). Reciprocal teaching procedures and principles. *Teaching and Teacher Education, 19*(3), 325–344.

Simon, S. B., Howe, L. W., & Kerschenbaum, H. (1995). *Values clarification. Practical strategies for teachers and students.* New York: Warner Books.

Snowman, J. & Biehler, R. F. (2008). *Psychology applied to teaching,* Ninth Edition. Boston: Houghton Mifflin.

Strauss, V. (2001, March 13). Brain research oversold, experts say. *Washington Post,* p. B6.

Viadero, D. (1996, May 22). Debate over how children learn is reignited. *Education Week, 15*(35), 5.

Walberg, H. J. (1986). Synthesis of research on teaching. In M. C. Wittrock (Ed.), *Handbook of research on teaching* (pp. 214–229). New York: Macmillan.

Willingham, D. (2004, Spring). Practice makes perfect: But only if you practice beyond the point of perfection. *American Educator Online.*

Willis, J. V. (2007, May). Which brain research can educators trust? *Phi Deltan Kappan, 88*(2), 699.

Wolfe, P. (2001). *Brain matters: Translating research into classroom practice.* Alexandria, VA: Association for Supervision and Curriculum Development.

Getting to Know Your Students and Motivating Them to Learn

CHAPTER 5

Conversation Starters

How much of your time and attention should be given to understanding and motivating students?

Many teachers believe they are responsible for teaching the "whole child" (academically, emotionally, socially) and to do so they must know a great deal about what makes each child tick. These teachers want their lessons and interactions with their students to take into account who they are and what motivates them.

Although others may feel similarly, they realize that time is extremely limited and that teachers need to use all of it for teaching. Even out of classroom time is restricted since there are lessons to plan and student work to evaluate.

How important do you believe it is to know your students individually and know what motivates them to learn?

Two challenging tasks you face as a teacher are *getting to know your students* and *motivating them to learn*. With regard to the first, this chapter will help you learn many ways by which you can come to know your students. To assist you in meeting the second challenge, a review of research on motivating students to learn will be presented.

How You Can Get to Know Your Students

"A teacher who tries to grasp each child's uniqueness . . . lays the groundwork for a successful year" (Allen, 2003).

A major responsibility and delight for most teachers is getting to know their students. Experts concur: Knowing your students is extremely important if you expect to become an expert teacher. One of the things that normally separates novices from more experienced teachers is that new teachers do not know much about their students (Berliner, 1986; Borko & Livingston, 1989; Carter et al., 1987; Zheng, 1992). Among other things, knowing your students enables you to organize them into a functional class, to interact with them more sensitively, and to teach them more effectively (Airasian, 2007). Wagner (2001) feels even more strongly: "Knowing students deeply, teachers are far more able to coach, nurture, and demand excellence from each one. No student remains anonymous or falls through the cracks" (p. 56). No child is faceless nor left behind.

There are two formal ways by which you can get to know your students. First, you can utilize existing information that has been collected about each of them since they began kindergarten. A second source of information about your students is that which you can unearth or discover yourself. Let's look closely at these two ways so that you can use each effectively.

Before moving on, you might like to take a quick look at some of the informal ways teachers can get to know students, and they can get to know each other, at the "Teacher Vision" and "Scholastic" websites.

5.1 How important to you is getting to know students? What do you most need to know about them?

Web Link
Teacher Vision and Scholastic

Using Existing Records

CUMULATIVE RECORDS

Chris Zajac had received her fifth-grade children's cumulative records, which were stuffed inside salmon-colored folders. . . . For now she only [looked at] her new students' names and addresses, and resisted looking [at other information contained in the records]. It was usually better at first to let her own opinions form. But she couldn't help noticing the thickness of some of the "cumes." "The thicker the cume, the more trouble," she told [another teacher]. (Kidder, 1989, pp. 8–9)

The major source of information about your students is their cumulative or permanent school records. The **cumulative record** is a depository of information and documents that most school districts require for each child. That record begins when a student enters kindergarten and follows the learner until he or she leaves school or graduates. It contains a variety of data: *personal information* (address, age, place of birth, special interests, hobbies); *home and family data* (names of parents or guardians, their occupation(s); names and ages of siblings, unusual home conditions); *school attendance records; scores on standardized tests* of aptitude and achievement; *year-end academic grades, teacher anecdotal comments* on students and comments written following parent conferences; and miscellaneous information such as health data, psychological reports, and written communications between school and home.

Student information is mostly private and it must be obtained and used with care (see Highlight 5.1 on page 119). Take a look at the Baltimore, MD City Schools' policy on student records on the Baltimore City Schools website.

5.2 What other information would you like to have about your kids?

Web Link
Baltimore City Public Schools

"When my teachers told me that my records would follow me through life, I thought they were exaggerating."

Five cumulative records are located at the end of this chapter. Two of the five students, Jack Brogan and Kathleen Glovak, are in fifth grade in a suburban school. The others, Benny Gamble, Julio Rivera, and Debbie Walker, are middle-school sixth graders in an inner-city school. Find the records and look them over. We will refer to them later. For now, let's consider two of the most important kinds of data contained in a "cume record"—scores on standardized tests and teacher anecdotal comments.

Standardized Test Scores   A **standardized test** compares a student's score on that test with the scores of a large number of similar students who have taken the same test. Thus, a standardized test score enables you to see how your students' scores compare to the scores of a larger sample of similar students, locally or nationally. Standardized tests that measure potential for learning are called aptitude tests. Those that measure how much students actually know are called achievement tests.

Aptitude Tests   **Aptitude tests** that measure potential to learn are referred to as general ability tests, or intelligence tests. These tests provide comparative information about such things as a student's ability to deal with abstractions and to solve problems. Look at Jack Brogan's cumulative record (at the end of this chapter). He has taken two mental ability tests. His scores of 103 and 104 become meaningful only when compared against the national average of 100 on the same tests. All students whose records appear in the appendix score about average on their mental ability tests. Scores 20 or more points higher or lower than 100 are usually indicative of higher- or lower-than-average learning potential. Thus, Jack's scores are quite average.

For the past few decades, there has been increasing debate over the use of general ability tests. Some argue the tests are culturally biased favoring white, middle-class kids—that the tests are written so that nonwhite and/or low SES students are less likely to do well on them. Most school districts, however, continue to use aptitude tests, although they caution against placing too much confidence in such scores by themselves.

In Chapter 3, we learned about multiple kinds of intelligence (Highlight 3.7), including interpersonal insight, physical aptitudes, and the ability to learn in specific fields such as music. In this chapter's appendix, you may notice that the Madison School District students (Jack and Kathy) also took a musical aptitude test. Both scored at the 6th percentile, which means they did as well as or better on this test than only 6 percent of students who have taken it. Based on the test result alone, they would seem to have limited musical aptitude or potential.

Achievement Tests   Standardized tests are also used to measure achievement, that is, how much a student knows compared to similar students. Again, turn to Jack Brogan's record (page 140). He took achievement tests in grades 1 through 4. In grade 1, he received a score of B (high normal) in readiness to read. In grade 2, Jack scored at the 40th percentile, which means his reading score was the same as or better than 40 percent of other students who have taken this test. In grades 3 and 4, Jack's standardized test scores are presented in another way. This form is called the grade level, or grade equivalent, score. A grade equivalent score is one that represents the pupil's level of performance relative to pupils in his or her own grade (Airasian, 2008). An example will make this definition clear. In fourth grade, Jack received a score of 4.2 on the "Middle Grades Achievement Test." What does 4.2 mean? A grade level or grade equivalent score of 4.2 means that, compared to other fourth graders for whom the test was intended and on whom the test was "normed," Jack is average. Let's look at Benny Gamble's record (page 149). In grade 3, he took the "Metropolitan Achievement Test" in several subjects. In reading, his grade equivalency score was 5.3. This means that, compared to other third graders for whom the reading test was intended, Benny did very well; it does *not* mean that Benny necessarily is reading at a fifth-grade level, as the 5.3 might seem to indicate. Standardized tests are discussed further in Chapter 9.

Teacher Anecdotal Comments   A second kind of information found in cumulative records and on report cards are teachers' **anecdotal comments** about students.

When you look at the "teacher comments" and "personal comments" on the five appended cumulative record cards, here are some things teachers felt were worthy of recording.

- A student's learning characteristics (Jack Brogan has a "short attention span").
- A student's work habits (Jack is "not finishing his work").
- A student's social and personality characteristics (Jack "is quite immature, constantly talking, fools and daydreams," and so on).
- A student's achievement (Kathy Glovack "is doing strong average work, does very well in school").
- A student's problems ("Kathy doesn't like the student teacher").
- A student's maladies (Benny Gamble "complains of illness").
- A student's interests (Julio Rivera "likes science and music").
- A student's family (Debbie Walker's "stepfather has left home and is trying to get the baby daughter from the mother").

For suggestions about writing comments on report cards, see Highlight 5.2. A PowerPoint presentation "Anecdotal Records" is available at the Literacy Council website. Click on PowerPoint Presentation.

Web Link
U.S. Dept. of Education
Family Policy Compliance
Office

5.3   How might you be affected by reading the student folders in the chapter's appendix?

Try Activity 5.1

Web Link
Literacy Council

5.4 Remember Teacher Chris Zajac (p. 109) resisted looking at her students' cumulative files until she had formed her own opinions. What do you think are the advantages and disadvantages of learning about students from school records?

Use the following guidelines for writing anecdotal comments when describing an *event*:

- Cover only a single incident or event in the anecdote.
- Record it as soon as possible, with the date and time indicated.
- Begin with a description of the place where the situation occurred, the people who were involved, and the circumstances.
- Describe what transpired (events, reactions, responses—use direct quotes if possible). Try to write in a reportorial style; that is, describe, but do not interpret or editorialize, what you viewed. Be objective—avoid personal judgments.
- Describe how the episode concluded.
- If the episode is related to other episodes, state how and why (American Association of School Administrators, 1992; Touliatos & Compton, 1983).

 Web Link
Manitoba Education

Individual Education Plans (IEPs)   In Chapter 3 you learned that, at times, detailed instructional plans are developed for children with special needs. Sometimes they become part of a learner's folder. Examples of IEPs are very hard to find since they are confidential. However, some are available at the Manitoba Education website. Enter the search term "iep samples," and you will be directed to four.

Unearthing New Information about Students

There may be occasions when there are no cumulative records or they are inadequate. At such times, you may want to find out some things about students yourself. There are several ways you can do so. *However, check with your principal beforehand to make sure your approach aligns with your school district's policy on student privacy.*

OBSERVING STUDENTS

Observation is an excellent way to learn about students. You can observe them talking, reading, working independently and in groups, listening, and so forth. These observations can be either formal or informal.

Formal observation involves carefully planned efforts to obtain information about a target student. The use of a carefully designed observation instrument permits you to formally observe a student. Conversely, informal observation refers to casual, unplanned observations done incidentally. Such spontaneous observations are nonetheless valuable to teachers.

Examples may make the distinction between formal and informal observation clearer. Suppose Jack Brogan is your target student. You note from comments in his cumulative record (pages 140–144) that he has difficulty interacting with other students ("minds other people's business, bothers people, has become sullen with other students"). To get a more complete profile of Jack, you decide to observe him. Now the choice of formal or informal observation comes into play.

If you observe Jack formally, you need to specify what you intend to look for. You must also decide how, when, and under what conditions you will make these observations. You might decide to observe his interactions with other students for one complete day: before he enters the building; when he enters and goes to his room; during the time before class begins; during class activities, recess, and lunch; and as he leaves the class and the building. You might even want to make up your own observation instrument or checklist (see Chapter 9 "Observational, Performance, and Authentic Assessment"). The following are questions you could use to focus your observation:

Try Activity 5.2

- With whom does Jack interact most and least?
- What circumstances surrounded positive interactions?
- What circumstances surrounded negative interactions?
- With whom were the positive, neutral, and negative interactions?
- Were the different kinds of interactions (positive, neutral, negative) related to different times of day, different activities, or other factors or circumstances?

Since formal observation is labor and time-intensive, most teachers reserve it for special circumstances, such as when a student needs academic or social help.

On the other hand, if you observe Jack informally, your observations will not be systematic. You will only be describing spontaneous events and situations that you feel are interesting or important. Thus, informal observation is casual, impromptu, and general. Teacher comments made on cumulative record cards and on report cards (see, for example, pages 142–143) are usually the result of informal observation.

INTERVIEWING STUDENTS

Certainly, one way to find out about persons is to talk with them directly, the way a talk show host would.

Likewise, teachers can find out about students either by talking casually with them or by formally interviewing them. Interviews are particularly useful in uncovering personal information that cannot be obtained through observation. For example, you can observe Jack Brogan to deduce possible causes of his unsatisfactory interaction with his peers, or you can interview him in an attempt to uncover the cause.

5.5 If you were Kathleen Glovack's student teacher, why might you want to interview her?

Like observations, interviews can be formal or informal. A **formal interview** is a structured, face-to-face meeting to obtain specific information about the interviewee's experiences, views, likes, and so forth. The key characteristics of a formal interview are *purpose* and *structure*. There are particular things you wish to find out, and in order to do so, you must frame your questions accordingly.

An **informal interview** is a face-to-face meeting that is more like casual conversation. The intention is to allow talk to flow naturally and spontaneously in more or less any direction.

What procedures are teachers expected to follow? Here are some guidelines; think about how you might follow them if you were interviewing Jack, Kathy, Benny, Julio, or Debbie.

- *Be prepared.* If you are conducting the interview for a specific purpose it must be carefully structured. In Kathy's case, you may want to find out how she feels about her student teacher and why. Have explicit, thoughtfully constructed questions ready.
- *Put the student at ease.* Begin by establishing a friendly, relaxed atmosphere. Use a warm-up period to talk for awhile about pleasant, nonthreatening things.

Try Activity 5.3

- *Guide the student.* Once you seem to be comfortable with each other, gently lead the child through your thoughtfully planned questions and probe for further, related information if that seems prudent. However, do not push too hard. You may recall times when teachers or parents "interviewed" you and perhaps met with resistance.
- *Know when to quit.* You may have to back off or stop if the interviewee feels threatened.

A teacher describes how he interviews in Highlight 5.3.

You can also obtain much useful information about a student through interviewing other teachers and through parent conferences. As with student interviews, the amount of useful information you obtain will be directly related to how well you prepare and how skillfully you follow good interviewing procedures.

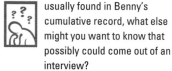

5.6 Beyond the information usually found in Benny's cumulative record, what else might you want to know that possibly could come out of an interview?

USING QUESTIONNAIRES

Another way you can acquire student information is to have students complete questionnaires such as the one below. (Of course, questions would be modified according to the student's developmental characteristics, such as age.)

5.7 What from this list would you want to know that could be discovered through a questionnaire?

- What are your favorite activities, games, hobbies, TV shows, videogames, websites? If you could do just two things, what would they be?
- What don't you like to do, and why?
- What is your favorite place, and why?
- What is your least favorite place, and why?
- What are your favorite school subjects, and why?
- What do you like and dislike most about school, and why?
- Is the work in school too easy, too difficult, or just right? How hard do you work in school?
- What kind of teacher do you like best?
- How do you think others (classmates, friends, your parents,) would describe you?
- How well do you usually get along with your classmates?

Try Activity 5.4

- What is it like for you at home?
- What is most upsetting to you? (Some things causing stress in kids are found in Spotlight on Research 5.1 on page 124.)
- If you had a magic wand, what would you change?
- What else do you want me to know that might help me help you?

Some questions were inspired by Rock (2004).

USING SOCIOMETRY

Sociometry is a technique used to obtain information about the social relationships of individuals within a group. A sociogram is a diagrammatic representation of the social relationships that exist within a group at a *particular point in time* (see Figure 5.1 on page 125).

It is often difficult to make a connection with a kid who is all tied up in knots, nonverbal, or oppositional. Trying to have a useful conversation with an angry adolescent makes party small talk seem easy. But asking the student question after question about him or herself seems to release something inside that starts them talking. It turns out that kids like talking about themselves almost as much as adults do.

I usually start with the most basic questions about age, living conditions, relatives, where they grew up, etc. After I have collected that batch of monosyllabic answers, I crank it up a notch and start asking them questions about their personal interests. I ask what their schedule is and which is their favorite class. I ask about hobbies, travel, outside of school experiences. I ask about pets, friends, relatives, and work. I ask and ask and ask until the kid has become used to talking.

Then I move into the really important questions.

I ask how they feel. I ask them about problems with learning. I ask them health questions, and I ask them about future plans. After a while, it doesn't really matter what I ask them. They have an adult in front of them who cares about what comes out of their mouth, and almost without fail, they will spill their guts. Give them time to get past the "I'm too cool to talk with teachers" phase and most students will open up.

The trick is to avoid telling them anything. Don't talk about yourself. Don't suggest any good ideas. Don't offer wisdom or advice. Just ask question after question and listen to what they say. There will be time later for all of the usual education objectives, but in the beginning simply ask them questions and let them talk.

Talking to adults is something most kids . . . avoid. But despite all the drama, they love to do it. I have found that talking to adults, especially to teachers, feels good to them. Talking releases tension, lowers frustration levels, eases fear, and generally makes kids feel important. What could be better than helping a kid release a little steam and increase self-esteem?

Teaching them anything after that will be easier, and you may find out something important that has been locked up inside. Maybe you will be the first adult to ask the kid any questions.

And don't forget; if you ask a bunch of questions, your student will walk away thinking you are really nice and very smart.

Source: Simpson (2005).

Suppose you are the teacher of Jack Brogan and Kathleen Glovack. Furthermore, assume you wish to know more about how their peers feel about these students, and how the students feel about their peers. If so, you might ask each class member to name three students they would like to sit near. As Figure 5.1 shows, the responses of the 29 students in Jack and Kathleen's class reveal that

- no one chooses Jack.
- four students would like to sit near Kathleen (three girls, one boy).

Ronald, the most nominated student in the class, was selected nine times. Five students other than Jack were not selected by anyone. Can you identify them?

Beyond frequency of nomination (popularity), teachers are also interested in attractions. Who nominated whom? Who chose each of the students? To what extent are the choices mutual? Are there cases of "unrequited love" or instances when students choose others who reject or spurn them?

Although sociometric nominations are one of the most dependable rating techniques, caution is urged when interpreting sociometric data (Anastasi, 1997; Poulin & Dushion, 2008). The information actually may indicate desired rather than real associations among class members, and "too often high sociometric status is interpreted to mean leadership ability and good personality adjustment, while receiving no sociometric choices is commonly equated with maladjustment. Receiving many choices actually could mean high conformity to the group, and isolation could be a sign of independence and creativity." Interested in sociometry? Visit these websites: Walsh's Classroom Sociometrics or Sherman's link in the Miami University of Ohio website.

5.8 How might you put sociometric information to good use?

Try Activities 5.5 and 5.6

OLC Web Links
Walsh's Classroom
Sociometrics
Sociometry in the Classroom

CHAPTER 5
Getting to Know Your Students
and Motivating Them to Learn

What is most upsetting to kids? Predominantly white, mostly middle-class 9- to 13-year-old city kids report the following stressors, listed in order of the percentage of kids bothered by each. For example, "grades, school, and homework" bothered 36 percent of students participating in the study.

Girls are more upset over family issues, siblings, and fighting. Boys are more troubled by sports-related matters.

Older children are more likely to be upset by grades, school, and homework. Younger kids are more upset by siblings and getting in trouble.

To handle stress, these children often use distractions (playing, listening to music, watching TV, playing videogames). Boys and girls differ in coping strategies.

Source: Brown (2005).

STRESS-CAUSING FACTOR	PERCENTAGE OF KIDS BOTHERED
Grades, school, and homework	36
Family	32
Friends, peers who tease, lie, gossip about me	21
Brothers and sisters	20
Mean or annoying people	20
Parents	14
Yelling or loud noise	9
Fighting	9
Sports	8
Not being allowed to do something	7
Getting in trouble	7
Being exhausted, tired, overextended	6
Doing something wrong or failing	5
Video or computer games	4
Chores	4
Lies and stealing	4
Confusion and/or bad memory	4
Being unwell	3
Being ignored	3
Animals or pets	2
Sleep issues	1
Death	1
Upsetting people	1
Phobias	1

USING AUTOBIOGRAPHY

Another way to obtain information about students is to ask them to write about some aspect of their lives. However, use of this technique is limited since it depends on students' verbal and writing ability. Additionally, it is time-consuming for the writers. Therefore, should you wish to obtain autobiographical information, limit the focus of the story. Ask students to recall and write about such topics as:

5.9 How would your teachers benefit from autobiographical information about you? What kinds of information would you want them to have?

- Who am I?
- The best day I ever had.
- My favorite year in school.
- My favorite teacher.
- My life at home.
- My life in the neighborhood.
- My life at school.
- My most memorable experience.
- My favorite things.

Try Activity 5.7

USING PARENTS AND GUARDIANS AS SOURCES

Parents and caregivers are important sources of information about students. Normally, parents know more about their children than anyone, and most

FIGURE 5.1 Sociogram

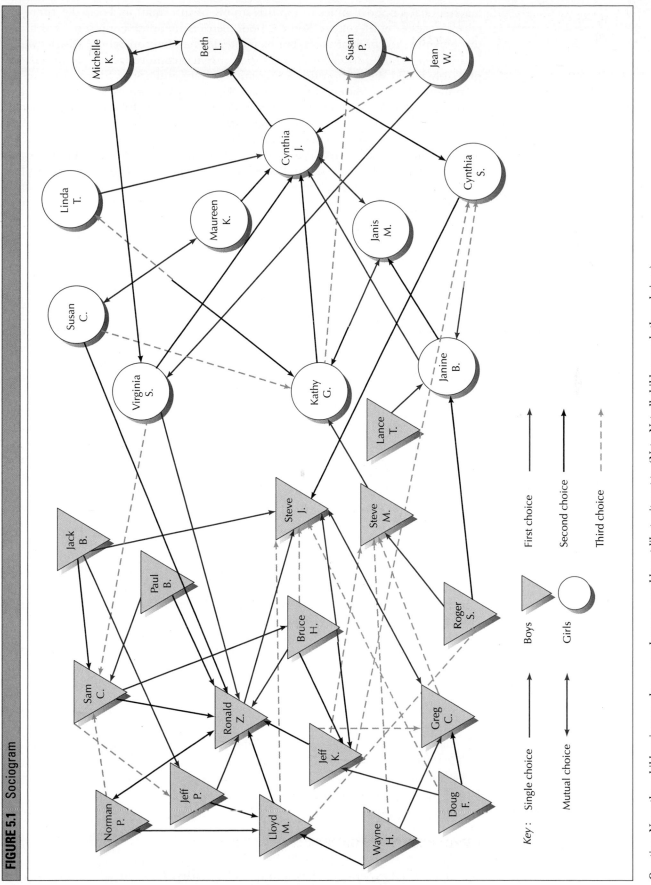

Key: Single choice ——→

Mutual choice ←——→

Boys ◢

Girls ◯

First choice ——→

Second choice ——→

Third choice – – – →

Question: Name three children in your classroom whom you would most like to sit next to. (Note: Not all children made three choices.)

teachers have opportunities to tap this supply of information. Formally, there are parent-teacher conferences. Some school districts mandate conferences and give teachers time to conduct them. For example, in the Madison School District where Jack Brogan and Kathy Glovack are students, yearly conferences are required. You probably noted the section titled "Parent-Teacher Conference Summaries" in the cumulative record folders. In the Urban School System where Benny, Julio, and Debbie are students, conferences are not required, and the folders have no specific place to record them. Of course, Urban teachers do confer with parents. You will note in Debbie Walker's folder that there is a request from her third-grade teacher for a parent conference or a follow-up letter from the parent. Mrs. Walker indicated she had received the request, but there is no evidence that a conference took place or that she responded with a letter.

Unfortunately, most parent-teacher conferences are held only to provide information to parents and not also to obtain information from them. Certainly, it was important for Kathy Glovack's fourth-grade teacher to learn that Kathy didn't want to come to school because she didn't like the student teacher. Also, Kathy's third-grade teacher learned from Mrs. Glovack that there was a new baby in the home. This is potentially useful information. In Jack Brogan's case, parent conferences revealed that his father is strict, that his parents want him to behave and learn, and that they are cooperative and helpful.

What might teachers need to know about students that could be learned from parents and guardians? Parents can tell teachers about a student's behavior at home, about his or her likes and dislikes, habits, responsibilities, and so forth. While parents do not know everything about their children, they can aid you tremendously in getting to know your students needs' and abilities.

What might teachers need to know about parents and guardians that, in turn, would help them understand more about their students? Touliatos and Compton (1983) suggest the following: parental background and current family status, personal characteristics of parents ("the Brogans are strict"), parental perception of their relationship with each other and with the student, the roles of both parents and students in the home, and parental attitudes toward the student and any siblings. To find out about the personal characteristics of parents and other family members, teachers might ask them to tell what they are like as people and as parents, then ask how that may affect their son or daughter. To know how parents perceive their own and their children's roles and relationships in the home, teachers might ask them how family responsibilities and decisions are shared.

It is particularly useful to know how parents or guardians feel toward parenting and child rearing. You might consider asking them what it is like to be parents or guardians, how being a parent has affected their lives, what it is like to be the target student's parent or guardian, what they believe in as parents or guardians, and so on.

Here are some other questions that you might put to parents and caregivers.

- Describe what your child is like at home. What does he do—not do, like—not like. What responsibilities does your child have?
- What is it like to be his parent? Are there any concerns you have that you would like to share?
- How would you describe your child's well-being, physical and emotional?
- What does your child think of himself?
- What does your child think of school? What does he like, dislike about it?
- How does your child get along with others?
- What are your child's strengths and weaknesses?
- What special experiences has your child had either in or outside school?

5.10 What do teachers absolutely *need* to know about a student's family background? What might they *want* to know that isn't absolutely necessary? What kinds of information are helpful? What family information is no one else's business?

"I said, 'Your son doesn't seem to listen very well'."

Try Activity 5.8

- Has your child ever received any special help?
- How can I best help your child? What are some best ways to work with him?

USING CASES

The **case approach** pieces together all existing information to form a comprehensive profile of the target student. Thus, a case pulls together information from cumulative records, observations, interviews, questionnaires, sociometric studies, autobiographies, parent conferences, and any other source and synthesizes it.

Normally, the best existing source of case history information is the cumulative record since it contains several kinds of information and is updated from time to time. When other data are available to fill in the blanks, teachers are able to complete the case. If other data are not available, they must collect the missing information.

To have an overall picture of a student, you need the following data (Touliatos & Compton, 1983):

- Identifying information (name, address, telephone number, age in years and months, place of birth, gender, grade, race, nationality, religion).
- Family history (relationship of the parent, guardian, or caregiver to the student; parents' age, race, nationality, religion, cultural background, and language spoken in the home; family physical and health concerns; education; present work status; homeowner or renter; adequacy of housing; interests; pastimes).
- Student's medical history (general health, record of prominent illnesses and injuries).
- Student's school history (schools attended, level of performance in general and in specific subjects such as reading and math, aptitude test scores, achievement test scores, special interests, attitudes, relationships with others, friends).

A teacher-written case study of Debbie Walker is contained in **Case 5.1.** Her cumulative record folder is appended at the end of the chapter.

Some schools store cumulative record information electronically. (See Highlight 5.4 on page 129.)

5.11 Would you like to have a complete profile of all the students you teach? What benefits would this offer?

Try Activity 5.9

Evaluating and Using Information

It is one thing to need or want accurate student information to aid you in your teaching. It is another thing to understand and to use it wisely.

EVALUATING INFORMATION

Several questions arise when you examine student data: *Is this information suitable for my purpose?* Just what is it that I want to know? Does this information supply the answers? Suppose you want to know about your students' aptitude for learning: to what extent are they likely to be able to deal with abstractions, solve problems, and learn? In this case you need to have the results of a standardized test that measures learning aptitude. On the other hand, a standardized test that measures student achievement—what a student already knows—would not be suitable for that purpose. Although students' scores on achievement tests are often closely related to their scores on learning aptitude tests, these tests measure different things. A student may perform well on a learning aptitude test, thus revealing the potential to learn, yet may not do well on an achievement test. Conversely, another student may earn a high achievement test score but a low learning aptitude test score. Can you see how this could happen? Since standardized tests have been carefully developed to measure what they are supposed to measure, make certain that you have the right test results for your needs.

Debbie Walker, Grade 5, Edison School. One November morning, Debbie Walker, a transfer student from Baker Middle School, arrived hobbling on crutches and accompanied by her mother. Mrs. Walker explained that Debbie had broken her leg while helping carry furniture into the house from a moving truck. As a result of the accident, Debbie had missed almost two months of school. As soon as she entered our classroom, the children immediately accepted her. This was probably partially a result of her incapacitation. Lynette Overmire and several other children were anxious to help and made plans to escort Debbie to and from classrooms and to her home. This was the first indication that Debbie was able to exert a subtle yet profound effect on the behavior of her peers.

Debbie Walker was born in the city of Urban and has lived in inner-city ghetto areas all her life. During this time, she has attended eight different schools and has been a pupil in 18 different classrooms. As a result of this continuous shifting, Debbie has never experienced any sense of security or permanency. Her home conditions (the family has 14 children) are in a constant state of turmoil. In a fatherless home until recently, Debbie and her siblings have moved from one area of the inner-city ghetto to another. Often, the only concern of such families is to eke out a day-by-day existence.

Until recently, Debbie lived only with her mother and six of her twelve siblings. However, within the last two years she also had a "stepfather." More recently, the stepfather left the home and is seeking court action to obtain custody of his baby daughter. Debbie knows nothing of her biological father. She does not even remember one. She has grown up on public assistance. This family has packed up its belongings and criss-crossed the city almost as many times as Debbie has counted birthdays.

Physically, Debbie is relatively tall for her age. She is an African-American and a member of the Baptist church. Her personal appearance varies from one day to the next. She does not seem to know how to be neat, clean, and well groomed.

Debbie's general attitude has been pleasant until recently. She has enjoyed helping in the classroom and about the school, and the children elected her to the position of class treasurer. Debbie has been assisting in the arts and crafts program in our after-school program at the Social Center. The arts and crafts teacher has praised Debbie's work.

Very recently, however, Debbie appears to be disturbed. Just last month, she was suspended from school for two days for encouraging two girls to fight each other outside the school building during lunch period. As a result of her suspension, she became sullen and would not complete her academic assignments. Now she has had her school and after-school responsibilities taken away from her.

Debbie had been relatively happy in school until these events occurred. This was reassuring, since she has been retained in the first, third, and fifth grades. She seems to enjoy art, music, and arithmetic the most. However, she claims she likes all her subjects.

Debbie uses fair Standard English. The mark of inner-city linguistic characteristics is evident in her speech pattern.

In a recent conversation with Mrs. Walker, we discussed Debbie's attitudes, general behavior, and failure to follow through with classwork. I indicated that this behavior was jeopardizing Debbie's school success. Her mother thinks that her friendship with Felicia Ault is the reason behind her change for the worse. It is true that Debbie and Felicia are close and have a somewhat negative influence upon each other and the other children. As mentioned earlier, Debbie is able to affect the behavior of her classmates through manipulation and subtle pressure.

Debbie's school achievement has been weak. She has taken three Kuhlman-Anderson IQ tests. The results reveal an IQ range from 86 to 103. Her achievement test scores are recorded on her cumulative record folder and should be interpreted according to her age and grade rather than just grade alone.

One hopes that Debbie's recent failure to complete her work and to behave in more appropriate ways in the school setting may pass. Now that she is encountering more homework, some provisions will have to be made for a quiet place at home for her to study. In a family as large as hers, this circumstance is improbable. Coming to school as she has recently with unfinished assignments may well have led to her frustration and antisocial behavior. Debbie must be continually encouraged to do her best to complete her work and to complete it on time. If she is able to develop this habit, she may soon be eligible to become a hall guard. This status, if attained, may ease her frustrations.

This case report was in the student's cumulative folder (see the Appendix).

INVESTIGATING AND SOLVING THE CASE

1. What factors seem to impact Debbie?
2. How do you feel about her teacher's assessment of Debbie's situation?
3. How would you help Debbie?

HIGHLIGHT 5.4
Electronic Student Information Retrieval Systems

Much student information can be entered into and retrieved from computerized student information systems (SIS) such as *PowerSchool* and *School Master*. They permit electronic storage of all kinds of information including student attendance, grades, cumulative record-like information such as teacher comments, and more. Their use eliminates the need for paper copies of cumulative and other kinds of student records.

They also allow parents access to their child's attendance and progress via the Internet. Additionally, they contain an e-mail feature permitting teachers and parents to communicate. Visit the PowerSchool website for a demonstration.

A second question related to student data involves correctness. Here you need to ask: *Is this information really accurate?* Two major factors can contribute to inaccuracy. One relates to whether the information is biased, while the other relates to whether the information is stable. For decades, certain standardized tests have been criticized as biased, usually in terms of culture or gender considerations. As previously mentioned in the section on aptitude tests, some tests appear to be easier for students brought up in white, middle-class communities because they use Standard English and draw from typical middle-class experiences. Others supposedly exhibit gender bias, usually meaning they are easier for males than females. To the extent that such tests are biased, it is impossible to obtain truly accurate student scores. School districts are increasingly aware of the need to find objective tests that provide unbiased, culture- and gender-fair results.

Unfortunately, some degree of bias exists in everyone. Accordingly, be cautious about accepting any interpretation of student data provided by others, including teachers. Although most teachers have no intention of providing slanted information, they naturally become attracted to certain students and are put off by others. They tend to identify with and praise the "attractive students" and to reject and punish the "unattractive" ones. To some extent, the attraction teachers feel toward certain students is a function of their own background and personality. Generally, we tend to like those who are like us. We feel more comfortable around them (the "birds of a feather flock together" syndrome).

Teacher bias is particularly evident when such things as race, nationality, gender, looks, and dress unfairly and incorrectly influence the teacher's perception of students. Can you recall instances of possible teacher bias toward you or a friend based on one of these factors?

Teacher bias also can be positive but inaccurate. Each of us has a friend or relative whom we are attracted to for some particular reason. Sometimes we admire that person so much for one or two positive qualities that we overlook any negative qualities he or she may have. To us, that individual wears a halo. You will find certain students seem to wear halos, too. They can do no wrong. This bias phenomenon is aptly termed "the halo effect." Although it is difficult to detect and control, you must strive to observe and report the truth, the whole truth, and nothing but the truth about learners. This is a tall order.

Inconsistent information about students also presents a problem. Consider Benny Gamble's "general ability tests" (page 152). He took these aptitude tests in grades 1, 2, and 3 and received intelligence scores ranging from 97 (about average) to 116 (above average). Similarly, you might receive conflicting perceptions of a student from different teachers. One might report an eager hand-raiser as an aggressive attention seeker, while another might interpret the same behavior as that of a motivated learner. Which should you believe? Generally speaking, when

OLC Web Link
PowerSchool Website

5.12 How will you become aware of your personal biases? How will you deal with them?

information about a student is inconsistent, err on the positive side: Accept Benny's high score as indicative of what he can do under optimal conditions. And, for the same reason, believe the best about any learner with mixed credentials.

In summary, if you are to be effective, you must learn to obtain and use only the information about students that suits your purpose, is unbiased, and is consistent or stable.

USING INFORMATION PROPERLY

The student information we obtain affects the perceptions and expectations we have of them. Moreover, some types of information are more influential than others. Dusek and Joseph (1983) identified and compared the results of 77 studies that were conducted to find out what most influences the academic and personal expectations teachers have for their students. The investigators looked for relationships between teachers' expectations and student gender, gender-role behaviors, physical attractiveness, race and social class, name stereotypes, conduct, and the teacher's previous experiences with a sibling. Five of these factors seem to significantly influence a teacher's judgment: student attractiveness, class conduct, race, social class, and cumulative record information, particularly test scores and teachers' anecdotal comments. To see how, turn to Spotlight on Research 5.2.

In contrast, Dusek and Joseph note that it is unclear whether a student's name (desirable versus undesirable), gender-role behaviors (whether their behavior follows a gender-role stereotype), or a teacher's previous experiences with a student's sibling influence teacher expectations. The researchers conclude that teachers, on average, are not influenced by a student's gender. Although a student's gender does not seem to influence the teacher's academic and personal expectations of that student, we learned in Chapter 3 that teachers still treat boys and girls differently. To explain this seeming contradiction, consider two friends—one male, one female. Could you hold similar academic and personal expectations for them and still treat them differently?

Since certain information about students influences the perceptions and expectations of teachers, just how much should they read or hear about their students *before* classes begin? Airasian (2008) says that in the course of interviews with teachers, he found most of them wanted at least three kinds of information early on. They want to know about (1) any physical or emotional problem, (2) learners' special needs, learning problems, or disabilities, and (3) problematic or atypical parent custodial arrangements.

Fortunately, many teachers adjust their perceptions and expectations of students after working with them, after getting to know them. Yes, as teachers we tend to believe what we read, but we change those impressions in light of our experience.

5.13 Are you able to change your mind about people?

Motivating Students to Learn

Try Activity 5.10

In addition to knowing your students, you must be able to motivate them to learn. Some teachers seem to come by this ability naturally. However, most of us have to learn how to motivate. Fortunately, knowledge about motivation is abundant. Alderman (2004), Anderman et al. (2009), Brophy (2004), Dweck (2010), Fredericks et al. (2004), and Seifert (2004) have reviewed that knowledge and offer the following advice. The advice is applicable when we plan, teach, or evaluate students.

- Establish a classroom environment that is conducive to learning. How? *First,* make yourself "attractive" and engaging to your learners. It helps when students feel positively toward you. (See Chapter 10 on effective teachers.) Communicate that you care and will help. *Second,* focus their attention on achieving goals—individual student goals and/or group goals. It helps when learners know what is to be done and, if possible, why. (See Chapter 4, "Cognitive Approaches to

Variables	Type of Influence
Student attractiveness (physical)	Influences teachers' expectations for both academic achievement and social-personal relationships.
Student classroom conduct	Influences teachers' expectations of future conduct.
Race	Generally, white students are expected to outperform non-white students.
Social class	Generally, middle-class children are expected to perform better than lower-class students.
Cumulative record information	Teachers' expectations are influenced mainly by test scores and other teachers' comments.

Source: Dusek & Joseph (1983).

Teaching and Learning.") *Third,* teach what is worth learning, and teach it in ways that help students appreciate its value.

- Maximize the likelihood that learners will make an effort to learn. Students are more likely to make an effort to learn when (1) they believe they are *competent* and can perform a task successfully and will feel rewarded, (2) they believe they have the power to succeed (a sense of *control* or **efficacy**), and (3) they believe they will receive the support necessary to succeed.

- Make special efforts on behalf of students who lack confidence and thus are reluctant to engage in learning. Make challenging but ability-related demands on them. Help them see that they can succeed with reasonable effort. Should they fall sort, help them understand why and show them how they can succeed. (See Spotlight on Research 5.3.)

- Make special efforts with students who have low expectations for themselves and readily accept failure. Provide them with continuous reassurance that they can succeed. Provide whatever support is needed. *Praise effort* and *accept progress. Individualize* as required. Collaborate with family and caregivers.

- Make special efforts with apathetic and disengaged students. Help them appreciate how learning will empower them and make them more satisfied with themselves. Such students can benefit from use of incentives and by use of signed agreements or contracts (see Chapter 7, "individualized instruction") that spell out learning goals and rewards for success. Encourage learners by being patient yet determined for their success. Build on existing learner interests and make learning tasks as satisfying as possible (see Spotlight on Research 5.3).

- Use both *extrinsic* and *intrinsic* reward as suitable (see Highlights 5.5 and 5.6 on pages 132 and 133 respectively). However, it is better to have learners engage in activities for their own reasons and their own fulfillment (intrinsic), rather than do something to please others, to obtain a material reward, or to avoid a punishment (extrinsic). Always try to focus student attention on what they personally are accomplishing or will accomplish by learning. To increase intrinsic motivation: (1) encourage autonomy by giving learners frequent opportunities (within the boundaries of the curriculum) to make decisions about what they will learn and how, (2) match learning tasks to the ability of each student, (3) use as many activity-oriented projects as possible and provide learners with immediate knowledge of how well they are doing, (4) try to use *authentic* activities—those that have a relationship to and application in the real world, (5) adapt the activities, when logical, to meet the interests of students, (6) personalize learning and try to make it emotionally or affectively engaging, and (7) avoid boring and aversive tasks. Also see Providing Feedback and Reinforcement, in Chapter 11.

5.14 How did your teachers maximize your interest in learning?

Try Activity 5.11

5.15 When and why have you experienced a lack of motivation to learn?

SPOTLIGHT ON RESEARCH 5.3
Motivating Reluctant Learners

There are students in almost every classroom who are academically unmotivated, referred to as *reluctant learners* or *tough teaches*. Perhaps, you can recall some. In fact, you may have been one yourself until someone or something turned you around. Some tactics that have been found useful to "catch and hold" the attention of the academically unmotivated include:

Make certain that what students are to read is easily comprehensible.

Additionally, try to find reading that contains novelty and surprise.

Give students choices. Even when seemingly trivial they seem to enhance student interest.

Consider single-gender groups or classes for some things that seem more difficult for either boys or girls. For example, it has been found that girls show higher levels of interest in physics when in a single-gender class.

Help students figure out how to make certain tasks less boring and more interesting. For example, "How can we make this more fun?"

Make students socially responsible. For example, utilize cooperative learning (presented in Chapter 8) where, in some cases, each learner in a small group must become expert on a topic and share that expertise with peers.

Source: Hidi and Harackicwicz (2000)

HIGHLIGHT 5.5
Paying for Performance?

Extrinsic rewards are items of value to kids, given to them for doing a good job. Putting smiley faces on student work is a simple example. However, there is now a movement to hand over cash or gifts. For example, the Earning by Learning program in Dallas uses cash incentives to encourage students to read. Other

districts offer items such as MP3 players and cell phones in return for improved academic performance.

Opponents line up on both sides of this issue. Some say it's worth a try especially for kids with a low SES who, through hard work, may be able to obtain something they value. Others

say that extrinsic rewards only work in the short term and that kids need to internalize the importance and fun of learning. Learning is an end in itself. Research results are mixed. If you were on the jury, how would you vote?

Source: Henderson (2009)

Try Activity 5.12

- Engage learners in tasks that permit them to accomplish curriculum goals and at the same time satisfy their own personal and social goals. Everyone wins.
- Encourage students to value learning. Do this by being an enthusiastic learner yourself, by treating students as eager learners, by avoiding classroom practices that cause student anxiety, by causing learners to think deeply, and by attaching learning to students' life experiences.
- Encourage students to support each other (see Chapter 8, "cooperative learning").

Some Final Thoughts

As we have seen, sizing up students has its benefits and pitfalls. We have already alluded to the potential danger of relying exclusively or too heavily on certain kinds of information, such as standardized test scores and teachers' comments. Airasian

Orlando Martinez who teaches third grade was devastated that on the first day of school most of his students couldn't write a paragraph or even a complete sentence. However, rather than give up on his kids, Martinez went to work looking for ways to motivate them to learn and to behave in ways that promote learning.

He gave each of them a cutout of either Spiderman or Spiderwoman. When a behavior occurred that interfered with learning, the Spiderman or Spiderwoman figure was lowered toward an illustration of their arch villain Scorpion. Following a second ill-advised behavior, they had to answer to Dr. Octopus. The ultimate penalty was to face the Green Goblin. Kids being kids, they all wanted to be Spiderman or Spiderwoman. However, they did not want to find themselves in the grasp of Scorpion, Dr. Octopus, or Green Goblin who had some form of corrective behavior to mete out.

The system seems to work, and the classroom walls are filled with posters of various super heroes that serve as role models. Besides the super heroes, there are also imaginary creatures and monsters the children created.

Martinez feels that "teachers are super heroes too, being with kids all day, serving as baby sitters, counselors, mentors, everything."

Besides using super heroes to motivate, Martinez has students work in pairs to provide encouragement and support for one another. He also divides the students into groups who vie for pretend prize money they get for academic achievements and good behavior. The phony money can be used to buy privileges or other benefits.

Martinez feels that making school fun is important, and his students and former students seem to agree, describing him as someone who is interested in them and their interests, someone who "goes the extra mile for the kids, parents and community."

Source: Zayas (2004).

(2008) offers suggestions on how teachers can overcome these and other possible problems. Our modifications of his suggestions follow:

- Be sensitive to the possibility that you will make poor initial judgments about students from biased, incomplete, or erroneous information or from having a poor first impression. Give each student a second chance to make a good impression.

- Do not rush to judgment about what any student is like. Over time, collect as much information as you can in order to find out who that person really is.

- Rather than relying on recorded information, how the student dresses or looks, and what others say, observe the student and try to get close enough to find out the truth for yourself. Looks can be deceiving!

A large number of formal instruments have been developed for assessing students. Using them can provide knowledge about your students' (1) cognition (intelligence, readiness to learn, maturation, language and number skills, cognitive style, and so on), (2) personality and emotional characteristics, (3) perceptions of the environment, (4) self-concept, (5) attitudes and interests, and (6) social behavior. These instruments are well described in a two-volume set edited by Johnson (1976).

On the other hand, the use of motivation has only benefits. Therefore, work toward improving your motivational prowess. The following quotations by famous motivators provide additional ideas about how to be a skillful motivator yourself:

- The important thing is not so much that every child should be taught, as that every child should be given the wish to learn. (John Lubbock)

- A teacher who is attempting to teach without inspiring the pupil with a desire to learn is hammering on cold iron. (Horace Mann)

- Above all things we must take care that the child who is not yet old enough to love his studies, does not come to hate them and dread the bitterness which was once tasted, even when the years of infancy are left behind. (Marcus Fabius Quintilianus)
- That which anyone has been long learning unwillingly, he unlearns with proportional eagerness and haste. (William Hazlitt)

CHAPTER SUMMARY

SUPPLEMENTAL RESOURCES

Go to the text's Online Learning Center at www.mhhe.com/cruickshank6e to access the chapter's **study tools** including web links practice for Praxis™ case studies, and video clips.

- Getting to know students is important to teachers. Expert teachers seem to know far more about their students than novice teachers do.
- While there are many ways to get to know students, the information they yield falls into two main categories: information obtained from existing student records and information teachers can obtain for themselves.
- The major source of existing information is the cumulative ("cume") records or folders (five examples are in the chapter appendix). Cumulative records normally contain personal information about a student, home-family information, school attendance data, academic grades, standardized test scores, teacher comments, and so forth. Generally, teachers seem most interested in obtaining standardized test scores and reading former teachers' comments.
- To interpret standardized test scores, it is necessary to know what the test attempts to measure and to understand terms such as *standardized test, percentile,* and *grade equivalent.* To judge teachers' comments, it is necessary to know something about the people who made them and how they reached their conclusions about the student. Teachers' comments are often brief, incomplete, and, at times, inaccurate.
- A second source of information about students is knowledge teachers obtain from observations, interviews, questionnaires, sociometrics, autobiographies, parents, and cases.
- Student observations can be formal (intentionally planned and carried out) or informal (spontaneous and unplanned). Formal observation requires the teacher to specify who will be observed and how the observation will take place. Informal observation requires only occasional and impromptu records of whatever catches the teacher's attention. Most teacher observations are informal.
- Interviews allow teachers to collect information that is difficult to gain through mere observation. Interviews also can be formal or informal. Following certain interviewing procedures increases both the amount and the quality of information obtained.
- Questionnaires are structured using either open- or closed-ended questions. Open-ended questions ask students to broadly describe their perceptions of themselves, their relationships with peers, and their school and home lives. Closed-ended questions force students to answer according to some preconstructed scale or by responding yes or no; they permit no elaboration.
- Sociometry is used to find out how students perceive their social and/or work relationships with peers. A sociogram is a visual representation of those relationships.
- Autobiographical writing provides students with the opportunity to tell about themselves. Use of autobiographical writing is somewhat limited because of the literacy demands it places on some students.
- Parents and caregivers can tell teachers much about their charges, and the teacher should tap them for this information. Knowledge of parents and family also helps us understand students.
- The case approach is a technique used to bring together all information about a student in order to create a more complete picture. Thus, a good case

contains a mixture of information obtained through all the techniques just mentioned.

- Teachers must be able to evaluate information about students. Of prime importance is how closely the available information relates to the decisions teachers must make. Information that fits the purpose is valid information. Also important is the accuracy and stability of information, which is referred to as its *reliability*. Being able to judge the validity and reliability of information is crucial to using it in decision making.

- Certain types of information influence teachers' perceptions and expectations of students more than other kinds. The most influential types of information seem to be class conduct, student attractiveness, social class, race, and cumulative records. All teachers seem to want to gain information about learners' physical, emotional, learning, or home problems early on. Fortunately, teachers adjust their early impressions of students based upon long-term, daily experience with them. Airasian (2001) offers suggestions for overcoming the tendency to think and act on first impressions.

- Teachers must be able to interest students in learning. Some of us are more able to do this than others.

- Student interest increases when we establish an attractive learning environment by displaying personal characteristics students find engaging, letting students know what the lesson is trying to accomplish, and making the lesson worth learning.

- Students are more likely to undertake learning when they think the task is within their ability, they feel they can succeed, and they believe you will assist them as necessary.

- Students either lacking confidence or reluctant to learn are helped when you provide ability-related, yet challenging tasks on which they can succeed with reasonable effort.

- Students with low expectations for themselves should be given regular assurance that they can succeed and should be praised for effort and progress.

- Apathetic students are helped when they understand the personal value of learning, when they face tasks related to their interests, and when incentives are provided. Intrinsic incentives or rewards are preferable.

- Be enthusiastic about learning and an enthusiastic learner yourself, and treat students as such.

KEY TERMS

Cumulative record, 117

Standardized test, 118

Aptitude test, 118

Achievement test, 119

Anecdotal comments, 119

Student observation, 120

Student interview, 121

Student questionnaire, 122

Sociometry, 122

Student stressors, 124

Autobiography, 124

Case approach, 127

Motivation to learn, 130

Efficacy, 131

ISSUES AND PROBLEMS FOR DISCUSSION

ISSUES

1. When should teachers read cumulative record information?
2. What kinds of information about students *must* a teacher have? What kinds *shouldn't* a teacher have?

3. How much confidence should teachers place in standardized tests? How should teachers use test data?

4. What are the advantages and disadvantages of showing students and parents standardized test results?

5. How can a teacher reduce his or her bias toward certain students?

6. Are parents and caregivers or teachers more responsible for creating student interest in learning?

7. How can what is known about student diversity (Chapter 3) be applied to student motivation?

8. How does each school of thought about learning (Chapter 4) apply to student motivation?

9. How can what we know about our students be used when motivating them?

10. What do you think are the three most important principles of motivation?

PROBLEMS   Following are some problems teachers have shared with us that relate to this chapter. What would you do in each case?

Problem 1:   A friend who just completed student teaching laments, "When I finished student teaching, I realized that I didn't know my students very well. It makes me sad because, as a teacher, you don't get to know your students as well as you would like. In a classroom setting, you are one teacher with at least 20 kids. Your main goal is to help each student grow academically, and in order to do this, you have to sacrifice some of the personal time with students."

Problem 2:   A parent really confused me when she said, "I know that the school keeps records on [my child]. I know those records have a lot of negative stuff in them. I don't want you be influenced by that stuff, so I would appreciate it if you would not look at them."

Problem 3:   "I wonder about the value of my colleagues' comments in cumulative folders. When I get some of these children I feel very differently about them than their former teachers felt."

Problem 4:   Hombo has a history of being absolutely disinterested in school, and now he is in my class.

THEORY INTO ACTION: ACTIVITIES FOR PRACTICE AND YOUR PORTFOLIO

ACTIVITY 5.1: Review Some Cumulative Records   If you are in a field experience, ask your mentor teacher if you can see the cumulative records for that class. If so, make a list of the kinds of information they contain. Make a second list of other kinds of information about students that might be helpful to you.

If you are not in a field experience, study the five cumulative records in the appendix and make the same two lists. What else do you need to know in order to understand or interpret specific information contained in the records? Be prepared to share your investigation with other students in this course.

ACTIVITY 5.2: Plan and Conduct a Formal Observation   If you are in a field experience, ask your mentor teacher if you might formally observe a student. Ask your teacher to help you identify the target individual. Then, prepare for the observation by answering the following questions.

- Who is the target student, and why has he or she been targeted? What is the concern or problem?
- What useful information might be gained by watching and listening to the student?
- Specifically when will the student be observed?
- What will be recorded? A list of questions or a checklist is usually required.

ACTIVITY 5.3: Plan and Conduct an Interview   If you are involved in a field experience, you may be able to plan and conduct an interview with a student.

Use these questions to guide you in preparing the interview:

- Who will the target student be?
- Specifically why was this student chosen? What is the interest or concern?
- What useful information might be gained by conversing with the student?
- When and where will the interview take place?
- What questions will you need to ask to obtain the critical information?

ACTIVITY 5.4: Develop and Use a Questionnaire   You might enjoy constructing your own questionnaire in order to find out more about students. If you are in a school, begin by finding out what student information is already available. You can determine this with the help of your mentor teacher. If you are not in a school, use the five cumulative record cards in the chapter appendix.

Third, construct the questionnaire items. These may be either open- or closed-ended. Keep the items few in number, short, clear, and as nonthreatening as possible. For example, if you wish to gain information about the student's attitude toward school or home, use open-ended questions like those on the left rather than closed-ended questions like those on the right:

"What are your most enjoyable moments at school?"	versus	"Do you enjoy school?"
"What are your most enjoyable moments at home?"	versus	"Do you enjoy being at home?"

After completing your questionnaire, have a few peers look it over, and then share it with your mentor teacher and university instructor. Finally, decide if, or how, you or your mentor teacher should or could collect and use the new information.

ACTIVITY 5.5: Study a Sociogram   If you are in a field experience, ask your mentor teacher if he or she has made a sociogram of the present class. If so, ask if you could see it and find out how it was done. Ask your mentor teacher to discuss the results. Were they as expected? How were they used? You may wish to make a transparency of the sociogram to share with others in this course.

ACTIVITY 5.6: Develop and Administer a Sociogram   If you are in a field experience, see whether you may develop and administer a sociogram. If so, follow this procedure or one similar to it:

1. Select one student question from the following:
   a. "Which two persons in the class are your closest friends?"
   b. "If you were working on a group project that would receive a grade, with which two persons would you want to work?"
   c. "If you were in some kind of difficulty, which two persons in the class would most likely help you?"
2. Explain to the students that you are trying to find out more about the class in order to be a better teacher.
3. Ask the students to privately answer the question you have selected (a, b, or c).

4. Record the choices each student has made on a chart similar to this one:

Respondent's Name	First Choice	Second Choice
a. Julio		
b.		

5. Record who chose each student.

    a. Julio was chosen by Robert and Malcolm.

    b.

6. Select symbols to represent males and females (see Figure 5.1).

7. Place the symbols representing the most oft-chosen students toward the center of the page and those least chosen toward the outer edges. Since males often choose males and females choose females, it may be helpful to place boys on one half of the page and girls on the other (see Figure 5.1).

8. Draw different colored lines with arrows to represent first choices, second choices, and mutual choices (arrows go both ways—see Figure 5.1).

ACTIVITY 5.7: Obtain Autobiographical Information   If you are in a field experience, you may be able to gain some idea of how autobiographical information is obtained and used. Ask your mentor teacher if he or she obtains student information by way of autobiography. *If so,* find out what the teacher obtains and how. Also, ask how that information is most useful. *If not,* try to obtain permission to collect some. Then, decide what you most need to know and the subsequent topic or topics students should address. For example, assuming you want to know what their lives are like outside school, you might ask them to write about "My Afternoons and Evenings" or "My Weekends."

ACTIVITY 5.8: Use Parent-Supplied Information   If you are in a school assignment, ask your mentor teacher how he or she has used parent contacts to find out about students and their families. What has the teacher found out? Where is it recorded?

    If such data are recorded in cumulative records, you may be able to read and reflect on them. What kinds of information have teachers obtained? What additional information could be useful?

ACTIVITY 5.9: Reading Cases   You may be able to obtain access to one or more cases. If you are involved in a field experience, ask your mentor teacher whether he or she has written any. Ask what caused the teacher to write the case and how he or she did it. Also, ask about the value of these cases. Perhaps you can share one of the cases with your peers in this course without revealing the student's identity.

ACTIVITY 5.10: Motivation in the Classroom   Perhaps you have an opportunity to observe a K–12 classroom teacher. If so, ask the teacher how he/she motivates students to learn, or observe and make a list of ways that the teacher uses motivation. Be prepared to share what you find out with your peers in this class.

ACTIVITY 5.11: Plan to Motivate   Select a topic that you might well teach. Describe specifically what you would do in order to motivate learners including those who lack confidence, have low expectations for themselves, and who are apathetic or reluctant to learn.

ACTIVITY 5.12: Motivational Techniques   Make a list of motivational techniques your teachers have used or create some of your own.

Airasian, P. W. (2008). *Classroom assessment.* New York: McGraw-Hill.

Alderman, M. (2004). *Motivation for achievement.* Mahwah, NJ: Lawrence Erbaum Associates.

Allen, R. (2003). Different starting points. *Education Update, 45*(5), 1, 3, 6–8.

American Association of School Administrators. (1992). *The nongraded primary school.* Arlington, VA: The Association.

Anastasi, A. (1997). *Psychological testing.* Sixth Edition. New York: Macmillan.

Anderman, E. M., Anderman, L., & Anderman, E. (2009). *Classroom motivation.* Upper Saddle River, NJ: Prentice-Hall.

Berliner, D. C. (1986). In pursuit of expert pedagogy. *Educational Researcher, 15*(7), 5–13.

Borko, H., & Livingston, C. (1989). Cognition and improvisation: Differences in mathematics instruction by expert and novice teachers. In T. Russell & H. Munby (Eds.), *Teacher and teaching: From classroom to reflection* (pp. 49–70). London: Falmer Press.

Brophy, J. (2004). *Motivating students to learn.* Mahwah, NJ: Lawrence Erlbaum Associates.

Brown, L. (2005). *KidsHealth KidsPoll—Coping Poll: Summary of Findings,* Carbondale, IL: Southern Illinois University. Access: www.nahec.org/KidsPoll/stress/Stress_Summary_of_Findings.pdf

Brualdi, A. (1998). *Teacher comments on report cards* (ERIC Reproduction Services ED 423 309).

Carter, K., Sabers, D., Cushing, K., Pinnegar, S., & Berliner, D. (1987). Processing and using information about students: A study of expert, novice and postulant teachers. *Teaching and Teacher Education, 3,* 147–157.

Dusek, J. B., & Joseph, G. (1983). The bases of teacher expectations: A meta-analysis. *Journal of Educational Psychology, 75*(3), 327–346.

Dweck, C. (2010, September). Even geniuses work hard. *Educational Leadership, (68)*1, 16–20.

Fredericks, J., Blumen Feld, P., & Paris, A. (2004, Spring). School engagement. *Review of Educational Research 74*(1), 59–109.

Henderson, J. (2009, March). Paying for performance. *Education Update,* 51(3), 1, 6.

Hidi, S., & Harackiewicz, J. (2000, Summer). Motivating the academically unmotivated. *Review of Educational Research, 70*(2), 151–179.

Johnson, O. (1976). *Tests and measurements in child development: Handbook II. Volumes 1 and 2.* San Francisco: Jossey-Bass.

Kidder, T. (1989). *Among school children.* Boston: Houghton Mifflin.

Lewis, J. L. (1986). Failing students: Can we identify them in advance? Paper presented at the annual meeting of the American Educational Research Association. San Francisco, CA (ERIC Document Reproduction Services ED 278 145).

Poulin, F. & Dushion, T. (2008, May). Methodological issues in the use of peer sociometric nominations with middle school youth. *Social Development, 17*(4), 908–921.

Rock, M. (2004, May–June). Transfiguring it out: Converting disengaged learners to active participants. *Teaching Exceptional Children, 36*(5), 64–72.

Seifert, T. (2004, Summer). Understanding student motivation. *Educational Research, 46*(2), 141–149.

Simpson, S. (2005, June 6). Getting kids to talk. *Ed. Net Briefs.* Simpson Communications, Box 325, 7829 Center Blvd. SE, Snoqualmie, WA 98065.

Touliatos, J., & Compton, N. H. (1983). *Approaches to child study.* Minneapolis: Burgess.

Wagner, T. (2001, December 5). The case for "New Village Schools": *Education Week, 21*(14), 42, 56.

Zayas, A. (2004, Feb. 26). Speaking the language of super heroes helps Blue Lakes Elementary teacher Orlando Martinez reach his third graders. *Miami Herald.* Access: heraldsuperteacher@yahoo.com.

Zheng, J. (1992). An exploration of the pedagogical content knowledge of beginning and experienced ESL teachers. Master's thesis, Queens College of the City of New York. New York, NY. (ERIC Document Reproduction Services ED 343 903).

PERSONAL DATA

Student's Name BROGAN, Jack Robert

Present Address 280 Falcrest Rd.

Telephone 354-7520

Present Age 9 years 11 mos.

Proof of Age Birth certificate

Place of Birth Monroe

Most Recent Picture

Special Activities, Interests, and Hobbies
Enjoys mythology

Special Health Conditions

TRANSFER RECORD

Transferred to M.S.D. from
Grade left M.S.D.
Transferred to Lakeside for grade 2
Reason
Reentered from Lakeside in grade 4

The name and data in this student record folder do not apply to the student's picture except for purposes of the teacher-training program.

FAMILY DATA

Father's Name Maxwell   Mother's Name Helen

Birthplace Elton   Bloomington, IN
Occupation laboratory technician retail sales
Employer   Harley-Ryan Talbot's

OTHER CHILDREN

Name	Present age
1. Cheryl	8
2.	
3.	
4.	
5.	
6.	
7.	
8.	

SPECIAL HOME CONDITIONS

Grandmother (maternal) living in the home

MADISON SCHOOL DISTRICT

Longacre ____ School

Student's Name ___ BROGAN, Jack Robert

ACHIEVEMENT

Primary
V—Very good progress
G—Good progress
N—Needs to improve

Grades 2-8
A—Excellent
B—Above average
C—Average
D—Below average
E—Failing

SUBJECT AREAS	1	2	3	4	5	6	7	8
English	G	B	C	C				
Social Studies		B	C	C				
Science		C	C	B				
Mathematics	G	B	C	C				
Reading	G	C	C	C				
Spelling		B	C	B				
Writing	V	B	C	C				
Teacher's initials	MC	HM	JH	FM				
PROMOTION	A	A	S	A				

PROMOTION
F—Fast
S—Slow
A—Average
U—Unearned

ATTENDANCE RECORD

	Kdg.	1st	2nd	3rd	4th	5th	6th	7th	8th
Total days present	170	180	182	179	183				
Possible no. of days attendance	185	185	185	183	183				

TESTING PROGRAM

Ability Tests

Grade	Test Given	Age	IQ
1	Mental Ability	6	104
3	Mental Ability	7	103
4	Musical Aptitude		
	(raw score 260/137 6 %ile)		

Reading Tests

Grade	Test Given	Score
1	Readiness Test	B (high normal)
2	Primary Reading	40 %ile

Other Achievement Tests

Grade	Test Given	Score
3	Upper Primary	2.8
4	Middle Grades	4.2

Needs to control his loud voice. Still immature. Attention

span improving; good progress in reading and writing!

    Maria Carrillo—grade 1

Sometimes fails to finish work because he fools and

daydreams. Minds others' business more than his own.

Too talkative. Forgets to wait his turn to speak.

    Holly Maybee—grade 2

Jack shows little improvement in finishing his work. He

still bothers other people. He does respond well when I

ask him to take on a special responsibility or give him

some extra attention. I would like to see him take more

responsibility for his work and behavior.

    Janice Hsieh—grade 3

Jack has shown slight improvement in completing

assignments. He still needs an extra push most of the

time. Is occasionally sullen with other students, but

shows improvement in solving problems with his classmates.

    Frances Markle—grade 4

PARENT-TEACHER CONFERENCE SUMMARIES

Grade	
K	Short attention span. Work is quite immature. Father is very strict. Sharon Wertz
1	Parents are disturbed because Jack is not finishing all his work and is a behavior problem because of constant talking. They want unfinished work sent home to do. They say they will follow through at home. Maria Carrillo
2	Parents very cooperative. Jack needs to be given responsibilities for jobs he can do for himself and needs discipline to follow up. Holly Maybee
3	I had a parent conference with Mr. and Mrs. Brogan. They were told Jack was not finishing enough work to keep up with his classmates or to be as successful as he should be in fourth grade. The difficulty seems to be immaturity, short attention span, and his tendency to daydream. He is too talkative and does not seem mature enough to follow directions and accept third-grade responsibility. I worked on giving Jack some responsibilities at school, and he picked up and improved the last month of school. His parents are encouraged. Janice Hsieh
4	Jack is still immature. Work not always completed without an extra "push." An assignment book is to be used so parents can check work not completed at night, and I will check it each morning. Both parents are very willing to help. Frances Markle

STUDENT'S NAME   *Brogan, Jack*

GRADE   *3*

SCHOOL   *Lakeside*

CLASSROOM TEACHER

DISORDER   *Interdental lisp - tongue thrust. Distorted sh sounds. No conference.*

WORK DONE IN SPEECH CLASS   *Jack was in a group of five third grade children who worked for correction of the s sound. The s in isolated words is now quite good. Jack can make the (below)*

DISPOSITION OF CASE   *Continue if fall reevaluation shows the need. There may be continued improvement over the summer.*

Speech Therapist

correction nicely. In conversation he is using quite good carryover. However, some s sounds are now a distortion in place of a lisp.

Jack has five s words which he thinks he will use frequently this summer. He is to try to say them right always.

PERSONAL DATA

Student's Name   GLOVACK, Kathleen

Present Address   142 Sellers Rd.

Telephone   359-9874

Present Age   10   years   1   mos.

Proof of Age   Birth certificate

Place of Birth   Elton

Most Recent Picture

Special Activities, Interests, and Hobbies

Special Health Conditions

TRANSFER RECORD

Transferred to M.S.D. from   Elton in grade 1

Grade left M.S.D.

Transferred to

Reason

Reentered from   in grade

The name and data in this student record folder do not apply to the student's picture except for purposes of the teacher-training program.

FAMILY DATA

Father's Name   Donald   Mother's Name   Virginia

Birthplace   Elton   Columbus, OH
Occupation   machinist   parapro
Employer   Elton Goods   M.S.D.

OTHER CHILDREN

	Name	Present age
1.	Roberta	14
2.	Todd	9
3.	Teresa	4
4.	Nicky	1
5.		
6.		
7.		
8.		

SPECIAL HOME CONDITIONS

MADISON SCHOOL DISTRICT

Longacre School

Student's Name: **GLOVACK, Kathleen**

ACHIEVEMENT

Primary
V—Very good progress
G—Good progress
N—Needs to improve

Grades 2 - 8
A—Excellent
B—Above average
C—Average
D—Below average
E—Failing

SUBJECT AREAS	1	2	3	4	5	6	7	8
English	G	B	B	B				
Social Studies	G	C	B	B				
Science	G	C	B	B				
Mathematics	G	B	B	A				
Reading	G	C	A	B				
Spelling	G	C	B	A				
Writing	V	A	A	B				
Teacher's initials	RP	MG	DA	FM				

PROMOTION
F—Fast
S—Slow
A—Average
U—Unearned

	1	2	3	4	5	6	7	8
	A	A	A	A				

ATTENDANCE RECORD

	Kdg.	1st	2nd	3rd	4th	5th	6th	7th	8th
Total days present		168	175	176	172				
Possible no. of days attendance		185	185	183	183				

TESTING PROGRAM

Ability Tests

Grade	Test Given	Age	IQ
1	Mental Ability	6/3	97
3	Mental Ability	8/2	99
4	Musical Aptitude (raw score 260/137 6 %ile)		

Reading Tests

Grade	Test Given	Score
1	Reading Readiness	B (high normal)
2	American Reading	2.4
2	American Reading	4.3

Other Achievement Tests

Grade	Test Given	Score
3	Middle Grades	5.5
4	Middle Grades	5.4

TEACHER COMMENTS

Kathy is a good average worker. Sometimes she is too thorough and has trouble finishing the work. She is quiet, but pleasant.

    Ruth Parks--grade 1

Very quiet, dependable. Good worker. Always smiling!

    Margarita Gascona--grade 2

Kathy is a quiet, but very good student. She is very polite and pleasant.

    Donna Amity--grade 3

Kathy is an excellent student. Very dependable; lovely child. Beginning to overcome her shyness.

    Frances Markle--grade 4

PARENT-TEACHER CONFERENCE SUMMARIES

Grade _____

1   With Mrs. Glovack. Progress report. Kathy doing strong

    average work. Ruth Parks

2   Conference with Mrs. Glovack. Kathy is doing well. Should

    speak up so she can be heard; rather shy. Mother is

    pleased with good work habits. Margarita Gascona

3   No conference—new baby in home—but discussed Kathy's

    good progress with mother at PTA. Donna Amity

4   Conference with mother. Kathy does very well in school.

    For a while, Kathy didn't want to come to school each

    morning. In speaking with her, we found she didn't like

    our student teacher. After our talk, she was fine. She

    has had some problems lately with her best friend, Janis

    Murdock, who has buddied up with Cynthia Jordan.

    Frances Markle

URBAN PUBLIC SCHOOL CUMULATIVE RECORD

Name _Gamble   Benny_   I.D.# _1092056_
　　　(Last)　　　　(First)　　　(Middle)

Present age __11__ yrs. __1__ mos.

Place of Birth _Urban_

Pupil lives with ☐ Both parents ☒ Mother ☐ Father

☒ Other (explain) _grandmother_

Father's name _Morris_   Employer _Post Office Department_

Mother's name _Lydia_   Employer _____

Address	Phone	Address	Phone
3526 Seneca Parkway	343-6580	5106 Hertel	266-4843
998 35th Street			
3526 Seneca Parkway	343-6580		
5245 College	266-4843		

Siblings　(List names of brothers and sisters in order of birth. Indicate sex by G for sister, B for brother. Express age differences as plus (+) or minus (−). Examples: +5 means five years older, −5 means five years younger.)

Sibling's Name	Sex	Age	Sibling's Name	Sex	Age	Sibling's Name	Sex	Age
None								

In case of emergency notify:

Name _____   Phone _____

Address _____   Relationship _____

ELEMENTARY AND MIDDLE SCHOOL PROGRESS RECORD

Reporting Code

ACHIEVEMENT: The letter represents the degree to which the child has met the grade standards.

E = excellent	U = unsatisfactory
G = good	GL = grade level
F = fair	BL = below grade level

EFFORT: The numeral indicates the effort the child is making.

1 = doing his best
2 = could work harder
3 = making little effort

Progress Record, Grades K-2

Semester Beginning	Grade	Weeks in Grade	Days Present	Promoted to Grade	Reading	Oral Language	Composition	Spelling	Handwriting	Social Studies	Arithmetic	Science	Art	Music	Physical Education	Conduct	School	Room No.
FALL	Kdg	20	85	Kdg												F	COLERIDGE	108
SPRING	Kdg	20	83	1			FAIR PROGRESS									F	CLERIDGE	107
Fall	1	20	65	1A	E	F			E	G	G	G	E	F		G	Coleridge	205
Spring	1A	20	80	2	E	E			G	G	E	G	E	F		G	Coleridge	205
Fall	2	20	80	2	G	G	G	G	G	G	G	G	G	G	G	G	Coleridge	120
Spring	2	12	53	2	G	G	G	E	G	G	G	G	G	G	G	G	Coleridge	120
SPRING	2	8	34	3	E	G	G	E	G	G	E	E	G	G		E	COLERIDGE	209

Progress Record, Grades 3-6

Semester Beginning	Grade	Weeks in Grade	Days Absent	Promoted to Grade	Reading	Reading Level	Math	Math Level	Listening	Speaking	Writing	Spelling	Science	Social Studies	Art	Music	Physical Educ.	Conduct	School	Room No.
FALL	3	20	9	3	G	G	G	G	G	G	G	E	G	G	G	G	/	G	ALEXANDER	205
SPRING	3	12	7	3	G	G	G	H	G	G	G	E	G	G	G	G		G	"	"
Spr.	3	7	1	4	E	G	F	G	G	F	F	E	F	F	F	F	F	F	EDISON	204
Fall	4	20	7	4	E		F	G	G	G	G	E	G	G	G		F		Edison	106
Spring	4	20	4	5	E		F	G	F	F	G	E	G	G	G	F		F	Edison	106
	5				attending school in the south (U.S.A.)												– – – –			
	5	21	12	6	E_2	G_1	F_2	GL	E_2	E_2	E_2	E_2	G_2	G_2	E_2	E_2	F_2	F	Edison	209

www.mhhe.com/cruickshank6e

General Ability Tests

Gr.	Name of Test	Form	C.A.	M.A.	I.Q.
1	KA		6.3	7.3	116
2	KA		7.1	7.8	110
3	KA		8.1	7.9	97

Bureau of Child Study Individual Exam Data

Gr.	

Personal Comments

Gr.	Remarks
2	Often complains of illnesses.
5	Claims pains in his back.

Achievement Test

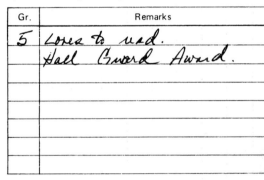

Gr.	Name of Test	Subtest	Score
1	Metropolitan Readiness		82%ILE
3	Metropolitan Achieve.	Reading	5.3
		Spelling	5.1
		English	4.1
		Arithmetic	3.6

Special Activities, Abilities, Honors

Gr.	Remarks
5	Loves to read. Hall Guard Award.

Other Pertinent Information

Name ___ Gamble, Benny ___

All data pertaining to this student study are based on actual files; however, the names, dates, and locations have been changed and the person pictured is a child actor/model.

ID# ___ 1092056 ___

Gr.	Examination	Evaluation	Gr.	Examination	Evaluation
1	Vision	Should wear glasses and be given front seat placement.			
1	Hearing	Pass			
4	Hearing	Pass			
5	Hearing	Pass			

Notes:

_____

_____

_____

_____

_____

_____

_____

_____

_____

_____

_____

_____

_____

_____

Name <u>Rivera</u>   <u>Julio</u>   <u>Jesus</u>   I.D.# <u>2783168</u>
           (Last)   (First)   (Middle)

Present age <u>11</u> yrs. <u>9</u> mos.

Place of Birth <u>Puerto Rico</u>

Pupil lives with [X] Both parents [ ] Mother [ ] Father

[ ] Other (explain) _____

Father's name <u>José</u>   Employer <u>Lakeside Metals</u>

Mother's name <u>Juanita</u>   Employer <u>Barkley Fish Co.</u>

Address	Phone	Address	Phone
1241 Yale	273-7408		
12 Sword			
5142 Aldine	641-1059		

Siblings   (List names of brothers and sisters in order of birth. Indicate sex by G for sister, B for brother. Express age differences as plus (+) or minus (−). Examples: +5 means five years older, −5 means five years younger.)

Sibling's Name	Sex	Age	Sibling's Name	Sex	Age	Sibling's Name	Sex	Age
Maria	G	-2						
Luchina	G	-5						
Felice	G	-8						

In case of emergency notify:

Name _____   Phone _____

Address _____   Relationship _____

CHAPTER 5
Getting to Know Your Students
and Motivating Them to Learn

ELEMENTARY AND MIDDLE SCHOOL PROGRESS RECORD

Reporting Code

ACHIEVEMENT: The letter represents the degree to which the child has met the grade standards.

E = excellent   U = unsatisfactory
G = good   GL = grade level
F = fair   BL = below grade level

EFFORT: The numeral indicates the effort the child is making.

1 = doing his best
2 = could work harder
3 = making little effort

Progress Record, Grades K-2

Semester Beginning	Grade	Weeks in Grade	Days Present	Promoted to Grade	Reading	Oral Language	Composition	Spelling	Handwriting	Social Studies	Arithmetic	Science	Art	Music	Physical Education	Conduct	School	Room No.
FALL	K	20	92	K	— Good —											F	McNULTY	104
SPRING	K	20	94	Prim 1	— Good —											G	McNULTY	104
Fall	Pri 1	5	23	1B	— Good —											G	McNULTY	106
Fall	1B	20	91	1	G	G			E	G	G		G	F		E	University	4
Spring	1	20	90	2	G	G			G	G	G		G	F		F	University	4
Fall	2	20	88	2	F₃	F₃			U₃	F₂	G₂		G₂	F₁	F₁	F₂	F	University	10
Spring	2	20	95	3	G₂	G			G	G	E	E₁	E	E	G	G	F	University	10

Progress Record, Grades 3-6

Semester Beginning	Grade	Weeks in Grade	Days Absent	Promoted to Grade	Reading	Reading Level	Math	Math Level	Listening	Speaking	Writing	Spelling	Science	Social Studies	Art	Music	Physical Educ.	Conduct	School	Room No.
Fall	3	20	2	3	G₁	G	G₁	G	G₁	G	G₂	G	G	G₁	E	G	G₂	F	University	16
Sp.	3	20	1		G	E₁	G	G₂	G	G₂	G₂	G₂	G	G₁	G	G	G₁	F	Unvesity	16
Fall	4	20	0	1	F₂	BL	F₃	GL	F₂	F₂	F₂	F₃	F₃	U	G₂	G₂		F	Edison	202
Spring	4	20	2	5	G₂	GL	F₃	GL	F₂	F₂	F₂	G₁	F₃	F₃	E₂	E₂	G	F	Edison	202
	5	40	4	6	F₁	BL	F₃	BL	F₂	G₂	F₂	G₂	E₁	F₂	E₂	E₂	G	F	Edison	209

General Ability Tests

Gr.	Name of Test	Form	C.A.	M.A.	I.Q.
1	KA		5-11	6-0	104
3	KA		9.4	8.6	91

Bureau of Child Study Individual Exam Data

Gr.	

Personal Comments

Gr.	Remarks
5	Interested in science and music. Will need to watch carefully or else he will run around the room or the building or sneak out. Motivation hinges on praise and close supervision. Wants to please

Achievement Test

Gr.	Name of Test	Subtest	Score
1	Metropolitan Readiness		60%ile
3	METROPOLITAN ACHIEVEMENT	WORD KNOWL.	3.6
		WORD DISCRIM	3.2
		READING	2.6
		SPELLING	4.0
		LANG.	3.2
		COMPUT.	3.0
		PROBLEM SOLVING	2.7

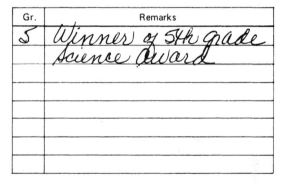

Special Activities, Abilities, Honors

Gr.	Remarks
5	Winner of 5th grade Science Award

Other Pertinent Information

Name Rivera, Julio Jesus

All data pertaining to this student study are based on actual files; however, the names, dates, and locations have been changed and the person pictured is a child actor/model.

24

ID# 2783168

Gr.	Examination	Evaluation	Gr.	Examination	Evaluation
2	Teeth	Oral hygiene fair. Dental care needed.			
2	Hearing	Pass			
4	Hearing	Pass			

Notes:

_____

_____

_____

_____

_____

_____

_____

_____

_____

_____

_____

_____

_____

_____

REFERRAL FOR PUPIL HEALTH SERVICES

Pupil's name Julio Rivera   Date   10/16

Address 5142 Aldine

School   Edison

Room   209

Reason for Referral:

      Julio has trouble seeing the chalkboard assignments

      in the classroom. He complains of headaches.

Report: Eye referral given to pupil to take home for vision test.

             Teacher Nurse   **Mary Martin**

CHAPTER 5
Getting to Know Your Students
and Motivating Them to Learn
www.mhhe.com/cruickshank6e   **157**

Vision Record on Child not Wearing Glasses

Urban Public Schools

Child's name Julio Rivera   Date 10/16

Address 5142 Aldine   Age 11

Parent's name Juanita   Grade five

School Edison

To the Doctor:

    Please fill in the following for the guidance of the class-
room teacher.

1. Should the child wear glasses?   Yes X   No ___
    If so, when   constantly

2. Should the child wear an occluder? Yes ___   No X
    If so, over which eye_____ when _____ duration _____

3. Should the child have front seat placement?
                                        Yes ___   No X

4. Should the amount of close work done by the child be
    limited?   Yes ___   No X
    If so, to what extent? _____

5. Vision test
    Uncorrected visual acuity   R 20/60   L 20/40
    Best corrected visual acuity R 20/25   L 20/25

                    Doctor's Signature

                    R. J. Manville

URBAN PUBLIC SCHOOL CUMULATIVE RECORD

Name <u>Walker　　　Debbie</u>　　　　　　　　　　　I.D.# <u>2585866</u>
　　　　(Last)　　　　(First)　　　(Middle)

Present age <u>14</u> yrs. <u>1</u> mos.

Place of Birth <u>Urban</u>

Pupil lives with ☐ Both parents　☐ Mother　☐ Father

[X] Other (explain) <u>Mother and stepfather</u>

Father's name <u>Gilliam</u>　　　　　Employer _____

Mother's name <u>Janice</u>　　　　　Employer <u>public assistance</u>

Address	Phone	Address	Phone
5924 Brass	278-8113	3708 Park	
1343 New York	215-7788	1260 52nd Street	542-2275
702 31st Street			
947 33rd Street			

Siblings　(List names of brothers and sisters in order of birth. Indicate sex by G for sister, B for brother. Express age differences as plus (+) or minus (−). Examples: +5 means five years older, −5 means five years younger.)

Sibling's Name	Sex	Age	Sibling's Name	Sex	Age	Sibling's Name	Sex	Age
Dewey	B	+10	Scott	B	+5	Melanie	G	−1
Carlton	B	+8	Gary	B	+4	Bishop	B	−4
Donald	B	+7	Louise	G	+3	Keith	B	−5
Douglas	B	+6	Todd	B	+2	Richard	B	−6
						Lori	G	−12

In case of emergency notify:

Name _____　　　　Phone _____

Address _____　　　Relationship _____

ELEMENTARY AND MIDDLE SCHOOL PROGRESS RECORD

Reporting Code

ACHIEVEMENT: The letter represents the degree to which the child has met the grade standards.

E = excellent	U = unsatisfactory
G = good	GL = grade level
F = fair	BL = below grade level

EFFORT: The numeral indicates the effort the child is making.

1 = doing his best
2 = could work harder
3 = making little effort

Progress Record, Grades K–2

Semester Beginning	Grade	Weeks in Grade	Days Present	Promoted to Grade	Reading	Oral Language	Composition	Spelling	Handwriting	Social Studies	Arithmetic	Science	Art	Music	Physical Education	Conduct	School	Room No.
Fall	K	13	48	/			Satisfactory									E	Edison	120
Fall	KB	6	27				satisfactory									G	Seward	107
Spring	KB	9	90	/B			satisfactory									G	Seward	107
FALL	1B	17	31	U	F			F	U							G	SEWARD	117
FALL	1B	3	9	retain U	F			F	U							G	LASALLE	215
Spring	1B	12	56	/	G	G		G	G							G	LaSalle	105
SPRING	1B	8	38	1A	G	G		G	G							F	LaSalle	103
FALL	1A	15	58	2B E	G			G	E							U	LASALLE	109
Fall	1A	5	33	2B	G	G		G	G							G	Martin	101
Spring	2B	20	91	CDP	Promoted to Primary Continuous Development Program											F	Martin	101
Fall	2A	20	96	3B	G	G	F	F	G		U					F	Martin	203

Progress Record, Grades 3–6

Semester Beginning	Grade	Weeks in Grade	Days Absent	Promoted to Grade	Reading	Reading Level	Math	Math Level	Listening	Speaking	Writing	Spelling	Science	Social Studies	Art	Music	Physical Educ.	Conduct	School	Room No.
SPRING	3B	20	97	3A	F	BL	F	BL	F	G	U	U	F	F	F	F	F	F	MarkJm	212
Fall	3A	8	32	retain	F	BL	U	BL	F	F	F	F	F	F	F	F.		F	Markum	302
Fail	3a	12	54	3a	7	BL	U	BL	7	7	7	U	7	U	7	E	U	7	Corcoran	309
Spg	3A	10	45	retain	7	BL	U	BL	7	7	7	U	U	7	7	E		7	Corcoran	208
SPRING	3a	9	44	4	U	BL	U	BL	F	F	U	7	F	U	g	g		g	Hess	205
Fall	4	20	3	4A	F	BL	F	BL	G	G	G	G	G	G	G	G	G	6	Hess	310
Spring	4A	20	4	5B	F	BL	F	BL	G	G	G	G	G	G	G	G	G	Hess	310
	5B	16	10		F	BL	F	BL	F	F	F	G	F	F	G	G	G	F	Hess	318
	5	4	3		No grades given due to late entrance.														Baker	316
	5	20	5		U	BL	U	BL	U	U	U	U	U	U				E	Baker	316
	5	29	11	6	C_2	U	G_2	U	E_2	G_2	G_2	E_2	G_2	G_2	E_2	E_2	E_2	F	EDISON	209

General Ability Tests

Gr.	Name of Test	Form	C.A.	M.A.	I.Q.
1	KA		6.0	5.8	94
1	KA		6.5	6.7	103
3	KH		9.2	7.11	86

Bureau of Child Study Individual Exam Data

Gr.	

Achievement Test

Gr.	Name of Test	Subtest	Score
3	Stanford Pri. "M"	Rdg	2.9
3	Metro Achievement	Reading	2.6
		Spelling	2.4
		Comp.	3.1
		Prob Slv.	2.8
4	METROPOLITAN ACHIEVEMENT	WORD KNOWL.	3.8
		WORD DISCRIM.	4.1
		READ'G	3.6
		SPELLING	4.6
		COMPUTE	4.1
		PROB. SOLVING	4.3

Personal Comments

Gr.	Remarks
5	FAILING TO COMPLETE ASSIGN-MENTS. SUSPENSION FOR TWO DAYS. STEPFATHER HAS LEFT HOME AND IS TRYING TO GET BABY DAUGHTERS FROM THE MOTHER. CASE IS PENDING IN COURT.

Special Activities, Abilities, Honors

Gr.	Remarks

Other Pertinent Information

Name ___ Walker, Debbie

All data pertaining to this student study are based on actual files; however, the names, dates, and locations have been changed and the person pictured is a child actor/model.

31

ID# 2585866

CORCORAN SCHOOL

Date Jan. 14

Dear Parent:

Your child Debbie Walker   is doing failing work X
            (grade 3)   poor work ___

in the following subjects:

Reading ____X_____   Social Studies_____

Arithmetic X_____   Spelling _____

Science _____   Penmanship_____

I believe this condition is caused by:

Inattention in class_____X_____

Poor conduct_____X_____

Poor study habits_____X_____

Health reasons _____

Absenteeism_____

I am available each school morning at 8:30 o'clock. You
may come to see me if you wish or you may write me a letter
telling me your plan to help your child.

Please sign this letter and return it to me.

Mrs. Janice Walker   *Geraldine Phillips*
_____   _____
Parent's Signature   Teacher's Signature

                Lois Enright
                _____
                Principal

HESS ELEMENTARY SCHOOL

September 23

Dear Parents:

Hess School is one of the schools in District 21 which has been selected to provide after-school instruction in reading for pupils who need such help. We are recommending that your child, <u>Debbie Walker</u> take part in this program.

These classes are to be held from 3:30 p.m. to 4:30 p.m. on Mondays, Tuesdays, Wednesdays, and Thursdays, from September 27 to June 23. Will you please remind your child that there will be no patrol boys on duty at 4:30 p.m. and that he/she should be especially careful when returning home.

We sincerely hope that you will take advantage of this opportunity for your child. Please sign the lower section of this letter immediately.

Very truly yours,

Geo. Mancuso

George Mancuso
Principal

. . ..

Date _____

I hereby give my permission for my child, <u>Debbie Walker</u> to be enrolled in the after-school classes at Hess School on Mondays, Tuesdays, Wednesdays, and Thursdays, from 3:30 to 4:30 p.m. beginning September 27, to June 23. I will remind my child that there will be no patrol boys on duty at 4:30 p.m. and that he/she should be especially careful when returning home.

Present Room <u>318</u>   Grade <u>5</u>   _____

Signature of Parent

After-school Room

I do not want Debbie to go because I an going to the hospital every day now. Mrs Janice Walker

_____

*Dear teacher,
Debbie has my permission to go to reading class.
Thank you
Her mother   Mrs Janice Walker*

31

Gr.	Examination	Evaluation	Gr.	Examination	Evaluation
1	Hearing	Pass			
1	Teeth	Carious			
2	Hearing	Pass			
3	Hearing	Pass			
4	Hearing	Pass			

Notes:

Needs to work on personal grooming and hygiene

The Act of Teaching

PART TWO

2

Teaching should be a conscious, deliberate act resulting from thoughtful decision making about what to teach and how students learn best. The four chapters in Part Two are intended to help you become an accomplished teacher. Chapter 6, Planning Instruction, will make you aware of factors that influence what is taught. Mostly, however, it concentrates on showing you how to make good decisions about planning *what* and *how* you will teach. Chapter 7, Four Instructional Alternatives, and Chapter 8, Four More Instructional Alternatives, contain readily usable information about eight prominent teaching strategies, as well as brief references to many others. Chapter 9, Evaluating Students' Learning, will inform you of the importance of assessing student learning and show you how you can do so effectively.

Planning Instruction

Conversation Starters

To plan or not to plan, is that the question?

Normally considerable attention is devoted to ensuring that pre-service teachers know how to plan instruction in great detail. However, detailed planning takes a lot of time and practicing teachers say that with so many things to teach they can't do that. Some admit to only sketchy planning. Others say that they only do detailed planning the first time they teach something. *So, how much teacher preparation time should be devoted to having the knowledge and skill to plan successful learning experiences? How important is it to have this knowledge and skill?*

Do you plan the events of your life or just let things happen to you? For example, when you take a vacation do you plan it or is it just a "happening"—whatever happens, happens?

When you assume responsibility for teaching, you do not have this choice. Regardless of your personal predispositions, you will be expected to plan lots of things including *classroom arrangement* (placement of furniture, equipment, materials, displays), *classroom routines and rules* (student movement, how materials will be distributed, how attendance will be taken), but most importantly, *learning experiences.*

This chapter is intended to help you plan worthwhile learning experiences. It will address some pretty important topics including the curriculum, instructional objectives, and long- and short-term instructional planning. We hope you see the many benefits of good instructional planning, how what gets taught is decided, what instructional objectives are and how to create them, and how to prepare instructional plans of different duration.

6.1 How do you use planning in your life?

Pros and Cons of Instructional Planning

Instructional planning is the process by which teachers decide (1) what to teach, (2) how to teach it, and (3) how they will determine whether students learned and were satisfied.

Some of us will be more inclined to plan than others. Here are some possible reasons. Check those applying to you.

6.2 How do you feel that planning instruction will benefit you?

☐ I am inclined to carefully plan most things in life.

☐ I want to feel as secure and organized as possible when I teach.

☐ I believe that good instructional planning results in greater learning.

Others of us are less inclined to plan.

☐ Planning is not one of my strong suits.

☐ A plan doesn't necessarily make me feel more secure or organized.

☐ I don't believe that planning necessarily results in better teaching and more learning.

☐ I believe that planning stifles spontaneity.

What other pros and cons can you add?

A serious constraint on planning is available time. If you have a number of subject preparations, as elementary teachers and some middle and secondary teachers do, then you will struggle to find time. "Finding time to get things done" is one of the five most challenging problems reported by teachers (see Chapter 13).

An often unsatisfactory solution to the planning time constraint is simply to sequentially cover material in a single textbook or use commercially marketed worksheets (see Highlight 6.1).

Businesslike and adaptable/flexible teachers, described in Chapter 10, seem to obtain greater student achievement through either more *precise or flexible planning.* The former direct student learning toward the efficient attainment of clearly defined learning goals. The latter are flexible when they implement lessons. If the lesson isn't working, they make adjustments.

Planning Is Especially Beneficial for New Teachers

Expect to spend a lot of time and energy planning instruction. Here are four reasons why. First, you will have little or no teaching experience to draw upon. Second, and understandably, you will be apprehensive and unsure of yourself and your teaching skills. Well-conceived plans provide a great deal of personal security and confidence

Textbooks and supplementary materials accompanying them (e.g., worksheets and tests) have great influence on teacher planning and what is taught. Estimates are that 75 percent of teacher and student class time is taken up by their use.

Textbooks are popular because: (1) lessons can easily be prepared from them, (2) they seemingly provide all the information needed, (3) other learning resources may not be available—for example library or Internet access, (4) teachers may feel they lack time to develop their own learning resources, (5) they are accepted as written by experts, and (6) they are readily available.

Beginning teachers are particularly vulnerable to over-reliance on them since most have not yet found or developed alternative instructional resources. No one would deny the value of textbooks, only over-dependence on them to the exclusion of other types of learning experiences that can be more meaningful.

It is important to remember that most textbooks are intended to be used by all students, anywhere. Consequently, when using them as a main resource, (1) determine their appropriateness for your learners and (2) make certain their contents focus on what your students must know and be able to do—the required curriculum.

6.3 Which reasons for instructional planning most appeal to you?

and even add to your enthusiasm. You feel relaxed and good to go! Third, you likely will not know what students are expected to know and do. Finally, given time to think and plan, teaching will be more creative and fun. Corny, but remember, only birds can wing it.

Generally, student teachers agree that planning makes a huge difference. Here is what one writes:

> I have come to truly appreciate the importance, difficulty, and necessity of effective . . . planning and preparation. With a limited time to reach students who have a limited attention span, lessons must be properly designed to engage students and carry them along to reach predetermined goals. Merely covering content, without specific objectives and a well-designed path to meet them, will result in wasted time and a lack of student engagement. (Galvin, n.d.)

Remember: Failing to plan is planning to fail!

Planning May Be Mandated   Planning instruction is deemed so important to the success of student teachers and first-year teachers that they often are required not just to plan but to submit those plans for reactions from mentor teachers during student teaching and from supervisors or principals during the early classroom years. Some principals require beginners to periodically submit *plan books* spelling out lessons one or two weeks in advance so that they are assured teachers have thought

6.4 Do you think planning instruction should be mandated?

6.5 What is your reaction to advice about planning?

carefully about what they will do and how they will do it. Good principals are good instructional leaders and want to help novice teachers as much as possible. Additionally, "plan books" are useful when supervisors observe beginning teachers and to ensure continuity of instruction when substitute teachers are needed. Some school districts go so for as to provide lesson plans (see Highlight 6.2).

"Are we that desperate for substitute teachers?"

How would you like it if your school district provided all the lesson plans you would need? Some school districts are beginning to do so. For example, Chicago teachers can receive detailed daily lesson plans in each subject they teach. The plans, developed by a team of about 100 top Chicago teachers, are offered for several reasons: to help teachers see what needs to be taught for K–12 students to cover the information they are supposed to learn each day at each grade level; to help new teachers acclimate faster; and to guarantee a level of quality instruction systemwide. Meanwhile the Miami school district gives detailed lesson plans for the first 10 days of school to every teacher of every class. In this case, they are provided so that teachers can begin teaching from the get-go. Officials believe that the plans may help new teachers ease into teaching and increase the time devoted to instruction during the early days of school. Use is voluntary (Pinzur, 2006). Teachers' reactions to lesson plans written by others vary. Opponents call it a "cookie cutter curriculum." Proponents say the plans are a boon for new teachers and teachers experiencing difficulties and a good guide and reference (Johnston, 1999).

In conclusion, since planning instruction is considered so important, student teachers and beginning teachers are advised to plan teaching events in considerable detail, leaving little or nothing to chance. Probably a good motto in the early stages of your career is, "Overplan." Later, as a seasoned teacher, you can and probably will rely more on experience and expertise. However, even then you will need to carefully plan instructional activities that are either new to you or have been troublesome in the past. Remember, plans are not mere window dressing or hoop jumping. They are a vital part of the act of teaching.

Deciding What to Teach

(The main ideas in this section are diagrammed in Figure 6.1.)

Of the planning decisions teachers make, the first is *determining what to teach*. That choice is pretty much fixed by the state and the school district in which you work. However, as you will see later, teachers occasionally have their way.

STATE STANDARDS AND HOW THEY ARE DEVELOPED

States have legal responsibility for education and each formulates standards or requirements regarding what K–12 students should know and be able to do. These standards are periodically reviewed by statewide committees made up of parents, teachers, school administrators, university faculty, subject matter experts, curriculum specialists, and persons representing business and economic interests such as textbook publishers. To find standards for your state, go to Academic Benchmarks and search "State Standards."

Factors Influencing State Requirements Naturally, the standards the committees set are influenced by the groups they represent—teachers representing teachers and so on. Additionally, the standards are influenced by three general factors: societal expectations, the nature and needs of children, and advice from professional education societies.

"And then, of course, there's the possibility of being just the slightest bit too organized."

Web Link
Academic Benchmarks

6.6 What recent events seem to be influencing what gets taught?

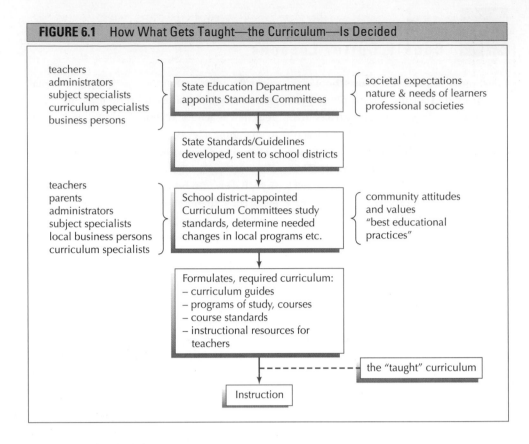

FIGURE 6.1 How What Gets Taught—the Curriculum—Is Decided

teachers
administrators
subject specialists
curriculum specialists
business persons

State Education Department
appoints Standards Committees

societal expectations
nature & needs of learners
professional societies

State Standards/Guidelines
developed, sent to school districts

teachers
parents
administrators
subject specialists
local business persons
curriculum specialists

School district-appointed
Curriculum Committees study
standards, determine needed
changes in local programs etc.

community attitudes
and values
"best educational
practices"

Formulates, required curriculum:
– curriculum guides
– programs of study, courses
– course standards
– instructional resources for
  teachers

the "taught" curriculum

Instruction

Societal Expectations   Social expectations often result from national and international events. Thus, after the Soviet Union beat the United States into space by launching the first satellite in 1957, there was great scurrying about to raise standards in math and science. Today, students from many countries are outperforming Americans on math and science tests, so once more the heat is on to beef-up requirements in those subjects.

The Nature and Needs of Learners   The nature and needs of learners also are considered when standards are set. After all, schools are about and for youth so their consideration is essential. As noted in Chapter 2, Teaching in a Changing Society, minority population is growing, families are in flux, and children increasingly encounter negatives such as economic disadvantages, lack of supervision, and abuse and neglect. Furthermore in Chapter 3, Teaching Diverse Students, we found that learners differ in multiple ways including culturally, by gender, and by development. These conditions are kept in mind when standards are debated.

6.7 How should schools be responding to the nature and needs of learners?

Professional Societies with Interests in Education   Such professional societies as The American Association for the Advancement of Science work diligently toward improving learning in their subject field. Moreover, there is at least one professional society or organization representing each subject area. Each wants to ensure that K–12 students are exposed to the latest knowledge and ideas in that field. Table 6.1 lists the common subjects taught and the names of documents published by selected professional societies. Many of the documents are available as noted online. These reports often are distributed to members serving on state standards committees.

Several national education organizations (learned societies) have taken on the challenge of creating educational standards or guidelines to be used at national, state and local levels. They are listed below by subject field. To view selected organization's standards go to the websites noted in the page margin.

 Web Links

Subject Fields		Web Links
Arts	National Standards for Arts Education MENC Publications, 1806 Robert Fulton Drive, Reston, VA 22091	National Arts and Education Network: ArtsEdge
	National Arts and Education Network: ArtsEdge Kennedy Center for the Performing Arts 2700 F Street NW Washington, DC 20566	
Civics	National Standards for Civics and Government Center for Civic Education, 5146 Douglas Fir Rd., Calabasas, CA 91302	Center for Civic Education
Economics	Voluntary National Content Standards in Economics National Council on Economic Education, 1140 Avenue of the Americas, New York, NY 10036	National Council on Economic Education
English and Language Arts	Standards for the English Language Arts National Council Teaching of English, Urbana, IL	National Council of Teachers of English
	Standards for the Assessment of Reading and Writing International Reading Association, 800 Barksdale Rd., P.O. Box 8139, Newark, DE 19714-8139	
Foreign Languages	National Standards for Foreign Language Learning National Standards for Foreign Language Education, Lawrence, KS	American Council on the Teaching of Foreign Languages
	Foreign Language Learning in the 21st Century American Council on the Teaching of Foreign Languages	
Geography	Geography for Life National Geographic, P.O. Box 1640, Washington, DC 20013-1640	National Geographic Society
Health	National Health Education Standards Association for Advancement of Health Education, Reston, VA	American Association for Health Education
History	National Standards for History National Center for History in the Schools, 10880 Wilshire Blvd., Suite 761, Los Angeles, CA 90024-4108	National Center for History in the Schools
Mathematics	Curriculum and Evaluation Standards for School Mathematics Principles and Standards for Teaching Mathematics NCTM, 1906 Association Drive, Reston, VA 22091-1593	National Council of Teachers of Mathematics
Physical Education	Content Standards and Assessment Guide for School Physical Education NASPE, 1900 Association Drive, Reston, VA 22091	National Association for Sport and Physical Education
Science	National Science Education Standards National Research Council	National Science Education Standards
Social Studies	National Council for the Social Studies 8555 Sixteenth St. Suite 500, Silver Spring, MD 20910	National Council for the Social Studies
	Expectations of Excellence: Curriculum Standards for Social Studies Fulfillment House, Whitehurst & Clark, 100 Newfield Ave., Raritan Center, Edison, NJ 08837	
Technology	National Educational Technology Standards (NETS) International Society for Technology in Education (ISTE)	International Society for Technology in Education

In review, state committees representing stakeholders in education and influenced by what is going on in the world, what is known about children and their needs, and the best advice of professional societies, engage in developing standards or descriptions of what learners should know and be able to do. Not an easy job. However, after much deliberation, standards emerge.

WHAT STATE STANDARDS LOOK LIKE

Standards differ in several ways from state to state. As an example, some are general and others specific. Let's take a look at a couple of standards in writing and math.

Writing   California has a set of K–12 writing standards. Among them is a second grade standard paraphrased as follows: "*Students write compositions that describe familiar objects, events, and experiences. The writing demonstrates a command of standard English . . .*" Following that standard are two **benchmarks** or indicators describing precise student accomplishments that make it clear they have reached the standard. The term *benchmark* is synonymous with *instructional objective,* described on page 174.
   Students can:

2.1 write brief narratives based on their experiences that move through a logical sequence of events and that describe the setting, characters, objects, and events in detail.
2.2 write a friendly letter complete with date, salutation, body, closing, and signature.

Mathematics   Arizona in its "grades 1–3 level" has a standard that reads:

Students represent and use numbers in equivalent forms through the use of physical models, drawings, word names, and symbols.

Following that standard are some indicators or benchmarks which include students' ability to:

Construct equivalent forms of whole numbers (e.g., 15 + 5 = 10 + 10), and Identify a given model that is divided into fractional parts (thirds, halves, and fourths).

THE POWER OF STATE STANDARDS

State standards are powerful in two ways. First, many states have **proficiency tests** that measure the extent to which students at various grade levels have attained the standards, such as those above. Proficiency tests understandably are often derived from or influenced by state standards. Ohio, for example, requires a statewide test in third grade in reading; tests in fourth, sixth, and ninth grades in reading, writing, math, citizenship, and science; and a tenth grade test in reading and math. Passing the ninth grade test is a requirement for high school graduation while the results of other tests are used to identify learners who might be non-promoted or need help. Second, as noted in Figure 6.1, the standards flow down to school districts and influence the curriculum, or what is taught.

WHAT HAPPENS AT THE SCHOOL DISTRICT LEVEL

At the district level, representative teachers, administrators, and others with educational interests periodically are convened in curriculum development committees. Goals of a curriculum development committee can include:

- Developing a vision for a high quality school curriculum.
- Determining programs of study (English, math, social studies, etc.).
- Determining courses within each program of study and describing general course content.
- Identifying useful instructional materials related to courses.
- Ensuring that the present or proposed curriculum is aligned with state standards and state testing.

   In the course of the above activities, school district personnel produce curriculum guides or handbooks that describe what students are expected to study and learn in each subject at each grade level. Such materials can also list and describe useful instructional resources such as textbooks, reference materials, and films, videos, or CDs. Consider curriculum guides a blueprint to follow. Unfortunately, new teachers lament that such blueprints fail to reach their hands (Public Education Network 2003). Consequently, you may have to ask for copies of them before you can begin to prepare educational experiences for your learners. Otherwise you will be like a ship without a rudder.

Reaching decisions about what should be taught and how sometimes is highly political in that members of a community often hold different values regarding a number of things. For example, controversy exists about what to teach regarding the nature of the universe: did it "evolve" or was it "created"? Other sticking points in communities may be what foreign languages to teach, whether to engage in bilingual education, and what to do about sex and substance abuse education.

Decisions regarding what gets taught also are affected by what research seems to indicate is best practice in various subject areas. For example, after reviewing research on best practices, New York City Schools decided to implement, among others, a phonetics approach to teaching reading and The University of Chicago Mathematics Program for schools.

For further understanding of local curriculum development see Danielson (2002).

6.8 What was a controversial part of the curriculum in your schools?

Summary   States establish guidelines or *standards* indicating what students should know and be able to do. Furthermore, most states require students to pass *proficiency tests* based on the standards. Failure to pass a test can result in non-promotion.

At the school district level, the standards are fine-tuned and implemented as curriculum. Based on the standards, programs and courses are set, and instructional materials helpful to teachers are located and/or created. Through study in the courses, students have *opportunity to learn* what is required in order to pass the proficiency exams. When students have opportunity to learn required material, it is said that the state standards, the state tests, and the school curriculum are aligned. When a goodly number of students do not pass a test it may be that what is learned and what is tested are different: there is lack of **alignment.**

THE FORMAL AND TAUGHT CURRICULA

So far, this discussion has been about the state and local school districts and what they require that learners must know and be able to do, and that is a lot (see Spotlight on Research 6.1). This is the **formal curriculum.**

However, teachers may or may not teach all of the formal curriculum. In place of, or in addition to it, they sometimes enlighten children about other matters. Porter (2003) notes "Teachers [and circumstances] are the ultimate arbiters of what is taught and how." Here are some examples of circumstances that result in departures from the formal curriculum.

- A teacher has an abiding interest and in-depth knowledge of some aspect of the curriculum: perhaps he knows a lot about plant life. Consequently, he takes the students into more depth in that area of study.

- An event has occurred that is compelling in its importance: The Supreme Court renders judgment on a controversial matter. This event creates an opportunity to learn something of importance, a "teachable moment."

- A parent has expertise that she is willing to share that is of great interest and use to students although it falls outside the formal curriculum. For example, expertise related to computer usage.

6.9 How will you balance the many curriculum demands made on your learners?

- Something of importance is happening in the life of a student: e.g., a child is selected to go to the History Day district finals. This provides opportunity for the class to help her consider how to make a good presentation.

School life is enriched by such interests and events and the variety and spontaneity they provide.

Students are supposed to know and be able to do a lot. In one study K–12 teachers were asked to estimate the amount of time it would take to address the curriculum content for which they were held responsible. Their aggregated estimate—15,465 hours. Assuming 13 years of instruction, the average length of a school year (180 days), and the average length of the school day (5.6 hours), teachers have 13,104 hours without subtracting significant amounts of time lost to classroom disruptions and other noninstructional events. Estimates run from 21 to 69 percent (Kendall & Marzano, 2000). Clearly, this curriculum is not viable if students lack time to learn it.

Recognizing the shortfall, Marzano (2003) suggests that schools:

- increase the amount of time available for instruction (research generally supports the positive impact of increasing instructional time) *or*
- drastically reduce the amount of content teachers are expected to cover. Get down to the essentials;
- sequence and organize the essential content logically so that it can best be learned;

- make sure that the essential content is being taught—that students have the opportunity to learn it;
- protect the available instructional time: cut classroom interruptions which tend to be numerous, be efficient about recess, lunch, time between classes.

To the extent students have the opportunity to learn the essential parts of the curriculum they will. Achievement test scores will verify that.

6.10 In your experience, when your teachers departed from the formal curriculum, how did you feel about it?

Thus, there are two kinds of curriculum: (1) the **formal,** required kind following from work done by state standards and school district curriculum committees and resulting in documents such as state guidelines, local curriculum guides, and other documents and (2) the **taught curriculum** that includes items from the formal curriculum teachers actually teach plus anything else deemed important by the teacher.

THE POWER OF THE CURRICULUM

What is to be taught and learned—the curriculum—drives life in classrooms. To the extent that it is presented in meaningful ways (see "Meaningful Learning" in Chapter 4) and authentic (related to the learner's real world [see authentic learning in Chapter 4]), your students are more likely to learn and be satisfied (see Case 6.1).

Instructional Objectives

Having access to state standards or guidelines, local curriculum guides, and a wide range of teaching and learning materials is prerequisite to planning your teaching. With these resources at hand you are poised to make learning come alive.

The first step is to prepare instructional objectives that will lead to meaningful, authentic kinds of learning experiences.

WHAT INSTRUCTIONAL OBJECTIVES LOOK LIKE

Regardless of whether a course, unit, or lesson is being planned, instructional objectives must be set. An **instructional objective** describes what learners must know and be able to do. Specific objectives are much like benchmarks (see page 172). When one is developed that allows a learner's progress to be precisely observed and measured, then objectives and benchmarks become identical.

First-Year Teacher: "Good Curriculum Avoids Discipline Problems"

Kelley Dawson learned early that if you don't plan "good curriculum," kids can really get out of control. "I tried everything to get my [fourth grade] students to behave: incentives, threats, punishments, being strict, being friendly, yelling, reasoning, sweet talking, and pleading for sympathy." Kelley was desperate.

Fortunately, after reflection, she realized that she shouldn't have to get the students under control to start teaching. Rather, it was the other way around. "You have to start by teaching interesting, engaging content." She asked herself

what she was doing that made students so bored and disruptive and concluded that she was making them plod through poor textbooks and other materials, disconnected from their lives. Consequently, Kelley began to find more interesting materials than the texts (some she made herself) and to relate what was to be learned as much as possible to students' experiences and interests.

Several years later, Kelley still struggles to provide a *curriculum that motivates*. But the struggle seems worthwhile. Beyond fixing disciplinary headaches she notes a good curriculum "gets kids

to think deeply, care about our world, and help them to make positive changes in it."

Source: Dawson (2002).

> **INVESTIGATING AND SOLVING THE CASE**
>
> 1. What did Kelley finally do that is consistent with what we know about learning as noted in Chapter 4?
> 2. What else would you have done?

Below are four illustrative, *general* objectives teachers may want to accomplish, each with a parallel, *specific* objective in italics.

- You want students to understand that a newspaper contains a number of parts and that each part contains different information:
  Given the daily newspaper, students will correctly list the main sections it contains and the contents of each section.
- You want students to know how waste can be recycled and to have practice using the Internet to find related information:
  Given access to the Internet, students will locate at least three websites related to recycling waste and prepare a list of at least five recycling suggestions.
- You want students to be able to appreciate that people have different values and attitudes that affect their behavior:
  Given a Harry Potter book, students will describe different attitudes and values held by three characters, how they are alike and different, and how they affect the characters' behaviors and interactions with other characters.
- You want students to practice their soccer dribbling skills:
  Given a soccer ball, students will practice dribbling by weaving around obstacles without hitting any of them.

6.11 Think of something you would want your learners to know or be able to do. Next, think of a specific instructional objective you could use to determine its acquisition. How do you feel about making objectives more specific and clear?

INSTRUCTIONAL OBJECTIVES DIFFER IN TWO WAYS

You can readily see the difference between a general instructional objective (a "want") and a specific one. Additionally, you probably noticed the four specific instructional objectives inspire different kinds of learning—cognitive, humanistic, and behavioral—as noted in Chapter 4. The first two are aimed toward *cognitive learning*, the third toward *humanistic learning*, and the last *behavioral learning*. They also differ in terms of the level of thinking or doing required of the learners. For example, the first objective requires learners to engage in basic knowledge acquisition (How is a newspaper divided into parts and what is in each part?). The last asks them not to acquire a skill but to become more skill proficient (Dribble around obstacles). To review, instructional objectives differ in *specificity*, *kind*, and *level*.

SOME OBJECTIVES ARE GENERAL, OTHERS ARE SPECIFIC

For decades, educators have argued over exactly how precise objectives should be. Early in the twentieth century, teachers were required to write objectives with great detail and specificity. An example might be "Learners will know 6 sevens are 42." You can imagine the results—literally thousands of detailed objectives! By 1930, an overcorrection occurred, and objectives were written very broadly and unclearly. An example of an overly broad and unclear objective might be "Learners will be able to think independently."

Both general and specific objectives are valid and have their place. Since general objectives are more skeletal in nature, they make more sense when people are discussing the broad goals or aims of education or instruction. For example, general objectives are useful at the national and state levels, where the intention is to broadly define what schools should teach. Consider, for example, one of the six educational goals set by state governors and the first President Bush in 1990 for America to attain by the year 2000:

> By the year 2000, American students will leave grades 4, 8, and 12 having competency in English, math, science, history, and geography; they will learn to use their minds, will be prepared for responsible citizenship, further learning, and productive employment. (National Governors' Association, 1990)

Unfortunately, due to their skeletal nature, general objectives are written using terms that are open to interpretation. In the goal statement above, "having competency" and "being prepared" are examples of general objectives. How will the nation know whether American students are "competent"? Specifically what must they know and be able to do in each subject area? Moreover, how will we determine whether students can "use their minds" and are "prepared for responsible citizenship" and so on?

While such objectives indicate what the learners will do, they do not explicitly indicate what pupils are to learn. This is unfortunate since it focuses attention on the means of instruction (what the teacher or students will do), not on the ends (what learners will learn). Activities are not ends in themselves, but a means to an end. *The real purpose of instruction is to change pupils' behavior and enable them to do things they couldn't do before instruction occurred.* To help keep the real purpose of instruction in mind, teachers should write statements that describe the behaviors instructional activities are intended to help pupils learn (Airasian & Russell, 2008).

Again, general objectives are useful when making a skeletal outline of what students are to accomplish. Often teachers write them when engaged in long-range planning for the semester or year or when deciding what to accomplish during a month-long unit of instruction. Following are three more examples of general objectives:

- Students will know what a verb is.
- Students will enjoy music.
- Students will be able to swim.

THE KINDS OF OBJECTIVES WE USE RESULT IN THREE DIFFERENT KINDS OF LEARNING: COGNITIVE, AFFECTIVE, PSYCHOMOTOR

Bloom (1989) studied numerous educational objectives and saw that they all fall within "the three schools of thought about learning." However, he referred to the three schools as "three domains of learning" and labeled them "cognitive, affective, and psychomotor."

Cognitive Domain Educational objectives in the cognitive domain cause learners to engage in mental or intellectual tasks. Thus, a learner might be expected to *recall* the sum of the angles of a triangle, to *analyze* the events surrounding Columbus's voyage to America in 1492, or to *identify* and discuss the themes found in Jane

Austen's novels. Within Bloom's cognitive domain there are six levels of cognitive complexity. They are from simplest to most complex:

1. *Knowledge.* Learners have knowledge of and the ability to recall or recognize information. Example: The learner can recite multiplication facts.

2. *Comprehension.* Learners understand and can explain knowledge in their own words. Example: The learner can explain why 6 sevens and 7 sixes are equivalent.

3. *Application.* Learners apply knowledge, that is they are able to use it in practical situations. Example: The learner can calculate the cost of purchasing six envelopes costing seven cents each.

4. *Analysis.* Learners are able to break down complex concepts or information into simpler, related parts. Example: The learner can break the numeric statement "6 × 7" into subparts or possible combinations (for example, 3 × 2 × 7).

5. *Synthesis.* Learners are able to combine elements to form a new, original entity. Example: The learner can hypothesize that if 6 sevens are 42, 7 sevens can be determined by adding another 7 to 42.

6. *Evaluation.* Learners are able to make judgments. Example: The learner can devise a strategy for evaluating the accuracy of solutions to multiplication problems with 7 as one integer.

Many educators believe that, unfortunately, teachers require mostly lower-order types of learning (knowledge and comprehension): When did Columbus reach America? Teachers much less frequently seem to prod students to develop higher-level, or higher-order, thinking (application, analysis, synthesis, and evaluation): Why did Europeans come to America in 1492? Although low-level knowledge is an essential foundation for higher levels of thinking, it is important that teachers develop objectives and prepare lessons that challenge students to reach all levels of cognitive ability (see Highlight 6.3).

6.12 When might you intentionally engage students in lower-order cognitive activity?

Affective Domain Bloom calls a second type or domain of learning outcomes "affective." The affective domain deals with attitudinal, emotional, and valuing goals for learners. Although teachers most often associate their instructional outcomes with the cognitive domain, almost all teachers try to promote some change in student affect. For example, most teachers hope that their students come to enjoy and value the subject they teach, as well as learning in general.

Bloom organizes the affective domain into five levels of complexity as follows:

1. *Receiving or attending.* Learners are willing to attend to, concentrate on, and receive information. Example: The learner listens attentively to Marjorie Kinnan Rawlings's story, *The Yearling.* (*The Yearling* is a novel about a young boy, Jody, who lives in the scrub and swamp of the hammock country of Florida. To survive, the family depends on a meager crop. Jody becomes attached to a tame fawn, Flag. However, to protect their crop from Flag, his parents are forced to kill the yearling.)

2. *Responding.* Learners respond positively to the information by actively engaging with it. Example: The learner participates in a discussion of *The Yearling.*

3. *Valuing.* Learners express an attitude or belief about the value of something. Example: After reading *The Yearling,* the learner may express the belief that life can be unfair and cruel and that what life is worth is sometimes lessened by unkind circumstances.

4. *Organization.* Learners compare and integrate the attitude or value they have expressed with attitudes and beliefs they hold, thus internalizing the value. Example: The learner considers whether the attitudes or values they expressed after reading *The Yearling* are consistent with other values they or others hold.

All learners, to varying degrees, possess four cognitive abilities (Sternberg, 1997). They are the ability *to memorize* or remember information, *to analyze* it, to take information and *to create* something further from it, and *to apply* or put information to use. These four abilities equate to Bloom's knowledge, analysis, synthesis, and application. Sternberg believes that when we teach, unfortunately, we ask students to utilize only the first two—memory and analysis. For example, when teaching social studies, we may ask learn-ers to "remember factors that have led to troubles in the Middle East," and we may then ask them to "analyze how or why different countries chose sides in this conflict."

But what about creativity and appli-cation? Sternberg observes that we less often ask learners to use these abilities. In order to help learners reach full intel-lectual potential, there is a critical need to teach in ways that require them to use all four abilities. "By exposing students to instruction emphasizing each type of ability, we enable them to capitalize on their strengths while developing and improving new skills" (p. 23).

How might learners extend the use of knowledge about the post World War II Middle East into the realms of creativity and application? In the first instance, we might ask them to "consider how the troubles might be resolved." To engage learners in use of their ability to apply information, we might ask them "what lesson nations should learn from conflict."

5. *Characterization.* Learners act out their values. Example: The learner behaves in ways consistent with espoused values. If the learner believes that life is valuable but is often treated as a cheap commodity, he or she may join some group concerned with the preservation of life, such as the Society for the Prevention of Cruelty to Animals.

Psychomotor Domain   According to Bloom, objectives in the third, or psychomotor, domain relate to learning physical skills. Courses in child or adolescent psychology taught you that as children grow, they are able to accomplish successively more com-plex physical tasks. For example, early on students learn how to hold a large crayon, then to hold a thinner pencil. First, they learn to print, then to write. Later, they learn to type and to use a word processor. Most subjects require some degree of psychomotor learning. In science, students learn how to organize and manipulate laboratory equip-ment. In music, they may learn how to use their voice or play an instrument.

Seven levels of the psychomotor domain have been identified (Simpson, 1972). Following are illustrations of possible objectives in this domain.

6.13   To which "school of thought about learning" are you mostly drawn? Why?

1. *Perception.* Learners use sensory cues (such as vision) to guide their later attempt to perform a skill. Example: The learner notices how to hold and move a brush to create a particular brushstroke.

2. *Set.* Learners are ready to perform a skill or an action. Example: The learner is mentally, physically, and emotionally prepared to perform the brushstroke.

3. *Guided response.* Learners practice the skill under the supervision of an expert. Example: The learner practices while the instructor coaches.

4. *Mechanism.* Learners become more proficient in the skill through practice. Example: The learner becomes more confident as the skill becomes second-nature or habitual.

5. *Complex or overt response.* Learners perform the skill with a high degree of proficiency. Example: The learner makes a great number of brushstrokes accurately and quickly.

Try Activity 6.1   6. *Adaptation.* Learners modify previously learned skills to perform related skills. Example: Building on previous skill, the learner creates different kinds of stan-dard brushstrokes.

7. *Origination.* Learners create new, original performances based on previously learned skills. Example: The learner creates brushstrokes the teacher has not demonstrated or suggested.

Please note that Bloom's taxonomy has been somewhat revised for additional uses (Krathwohl, 2002).

ANOTHER WAY OF CLASSIFYING LEARNING OUTCOMES

Gagné and others (2004) provide another arrangement for thinking about and classifying learning outcomes, or objectives. Their system contains five groups of learning outcomes compared to Bloom's three:

1. *Verbal information.* This term is used to describe the vast amount of information obtained and stored in our memory. It is similar to the knowledge level in Bloom's cognitive domain. Example: Pupils learn factual information such as principles of physics or chemistry that they can retrieve as needed. Cognitive scientists refer to this as declarative knowledge.

2. *Intellectual skill.* This refers to learning how to do something mentally. It encompasses knowing how to do something rather than merely knowing about something. Example: Learners are able to create a balanced menu or devise a scale model based upon what they know about nutrition or about the object the model is based on. Cognitive scientists refer to this as procedural knowledge.

3. *Cognitive strategies.* This refers to learning ways of thinking and solving problems, including learning how to learn. Example: Learners learn to use an inductive approach to solve problems. Thus, knowledge of how to use induction would be a cognitive strategy. Problem solving usually combines the use of declarative and procedural knowledge.

4. *Motor skills.* Although Gagné does not refer to the Bloom or Simpson designations of psychomotor skills, they seem to be the same type of learning outcome as Gagné's motor skills.

5. *Attitudes.* Gagné likens attitudes to Bloom's affective domain.

Writing Specific Objectives

Another thing you must decide when writing instructional objectives is what information to include in them. Many educators believe that a good objective tells learners exactly what they are expected to know and be able to do. For example, "Given a paragraph, the learner will identify every verb by circling it correctly." This objective does just that: It tells the learners what they are expected to know (what is a verb) and what they are expected to do (find and circle each one correctly in a given paragraph).

A method has been developed to assist beginning teachers in writing such specific objectives. It goes like this:

Every objective should contain an A, B, C, and D where

- A stands for the audience the objective is written for. In the objective above, the audience, A, is the learner.
- B stands for the behavior expected of the learner. In the objective above, the behavior, B, is the learner who will identify every verb. Table 6.2 contains a list of verbs that can be used to attain learning outcomes at various levels of each of Bloom's three instructional domains.
- C stands for the condition under which the learner identifies every verb. In the objective above C is "Given a paragraph."
- D stands for the degree of proficiency or correctness that the learner must display. In the objective above the degree of proficiency, D, is circling each verb correctly.

6.14 How do you feel about preparing instructional objectives in each domain of learning and at various levels?

Web Link
Bloom's Revised Taxonomy

6.15 Why do you prefer the Bloom or Gagné schema for arranging instructional objectives?

TABLE 6.2 Verbs to Use When Writing Objectives at Various Levels of Bloom's Three Domains of Learning

1. **Cognitive domain**
   a. *Knowledge level*
      1. Objective: to know about
      2. Verbs to use: list, tell, define, identify, label, locate, recognize, describe, match, name, outline, reproduce, state
   b. *Comprehension level*
      1. Objective: to understand
      2. Verbs to use: explain, interpret, illustrate, describe, summarize, expand, convert, measure, defend, paraphrase, rewrite, apprehend, comprehend
   c. *Application level*
      1. Objective: to use knowledge and understanding
      2. Verbs to use: demonstrate, apply, use, solve, choose appropriate procedures, modify, operate, prepare, produce, construct
   d. *Analysis level*
      1. Objective: to break down
      2. Verbs to use: analyze, debate, differentiate, generalize, conclude, organize, break down, dissect, diagram, separate, subdivide, relate
   e. *Synthesis level*
      1. Objective: to combine, to create
      2. Verbs to use: create, combine, plan, design, produce, compile, develop, compose, devise, modify, organize, rearrange, reconstruct
   f. *Evaluation level*
      1. Objective: to judge
      2. Verbs to use: judge, evaluate, conclude, contrast, develop criteria, appraise, criticize, support, decide, compare

2. **Affective domain**
   a. *Receiving level*
      1. Objective: to be willing to attend to and to receive information
      2. Verbs to use: listen, be aware of, observe, be conscious of, recognize, realize, be tolerant
   b. *Responding level*
      1. Objective: to be willing to respond
      2. Verbs to use: respond, cooperate, appreciate, find pleasure in, comply, discuss
   c. *Valuing level*
      1. Objective: to develop attitudes and beliefs
      2. Verbs to use: value, opine, appraise, estimate, approve, appreciate, assess, believe, size up (See also "Evaluation level" under "Cognitive domain.")
   d. *Organizational level*
      1. Objective: to act out values
      2. Verbs to use: demonstrate, perform, act out, engage in, uphold

3. **Psychomotor domain**
   a. *Perception level*
      1. Objective: to notice, recognize, sense
      2. Verbs to use: notice, recognize, sense, perceive, detect
   b. *Set level*
      1. Objective: to be ready to try
      2. Verbs to use: be ready, be prepared, take steps, make preparation, desire
   c. *Guided response level*
      1. Objective: to try
      2. Verbs to use: try, perform, practice
   d. *Mechanism level*
      1. Objective: to improve
      2. Verbs to use: improve, become proficient, change, increase, decrease
   e. *Complex or overt response level*
      1. Objective: to be proficient
      2. Verbs to use: excel, master, perfect
   f. *Adaptation level*
      1. Objective: to adapt
      2. Verbs to use: adapt, adjust, accommodate, modify, modulate
   g. *Organization level*
      1. Objective: to create
      2. Verbs to use: create, originate, produce

Thus, if you want to be precise about your instructional objectives and want to write them as specifically as possible, you can follow this method. Here are examples, including the objective used above, of specific objectives coded with A, B, C, and D.

1. When given a paragraph, the learner will identify every verb by circling it correctly.
   (C)   (A)   (B)   (D)

2. Given ten sentences containing 20 misspelled words, the learner will
   (C)   (A)

   underline at least 16 of the misspellings.
   (B)   (D)

3. The learner will solve at least eight of ten binary addition problems.
   (A)   (B)   (D)   (C)

4. Given a 100-word speed test in class, the student will type at a rate of no less
   (C)   (A)   (B)

   than 30 words per minute with fewer than four errors.
   (D)

5. When presented flash cards of words containing the letter combination "ph,"
   (C)

   the student will pronounce the words on at least 18 of 20 cards
   (A)   (B)   (D)

   correctly.

THE VALUE OF SPECIFIC OBJECTIVES

It is beneficial to *have clear, specific learning objectives in mind* and, as mentioned in Chapter 4, to *communicate them to learners* so that they are aware of what they are expected to know and be able to do. If you do, students will learn more (Marzano, 2009). Additionally, such careful attention to detail will give you greater security, especially in your first years of teaching.

Counterpoint Not all educators think teachers should use specific instructional objectives. On the contrary, they believe use of such objectives may be counterproductive. Among potential negative consequences, they cite the following:

- Specific objectives, because they are so precise, are difficult to write. They are easiest to write when the learning outcome is at the lower levels of any of Bloom's three domains of learning. For example, it is easier to write a specific objective in the cognitive domain for "knowledge" than for "synthesis" or "evaluation." Look at the first objective above. You can see it is fairly simple to write an objective that calls for identification or recall of something. Try to write a specific objective that would call for learners to analyze the characteristics of verbs. That's not so easy. The negative consequence of such objectives may be that students are challenged to learn mostly simple and factual information instead of engaging in higher-order thinking.

- Evidence exists that, in general, when teachers teach to precise objectives learners are more likely to attain the specified knowledge, skills, or attitudes but fail to learn other, worthwhile related material. Marzano, Pickering, and Pollock (2001) note, "This phenomenon might occur because setting a goal focuses students' attention to such a degree that they ignore information not specifically related to the goal" (p. 94). The negative consequence of teaching to set, and especially specific objectives, is that learners may miss something of the bigger picture.

- There are times when students should be given learning situations without predetermined, specific learning objectives. For example, taking a walk through the school neighborhood could be a very different experience for each learner. Why expect each one to concentrate on coming away with similar observations and impressions? Comparing uniquely individual observations and impressions after the walk might lead to knowledge and insights that could not possibly have

Try Activity 6.2

6.16 How specific do you think your instructional objectives will be?

been forecast. The negative consequence of specific objectives here may be that spontaneity of learning can be lost.

- Experienced teachers seldom write specific instructional objectives. In fact, they seem to do much instructional planning by mentally making only brief notes of the procedures they will follow. The negative consequence of specific objectives in this case may be that time devoted to writing specific objectives might not have much transfer to classroom teaching.

Some additional, related research findings are presented in Spotlight on Research 6.2.

WHEN ARE OBJECTIVES GOOD?

When developing any instructional plan, you prepare a sequence of related instructional objectives. However, it is essential that you also stop and reflect on those objectives to judge their appropriateness to the curriculum and your learners. You can judge instructional objectives by asking yourself the following questions:

- Are the objectives relevant to the curriculum for which students will be held accountable?
- Do the objectives promote learning outcomes across learning domains where appropriate (cognitive, affective, psychomotor)?
- Do the objectives promote a range of levels of understanding or performance (low or high) within each domain?
- Are the objectives written in terms of what learners are expected to know or do? Are they specific enough that students will be aware of exactly what they need to know and do?
- Can this group of students achieve the objectives? Do the objectives correspond to the readiness and ability levels of students? Do the objectives take individual differences into account?

Research findings related to instructional objectives are presented in Spotlight on Research 6.2.

Preparing Instructional Plans of Varying Duration

Once you have decided what to teach and have prepared good instructional objectives, you need to ask yourself, *How much* and *what kind* of instruction do students need to accomplish these objectives? This question could be asked in reverse order as well. For example, do you first decide how learning should take place and then allocate sufficient time as if the latter were variable? Or, conversely, do you decide how much time you have as if time were a constant and then decide how much or in what manner you can teach within that time span? Since the allocation of time to instruction or of instruction to time is often a burning issue, you may wish to discuss it in class. Perhaps you recall a course you were enrolled in, or a trip you took, that ran out of time and was not completed.

THE "LONG AND SHORT" OF PLANNING

As a teacher, you will regularly engage in long-, intermediate-, and short-range planning. An example can be used to illustrate this. You and your friend plan a vacation in Canada. This was your long-range plan. Then you determine the cities you will visit, the route you will take, and approximately how many days you will spend at various sites. This was the intermediate-range plan. Finally, for each day and site, you decide which specific things you want to do or see. Thus, you are also concerned with the daily and hourly routine. This was your short-term plan.

According to Snowman and Biehler (2005), the following conclusions can be drawn from the research on instructional objectives:

1. Objectives seem to work best when learners are aware of them, when learners treat the objectives as guides to learning specific sections of material, and when learners feel the objectives will aid learning.
2. Objectives seem to work best when they are clearly written and when the learning task is neither too difficult nor too easy.
3. Students of average ability seem to benefit more when they know what the objectives are than do those of higher or lower ability.
4. Objectives improve intentional learning but lead to a decline in unintentional or incidental learning of things that go unstressed. Incidental learning is more likely to occur when general rather than specific objectives are used.

Slavin (2008), who also reviewed research on instructional objectives, notes that communicating objectives to students has never been found to reduce student achievement and often has been found to increase it. He suggests that objectives communicated to students be general enough to encompass everything the lesson or course is supposed to teach in order to prevent students from focusing too narrowly, thus excluding much important information.

Similarly, as a teacher, you will engage in long-range, intermediate-range, and short-term instructional planning for your students.

When teachers engage in long-range planning, they are deciding how generally to approach teaching either for an entire year or for a semester-long course. Teachers doing long-range planning first must choose a focus. The focus might be local history, American or Canadian literature, or fourth-grade arithmetic. Second, the teacher needs to determine how many weeks, days, or hours are available for instruction. Interruptions such as holidays, vacations, or exam weeks are taken into account. Third, the teacher must select the content of instruction. For example, long-range planning for an American history course involves deciding which topics and information should be included in this course, given the time available.

Intermediate, middle-range, or **unit planning** involves decisions about how courses can be broken into chunks, parts, or units, each with a particular theme. In intermediate or unit planning, teachers arrange units or topics in a meaningful order, thus determining the sequence of the course. The history course could be broken into historical periods that students can examine chronologically. Arithmetic for fourth graders might be broken into a series of units on arithmetic processes that are sequenced from simple to complex. A university course outline or syllabus provides an example of long-range and intermediate-range planning.

Once intermediate planning is completed, teachers next plan for the short range; that is, for the week and for daily lessons. During short-range planning, you decide in detail what students must learn and how that can most effectively be accomplished. It is at this level of planning that specific instructional objectives are needed.

6.17 How will you use long-, intermediate-, and short-range planning?

Figure 6.2 depicts plans of different duration (long-range, intermediate-range, and short-range), while Figure 6.3 shows the relationships among subjects, courses, units, and lessons.

PREPARING LONG-RANGE PLANS: YEARLY AND SEMESTER PLANS

As you have learned, teachers do long-range planning to determine what a year-long or semester-long course should include and how it may be taught. As mentioned, developing a long-range plan for teaching a course is similar to developing a vacation plan. Once you have a general vacation destination in mind, you start to collect ideas.

FIGURE 6.2   Plans of Different Duration

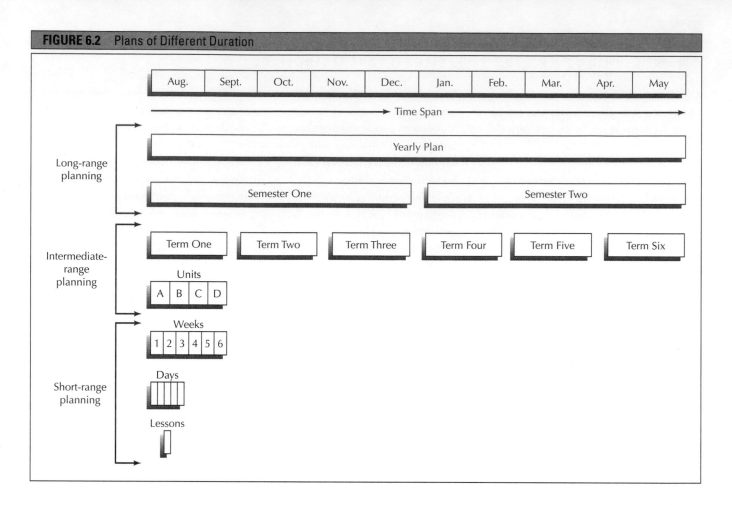

| Aug. | Sept. | Oct. | Nov. | Dec. | Jan. | Feb. | Mar. | Apr. | May |

Time Span

Long-range planning
- Yearly Plan
- Semester One | Semester Two

Intermediate-range planning
- Term One | Term Two | Term Three | Term Four | Term Five | Term Six
- Units: A B C D

Short-range planning
- Weeks: 1 2 3 4 5 6
- Days
- Lessons

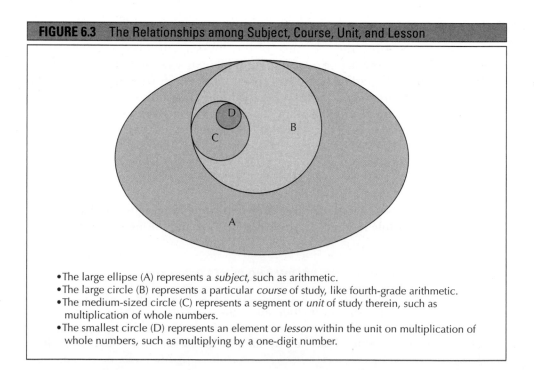

FIGURE 6.3   The Relationships among Subject, Course, Unit, and Lesson

- The large ellipse (A) represents a *subject*, such as arithmetic.
- The large circle (B) represents a particular *course* of study, like fourth-grade arithmetic.
- The medium-sized circle (C) represents a segment or *unit* of study therein, such as multiplication of whole numbers.
- The smallest circle (D) represents an element or *lesson* within the unit on multiplication of whole numbers, such as multiplying by a one-digit number.

Many will come from books and travel brochures. Other ideas may come from talking with people who have taken similar vacations. You use these ideas and materials as resources. You sit down with them and consider things such as:

1. *Your objective.* Where specifically do you want to go and what do you want to accomplish? Is your aim to spend considerable time at a few sites, to see all the sites you can, or to experience the local culture?

2. *Your timeline.* How much time can you spend in each place you wish to visit? Where do you want to be by certain dates in order to get everything done?

3. *Needed resources.* What will you need to take along or secure along the way to ensure that the vacation is successful?

In other words, you take into account your goals, the order in which you think they can best be achieved, the time required, and the resources needed.

Similarly, when developing a course, you consider what it is your students are expected to know and to be able to do; what activities they might engage in and in what order; how much time is available (weeks, days, hours) to be divided among the various activities; and, finally, what resource materials are at hand. When engaged in long-range planning you should keep in mind that:

- The course primarily should be derived from the established, formal curriculum; that is, it should fit into state and school district curriculum plans.

- The course should be developed to reflect what is known about the subject area. Thus, the content of the course should be up to date and reflect what experts in the field think is important.

- The course should be developed to take into account what you know about your learners. To some extent, then, each course you teach will be custom made. There is no one course that is good for all students because of the differences among learners noted in Chapter 3. Unfortunately, since you will not know your new students, plan revisions are necessary.

- Decisions regarding what to teach are value laden. Consequently, you must constantly guard against teaching only personal beliefs or biases about a subject or issue. Likewise, guard against teaching what seems to be "politically correct," that is, presenting a position or information that presents only what special-interest groups regard as true or valid while ignoring or depreciating what others of different persuasions believe or know.

Glatthorn (1987) presents a model to follow when developing a course. At this point, you might try your hand at constructing a long-term plan. If you'd like to do so, turn to Activity 6.3 at the end of this chapter.

Try Activity 6.3

PREPARING UNIT PLANS

Once you have created a long-range plan for the course, the intermediate stage of planning begins. Ultimately you must divide the course into parts, or units; then you must plan the units. A unit or unit plan is a more detailed plan for teaching a major section or topic within a course. At the secondary level, units normally are taught over a period of weeks and are limited to one topic. For example, in an American history course, the content might be divided into topics based on chronological periods such as the colonial, federal, and early industrial eras. Several weeks would be allocated to learning about each period. Units developed for elementary grades are often shorter, only a few days or weeks long.

As a teacher, you will likely find or develop several types of units:

- *Resource units* are mostly prepared by and are available at minimal or no cost from state education departments, special interest groups, government agencies, and businesses. Consequently, they must be adapted to the particular classroom they are used in to ensure that the level of difficulty and the general appeal are appropriate. An example of a science resource unit is a package that might contain a set of lesson plans, slides, transparencies, student worksheets, and a teacher's guide on natural gas produced by the regional gas company. Of course, resource units are likely to favor the viewpoint of the governmental or commercial group that produced them. They may possess a subtle, "hidden" curriculum bias.

- *Teaching units* are prepared by a teacher or teachers for use with a particular group of learners. Ideas may come from resource units, but they primarily arise from the teachers and from learners who may help develop the unit. Although teaching units, like resource units, are prepared before teaching occurs, they are flexible and often modified in use.

- *Experience units* are more of a "happening" than a preplanned unit. No one defines in advance what students are to learn. Teachers and students merely decide what they will generally do from day to day and from lesson to lesson. The learning experiences evolve. An experience unit might revolve around the theme "Sound Surrounds Us." What the students are experiencing is of the greatest importance, so students keep journals of what they have learned as their adventure with sound unfolds. Experienced teachers are more comfortable and adept with experience units.

- *Integrated units* are especially appropriate at the elementary level. Integrated units combine study from several fields such as social studies, language arts, science, and art around a central theme or topic. For example, an integrated unit on the Crusades might combine a historical and cultural study of that period. Students might also read translated literature from that era, study life and customs during the Crusades, and depict them through art.

Parts of a Unit Plan Although there are many types of units and unit plans, the typical unit plan includes the following parts or sections:

1. The *title* denotes the topic or theme under study, for example, "Sports in America or Canada." The topic usually is one the school district's curriculum or course of study requires. However, it may be one introduced for enrichment.

2. The *introduction* provides the rationale or reason why the unit is important to the course and in its own right. It should explain, in terms meaningful to students, why this unit is important, answering the ubiquitous student question: "Why do *we* have to know this?" The introduction also presents the parameters or scope (breadth) and sequence of the unit. By reading the introduction, one should be able to discern what main ideas or subtopics are addressed in roughly what order. The scope and sequence show how the main ideas build on each other and how the unit flows.

3. The *general objectives and preassessment of student prior knowledge* broadly state the knowledge, skills, or attitudes students will acquire as a result of engaging in this unit. You need to find out what your students already know about the topic at hand so that the unit is neither too familiar nor unfamiliar, neither too easy nor difficult. Preassessment also enables you to remediate weaknesses or gaps in students' understanding of the topic and to increase the unit's appeal by building it around students' interests and perceived needs. You can preassess students in a number of ways, including informal observations, discussion, or questioning; formal pretesting of skills, knowledge, and attitudes; or examination of the curriculum previously studied by this group of students.

4. The *body* contains the unit's content, activities, and sequence of instruction. Included are a topical outline, activities, resources, and a time frame.
   - The *topical outline* presents the main points and supporting points of the content. A detailed outline can become the wellspring for daily lessons.

- The *activities* section denotes in general what the class or individuals can do in order to accomplish the unit objectives. What activities might they undertake to engage in learning the skills, knowledge, and attitudes the unit encompasses?
- Also included in the body is the list of instructional materials and other *resources* that might be useful.
- A *time frame* describes when the unit will begin and end and when students will undertake particular activities.

5. The *assessment* section describes how learners will be evaluated in terms of achievement and satisfaction. To what extent do they know what they are expected to know? Can they do what they are expected to do?

6. A *bibliography* presents a list of resources useful to teachers in preparing and teaching this unit. A second list of references useful to students also should be prepared. If the unit will likely be revised and used again, it is a good idea to provide complete bibliographic references. In addition, it is helpful to make a note of where you obtained the resource (that is, your personal library, the school library, a friend's collection, or some other source) so that you can find it again.

Highlight 6.4 describes how to write a unit that is based on a state standard. Highlight 6.5 on page 189 is a sample abbreviated unit plan.

Online samples of units are available at the Teacher Carnegie Foundation, the Educators' Reference Desk (search both for "unit plans"), the Beacon Learning Center, and Inside Teaching websites.

Try Activity 6.4

 Web Link
Teacher Carnegie Foundation
Educators' Reference Desk
Beacon Learning Center
Inside Teaching

Benefits of Unit Planning   Developing a unit or several unit plans, especially early in your teaching career, can be time consuming. However, it also tends to be an engaging and worthwhile exercise because of the flow of ideas and resources generated. Many benefits result from preparing and using units:

- Once completed, unit plans give clear direction for short-term planning—for a week, day, or lesson. An ounce of unit planning now may save a pound of work and classroom anxiety later.
- Good unit planning makes you more aware of your learners' unique qualities.
- Unit planning causes you to think imaginatively about how to get the job done using a variety of instructional materials and activities. It weans you away from mere textbook teaching.
- Unit planning asks you to consider how to help students study some topic or phenomenon in an *interdisciplinary*, or holistic, way. Through use of units, you can incorporate writing, reading, reporting, and so forth into learning activities.

PREPARING LESSON PLANS

To begin, look at Spotlight on Research 6.3 on page 190 to see what makes a good lesson.

A **lesson plan** describes specifically what and how something will be learned within a brief period, usually one or a few class hours. Consider an analogy of vacation planning. The long-range plan is to tour the Eastern United States. The intermediate plan could be to visit Boston and would cover what you want to accomplish only within that part of the trip. The short-term plan is the day-to-day, hour-to-hour formulation of what you would do: for example, a daily plan could be to walk the Freedom Trail during the day Monday, attend a Boston Pops Concert Monday evening, shop Tuesday and see a Red Sox game, and so forth.

Lesson planning further defines a daily plan. It is even more detailed. It is an effort to ensure that on that day, every activity will go well.

1. Select a state standard(s). What standard(s) will be addressed?

2. Decide on the specific outcomes students will achieve as a result of instruction. Sometimes general state standards are accompanied by specific, related objectives or benchmarks (see previous section, "What State Standards Look Like"). In any case, what should students know and be able to do at the end of the unit?

3. Decide how those ideas will be assessed at the end of instruction. How will students show what they know and can do?

4. Give a preassessment and focus instruction appropriately. What do students know already? What are they ready to learn?

5. Develop and sequence the specific lessons and activities that will make up the unit. What will students be taught? What instructional strategies will be used?

6. Assess and analyze the results, reflect, and reteach as necessary to help all students meet the outcomes. Did students learn what was expected? What additional instruction is necessary? How could instruction be modified in the future?

Source: Adapted from Ohio Department of Education Online.

Parts of a Lesson Plan   Many formats for lesson plans are used. A sampling is shown in Table 6.3 on page 190. By comparing the formats, it is obvious that they have a lot in common. The lesson plan format we like appears in Table 6.4 also on page 190. Keep in mind that eventually you will need to choose your own lesson plan format unless your school district prescribes one.

Let's consider each part in our recommended lesson plan format:

Try Activity 6.5

1. *Objectives.* The challenge here is to write objectives at the lesson level that meet as many of the criteria for good objectives as possible. Remember, the objectives should be relevant to the curriculum; promote learning outcomes across the cognitive, psychomotor, and affective domains; reasonably promote a range of levels of understanding (low and high) within each domain; be written specifically enough that it is clear what each student must know and be able to do; and be achievable by your students.

2. *Resources.* What is available to assist learners? Assemble all the available human and material resources that might be used to help your learners gain the objectives. Many will be noted later in the section entitled "Resources Useful When Planning." In practice, many teachers do this step first, before they write specific objectives. In any case, the lesson plan should specifically denote which resources you and the learners will use in order to accomplish the specific instructional objectives.

3. *Set induction.* How will learner interest be obtained? **Set induction** or anticipatory set are terms used to indicate the need to start the lesson by capturing learner attention and interest. During this part of lesson planning, we must think of ways to do so. One idea is to relate what is to be learned to what learners are interested in and/or have previous knowledge of. It has long been assumed and has now been confirmed that people work harder on tasks related to their knowledge and interests (Renninger, Hidi, & Krapp, 1992). Interest contributes to learning because, among other things, it stimulates a personal, emotional network of associations. By relating new learning to prior knowledge, associations, and connections also are more apparent. Chapter 11 details how to provide set induction, while Unit 1 (Microteaching Lesson Two) in the Practice Teaching Manual provides a practice exercise.

Title: Explorers of North America

Introduction: Everyone is interested in other people, especially the famous. We find out about them in the news, in movies, and on television. When someone writes about another person's life that is called biography. Biographies sometimes are about good role models such as Anne Frank, Abraham Lincoln, and Martin Luther King. Sometimes they are not. In any case, they increase our knowledge of history.

The biography we will look at in this unit focuses on explorers of North America. They are important to us since they blazed the trails that made settlement of this continent possible. Some explorers were good role models. As you will see, others were not.

Both the study of biography and explorers are important to educated persons and as such are part of the K–12 curriculum.

General objectives: We want you to find out about an explorer of North America, summarize what you found out, and put that information on a trading card that you can share with the class.

Pre-assessment: Find out what students already know about explorers of North America, how to summarize, and how to use the computer to prepare an illustrated trading card.

Outline:
  i. Explorers of North America
 ii. Locating biographical information
iii. Summarizing
 iv. Computer graphics
  v. Presentations: PowerPoint for PCs, Presentation for Mac

Activities (others may be necessary)
  i. Lesson 1: Explorers of North America. Students will find out who they were and, in general, what each did. Students will choose an explorer to study.
 ii. Lesson 2: Locating biographical information. Students will identify information on their target explorer using a variety of library and Internet resources.
iii. Lesson 3: Summarizing. Class will decide what information is of most interest, and students will read and prepare brief summaries.
 iv. Lesson 4: Computer graphics. Students will learn to and will create a trading card.
  v. Lesson 5: Presentation. Students will learn to and will prepare computer presentations containing the trading card they have developed.

Resources: Librarian and I will identify materials and websites children may use.

Time frame: Project time needed will be five class days plus independent work. Additional time will be needed to share presentations.

Assessment: Valued will be student ability to prepare a biographical summary, to create a computer graphic, and to present the material effectively.

Bibliography (initial): social studies textbooks, library materials, Internet resources will be searched. Initially I have found the following to be potentially very useful:
  i. Infoplease: Biographies of Notable Explorers.

4. *Methodology.* How will teaching and learning proceed? Here you describe how learning will take place. Chapters 2 and 3 on student diversity and 4 on learning should be particularly useful in planning your methodology because they describe what is known about students and how they learn. Chapters 7 and 8 on instructional alternatives also are very relevant.

5. *Assessment.* How will learning be determined? This includes two things: how you plan to monitor students' learning during instruction and how you plan to evaluate learning at the lesson's conclusion. While instruction is ongoing, a teacher should "read" the students. To what extent does each one seem interested and engaged? Is the pace of the lesson appropriate? Are students learning? Your plan should include how you will determine such things. Informal indicators of interest and engagement might include facial expression, body language, and verbal responsiveness. Informal assessments can also be made by asking questions that check understanding and by observing how well and how

Web Links
Infoplease: Biographies of Notable Explorers

Cooper and McIntyre (1994) wanted to find out what a good lesson was like in the eyes of teachers and their students. Thus, they interviewed 13 teachers and 325 students, the latter 11 or 12 years old. Teachers and students generally agreed on what constitutes a good lesson:

- Specific knowledge or skills are acquired.
- Students work on and complete the tasks.
- Students engage in deep reflection and produce new insights.
- Students are involved in and enjoy the learning activity.
- There is a low incidence of disruptive behavior.
- There is cooperation and harmony between teacher and student and among students.
- Teaching methods are considered effective.

TABLE 6.3 Selected Formats for Lesson Plans Listed by Author or Source

El-Tigi (2001)	Hunter (2004)	Jacobson et al. (2009) Moore (2000)	NY Times (nytimes.com/learning/teachers/lessons/archive.html)
1. Objectives	1. Objectives	1. Determine content	1. Lesson overview
2. Assess learner preparedness	2. Set induction	2. Objectives	2. Time needed
3. Resources needed	3. Input and modeling	3. Introduction	3. Objectives
4. Lesson description/procedure	4. Checking for understanding and guided practice	4. Instructional method	4. Learning resources
5. Closure	5. Independent practice	5. Lesson closure	5. Activities, procedures
6. Assessment/evaluation		6. Learner assessment	6. Assessment
			7. Extended activities
			8. Relationship to other subjects
			9. Relationship to standards

TABLE 6.4 Our Recommended Lesson Plan Format

1. Objectives—Indicate the lesson's objectives
2. Resources—Denote resources and materials to be used
3. Set Induction—Describe how the lesson will be introduced
4. Methodology—Describe how teaching and learning will take place
5. Assessment—Make clear how student learning will be determined
6. Closure—Provide for lesson ending
7. Reflection—Conside the lesson's effectiveness

6.18 What format inspires you? Why?

frequently students apply what they have learned. Formal assessments, frequently used at a lesson's conclusion, include worksheets, homework, and quizzes. No matter which assessment technique you use, remember that it must provide evidence of the students' progress toward the lesson's objectives. See Chapter 9.

6. *Closure.* How will the lesson be concluded? All lessons need a good finish. But what is a good finish? Normally it takes the form of a review that gets students to summarize what they have learned and connect it to prior and future learning. In Chapter 4, you saw that when information is well-organized and connected to students' prior knowledge, it likely enters their long-term memory. You also learned that a review should require learners to think about the new information,

to reflect on its application and its personal meaning. Many teachers conduct their review by asking students what they have learned or discovered.

7. *Reflection*. Now it's time to consider the experience you and your students have had and to learn from it. Following teaching, effective teachers ask questions such as:

- Did the students learn and were they satisfied? What might have been done to increase achievement and satisfaction?
- What are some things I learned from this teaching experience?

Chapter 14 provides considerable help if you wish to become a reflective, thoughtful teacher.

Highlight 6.6 contains an abbreviated lesson plan designed to help learners discriminate between the terms *theme* and *variation*. How would you improve the lesson if you were teaching toward the same objective? Eight more lesson plans are in Chapters 7 and 8. Highlight 6.7 on page 193 provides a sample of a plan for teaching computer functions.

You eventually need to develop your own style of lesson format unless the school district in which you teach mandates a particular one. Kagan and Tippins (1992) followed elementary and secondary student teachers into their classrooms to find out how they planned. Their study is reported in Spotlight on Research 6.4 on page 193.

Although instructional planning is a centerpiece of teacher preparation, it has not been the subject of much recent study. A few things we know about planning are found in Spotlight on Research 6.5 on page 194.

EVALUATING LESSON PLANS

An Instrument for Use in Assessing Your Lesson Plan   Given all that has been said in this chapter, here is a twenty item checklist that might be useful should you be challenged to prepare a lesson plan and evaluate it.

- ☐ 1. The lesson plan ties in with the curriculum.
- ☐ 2. The objectives are clear and measurable.
- ☐ 3. The objectives promote learning across the cognitive, affective, and psycho-motor domains when appropriate.
- ☐ 4. The objectives promote the highest reasonable level of learning in a given domain.
- ☐ 5. The objectives are appropriate to the diversity of the learners.
- ☐ 6. There are provisions in the lesson for informing learners of the objectives.
- ☐ 7. Instructional resources are available, appropriate, rich, and varied.
- ☐ 8. Technology resources are appropriate.
- ☐ 9. *Set induction* is provided.
- ☐ 10. The learning activities are clear.
- ☐ 11. The learning activities take into account what we know about learning.
- ☐ 12. The learning activities are appropriate for all learners.
- ☐ 13. The learning activities will likely result in learners meeting the lesson objectives.
- ☐ 14. There is a plan for ongoing monitoring of student learning.
- ☐ 15. There is a plan for assessing learner accomplishments at the lesson's conclusion.
- ☐ 16. Provisions are made for summarizing what has been learned, how it connects with past and future learning.
- ☐ 17. The lesson is achievable in terms of available time and space.
- ☐ 18. The plan takes into account what we know about good lessons. (See Spotlight on Research 6.3.)

Try Activities 6.6 and 6.7

Objectives

1. Given several objects of a common kind or theme—for example, automobiles or sunglasses—the learner will see likenesses and differences among them.
2. The learner will demonstrate understanding of *theme* by drawing six objects with the same shape.
3. The learner will demonstrate understanding of *variation* by varying characteristics of the objects.

Resources

1. Pictures of a variety of automobiles
2. A variety of sunglasses
3. Paper, crayons, or markers

Set Induction (preparing learners to grasp the concepts *theme* and *variation* by causing them to think of themes and variations within their personal experience)

1. Show pictures of automobiles. "What is the same about each object in our pictures?" (all are automobiles) "What is different about the automobiles?" (color, shape, size)
2. Show sunglasses "What is the same about these objects?" (all are sunglasses) "What is different about them?" (color, shape, size)

3. "Can you think of other objects that have something in common yet are somewhat different?" (people, animals, toys)
4. "Today, we are going to learn two new words we can use to describe things that have something in common yet are somewhat different."

Methodology

1. "The two new words we want to explore are *theme* and *variation*. Print words on chalkboard.
2. "If I said that these pictures [hold up automobile pictures] have a common theme, what do you suppose I mean?" (They are alike in some way.) "What is the common theme?" (They are all automobiles). Underneath the word *theme* on the chalkboard, write *automobiles*.
3. Repeat steps 1 and 2 with sunglasses.
4. "We know that things with something in common can also be different, or vary, in certain ways. As you said, automobiles and sunglasses have variations." Point to the word *variation* on the chalkboard. "How did you say they vary?" (They vary in size, shape, color.) Write *size, shape, color* underneath the term *variation* on the chalkboard.

5. "Do you think you can show that you understand the words *theme* and *variation?* Draw a group of objects that have a common theme but also show variation. Perhaps you could draw six leaves or six books or anything else that comes to mind."
6. "What ideas do you have for showing *theme* and *variation*, or what we call 'variations of a theme'?"
7. Pass out paper. Instruct students to fold paper into six sections and to draw one object in each section.
8. Circulate to guide, monitor, and assess understanding. Ask individuals, "What theme are you using?" and "What variation?"
9. Ask learners to share their themes and variations.

Assessment

1. See Methodology steps 8 and 9.

Closure

1. "What two new words did you learn today?"
2. "What does each word mean?"
3. "Why do you think these words are important? Why is it important to be able to notice likenesses and differences?"

☐ 19. Thought has been given to what might go wrong.
☐ 20. I will like teaching to my plan and learners should learn and be satisfied.

Lesson Plans Online For a list of online resources for lesson plans on a variety of topics, see Highlight 6.8 on page 194.

THE "BACKWARD DESIGN" IDEA OF LESSON AND UNIT PLANNING

The processes we have just described for planning lessons and units are characterized as backward planning in that, when designing an instructional event, you are asked *to begin at the end*—to set learning objectives describing exactly what learners should know or be able do to at the completion of instruction. However, an entire

HIGHLIGHT 6.7
A Framework for Use When Planning Lessons on Computer Functions

Here is another lesson plan format. This one intends to help specifically when you want students to learn how to use any major computer function (word processing, reports, spreadsheets, databases, graphics, presentations, or Internet searches).

NTeQ (iNtegrating Technology for inQuiry) provides a unique lesson plan format that helps design learning activities promoting computer use and literacy. Its lesson plan steps have been modified for inclusion as follows:

- *Setting Objectives:* What should learners know and be able to do?
- *Matching objectives to computer functions* such as word processing, spreadsheets, databases, presentations, or Internet searches. Which objectives can be

accomplished using which computer function(s)?
- *Using the functions:* How specifically will learners use the computer functions to reach objectives? Will they create a word processing document, create a spreadsheet, create a database, prepare a report, or navigate websites?
- *Presentation of results:* How will learners present the results of their work (written, slide show, poster. . .)?
- *Activities prior to using the computer:* What will learners need to do in preparation to using the computer?
- *Computer activities:* What will learners do at the computer? (For example, learners will look for Internet sites related to the objective.)

- *Activities after using the computer:* What will learners do after using the computer? (Will they compile information, prepare a report?)
- *Evaluation:* How will student success be measured?

NTeQ has a website with links to a related book by Morrison & Lowther (2001), PowerPoint presentations, and a "lesson planner" where you can see samples of plans for all grade levels and subjects wherein computers are used as a primary learning tool. Go to Integrating Computer Technology in the Classroom website.

 Web Link
Integrating Computer
Technology in the Classroom

SPOTLIGHT ON RESEARCH 6.4
Three Things We Know about Teacher Planning

1. Preservice teachers are encouraged to use the *objectives-based planning model*, a modification of which is described in "Parts of a Lesson Plan." However, classroom teachers generally do not use that linear planning model. Rather, they focus on what content is to be taught and how it can best be learned, student needs and interests, and available teaching resources.

2. Teacher planning is very idiosyncratic, varying from teacher to teacher. It is affected by, among other things, the teacher's experience; age, experience and interests of the students; the nature of the subject matter (whether it is language arts or math); the availability of teaching and learning materials and resources; administrator demands; and time.

3. Typically, teachers devote 12 hours per week to instructional planning. Most of the planning of instruction resides in teachers' heads rather than in detailed lesson plans. Experienced teachers are less likely to see the benefits of written plans. However, teachers who have daily plans have higher student achievement (Ball, 2007).

---

related school of thought called **backward design** has emerged and asks more (Wiggins & McTighe, 2001). Here is a description of that process.

Stage 1 requires that the lesson or unit's objectives focus on six particular "understandings" similar to some of Bloom's higher-order thinking skills noted in Table 6.2. Namely, learners should

- be able to explain: Cognitive domain, "Comprehension"
- be able to interpret: Cognitive domain, "Analysis"

Kagan and Tippins (1992) asked five elementary and seven secondary student teachers at the University of Georgia and the University of Alabama to assist them in answering this question. Because they wanted to see what would happen naturally, the researchers asked the cooperating teachers not to require their student teachers to use any particular lesson plan format. However, Kagan and Tippins gave the student teachers a format with six components: objectives, motivation, major activities, closure, student evaluation, and homework or follow-up. They then asked the student teachers to modify the format so that it worked for them.

As the semester went on, Kagan and Tippins found that (1) elementary teachers' plans became briefer and less detailed, while secondary teachers' plans became more detailed; (2) elementary teachers' plans focused more on learning activities, while secondary teachers focused more on incorporating an outline of a lecture into their plan, and (3) elementary teachers regarded written plans as ways of organizing for the lesson, but preferred to behave spontaneously rather than according to a "script."

The investigators cite the limitations of their study, particularly that only twelve student teachers were involved.

However, they conclude that lesson plan formats probably differ not only between novice elementary and secondary teachers but also as a function of the lesson's academic content. Furthermore, Kagan and Tippins suggest that "it would probably be more productive to define lesson plans as lists of major instructional procedures" (p. 487) and that planners should not be required to list "objectives" and "materials" if they are self-evident in the instructional materials. They also suggest that requiring a section on "evaluation" may promote overuse of formal testing.

Planning successful lessons is a challenging daily activity. Following are some websites that provide access to thousands of lesson plans that might be useful to you. Remember, however, that any plan developed by another teacher for another group of students will need to be modified to meet your curriculum and your learners' needs.

- Lesson Plan Page
- Educator's Reference Desk—Lesson Plans
- Yahoo: Education K–12
- Columbia Education Center
- The Gateway: Collections List
- Lesson Plan Archive
- New York Times Learning Network
- Discovery Education
- Lesson Plan Library
- Teachers Net

Web Links

Lesson Plans Online

- be able to apply: Cognitive domain, "Application"
- have perspective: Cognitive domain, "Evaluation"
- be able to empathize: Affective domain, "Valuing"
- have self-knowledge: Affective domain, "Organization"

Having established the lesson or unit's objectives at a high level, in stage 2 you must determine how you will know learners have accomplished them. To do so, you prepare an assessment or test characterized by performance measures that require learners to demonstrate the above listed six understandings. (Look at the end-of-chapter activities. Which of them are performance measures of the six understandings?)

Stage 3 coincides with normal planning procedure in that it asks: What must learners do to produce the required performances? How can they learn best?

What distinguishes backward design is its focus on using the six understandings and preparing a lesson or unit assessment procedure in advance of teaching. School districts are trying to use backward design with mixed results (Greece Central School District, Ravenswood Heights). The Teaching Today website demonstrates backward design.

RESOURCES USEFUL WHEN PLANNING

As you make either long- or short-range plans, you will need to locate and use two kinds of resources, *curriculum guides* and *instructional material.*

Curriculum Guides   A *curriculum guide* will tell you what you are expected to teach. In a previous section, The Formal Curriculum, you learned that such guides prescribe what the state and your school district want students to know and be able to do.

A detailed "Guide to Curriculum Development" is available at the Connecticut State Department of Education website. To check out actual guides related to state standards in several subject matter areas search "Connecticut Curriculum Frameworks."

Instructional Material   *Instructional materials* include those things that assist student learning of the curriculum. They include:

- Resource units, which often are available from your state education department, federal agencies, professional associations, and special interest groups including business and industry. A resource unit is a plan for teaching something in the curriculum, for example, the Constitution.
- Textbooks and other print material.
- Nonprint material, for example illustrations, audio and videotapes, and computer-related material as instructional software.

Resources useful when planning instruction are available in your college or education libraries, at school district locations, and at state education departments. Another way to find instructional material is to search online using the Educational Resources Information Center (ERIC). ERIC is a national information network designed to provide you with ready access to educational literature such as curriculum guides, unit plans, lesson plans, ideas for innovative instruction, descriptions of promising practices, and so forth.

For your use we have added selected websites for many subject areas in Highlight 6.9.

Finally, don't forget that knowledgeable parents and community persons can be great resources for some areas of study.

COLLABORATIVE, COOPERATIVE, OR TEAM PLANNING

Normally, you alone will plan what and how your students will learn. However, at some time when planning, you will solicit the assistance of other teachers or your students. You will use either teacher-team or teacher-pupil planning.

Teacher-team planning often occurs when courses of study or units are being prepared. The principal benefit is that two or more teacher heads often are better than one. Team planning results in sharing purposes, materials, expectations, and instructional ideas. Since teachers tend to be social and gregarious, team planning also can satisfy the need for affiliation and interaction, discussed in Chapter 13.

Teacher-pupil planning is based on the notions that students should learn how to guide or direct their own learning and that they have the motivation and ability to do so. Teacher-pupil planning derives credibility from the fact that pupils are more likely to be responsive to events they helped plan than to events planned for them. Teacher-pupil planning provides the opportunity to plan activities that students perceive as more engaging and interesting. Last but not least, advocates note that the process can be an exercise in citizenship and responsibility.

 Web Links
Greek Central School District
Ravenswood Heights
Teaching Today

 Web Links
Connecticut Curriculum
Frameworks

 Web Link
Educational Resources
Information Center

Go to the Online Learning Center to connect with these sites.

ART
Art Cyclopedia
Incredible Art Department
The Getty

ENGLISH/LANGUAGE ARTS
Awesome Library: English
English Starting Points
National Council of Teachers of English

FOREIGN LANGUAGE
American Council of the Teaching of Foreign Languages

Annenberg Media Learner (good for all subject areas)
Foreign Language Teaching Forum

HEALTH
Great Sites for Teaching About Health
Resources for Teaching Health

MATH
The Access Center
Arithmetic Classroom Materials
Elementary School Teachers' Place
Mega Math
Open Directory

MUSIC
Children's Music Web
Music Education Online
Music Teachers' National Association

SCIENCE
National Science Teachers Association
Science Spiders
Understanding Science

SOCIAL STUDIES
History/Social Studies Website for K–12 Teachers
National Council for the Social Studies

A few cautions about teacher-pupil planning. Such planning should not stray too far from course, unit, or lesson objectives. Consequently, a secure teacher who can hold students to responsible, reasonable boundaries and standards should monitor and guide the planning process. Not all classes and students may be ready for this responsibility, and teacher-pupil planning must be tempered accordingly. While time-consuming on the front end, advocates claim it results in greater student interest and time-on-task.

Overall, teacher-pupil planning requires skill and considerable forbearance. Teachers who use this technique must be able and willing to provide time, support, guidance, ideas, and resources. Time and effort aside, assisting students in planning what and how they may learn makes a great deal of sense if one of our goals as teachers is to help students become self-directed learners.

6.19 What do you feel are the advantages of collaborative planning?

COMPARATIVE PLANNING

It is interesting and informative sometimes to compare educational practices across cultures; for example the ways Chinese teachers plan as compared with the way we do it. See Highlight 6.10.

Some Final Thoughts

Anything important deserves to be planned. Teaching is so important it deserves to be well-planned! Furthermore, studies make clear that if you are a businesslike yet flexible planner then you and your students are more likely to enjoy achievement and satisfaction. However, some of us are planners and some are not. Whatever the case, your planning habits are well ingrained, and you will bring them to the classroom. Take heart. You can overcome. If you are not a natural planner, knowledge of planning and determination to plan can serve you well.

There are no absolutes about instructional planning, for example how to plan a unit or a lesson, and most schools will not prescribe how those things must be done. Your challenge is to find out what kind of planning serves you and your learners best.

Chinese teachers first map out the content they must teach for the semester. They then plan units of work and finally individual lessons. When planning individual lessons, teachers are expected to make sure the lessons relate directly to the larger unit and the semester content.

A lesson plan contains these parts: cognitive and affective objectives, key content to be taught and learned, and anticipated difficulties students may encounter. The plan also outlines the lesson flow—how the lesson will be introduced, how the knowledge will be presented, and how the knowledge will be applied by students, along with a summary and homework assignment. Every effort is made to connect each lesson to students' everyday lives. Before the lesson is taught, teachers select teaching materials and aids. During and following the lesson teachers takes notes for later reflection and improvement.

Chinese teachers share and study each others' plans and seek input from their colleagues. They also observe each other teaching.

An elementary teacher in China has at least two periods daily to prepare lesson plans. Secondary teachers have more time.

Chinese teachers complain that so much emphasis on planning detracts from other important professional responsibilities. (Shen, Poppink, Cui, & Fan, 2007)

Compare and contrast planning by Chinese and American teachers. What are the plusses and minuses of each?

You will be OK if you regularly demonstrate that you know what your students must know and be able to do and that you have deliberate plans to get them there.

Part of instructional planning, especially short-range, is selecting ways of teaching a lesson that are most likely to be effective. In the next two chapters you will learn about eight ways of teaching that are best known and powerful.

CHAPTER SUMMARY

- Thoughtful instructional planning is extremely important for you and your learners. It will likely ensure that you will teach with greater confidence and more creativity. And, importantly, it should assure that you will accomplish your instructional purposes. Thoughtful planning is important to students because you will have taken into account their diversity, how they learn best, and what interests and motivates them. Thoughtful planning is the prelude to good teaching.

- The first task of planning is determining what it is that you are responsible for helping students to learn. That curriculum results from your state education department which establishes state standards and from your local school district that uses the standards to prescribe what is taught in schools. School districts prepare curriculum guides for teachers showing what is to be taught in each subject at each grade level. Teachers use these guides to develop long- and short-range instructional plans.

- The second task of planning is the preparation of instructional objectives that clearly indicate what students are expected to know and be able to do. There are three commonly used domains of instructional objectives: cognitive, affective, and psychomotor. When possible, effective instruction draws upon each. When possible, effective instruction encourages learners to function at the highest levels within each domain.

- Teachers are advised to prepare specific objectives as part of their instructional plans because they can be used to let learners know exactly what they are expected to know and be able to do. Such instructional objectives contain

SUPPLEMENTAL RESOURCES
Go to the text's Online Learning Center at www.mhhe.com/cruickshank6e to access the chapter's **study tools** including web links, practice for Praxis™ case studies and video clips.

four kinds of information. They designate the target audience, the learning outcomes expected of the audience, the conditions under which the audience is to exhibit the learned abilities, and the degree or amount of proficiency expected.

- Instructional objectives are good when they are relevant to the curriculum for which learners are held accountable; achievable by your learners; promote learning in as many of the three domains as feasible; and pursue higher-order cognition, affective, or psychomotor skill.

- Research supports that learners benefit when they know what the instructional objectives are and when they result in learning experiences that are neither too easy nor too difficult.

- Instructional plans are of varying duration: long-range (semester, year), intermediate-range (monthly, weekly), short-range (daily, lesson). Since all are important and useful, teachers should be able to craft each.

- Lesson plans are critical. There are many formats for use in writing them and unless required to use one, you should find a model that you like. The format we like has seven parts: objectives, resources, set induction, methodology, assessment, closure, and reflection. As teachers gain classroom experience and wisdom, plans are more brief and focus more on the learning activities (methodology).

KEY TERMS

Benchmarks, 172	Instructional objective, 174	Lesson plan, 187
State standards, 172	Cognitive domain, 176	Set induction, 188
Alignment, 173	Affective domain, 177	Anticipatory set, 188
Formal curriculum, 173	Psychomotor domain, 178	Backward design, 193
Taught curriculum, 174	Unit plan, 183	

ISSUES AND PROBLEMS FOR DISCUSSION

ISSUES   Here are some questions worthy of debate in your class.

1. What are the major obstacles you see to good instructional planning?
2. Should written plans be mandated?
3. What must a teacher think about when planning instruction?
4. What kinds of persons under what circumstances might be able to teach off-the-cuff, that is, without a plan?
5. Should lessons be standardized across teachers to ensure they are on target and well-formulated? (See Highlight 6.2.)

PROBLEMS   Following are some planning problems teachers report. What would you do in each circumstance?

Problem 1.   "What a mess! Some students finished the task in 10 minutes, some are still working on it and half an hour has passed. There are two or three that won't finish if they have another half hour. It's getting dicey."

Problem 2.   "I try to get the kids to use a lot of different resource materials. Many of them can't find anything related to their topics. Some who find stuff can't understand most of it. Lots of times I think we should just stick to the text. It's handy and readable."

Problem 3. "My principal wants to see a week's lesson plans each Friday. She says she wants to see how I am doing and offer suggestions. Maybe, but I am swamped and don't know how I can do this and keep my sanity. I need the weekend to plan what I am going to do the next week."

Problem 4. "Wouldn't you know. Now we are supposed to show how each one of our lessons is 'aligned' with some state standard and 'benchmark.' Teaching is getting pretty prescriptive. I can remember when other countries used to follow our lead. It seems we are teaching what they were 20 years ago. What happened to helping kids become more creative?"

Problem 5. "Technology. Wonderful, when it works. Spent beau coup time planning a lesson that students would do online. Computers are down. Just like the TVs that don't work. I am up the creek without a paddle. We need a school tech person."

Problem 6. "Today students were removed from the room in groups to take hearing tests. I could not continue with my plans because so many children were continually gone. Then, many of the children had to be retested because the tests were invalid. My daily plans were completely altered, and I accomplished very little teaching."

Problem 7. "Our lesson required use of the textbook and a state map. Many pupils arrived without one or the other, claiming they had forgotten them."

THEORY INTO ACTION: ACTIVITIES FOR PRACTICE AND YOUR PORTFOLIO

ACTIVITY 6.1: Recognizing Domains and Levels of Instructional Objectives Given the following specific objectives, identify the level of each according to Bloom or Simpson by placing an X in the correct boxes.

1. Given a list of spelling words, each learner will use each word in a sentence and spell it correctly.
   Domain: ☐ cognitive   ☐ affective   ☐ psychomotor
   Level: ☐ knowledge   ☐ comprehension   ☐ application
   ☐ analysis   ☐ synthesis   ☐ evaluation
2. Given a reading assignment in Rawlings's novel *The Yearling*, each learner will make a judgment about the correctness of the Baxters' decision to kill Flag the fawn.
   Domain: ☐ cognitive   ☐ affective   ☐ psychomotor
   Level: ☐ receiving/attending   ☐ responding   ☐ valuing
   ☐ organization   ☐ characterization
3. At the conclusion of the typing course, each learner will demonstrate proficiency by typing 60 words a minute with five or fewer errors.
   Domain: ☐ cognitive   ☐ affective   ☐ psychomotor
   Level: ☐ perception   ☐ set   ☐ guided response   ☐ mechanism
   ☐ complex or overt response   ☐ adaptation   ☐ origination

ACTIVITY 6.2: Recognizing Well-Written Specific Instructional Objectives Read each of the following objectives and determine whether it is well-written. If it is, label the parts A, B, C, D. If it is unclearly written, rewrite it as a good-quality specific instructional objective and label the four parts.

- When dissecting a frog, the student will identify organs of the digestive system.
- Given a worksheet containing 20 addition examples requiring regrouping, the student will correctly complete 17.
- The class will know how to use a dictionary for an in-class oral quiz tomorrow.
- Students will be able to list and describe four types of soccer kicks or passes with 100 percent accuracy.

ACTIVITY 6.3: Developing a Long-Range Plan Do the following to learn more about long-range planning.

- Talk with classroom teachers or your college instructors about how they plan for a year-long or semester-long course.
- Look through state or local school district courses of study, curriculum guides, and subject matter curriculum standards (Table 6.1) to see how they can help you in course planning.
- Develop a long-range plan for something you likely will teach during your field experiences or that you hope to teach as a beginning teacher. As part of that long-range plan, it might be helpful to

  a. consult the state or school district course of study to learn the requirements for such a course.
  b. talk with teachers who teach this course to determine what they include in the course and how and why they make those decisions.
  c. collect and file as many related resources (print and nonprint) as you can.
  d. determine the main topics the course will include and establish the order in which you will present them.
  e. think about who the learners will be in the course and their interests, aptitudes, and past experiences.
  f. write *general* objectives you want to accomplish in the course.
  g. subdivide the course topics into parts or units and assign a time for each.
  h. decide how you will be able to tell whether learners have accomplished the course goals and are satisfied with the course.

ACTIVITY 6.4: Developing a Unit Plan Do the following activities to learn more about unit planning.

- If you are working in a school, talk with your mentor or cooperating teacher about unit planning. How does he or she organize various activities, experiences, and types of learning around topics, central problems, or areas of interest?
- Look over units your mentor teacher or university professor may have. Also, check to see if any are available through the professional education library or a materials resource center on campus.
- Develop a unit plan that contributes to the long-range plan you developed for Activity 6.3. If you didn't design a long-range plan, design a unit on some topic you probably will teach.

ACTIVITY 6.5: Recognizing Variations on the Theme of Lesson Planning Look at different lesson plans that are available to you from your mentor teacher, education instructor, or other professional education students.

- What format similarities do they share?
- What is different about each lesson plan?
- Which format would be most useful to you when teaching?

ACTIVITY 6.6: Obtaining Classroom Teachers' Views of Lesson Planning If you are doing fieldwork, talk with your mentor teacher about how he or she plans a lesson. You might consider asking some of the following questions.

- When do you develop your lesson plans? How much time does it take each day or each week?
- What information do you write out in the lesson plan?
- Do you have the lesson plan in front of you when you teach?
- How do you know when to change or vary the lesson you have planned?
- What advice would you give a new teacher about planning?

ACTIVITY 6.7: Observing the Implementation of a Lesson Plan Observe a fellow student or teacher implementing a lesson. Did the teacher provide for each of the following? If so, describe briefly what the teacher did with regard to each:

- Set induction.
- Communication of objective(s).
- Methodology.
- Provision for diverse students.
- Closure or summary.
- Assessment.
- Practice.

ACTIVITY 6.8: Developing and Evaluating a Lesson Plan Develop a lesson plan for something you likely will, or hope to, teach. If you have developed a unit plan, as suggested in Activity 6.4, plan a lesson for use within that unit. Or you might develop a lesson plan for one of the Reflective Teaching Lessons contained in Unit 2 of the Practice Teaching Manual. Follow the format for lesson plans presented in this chapter. Be sure to include all the essential parts.

When you have completed the lesson plan, use the checklist on pages 191–192 to evaluate it.

REFERENCES

Airasian, P. W., & Russell, M. (2008). *Classroom assessment.* New York: McGraw-Hill.

Ball, A. L., Knobloch, N. A., & Hoop, S. (2007). Instructional planning experiences of beginning teachers. *Journal of Agricultural Education, 48*(2), 162–169.

Bloom, B. (Ed.). (1989). *Taxonomy of educational objectives. Handbook I: Cognitive domain.* Upper Saddle River, NJ: Allyn & Bacon.

Cooper, P., & McIntyre, D. (1994). Patterns of interaction between teachers' and students' classroom thinking, and their implications for the provision of learning opportunities. *Teaching and Teacher Education, 10*(6), 633–646.

Danielson, C. (2002). *Enhancing student achievement.* Alexandria, VA: Association for Supervision and Curriculum Development.

Dawson, K. (2002, Fall). Best discipline is good curriculum. *Rethinking schools online: An urban education resource, 17*(1).

El-Tigi, M. (2001). How to develop a lesson plan. An AskERIC write-a-lesson plan guide. Access: http://eric.syr.edu/Virtual/Lessons/Guide.html

Gagné, R., Wager, W., Golas, K., & Keller, J. (2004). *Principles of of instructional design.* Belmont, CA: Wadsworth.

Galvin, B. (n.d.). *Reflections on teaching: Reflective writing task.* Ann Arbor:

University of Michigan. Access: #1.http://sitemaker.umich.edu/brian.galvin/reflective_writing_task_1

Glatthorn, A. (1987). *Curriculum renewal.* Alexandria, VA: Association for Supervision and Curriculum Development.

Greece Central School District, Backward Design website. Access: www.greece.k12.ny.us/instruction/ela/6-12/BackwardDesign/BDstep4.htm

Hunter, R. (2004). Mastery teaching. El Segundo, Thousand Oaks, CA: Sage Publications.

Jacobson, D., Eggen, P., & Kauchak, D. (2009). *Methods for teaching.* Ramsey, NJ: Allyn & Bacon.

Johnston, R. (1999, October 13). In Chicago, every day brings a new lesson plan. *Education Week, 19*(7), 1, 10–11.

Kagan, D. M., & Tippins, D. J. (1992). The evolution of functional lesson plans among twelve elementary and secondary student teachers. *The Elementary School Journal, 92*(4), 477–490.

Kendall, J., & Marzano, R. (2000). *Content knowledge.* Alexandria, VA: Association for Supervision and Curriculum Development.

Krathwohl, D. (2002, Autumn). Revision of Bloom's taxonomy. *Theory into Practice, 41*(4), 212–219.

Marzano, R. (2003). *What works in schools.* Alexandria, VA: Association for Supervision and Curriculum Development.

Marzano, R. (2009, September). Setting the record straight on "high yield" strategies. *Phi Delta Kappan, 91*(1), 30–37.

Marzano, R., Pickering, D., & Pollock, J. (2001). *Classroom instruction that works.* Alexandria, VA: Association for Supervision and Curriculum Development.

Moore, K. (2000). *Classroom teaching skills.* New York: McGraw-Hill.

Morrison, G., & Lowther, D. (2001). *Integrating computer technology into the classroom.* Upper Saddle River, NJ: Prentice-Hall.

National Governors' Association. (1990, February). Report adopted by members of the National Governors' Association.

Ohio Department of Education Online. Access: http://ims.ode.state.oh.us/ODE/IMS/Lessons/default.asp

Pinzur, M. (2006, August 7). Lesson plans aim for smooth start. *Miami Herald online.* Access: www.miamiherald.com

Porter, A. (2003). *Measuring the content of instruction.* Madison, WI: Wisconsin Center for Educational Research.

Public Education Network. (2003). *Voice of the new teacher.* Washington, DC: The Network.

Ravenswood Heights [School], Tasmania, Australia. Access: www.Itag.education.tas.gov.au/transschools/ravenswd.htm

Renninger, K. A., Hidi, S., & Krapp, A. (1992). *The role of interest in learning and development.* Hillsdale, NJ: Erlbaum.

Shen, J., Poppink, S., Cui, Y., & Fan, G. (2007, Summer). Lesson Planning: A practice of professional responsibility and development. *Educational Horizons, 85*(4), 248–256.

Simpson, E. (1972). *The classification of educational objectives: Psychomotor domain.* Urbana: University of Illinois Press.

Slavin, R. (2008). *Educational psychology,* Eighth Edition. Boston: Allyn & Bacon.

Snowman, J., & Biehler, R. (2005). *Psychology applied to teaching.* Eleventh Edition. Boston: Houghton Mifflin.

Sternberg, Robert J. (1997, March). What does it mean to be smart? *Educational Leadership, 54*(6), 20–24.

Wiggins, G., & McTighe, J. (2001). *Understanding by design.* Upper Saddle River, NJ: Prentice-Hall.

Yinger, R. (1980). A study of teacher planning. *The Elementary School Journal, 80,* 114–115.

Four Instructional Alternatives: Presentation, Discussion, Independent Study, and Individualized Instruction

Conversation Starters

How to teach? Let me count the ways.

There are dozens of ways to teach called instructional alternatives.
How do you think teachers should teach? How do you think you will teach?

When planning instruction, decisions are made regarding *what to teach, how to teach it,* and *how learning will be assessed.* Chapter 6 focussed on the first challenge. It described how what is taught is determined, how that curriculum is translated into objectives students are expected to accomplish, and how instructional plans such as units of work and lessons are prepared to accomplish those objectives.

This chapter and the next look at the second challenge, that is *how to teach.* Over time, a number of ways of teaching have been developed, modified, and even combined. We call these ways of teaching **instructional alternatives.** Thirty-one are displayed in Figure 7.5 on page 246. Instructional alternatives can be classified as either *teacher* or *learner* centered. *Teacher-centered strategies* assume that learning is best accomplished when teachers provide learners with knowledge: facts, concepts, and understandings. Students learn by listening to the teacher, reading texts, practice, drill, and answering related questions. On the other hand, *learner-centered strategies* are based on the belief that students learn best through discovering or coming to know things for themselves and through problem solving. Some instructional alternatives are clearly one or the other. As you will see, others are hybrids.

As a novice teacher, you are not expected to be knowledgeable of and proficient in each or even most of them. However, over time, instructional variety will serve you well. Surely you can recall teachers who kept classes interesting and lively by engaging students in many kinds of learning activities such as demonstrations, debates, and simulations. These teachers, like acclaimed actors, were multitalented. Their classes were stimulating and fun to be in. You will learn more about the importance of using variety in Spotlight on Research 7.1 and in Chapter 11.

In order to start you down the road to becoming a multitalented, versatile teacher, in this chapter and the next, you will take an in-depth look at eight instructional alternatives. Particularly helpful should be the tables that summarize what is known about each, the sample lesson plans, and the end of chapter Theory Into Action activities that allow you to prepare different kinds of lessons and perhaps teach them to your peers.

We begin our quest to become multitalented teachers by investigating four commonly used instructional alternatives: *presentation, discussion, independent study,* and *individualized instruction.*

CHAPTER 7

Presentations: Teaching as Telling and Showing

WHAT IS A PRESENTATION?

A **presentation** is an informative talk a more knowledgeable person makes to less knowledgeable persons. You present when you tell less informed students when to use a semicolon, why the seasons change, or how to multiply fractions.

Presentations are akin to what cognitive learning theorists call "expository teaching" and "reception learning"—expository because the teacher is "putting on a show," reception learning because students are its recipient. (See Chapter 4, "Cognitive Approaches to Teaching and Learning.")

Showing can enhance telling, so teachers often accompany their talks with demonstrations. For example, in addition to telling students why the seasons change, you might also use a film, videotape, computer graphic, or a mechanical model to provide a visual demonstration.

PURPOSE AND CHARACTERISTICS OF TEACHER PRESENTATIONS

The purpose of a presentation is *to inform an audience of certain facts, ideas, concepts, and explanations.* However, talks can be very different in terms of length, formality, and who does the talking. Think of the many different kinds you have experienced.

7.1 Think of presentations you have experienced. What made some good and some bad?

Students benefit when teachers use a variety of instructional strategies. Wasley and her colleagues (1997) reached this conclusion after following high school students for three years and finding that students whose teachers' use instructional variety are more interested in school and more likely to invest their time in academics.

Typically, at the beginning of a year she found students were enthusiastic about school. However, by midyear they displayed frustration with the routines and sameness of instruction. They wanted to "cut-out"—to depart from the lock step of learning they felt controlled by. Fortunately, the researchers found some teachers who used instructional variety that kept learners with them, interested, and intellectually challenged.

Wasley (1999) believes that most teachers do not demonstrate instructional variation because they have limited images of good teaching and have not learned a variety of instructional strategies or had the opportunity to practice them.

Chapter 11 clearly shows how and why using variety results in increased learning and learner satisfaction and why.

In terms of length, some were long and some were short. At times, a teacher presented or talked for a whole class period, without interruptions or questions. Perhaps the teacher said he would answer your questions at the end, but by then you had forgotten what to ask. Other talks were of short duration.

Teacher presentations also vary according to degree of formality. Speeches are, of course, more formal than talks, and talks interspersed with teacher questions or student questions are even less formal. When teachers talk in order to force students to think or reflect, they are practicing a version of what is called the Socratic technique. The Greek philosopher Socrates taught by questioning his listeners about their views and opinions (What do you think?) and then interrogating them further about what they said (Why do you think that?). He talked in order to probe his listeners' minds and to force them to confront their thoughts and ideas.

A third dimension of teacher presentation has to do with the presenter. Is she the teacher, a guest (perhaps another teacher, or a parent or community figure), or a student? Teachers working together to share their expertise engage in what is called **team teaching** or collaborative teaching. Sometimes the collaborator isn't even present. An image and voice may reach us by television, computer, radio, or telephone. When prerecorded presentations are used as part of individualized, self-paced instructional programs, they are referred to as audio, or audiovisual, tutorials. To illustrate, students in Spanish might watch a videotaped analysis of a classic novel such as Cervantes's *Don Quixote*.

Figure 7.1 reviews the purpose and key attributes of a presentation.

"Before giving my report, I want to say my dress is by Vivace, my shoes by Gelding and Strauss, my accessories by the Shantz Collection, and my hair and make-up is by J. Cuthright."

FIGURE 7.1   Purpose and Key Characteristics of a Presentation

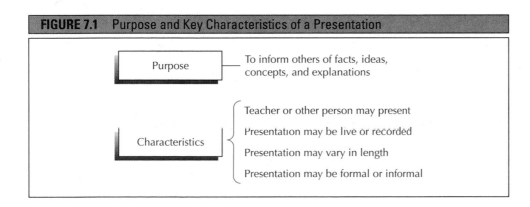

Purpose	To inform others of facts, ideas, concepts, and explanations
Characteristics	Teacher or other person may present
	Presentation may be live or recorded
	Presentation may vary in length
	Presentation may be formal or informal

CHAPTER 7
Four Instructional Alternatives:
Presentation, Discussion, Independent
Study, and Individualized Instruction

www.mhhe.com/cruickshank6e

205

GOOD PRESENTERS

Before making a presentation, you must believe that your learners can best gain particular knowledge or skill by attending, looking, and listening to you or another presenter. There is no other, better way by which the learner can learn. For example, say your students need to learn how to divide fractions. After looking at instructional resources that students might use to accomplish this goal, you conclude that you can best teach the process yourself and perhaps do it in less time.

In addition, you believe that when giving a presentation you can better monitor how well students are learning: you can observe the extent to which the students seem to grasp what they need to learn. Finally, and importantly, you believe that you are a good presenter.

7.2 Given the characteristics of good presenters, which do you feel you have and which must you further develop? How might you do so?

What are good presenters like? How can you become one? On a personal level, you should be friendly, humorous, enthusiastic, verbally fluent (in other words, talk effortlessly and smoothly), and clear (Wilen & Kindsvatter, 2004). Unfortunately, while such characteristics are helpful, they are not sufficient to make you a good presenter. You must also possess knowledge of your students (particularly with regard to their diversity) and, of course, have mastery of the subject you are presenting. In short, being a friendly, funny, dynamic, and talkative person will not do the job if you don't know your audience or what you are talking about. Don't be alarmed! Few people have all or even most of these desirable qualities. So everyone simply has to make the best of what they have and keep trying to improve. You cannot learn to teach overnight or even during your university preparation; it is a lifelong affair. You will find out how to be more humorous, enthusiastic, and clear in Chapters 10 and 11.

GOOD PRESENTATIONS

Persons who have thought about and studied the quality of teacher presentations tend to analyze them according to three primary factors: preparation, delivery, and closure (Bligh, 2000; Brown, 1987; Gage & Berliner, 1976; Rosenshine & Stevens, 1986). The following discussion centers on these three characteristics.

7.3 What, to you, are the most important characteristics of a good presentation?

Preparation   Getting ready for the presentation is key. First, establish the topic and the objectives learners need to achieve. Next, collect, review, and organize the available subject matter resources. Look for software, books, articles, films, videotapes, models, exhibits, and pictures. The use of visual aids can particularly increase students' interest and learning since we live in a visually-oriented society. Sources of such instructional materials include the classroom, school library, public library, Internet, museums, and students. Table 7.1 suggests how selected visual aids can improve presentations.

Try Activity 7.1

Suppose the topic is "Roman Numerals." What are the objectives of the presentation? Do students need to be able to read and write Roman numerals, know how Roman numerals are used today, know how the Romans used fractions, or compare and contrast Roman numerals with the decimal numeration system? Let's say your objectives are to ensure that learners recognize the basic Roman numerals (I, V, X, C, D, and M) and be able to use rules for creating other numerals from them such as II, IV, VI, IX, XI, and so forth.

Objectives in mind, you should ask, is a presentation the best way for students to accomplish the objectives or is there a better instructional alternative? Being able to answer the question affirmatively is critical. Why provide a presentation if students can learn better another way? Perhaps at this point, you see that it might be better to give your presentation a "discovery" twist. Maybe given the basic numerals, students can discover for themselves the rules used to construct other numerals from them.

TABLE 7.1 Improving Teachers' Presentations with Visual Aids

Visual Aids	Uses
Printed material that serves as advance organizers: handouts, outlines, "questions to think about"	Give these to your students before you begin your presentation to help students focus their attention and to guide their note taking during the presentation.
Overhead transparencies: outlines, drawings, charts, diagrams, maps, cartoons, quotes, key words and ideas	Use these at key times in your presentation to emphasize a point, to review, to organize and categorize information, to stimulate interest, to add a touch of humor, and to summarize.
Pictures and prints: photographs, paintings, posters, slides	Photographs or posters of important people, places, objects, and artwork can greatly aid student comprehension and stimulate interest.
"Clips" on videotape	Showing a segment of a newscast or some televised special can bring events and people to life.
Maps, wall charts, and globes	These can be especially useful if students have desk-size versions or their own small copies.
Concrete objects (manipulatives)	When possible, have examples for students to look at and handle. A lesson on trees could include different types of leaves and bark.

Source: The content of this table is attributed to Dr. Jeffrey Peck, Bethel College.

For our purposes here, let's consider the presentation approach is best.

With topic and objectives in mind and resources collected, you are now ready to review your subject and create a plan for your talk. Keep in mind the diversity of your students—their interests, abilities, and background knowledge. Be especially prepared to introduce concepts or ideas new to them. Perhaps besides introducing the concept of Roman numeration, you will want to introduce the underlying concept of "numeration systems." Highlight 7.1 provides suggestions about how to teach a new concept.

In summary, preparing a presentation includes (1) establishing the topic for the presentation and the learning objectives, (2) collecting and reviewing information to be presented, and (3) organizing or planning delivery.

Delivery When we talk about "delivery," we are talking about a teaching performance, about the presentation itself.

As noted earlier, presentation is akin to what cognitive learning theorists call *expository teaching* and *reception learning*. Certain rules apply. The rules, with illustrative examples for a lesson on Roman numerals, follow.

- *Focus student attention* (**set induction**). (Holding up pictures containing Roman numerals, the teacher asks, "Here is a 'code' that was invented long ago but is still used today. Does anyone know what this code might be? Where did it come from? Where have you seen it used?") Set induction was introduced on page 188 and is fully discussed in Chapter 11.

- *Present learners with the learning objectives*—tell them what they are expected to know and to be able to do and why that is important. ("We will learn about Roman numerals. You will recognize the basic numerals and understand rules for creating others.")

- *Use an advance organizer* (see Highlight 7.2 on page 209). Link what is to be learned to what students already know. ("What do you know about Roman numerals?")

- *Present information in an organized, step-by-step manner.* The better structured the lesson, the greater likelihood it will be followed and understood. ("First

CHAPTER 7
Four Instructional Alternatives:
Presentation, Discussion, Independent
Study, and Individualized Instruction

www.mhhe.com/cruickshank6e

207

The term *concept* is used to refer to a group of ideas or objects that are alike and thus share a common name or label, such as tables, clouds, dogs, or dinosaurs. We learn many concepts through everyday experience rather than in school. Examples include hot, cold, wet, dry, loud, and quiet. However, a major function of formal education is to teach concepts. Remember when you were taught such concepts as "a meter," "carbon dioxide," "poetry," "the color wheel," "treble," and "long jump"? If your concepts were well taught, you learned and remembered them.

Teachers present concepts in at least two ways. Sometimes they describe a concept by presenting examples or illustrations. For example, you could tell students what a *peninsula* is—a peninsula is a long projection of land into water. Conversely, sometimes teachers ask students to discover what a concept is. In this instance, you could show students different peninsulas without describing their character and have students analyze what they have in common—peninsulas are large land masses that extend into water.

Since this section of the chapter is about presentations, the following is an example of how a teacher might use a presentation or expository technique to teach the peninsula concept. In the next chapter, when you get to the section on *discovery learning*, think about how you could teach concepts in *that* way.

1. Begin with a clear definition that describes the attributes of the concept: "A peninsula is a *land area almost entirely surrounded by water* and *connected to the mainland* by a single strip of land or isthmus." (The attributes are in italics.)

2. Next, provide examples of the concept and relate the examples to the definition: "Look at the map. Arabia and Alaska are the largest peninsulas in the world. India is a peninsula with a very large mainland connection. The Baja Peninsula in lower California is a typical peninsula. Florida is a peninsula. Each is an area of land almost circled by water."

3. Now provide nonexamples or negative examples: "Mexico is not a peninsula. It is connected to land on two sides. Australia is not a peninsula. It is completely surrounded by water."

4. Check for understanding: "Which of the following are peninsulas? Korea, Turkey, Italy, Scandinavia, Newfoundland, Greenland, South America? Why?"

---

we will learn the basic numerals and then how to combine them to form new ones.")

Try Activity 7.2

- *Provide explanations that are complete, accurate, and clear* (see Highlight 7.3). ("There are two rules for creating other numerals from the basic ones. They are . . .") Relatedly, don't overwhelm or underwhelm learners.

- *When teaching a new idea or concept, use both examples and non-examples of it.* ("Which of these are examples of Roman numerals and which are not? I, B, V, X, L, C, D, M, Y?") (See Highlight 7.1.) Use of examples and illustrations make concepts more clear and interesting. For example, you could use pictures containing examples of Roman numerals in order to reacquaint learners with them and to show that they are used in books, on watches and clocks, on buildings, and so forth.

- *Keep presentations short.* If longer than 20 minutes, change things by introducing variety or have learners review what has been presented.

- *Expect and solicit pupil interaction in the form of questions and comments.* ("Learning a code is never easy, so I expect you will have lots of questions. As we go along you may also have feelings about how the numeral system we use compares with what the Romans used.")

Support for these rules is found in Marzano and others (2004) and at the Center for Teaching website. Spotlight on Research 7.2 (on page 210) presents research findings on effective presentations.

OLC Web Link
Center for Teaching

HIGHLIGHT 7.2
"Advance Organizers" Help Students Learn

Prepare learners for receiving new information using advance organizers. Ausubel (2002) and Leinhardt (1992) describe four kinds. The best preparation occurs when we relate new information to information learners already know—when we connect the new with the old. For example, "Yesterday we talked about the election process for choosing a president. What did we learn? . . . Today we are going to learn about the part the electoral college plays in the process."

A second kind of advance organizer gives learners background knowledge needed in order to understand new knowledge. For example, "Today we are going to learn about word processing. However, before we can do that we need to know some things about how a computer works."

A third kind of advance organizer prepares learners to focus their attention on specific things so as to notice and understand them better. For example, "In this basketball film, pay particular attention to the defensive players. Notice what they do in common."

A fourth type of advance organizer helps learners follow your lesson. For example, if you give a lesson on rain forests, give them a skeletal outline to fill in as the lesson unfolds.

To see videos of teachers using different kinds of advance organizers, go to the Digital Edge Learning Interchange>advance organizers

 Web Link
Digital Edge Learning Interchange

HIGHLIGHT 7.3
Making a Good Explanation

Teachers use explanation for at least two purposes. In one case, we explain a concept (see Highlight 7.1), idea, procedure, or rule so as to make it understandable. Thus, we explain a concept (global warming), a procedure (how to subtract), or a rule (we raise our hand to be recognized). In a second case, we explain something in order to account for its occurrence: why global warming occurs, how the subtraction algorithm works, or why the class must raise hands. Here explanation is akin to giving reasons.

A good explanation has three characteristics: It must be

- complete,
- accurate, and
- clear

When you give an explanation, remember C-A-C.

Of course, students should be called on to give explanations too. The quality of their explanations can also be judged according to C-A-C guidelines.

Source: Cruickshank & Metcalf (1995).

Handouts You have undoubtedly attended presentations where the presenter distributed handouts containing an outline or related information. You probably found them helpful when they did any or all of the following: (1) made clear the purpose of the talk and what you were expected to know or to be able to do, (2) provided questions that helped you focus on important points, (3) contained an outline of the main points, or (4) included a quiz to check your understanding.

A compilation on making presentations is available from McMaster University.

 Web Link
McMaster

Closure How should you conclude the Roman numeral presentation? Several recommendations are consistent with what we know about short- and long-term memory and reception learning. Since you told learners what they *would learn* at the outset,

www.mhhe.com/cruickshank6e

CHAPTER 7
Four Instructional Alternatives:
Presentation, Discussion, Independent
Study, and Individualized Instruction

209

Studies of teacher presentations have been done at all educational levels (Doherty, 2004; McLeish, 1975). Findings include:

- The presenter's style increases retention. Presenters should be forceful and dynamic; they should use concrete objects and illustrations, simplify the complexity of what is to be learned, and present information slowly.

- For some students, attention falls off rapidly after the first 15 minutes of a presentation. At the 30- to 40-minute mark, the amount of information absorbed can be very low.
- Having students take notes during a presentation helps long-term but not short-term recall of information.
- For younger kids, speak slowly.
- Presentations are better than discussions for transmitting information but not as good for

promoting student thought or reflection.
- Learners prefer small- to large-class presentations.
- Underachieving learners (students who should be performing at a higher level) are helped by being given supplementary assignments that engage them in some form of related activity and provide them with knowledge of how well they understand.

now remind them of what they *have learned*. Review and summary are appropriate. Reiterate the major concepts, facts, and generalizations that you want learners to recall. Of course, you might consider drawing this information out of your students by way of questioning or recitation. Make them rummage around in their minds.

Next, connect what students have learned about numeration to what they knew prior to the presentation ("This is what you knew then. This is what you know now."). Help students see how their knowledge has grown with regard to what a numeration system is. Remember, this effort to tie new information to old enhances long-term memory and information retrieval.

Finally, check for understanding. Be especially sensitive to whether your students can use the information at the higher cognitive levels; demonstrating application, analysis, synthesis, and evaluation described in Chapter 6.

A summary of the qualities of good presenters and good presentations is contained in Table 7.2. This is one of several tables contained in this and the next chapter that you will want to keep handy for future reference.

A presentation lesson plan on Roman numerals appears as Lesson Plan 7.1 (on page 212). A presentation on the newspaper appears in Lesson Plan 7.2 (on page 213).

COMPUTER PRESENTATIONS: PROS AND CONS

Computer programs are available that permit teachers to add all kinds of visual and auditory aids to a presentation. Two such programs are Microsoft *PowerPoint* and *Mac Keynote*. You can go through an eight-unit tutorial on PowerPoint on the PowerPoint website. Catalyst also has a tutorial on its website. Click on Quick Links > Create a PowerPoint Presentation.

Increasingly, teachers are using one of these presentation aids. The teacher in Lesson Plan 7.1 could have made a computer presentation. If so, she might have used several slides: Slide 1 containing the lesson's objectives, Slide 2 containing questions such as What is a code?, Slide 3 containing examples and illustrated of Roman numerals, and so forth.

When students are asked to make presentations, they often are expected to make them via the computer. Microsoft provides an example.

> Seth, an eighth grader, is preparing a presentation on "earthquake preparedness." PowerPoint guides him step-by-step in developing an outline. Seth then considers how he will present the material in his outline on six slides. Then he plans a "title" slide,

OLC **Web Links**
PowerPoint Tutorial

Catalyst

Try Activity 7.3

7.4 What has been your experience with PowerPoint or other forms of computer-enhanced presentations?

TABLE 7.2 Qualities of Good Presenters and Good Presentations

Good Presenters Are . . .	Good Presentations Include . . .
• Knowledgeable about the subject matter • Aware of learner diversity • Friendly • Humorous • Enthusiastic • Verbally fluent and audible	*When preparing:* • Choose the topic • Set specific learner objectives • Collect, review subject matter and useful material • Plan the presentation • Prepare handouts *When delivering:* • Get students' attention • Tell students what they will learn and what they must be able to do • Relate new information to that already known • Present information step by step • Move from the general to the specific • Don't overwhelm or underwhelm • Emphasize important points • Use examples and illustrations to make things clearer • Use variety, such as visual aids, to maintain attention • Monitor understanding by promoting questions, comments • Avoid digressions *When closing:* • Review and summarize important points • Secure new learning to previous knowledge • Check for ability to apply what was learned and to use new knowledge at a higher cognitive level

and the last slide he will label "Questions?" Seth keeps in mind that the slides must be easy to read and uses color for contrast. (PowerPoint website)

Critics of computer presentations warn that they can be overused; be too similar to one another in style and look; and cause teachers to jam complex thoughts into brief snippets that fit onto a screen. Furthermore, although good for making points, they are not so good for introducing and encouraging reflection and discussion (Keller, 2003). Another way to say it is that caution must be taken to ensure that computer presentations aren't too packaged or too confining.

7.5 Which characteristics of good presenters do you possess? Which do you need to develop?

WHEN TEACHER PRESENTATIONS SHOULD BE USED

It is most appropriate for you to present knowledge to your learners when (1) they don't know much about what is to be learned, (2) the new knowledge is not available in a better, more understandable form (e.g., in a book), (3) the knowledge need not be remembered for a long time, or (4) the knowledge is a basis for what will be explored later in depth.

Most knowledge transmission takes place in literacy and mathematics classes. Examples in literacy are telling students what the parts of speech are or how to use a dictionary. An example in math is telling students how to do long division. Presentations also are used in the early stages of science and social studies lessons to provide a basis for later processing-using-applying the new knowledge. For example, in science students might be told what the scientific method is and then be asked to apply it. In social science, learners are told about Christopher Columbus and then are asked to think about the consequences of his explorations (Brophy, 2006; Gage & Berliner, 1998).

Although these factors define when presentations should be used, in actuality you will probably make use of them (1) if your former teachers frequently presented, and for the most part you liked and learned from them, (2) if you have

LESSON PLAN 7.1

Abbreviated Presentation Lesson: Roman Numerals

Curriculum tie-in: This lesson may be linked to the study of Roman civilization or the study of numerical systems.

OBJECTIVES

1. Learners will recognize the basic Roman numerals (I, V, X, L, C, D, and M) and know their values.

   Specific objective: Given a list of Roman numerals, learners will correctly identify and circle all basic numerals.

2. Learners will understand two rules for creating other numerals.

   Specific objective: Given a list of Arabic numerals, using the rules, learners will correctly translate all of them into Roman.

RESOURCES

1. Pictures of or documents containing Roman numerals (book preface pages, book chapter numbers, watch and clock faces, building cornerstones, inscriptions on statues, outlines).

2. Supplementary materials on Roman numerals contained in texts, encyclopedias, journals, and so forth.

3. Websites on Roman numerals.

4. Lesson plans on Roman numerals contained on the Web.

METHODOLOGY

1. *Set induction.* "I am going to show you a secret code. What is a code?" (Show resource objects and pictures containing Roman numerals.) Ask, "What is this code called? Where did this code come from? Where have you seen it?"

2. Inform learners of what they will learn and be able to do as a result of the lesson (see Objectives).

3. Find out what learners know about Roman numerals. Ask, "What are some things you know about Roman numerals?"

4. Present/review the lesson information.

   a. There are only a few basic numerals (I, V, X, L, C, D, M).

   b. Other numbers are *mostly* created by either

   (1) Putting a number(s) of lesser value after one of greater value, e.g.,

   VI = 6, XII = 12, LXXVII = 77 or

   (2) Putting a number(s) of lesser value *before* one of greater value, e.g.,

   IV = 4, IX = 9, XL = 40.

ASSESSMENT

1. Given a list of fourteen Roman numerals, learners will circle only the seven basic ones.

2. Given a list of Arabic numerals, learners will convert them to Roman equivalents.

3. Reteach as necessary.

CLOSURE

1. Have students write summaries of what they know about Roman numerals and have them share their knowledge: e.g., Where are they found? What are the basic numerals? What are the rules for making others from them?

If more is to be learned about Roman numerals and their use:

2. Have interested students locate examples of uses of Roman numerals.

3. Have interested students locate additional information on Roman numerals.

prior knowledge about the topic or subject, (3) if you like to talk and have a knack for it, (4) if you believe your students will learn the material best this way, (5) if you have few related instructional resources, (6) if you lack time or competence to facilitate learning in another way, and (7) if presentations meet your personal and professional needs.

LIMITATIONS OF PRESENTATIONS

Of course, presentations have shortcomings. Among others, teachers may not know the content sufficiently to present it, presentations often do not involve learners enough, and they may be overwhelming, underwhelming, or boring. For these reasons they may trigger frustration in learners who do not have good attention, note-taking, or memory skills (Freiberg & Driscoll, 2004).

What if you don't have adequate knowledge to make a presentation in some area that you are responsible for teaching? What can you do? Good (1995) suggests some possible ways to overcome that shortcoming, including finding and using material to increase your knowledge, bringing in guest speakers including other

LESSON PLAN 7.2

Abbreviated Presentation Lesson: The Newspaper

Curriculum tie-in: This lesson may be linked to the study of social studies and communication.

OBJECTIVES

1. Learners will know some functions of a newspaper: to report news, opinions, or commentaries, weather, entertainment, and television schedules.
2. Learners will be able to locate the above functions in both hard copy and electronic versions of newspapers and know their usual placement.

RESOURCES

1. Multiple copies of a daily newspaper
2. Computers and the website of a daily, preferable local, newspaper

METHODOLOGY

1. Set induction. "What do you and your parents read to find out what is happening?" (Responses probably will include newspapers and magazines. Some may mention web sources.) "How many of you use the newspaper?"
2. Inform learners of what they will learn and be able to do as a result of the lesson (see Objectives).

3. Find out what learners already know about newspaper. Ask, "What do you know about a newspaper?"
4. Present lesson information:
   a. Newspapers serve a number of purposes.
      (1) They report national, state and local news. Ask, "What might be examples of national . . . state . . . or local news?"
      (2) They provide opportunity for people to comment on things that are happening at the national, state, and local levels. Ask, "What are some happenings that you would like to express your opinion about?"
      (3) They print weather forecasts. Ask, "When do you like to have a weather forecast?"
      (4) They provide entertainment and television schedules. Ask, "What kinds of entertainment do you like and how do you find out about them?"
   b. Review the purposes of newspapers and extend them to include others.

   c. Distribute newspapers and direct learners to find sections that provide national news, state news, local news, opinion or commentary, weather, and entertainment.
   d. Emphasize that these sections are generally in the same place each day.
   e. Direct students to the computers and to the website for a newspaper and guide them through the electronic version.

ASSESSMENT

Have learners address:

1. What are five major things that a newspaper provides its readers?
2. The parts of a newspaper are usually found in a particular order. In the newspapers we have used, what has the order been?

CLOSURE

Review and summarize important points you have made about newspapers. Make related assignments as necessary.

---

teachers, and telling students that this is an area about which you are still learning. An obvious, other suggestion is to use a different instructional alternative that does not rest on the teacher knowing the material quite so extensively.

SUMMARY ON PRESENTATION

You have learned that informative teacher talks are common occurrences and that they differ in many respects. For example, they differ in degree of formality and length, with informal and shorter talks generally preferable. Presentations also differ according to whether they are live or recorded. To conduct a good presentation, the presenter should demonstrate certain qualities and follow certain procedures, as Table 7.2 noted. Like all instructional alternatives, teacher presentations have advantages and disadvantages for both teachers and learners. In general, when dissemination of information is the goal, they are efficient and economical. Like any instructional alternative, teacher presentations have their place and contribute to learner achievement and to teacher and learner satisfaction.

Try Activity 7.4

7.6 How do you feel about presentation as a way of teaching?

7.7 What factors in Chapter 1 may influence how you feel about using presentation?

CHAPTER 7
Four Instructional Alternatives:
Presentation, Discussion, Independent
Study, and Individualized Instruction

www.mhhe.com/cruickshank6e

213

Discussion: Learning through Informative Interaction

Do you think teachers talk too much? Scholars have provided evidence that teachers talk two-thirds of the time that class is in session. Do you get tired of constantly hearing what someone else has to say? Do you get squirmy if you have to sit and listen too long? To make matters worse, you may already have acquired from books or other teachers some of the information you are hearing. Listening can become boring, boring, boring! "Why doesn't the teacher let us talk about what we know and how we feel?" Despite the plethora of teacher talk, the track record for using discussion is poor. For example: in classrooms where discussion might be expected to be used almost none occurs; in classrooms where it might be expected to be used *and is,* on average, the discussions last a mere 30 seconds. Sadly, discussion is mostly used in honors programs and even then sparingly: advanced placement classes can be as discussion free as any class (Parker, 2006).

WHAT IS A DISCUSSION?

7.8 How do you like discussions? What have been your experiences with them, good and bad?

A **discussion** is a situation wherein students, or students and a teacher, converse to share information, ideas, or opinions or work to resolve a problem. Conversely, a discussion is not a situation wherein a teacher asks a question, a student or students answer, and then the teacher asks another question. This question-answer-question format is called **recitation.** Its purpose is mainly to quiz students to determine what they know or understand. Often teachers who claim they are leading a discussion, when observed, are leading recitations (Parker, 2006). Some differences between a true discussion and a recitation are illustrated in Table 7.3.

PURPOSES AND CHARACTERISTICS OF DISCUSSION

Students preparing to be teachers want to know the purposes, characteristics, and procedures of discussion (see Spotlight on Research 7.3). Hopefully, what follows will meet these desires.

Purposes of Discussion   A discussion can serve a variety of purposes (Gall, 1987; Gall & Gall, 1990; Goldenberg, 1991; Larson, 2000; Spiegel, 2005). One purpose is

TABLE 7.3 Discussion and Recitation Compared		
	Discussion	**Recitation**
Definition	When a student or students and a teacher converse to share information, ideas, and so forth	When a teacher asks students a series of relatively short-answer questions
Purpose	To review what students have learned, encourage students to reflect on their ideas or opinions, explore an issue, resolve a problem, or improve face-to-face communication skills	To determine what students remember or understand
Conceptual level	Discussion usually is at a higher cognitive level or may be in the affective domain. *Examples:* "What leads to exploration and discovery?" "Are exploration and discovery bad or good?" "If we find life on another planet, should we try to improve it?"	Questions are usually lower-level, cognitive domain. *Examples:* "When was America discovered?" "What is the sum of the angles of a triangle?" "What are the themes of Fitzgerald's novels?"
Role of the teacher	Facilitator-moderator, participant, or observer-recorder	"Quizmaster"

Two college instructors conducted a study to see if they could help their student teachers feel more comfortable when using discussion in their classrooms (Parker & Hess, 2001). Their method was to engage the student teachers in good, meaningful discussions and then have them analyze what happened. Unfortunately, the students did not seem to benefit from this immersion procedure as much as the instructors had hoped. As Lisa, one student teacher, said afterward, she "really [still] had no idea how to lead a discussion herself" (p. 273). The professors agreed that she spoke for all the student teachers involved in the study. The problem seemed to be that involvement in and analysis of good discussion is necessary but not sufficient. Students wanted and needed to know more about discussions. Consequently, the professors modified their approach to ensure that student teachers not only engaged in good discussions and analyzed them but also knew the value, purposes, types, and procedures of discussion and discussion methodology.

---

to review and extend what students have learned in order to *ensure their mastery of a subject*. Hill (2000) presents us with a discussion model for subject matter mastery that follows certain steps. First, your students see, hear, or read something. Perhaps they view a documentary on using animals in medical research. Then they discuss what they have seen and heard. Among other things, they give attention to terms and concepts that need explanation, to the major ideas presented, and to the major message. Of course, the discussion could go well beyond merely processing (clarifying and rehearsing) the information received. You could, Hill advises, engage students in higher-order thinking by getting them to talk about the authenticity of the message or its effect if carried out. Such discussions primarily help us learn through rehearsal, that is, recalling and talking about things so they become more firmly fixed in our memories.

A discussion can also be held when the purpose is *to have students examine their ideas or opinions*. After studying about the use of animals in medical research, students could be asked to share their views about its appropriateness.

A third purpose a discussion might have is *to solve a problem*. Students are presented with political, economic, or social problems to discuss and resolve, such as these: How can better relationships be established with North Korea? How can we reduce the national debt? How can violence by children be reduced? Closer to home, you and your classmates could address such questions as how to work with students at risk, how to locate instructional resources, or how we can become better classroom problem solvers.

Sometimes a discussion can help students *to improve their face-to-face* or *interpersonal communication skills*. The purpose is for learners to become better at being good contributors and active listeners, making a point, handling disagreements and conflicts, overcoming fear of speaking in public, and so forth.

Certainly, these are four good reasons for including discussion in your teaching repertoire. Can you think of others?

Characteristics of Discussions   We can consider discussions on the basis of a number of attributes or characteristics: the interaction pattern, group size and composition, and group arrangement.

Interaction Pattern   Discussion differs from recitation, or the teacher question–student answer technique. Interaction during discussions is less formal and more conversational. Moreover, the conversation can occur among students as well as between students and teacher. In the most lively discussions, everyone is an active

CHAPTER 7
Four Instructional Alternatives:
Presentation, Discussion, Independent
Study, and Individualized Instruction

www.mhhe.com/cruickshank6e

215

participant. Simich-Dudgeon (1998) reviewed research on "collaborative talk" or discussion among students and tells us it contributes to student success.

Group Size and Composition   The whole class can engage in a common discussion, or it can be divided into groups. All other factors being equal, small groups are preferable since they allow more potential for participation. The composition of a group is also at issue. That is, should members be similar (homogeneous) or dissimilar (heterogeneous)? Arguments can be made for either position.

Group Arrangement   One rule seems to hold: To converse, participants should be face to face. Thus, arranging discussion participants in a circle is a common occurrence. On occasion, a panel discussion makes sense. A panel discussion is carried on when a preselected group of students discusses in front of others who observe. Students on the panel should be arranged face to face. Students who observe might surround the panel. This procedure and arrangement is referred to as a fishbowl—everyone is watching the panel or "fish."

Role of the Teacher   Of course, the interaction pattern suggests a number of different teacher roles and responsibilities. If the interaction is strictly among students, the teacher serves as observer, recorder, and perhaps arbitrator. At other times, you will want to be a member of the discussion group but not its official leader—you merely want to participate. Other occasions may call for you to be the facilitator-moderator. In this case, the duty of the teacher is to "enable learners to reflect critically on their experiences . . . to explore different perspectives, to consider how their knowledge is rooted in personal experiences" (Van Ments, 1981 p. 12). The role you choose to play—observer, participant, or facilitator—will vary according to circumstances such as the purpose of the discussion and the maturity and experience of the students. Another role: to ensure that group members feel safe and comfortable with each other (Spiegel, 2005).

For a visual summarization of the purposes and key characteristics of a discussion, see **Figure 7.2.**

7.9   When, in your opinion, might it be preferable to form heterogeneous and homogeneous groups?

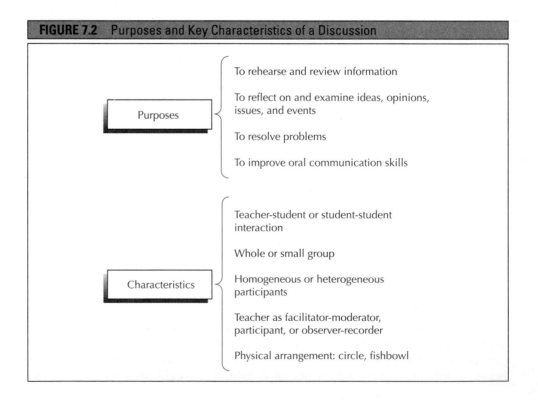

FIGURE 7.2   Purposes and Key Characteristics of a Discussion

Purposes
- To rehearse and review information
- To reflect on and examine ideas, opinions, issues, and events
- To resolve problems
- To improve oral communication skills

Characteristics
- Teacher-student or student-student interaction
- Whole or small group
- Homogeneous or heterogeneous participants
- Teacher as facilitator-moderator, participant, or observer-recorder
- Physical arrangement: circle, fishbowl

GOOD DISCUSSION LEADERS

What does it take to be a good discussion leader? We believe you need to possess an assortment of beliefs and skills. First, let's look at four beliefs. Basically, discussion leaders should believe that students, like most persons, desire to communicate with others. We noted previously that teachers like to talk. Well, students like to talk, too, don't they? Persons who utilize discussion as an instructional alternative use it in part to legitimatize classroom conversation, that is, to make it acceptable and purposeful.

Teachers who use discussion also believe in the purposes of discussion: review and extension of what students have learned, examination of ideas and opinions, problem solving, and increased interpersonal communication skills. Democratic forms of government depend on persons so educated (Cook & Tashlik, 2004).

In addition to believing in the purposes of discussion, discussion users must have confidence in their students' capacities to think effectively. They have faith that, with guidance, students will employ higher-level cognitive skills such as application, analysis, synthesis, and evaluation. Discussion users also believe that by engaging students in discussion, they can accomplish many affective goals, such as encouraging students to respond and value. You may recall that these terms were introduced in the section entitled "Writing Specific Objectives" in Chapter 6.

A fourth belief held by persons who favor discussion is that involving students in a well-conceived group experience will enhance their psychological and social growth. In such situations, they can learn to feel good about themselves and to accept others. In addition, shy students can often be encouraged to participate, especially in smaller discussion groups. Good discussion leaders encourage and enhance student pride, dignity, sense of efficacy or personal power, and caring.

 7.10 Which of the four beliefs of good discussion leaders do you hold?

Beyond holding to these beliefs, you will be a better discussion leader if you have related skills. Can you frame good questions that promote higher-order thinking as noted in Table 6.2 and in Chapter 10? Can you limit your own talk? Remember, this is the students' conversational opportunity. Persons who have observed discussion remind us that frequently teachers talk too much even during discussions (Dillon, 1985, 1988). Could it be that many of us simply need to rein in our compulsion to talk? We must learn how to get *students* to ask more questions, explore and speculate more, make more references to *their* personal experiences, and so forth.

Additionally, you must be a facilitator, human relations expert, clarifier, and summarizer. As a *facilitator*, you are responsible for beginning the discussion, moving it briskly, and keeping the group on task and attentive. As a *human relations expert*, your job is to make everyone feel comfortable and important and to encourage full and equal participation. You must also moderate differences of opinion. As a *clarifier*, you must ensure that everyone's message is heard and understood. This might require that certain students' comments be limited, rephrased, or probed. Finally, as a *summarizer*, you need to be skillful in drawing the conversation together and ensuring that everyone sees the progress they have made toward the stated goal.

7.11 How do you feel about your abilities as a facilitator, human relations expert, clarifier, summarizer, and teacher of communication skills?

You also need skill in teaching three kinds of communication skills to your students (Bridges, 1988; Brookfield & Preskill, 2005). You must be able to help them know how to make remarks that are reasonable, to know when and for how long to speak, and to know how critical they should be of the remarks others make.

GOOD DISCUSSIONS

Can you recall thinking to yourself, Wow! That was a good discussion! What makes a discussion good? As is true of any instructional alternative, a discussion is good when it results in learning and satisfaction. Both of these outcomes depend on how the discussion was prepared, presented, and concluded (Bridges, 1988;

www.mhhe.com/cruickshank6e

CHAPTER 7
Four Instructional Alternatives:
Presentation, Discussion, Independent
Study, and Individualized Instruction

217

Brookfield & Preskill, 2005; Dillon, 1988, 1995; Gall, 1987; Goldenberg, 1991; Muller, 2002).

Preparation   First, you need to decide whether you should use a discussion and why you want to use one. Do you remember the four purposes—to review and extend knowledge, examine ideas, solve problems, and improve communication skills? For illustration, let's say your purpose is to review what students have learned and to extend that knowledge. More specifically, let's say your goal is for students to review and extend what they have learned about dinosaurs from reading an article called "The Age of Dinosaurs" in *National Geographic World,* a magazine written for students. From the article, the students ascertain how scientists learn about dinosaurs and what they have learned. Consequently, students could discuss a number of things. Some are basic and factual. When did dinosaurs live? Where did they live? What kinds of dinosaurs existed when? How did dinosaurs live? How do scientists study dinosaurs?

At a higher level, you can ask participants to analyze, synthesize, and evaluate using the following ploy: "Dinosaurs haven't really become extinct—birds belong on the dinosaur family tree. So, you have a dinosaur bath in your backyard, you dine on roast dinosaur at Thanksgiving, and you munch on dinosaur nuggets at McDonalds. . . . What is a family tree? How do you suppose paleontologists decided birds and dinosaurs are related?" Another premise for discussion might be this: "Finding out about dinosaurs is both very time-consuming and expensive. Why is it so important? Couldn't the time and money be spent on other things society needs more urgently?" The last questions move the discussion into the realm of reason seeking and addressing an issue.

Another early consideration when preparing for a discussion relates to student preparation. Are they ready? Perhaps you will need to remind the class or individuals about the need to listen, to take turns, and to be clear, reasonable, considerate, and so forth. Some older children may have watched *Meet the Press* or *The McLaughlin Group* on television. As a result, they may believe a discussion is a verbal "knock-em-down" that stops just short of mental, if not physical, fisticuffs. Of course, if students have already been involved in discussions with good leaders, they should be more effective participants.

Try Activity 7.5

Next, you must think about your role, which raises questions about grouping, physical arrangements, and time management. If your students are not familiar with discussion, you will have to play the role of facilitator-moderator. Relatedly, you may want to hold a *whole-class* discussion with a less experienced group. That way you can exercise more control over such matters as staying on task, providing for equitable participation, and ensuring that everyone enjoys psychological safety. Students more experienced and mature in discussion enable you to take less dominant, directive roles.

Delivery   Once you have determined your purpose, students' readiness, your role, group arrangements, and time constraints, you are now ready to deliver. This means (1) making certain your students understand the purpose of the discussion ("Let's think further about the material on dinosaurs we have read"); (2) ensuring that you have related the discussion to something students previously learned or to something upcoming; (3) informing them of the discussion questions and potential information sources they can use in preparation ("Some discussion questions can be answered directly from the reading; for others, you will need to come up with your own answers or opinions"); reminding them of discussion rules (perhaps by handing out or posting a set of guidelines such as those in **Table 7.4**); and (4) organizing the participants. If several small groups will discuss, you may want to appoint or ask each group to select a facilitator and a recorder, and, of course, the students in these roles must know what is expected of them.

TABLE 7.4   Discussion Guidelines for Students

- Everyone should have an equal opportunity to contribute.
- Encourage your classmates to join in.
- Ensure that everyone contributes by waiting his turn and taking part about as much as everyone else.
- Listen carefully to what others say and feel.
- Work to understand and, whenever possible, to support what others say and feel.
- Understand that your knowledge and ideas may not always be right.
- Stay on target and help others do the same.
- Be gracious with your peers.

Throughout a discussion, effective performance of your role as either facilitator-moderator, participant, or observer-recorder is critical. You will especially need to remember that this is the students' time to talk: Your role is to encourage participation and elevate the cognitive or affective level of the discourse. *Give the discussants a purpose, a plan, and freedom to operate.*

Use of discussion as an instructional technique draws support and direction from various learning theories (described in Chapter 4), depending upon the purpose of the discussion. To illustrate, suppose the purpose of the discussion is to rehearse or practice. Such learning tasks are easier for students when teachers put to work beliefs and findings related to information processing and behaviorism. Or, suppose the purpose of the discussion is to reflect on events, ideas, or opinions. In such cases, we would want to apply the beliefs and findings from the humanistic school, particularly those relating to values clarification. If the purpose is to engage in problem solving, we might want to use what researchers know about meaningful learning.

7.12 What factors from Chapter 1 may influence how you feel about using discussion?

Try Activity 7.6

Closure   At the appropriate moment, the discussion should end. Sometimes it is fitting to close a discussion earlier than planned—for example, when the discussion has accomplished its purpose or when it is failing to do so. In any case, with the possible assistance of the participants, you need to pull the learning together. At this stage, review with students the extent to which they accomplished the purpose of the discussion. Point out where they need to go from here, that is, how the discussion will tie in with future work. A summary of the qualities of good discussion leaders and good discussions appears in Table 7.5.

A sample discussion lesson plan appears as Lesson Plan 7.3 (on page 221).

WHEN DISCUSSIONS SHOULD BE USED

A few guidelines will help you know when to select the discussion alternative from your teaching repertoire, dust it off, and put it to use. As a general rule, you should use discussion when any of its purposes coincide with yours. Consequently, engage students in discussion when your purpose is to review information, examine ideas and opinions, solve problems, or improve oral communication skills. You should also use discussion when you are more interested in long-term memory, higher-order thinking, motivation, attitude change, or moral reasoning. Finally, use discussion when it best meets your students' social and psychological needs. Discussion is effective when students have been mostly inactive listeners, when a more relaxed atmosphere is warranted, and when it would be beneficial to enhance student-to-student friendships and affiliation.

Since there is no research evidence on when or how teachers actually use discussions, our guess is that teachers initiate discussions mostly when pursuing the above goals. However, we are sure you will be guided by other things in your selection of discussion. One is your past experience. Have you been involved in many

www.mhhe.com/cruickshank6e

CHAPTER 7
Four Instructional Alternatives:
Presentation, Discussion, Independent
Study, and Individualized Instruction
219

TABLE 7.5 Qualities of Good Discussion Leaders and Good Discussions

Good Leaders	Good Discussions
• Believe students want and need to engage in purposeful talk • Believe students should be asked to review and use information, explore issues, and resolve problems • Believe students are capable of thinking and doing for themselves • Believe students can be helped to develop via discussion • Control their own talk • Get students thinking • Get all learners involved • Serve as skillful facilitators, human relations experts, clarifiers, and summarizers • Are skillful in teaching communication skills	*When preparing:* • Establish the general purpose • Set specific learner objectives • Consider the readiness of the class and individuals for discussion • Decide what role you will play, the class grouping, physical arrangements, and time allowance *When overseeing:* • Get students' attention • Ensure that participants understand and see the value in the purpose and objectives • Relate the goal and task to previous knowledge and future work • Set out the specific questions or statements to be discussed • Remind participants of discussion rules • Monitor to ensure on-task behavior, balanced participation, and understanding • Encourage participants, elevate the level of discourse *When closing:* • Do so at the most appropriate time rather than at a specific time • Summarize progress toward the purpose and objectives • Tie new learning to previous knowledge • Establish what the participants might do next

7.13 What do you think are the most important characteristics of a good discussion?

discussions, and are your remembrances of those experiences positive? Second, how adept are you as an interaction leader, facilitator, or participant? Are you pretty skillful with group interaction? Third, what is your willingness to give up or share the "chalk and talk"? Many teachers, and not just novices, are afraid to let students participate for fear of losing their intellectual or even managerial authority.

RESEARCH ON DISCUSSION

A number of advantages result from engaging in a good discussion. Namely, it promotes knowledge retention, higher-order thinking, positive attitude change, enhanced moral reasoning, and increased motivation. On the downside, discussion is less effective than presentation in helping students acquire factual knowledge. For a more complete set of data, see Spotlight on Research 7.4 on page 222. For a look at what students say about discussion, see Spotlight on Research 7.5 on page 223.

LIMITATIONS OF DISCUSSIONS

Although discussion has a goodly number of benefits, it also has shortcomings. Think and be prepared for these. What if the learners do not seem to know what they are supposed to do? What if learners do not know enough or are not mature enough to engage in the discussion? What if learners digress? What if the discussion is dominated by a few? What if some learners are reluctant to participate? As you learned from Table 7.5, you must follow good discussion procedures in order to avoid the above problems.

LESSON PLAN 7.3

Abbreviated Discussion Lesson Plan: Elephants

Curriculum tie-in: This lesson may be linked to the study of Africa, India, Southeast Asia or preservation of wildlife.

OBJECTIVE

1. Learners will find out, discuss, and organize what is known about elephants. *Specific objective:* Given material containing information about elephants, learners will create semantic maps that organize the knowledge into categories (see Methodology below).

2. They will also correct misconceptions they may hold about elephants, e.g., that male elephants rule the herd.

RESOURCES

1. Print and nonprint material on elephants.

2. Websites on elephants.

METHODOLOGY

1. *Set induction:* Ask learners, "What do you know about elephants?" Allow them to review that knowledge and list it on the chalkboard. DO NOT correct misconceptions at this point. See Closure below.

2. Inform learners of what they will learn and be able to do as a result of this lesson.

3. Inform learners that they (a) should locate knowledge about elephants, (b) list the knowledge on paper as you did at the chalkboard, (c) be prepared to share the knowledge with the class, and (d) be prepared to organize the knowledge in some way.

4. Following the independent work, learners discuss what they found and discuss how they think that knowledge can be organized.

5. The learners are guided as they discuss how the knowledge can be organized using semantic mapping. Put the term elephant on the chalkboard. Have students discuss what they have found out about elephants that can be categorized and into what categories the information seems to fit. Examples include:

- Where elephants are found.
- An elephant's characteristics.
- What elephant families are like.
- Elephant food.
- Importance of elephants.
- Elephant enemies.

ASSESSMENT

1. Move around the room to monitor progress toward the following:
   Are learners knowledgeable about elephants?
   Are they able to construct semantic maps of the knowledge they have gained?
   Are they finding that certain things they believed true about elephants may not be so?

2. Reteach as necessary.

CLOSURE

1. Have learners discuss what they have learned and to what extent it is consistent with what they previously knew or thought they knew.

Discussions will be a disappointment if they are poorly conceptualized, poorly conducted, or when learners are not ready to participate in them successfully (Battistich, Solomon, & Delucchi, 1993).

SUMMARY ON DISCUSSION

Discussions serve at least four purposes: they can review and extend knowledge, examine ideas and opinions, solve problems, and improve oral communication skills. Most classroom discussions serve the first purpose; that is, students review information they have previously learned from a presentation or from reading. Even then, however, students should review the material at the highest cognitive level. They should be prompted to analyze, synthesize, and evaluate information rather than merely be asked to respond to lower-level, factual questions as in a prototypical recitation.

In addition to their many purposes, discussions are characterized by multiple interactions with the teacher assuming the role of either facilitator-monitor, participant, or observer-recorder. Discussions may be whole-class or small-group in nature, and groups may vary in size and composition. For maximum effectiveness, participants must be arranged face to face.

Good discussion leaders need to hold certain beliefs and possess special abilities which are summarized in Table 7.5, column 1. Discussions can be improved by following the guidelines for preparation, delivery, and closure found in Table 7.5, column 2.

Try Activity 7.7

What We Know about Classroom Discussion

Research on discussion has taken place in elementary and secondary classrooms as well as with university students, workers in business and industry, and adult volunteers. Here is a summary of findings. Interpretations and explanations, if any, are ours.

- Discussion generally is more effective than teacher presentation or lecture for promoting retention of knowledge and higher-level thinking (such as analysis, synthesis, and evaluation). This likely is true because the opportunity for rehearsing or using information is greater during discussion.
- Use of discussion generally results in increased motivation to learn. This probably is because engagement in discussion meets the personality needs of many students.
- Discussion is effective in changing attitudes and, to some extent, in advancing moral reasoning. Discussion can create a forum for ideas and idea changes.

- Discussion is less effective than presentation in helping students acquire factual knowledge. Presentations appear to be superior for sheer communication of information.
- After a discussion group reaches consensus, it tends to disregard any further, high-quality ideas that are presented. The group probably has struggled to reach a consensus and fears that new ideas would distract from it.
- Socially aggressive and/or less capable persons may dominate discussion.
- Small group size results in more participation, increased satisfaction among members, and greater academic achievement.
- Groups in which members are more alike or homogeneous are more cohesive, communicate more, and experience greater self-esteem. Heterogeneous groups may be more effective in performance. "Birds of a feather" may feel more comfortable together, but they may

not challenge or assist one another sufficiently.

- Groups without a teacher leader or assertive members interact more often. They also achieve greater satisfaction from the discussion and are effective in handling complex tasks.
- Students who engage in conversation/discussion of literature identify more closely with it, are more motivated, and learn more.
- Even with use of discussion, teachers may hold students responsible for lower levels of knowledge, such as facts.
- Teachers sometimes do most of the higher-order thinking for the group(s): making generalizations, hypothesizing, and synthesizing.
- Teachers sometimes do most of the talking.

Sources: Doherty (2003); Gall (1987); Langer, Nystrand, & Gamoran (2003); Watson (1983).

Independent Study: Teaching as Giving and Guiding Seat Work and Homework Assignments

WHAT IS INDEPENDENT STUDY?

7.14 What personal school experiences come to mind when you think of independent study?

Independent study is any assignment learners complete more or less on their own. Examples of independent study include; reading, writing a composition, rehearsing words for a spelling test, and preparing a report. If done in school, the assignment is referred to as *seatwork:* if done at home, *homework*. Estimates of time spent doing seatwork are as high as 70 percent. Estimates of daily homework time vary from between 53 minutes for elementary to 104 minutes for high schoolers (Linver et al., 2005).

PURPOSE AND CHARACTERISTICS OF INDEPENDENT STUDY

We can describe independent study according to purposes, type, teacher role, and the context in which it takes place.

When researchers at Stanford University asked high school students questions about their school experiences, they received many comments on both teachers and teaching. From these comments, the researchers concluded that "both high- and low-achieving students prefer teachers who draw them into the learning process by holding discussions in which ideas are explored and thoughts, feelings, and opinions are shared" (p. 700). Furthermore, the researchers concluded from students' remarks that during discussions, learners feel important and feel that what they think counts. Students are particularly complimentary of teachers who make the classroom a place where they feel comfortable in expressing themselves. As one student reported,

[The teacher] makes the class feel comfortable talking about themselves and really expressing their feelings. Like if you read something and everyone interprets it differently, she wants to hear everyone's opinion. (Phelan, Davidson, & Cao, 1992, p. 700).

Purposes of Independent Study   Teachers use independent study for many reasons, some more justifiable than others. It is most justifiable *when students need to rehearse or practice something;* for example rehearsing a play or practicing long division. In Chapter 4, you saw how important it is for learners to rehearse what they are learning by thinking about it or repeating it. Rehearsal is part of information processing: It gets information into our long-term memory.

As a teacher, you will probably use independent practice when you want to be certain that your learners gain specific knowledge or skills. Thus, if you are an elementary or middle school teacher, your students definitely will rehearse or practice reading comprehension skills, language arts skills such as writing paragraphs, and mathematics skills such as solving story problems and computation. Secondary teachers provide students with practice too, as do athletic coaches. If you have participated in sports, think of the innumerable times you have practiced shooting foul shots, dribbling a soccer ball, or flutter kicking until these acts became part of your motor memory.

The second purpose served by independent study is to encourage students to acquire study skills that will serve them throughout life. These skills include how to locate, analyze, synthesize, and evaluate information. The more opportunities learners have to dig out, judge, and use information, the better equipped they will be to learn on their own. The curious child who was helped to learn about life in a pond at age 10 is more likely to want and be able to find out about our disappearing wetlands at age 20.

Independent study is also used, and occasionally misused, as a means to other ends. For example, teachers can use it for convenience. This would be the case when learners are given work to keep them busy ("busywork") because their teachers must do something else. The something else might be working with other students or simply taking a breather. Working with other students, of course, is necessary and therefore justifiable.

Unfortunately, independent study can be misused. Here is a case. Teacher Stanley loved to read. In fact, he often gave his middle school students independent work so that *he* could read. After giving his class the assignment, Stanley went to his desk, sat down, and opened the middle drawer where he always kept a novel. Students were not permitted to interrupt or to come to his desk.

It may take learners a while to catch on to the misuse of independent study or practice, but they can and do, as evidenced from the student's comment in Case 7.1.

"It's moments like this—when they're all so very, very quiet—that I get a strange, uneasy feeling."

www.mhhe.com/cruickshank6e

CHAPTER 7
Four Instructional Alternatives: Presentation, Discussion, Independent Study, and Individualized Instruction

223

I remember a history teacher in high school. I really liked her because her class was so organized and orderly. When we came in there were *x* number of questions on the chalkboard. We read a certain section of the book and wrote out the answers. When time ran out she would ask, "Do you have any questions?"

As she said the word *questions*, the bell always rang. Now I've figured out she taught that way just to keep us busy. We didn't have time to do anything but write out answers. That wasn't really teaching! There was no interaction of ideas and people. No real class.

Source: Bower (1973).

INVESTIGATING AND SOLVING THE CASE

1. What in this chapter provides insight into this situation?
2. What would be required for "real teaching"?

Types of Independent Study By *type* of independent study, we refer to whether the teacher prescribes the work assignment or learners freely choose it. Teachers normally determine the material to be rehearsed. However, when the purpose is to provide opportunities to develop and practice independent study skills, students could select the work. For example, suppose you are teaching a unit on biography. Students could read a common biography you assign, or they could select one of personal interest.

Teacher's Role As with presentation and discussion, the objective of independent study is to facilitate students' learning and satisfaction. Clearly, learning and satisfaction during independent study are in jeopardy if you are not available to guide and monitor your students' work. Effective teachers always monitor student progress (see Chapter 11). Students left entirely on their own may not only fail to learn but also learn incorrectly. Of course, when independent study takes the form of homework, monitoring is not possible; even then, it must be checked. Increasingly, parents are being asked to supervise and assist students with their homework. Unfortunately, parental availability, interest, and capacity to assist students vary. Some may be better teachers than we are; others might not have a clue about helping a child.

7.15 Which beliefs about use of independent study do you hold?

Context We have already alluded to the fact that students can do independent work either in school or as homework. In-school assignments can be accomplished at a variety of times and in different places. Students reading biographies could work on them during class, during study or library periods, or after other class work has been completed. Some schools even have before- and after-school arrangements that give students an additional time and place to do independent work.

Figure 7.3 reviews the purposes and key characteristics of independent study.

GOOD INDEPENDENT STUDY LEADERS

If you are going to use independent study well, you must believe in its purposes and values, particularly as a way to provide rehearsal or practice and as a way to help students learn how to learn. Furthermore, you must have confidence in your students' ability to work alone.

Additionally, you must know how to get and keep learners involved in worthwhile independent activities. Kounin (1977) is most helpful here. He and his colleagues observed the behavior of teachers whose students stayed engaged in their seatwork assignments. The teachers had several things in common. They demonstrated valence and challenge arousal, variety and challenge, withitness, and overlapping. Since these terms are Kounin's inventions, they require definition.

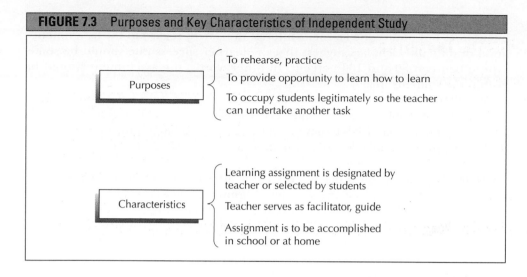

FIGURE 7.3 Purposes and Key Characteristics of Independent Study

Purposes
- To rehearse, practice
- To provide opportunity to learn how to learn
- To occupy students legitimately so the teacher can undertake another task

Characteristics
- Learning assignment is designated by teacher or selected by students
- Teacher serves as facilitator, guide
- Assignment is to be accomplished in school or at home

Valence and challenge arousal is the ability to engender curiosity and enthusiasm in students and to get them involved in the independent work. Obviously, teachers who are enthusiastic themselves are more likely to beget enthusiasm in their learners. In Chapter 10, you will learn more about teacher enthusiasm.

Variety and challenge involves the ability to identify and assign independent study assignments that vary enough to be interesting and are challenging enough to maintain attention. Such assignments need to be demanding but not defeating. What we know from Chapter 4 about gaining and holding attention applies here.

Withitness is the ability to communicate to learners that we know what they are doing even when we are not nearby or looking at them. Perhaps you can recall teachers who seemed to have eyes in the back of their heads. Withitness is this kind of sixth sense.

Overlapping is the teacher's ability to attend to more than one thing at a time. In a sense it is akin to being a juggler. This ability is especially important when working with one or more students, such as when you are directing a group activity while the rest of the class works independently. In such cases, you work with one group while simultaneously monitoring the other students. You will learn more about overlapping and withitness in Chapter 12.

7.16 How do you feel about your ability to use *valence and challenge arousal, variety and challenge, withitness,* and *overlapping?*

GOOD INDEPENDENT STUDY

Considerable agreement exists about what must be done to ensure good independent study (Anderson, Brubaker, Alleman-Brooks, & Duffy, 1984; Brophy & Good, 1986; Emmer et al., 1981; English, 1984; Gilstrap & Martin, 1975; Rosenshine, 1980; Rupley & Blair, 1987; Slavin, 2008). Let's review that opinion in terms of the preparation, delivery, and closure of independent study assignments.

Preparation After determining a general purpose and specific instructional objectives, you must determine whether independent study is the instructional alternative of choice. As mentioned earlier, independent study seems preferable when the purpose is to have learners (1) practice or rehearse information, (2) acquire better self-study or learning skills, or (3) remain occupied in some legitimate way so you can undertake another teaching task, perhaps work with students who need help.

Next, determine the assignment type. Should all students receive a standard assignment, or should they be able to select one of their choice? In either case, we are advised to make sure their assignments are interesting, concise, and at the correct level of difficulty. Of course, older students can work independently for

Try Activity 7.8

CHAPTER 7
Four Instructional Alternatives:
Presentation, Discussion, Independent
Study, and Individualized Instruction

www.mhhe.com/cruickshank6e

225

longer periods of time than younger ones, but it is wise to ensure that the assignment does not outlive the learner's interest in it. With regard to the assignment's level of difficulty, scholars suggest that the learner success rate should be somewhere between 80 and 100 percent. In other words, the assignment should be within the students' reach.

Whether the assignment is teacher-mandated or learner-selected, resources must be available so that students can undertake the task comfortably and successfully. If your assignment of choice is to have each student read a biography, a large assorted collection must be available so that the needs of diverse students are met.

Delivery   Delivery involves making the study assignment and guiding it to a satisfactory conclusion. When making the assignment, attention, valence and challenge arousal, and clarity are most important. Clarity is discussed in Chapter 11. Clarity requires that you inform learners of the lesson's importance. To be clear, you must also ensure that students know specifically what they are to do and how to accomplish it. Instructions should also include time limits and indicate what students must or may do if they complete the assignment early. Learners should also be told precisely when and how they may get help. Can you remember times when you couldn't get help and how debilitating that was? This often happens when the independent work is to be done outside class.

What is your role during independent study? Foremost, it is to actively guide and facilitate learning. This cannot be done as novel-loving teacher, Stanley I., did. Rather, you must be alert ("withit") and, whenever possible, be on your feet, moving, monitoring, interacting with individual learners, and diagnosing their progress. Even when you assign independent study in order to work on another teaching task, you cannot closet yourself from your students or shirk the responsibility of making sure they are doing all right. Thus, as Kounin (1977) notes, you need to have or to develop the capacity of overlapping—the ability to deal with more than one thing at a time. Finally, if your students are to be on task in their independent work, you must protect them from each other's needless, distracting interruptions. Properly delivered, independent study may require more of you than giving a presentation or guiding a discussion. Giving students something to do and ensuring their success is not that simple.

Try Activity 7.9

Like presentation and discussion, independent study draws support from learning theory. When its purpose is to rehearse or practice, follow the principles outlined in Chapter 4 for information processing and behaviorism. However, when the purpose is to help students learn how to learn, you will find assistance in the cognitive and humanistic or affective schools of thought. To illustrate, if you want students to independently learn something that is mostly cognitive, or knowledge-related, key principles from the cognitive school of thought should guide them. When they are to learn something mostly affective or relating to attitudes or values, the beliefs and findings of the humanistic school apply.

7.17   Now that you are aware of what it takes to have good independent study, what would you suggest the teacher in the Case 7.1 scenario needs to do?

Closure   A major error many teachers make is to underestimate the importance of correctly closing a lesson. An independent study assignment is no exception. You cannot just create a worthwhile assignment, give it, and then forget it. You have to "close the deal." But what does that mean? Experts say you must collect the assignment, assess it, count it, and give learners feedback on how well it was done. Reteaching may also be in order. Reteaching is not done enough. Failure to do any of these things sends a message that independent work is not serious business—just busywork intended to occupy the learner's time. Remember the teacher (Case 7.1) who left no time at the end of class for students' questions? Perhaps you can recall teachers who gave you busywork. Without a doubt, students eventually catch on. When they sense that your assignment doesn't count, don't expect them to take it seriously. Would you?

Expect and collect the assignment on time, holding the learner accountable. Assess the assignment, and go over it with students as soon as possible. Some whole-class, in-class assignments can be reviewed immediately. For example, if students take time for in-class practice in mathematics, go over the answers with them right away. Provide immediate feedback. And, don't forget to count independent study assignments as part of the grade. Walberg (1984) finds that when homework assignments are graded, student achievement improves.

When a student does not complete seatwork or homework, look to the Education World website and search "homework" for ideas. A summary of the qualities of good independent study leaders and good independent study is contained in Table 7.6. Spotlight on Research 7.6 also explores what makes for good independent study. A sample independent study lesson plan is contained in Lesson Plan 7.4 (on page 229).

OLC Web Link
Education World

WHEN INDEPENDENT STUDY SHOULD BE USED

To reiterate, independent study should mostly be used (1) when learners need to rehearse or practice information or a skill to get it into long-term memory or (2) when learners need to learn how to learn independently. In the first case, we are saying that students need to practice: Remember the adage "Practice makes perfect." In the second case, we are saying that a major, if not the ultimate, goal of education is to assist students in learning *how* to learn so that they no longer need schools and teachers. *They* are empowered!

Although we lack evidence to support our assumption, we believe independent study is used mostly in K–12 schools as a means to practice or rehearse. We think

TABLE 7.6 Qualities of Good Independent Study Leaders and Good Independent Study	
Good Leaders	**Good Independent Study**
• Believe independent study enhances learning through rehearsal/practice • Believe independent study enhances learning how to learn • Believe students can work successfully independently • Exhibit clarity, valence and challenge arousal, variety and challenge, withitness, and overlapping	*When preparing:* • Establish the general purpose • Set specific instructional objectives • Consider the ability of individual learners to work independently • Plan the assignment so that it is interesting and at the optimal level of difficulty and length • Collect, prepare instructional resources *When delivering:* • Get students' attention • Inform learners of the rationale for the assignment and of the objectives • Relate assignment to previous and upcoming work • Make sure learners know what to do and how to do it before work begins • Make certain learners know when and how they may get help • Make sure learners know what to do if they finish early • Be alert, move about to monitor and interact with learners • Diagnose students' progress and provide assistance when needed *When closing:* • Collect assignments • Assess assignments • Provide feedback to students • Count assignments toward the grade

7.18 What do you think are the most important elements of independent study?

CHAPTER 7
Four Instructional Alternatives:
Presentation, Discussion, Independent
Study, and Individualized Instruction

www.mhhe.com/cruickshank6e

227

Fortunately, more research on this instructional alternative is available than is available for either discussion or presentation. The studies have taken place in K–12 schools, although mostly in elementary and middle grades. While Scott (1989), Anderson (1995), and Cooper and others (2006) provide the most recent general literature review, the individual studies of Emmer, Evertson, Sanford, and Clements (1982), Fisher and others (1980), Good and Grouws (1975), Gump (1967), Kounin (1977), Gartland (1986), and Rosenshine (1980) are most helpful. Most investigators have looked at independent study when its purpose is to rehearse or practice information just received through presentation or recitation.

Gump reports on the incidence of independent study, a strategy he finds commonly employed in elementary school classrooms. Rosenshine notes that independent assignments are usually both appropriate and at the correct level of difficulty. As we have already learned, Kounin finds that learners are more likely to be on task during independent study when teachers demonstrate valence and challenge arousal, variety and challenge, withitness, and overlapping (see pages 224–225). Several scholars found that the ingredients of good independent study are clarity of purpose, assignment, and procedures; good monitoring; and the provision of immediate feedback to learners (Emmer et al.; Fisher et al.).

With regard to monitoring, Fisher and others found that when teachers interact briefly but meaningfully with students during independent work, the students' on-task time increases by about 10 percent. Relatedly, Good and Grouws report that teachers whose students achieve more have more contacts with learners at work. Furthermore, these teachers take monitoring opportunities to give students relevant feedback and so help them be successful. Finally, Gartland finds that teachers should not provide students with more whole-class practice during a teacher presentation but instead should provide them with more monitored independent practice.

it is used much less to prepare students for lifelong learning, although everyone recalls working on self-propelling independent reports. We also believe many teachers use this practice for a third purpose: to keep some students legitimately occupied so that teachers can work with other students in, say, a reading or math group. The key word is *legitimately*. Unfortunately, it is too easy to give students work that is nothing more than busywork; in other words, its sole intention is to keep students occupied.

One of the authors recalls visiting in a daughter's first-grade classroom on parents' night. The teacher was entertaining questions. One mother asked, "Why do the children spend day after day coloring worksheets and cutting them out?" The teacher, stymied for a moment and perhaps feeling found out, stammered a possibly suitable but unlikely answer: "To improve eye-hand coordination."

7.19 What factors in Chapter 1 may influence how you feel about independent study?

LIMITATIONS OF INDEPENDENT STUDY

Perhaps the greatest drawback to independent study is not with the technique itself but with its intentions, conduct, and assessment. If the intentions of such study are not clear and reasonable, students may resist the assignments or exert minimal effort. Said another way, when learners do not perceive the task as meeting some need or having value, they will not honor it.

7.20 How do you feel about the use of independent study?

In terms of the conduct of independent study, be forewarned that you must monitor the study, provide feedback, and help students see that the assignment is as valuable as other work (Anderson, 1981; Anderson, Brubaker, Alleman-Brooks, & Duffy, 1984; Dembo, 1994; Seifert & Beck, 1984).

MAKING GOOD HOMEWORK ASSIGNMENTS

Homework assignments are a form of independent study. Therefore, almost all the information in the section on independent study applies here. However, there

Curriculum tie-in: This lesson may be linked to studies in almost any subject field.

OBJECTIVE

1. Learners will collect and synthesize biographical information, then prepare a brief, written biography. *Specific objectives:* Learners will:

   a. Select a target person for whom a biography will be prepared.

   b. Establish what they want to learn about the person.

   c. Collect related information utilizing resources such as print material, electronic encyclopedias, the Internet, and the like.

   d. Organize found information into categories determined in *b* above.

   e. Synthesize the most interesting, useful information in each category.

   f. Prepare a written story of the target person's life that is organized, interesting, and follows the rules for spelling, grammar, and capitalization.

RESOURCES

1. Print and nonprint biographical resources: books, periodicals, electronic encyclopedias, and Internet sites on biography.

2. Activity sheet to be prepared that illustrates the categories of information that learners might seek about their target person.

METHODOLOGY

1. *Set induction:* "Have you ever seen the television show *Biography*? What is a biography? What biographies have you read or seen? Why do you suppose biographies are so interesting and helpful? How might learning about a person who is related to what we are studying be interesting and helpful?"

2. Inform learners of what they will learn and be able to do as a result of the lesson (see Objective above).

3. Get learners to consider the process of writing a biography: "How do you suppose a biography is written? What steps would need to be followed?" List steps on the board.

4. Have learners make a list of questions, the answers to which they think would provide the basis of an interesting (rather than boring) and informative biography.

5. Set parameters for the task: deadlines for selecting target person, for completing information collection and organization, for story length, and completion.

6. Make certain learners know from whom and how they can get help.

7. Tell students that it is important that you monitor their progress and how you will do so.

ASSESSMENT

1. Learners will prepare a brief biography that targets a key person (one related to the study at hand) and that shows evidence of careful planning, organization, and good presentation as noted in the Objective.

CLOSURE

1. Have learners review the purpose of the task and how it will be accomplished.

2. Discuss ways by which the biographies will be used in class: oral presentations, classroom exhibits, placing them on the class or school website.

---

are some additional tips that apply specifically when homework assignments are used (Cooper & Valentine 2001; District Administrator, 2004; Feldman, 2004; Matthews, 2003; Paulu, 1998; Vatterott 2010).

- Let learners, parents, and caregivers know when and how often assignments will be made and approximately how long they will be. Rules of thumb for most learners are as follows: for young children, no more than 20 minutes a *school day;* for fourth through sixth graders, 20 to 40 minutes; for seventh through ninth graders, two hours; for older students two and a half hours.

- Make sure that assignments serve a good purpose. They permit learners to review or practice what they are studying, allow learners to explore something in greater depth or breadth, get learners ready to learn something in the next day's class, or teach learners how to use learning resources such as libraries and reference materials. Never use homework for punishment (a bad purpose since it then is thought of in negative terms).

- Make certain that learners understand the good purpose and meaning of the assignment and that they have resources necessary to succeed.

"When do you get to start leaving your work at the office?"

- Ensure that the assignment is clear and that learners know both what is to be accomplished and how.

- Make assignments that are neither too easy nor too difficult. Make absolutely certain that learners are capable of successfully accomplishing the work *before* they leave you.

- Vary assignments. Try to create assignments that provide for individual differences in how students learn (see "Learning Style Differences" in Chapter 3). Take into account that your learners have different ability and attention differences (see "Learning Aptitude Differences" in Chapter 3).

- Teach school study habits that transfer to homework assignments (such as the need to eliminate distractions and the need to make certain materials necessary to complete the assignment are available).

- Provide learners with feedback on their work. Learners must have knowledge of results. What did they do well and not so well? Provide help (reteaching) as needed. Unexamined assignments are useless to the learner and convince students that they were just busywork. Worse yet, student errors go uncorrected, and thus are learned.

- Work with parents and caregivers to ensure that home assignments are meeting your expectations and theirs in terms of quality and length and find out what effects (positive and negative) they are having on a learner's home life.

Remember, good homework, like a good school assignment, encourages love of learning while bad homework is destructive.

Spotlight on Research 7.7 presents what research tells us about homework.

SUMMARY ON INDEPENDENT STUDY

Try Activity 7.10

Independent study is an excellent instructional alternative that serves several important purposes. Mostly teachers use it for practice or rehearsal of information. However, it also helps students acquire study and inquiry skills that will serve them throughout life. During independent work, your role is to facilitate and guide learning. To do so, you must not only be available, but also must actively monitor. When you are not available or cannot monitor, as with home assignments, you must find someone else to fill this role.

Since considerable consensus exists regarding the benefits of independent study and how to conduct good independent study assignments, you should make use of this instructional alternative. Doing so will make you a better teacher and help your students achieve and be satisfied.

Go to the "Instructional Strategies: Independent Study" website for more information.

OLC Web Link
Instructional Strategies:
Independent study

7.21 How do you feel about individualism as opposed to conformity? To what extent should teachers tailor instructions to fit individuals?

Individualized or Differentiated Instruction: Tailoring Teaching

WHAT IS INDIVIDUALIZED INSTRUCTION?

Individualized instruction and **differentiated instruction** are terms used to refer to any instructional maneuver that attempts to tailor teaching and learning to a learner's, or a group of like-learners', unique strengths and needs. Said another way, individualized instruction means responding educationally to *individuals*. In Chapter 3, we found out that teachers must, according to the Individuals with Disabilities Education Act, develop an individualized educational plan (IEP) for each student with educational challenges or handicaps. Of course, to a lesser extent, teachers try to meet the special needs of all children. You can probably recall some teachers who, more than others, took into account your strengths and needs.

How do students feel about homework? What is its effect on them? The majority of students rate homework among their least favorite things. Only having to hold a job rates lower. Nevertheless, they report it is valuable and that they have time to do it. Those kids who report they have too much homework, or not enough time to do it, are less likely to finish their assignments, less likely to believe homework is important, and more likely to have lower grades.

What distracts students from doing homework? Educators report the following, in order of importance, interfere with homework completion: distraction of technological devices and social networking, poor learner organizational skills, lack of parental support, lack of motivation, lack of time, home responsibilities, not understanding the assignment or having necessary skills to do it, not seeing the value or purpose, not knowing where and how to get help, extracurricular involvement, feeling overloaded, and noise at home.

How do parents feel about homework? The majority of parents feel homework is a good thing, that teachers assign the right amount, and that kids have time to do it. Minority parents especially are convinced of its importance. However, most parents are not sure of the quality of the assignments. Many believe much of it is busywork.

What is the result of parent involvement in homework? When parents are trained to help kids with homework, the latter complete more homework, have fewer related problems, and, with the exception of middle school students, tend to perform better. Parents not supportive of homework are less connected to schools.

Why do teachers assign homework? Teachers use homework to give students practice using something learned in class, to prepare them for tests, to create interest in a new topic, and to develop work habits and responsibility.

How do more experienced teachers think about and treat homework? Highly experienced teachers believe it is more important; they provide students with more homework feedback; and they feel better prepared to give good assignments.

What is the effect of homework on student achievement? Homework has positive effects on achievement in most cases, even when only an "average amount" is done. When the homework is evaluated by the teacher the result is even better.

How much homework should be assigned? More is usually better *but* to a point. These variables need to be taken into account: homework difficulty; learner ability and disposition; time available to the learner to do the task; and time available to the teacher to judge it and provide students with feedback.

Who does and doesn't do homework? About two-thirds of K–12 students report doing homework daily. Most likely to have and do homework are kids in upper elementary school, high school girls, and students whose parents are more highly educated and affluent. Interestingly, students in one-parent households whose parent works are likely to do homework. Most unlikely to do it are upper elementary and junior high minority children, children in larger families, and those with siblings in the home. Minority children who have or do homework are more likely to spend more time on it.

Sources: Cooper, Robinson, & Pattal (2006), Metlife Survey (2007), Pattall, Cooper, & Robinson (2008)

As you will see, various types of individualized instruction exist. Each more or less individualizes instruction. By "more or less," we mean some types do more than others in addressing learners' strengths or meeting learners' needs.

The concept **differentiated instruction**—teachers working to accommodate and build on student's diverse learning needs—is not new. Rather, it is an outgrowth and elaboration of individualized instruction. Tomlinson shares her perspective in Rebora (2008).

PURPOSE AND CHARACTERISTICS OF INDIVIDUALIZED INSTRUCTION

Individualized, personalized instruction has unique attributes. As the name implies, its most unique purpose is to tailor teaching to an individual's peculiar strengths and needs. No other instructional maneuver does just that.

The characteristics of individualized instruction also set it apart. Consider the role of the teacher. When individualizing instruction is the goal, the teacher's role is to know and care about individuals, about the diversity of students. The teacher can't teach the class as though everyone in it is alike (one size fits all)

CHAPTER 7
Four Instructional Alternatives:
Presentation, Discussion, Independent
Study, and Individualized Instruction

www.mhhe.com/cruickshank6e

231

any more than parents can treat their children as if they are all the same. It just won't do.

Another characteristic that sets individualized instruction apart is the unique way in which it deals with five variables: the *goals of instruction, learning activities, resources, mastery level,* and *time.* When learners have a great deal of autonomy in regard to these five factors, we can say that instruction really has been *tailored, differentiated, customized,* or *personalized.* Let's consider each variable.

Goals of Instruction As we learned in Chapter 6, the "formal curriculum" is set by the state and local school district. For the most part, teachers teach that curriculum. Perhaps all fourth grade classrooms study the history of Native Americans, while in the tenth grade everyone studies American government. However, what if one or more fourth graders is interested in learning about the discovery of gold in California and Alaska or some tenth graders want to study African-American history? To the extent that teachers allow students to choose the topic or subtopic of study, they are individualizing instruction, that is, meeting individual needs.

Learning Activities In most classrooms, all students are asked to follow a similar learning procedure. For example, if the teacher's goal is to study the history of Native Americans, the teacher usually spells out how the class will do this. However, the teacher, after setting the goal, could permit a good deal of autonomy with regard to how individual students might attain the goal. In this case, the instructor could say, "We are going to study Native Americans. How would you like to do this? Would some of you prefer to read? To look at recorded documentaries? To interview Native Americans?" The greater the instructional autonomy teachers grant, the more they are individualizing and personalizing. This should put you in mind of the idea of multiple intelligences presented in Chapter 3. Teacher Laurie Biser in Case 7.2, How Teachers Individualize, allows her learners this freedom of choice.

Resources Even though individual students have preferences about how they want to learn, they need further individualization. For example, if several students want to learn about Native Americans through reading, a number of different kinds and levels of reading material must be made available. Teacher Rob Frescoln in Case 7.2 makes such provision. Providing autonomy to choose how to learn carries individualization only so far. Providing a variety of resource materials for different ability levels takes it further.

Mastery Level Another way you can individualize is to accept different levels of performance from different students. This is complicated because you also need to have high expectations for all. Perhaps the best way to put it is to have high expectations for all learners but even higher expectations for some. Thus, you might want all children to achieve at some agreed-upon level but want others to surpass that level—to excel. In studying the history of Native Americans, children with little previous related knowledge could be expected to reach level X, while children who have had a keen interest in and prior knowledge of Native Americans could be expected to reach level Y. As Brophy and Evertson (1976) note, "The very idea of individualized instruction implies that there is a certain level of difficulty or content specificity that is optimal for each student" (p. 61). Teacher Pat Rutz in Case 7.2 provides different mastery levels.

7.22 In which ways are you most likely to individualize instruction?

Time The final variable that can be manipulated for individuals is time. You can, as is usually the case, expect all students to accomplish the goal in the same amount of time. Or time can be flexible, with some students taking more than others.

CASE 7.2
How Teachers Individualize

Willis and Mann (2000) provide illustrations of how teachers individualize instruction.

Pat Rutz, an East Hanover, New Jersey, primary teacher, differentiates learning activities for kids strong in math by allowing them to pursue higher-level math independently. For example, if some learners know the concept of place value, they are challenged by other related activities while she teaches the basic concept to the rest of the class.

When Ann Arbor, Michigan, fourth-grade teacher Laurie Biser teaches the multiplication facts, she is very aware that her students will learn them best when a variety of approaches are permitted. So, she expects them to learn using drawing, flash cards, or manipulatives (objects that may be arranged and rearranged such as coins and collector cards). Biser also uses contracts that permit students to choose from a variety of spelling activities worth different point values depending upon the level of difficulty. (See *contracts* in the section below, The Dalton and Winnetka Plans.)

Seventh-grade Chapel Hill, North Carolina, teacher Rob Frescoln accepts that his students differ greatly in their reading and writing skills. Thus, when they do research papers he provides a variety of texts at different reading levels. Furthermore, he has students work in mixed ability groups, each reading at his own level and then sharing what has been learned with the others. Frescoln believes that this approach helps all students to push themselves just a bit further.

Gaithersburg, Maryland, secondary social studies teacher Leon Bushe likes to engage students in mock trials. He divides his class of 30 into three groups of 10 and gives each group a court case involving a legal concept such as "beyond a reasonable doubt." Learners choose the role they wish to play (lawyers, witnesses, judge, etc.). To prepare for their roles in the trial and the trial itself, students must complete individualized reading and writing assignments.

Additional examples of how teachers differentiate instruction are presented in Tomlinson (1999).

Source: Willis & Mann (2000).

INVESTIGATING AND
SOLVING THE CASE

1. How have teachers Rutz, Biser, Frescoln, and Bushe made use of individualization?

2. Which of the several approaches they use appeal most to you?

To repeat, individualized instruction has a unique purpose and characteristics. Its purpose is to serve the individual rather than the entire class. Consequently, the teacher is expected to know and care about student diversity. The nature or character of individualized instruction is a function of several factors. It can differ according to the amount of autonomy given students to select what they will do and how they will do it. It can also differ according to the resources they have available, the level of mastery expected, and the time they are given to complete the task. Figure 7.4 depicts the key characteristics of individualized instruction.

Spotlight on Research 7.8 describes how teachers let students choose what and how they will learn.

TYPES OF INDIVIDUALIZED INSTRUCTION

We have identified a number of procedures and programs that have been generated to individualize instruction. As you read about each, ask yourself, "To what extent does this idea really get at individual strengths and needs?"

Contracts Contracts are signed agreements in which learners promise to perform specific academic work—perhaps read a book and write a synopsis of it. Usually, contracts describe precisely what will be done, how, at what level of achievement, and within what time frame. The task may be learner selected; for example, the student decides what book to read. The task may be contracted at various levels of difficulty; for example, the book may be an original text or a popularized version. Work that is contracted at a high level and completed successfully results in a high

7.23 Which of the various forms of individualized instruction have you experienced? What were they like for you?

www.mhhe.com/cruickshank6e

CHAPTER 7
Four Instructional Alternatives:
Presentation, Discussion, Independent
Study, and Individualized Instruction

233

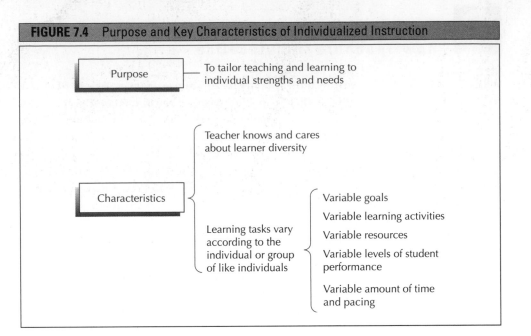

FIGURE 7.4 Purpose and Key Characteristics of Individualized Instruction

Purpose — To tailor teaching and learning to individual strengths and needs

Characteristics

- Teacher knows and cares about learner diversity
- Learning tasks vary according to the individual or group of like individuals
  - Variable goals
  - Variable learning activities
  - Variable resources
  - Variable levels of student performance
  - Variable amount of time and pacing

SPOTLIGHT ON RESEARCH 7.8
What Kind of Learning Choices Do Teachers Give Students?

Teachers report that they individualize or differentiate instruction in several ways. Mostly they give students choices of what content they can study or how (see Case 7.2 above). Additionally, it is common for teachers to provide variety with regard to homework and the use of in-class free time, and provide alternative ways students can show their knowledge. Students are less often given choices regarding how they will be tested.

More choices are given to older learners, those of higher ability, and those who are high achievers.

Overall, teachers in the study believe it is important that all students be given some choices so that they can practice self-determination and decision making and because choosing increases interest and engagement. (Flowerday and Schraw, 2000.)

grade. Work contracted and successfully completed at a lower level, perhaps by a challenged learner, might be graded satisfactory, etc. One format for a contract appears in Highlight 7.4.

Programmed and Computer-Assisted Instruction These are described in Chapter 4 as examples of instruction following the behavioral school of thought.

Both programmed instruction (PI) and computer-assisted instruction (CAI) use self-instructional formats. The material to be learned is broken down into small, easily learned segments. When students finish one segment correctly, they go to the next. If a student does not understand, he is redirected to try again or is provided additional information that facilitates understanding. Newer programs actually diagnose students' mistakes and provide them with highly individualized feedback. Some computer-assisted instruction is very creative (see Case 7.3 on page 236).

Individually Prescribed Instruction (IPI) IPI is described by Jeter (1980). At the beginning of a school year students are pretested in several subject areas to find out what they already know. According to the results, students are assigned work at appropriate academic levels. Students do not necessarily work alone; they may be given tasks to complete with other learners who are at the same level. At set intervals in the curriculum, learners take tests. If they are successful, they move on. If not, instruction is repeated.

Individually Guided Education (IGE) IGE is another form of individualized instruction. A major difference between IGE and other systems is that IGE is done in a "nongraded" school. A **nongraded school** is one in which grade levels are blurred or nonexistent. In IGE schools, several teachers may be assigned to a unit of 100 to 150 students who would typically span several grade levels in achievement. The team of teachers develops and evaluates an instructional program for each child. Each child's program is based on how and at what pace he learns best, and where he stands on mastering specific skills and concepts. Pavin (1992) provides a review of the benefits of nongraded programs, while Gutierriz and Slavin (1992) describe types of nongraded schools and their respective effectiveness.

Tutoring Tutoring, or coaching, is perhaps the oldest and best-known means of individualizing instruction. It is used either to give remedial instruction to a student or to provide supplementary information. In the first case, a child could be tutored if she or he couldn't count to 100 by an appropriate age or developmental level. In the second case, a child might be instructed as to how to create a crossword puzzle.

CHAPTER 7
Four Instructional Alternatives:
Presentation, Discussion, Independent
Study, and Individualized Instruction

www.mhhe.com/cruickshank6e

235

Ameritech is one of several companies supporting computer instruction in America's classrooms. It has a traveling display that demonstrates newer ways computers can help students learn. Stratton (1993) describes three of them.

Jason, a high school freshman, opened a computer window and looked inside a storm cloud. The cloud was a model projected on the screen. Jason could rotate the image so he could see the column of heat in the cloud's center.

Furthermore, he would vary the temperature or wind speed to see how the cloud would react.

Ten-year-olds Teruko and Sam talked to each other over speakerphones while viewing a world map on their separate computer screens. In this way, they could collaborate on a homework assignment on mapping.

Pupils in two Ohio cities were connected by a large-screen computer and telephone that enabled them to jointly study tissue and genetics. They could not only see and hear each other but also see and hear the teacher and see slides and other materials the teacher used.

> **INVESTIGATING AND SOLVING THE CASE**
>
> 1. In what ways have you experienced computer classrooms?
> 2. What were the good and bad of them?

Many different persons serve as tutors, including teachers, teacher aides, students, and parents. Peer assisted learning (PAL) occurs when students tutor classmates (see Spotlight on Research 7.9).

Distance Learning This is another variation of individualized instruction. As the name implies, the intention is to make education more accessible to persons not located near an instructional facility such as a public school. Distance education programs have long been used to serve children in remote areas in Alaska, Canada, and Australia. Traditionally instruction has been provided via telephone, radio, television, and printed materials such as texts and guidebooks. Most of us are familiar with the concept of correspondence courses and correspondence study.

The advent of the computer has made it possible to increase the incidence and quality of distance education. Moreover, it is commonly called upon to provide a complete or nearly complete education to kids who are home schooled. There are thousands of **virtual, online, or e-schools** that provide an entire curriculum for students. Students "attending" virtual schools full time receive a computer and have access to many software programs especially designed for individualized use. They go through the courses at their own pace and have assistance available from online instructors and their home school teacher.

Beside serving home schooled children, cyber-based schools also provide advanced and enrichment courses that might not otherwise be available at a child's school of attendance.

Here are some positives about virtual education.

- It is popular both with high- and low-achieving students. The latter seem to benefit from the one-on-one instruction it can provide.
- It can make an otherwise unavailable course available. For example a student in a rural school might have access to an online AP class her school could not offer.
- Students can have access to quality online teachers who interact with them in discussion groups and via e-mail and instant messaging (Fording, 2004).

Following are some good, related websites to explore. You can link to them directly from the Online Learning Center.

SPOTLIGHT ON RESEARCH 7.9
Peer Assisted Learning Works

After looking at over 80 studies on peer-assisted learning (when students help one another), researchers concluded that it works. It is particularly effective with younger children, urban children, low-income and minority kids. It works best when "peer assisted strategies" are carefully implemented (Rohrbeck et al., 2003).

The peer assisted learning strategy (PALS) is described on its website as follows.

PALS is a version of classwide peer tutoring. Teachers identify which children require help on specific skills and which children might help them learn those skills. Using this information, teachers pair students in the class, so that partners work simultaneously and productively on different activities that address the problems they are experiencing. Pairs are changed regularly, and over a period of time as students work on a variety of skills, all students have the opportunity to be "coaches" and "players."

PALS creates 13 to 15 pairs in a classroom, each geared to the individual student's needs, instead of a single, teacher-directed activity that may end up addressing the problems of only a few children. The strategy also creates opportunities for a teacher to circulate in the class, observe students, and provide individual remedial lessons.

 Web Link
Peer Assisted Learning

- *American School Board Journal online* (September 2002) for a special report "Learning Without Walls." Click on "A new kind of school" to find out about e-learning. Click on "A virtual tour of virtual schools" to visit some.
- British Broadcasting Company.
- Connections Academy.
- Electronic Classroom of Tomorrow and click on "Curriculum" where you can engage in some of the programs used with children.
- The Ohio Virtual Academy.

7.24 What has your experience been like with online learning?

The Project Method: Self-Directed Learning The Project Method is defined as: Teaching by engaging students in a long-term activity in which they gather information and develop a product of some kind, such as a written report, oral presentation, or model. Some educators believe that students learn more, understand the content more thoroughly, and remember information and skills longer when they work on a project (ASCD Lexicon of Learning).

Where individualization is the goal then the project, often undertaken by a group, is self-selected and focuses on real world problems. An example may clarify. The curriculum for Ms. Garcia's class requires learning ways to encourage energy conservation. Students may rummage around and find related topics of interest including energy conservation in the home, in school, in transportation, and so forth. That done, they decide to work on a topic individually but more commonly in small groups. Ms. Garcia is the facilitator, helping learners to frame worthwhile questions to answer, structuring the work to be done, coaching, and so forth. However, learners are mostly responsible for seeking solutions to the problem and to present them to the whole class for inspection and discussion (Abdullah, 2001; David, 2008).

Projects can be assigned but learners may decide how to do them. Web Quests are an example. They require students to work in groups. To illustrate, one Web Quest asks students to write and produce an old-time radio program. To do so they are given a website address on old-time radio where they can collect useful information. Go to the OLC Web Link "Web Quests" to see their potential.

Blogger Matthews reflects on self-directed learning in Highlight 7.5.

Individualization, then, is not any one kind of program. It eschews whole-class or mass teaching and embraces instead *differentiation, adaptation of subject matter to the individual,* and, at its extreme, the *emancipation of students from the constraints of the curriculum planned by others.* Its tenets include self-direction, initiative, freedom,

 Web Link
Web Quests

CHAPTER 7
Four Instructional Alternatives:
Presentation, Discussion, Independent
Study, and Individualized Instruction

www.mhhe.com/cruickshank6e

237

Experiential learning, though underutilized, is by far, the most effective [teaching] method. . . . [Here is my explanation for] why I believe educators shy away from it in favor of lectures and worksheets. Many people who choose teaching as a career do so because they are very comfortable with a highly structured environment; the schedules, the bells and the rules. Experiential learning, especially when self-directed, asks teachers to step outside of a comfort zone and into a situation where they are not always in control of the outcome. That can be very scary for some folks.

I am not a person with control issues, in fact I have a sign in my office with a quote by poet Wistawa Szymborska that says: "I prefer the hell of chaos to the hell of order."

I try to give my students as many experiential learning experiences as I can, but I am not always successful with a self-directed approach. Although I am comfortable relinquishing control of an outcome, often my students find self-direction confusing. They like recipes, they like specifics, they like to be told exactly what to do. It is easier for them. Creativity requires thinking: it requires work.

Ambitious students will take a self-directed assignment and fly with it. [Less ambitious] students will more than likely give up and fail. It is extremely hard for those kids who were never expected to think for themselves, to be expected to make their own decisions.

It is up to me to open the door and give them permission to explore. Some of them will eventually find the courage to step outside, others may need a push, but sadly there will always be those who will flat-out refuse, never leaving an environment that tells them what to think and how to live.

Source: Matthews (2006).

responsibility and a preference for constructivist learning theory, and learning by doing rather than by listening.

GOOD USERS OF INDIVIDUALIZED INSTRUCTION

7.25 What values, knowledge, and abilities do you have that would help you implement individualized instruction?

To be really good at individualizing instruction, you must have particular values, knowledge, and abilities. Foremost, you must prize diversity. "You must comprehend, accept, value, and affirm respect for all people regardless of sexual, racial, cultural, ethnic, religious, and physical differences" (Heck & Williams, 1984, p. 53). Relatedly, you must value individualism by encouraging your students to think and do for themselves.

Gaining knowledge of your students is essential. The more you know about them, the better your potential to address their strengths and needs. Therefore, you must be inclined toward being a diagnostician and clinician. Chapter 5 provides suggestions for getting to know learners better.

You also need knowledge of and ability to use the various types of individualized instruction. Finally, you will need interpersonal skills, including the ability to listen, to accept, and to encourage.

GOOD INDIVIDUALIZED EDUCATION PROGRAMS

7.26 Which advantages of individualized instruction are most important in your eyes?

Given the definition of individualized instruction and its purpose and characteristics, the following criteria should help you decide how good an individualized program really is.

- Is the program tailored to meet learners' unique strengths and needs?
- How much autonomy do learners have with regard to the goals of instruction, the learning activities, resources, and time?
- Does it result in equity (academic, social, emotional) without hurting participants by stigmatizing, causing loss of self-esteem, or restricting friendships?

Yes, individualized education, done well, has lots of potential advantages. Among other things, it can allow learners to pursue their interests, help them to take responsibility for learning, allow them to utilize their preferred learning style, expose them to a wide variety of educational resources geared to their ability level, challenge them to be as good as they can be, and permit them to work at their own best pace. Such advantages should make your class more attentive, enthusiastic, independent, and, of course, academically able.

A summary of what good users of individualized instruction and good programs are like appears in Table 7.7.

A brief individualized instruction lesson appears as Lesson Plan 7.5.

WHEN INDIVIDUALIZED INSTRUCTION SHOULD BE USED

Obviously, individualized instruction should be used whenever teachers hope to serve a student's unique strengths and needs. "OK," you say, "but isn't that all the time?" Of course, but human and material resources are not available to meet this ideal. Thus, you will need to compromise, using individualized, personalized instruction whenever a child is at risk of school failure and beyond that as often as possible.

From your experience, you know that, in almost all classrooms, teacher presentations and recitations prevail. In some instances, discussion is an occasional alternative of choice. Most likely, individualized instruction is underutilized, even with children at risk. The only pervasive effort to compel its use is contained in the Individuals with Disabilities Act, that requires Individual Educational Plans (IEPs) be drawn up and followed for students with disabilities. That is not to say that teachers are unaware of the needs and strengths of individual students, nor that they totally ignore such information. Rather, for the most part, teachers do not in a regular and conscious fashion individualize. What they tend to do is ability-group children with similar needs or similar strengths. However, and sometimes unfortunately, the practice of homogeneous grouping is drawing fire from those who claim it has negative side effects such as stereotyping students in the less advanced groups.

Spotlight on Research 7.10 (on page 241) summarizes the research findings on individualized instruction.

LIMITATIONS OF INDIVIDUALIZED INSTRUCTION

The overwhelming disadvantage of individualization is that when done properly, it is very time-consuming. You cannot just give students any old thing to do, even on an attractive computer. Neither can you simply allow students to do whatever they please. Individualizing means responding responsibly to each individual as a person with unique educational needs. That is compounded by large class size.

TABLE 7.7	Qualities of Good Users of Individualized Instruction and of Good Individualized Programs

Good Users . . .	Good Programs . . .
• Prize diversity	• Are tailored to meet individual learners' strengths and needs
• Value individualism	
• Know learners' strengths and needs	• Permit considerable learner autonomy with regard to goals, means, resources, time
• Have knowledge of and ability to implement such programs	• Result in greater equity
• Have strong interpersonal skills	• Have no damaging side effects

Curriculum tie-in: This lesson may be linked to reading and literature.

OBJECTIVES

1. Learners will engage in reading books and periodically choose a favorite.
2. Learners will share the criteria used in selecting their periodic favorite. *Specific objective:* Learners will be consciously aware of their book reading and liking motives.
3. Learners will report on the book. *Specific objective:* Learners will determine what they think others would want to know about the book and subsequently prepare a report for class presentation and placement in a class "Favorite Books Folder." The report should include the reasons why the book was so appealing to the reader.

RESOURCES

1. Books on the Internet.
2. School and community libraries.
3. Bookstores.
4. Home.

METHODOLOGY

1. *Set induction:* "What is the most favorite book you have ever read? Why did you enjoy it so much? When you read a good book do you like to share the story with your friends, relatives, or parents? I thought you would, and therefore I thought you might like to start a Favorite Book Club in our class."
2. Establish guidelines:
   - A folder will be kept containing what you want to tell others about your favorite new book. That might include the name and author of the book, the reasons why you chose to read it, what you think would interest others in reading the book, and anything else you might want to include. Perhaps you would want to include an illustration you make or the tape-recorded dialogue you make of some interesting passage you would like others to hear. What else you place in your book folder is up to you.
   - You may read the book(s) at home or in class—anytime your work is done.
   - You may choose a book of any length or on any topic that is in good taste.
   - You may submit a folder once a month, more than once a month, or less than once a month. How often you choose a favorite book will depend upon the books you choose (some you read may not be favored), the amount of time you have available to read, and other factors. The major goal is to locate and read material you truly enjoy and to share both our motives for reading and our discoveries.
   - Periodically, you will be asked to share your results in class.

ASSESSMENT

1. What have you found out about your reading interests? What kinds of books do you seem to like and why?
2. What do you believe your classmates most want to know about a book? How did you decide? Were you right?

CLOSURE

1. As a class, have students review what they have learned about how people choose books to read and how that is reflected in libraries.

SUMMARY ON INDIVIDUALIZED INSTRUCTION

As we have seen, individualized instruction takes many different forms. Most of the forms in use are fairly prescriptive and controlled: students have little or nothing to say about what or how they will learn. The only part of individualized instruction that may be truly individualized is the time needed to learn. The forms are often tight programs that students move through as quickly as they can. However, in terms of student learning, these programs seem to work.

Try Activity 7.11

Few forms of individualized instruction allow students any real autonomy in deciding what they will learn and/or how. We mentioned one exception: the Project Method, a standby for generations, that seems to work for teachers and learners alike. You will see many classrooms, particularly in elementary and middle schools, where individuals or groups of children address themselves to topics they have an interest in and decide how they will learn about some aspect of the topic.

We have said that when teachers instruct students one on one, they must know the students and accept and prize their diversity. Furthermore, they have to value

There are so many variations on the theme of individualized instruction that it is difficult to generalize about its success. Walberg (1984, 1991) looked at the results of nearly 3,000 studies covering a variety of educational practices; included among them were studies of several forms of individualized instruction. In order of effectiveness, they include acceleration (that is, advancing students academically), science mastery learning, personalized instruction, adaptive instruction, tutoring, individualized science, diagnostic prescriptive methods, individualized instruction, and individualized mathematics. Obviously, some of these forms of individualized instruction are not well known. It will suffice to say,

however, that they all are arrangements that customize teaching and learning in some way to better serve students.

Ellson (1986) is another scholar who has studied educational practices to determine their effectiveness. Among those he reports as most beneficial are so-called nonconventional alternatives, including programmed instruction and performance-based instruction in which learning is constantly monitored and instruction regularly altered to help the learner succeed.

Slavin and Madden (1989) believe that good instruction for children at risk of school failure must entail individualization. They find support for and advocate using one-on-one tutoring,

individually adopted computer-assisted instruction, frequent monitoring of individual student progress, modification of instruction and grouping arrangements to meet individual needs, and having and using a wide range of instructional resources.

Finally, the U.S. Department of Education in a publication called *What Works* (1986, 1987) names several forms of individualized instruction among its findings on how best to teach and improve learning. The forms are having parents read to children, tutoring, and acceleration of gifted students.

Given these research findings, it would seem that individualizing instruction is well worth the extra effort required.

individualism and have good interpersonal skills, especially the ability to listen and encourage. If the individualized program you use is a good one, it will be tailored to each learner's strengths and needs, give students as much autonomy as possible, and help children achieve without causing personal embarrassment.

Good individualized instruction seems to be a standout approach. It can meet a great many personal, professional, and educational needs for teachers and students. This instructional alternative also has good support from research.

Matching Instructional Alternatives to Learners

What do teachers think are the best instructional alternatives for different kinds of students? Are certain ways of teaching better suited to high- or low-ability learners? Are some better suited to independent versus (as opposed to) conforming learners? Shuell and his colleagues undertook two studies in order to find answers (Shuell, Brown, Watson, & Ewing, 1988).

In the first study, 91 suburban elementary teachers received information about four different kinds of hypothetical students. The information portrayed each of the students as either (1) high ability–independent, (2) high ability–conforming, (3) low ability–independent, or (4) low ability–conforming. For example, the hypothetical high ability–independent learner was characterized as follows:

> Robby is an independent, productive worker. He is doing very well in all his subjects, and is usually ahead of [them] in tasks requiring complex verbal skills. His classmates look up to him for leadership. The teacher has assigned the class to read Black Beauty and asked them to be ready for a quiz. (p. 354, paraphrased)

After reading the four hypothetical student characterizations, the 91 teachers were asked to decide which of several instructional alternatives would be best suited for each student when engaged in a verbal learning task such as reading.

www.mhhe.com/cruickshank6e

CHAPTER 7
Four Instructional Alternatives:
Presentation, Discussion, Independent
Study, and Individualized Instruction

241

The instructional alternatives teachers were to consider were lecture/explanation, seat work (supervised study), discussion, one-to-one teaching (individualized instruction), peer tutoring (individualized instruction), homogeneous grouping, or praise. We do not consider the last two areas to be instructional alternatives, and the investigators did not claim "praise" was one either. Still, it was included.

In the second Shuell study, 20 fourth- and fifth-grade teachers participated. First, they were asked to think about each of their present students with regard to five attributes: general academic ability, achievement orientation, classroom participation, motivation, and prior knowledge. Next, the teachers were asked to describe which instructional alternative was most appropriate for each student when engaged in a verbal learning task. The instructional alternatives teachers could choose among were the same as in the first study except that "homogeneous grouping" was replaced by "games," and "small-group work" displaced "discussion."

The investigators acknowledge that the two studies differ somewhat but believe the following conclusions are in order:

- Teachers believe different instructional alternatives work best for different learners.

- Teachers consider lecture/explanation and seat work most beneficial for high-ability students.

- Teachers consider one-to-one work, peer tutoring, and praise more appropriate for children of low ability.

- Teachers present mixed perceptions with regard to discussion. In study 1 (the hypothetical students), they felt it was equally inappropriate for either high- or low-ability learners. In study 2 (real students), they reported it appropriate for high-ability students.

7.27 How do you think these factors will influence how you will teach during student teaching?

Shuell and associates conclude that teachers do have definite ideas regarding how best to teach different learners and that, generally, these ideas are consistent with what we know about learning and teaching.

In Spotlight on Research 7.11 student teachers describe five factors that influence their choice of teaching method. One is the developmental ability of the learner.

Overview of 31 Instructional Alternatives

At the beginning of the chapter, we indicated that a brief overview of 31 instructional alternatives would follow the in-depth information on presentation, discussion, independent study, and individualized instruction. Here they are, presented alphabetically. You will note that some have characteristics in common with others. For example, presentations and recitations are both normally led by the teacher.

- **Academic games or competitions**—Learners compete with each other one to one or team to team to determine which individual or group is superior at a given academic task such as in "spelldowns," anagrams, or project completion. Some well-known commercially available academic games include *Probe* (vocabulary and spelling) and *Rook* (mathematics). Cooperative learning, presented in the next chapter, may incorporate games and competition.

- **Brainstorming**—To generate creative ideas, learners are asked to withhold judgment or criticism and produce a very large number of ways to do something, such as resolve a particular problem. For example, learners may be asked to think of as many ideas as they can for eliminating world hunger. Once they have generated a large number of ideas, the ideas are subjected to inspection in respect to their feasibility.

Student teachers tell us the following factors influence how they teach.

- *Subject matter.* They believe some subjects (science and social studies) are best taught using indirect, student-centered teaching, while others (math and reading) are best taught using direct, teacher-centered instruction.
- *The developmental ability of learners.* Student teachers believe that certain instructional approaches are best suited to learners because of age, ability, and maturity. They believe certain learners need structure and feel more comfortable using direct teaching with them. They also believe direct, structured teaching results in better classroom control.
- *Status as a student teacher.* Student teachers are more likely to try different approaches to teaching when encouraged by mentors. Those with more self-confidence are more likely to try different instructional approaches.
- *Knowledge of and skill in instructional alternatives.* Student teachers use instructional alternatives they know most about and are comfortable with or those their mentor teachers use.
- *Knowledge of subject matter.* Student teachers are less willing to use indirect teaching of content that they don't know much about. For example, if they don't understand math well themselves, they are less likely to teach it indirectly when students are expected to explore the subject more deeply.

Source: Gerges (2001).

- **Cases**—Students make detailed analysis of some specific, usually compelling, event or series of related events so that learners will better understand its nature and what might be done about it. For example, learners in a science class might investigate the occurrence of El Niño, or a disaster of human origin such as the infiltration of the zebra mussel in the Great Lakes.

- **Centers of interest and displays**—Collections and displays of materials are used to interest learners in themes or topics. For example, children may bring to school and display family belongings that reflect their ethnic heritage. The intention may be to interest the class in the notion of culture. Or, the teacher might arrange a display of different measurement devices to prompt interest in and exploration of that topic.

- **Colloquia**—A guest or guests are invited to class to be interviewed. Thus, a guest musician might serve as a stimulus for arousing interest in music and musical performance.

- **Constructivism**—Learners coming to learn through purposeful experiences (see Chapter 8).

- **Contracts**—Written agreements students and teachers may enter into describe the academic work students plan to accomplish in a particular period of time such as over a week or month.

- **Cooperative learning**—AKA *student-team learning*. Students working in groups are rewarded for collective effort (see Chapter 8).

- **Debates**—In this form of discussion, a few students present and contest varying points of view on an issue. For example, students could debate the issue "Is current criticism of Christopher Columbus fair?" (Barlowe 2005).

- **Demonstrations**—In this form of presentation, the teacher or learners show how something works or operates, or how something is done. For example, a teacher could demonstrate how to use a thesaurus, how to operate a handheld calculator, or what happens when oil is spilled on water (as when an oil tanker leaks).

CHAPTER 7
Four Instructional Alternatives:
Presentation, Discussion, Independent
Study, and Individualized Instruction

www.mhhe.com/cruickshank6e

243

"It was a very successful field trip. I managed to lose five of them."

- **Direct instruction**—A teacher gives explicit, step-by-step instruction (Rosenshine, 1987) (see Chapter 8).

- **Discovery**—In discovery learning, students are encouraged to derive their own understandings or meanings (see Chapter 8).

- **Discussion**—Described in this chapter, discussions occur when a group assembles to communicate with one another by speaking and listening about a topic or event of mutual interest.

- **Drill and practice**—In this form of independent study, the teacher explains a task and then learners practice it. After students learn how to use a thesaurus, for example, they could be asked to locate and use synonyms.

- **Field observation, fieldwork, field trips**—Students make observations or carry out work in an outside-the-school setting. Students might visit the local museum of natural history to see displays about dinosaurs, or they might begin and operate a small business to learn about production and marketing.

- **Independent study or supervised study**—Described in this chapter, independent study requires learners to complete a common task at their desks or as a home study assignment.

- **Individualized instruction**—Described in this chapter. Any of a number of teaching methods that tailor teaching and learning to meet a learner's unique characteristics.

- **Learning modules**—These are a form of individualized instruction that allow students to use a self-contained package of learning activities. The activities guide learners to know or to be able to do something. Students might be given a learning module that contains activities intended to help them understand good nutrition.

- **Mastery learning**—As a class, students are presented with information to be learned at a predetermined level of mastery. The class is tested, and individuals who do not obtain adequate scores are retaught and retested. Those who pass undertake enrichment study while classmates catch up (see Chapter 4).

- **Oral reports**—Individuals or groups of learners are assigned or choose topics. For example, each may be asked to find out about one planet in our solar system. They share what they learn with other class members through oral presentations.

- **Presentations**—Described in this chapter. Students listen to a person who talks about a topic. The teacher, or a guest speaker, might tell the class all about the artist Dali, for example.

- **Problem solving**—Individuals or groups of learners are presented with a perplexing, difficult question or situation and are asked to think about and try to resolve it (see Chapter 4).

- **Programmed and computer-assisted instruction**—In this form of individualized instruction, students learn information in small, separate units either by reading programmed texts or by using computer-presented teaching programs. A correct answer to a question or problem enables the learner to advance, while an incorrect response requires repetition or relearning (see Chapter 4).

- **Project or activity method**—In this form of individualization, learners choose and work on projects and activities on related topics. Students might write on or present in graphic presentation "Life in the South" or "Life in the North during the Civil War." Learners not only choose topics but also the project that will show what they've learned. (See this chapter, "Independent Study.")

- **Protocols**—Learners study an original record or records of some important event and then try to understand the event or its consequences. They might

"Please feel free to call on me if any of you need individual attention."

watch a film depicting actual instances of discrimination and then consider its causes and effects.

- **Reciprocal Teaching**—Teacher gradually shifts teaching responsibility to learners (see Chapter 4 on learning style differences).

- **Recitation**—Students are given information to study. They then recite what they have learned when the teacher questions them. For example, students might read about what causes different weather patterns, and the teacher might then question them to determine the extent and nature of their knowledge and understanding (see Table 7.3).

- **Role playing**—Learners take on the role of another person to see what it would be like to be that person. Thus, a student could play the role of an imaginary student no one likes or the role of an individual with handicaps.

- **Simulation games**—Students play a specially designed, competitive game that mirrors some aspect of life. For example, they might play the *Ghetto* (Toll, 1969) to find out about the problems and pressures ghetto dwellers face and, relatedly, to sense how difficult it is to improve one's lot in life. Another commercially available simulation game is *Gold Rush* (life and adventure in a frontier mining camp). Some simulation games are computerized, for example, *Oregon Trail* and *Amazon Trail*.

- **Simulations**—Learners engage with something intended to simulate—to give the appearance or have the effect of—something else. Thus, students may engage in a simulation of the United Nations General Assembly in order to have "firsthand" experience with how the Assembly works and what its delegates do.

- **Student-team, pupil-team, cooperative learning**—Described in Chapter 8. Learners are placed in groups or teams of four to six. Sometimes the groups are as diverse or heterogeneous as possible. In such cases, team members are often rewarded for the team's overall success. Under one type of cooperative learning, student teams might see a teacher presentation on division of fractions. They would then receive worksheets to complete. Team members would work together to find the answers. Finally, team members would take a quiz on division of fractions, and the team members' scores would be added to make up a team score.

- **Tutoring**—In this form of individualization, either a teacher or a fellow student provides a learner or small group of learners with special help, usually because the student is not learning well enough with only conventional instruction (Medway, 1987).

7.28 Which instructional alternatives do you prefer? Why?

The instructional alternatives we have briefly described are depicted on the Wheel of Instructional Choice in Figure 7.5.

Using Technology in Teaching

Technology certainly has changed how students learn and teachers teach. Software programs have long been available that permit kids to learn online using *tutorials* (e.g., Spanish for young children), *practice* (e.g., multiplication), or engagement in a *simulation* (e.g., building a city).

Most people know about and use search engines to find out about almost anything. Furthermore, most are knowledgeable about PowerPoint presentations as computer techniques for presenting information.

Increasingly we are becoming knowledgeable about *blogs, wikis,* and *podcasts.* Blogs (web logs) are merely websites created by persons who wish to share experiences. You have examples of what teachers post on blogs in Highlight 5.6 and

FIGURE 7.5 Wheel of Instructional Choice

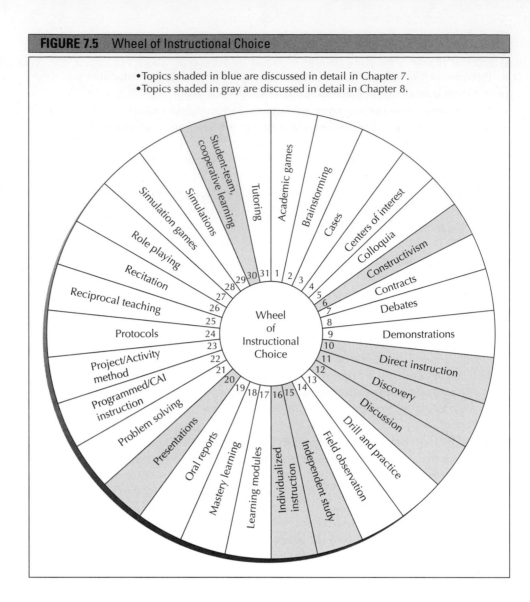

- Topics shaded in blue are discussed in detail in Chapter 7.
- Topics shaded in gray are discussed in detail in Chapter 8.

Wheel of Instructional Choice

Case 8.3 (next chapter). Middle school teacher Eric Langhorst created a class blog or online journal around the novel *Guerrilla Season*, which details Civil War atrocities committed by neighbors in Missouri. Students post their comments on the blog and author Pat Hughes responds to them (Bleimes, 2006).

A wiki is a collaborative website to which anyone belonging may edit something placed on that site. (*Wiki* means quick in Hawaiian.) A well-known example of a wiki is the online encyclopedia *Wikipedia*. Wikis permit collaborators to combine their knowledge and skill in order to produce something perhaps better than could be produced by a single person. Teacher Ben Sanoff has students put stories or essays on a class wiki site and they are edited by each other (Gillard, 2007). We cannot direct you to a class wiki since you need permission to be there.

Podcasts mostly are amateur radio recordings. For example, a student could create a talk show, presenting and commenting on news. Another might make an audio presentation of her report on My Family. A third might record an original story or poem. To learn more about podcasts, go to the website. (A tutorial is included.)

Take a look at Highlight 7.6 to see how teachers are employing some of these newer web tools. A number of online tutorials for teachers who plan to use technology when teaching is available at The Teacher Tap website.

Web Link

Podcasts

Web Link

The Teacher Tap

HIGHLIGHT 7.6
How Teachers Are Using Blogs, Wikis, and Podcasts

From blogs to wikis to podcasts, teachers in schools across the country are [using] Web tools to enhance student learning.

- Eric Langhorst's eight-grade American History students in Liberty, Mo., listen to his podcasts about the Boston Tea Party while . . . doing chores, or getting ready for bed.
- Ben Sanoff's World History students in Berkeley, Calif., discuss their

essays via instant messages before posting their final draft to the class blog . . . Later they return to the blog to read and discuss one another's work.

- Fifth graders in College park, Ga., create a wiki [that] in the first few days receives over 1,000 hits from as far away as Indonesia, Turkey, and Latin America . . . The [wiki], centered on an historical novel,

includes a slide show, maps, hsitorical background, and interviews.

Such [Web 2.0 interactive tools] are transforming how students learn and how teachers teach. [T]he use of Web tools in the classroom naturally propels teachers from lecturing at the front of the room to coaching from the back, a direction education professionals have been trying to steer teachers in for decades. (Gillard 2007).

SELECTING QUALITY SOFTWARE AND WEBSITES

The good news is that the software available in your classroom likely will be satisfactory with regard to both its quality and ability to help learners develop a range of lower- and higher-level thinking skills. The bad news is that the software often does not match the state and school district curriculum requirements for your subjects and grade levels. In other words, you may have top-notch software, but it doesn't necessarily teach what students are expected to learn. Thus teachers must often search long and hard for instructional software to fill specific curriculum needs.

Fortunately, educational software is reviewed both by public and private content evaluators. Some states provide public, formal evaluations on their websites. Among them are California and North Carolina. Journals also provide software reviews as do some professional associations. Sharp (2008) lists Internet sites that provide software reviews as does the Educational Software Directory (see Table 7.8).

Many teachers are using the Web as well as, or instead of, software to provide learning experiences. Websites may have the advantage of being interactive, and they are more likely up-to-date and free. On the other hand, some teachers don't like the Web. They feel it is too difficult to find good sites and then find ways to tie them into their normal lessons. They also worry that allowing students to explore the Web can result in their being distracted and that downloading website information can be a serious time constraint.

 Web Links
California Learning Resource

North Carolina Department of Public Instruction

UTILIZING DIGITAL CONTENT

Even though you may want to use digital content to improve learning, it will be a challenge. Teachers cite problems with expense, time, and preparation. Overwhelmingly, teachers who use software cite expense as a major concern. Most teachers note that there is not enough time to find and to use digital content. Finally, nearly half of teachers are concerned about the amount of preparation time required to use software and websites.

Some teachers and students don't restrict themselves to using existing digital content. They develop their own software and websites. This is possible through use of "computer tools" that include the following:

- *Word processing* that allows learners to write and revise with the assistance of spelling and grammar checkers.

7.29 How prepared are you to utilize digital content in your classroom? What further preparation do you feel you need? How might it be obtained?

CHAPTER 7
Four Instructional Alternatives:
Presentation, Discussion, Independent
Study, and Individualized Instruction

TABLE 7.8 Educational Software Reviews

A guide to educational software reviews on the Web can be found on the Educational Software Directory website.

- All Star Review—educational and entertainment product reviews.
- CALICO Review—language learning software reviews from the Computer Assisted Language Instruction Consortium.
- Children's Software Revue—attempts to help adults leverage the power of technology to support the development of children by providing timely, accurate reviews of commercial interactive products, including educational software, videogames, smart toys, and websites.
- Computing with Kids—weekly syndicated column by Jinny Gudmundsen which is published in over 80 newspapers and is also available as a free eZine.
- Cyber News and Reviews—monthly column by Howard Berenbon, developed to offer information on some of the best computer products available covering business, education, and entertainment software and hardware.
- Discovery School—reviews by DiscoverySchool.com.
- Epinions—reviews by the Epinions community.
- Game Zone's Kid Zone—children's software reviews.
- IT Reviews—reference software reviews by professional journalists.
- Kids Domain—more than 1,500 reviews of commercial software products by parents for parents.
- Learning Village—an independent review and advisory center for parents and teachers who are looking for credible information on educational software.
- LearningWare Reviews—reviews by Juline Lambert.
- Memorization Software Reviewed—reviews of over 200 computer programs for flash-card-based learning.
- The Review Zone—provides in-depth reviews on the best kids' and family edutainment software, hardware, computer books, and cutting-edge technology for parents and teachers.
- SuperKids—children's software reviews by teams that include educators, parents, and children from across the United States. Review teams include experts from Stanford, Harvard, and Northwestern universities.
- Teachers Evaluating Educational Multimedia (TEEM)—provides teachers with free access to independent, classroom-based evaluations of educational multimedia.
- Tech Learning Reviews—reviews by Tech Learning.
- World Village—reviews by World Village.

- *Spreadsheets* that permit adding up collected data, crunching statistics, and graphing.
- *Drawing/painting.*
- *Multimedia and presentation* tools that allow learners to create sophisticated class presentations.
- *Desktop publishing* that enables students to create materials for print or on the Web using scanning, design, and layout tools.

Teachers and learners who develop digital content are inclined toward discovery or inquiry-based learning (see "Facilitating Discovery Learning Online" in Chapter 8). Of course, in order to create digital content with your learners, you would need to be much more computer savvy than if you simply use already developed software. So, as your computer comfort level increases you will be more likely to try using some of the above tools with learners.

GET BETTER PREPARED FOR THE DIGITAL AGE

Obviously, you need all the preparation you can get in order to use digital technology. That preparation should include training on computers, in Internet basics, and in how to integrate technology into the classroom. It is the latter, integration, that presents the most problems. However, teachers who receive 11 or more hours of curriculum-integration training are five times more likely to feel much better prepared to integrate technology into their lessons than teachers who receive no such training. Presently, 42 states require teacher technology training, yet teacher preparation programs are finding it difficult to fit training into an already packed preservice curriculum. It is likely that you and subsequent generations of teachers are and will be better prepared to use digital technology because of your exposure to it when growing up. So, the problem may partly take care of itself.

Some Final Thoughts

This chapter is intended to put you on the road to becoming a more multitalented, versatile teacher. Now you are generally aware of 31 ways to teach, and you have special knowledge about four that are considered teaching staples. For these four, you have learned their purposes and characteristics, what you must do to excel at each, and what benefits research tells us will accrue. We hope you have the opportunity to try out each one and/or to observe a master teacher demonstrating each. Furthermore, we hope you have reflected on how you feel about them. Consider yourself partway out on the diving platform leading to successful teaching. After Chapter 8, we think you will be ready to take the plunge.

CHAPTER SUMMARY

- An instructional alternative is a way of teaching intended to facilitate student learning and satisfaction. The most familiar alternatives are presentations, discussion, independent study, and individualized instruction. Other notable alternatives (presented in the next chapter) are direct instruction, cooperative learning, discovery learning, and constructivism. As many as 31 instructional alternatives exist and are depicted on the Wheel of Instructional Choice (Figure 7.5).

- Presentations are informative talks a more knowledgeable person makes to less knowledgeable persons. These talks draw their strength from the cognitive school of thought, especially information processing and reception learning. They can be long or short, interrupted or uninterrupted, formal or informal, given by a teacher or by another person, and either live or recorded.

- Good presentations have three parts: preparation, delivery, and closure. Preparation requires the presenter to establish the general purpose and specific learning objectives, collect and review the information to be presented, and organize and plan delivery. Delivery requires the presenter to obtain students' attention, present the learning objectives and expectations, use an advance organizer, present the information in an organized, step-by-step manner, expect and promote pupil interaction, move from general to specific ideas, use examples and nonexamples when teaching new concepts, ask learners to reflect on what they have learned, and then ask them to use the information. Closure requires the presenter to review, summarize, and relate the new learning to what students already knew, and check learners for understanding.

- Research indicates that the presenter's style is important, that good presenters are often friendly, humorous, enthusiastic, and verbally fluent, that attention falls off rapidly after 15 minutes, that note taking aids long-term memory, that presentations are good for transmitting information and not as good for promoting students' thinking, and that underachievers need special consideration when using presentations.

OLC

SUPPLEMENTAL RESOURCES
Go to the text's Online Learning Center at www.mhhe.com/cruickshank6e to access the chapter's **study tools** including web links, practice for Praxis™ case studies, and video clips.

www.mhhe.com/cruickshank6e

CHAPTER 7
Four Instructional Alternatives:
Presentation, Discussion, Independent
Study, and Individualized Instruction
249

- A discussion is a conversation wherein students, or students and teacher, interact to share information, ideas, or opinions, or work to resolve a problem. Discussions also are guided by learning theory. However, the theory the discussion leader draws from will vary according to the discussion's purpose, that is, whether it is mainly cognitive, affective, or some combination of the two. Discussions may take place between teacher and students or solely among students, and the teacher may be actively involved as leader or participant or merely serve as the observer. Finally, a discussion may involve the whole class, small group, or a panel.

- Good discussion leaders usually believe that students' participation in purposeful conversation is normal and healthy, that students must think aloud about information, ideas, issues, and problems, that students are able to think effectively, and that by thinking and interacting effectively, students experience psychological and social growth. Additionally, good discussion leaders control their own talk and are skillful facilitators, human relations experts, clarifiers, and summarizers.

- Good discussions include preparation, delivery, and closure. Preparation requires the leader to determine the purpose and specific objectives; determine students' readiness for discussion, particularly this discussion; decide what kind of interaction is best (teacher-student, or student-student) and, relatedly, what the teacher's role should be (leader, participant, or observer); and decide whether the discussion should involve the whole class or a small group and what the time parameters should be. Delivery requires that the leader ensure that students understand the purpose and objectives of the discussion, set the task, remind students of guidelines for behavior during discussion, organize the participants, and let them "have at it" as the leader fulfills his or her role. Closure requires the discussion leader to summarize and organize findings, conclusions, solutions, or whatever the objectives called for as well as assess students' learning and satisfaction.

- Research on discussions shows, among other things, that they generally are motivating, promote retention, foster higher-order thinking, and are effective in altering attitudes and advancing moral reasoning.

- Independent study includes any school-related assignment students do more or less alone. It is guided mostly by information-processing and behavioristic theories. The purposes of independent study are to provide rehearsal and practice, opportunities to learn how to learn, and to occupy students legitimately so the teacher can perform other important tasks. Characteristics of independent study include the type (teacher-prescribed or student-chosen), the teacher role (the availability of the teacher to guide), and the context (in school or home).

- Good independent study leaders believe that the purposes of independent study are valuable. They have confidence in students' ability to work alone and are able to demonstrate valence and challenge arousal, variety and challenge, withitness, and overlapping.

- Good independent study includes preparation, delivery, and closure. Preparation requires the teacher to establish the general purpose and specific objectives, settle on the assignment's nature and type, and ensure that it is within learners' interest and ability. Delivery requires that the teacher be absolutely clear regarding the assignment's purpose, objectives, relationship to what has or will be learned, procedures, and time limit. Closure requires the teacher to collect, assess, and evaluate the work, giving learners specific feedback and reteaching when necessary.

- Research on independent study finds that it is commonly used, that it is more effective when teachers demonstrate certain leadership behaviors, and that its most important ingredients are (1) clarity of purpose, assignment, and procedures, and (2) monitoring, grading, and provision of immediate feedback.

- Research on well-conceived homework supports its use since it enhances learning.
- Individualized instruction refers to a number of instructional maneuvers that attempt to tailor teaching and learning to a learner's unique strengths and needs. There are many types of individualized instruction, including the Dalton and Winnetka plans, programmed and computer-assisted instruction, Individually Prescribed Instruction, Individually Guided Education, tutoring, and the Project Method. In some, individuals with like abilities are grouped.
- The teacher's role in individualized instruction is to know and care about the diversity of students and to see that the learning tasks are varied or modified for each individual. Good users of individualized instruction prize diversity, value individualism, know learners' strengths and needs, know about and have the ability to implement individualized instruction programs, and have good interpersonal skills.
- Good individualized instruction programs are tailored to meet individual learners' strengths and needs, permit considerable autonomy, result in greater equity, and have no damaging or harmful side effects on students.
- Research on individualized instruction makes it clear that its use is worth the extra time and effort. Its major limitation is that when it is properly conducted, it is very time-consuming.

KEY TERMS

Instructional alternatives, 204	Recitation, 214	Tutoring, 235
Presentation, 204	Independent study, 222	Distance learning, 236
Team teaching, 205	Homework, 222	Virtual, online, or e-schools, 236
Set induction, 207	Individualized or differentiated instruction, 230	Self-directed learning, 237
Advance organizer, 207		Wheel of Instructional Choice, 245
Explanations, 209	Contracts, 233	
Discussion, 214	Nongraded school, 235	

ISSUES AND PROBLEMS FOR DISCUSSION

ISSUES Several issues and problems are related to instructional alternatives. Here are a few you might like to discuss in class.

1. Which instructional alternatives should you be able to handle most skillfully?
2. Which instructional alternatives work best for which purposes?
3. When deciding which alternative to use, what is the relative importance of teacher versus learner needs?
4. How can you become more competent in using a given instructional alternative?
5. Why do you suppose there is a dearth of useful research-based knowledge about instructional alternatives?

PROBLEMS Teachers regularly report that they have difficulty "learning to use alternative methods of instruction" (Cruickshank et al., 1980). What would you have done in each of the following situations?

Problem 1: "I spent the whole weekend reading about Geronimo and preparing to tell the class about him as part of Cultural Awareness Week. I chose Geronimo

CHAPTER 7
Four Instructional Alternatives:
Presentation, Discussion, Independent
Study, and Individualized Instruction

www.mhhe.com/cruickshank6e

251

because there are no Native Americans in the class and I wanted to broaden the kids' perspectives. Well, I'll tell you, very few of the students had any interest whatsoever! Finally, I just cashed it in. So much for giving an 'interesting' talk."

Problem 2: "No matter how many times we use group discussion, the same old problems crop up. Rashawn and Lawrence think they know everything and won't let others talk or respect what others say. Melody, Arnold, Diane, and Mary won't participate, and Barney sleeps."

Problem 3: "Students really like to do individual study. They can't wait to get started. After that, some just sit, some carry on conversations with neighbors, some just copy word for word from a book. A few hurry through so they can fool around. Out of 26, I'd say I can count on 14."

Problem 4: "We have some pretty good software and audiovisual materials available. To add variety, I like to have the students use these resources instead of just listening to me. They waste so much time finding what they want and settling down that I usually wish I had done whole-class teaching."

THEORY INTO ACTION: ACTIVITIES FOR PRACTICE AND YOUR PORTFOLIO

ACTIVITY 7.1: Prepare a Presentation Utilizing what you now know about learning (Chapter 4), good presenters, and good presentations, prepare a brief presentation for a group of peers on a topic chosen from group A or B below. The presentation should be no longer than 10 minutes.

A. *Topics from this text*
  1. Attention
  2. Short-term memory
  3. Long-term memory
  4. Reception learning
  5. Bloom's taxonomy
  6. Writing a unit plan
  7. Writing a lesson plan
  8. (your choice)

B. *School curricula topics*
  1. Homophones
  2. Characteristics of Picasso's paintings
  3. The electoral college
  4. The musical scale
  5. Wilderness survival
  6. Peninsulas
  7. Triangles
  8. (your choice)

Assessment: Did you establish your general purpose, set specific learning objectives, collect and review related materials, and plan the presentation with student diversity in mind?

ACTIVITY 7.2: Deliver a Presentation Deliver your Activity 7.1 presentation to a small group of your peers.

Assessment: To what extent did you:

1. Obtain learners' attention and interest?
2. Inform learners of what they need to learn?
3. Relate new information to what they know?
4. Present information step by step?
5. Move from the general to the specific?
6. Provide just the right amount of information?
7. Emphasize important points?
8. Use examples and illustrations?
9. Use variety to maintain attention?
10. Ask questions and call for comments?

Were you:

1. Friendly?
2. Humorous?
3. Enthusiastic?
4. Fluent and audible?
5. Able to take learners' differences into account?
6. Knowledgeable?

How well do your learners feel you did these things?

ACTIVITY 7.3 PowerPoint Presentation On paper, create a six slide presentation you might use to present material in Lesson Plans 7.1 or 7.2.

ACTIVITY 7.4: Observe a Teacher Presentation Now that you have learned about presentations, it would be very helpful to observe one or more in a K–12 classroom. If you are enrolled in a field experience, find out when your mentor teacher will be giving a presentation. Talk with him or her about how it would help if you could see a presentation in action. If not so enrolled, perhaps you can obtain a videotape of a presentation made by a teacher or student teacher.

As you observe, record answers to these questions:

- What characteristics of a good presenter did the teacher demonstrate? (See Table 7.2, column 1.)
- What qualities of good presentations were evident in this one? (See Table 7.2, column 2.)
- Were any of the research findings on presentations borne out?

Additionally, talk with a student who was attentive and find out how he or she feels about presentations. Conversely, talk with another who was off-task or not attentive to determine his or her perceptions about this instructional alternative.

Finally, ask the teacher how well he or she felt the presentation facilitated learning and satisfaction.

ACTIVITY 7.5: Plan a Discussion Plan a discussion for this class focusing on any one of the following topics. Plan it so that it has one of the following purposes: to review information; to examine ideas, opinions, or issues; to solve problems; or to improve communication skills. Reread the section Good Discussions for assistance.

Topics from this text:

1. Factors influencing how we teach
2. The changing nature of childhood
3. Student diversity

CHAPTER 7
Four Instructional Alternatives:
Presentation, Discussion, Independent
Study, and Individualized Instruction

www.mhhe.com/cruickshank6e

253

4. Three schools of thought about learning
5. Presentations or discussions
6. (your choice of topic)

Assessment: Did you have a clear purpose and outcomes in mind, take into account learners' differences, decide what role you would play, work out the physical arrangement, and establish the time frame?

ACTIVITY 7.6: Conduct a Discussion   Conduct the discussion you planned in Activity 7.5.

Assessment: Did you:

1. Obtain learners' attention and interest?
2. Inform learners of the goal of the discussion and its value?
3. Relate what learners will discuss to their previous knowledge and experience and/or tie it to something they will learn?
4. Remind participants of the rules of (this) discussion?
5. Obtain a facilitator-moderator and recorder for each small group if small-group discussion was used?
6. Monitor understanding and participation?
7. Elevate the level of thinking and discourse?
8. Summarize?
9. Tie what was discussed to previous knowledge?
10. Connect the discussion to what will happen next?

Were you:

1. Able to get learners thinking?
2. Able to keep your own talk under control?
3. A facilitator, human relations expert, clarifier, or summarizer as necessary?
4. Able to improve group communication skills?

ACTIVITY 7.7: Observe a Discussion   Try to observe a discussion involving K–12 students. If you do not have access to a K–12 classroom, perhaps your college instructor has a videotape of one. As you observe, record answers to these questions:

1. Which of the four purposes of a discussion seemed to be in play—to review, to examine ideas and opinions, to solve problems, or to improve oral communication skills?
2. What were the characteristics of the discussion? Was the interaction between teacher and students or among students only? Was the teacher a facilitator-moderator, participant, or observer-recorder? Was it a whole-class or small-group discussion? If small group, what was the composition of the group? What was the physical arrangement?
3. What beliefs and abilities related to good discussion did the teacher demonstrate?
4. To what extent did the discussion bear out any of the research findings on discussion?
5. To what extent did student learning and satisfaction occur?

ACTIVITY 7.8: Plan an Independent Study   Using what we know about learning and independent study, prepare an assignment for a group of peers on a topic chosen from purpose 1 or 2:

1. *Purpose:* To have peers independently rehearse or practice what you have learned about:
   a. Presentation
   b. Discussion
   c. Independent study
2. *Purpose:* To have peers independently learn more about other instructional alternatives appearing on the Wheel of Instructional Choice (Figure 7.5).

In either case, did you establish your general purpose, set specific learning objectives, consider the diversity of the learners, and make the task interesting?

ACTIVITY 7.9: Conducting Independent Study   Conduct the independent study activity you planned in Activity 7.8.

Assessment: Did you:

1. Get student attention?
2. Present the assignment's rationale and objectives?
3. Relate the assignment to previous or upcoming work?
4. Ensure that students knew what to do and how to do it?
5. Tell them how they could get assistance?
6. Ensure that they had something to do when they finished?
7. Monitor and interact with learners?
8. Diagnose individual progress and provide assistance?
9. Collect assignments?
10. Provide students with specific feedback?
11. Give credit for the work?

ACTIVITY 7.10: Observe Independent Study   If you are enrolled in a field experience, arrange to visit a classroom to see a scheduled independent study.

1. Which of the purposes for using independent study seemed to be in play (to provide rehearsal or practice of information, provide opportunities to learn independently, or keep students legitimately occupied so the teacher could do something else)?
2. Which of the behaviors of good independent study leaders did the teacher demonstrate?
3. Which of the qualities of good independent study were present?
4. Which of the research findings on independent study was the teacher able to apply?

Additionally, talk to two students, one who seemed to be very much on-task and another who was more off-task. Ask them how they feel about studying alone. Finally, get the teacher's reactions to the independent study. You might ask, "Do you feel the students accomplished what you wanted them to?"

ACTIVITY 7.11: Observe Individualized Instruction   If you are presently involved in a field experience, find out if your mentor teacher or another teacher is using some form of individualized instruction. Should you be able to observe, answer the following questions.

• How would you describe the setting, the class, and the lesson?
• Which of the following were altered to meet students' strengths and needs?
  1. The goals and content of instruction.

CHAPTER 7
Four Instructional Alternatives:
Presentation, Discussion, Independent
Study, and Individualized Instruction

www.mhhe.com/cruickshank6e

255

2. Learning activities, or how students could choose to learn.

3. Materials and resources.

4. Mastery level, or how much students were expected to learn.

5. Pacing or time.

6. Other.

- To what extent did the lesson seem to accomplish the purpose of individualization, that is, to meet students' individual strengths and needs? Explain. Also, talk to the teacher and students. How do they feel about individualization of instruction?

REFERENCES

Abdullah, M. (2001). *Self-directed learning*. Bloomington, IN: ERIC Clearinghouse on Reading, English and Communication (ERIC Document Reproduction Services ED 459 458).

Anderson, L. M. (1981). *Students respond to seat work: Implications for the study of students' cognitive processing*. East Lansing, MI: Institute for Research on Teaching, Michigan State University.

Anderson, L. M. (1995). Assignment and supervision of seatwork. In L. W. Anderson (Ed.), *International encyclopedia of teaching and teacher education* (pp. 264–268). Oxford: Pergamon Press.

Anderson, L., Brubaker, N., Alleman-Brooks, J., & Duffy, G. (1984). *Making seat work work. Research Series 142*. East Lansing, MI: College of Education, Michigan State University.

ASCD (Association of Supervision and Curriculum Development). (n.d.). Project method. *Lexicon of Learning* online. Retrieved from http://www.ascd.org/Publications/Lexicon_of_Learning

Ausubel, P., & Ausubel, D. P. (2002). *Acquisition and retention of knowledge*. Boston: Kluwar Academic Publishers.

Barlowe, A. (2006). *Inquiry in action: Teaching Columbus*. New York: Teachers College Press.

Battistich, V., Solomon, D., & Delucchi, K. (1993, September). Interaction processes and student outcomes in cooperative learning groups. *The Elementary School Journal, 94*(1), 19–32.

Bleimes, A. (2006, November 14). Blogging now begins young. *USA Today*. Retrieved from http://www.usatoday.com/tech/news/2006-11-14-blogs-education_x.htm

Bligh, D. (2000). *What's the use of lectures?* San Francisco: Jossey Bass.

Bower, E. M. (1973). *Teachers talk about their feelings*. Rockville, MD: National Institute of Mental Health, Center for Studies of Child and Family Health.

Bridges, D. (1988). *Education, democracy, and discussion*. Blue Ridge Summit, PA: University Press of America.

Brookfield, S., & Preskill, S. (2005). *Discussion as a way of teaching*. New York: Wiley.

Brophy, J. (2006, July). Graham Nuthall and social constructivist teaching. *Teaching and Teacher Education, 22*(5), 529–537.

Brophy, J., & Evertson, C. M. (1976). *Learning from teaching*. Boston: Allyn & Bacon.

Brophy, J. E., & Good, T. L. (1986). Teacher behavior and student achievement. In M. C. Wittrock (Ed.), *Handbook of research on teaching*. Third Edition (pp. 328–375). New York: Macmillan.

Brown, G. A. (1987). Lectures and lecturing. In M. J. Dunkin (Ed.), *The international encyclopedia of teaching and teacher education* (pp. 284–287). Oxford: Pergamon Press.

Cook, A., & Tashlik, P. (2004). *Talk, talk, talk*. NY: Teachers College Press.

Cooper, H., Robinson, J., & Pattal, E. (2006, Spring). Does homework improve academic achievement? *Review of Educational Research, 76*(1), 1–62.

Cooper, H., & Valentine, J. (2001). *Homework*. Matwan, NJ: Earlbaum.

Cruickshank, D., Applegate, J., Holton, J., Mager, G., Myers, B., Novak, C., & Tracey, K. (1980). *Teaching is tough*. Englewood Cliffs, NJ: Prentice Hall.

Cruickshank, D., & Metcalf, K. (1995). Explaining. In T. Husen & T. N. Postlewaite (Eds.), *International encyclopedia of education*. Second Edition. Oxford: Pergamon Press.

David, J. (2008, February). What research says about project-based learning. *Educational Leadership, 65*(5), 80–82.

Dembo, M. H. (1994). *Applying educational psychology in the classroom*. New York: Dembo, Longman.

Dillon, J. T. (1985). Using questions to foil discussion. *Teaching and Teacher Education, 1*(2), 109–121.

Dillon, J. T. (1988). *Questioning and discussion: A multidisciplinary study*. Norwalk, NJ: Ablex.

Dillon, J. T. (1995). Discussion. In L. W. Anderson (Ed.), *International encyclopedia of teaching and teacher education* (pp. 251–254). Oxford: Pergamon Press.

District Administrator. (2004, February). *Taking a closer look at homework, 40*(2), 65.

Doherty, L. (2004, Nov. 1). Children drowning in a sea of blah. *The Age online*. Access: www.theage.com.au/articles/2004/10/29/1099028201302.html; oneclick=true

Doherty, O. (2003, November 26). Discussion in class found to boost students' literacy. *Education Week, 23*(13), 5.

Dunkin, M. (1987). Lesson formats. In L. W. Anderson (Ed.), *International encyclopedia of teaching and teacher education* (pp. 251–254). Oxford: Pergamon Press.

Ellson, D. (1986, October). Improving productivity in teaching. *Phi Delta Kappan, 68,* 111–124.

Emmer, E., Evertson, C., Sanford, J., & Clements, B. (1982). *Improving classroom management: An experimental study in junior high classrooms.* Austin: The University of Texas (ERIC Document Reproduction Services ED 261 053).

Emmer, E., Sanford, J., Evertson, C., Clements, B., & Martin, J. (1981). *The classroom management improvement study: An experiment in elementary school classrooms.* Austin: The University of Texas (ERIC Document Reproduction Services ED 226 452).

English, C. S. (1984). Measuring teacher effectiveness from the teacher's point of view. *Focus on Exceptional Children, 17,* 1–15.

Feldman, S. (2004, February). The great homework debate. *Teaching PreK–8, 34*(5), 1.

Fisher, C., Berliner, D., Filby, N., Marliave, R., Cahen, L., & Dishaw, M. (1980). Teaching behaviors, academic learning time, and student achievement: An overview. In C. Denham & A. Lieberman (Eds.), *Time to learn: A review of the beginning teacher evaluation study* (pp. 7–32). Washington, DC: National Institute of Education.

Flowerday, T., & Schraw, G. (2000, December). Teacher beliefs about instructional choice. *Journal of Educational Psychology, 92*(4), 634–645.

Fording, L. (2004, March 30). Education 21st century style. *Newsweek.*

Freiberg, H., & Driscoll, A. (2004). *Universal teaching strategies.* Boston: Allyn & Bacon.

Gage, N. L., & Berliner, D.C. (1976). The psychology of teaching methods. In N. L. Gage (Ed.), *The psychology of teaching methods* (pp. 1–20). Chicago: University of Chicago Press.

Gage, N. L., & Berliner, D.C. (1998). *Educational psychology.* Sixth Edition. Boston: Houghton Mifflin.

Gall, J., & Gall, M. (1990). Outcomes of the discussion method. In W. W. Wilen (Ed.), *Teaching and learning through discussion: The theory and practice of the discussion method* (pp. 25–44). Springfield, IL: Charles C. Thomas.

Gall, M. D. (1987). Discussion methods. In M. J. Dunkin (Ed.), *International encyclopedia of teaching and teacher education* (pp. 232–237). Oxford: Pergamon Press.

Gall, M. D., & Gall, J. P.(1976). The discussion method. In N. L. Gage (Ed.), *The psychology of teaching methods* (pp. 166–216). Chicago: University of Chicago Press.

Gartland, D. (1986). The effects of varying amounts of teacher-directed instruction and monitored independent seat work on the acquisition of syllabication rules by severely disabled readers. Unpublished doctoral dissertation. University Park: Pennsylvania State University.

Gerges, G. (2001, Fall). Factors influencing pre service teachers' variation in use of instructional methods. *Teacher Education Quarterly, 28*(9), 71–88.

Gillard., C. (2007, May/June). Better teaching with web tools. *Harvard Education Letter.* Access: http://www.edletter.org/part/issues/2007-mj/abstracts.shtml/#gillard

Gillard, D. (2007 May/June). Better teaching with web tools. *Harvard Educational Letter, 3*(5).

Gilstrap, R. L., & Martin, W. R. (1975). *Current strategies for teachers.* Pacific Palisades, CA: Goodyear.

Goldenberg, C. (1991). *Instructional conversations.* National Center for Research on Diversity and Second Language Learning. University of California, Los Angeles.

Good, T. (1995). Teachers' expectations. In L. W. Anderson (Ed.), *International encyclopedia of teaching and teacher education* (pp. 29–35). Oxford: Pergamon Press.

Good, T., & Grouws, L. (1975). *Process–product relationships in fourth grade mathematics classrooms.* Columbia: University of Missouri.

Gump, P. (1967). *The classroom behavior setting: Its nature and relation to student behavior.* Lawrence: University of Kansas (ERIC Document Reproduction Services ED 015 515).

Gutierrez, R., & Slavin, R. (1992). Achievement effects of the nongraded school. *Review of Educational Research 62*(4), 337–761.

Heck, S., & Williams, C. R. (1984). *The complex roles of the teacher.* New York: Teachers College, Columbia University.

Henke, K., Weber, B., Kneifel, S., Wiesner, H., & Buck, A. (1999). *Human hippocompus associates information in memory.* Proceedings of the National Academy of Science, USA, 96: 5884-5889.

Hill, W. F. (2000). *Learning through discussion: Guide for leaders and members of discussion groups.* Prospect Heights, IL: Waveland Press.

Jeter, J. (1980). Individualized instruction programs. In J. Jeter (Ed.), *Approaches to individualized education* (pp. 402–407). New York: Bowker.

Keller, J. (2003, February 10). Is PowerPoint the devil? *Chicago Tribune,* E1–2.

Kounin, J. (1977). *Discipline and group management in classrooms.* Chicago: Holt, Rinehart, and Winston.

Langer, J., Nystrand, M., & Gamoran, A. (2003, Fall). Discussion-based approaches to developing understanding: Classroom instruction and student performance in middle and high school English. *American Education Research Journal, 40*(3), 685–730.

Larson, B. (2000). Classroom discussion. *Teaching and Teacher Education, 16,* 661–677.

Leinhardt, G. (1992, April). What research on learning tells us about teaching. *Educational Leadership, 49*(7), 20–25.

Linver, M., Brooks-Gunn, J., & Roth, J. (2005). *Children's homework time.* Paper presented at the CDS II Early Results Workshop. Ann Arbor, MI: University of Michigan.

Marzano, R., Pickering, D., & Pollock, J. (2004). *Classroom instruction that works.* Association for Supervision & Curriculum Development.

Matthews, M. (2006, June 23). *Self Directed Learning: Reflection.* MB Matthews: Street Smarts blog. Access: www.mbmatthews.blogspot.com/

Matthews, J. (2003, February 18). *Class struggles: Is homework really so terrible?* WashingtonPost.com.

McLeish, J. (1975). The lecture method. In N.L. Gage (Ed.), *Psychology of teaching methods* (pp. 252–301). Chicago: University of Chicago Press.

Medway, F. J. (1987). Tutoring. In M.J. Dunkin (Ed.), *International encyclopedia of teaching and teacher education* (pp. 243–245). Oxford: Pergamon Press.

Metlife Survey of the American Teacher. (2007). *The Homework Experience*. New York, NY: Metropolitan Life Insurance Company.

Muller, H. (2002, November). Facilitating classroom discussion. Washington, DC: Paper presented at the National Communication Association Meeting (ERIC Document Reproduction Services ED 450 434).

Olson, L. (1993, February 17). Progressive-era conception breaks mold: NASDC schools explore "project learning." *Education Week, 12*(21), 6.

Parker, W. (2006, November). Public discourse in schools. *Educational Researches, 35*(8), 11–18.

Parker, W., & Hess, D. (2001). Teaching *with* and *for* discussion. *Teaching and Teacher Education, 17,* 273–289.

Patall, E., Cooper H., & Robinson, C. (2008, December). Parent involvement in homework. *Review of Educational Research, 78*(4), 1039–1101.

Paulu, N. H. (1998). *Helping your students with homework.* Washington, DC: Office of Educational Research and Improvement, U.S. Department of Education.

Pavin, R. (1992, October). Benefits of nongraded schools. *Educational Leadership,* (2), 22–25.

Phelan, P., Davidson, A. L., & Cao, H. T. (1992, May). Speaking up: Student's perspectives on school. *Phi Delta Kappan, 73*(9), 695–704.

Rebora, A. (2008). Making a difference: How differentiated instruction works. *Teacher Magazine, 2*(1), 26, 28–31.

Rohrbeck, C., Ginsburg-Block, M., Fantuzzo, J., & Miller, T. (2003, June). Peer assisted learning interventions with elementary school students. *Journal of Educational Psychology, 95*(2), 240–257.

Rosenshine, B. (1980). How time is spent in elementary classrooms. In D. Denham & A. Lieberman (Eds.), *Time to learn: A review of the beginning teacher evaluation study* (pp. 107–126). Washington, DC: National Institute of Education.

Rosenshine, B. (1987). Direct instruction. In M. J. Dunkin (Ed.), *International encyclopedia of teaching and teacher education* (pp. 257–262). Oxford: Pergamon Press.

Rosenshine, B., & Stevens, R. (1986). Teaching functions. In M. C. Wittrock (Ed.), *Handbook of research on teaching* (pp. 376–391). New York: Macmillan.

Rupley, W., & Blair, T. (1987, January). Assignment and supervision of reading seatwork: Looking in on 12 primary teachers. *The Reading Teacher, 40,* 391–393.

Scott, R. M. (1989). The relationship between elementary teachers' use of theoretical knowledge about seat work during reading instruction and students' on-task behavior. Unpublished doctoral dissertation. Columbus: Ohio State University.

Seifert, E. H., & Beck, J. J. (1984, September–October). Relationship between task time and learning gains in secondary schools. *Journal of Educational Research, 78,* 5–10.

Sharp, V. (2008). *Computer education for teachers.* Boston: McGraw-Hill.

Shuell, T. J., Brown, S., Watson, D. G., & Ewing, J. A. (1988, March). Teachers' perceptions of the differential appropriateness of various teaching methods. *The Elementary School Journal, 88*(4), 339–356.

Simich-Dudgeon, C. (1998). Classroom strategies for encouraging collaborative discussion. In P. DiCerbo (Ed.), *Directions in language and education.* No. 12, Washington, DC: George Washington University.

Slavin, R. E. (2008). *Educational psychology.* Eighth Edition. Boston: Allyn & Bacon.

Slavin, R., & Madden, N. (1989, February). What works for students at risk: A research synthesis. *Educational Leadership, 46,* 4–13.

Spiegel, D. (2005). *Classroom discussion.* New York: Teaching Resources.

Stratton, (1993, February 19). Pupils see computer's classroom potential in action. *The Columbus Dispatch,* p. D1.

Swang, J. (1993, April/May). Ensuring Success in Science. *Learning, 93,* 24–27.

Toll, D. (1969). *Ghetto.* Indianapolis, IN: Bobbs-Merrill.

Tomlinson, C. (1999). *The differentiated classroom.* Alexandria, VA: Association for Supervision and Curriculum Development.

U.S. Department of Education. (1986, 1987). *What works: Research about teaching and learning.* Washington, DC: U.S. Department of Education.

Van Ments, M. (1981). *Active talk.* London: St. Martin's Press.

Vatterott, C. (2010, September). 5 Hallmarks of good homework. *Education Leadership, 68*(1), 10–15.

Walberg, H. (1984, May). Improving the productivity of America's schools. *Educational Leadership, 41,* 19–27.

Walberg, H. (1991). *Effective teaching:* Current research. Richmond, CA: McCutchan Publishing.

Walberg, H., & Pascal, R. (1995). Homework. In L. Anderson (Ed.), *International encyclopedia of teaching and teacher education* (pp. 268–271). Oxford: Pergamon Press.

Wasley, P. (1999). Teaching worth celebrating. *Educational Leadership, 56*(8), 8–13.

Wasley, P., Hampel, R., & Clark, R. (1997). *Kids and school reform.* San Francisco: Jossey-Bass.

Watson, K. (1983). Some aspects of classroom discourse in English. Paper presented at the annual meeting of the Canadian Council of Teachers of English (ERIC Document Reproduction Services ED 233 365).

Wilen, W., & Kindsvatter, R. (2004). *Dynamics of effective secondary teaching.* New York: Allyn & Bacon.

Willis, S., & Mann, L. (2000, Winter). Differentiating Instruction. *Curriculum Update* (pp. 1–3, 6–7). Alexandria, VA: Association for Supervision and Curriculum Development.

Four More Instructional Alternatives: Cooperative Learning, Discovery Learning, Constructivism, and Direct Instruction

CHAPTER 8

Conversation Starters

How to teach? Different strokes for different folks.

Some of us prefer to learn by listening. Others prefer to learn by doing. Some of us prefer to learn in a large group. Others prefer to learn in small groups. Some of us enjoy competition in the classroom while others prefer cooperation.

How do you stand on these matters? Which is better: learning by listening or doing, telling students what they should know or helping them find it out for themselves, learning in large or small goups, student competition or cooperation?

Cooperative Learning: Teaching Learners to Like and Care for One Another

WHAT IS COOPERATIVE LEARNING?

8.1 How do you feel about classroom competition and cooperation?

In a number of classrooms in which you have been a student, there has probably been a degree, perhaps a high degree, of competition among your peers. After all, nearly everyone in a class wants to get a good grade, and usually there are not enough to go around. Competition for good grades, however, may result in jealousy, even hostility, among learners. In an effort to reduce or eliminate competition and, relatedly, to build a sense of community, educators have searched for less competitive, nonconfrontational instructional alternatives. Mostly, they find some form of group work a suitable alternative. The group work of choice now is cooperative learning which has been one of the most successfully implemented instructional alternatives of the past several decades (Johnson & Johnson, 2009).

Cooperative learning (formerly called student-team learning) is the term used to describe instructional procedures whereby learners work together in small groups and are rewarded for their *collective* accomplishments. Does that remind you of a team sport such as volleyball or soccer? The whole team does or doesn't do well depending on the contribution of each individual player and the extent to which they help one another. Cooperation is critical!

8.2 Have you ever experienced cooperative learning? What was it like for you?

In cooperative learning, the teams typically have four to six members. Their team task is to collectively learn or master content the teacher has previously presented or complete a teacher-assigned project. In the first case, learners might work together to master spelling words. In the second, sometimes referred to as *group investigation,* or *work groups,* they might work to learn about Native Americans of the Southwest or to solve a complex mathematical problem.

PURPOSE AND CHARACTERISTICS OF COOPERATIVE LEARNING

8.3 How important to you is the purpose of cooperative learning?

In contrast to the many other ways of teaching, cooperative learning encourages learners to work together for both the common and individual good. This purpose may remind you of the famous line d'Artagnon speaks in Alexandre Dumas's novel *The Three Musketeers,* "All for one, one for all, that is our device, is it not?" Highlight 8.1 contrasts competitive versus cooperative classrooms.

What are the key characteristics or attributes of cooperative learning systems? How is this "all for one, one for all" purpose achieved? Such systems are generally characterized by (1) the way the groups or teams are made up; (2) the kinds of tasks they do; (3) the groups' rules of behavior; and (4) their motivation and reward systems.

According to advocates, teams must be mixed in terms of gender, academic ability, race, and other traits. Heterogeneity is promoted for at least three reasons. First, cooperative learning is based partly on the humanistic school of thought about learning. That school of thought, as you recall from Chapter 4, focuses on the importance of personal and social development. One of its major objectives is to make students feel better about themselves and to be more accepting of others. Mixed groups offer a major means of achieving this goal.

A second reason to form heterogeneous teams is so that each member will have an equal opportunity to learn, since "talent" is about equally distributed to each group. Finally, heterogeneity is fostered because students with lower abilities are more likely to improve their achievement in mixed groups than in homogeneous groups (Fashella & Slavin, 1997; Gamoran, 2009; Slavin, 1995). Thus, heterogeneous teams would seem especially beneficial for students at risk of academic failure.

A second way cooperative learning can be characterized is by the kinds of tasks teachers typically assign to the teams. The most common assignment requires

Competitive classrooms Often teachers are heard to say, "Boys and girls, let's see who can do this the best or the fastest." Praise and accolades go to the winner. Moreover, the winner's circle is small, and the multitude who don't get in soon learn: not to try, to feel unworthy, to envy or dislike winners, or to feel that life is unfair. Competition, although a motivator for some, has serious limitations for others. Even top kids in whatever kind of competition may be embarrassed by their successes or become the target of the not-so-successful others. Although "competition brings out the best," it can also bring out the worst.

Cooperative classrooms In cooperative classrooms teachers want all kids to be their best. Students help each other to learn and succeed. They provide mutual support and celebrate each others' successes. They try to reduce others' failures. Teachers believe that successful classrooms like successful businesses must get individuals or groups of individuals to share and work together for the good of each and all.

Source: Block (2005).

---

each team to master material the teacher presented previously. For example, Mrs. Braggins does a presentation on why the seasons change. She then asks the teams to review and learn the material in preparation for a quiz. Another common task is to ask teams to work on projects. Mr. Cruz asks his teams to read about the settling of California and then to collaboratively compose a letter as if a settler were writing to relatives in Spain describing the conditions of mission life.

Third, cooperative learning is characterized by rules of behavior required of team members: individual responsibility and accountability to oneself and the team, support and encouragement of team members, peer helping and tutoring, and, of course, cooperation. You can see how well the "all for one, one for all" analogy fits.

Finally, cooperative learning is characterized by a unique system of rewards. Rather than a mark based on personal effort, the individual receives a mark based on the team's achievement. If the students studied for and took a quiz on why the seasons change, the team's mark may be the average score for all team members. In the letter-writing assignment, all team members receive the score the letter earns. Again, we can liken such a situation to a sport where the team has a collective score and thereby wins or loses. Of course, this arrangement usually arouses peer pressure to do well and to help others do well. Thus, we think cooperative learning also derives some of its ideas from the behavioral school of thought, particularly operant conditioning and social learning.

In some cases, as you will see, cooperative teams can compete against one another. In other cases, teams compete against themselves and get a better mark only when they surpass some earlier achievement. Figure 8.1 illustrates the purpose and key characteristics of cooperative learning.

SOME VARIATIONS ON THE THEME OF COOPERATIVE LEARNING

Student Teams, Achievement Divisions (STAD) Of the variations, the simplest to understand is STAD. In STAD, the student teams must master some content, usually presented by the teacher, perhaps new vocabulary. Students work in teams to ensure that all members can perform well on an upcoming vocabulary quiz. The STAD process involves teacher presentation, team study, individual quizzes, determination of team scores, and team reward or recognition. To arrive at a team score, an individual's score is often compared to past work she or he has done. If the work is better than comparable past work, the person earns "improvement points." The team score is the sum of the improvement points individual members earn. This

CHAPTER 8
Four More Instructional Alternatives:
Cooperative Learning, Discovery Learning,
Constructivism, and Direct Instruction

www.mhhe.com/cruickshank6e

261

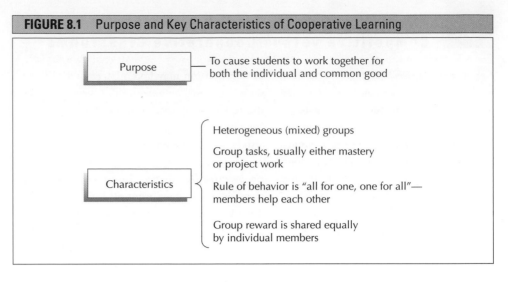

FIGURE 8.1 Purpose and Key Characteristics of Cooperative Learning

Purpose — To cause students to work together for both the individual and common good

Characteristics
- Heterogeneous (mixed) groups
- Group tasks, usually either mastery or project work
- Rule of behavior is "all for one, one for all"—members help each other
- Group reward is shared equally by individual members

kind of scoring is most easily done when students take quizzes in spelling, arithmetic, and other subjects with easily quantified scores.

Teams, Games, Tournaments (TGT) The procedure for TGT follows STAD except that, instead of an individual quiz being given, the teams compete against one another. Thus, the TGT procedure is teacher presentation, teamwork, team-versus-team competition, scoring, and team reward. In the team-versus-team competition phase, each member of a team is assigned to a table where he or she will compete against members from other teams. Top members from each team compete against one another in *equal competition;* the winner at each table is usually bumped up to the next higher level or table of competition. Think of this as comparable to the "ladders" used in sports competition—if you lose, you move down. Thus, competition always occurs among matched or somewhat like-achieving students. To some extent then, TGT loses the characteristic of heterogeneity, at least during academic competition.

Team-Assisted Individualization and Team-Accelerated Instruction (TAI) TAI combines the notions of cooperative learning and individually paced instruction. The latter means that students do not stay together academically, but instead learn or move through the material they are to master at their own pace. For instance, at the outset students take a proficiency test in arithmetic. Based on the results, they are placed on mixed-ability teams. However, instead of working together, each team member works on a different aspect or unit of arithmetic according to her or his needs. The unit usually contains some guide pages that provide information essential to completing the work. Thus, a unit on division of fractions would contain pages illustrating how to divide fractions. The unit also would contain practice exercises, a short test or tests, and an answer sheet. In TAI, team members check one another's work, and more advanced students serve as tutors. Rewards may be based upon the number of units each team has completed, the number of final tests they have passed, or other criteria. An important element of TAI is that while teams are at work, the teacher is free to pull together students working on similar units to diagnose their progress and further assist them.

Jigsaw A jigsaw group of students is given an assignment or puzzle to solve, for example "to learn about World War II." That assignment is broken down into smaller topics or puzzle pieces. Each member of the group is assigned or chooses a piece of the puzzle and investigates it. When the investigations are completed, members report what they have learned, and a more complete picture of the problem or puzzle emerges. Here is an example:

> Your thirty students are divided into five jigsaw groups with six students per group. The task is to learn about World War II. In every jigsaw group one person is responsible for researching Hitler's rise to power, a second to fact-find about concentration camps, a third to find out Britain's engagement, a fourth to study Russia's part, a fifth to uncover Japan's role, and the sixth to learn about the development and use of the atomic bomb. Thus, each jigsaw group member has counterpart members in other groups researching the same topic. For example, in group 1 Sara is responsible for looking into Hitler's rise, in group 2 the same assignment falls to Tyler and so on.
>
> Sara learns all she can about Hitler's rise to power. Then, before reporting to her personal jigsaw group, she meets with her counterparts (including Tyler) from other jigsaw groups. These "experts on Hitler" share what they have learned and discuss how they will present their findings to their jigsaw group.
>
> Eventually students return to their jigsaw group and present a well-organized report. Students are then tested on what they have learned about World War II from their fellow group members. (Adapted from The Jigsaw Classroom website.)

Web Link
The Jigsaw Classroom

Cooperative Integrated Reading and Composition (CIRC) CIRC is mainly used to teach reading and composition. In the typical CIRC procedure, the teacher sets a lesson in some specific area of reading or composition, for example, identifying the main characters and ideas in a piece of literature such as *Romeo and Juliet*. Student teams are then asked to read the story and to note the main characters and ideas. Team members, who may work in pairs, interact to check each other and gain consensus. They then may check their understanding with another pair on their team or against an answer sheet. While these paired and team activities are going on, the teacher convenes members from each team who are at a comparable proficiency or skill level in order to teach them a new reading skill, and the cycle continues. As with other forms of cooperative learning, points are given to teams based on individual members' performances on the activities and/or tests.

8.5 Which variation of cooperative learning appeals to you most? Why?

The five forms of cooperative learning described are compared in Table 8.1.

GOOD LEADERS OF COOPERATIVE LEARNING

Cooperative learning procedures demand a lot from teachers. These approaches, depending on the type, require teachers to be responsible for presenting information, creating suitable group and possibly independent work assignments, establishing and maintaining cooperating groups, monitoring individual and group progress, convening and teaching small groups of learners, devising and maintaining progress records, and providing rewards.

TABLE 8.1 Five Forms of Cooperative Learning and Their Individual Characteristics

STAD	TGT	TAI	Jigsaw	CIRC
		Proficiency testing of students, team assignment		
Presentation of information	Presentation of information	Individual but team-assisted study	Individuals work, experts plan and give presentations	Pairs work and teams work
Individual student quizzes	Team-vs.-team competition	Individual student quizzes	Individual student quizzes	Individual student quizzes
Team scoring	Team scoring	Team scoring	Team scoring	Team scoring
Recognition	Recognition	Recognition	Recognition	Recognition

Foremost, as the leader of any instructional alternative, you must believe in its purpose. You must have faith! In this case, you must subscribe to the "all for one, one for all" philosophy. Relatedly, you must be able to organize heterogenous teams and ensure that team members also value cooperative, collaborative learning. Also, since STAD, TGT, and CIRC incorporate teacher whole-class or small-group presentation, you must be a good presenter (see Table 7.2). Finally, since all these variations of cooperative learning utilize some amount of independent study, you will also need to be good at facilitating this (see Table 7.6).

All forms of cooperative learning call for teachers who have the organizational skills to plan, monitor, facilitate, and track the work of disparate groups. Monitoring and facilitation are best accomplished when you have diagnostic and clinical skills, that is, when you are able to identify and help students and teams as they encounter problems. You must be a good juggler.

A subtle, yet very real, challenge teachers face when they use small-group instruction is the need to ensure that high-achieving students do not dominate the heterogeneous groups they are in. In a study of cooperative learning, King (1993) reports that "high-achieving students assumed dominant roles in the undertaking of group tasks, in group decision making, and in the frequency and quality of contributions" (p. 399). To avoid passivity on the part of low achievers, King suggests that teachers must create positive expectations that low achievers "can do." As you can see, utilizing cooperative learning is not for the faint of heart.

8.6   What beliefs and abilities do you have that might help you implement cooperative learning? What might inhibit your use of it?

GOOD COOPERATIVE LEARNING

Since there are several forms of cooperative learning, each requires a somewhat different kind of teacher preparation, delivery, and closure. Therefore, we will restrict our comments to STAD since it is the simplest, best known, and most frequently used form. Furthermore, Slavin (1995) recommends it as "a good model to begin with for teachers who are new to the cooperative approach" (p. 54).

Preparation   STAD, you may recall, is the form of cooperative learning in which the teacher presents information and then places students in heterogeneous groups to learn or master that information. Thus, two kinds of preparation are essential: (1) you must be prepared to provide information in the most effective way, and (2) students must be prepared to engage in group work so they can master the information.

Since a teacher presentation is called for, the information on good presentations in the previous chapter is useful. You may recall from Table 7.2 that as you prepare for a presentation, you must establish specific learner objectives (what learners should know and be able to do as a consequence of receiving the information). Johnson and Johnson (1998) offer a few questions useful in guiding teacher planning. They include: What do I want students to learn? What cognitive and affective outcomes should they achieve? What are some learning activities that can best accomplish these ends? What resources and assistance will learners need? In addition, you must collect and review materials that provide the knowledge you will present and, having taken these steps, plan the presentation. Finally, since a team assignment is to be undertaken following the presentation, you must organize that assignment and be ready to deliver it. You also must create a quiz.

Try Activity 8.1

Students must also be oriented to engage in STAD. Prior to its first use they must be told why it is being used, how it works, and, particularly, what is expected of them. Thereafter, each time STAD is used, learners need to be organized into heterogeneous groups and motivated to help one another learn. In some cases, students will need to be taught or reminded of the social skills they need to use. Highlight 8.2 lists some of these skills and discusses their importance.

Johnson and Johnson (1989/1990) caution us that "people do not know instinctively how to interact effectively with others. Nor do interpersonal and group skills magically appear when needed. Students must be taught these skills and be motivated to use them. If group members lack interpersonal and small group skills . . . cooperative groups will not be productive" (p. 30).

The student skills Johnson and Johnson feel are most necessary are to:

- Know and trust one another.
- Communicate clearly and accurately.
- Support one another through praise and encouragement.
- Resolve conflicts constructively.

Delivery   Delivery of STAD involves two steps: (1) your presentation and (2) initiation and monitoring of the teamwork. Once more, the information on good presentations from Chapter 7 is applicable. To review, when delivering a good presentation you should get students' attention, tell them what they will learn and, as a result, what they should be able to do after learning; relate the new information to ideas learners already know; present the information in a step-by-step manner; don't overwhelm or underwhelm; emphasize the most important points students need to remember or use; use examples and illustrations to increase clarity; use variety to maintain attention; and make sure learners understand by asking them questions.

Following your presentation, teamwork begins. You must then accomplish the following:

1. *Set the team goals.* The major function of the team in STAD is to prepare its members to learn as much as possible in order to obtain a high team quiz score.

2. *Prepare students for teamwork.* In STAD, this requires forming them into heterogeneous groups, reminding them of the "all for one, one for all" philosophy of cooperative learning, communicating your expectations for individual and group behavior, and jogging their memories concerning the interactive or social skills they will need to use.

3. *Give the teams the assignment.* Depending upon the nature of the assignment, you may have prepared handouts, worksheets, or a practice quiz for the teams to work on collaboratively.

4. *Monitor the teams.* Although the intention is that students teach one another, be sure that this, in fact, is happening. Therefore, you must be up and about, observing and listening, and intervening when necessary. One of the biggest mistakes you can make is to assume students know what to do and to assume they are doing it correctly. An ounce of prevention is worth a pound of cure.

5. *Quiz the students.* At a previously designated time, individual team members take the quiz. Although students have worked together to get ready for the quiz, they must take it independently.

6. *Score the quizzes.* Students score one another's papers, or you may collect and score them yourself. (There are advantages and disadvantages either way. Can you think of some of them?) Once you have scored individual quizzes, calculate team scores. There are at least two ways to derive team scores. In one, you calculate an "improvement score" by comparing each learner's achievement on this quiz with her or his achievement on a similar, earlier quiz. If the score is better, the student receives improvement points. Then you add all individual improvement scores to get the team improvement score. Another way to calculate a team score is simply to add the members' scores together. Most

CHAPTER 8
Four More Instructional Alternatives:
Cooperative Learning, Discovery Learning,
Constructivism, and Direct Instruction

www.mhhe.com/cruickshank6e

265

advocates of cooperative learning procedures favor the use of improvement scores.

7. *Recognize team accomplishment.* When improvement scores are used, teams that have improved performance receive some recognition. Thus, teams compete with themselves to improve, rather than against other teams to win. This is more gentle than rewarding teams that outperform other teams. Forms of recognition and reward can include printed certificates of achievement, recognition as "super team" of the week, or special privileges. As mentioned earlier, cooperative learning draws from the behavioral school of thought and particularly from operant conditioning. If you do something well, you get rewarded.

8.7   What factors in Chapter 1 may influence your use of cooperative learning?

Try Activity 8.2

Closure   Little is said in the literature on cooperative learning about what, if anything, to do after you give grades and rewards. Considering what we know about short- and long-term memory (Chapter 4), we presume that students should be reminded of what they have just learned, the new information should be securely related and attached to what they already know or what they will learn next, and they should have the opportunity to apply the information in some way.

A summary of the qualities of good cooperative learning leaders and of the elements of good cooperative learning appears in Table 8.2. A sample cooperative learning lesson plan appears as Lesson Plan 8.1.

WHEN COOPERATIVE LEARNING SHOULD BE USED

Properly conducted, cooperative learning is an instructional alternative with strong support. It seems to reduce competition and increase cooperation and achievement. When should it be used? Our answer is, often—but not always. As indicated in Chapter 7, variety in instruction is extremely important. Teachers' comments

TABLE 8.2 Qualities of Good Cooperative Learning Leaders and of Good Cooperative Learning (STAD)	
Good Leaders of Cooperative Learning . . .	**Good Cooperative Learning (STAD)**
• Believe in the importance of getting learners to work together for the individual and common good • Are able to get diverse learners to work cooperatively • Are competent presenters and use independent study assignments effectively (see Tables 7.2 and 7.6) • Are especially effective organizers and coordinators of work • Are especially effective diagnosticians and clinicians, i.e., are able to identify and help students and teams having difficulty	*When preparing:* • Prepare the presentation utilizing elements of a "good presentation" (Table 7.2) • Prepare the team assignment (Table 7.6) • Prepare students for future engagement in cooperative learning by explaining effective interpersonal and interactive skills (see Highlight 8.2) *When delivering:* • Make the presentation utilizing elements of a "good presentation" (Table 7.2) • Set team goals • Prepare students for work with their team • Give the teams the assignment • Quiz the students • Recognize team accomplishments *When closing:* • Remind students of what they learned • Relate new learning to past or future learning • Provide opportunity for practical use of information

LESSON PLAN 8.1

Abbreviated Cooperative Learning Lesson Plan: Applied Arithmetic

Curriculum tie-in: This lesson allows learners to see how arithmetic computation is used in everyday life. It also complements the social relationships curriculum.

OBJECTIVES

1. Each team of learners will cooperate to build the tallest free-standing structure at the lowest cost.
   Specific objectives: Given resources, teams of learners will build a free-standing structure that is as tall and as inexpensive as possible; teams will engage in arithmetic computations to determine its cost.
2. Teams will encourage arithmetic contributions from each member.
   Specific objective: Given the task, each team should strive to record at least one arithmetic contribution from each member.
3. Teams will employ good interpersonal skills.
   Specific objective: Learners will display respect for and consideration of others.

RESOURCES PER TEAM (others may be substituted)

1. 20 plastic straws (value $1 each), 10 small paper clips (value $.20 each), 20 straight pins (value $.10 each), roll of masking tape (value $.20 for each inch used).
2. Yard or meter stick.
3. Calculator (optional).
4. Encyclopedia material on building construction.

METHODOLOGY

1. *Set induction:* "What are some of the tallest buildings in the country? How do you think they can be built so tall?"
2. Inform learners of what they will learn and be able to do as a result of lesson.
3. Establish *heterogeneous* groups of four to six learners and provide each with space and building materials (see Resources above).
4. Establish roles: *builders, mathematicians, scientists* (who list principles of building used), *reporter* who observes and prepares a report for the class that includes such things as how tall the structure was, how much it cost, what principles of building were used, what arithmetic was most valuable.
5. Have students discuss how they can encourage and respect the ideas and skills of other team members.
6. Provide time for teams to read about buildings and to plan and build theirs.
7. Have each team reporter tell the class what rules of construction were used, what the successes and failures were, how each member contributed mathematically, what math was most useful, and what the height and cost of the building was.

ASSESSMENT

Monitor all groups to determine
1. How well learners are able to employ arithmetic properly and correctly.
2. To what extent team members employ good interpersonal skills.
3. To what extent all learners are involved as contributors.

CLOSURE

1. Ask learners to tell what they learned about building, the value of arithmetic, and helping all to contribute.
2. Ask them how arithmetic is used in other occupations and how their caregivers may use it.

---

interspersed throughout Slavin's book (1995) indicate that although students do not seem to tire of cooperative learning, the possibility of boredom exists. Consequently, teachers who use this instructional alternative make certain adjustments. For example, they vary team membership, tasks, and rewards.

A second reason to avoid putting all our eggs into the cooperative learning basket is that different kinds of educational objectives are best achieved using different instructional alternatives. Supporting this view, Stallings and Stipek (1986) note that TGT does not seem to produce as much achievement when used in social studies. Furthermore, they cite Sharon (1980), who questions whether the use of cooperative learning, specifically STAD and TGT, can be as effective when the goal is to teach or use higher level thinking skills such as analysis, synthesis, and evaluation.

Keeping these restrictions in mind, cooperative learning is probably best utilized when the class needs to develop a sense of harmony and community building (all for one, one for all), when students are at risk or generally suffer from low self-esteem, and when teachers want to help integrate mainstreamed students.

CHAPTER 8
Four More Instructional Alternatives:
Cooperative Learning, Discovery Learning,
Constructivism, and Direct Instruction

www.mhhe.com/cruickshank6e

267

Teachers who select cooperative learning strategies probably believe in the "all for one, one for all" philosophy, feel they have good leadership and interpersonal skills, know that their organizational and monitoring abilities enable them to do more than one thing at a time (overlapping), and believe that this approach works.

Three kinds of students who seem to benefit from involvement in cooperative learning are described in Case 8.1.

The Concept to Classroom website provides a link to an online tutorial with video clips on cooperative-collaborative learning. The Cooperative Learning Center also maintains a website.

Web Links

Concept to Classroom

Cooperative Learning Center

LIMITATIONS OF COOPERATIVE LEARNING

The success of cooperative learning depends upon a number of conditions. First, research shows that for a cooperative learning activity to succeed, team members must not simply share answers but, more importantly, explain how they derived the answers and why they are correct (Slavin, 2008). Without this step, students are not able to apply or use the information later. Therefore, some students in each group must be "good teachers." Successful learning experiences also require that high achievers care for and help or nurture low achievers. The implicit assumption is that good students wish to help less able students.

A second important condition is that individual team members be accountable to the team. This "one for all" expectation is not what students have been accustomed to; what they are accustomed to is interpersonal competition.

Third, in order for cooperative learning to have a chance, team members must stay on task, since time on task is consistently related to students' learning (see Chapter 11). Students tend to get off task when the teacher is not present. Teachers must regularly monitor individual and small-group work during cooperative learning.

Fourth, in any team, individuals must get along with one another. In every classroom, certain students will find this difficult. There may also be students who will do less work or work less hard, thereby causing the team to suffer or cover up. Good and Brophy (2007) remind us that any form of small-group instruction is more difficult than teaching the class as a whole because these and other management problems are compounded (see Chapter 12).

Finally, teaching arrangements that encourage some children to provide assistance and others to receive it appear likely to increase dependency (Biemiller, 1993).

SUMMARY ON COOPERATIVE LEARNING

At the outset, we characterized cooperative learning as teaching learners to like and care for one another. We stated that the method is analogous to creating teams of musketeers who come to one another's assistance and who succeed together no matter what the circumstances. Cooperative learning seems to have a hint of romanticism about it when compared to its more common instructional cousins such as presentation, discussion, and independent study. In business jargon, it seems to have more "sizzle."

We also learned that there are a number of different cooperative learning approaches but that most have four characteristics in common (see Figure 8.1): (1) they utilize teams that are mostly heterogeneous in composition; (2) the task the teams undertake usually involves either mastering material presented by a teacher, mastering written materials, or working on a project; (3) accountability is twofold—to oneself and to assisting the team and its members; and (4) rewards are generally tied to overall team improvement.

As with any instructional alternative, teachers who use this approach need certain attributes. They need to be good presenters, to be insightful in developing worthwhile team assignments, and to be able to monitor teamwork, diagnose problems, and prescribe remedies. Since the various forms of cooperative learning

Three teachers provide sketches of a few kinds of students positively affected by cooperative learning (Augustine, Gruber, & Hansen, 1989/1990).

Andy is a low-achieving elementary school student. He was failing several subjects and needed supervision to stay on task until cooperative learning was introduced. The changes are astonishing. His grades have improved to the point where he is passing all subjects. Additionally, Andy has become a "cheerful, confident child."

Susan, a child with handicaps mainstreamed in a regular classroom, was placed in a cooperative learning group. The group's task was to prepare for a chapter test. When the group's study time was over, Susan still was not ready. Instead of taking recess, her group colleagues stayed to work further with her. They also helped her the next day before the test was given. On the test, Susan and all her teammates received perfect scores.

Angela, a gifted student, excelled at school and also in piano, gymnastics, and dance. Her parents questioned how working in a group where she would be held to a group norm would be beneficial.

After all, Angela did outstanding work on her own. After a conference, Angela's parents were convinced she might benefit from learning how to interact with less capable peers. Her group work has helped Angela become more tactful, respectful, and sharing.

INVESTIGATING AND SOLVING THE CASE
1. How has cooperative learning helped these students?
2. What other kinds of students might benefit from its use?

---

differ, each has a set of best procedures to follow. The qualities of good procedures for STAD appear in Table 8.2.

Like each instructional alternative on the Wheel of Instructional Choice (Figure 7.5), cooperative learning (student-team learning) has advantages and limitations. Its advantages mirror those offered by discussion, another student-centered alternative. However, cooperative learning seems to be better than discussion at meeting students' needs to achieve academically and socially.

Certain cooperative learning processes have been subjected to study, and most prove to contribute to student achievement and satisfaction (see **Spotlight on Research 8.1**). Little consensus exists concerning how frequently cooperative learning is used; estimates range from 7 to 20 percent of the time. However, we can assume from its repeated mention in the professional literature that cooperative learning is very much alive and well. One of its better known proponents sums it up, although perhaps a bit too optimistically: Cooperative learning seems to be an extraordinary success (Johnson & Johnson, 2009). It has an excellent research base, many viable, successful forms, and hundreds of thousands of enthusiastic adherents (Slavin, 1989/1990, p. 3).

Try Activity 8.3

Discovery Learning: Figuring Things Out for Yourself

WHAT IS DISCOVERY LEARNING?

You have probably heard of Sherlock Holmes, the famous detective created by Sir Arthur Conan Doyle. As you may recall, Holmes was regularly faced with baffling cases such as the mysterious death of Sir Charles Baskerville in the novel *The Hound of the Baskervilles*. According to his great friend Dr. Watson, Holmes—as was his custom—demanded the facts. After gathering them, he would retreat into seclusion in order to "weigh every particle of evidence, construct alternative theories, balance one against the other, and make up his mind as to which points were essential and which immaterial" (p. 35) to solving the mystery. Holmes was the consummate

www.mhhe.com/cruickshank6e

CHAPTER 8
Four More Instructional Alternatives:
Cooperative Learning, Discovery Learning,
Constructivism, and Direct Instruction
269

When academic achievement is the goal, then cooperative learning seems to be a good instructional alternative. After reviewing 158 studies of various kinds of cooperative learning that compared this teaching strategy with competitive and individualistic kinds of instruction, Johnson, Johnson, and Stanne (2000) report that *all* kinds had a more positive effect on student achievement regardless of whether students were in elementary, middle, high, or postsec-ondary school. However, they caution that many of the studies had limitations or shortcomings.

Slavin (1996) reports that 37 of 44 studies comparing cooperative learning methods with traditional instruction favor the former when "interdependent work" and "individual accountability" are expected of students. "There is widespread consensus [among researchers] that students benefit when they can help one another learn instead of hav-ing to work apart from or against one another" (Walters, 2000).

Cooperative learning seems to have benefits beyond academic achievement. Studies seem to show that it also encourages social and interpersonal development as students learn to appreciate cross-racial and other forms of diversity while they work together. African-Americans, in particular, often perform better in such groups (Hurley, Allen, & Boykin, 2009).

inductive reasoner, always "putting two and two together" in order to reach some logical explanation or conclusion.

Many times we, too, face situations where we have to figure things out for ourselves. What is the meaning of a new word we find in a sentence? How can we get the word processor to double-space? Why did we get a C in the course instead of a B? How can we get a B next time?

Psychologists and educators (Bruner, 2004; Dewey, 1997; Joyce, Weil, & Callahan, 2008; Strike, 1975; Suchman, 1961; Wolk, 2008) make the case that reasoning and problem solving skills—Sherlock Holmes's, or our students'—can be improved through use. They propose that we utilize discovery learning to give learners opportunities to collect, organize, manipulate, and analyze data. Discovery learning is the instructional alternative many educators tout as the choice for teaching social studies, science, and mathematics. It falls within the cognitive school of thought (see Chapter 4) under meaningful learning.

8.8 Do you prefer having someone tell you something or figuring it out for yourself?

Discovery or **inquiry learning** refers to learning that takes place when students are asked to find out or figure out something for themselves as Sherlock Holmes does. Here are some classroom examples. Rather than telling students using watercolors that if they want to create green they must mix blue and yellow, the teacher asks them to mix the two colors to find out the result. Rather than telling students the value of *pi,* the teacher asks them to measure spherical objects (such as a tennis ball) to find it out. Rather than telling students the life cycle of a frog, the instructor has learners observe and record it. Do you see how discovery learning or figuring things out for yourself might result in greater understanding and better recollection?

PURPOSES AND CHARACTERISTICS OF DISCOVERY LEARNING

Teachers use discovery learning to accomplish three educational purposes (see Figure 8.2). First, *they want learners to know how to think and find things out for themselves.* Conversely, they want them to be less dependent on receiving knowledge from teachers and accepting the conclusions of others. Secondly, users of discovery learning *want learners to see for themselves how knowledge is obtained.* Such teachers want students to be able to learn by collecting, organizing, and analyzing information to reach their own conclusions. Third, *these teachers want learners to use their higher-order thinking skills* described in Chapter 6. They want them to analyze, synthesize, and evaluate.

FIGURE 8.2 Purposes and Key Characteristics of Discovery Learning

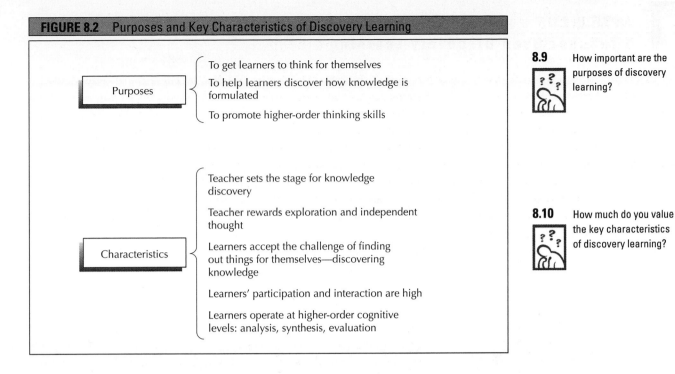

Purposes	To get learners to think for themselves
	To help learners discover how knowledge is formulated
	To promote higher-order thinking skills

8.9 How important are the purposes of discovery learning?

Characteristics	Teacher sets the stage for knowledge discovery
	Teacher rewards exploration and independent thought
	Learners accept the challenge of finding out things for themselves—discovering knowledge
	Learners' participation and interaction are high
	Learners operate at higher-order cognitive levels: analysis, synthesis, evaluation

8.10 How much do you value the key characteristics of discovery learning?

The above purposes of discovery learning result in its having unique characteristics (see Figure 8.2). To begin with, the role of the teacher is not to impart knowledge but rather to create classroom experiences in which learners engage in order to discover knowledge. Read **Case 8.2**, in which teacher Deb O'Brien found an alternative to telling her learners that clothing does not produce heat. Instead she engaged learners in finding out for themselves that that is a misconception.

A second characteristic of discovery learning is that as learners engage in inquiry, the teacher encourages them to think deeply. Deb probably asked, "What could we try to find out if clothes make heat?" She helps learners think through their ideas and helps them formulate experiences that might be undertaken.

A third characteristic is that learners accept the challenge of finding something out for themselves rather than having the teacher give them an answer. They feel empowered.

As the process of inquiry goes on, it is characterized by a high degree of learner participation and interaction. There are lots of ideas and lots of give and take.

Other excellent examples of discovery/inquiry learning are found in **Case 8.3** (on page 273) and in National Research Council (2000), pages 6–10, 40–46, 48–57, 60–64, and 66–72.

Finally, during the inquiry process, learners operate at high cognitive levels as the teacher asks questions such as, What do you think? How can we find out? How will we know? In teacher O'Brien's case the questions were "What is heat? How can we find out if it comes from clothing? Why do clothes make us feel warmer?"

Yes, the roles of teacher and learners change dramatically when you employ discovery learning. So does the process of learning.

GOOD FACILITATORS OF DISCOVERY LEARNING

To use discovery learning effectively, you must believe in its purposes. Do you think a major goal of education is to get students to think for themselves? Do you believe students have the ability to think for themselves? Even if you answer the first question affirmatively, you may be stymied by the second. After all, you have probably been in classrooms where some of your peers seemed less than able intellectually.

8.11 When your students don't understand are you more likely to give them the answer or help them discover it?

www.mhhe.com/cruickshank6e

CHAPTER 8
Four More Instructional Alternatives:
Cooperative Learning, Discovery Learning,
Constructivism, and Direct Instruction

271

A Teacher Uses Discovery Learning

Deb O'Brien introduced the new science unit on heat by asking her 9-year-olds, "What is heat?" She intended, through the question, to have them draw from their experiences, and this they did. They recalled that heat came from the sun and from fires, radiators, and assorted other sources. However, one boy posited that heat came from clothing such as coats and sweaters. His peers readily agreed. Deb recognized that to a 9-year-old, the observation seemed reasonable. After all, when they put "warm" clothing on, they were warmer. But how to correct this misconception? Should

she tell them the truth? No. She felt it more appropriate that they learn it for themselves. So the class constructed an experiment. They wrapped thermometers in coats and sweaters and assumed the temperature thereon should rise. When it didn't, they sealed the clothing and thermometers in plastic bags. Still the thermometers recorded no heat change.

After numerous failed efforts to prove that clothes gave off heat, the learners were willing to entertain an alternative hypothesis—that clothing merely holds or contains the heat given off by those

wearing it. These fourth-graders discovered for themselves knowledge about what causes and what contains or traps heat (Watson & Konicek, 1990).

> **INVESTIGATING AND SOLVING THE CASE**
> 1. What knowledge in this chapter is Deb O'Brien applying?
> 2. Think of something you may teach where principles of discovery learning would be very helpful.

However, keep in mind that the cause of their apparent ineptitude may stem from their never having the opportunity to build confidence in their own thinking ability. Belief in one's power to think must be planted and cultivated.

A second purpose of discovery learning is to get learners to find out how knowledge is constructed. Do you want them to know how concepts, facts, generalizations, rules, and laws are formulated? If you do, you have intellectual aspirations for your learners. You expect them to understand the very origin and nature of knowledge rather than just to memorize facts.

A third purpose of discovery learning is to get learners to develop their higher-order or critical thinking skills. Do you want them to know how to analyze, synthesize, evaluate, and solve problems? Can you encourage them to explore, investigate, observe, classify, measure, define, interpret, infer, predict, and hypothesize? If so, you will make an indelible mark on their minds and lives.

Aside from believing in the purpose of discovery learning, to be a good practitioner you need certain qualities. For example, you must enjoy inquiry yourself: You should be naturally curious and have "a strong interest in the discovery of truth by an empirical, critical, rational, 'intellectual' approach" (Anastasi & Urbana, 1997, p. 488). Relatedly, you should believe that your learners are or can be curious, too. Moreover, you should be nurturing, thoughtful, patient, and accepting of learners' ideas while holding high expectations for them.

8.12 What beliefs and abilities do you have that would help you to be a good practitioner of discovery learning?

GOOD DISCOVERY LEARNING

Suppose you are sold on discovery learning and feel you have the ability to pull it off. What process would you follow? Persons either reviewing or advocating this instructional alternative suggest several stages and steps (Joyce, Weil, & Callahan 2008; Kauchak & Eggen, 2006; Orlich, 2009).

Preparation   When preparing any learning activity, you should have some broad purpose in mind. Perhaps it is to have students learn about pulse rate or rate of respiration. With that in mind, you decide *specifically* what students should know

I've been meaning to write a little about my unit on Simple Machines, which is so much fun and feels like I actually know what I'm doing in the classroom, and might be useful for someone out there trying to teach this stuff.

We segued from reading about work and power and practicing our nonfiction reading skills into simple machines. They were completely confused about the idea that machines don't make less work, they just make work easier by changing the force, distance, and/or direction. I gave some examples and then asked them to trust me, that we'd see it in action over the next few days, and to ask again if they were still confused after doing some exploration. They decided to trust. . . . Some skills emerge from a bunch of playful explorations and a little explicit teaching.

For inclined planes, I set up three stations. I have six groups in my classes, so we had two of each station. It took two days to introduce each station and rotate through all three, about 25 minutes at each station. Then we took another period and just discussed what we learned. I had them read the textbook section on inclined planes for homework, and use their reading skills to "take useful notes." Most took pretty good-looking notes. . . .

The first station had them pull a block up a cardboard ramp to the seat of a chair. They pulled straight up, up a steep ramp, and up a gradual ramp, and they used a spring scale to measure the force needed, and a meter stick to measure the distance. The experiment was wildly imprecise but it consistently showed that the longer the ramp, the less force required.

The second station had them investigate screws. I put a bunch of screws in a tray and asked them to trace the threads with a finger and draw the shape of the threads—a spiral. Then they took triangular shaped pieces of paper and wrapped them around pencils, to see that the threads are formed by an inclined plane being wrapped around a cylinder. I had two different triangles for them to compare, to see what kinds of threads are formed by a "steep" triangle and a "gradual" triangle. Then I asked them to predict which type of screw would require more force to screw into a board, and which would need to be turned a longer distance. If I do this station again, I will have them actually test their prediction with a screwdriver. . . .

The third station made me very nervous, though the kids handled it extremely well. I had them look at wedges—doorstops and kitchen knives. They examined the shapes of these objects to see that they are inclined planes. Then they cut carrots and pushed the doorstop under the door, observing the direction of the input and output forces, to see that wedges take a force in one direction and turn it into a force in another direction. We use knives every day, but how often do you think that you are applying a downward force, and the knife is applying a horizontal force on the object you are cutting? I let the kids use pretty sharp knives—after all, they all have these things in their kitchens—but I kept close watch and set very clear expectations of how the knives would be handled. I think plastic knives and clay would work, though it would be a little harder to see the wedge-shape of the knife and to see the change in direction of the force.

Inclined planes are unique in allowing the middle school teacher to say "wedge" and "screw" about a hundred times a day and all in the same unit! . . . [Written by a middle school teacher]

Source: Msfrizzle (2006).

INVESTIGATING AND
SOLVING THE CASE

1. What principles or procedures of discovery learning did Ms. Frizzle use?

2. How would you teach simple machines?

---

about either or both. Let's say you want them to know the meaning of pulse and respiration (concepts), how pulse and respiration are measured (procedures), the range of pulse and respiration rates (facts), normal rates (facts), and conditions that affect the rates (generalizations). To ensure your own knowledge of these areas and to have related resources available, you need to collect material on these topics.

Now you are ready to generate the discovery lesson. How can you create situations where students can find out these things for themselves? And, importantly, how can you create interest? What do you want students to notice or discover? How

CHAPTER 8
Four More Instructional Alternatives:
Cooperative Learning, Discovery Learning,
Constructivism, and Direct Instruction

www.mhhe.com/cruickshank6e
273

Try Activity 8.4

can they do so? Here we take into account all we have learned about lesson planning from Chapter 6, Planning Instruction.

Finally, in the preparation stage you need to be sure your students are ready to use scientific methods such as observation, recording, and analyzing. If they have not previously had experience with inductive and deductive reasoning, you will have to provide greater guidance and simplification.

Delivery When you studied information processing in Chapter 4, you learned how essential it is to obtain and maintain students' attention. In Chapter 6, Planning Instruction, this message was reinforced by the concept of **set induction,** that is, doing something at the start of the lesson to grab the learners' attention. Can you think of something that would cause students to focus on learning about pulse and respiration? It could be a question such as, "What are some things our body must do to stay alive?"

Having gained your students' attention, you next might present a situation, real or hypothetical, that is challenging or baffling. Again, you can use questions such as "What do physicians do to find out if our systems are O.K.?" "How do they know?" "How do we know when our pulse rate and respiration are normal?" "What is normal? How can we find out?" "What might make our pulse and respiration rates change? How can we find out?" Depending on the specific objectives of your lesson, you would phrase questions that invite learners to discover answers. Getting them to phrase questions is even better. Table 8.3 reminds us of four forms of knowledge and provides examples of questions that promote each form.

Once you have presented students with a challenge, you need to ensure that they have a clear idea of how to investigate the question. "What can you do to discover the answers to these questions?" "Which ones might you be able to find out for yourselves without reading books?" "How could you do so?"

"How do you expect me to learn anything when you're the one who keeps asking all the questions?"

8.13 How would you help learners come to know any one of these concepts, facts, generalizations, or rules/laws?

TABLE 8.3 Four Forms of Knowledge and Illustrative Questions That Could Be Used to Promote Discovery of Each	
Form of Knowledge	**Questions That Promote Discovery**
1. *Concepts.* A concept is the name that describes a class of ideas or objects.	1.1 What is a mammal?
	1.2 What is luck?
	1.3 What is rap music?
	1.4 What is a democrat?
2. *Facts.* A fact is a truth.	2.1 What is the average pulse rate?
	2.2 What is the life history of the frog?
	2.3 What is the sum of the angles of a triangle?
	2.4 What happens when blue and red mix?
3. *Generalizations.* A generalization is an inference that may not be universally true but is widely supported.	3.1 How are families changing?
	3.2 How should lessons be prepared?
	3.3 What are the attributes of good teachers?
	3.4 Why do students go south for spring break?
4. *Rules/laws.* A rule or law is an unchanging principle that governs a particular situation or set of conditions.	4.1 How are words divided into syllables?
	4.2 How is table tennis played?
	4.3 How are fractions divided?
	4.4 Why do certain objects float?

When students are ready to proceed with their observation, data collection, analysis, and so forth, your task is to monitor and display the qualities of a good discovery learning teacher. These include holding high expectations that students can learn on their own, nurturing them, being patient and accepting of their ideas, and causing them to be thoughtful and reflective. It is particularly urgent that you develop a secure environment that supports risk-free thinking. Fear of ridicule, failure, or criticism must be removed or your learners may be intellectually paralyzed. This does not mean that the environment is evaluation-free. Rather, it means that judgments result from thoughtful consideration and perhaps from the testing of all ideas.

Closure Following open and substantial consideration of the data they have unearthed, learners need to draw conclusions. "After your investigation, what can you conclude about pulse and respiration rates?" Here your task is to help learners organize and phrase the discoveries. To ensure that the discovery has become embedded in long-term memory, you next need to provide an opportunity to use it. In the case of pulse and respiration, perhaps students could assess family members' pulse rates.

Table 8.4 summarizes qualities of good discovery learning teachers and good discovery learning procedures. An abbreviated discovery lesson appears as Lesson Plan 8.2.

A tutorial on discovery–inquiry learning is available at the Concept to Classroom, "Inquiry-based Learning" website.

8.14 What factors mentioned in Chapter 1 or Chapter 4 may influence your use of discovery learning?

Web Link
Concept to Classroom:
Inquiry-based Learning

TABLE 8.4 Qualities of Good Facilitators of Discovery Learning and of Good Discovery Learning	
Good Facilitators . . .	**Good Discovery Learning**
• Believe in the purposes of discovery learning	*When preparing:*
• Tend to be inquirers (curious) themselves	• Determine the general purpose of the lesson
• Are optimistic and confident in students' ability to inquire	• Determine the specific lesson objectives: identify the concepts, facts, generalizations, rules, or laws to be discovered
• Hold high expectations of students	• Collect useful resources and materials
• Are nurturing	• Plan the discovery lesson
• Are thoughtful	• Ensure that learners are ready to use inductive methods
• Are patient	*When delivering:*
• Accept students' ideas	• Obtain students' attention via set induction
• Are reflective	• Present the challenging or baffling situation
	• Utilize questions that will promote discovery (see examples in Table 8.3)
	• Ensure that learners know what they are supposed to do
	• Monitor and guide student activity and thinking
	• Encourage observation, collection and organization, manipulation, analysis of ideas and data, and so forth
	When closing:
	• Help learners to organize and phrase what they have concluded: the concepts, facts, generalizations, and so forth
	• Provide opportunity to use the new knowledge

www.mhhe.com/cruickshank6e

CHAPTER 8
Four More Instructional Alternatives:
Cooperative Learning, Discovery Learning,
Constructivism, and Direct Instruction
275

LESSON PLAN 8.2

Abbreviated Discovery Lesson: Secondary Colors

Curriculum tie-in: Art

OBJECTIVE

1. Learners will discover how to create secondary colors.
   Specific objective: Given the three primary colors (red, yellow, blue), learners will discover how they may be combined to form the secondary colors (orange, violet, green).

RESOURCES

1. Tempera paint: yellow, red, blue. One container of each per group of learners.
2. Water. One container per group of learners.
3. Paint brushes. One per learner.
4. Paper plates (glossy, nonabsorbent). One per learner.
5. Paper toweling. At least one sheet per learner.
6. Writing paper. One sheet per learner.

METHODOLOGY

1. *Set induction.* "Have you ever mixed things together? What have you mixed? What happened? Today you are going to discover what happens when certain colors are mixed."

2. "You will have three colors of paint: yellow, red, blue. How many combinations of these three colors can you make? (yellow with red, yellow with blue, red with blue) What colors do you think will result when you mix these three combinations? (orange, green, violet) Let's find out."

3. Place learners in groups of three to five around tables. On each place a container of yellow, red, and blue tempera paint, a container of water, paint brushes, paper plates, and paper toweling.

4. Provide directions such as the following:
   "We are going to do two things—experiment by mixing paint and make a record of what we discover. Here is the order of things we will do. Mix yellow with red on the paper plate then write on your paper the color you got. Wash the new color out of the brush and dry it on the paper towel. Mix red with blue and do likewise, record the new color, and wash the brush. Finally, mix blue with yellow . . ."
   (You may want to have the groups stay together, mixing only one combination and discussing the results.)

5. Discuss the following:
   What happened when you mixed combinations 1, 2, and 3?
   Why do you suppose that some of your secondary colors look a little different? (Perhaps students mixed a little more of one primary color than the other.)
   How can the primary colors we started with and the secondary colors we made be put on a chart, for example as a wheel or spectrum)?

ASSESSMENT

1. Learners are asked to take paper and create a picture containing grass, flowers, sun, and sky making sure they use the three primary and three secondary colors.

CLOSURE

1. Have students recall what they have learned: What are the primary and secondary colors? What happens when primary colors are combined? What happens when they are combined unevenly?

FACILITATING DISCOVERY LEARNING ONLINE

You can accomplish the outcomes of discovery learning by utilizing certain computer software programs and by using the computer to search for information. The Dalton School in New York City exemplifies how (Wallis, 1995).

A software program called *Archaeotype,* developed at Dalton, is a middle school level computer simulation of an archeological dig, complete with virtual excavation and shovel sounds. Groups of four or five students are assigned a "lot" to unearth at an ancient Syrian site. The purpose: to locate what is buried, analyze it, and create and defend a thesis about the site and its inhabitants. To support the theories generated, the group has online access to libraries and art museums containing stores of related information. Thus, rather than receiving information about life in ancient Syria, students discover the knowledge for themselves. Quite literally, they construct it.

Another class at Dalton, after reading Shakespeare's *Macbeth,* is able to delve more deeply into the text and its characters by connecting online to various databases containing related information. For example, a group of students working on a paper on Lady Macbeth is able to access illustrations of the character, scenes in which she is portrayed in motion pictures, and dozens of essays about her. Obviously, the information obtained is far more extensive than would otherwise be available, and having it permits the group to formulate knowledge, to derive their own meaning about who this person was.

To find out more about Dalton School curricular projects using discovery learning go to the Digital Dalton website and click "Projects."

Web Link
Digital Dalton

WHEN DISCOVERY LEARNING SHOULD BE USED

Given what we know, when should discovery learning be used? We believe it should be employed when your instructional goals coincide with its main purposes: (1) to get students to think for themselves (see Case 8.3), (2) to help them discover how knowledge is created, and (3) to promote higher-order thinking. Additionally, discovery learning should be used when it best serves the personal and educational needs of you and your learners. Finally, it should be used only when you have developed the qualities of a good facilitator and you know and can follow the regimen for good discovery learning.

Of course, all the above is based on the premise that your learning objectives can be most effectively gained using this alternative. If that is not the case, you must be convinced that the time and energy it demands are worth it. Said another way, the ends of discovery learning should justify it as the means.

Try Activity 8.6

All teachers probably use some modified or abbreviated forms of discovery learning because of the influence of educational philosopher John Dewey (2005) and psychologist Jerome Bruner (1961, 2004). Both theorists admonished teachers to get students to think for themselves. Consequently, when you observe a reading class in an elementary school, you will often hear the teacher ask students to figure out the meaning of a new word from the sentence and paragraph the word is embedded in. In another classroom, you might see students investigating the leaves of different trees. Joyce, Weil, and Callahan (2008) note, "Probably nothing has been more consistently pursued yet remains more elusive than the teaching of thinking" (p. 42). However, even though discovery learning is widely recommended for this purpose, most teachers use it incidentally, as a part of recitation or discussion. For the most part, teachers persist in telling students what to think.

LIMITATIONS OF DISCOVERY LEARNING

It is too bad that so promising an alternative also has formidable shortcomings. Most notably, not everything students must learn is amenable to classroom discovery. Students in most classrooms cannot be expected to discover chemical elements, the themes of famous writers and artists, or the way a computer works. Such knowledge is probably too complex for the minds of K–12 students. Even when they have the capacity to discover complex knowledge, there may not be sufficient time or appropriate resources to make the investigation. Perhaps that is why teacher presentations are still so common. They provide a fairly efficient way of getting complex knowledge to a large group of diverse learners.

Another shortcoming is that some teachers simply do not have the experience or aptitude for this approach (Tamir 1995). Neither do all students—it may just not be your or their "style." In this case, perhaps teachers and students would like it more if they simply tried it more. Maybe it just needs getting used to.

8.15 How formidable do the limitations of discovery learning seem to you?

Finally, discovery learning allows students to make errors. Unless these errors are corrected, serious confusion can result. Consequently, the teacher must closely guide and monitor the results of discovery learning.

SUMMARY ON DISCOVERY LEARNING

Almost every day, you are faced with perplexing academic and nonacademic situations and, for the most part, you must cope with them on your own. Thus, any previous experience you have had with inductive thinking should be of help. If you

www.mhhe.com/cruickshank6e

CHAPTER 8
**Four More Instructional Alternatives:
Cooperative Learning, Discovery Learning,
Constructivism, and Direct Instruction**
277

have had teachers who mostly told you what to do and think, you are disadvantaged. Such teachers may have given you much knowledge but not taught you how to think and to figure out things for yourself.

Discovery learning holds promise in ensuring that your learners will be able to think for themselves. To use this alternative effectively, you need to believe in its purposes; you must have certain qualities such as curiosity, optimism, and confidence in students' abilities to think and inquire; and you must have patience. Finally, you need to know and follow the discovery learning regimen or procedure illustrated in Table 8.4.

Discovery learning appears well-suited to certain teachers and students. It may be well-suited to others who have had little experience or bad prior experiences with the method. As teachers, one of our toughest jobs is to remediate bad past experiences students have had. Spotlight on Research 8.2 describes the negatives and positives of discovery learning.

Constructivist Teaching and Learning: Problem Solving under Teacher Guidance

WHAT IS CONSTRUCTIVISM?

Constructivism is a way of teaching and learning that intends to maximize student understanding. Like discovery learning, it is situated within *meaningful learning* in the cognitive school of thought (see Chapter 4). Constructivism is defined variously as teaching that emphasizes the active role of the learner in building understanding and making sense of information (Woolfolk, 2009); learners' construction of knowledge as they attempt to make sense of their environment (McCown, 2001); and learning that occurs when learners actively engage in a situation that involves collaboratively formulating questions, explaining phenomenon, addressing complex issues, or resolving problems (Gagnon & Collay, 2001). This way of teaching is utilized mostly in teaching science, social studies, and math.

Constructivist ideas come from many persons including Dewey, Piaget, Montessori, and Vygotsky and from educational movements such as progressive education, inquiry-discovery learning, open education, and whole language teaching (Gagnon & Collay, 2001; Good & Brophy, 2007).

As you will see, it is one of the most challenging yet rewarding approaches to teaching.

PURPOSES AND CHARACTERISTICS OF CONSTRUCTIVISM

The purpose of constructivist teaching and learning is to help students to acquire information in ways that make that information readily understood and usable.

To make learning activities most understood and usable, constructivists have collected a number of ideas and brought them together to form a mosaic. The ideas, among others, include

- *Active learning* (when students are directly involved in finding something out for themselves) is preferable to *passive learning* (when students are recipients of information presented by a teacher).
- Learning takes place best in *communities of learners,* that is, group or social situations.
- Learners should engage in *"authentic and situated"* activities, that is, the tasks they face should be real problems versus hypothetical ones: concrete rather than abstract.
- Learners should relate new information to that which they already have (called **bridging**).

What does research on discovery learning tell us? The results are mixed. Hofwolt (1984) reports that compared to more traditional teacher- and textbook-centered techniques, inquiry teaching produces significant learner achievement in science. Slavin, Karweit, and Madden (1989) find more direct forms of instruction better for teaching concepts. (The last section of this chapter will introduce direct instruction.) Klahr and Nigam (2005) report discovery learning and direct instruction are equally good while Kirscher (2006) questions its use in general.

Nuthall and Snook (1973) conclude that "it is still necessary to find the experimental evidence which demonstrates convincingly that the discovery procedure is superior [to expository teaching or teacher presentations]" (p. 63). Merwin (1976) puts it all in perspective when he writes, "The research related to discovery learning is neither conclusive nor convincing enough to warrant its universal adoption. . . . However, one cannot ignore the successful learning outcomes as recorded in several [research studies]. For many students and teachers, discovery learning provides an exciting and rewarding [experience]; for others, it is fraught with frustration and failure" (p. 391).

Mayer (2004) reviewed decades of research comparing *guided* discovery learning with unguided kinds. In the former, the teacher sets questions to be explored and guides learning activities. In the latter, students are allowed to learn with less or no direction. Mayer found that guided discovery is superior.

- Learners should reflect or think about what is being learned.
- Rather than present information to learners, teachers facilitate its acquisition.
- Teachers must provide learners with *scaffolding* assistance needed for them to progress (see Chapter 4).
- Students are expected to resolve what they thought they knew with new information that may be contradictory.

Purposes and key characteristics are reviewed in Figure 8.3. Research on constructivism is discussed in Spotlight on Research 8.3.

Look at Lesson Plan 8.3 (on page 281). Can you identify the characteristics of constructivism in it?

GOOD CONSTRUCTIVIST TEACHING AND LEARNING

Among suggestions about how to use constructivism as an instructional alternative are those of Brooks and Brooks (2002) and Gagnon and Collay (2001). We draw from both in the following discussion.

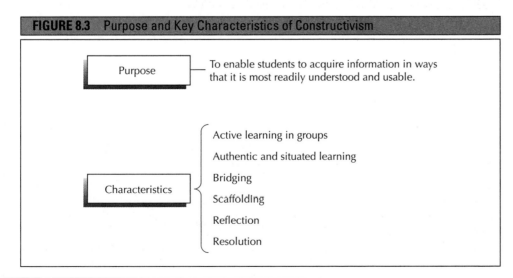

FIGURE 8.3 Purpose and Key Characteristics of Constructivism

Purpose — To enable students to acquire information in ways that it is most readily understood and usable.

Characteristics —
- Active learning in groups
- Authentic and situated learning
- Bridging
- Scaffolding
- Reflection
- Resolution

CHAPTER 8
Four More Instructional Alternatives:
Cooperative Learning, Discovery Learning,
Constructivism, and Direct Instruction

www.mhhe.com/cruickshank6e

279

Many teachers use *teacher-centered* instruction. They make predictable, controlled presentations or have students do so. Then they engage the class in rote learning and memorization. Recitation (Table 7.3) is often used to check student understanding. Learning is mostly passive and controlled. Other teachers prefer *learner-centered* teaching. They engage students in hands-on learning approaches such as constructivism, which promotes activity, authenticity, and reflection (Table 8.3). Being a learner-centered teacher is less predictable and thus more messy. In addition to being knowledgeable, teachers must be especially good at helping kids construct knowledge as opposed to feeding it to them.

But is the research case proven for learner-centered instruction, in this case constructivism? According to Brophy (2006a), teacher-centered, transmission techniques such as presentation and recitation are best used to communicate basic knowledge and procedures while constructivist techniques are best for developing higher-level thinking or skill. Notably, 25 percent of what kids retain after instruction is a function of interacting with other students. Nuthall's research led him to believe that constructivism should be used only in small-group settings and that it called for more teacher scaffolding or help and much less independent student activity than its proponents expect (Nuthall, cited in Brophy, 2006b). Apparently, although constructivism is good in many ways, it is not easy.

Try Activity 8.7

Preparation   Begin by identifying a relevant challenge for your learners—something that they should understand. Here we borrow from Gagnon & Collay's introduction and assume that the something to be understood is "the nature of fairy tales."

Rather than prepare a presentation on what constitutes fairy tales or have learners merely read about them, you decide that you want them to come to understand the concept as a result of examining personal experiences with them. With that goal in mind, you decide specifically what students should understand. You conclude learners should understand the core elements and characteristics of fairy tales (they contain one or more fairies or little people such as elves, goblins, leprechauns, poltergeists, or trolls; fairies mostly do good deeds, but often they play tricks).

Gagnon and Collay have established a nice framework for what they call a "constructivist learning design" or CLD. A CLD ensures that the key characteristics of constructivism are followed. Lesson Plan 8.3 is a modified version of their CLD for a lesson on fairy tales.

Try Activity 8.8

Delivery   Given the above CLD plan, its implementation in the lesson plan is fairly straightforward. You have provided for set induction by sharing your experiences with fairy tales and asking learners to share theirs. The most important teacher tasks during the lesson are to ensure that groups are functional (pursuing the hoped-for results or objectives and interacting humanely) and that learners are all on the same page and contributing.

Closure   It seems wise at the lesson's end to determine the extent to which learners have constructed improved, more thoughtful understandings. Using the fairy tale CLD in Lesson Plan 8.3, you might ask, how, if at all, students' understanding of fairy tales increased or changed?

GOOD FACILITATORS OF CONSTRUCTIVIST LEARNING

To be a constructivist teacher you must believe that your job is to ensure that learners acquire information in ways that make it readily understood and usable. Furthermore, you must believe that this can best be accomplished using constructivist principles including active learning, group learning, engaging learners in concrete rather than abstract tasks, helping them see the relationship between what they already know and new knowledge, helping them understand and make sense

LESSON PLAN 8.3
Constructivist Learning Design for a Lesson on Fairy Tales

Level: Middle school
Subject: Language arts
Title: Fairy tales
Designers: Ellen, Gail, and Sue

Describe the active learning *situation*— its purpose and how it will be accomplished:

- *Purpose of the lesson* is to have learners come to understand the concept and characteristics of fairy tales. *To accomplish this*, learners consider their personal experience with fairy tales, list their common characteristics, and define fairy tales. Then, learners compare what they think about fairy tales with information contained in resource material they are given.

Determine the *groups* and *group activities:*

- Learners form groups of three or four.
- Groups are provided with chart paper, marking pens, and tape for listing and posting the common characteristics of fairy tales and the group's definition of fairy tale.

Describe how new understanding will be connected or *bridged* to what learners already know:

- Briefly describe your experiences with fairy tales—perhaps with the *Tales of Mother Goose, Grimm's Fairy Tales*, or Barrie's *Peter Pan*.
- Have learners recollect their personal experiences with fairy tales in detail.

Provide questions to the groups:

- What experiences have you had with fairy tales?
- What are the common characteristics of fairy tales?
- How do you and your group define a fairy tale?
- How does your thinking about fairy tales compare with the material you just read?

Ensure that learners *exhibit* and share their understandings:

- Groups share their postings of common characteristics and definitions and try to reach agreement on the characteristics and definitions.

Reflection:

- Class was given print material about fairy tales and asked to compare what is written with their personally acquired understandings of fairy tales. Ask learners to describe how they felt and what they thought when their experiences and information differed from that of others— both peers and experts. How did they reconcile the differences? How has their knowledge been affected? What have they learned?

of new information (especially that which is discrepant), and considering the context, importance, and uses of newly acquired information (see Table 8.5).

WHEN CONSTRUCTIVISM SHOULD BE USED

Obviously, when you want to ensure that your students understand something well and can call upon it for later use, you need to use every possible approach. Many of the ideas about how learners come to understand best have been gathered by constructivists in the hope that you can and will use them. Most of us agree that our most memorable learning experiences were those in which we were immersed in a situation and learned from personal experience.

LIMITATIONS OF CONSTRUCTIVISM

Among the limitations to this approach to teaching are the following. It would be difficult for novices to learn how to do something if they do not have the needed prior knowledge. For example, if they were asked to construct a fairy tale (Lesson Plan 8.3) they would need to have experienced them—to know what they are. It also might be questionable to engage kids in a constructivist activity if they do not have the ability to work well with others, or the teacher has difficulty handling commotion. Moreover, teachers would need to be able to monitor and guide often free-flowing activity and to provide scaffolding or help momentarily.

SUMMARY ON CONSTRUCTIVISM

Understanding is the most important outcome of learning. Constructivists believe that to gain understanding requires students to engage in group experiences in

www.mhhe.com/cruickshank6e

CHAPTER 8
Four More Instructional Alternatives:
Cooperative Learning, Discovery Learning,
Constructivism, and Direct Instruction
281

TABLE 8.5	Qualities of Good Facilitators of Constructivism and Good Constructivist Learning	

Good Facilitators	Good Constructivist Learning
• Believe in the purpose of constructivism • Want learners to draw their own conclusions and form their own opinions • Have high respect for constructivist principles including active learning, concrete learning, group learning, and reflection • Are willing to help all students understand by intervening and providing support or scaffolding as needed	*When preparing:* • Determine the purpose of the lesson • Describe how the purpose will be attained • Decide how grouping will be used • Decide how to link new learning to old • Collect useful resource materials • Decide how reflection will occur *When delivering:* • Ensure groups are pursuing lesson goals and interacting humanely with others • Ensure learners are together and contributing *When closing:* • Determine what learners now understand and the extent to which the understanding is new or different in some way

which they learn through active involvement, by doing. In the process of learning by doing, the community of learners builds or creates new knowledge for themselves, connects that new knowledge to knowledge they already possess, and considers any discrepancies between the two. Learners also think about the new information they have come to understand and how it may be applied. Constructivists believe that the role of the teacher is to facilitate active involvement and to support groups and individuals to increase their likelihood for success.

Gagnon and Colloy maintain a website at the Prairie Rainbow Company where additional information about constructivism is available. The website provides a link to an online tutorial on constructivism: teacher comments, classroom videos, and ideas for constructivist lessons and lesson plans.

 Web Links
Prairie Rainbow Company
Concept to Classroom
Constructivism

Direct Instruction: Teaching in the Most Efficient and Effective Way

WHAT IS DIRECT INSTRUCTION?

Direct Instruction (DI) is a variation on the theme of teacher presentations in that it is teacher-dominated and directed. However, a striking difference is that the principles of DI derive exclusively from research on teaching and/or learning. In the first instance, "effective teachers," described as those who help students get higher test scores, are observed. The findings about these teachers and what they do are detailed in Chapters 11 and 12. In the second instance, what we know about human learning has been mined. The resultant "gold" is described in Chapter 4. Although DI probably is the instructional alternative with the most empirical support, it is disdained by many who feel that it has serious shortcomings and limitations, which are discussed later.

PURPOSE AND CHARACTERISTICS OF DIRECT INSTRUCTION

8.16 How important are the purpose and characteristics of direct instruction?

The purpose of direct instruction is to help students learn basic academic content such as reading, mathematics, and so forth, in the most efficient, straightforward way. The key characteristics of this way of teaching are teacher centrality or domination, task orientation, positive expectations, student cooperation and accountability, nonnegative affect, and established structure.

Teacher centrality means that teachers exert strong direction and control over what is to be learned and how. They are visibly in charge. **Task orientation** means that the primary task is academic learning of basics such as reading and math. **Positive expectations** indicates that teachers expect each child to be successful, and are deeply concerned about the progress of each child. **Student cooperation and accountability** means that students are held accountable for their academic work and, furthermore, they are expected to assist one another and to share materials. **Nonnegative affect** means teachers ensure learners feel psychologically safe and secure—that is, not threatened. Finally, **established structure** refers to the fact that teachers establish class rules and insist they are followed.

The purpose and key characteristics of direct instruction are illustrated in Figure 8.4.

EXAMPLES OF DIRECT INSTRUCTION PROGRAMS

Following are five examples of DI programs. The first three are based upon studies of what teachers—who are able to bring about significant student learning—do in their classrooms. The last two examples are based upon putting into practice what is known about learning.

Basic Practice Model   This kind of DI follows four steps: lesson introduction, lesson development, guided or structured practice of what is to be learned, and independent practice.

In the introductory, or orientation, phase, the teacher establishes the content area to be studied, the instructional objectives, and the procedures to be followed. Additionally, the teacher communicates expectations to the students.

During the development phase, teachers present the information to be learned (concept, fact, generalization, skill, and so on). Teachers increase clarity of presentation by demonstrating and by using examples. They also reinforce newly learned procedures and rules, and check students' understanding regularly to ensure progress.

Next, learners begin structured, controlled practice. Students try out or rehearse the information or skill the teacher has presented under the teacher's supervision. The teacher reinforces correct practice immediately and addresses incorrect practice, misunderstandings, and misconceptions as they occur.

After teachers are satisfied that learners know or can do what is expected of them, the learners are set free to practice independently. However, even then, teachers

---

FIGURE 8.4   Purpose and Key Characteristics of Research-Based Direct Instruction

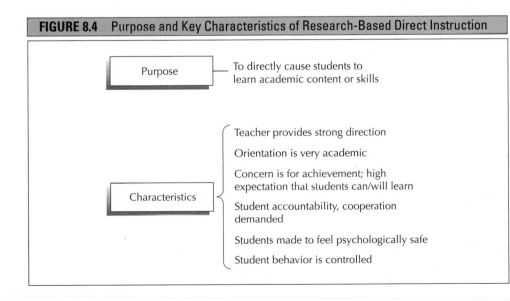

Purpose — To directly cause students to learn academic content or skills

Characteristics
- Teacher provides strong direction
- Orientation is very academic
- Concern is for achievement; high expectation that students can/will learn
- Student accountability, cooperation demanded
- Students made to feel psychologically safe
- Student behavior is controlled

www.mhhe.com/cruickshank6e

CHAPTER 8
Four More Instructional Alternatives:
Cooperative Learning, Discovery Learning,
Constructivism, and Direct Instruction
283

"Ms. Perkins certainly has a way with children."

move about the classroom, constantly monitoring and checking the work (Joyce et al., 2008; Murphy, Weil & McGreal, 1986).

Explicit teaching   Explicit teaching has six phases of instructional activity: review and check homework, present new content/skills, guide student practice, provide feedback and correctives, move to independent practice, and conduct weekly and monthly reviews.

First, teachers review the previous day's work and homework, if assigned, and reteach when needed. This review of prior learning ensures that students are ready for the presentation of new information or skills. Such reviews often take the form of teacher questioning and recitation.

In the presentation stage, teachers inform their learners of the lesson's objectives—that is, what learners must come to know or be able to do. Teachers provide an overview of what will happen during the lesson, and how. Then the presentation proper begins with the teacher proceeding in small steps but at a rapid pace. A rapid pace is also referred to as gathering and maintaining lesson momentum. The teacher provides many detailed examples and illustrations, highlights or reinforces major points to notice and remember, and regularly raises questions to check for understanding. Most importantly, throughout the presentation, the teacher must be clear.

Following the presentation and a quick check for understanding, teacher-guided whole-class practice begins. Guided practice often takes the form of a public recitation, whereby the teacher asks a question, a student or students answer, and then the teacher asks another question (see Table 7.3). The teacher directs the questions to all students and provides them adequate time to think (see the discussion on wait time in Conducting Interpretive Instruction in Chapter 11). When students have difficulty, the teacher prompts or helps them think aloud. Guided practice continues until the class and individuals are responding correctly over 80 percent of the time.

Providing feedback and correction are part of the presentation. Investigators who observe effective teachers report that they use specific praise in moderation ("That is a good answer because . . ."). Correction of misconceptions may require review, reteaching, or more practice.

Having determined that their learners seem to know or be able to do whatever is needed, teachers provide opportunity for independent practice. Their intention is to have students rehearse the information or skill to get it into long-term memory. Independent practice should continue until learners' responses are rapid, confident, and highly accurate. Teachers hold students accountable for independent work, and they monitor it whenever possible.

Finally, teachers periodically engage their learners in review so that the information or skill is further embedded in long-term memory (Joyce et al., 2008; Rosenshine, 1987; Rosenshine & Meister, 1995; Rosenshine & Stevens, 2001).

Highlight 8.3 provides an example of Explicit Teaching. Go to the Instructional Strategies website to learn more about explicit teaching.

 Web Link
Instructional Strategies Online

Active teaching   Active teaching results primarily from observations of effective mathematics teachers. It has five instructional phases: opening, development, independent work, homework, and continued review.

Opening refers to reviewing the concepts or skills recently taught, and collecting homework. During lesson development, effective teachers do a number of things. They ensure that students have the knowledge needed to understand the new information to be presented. They develop the new concepts and skills using numerous lively illustrations and explanations. They make skillful use of questioning, examples, and problems. And, importantly, they repeat and elaborate as necessary. Good and Grouws (1977) found that when fourth-grade teachers spend about half of the mathematics class time on lesson development and increase students' participation in the lesson, learning gains are dramatic.

The independent work stage is characterized by uninterrupted practice. Students are forewarned that their work will be examined. The difficulty level of assigned work is intended to produce 80 percent or higher accuracy. During independent practice, effective teachers are careful to keep everyone involved and on task.

Effective elementary school teachers give about fifteen minutes of homework each night, Monday through Thursday. The assignment allows students to practice newly acquired information and review the old. Finally, effective math teachers use continued review. They have students recall and use earlier learning by holding in-class weekly and monthly reviews (Good & Brophy, 2007; Good, Grouws, & Ebmeier, 1983; Joyce et al., 2008).

CHAPTER 8
Four More Instructional Alternatives:
Cooperative Learning, Discovery Learning,
Constructivism, and Direct Instruction

www.mhhe.com/cruickshank6e

285

HIGHLIGHT 8.3

Explicit Teaching: An Example of Direct Instruction

Explicit teaching requires that you provide very specific directions and guidance. In the following example, questions are asked to guide learners through the thinking process as the teacher models how to construct a main-idea statement from a given paragraph. If students falter, they are given hints (scaffolding).

Lesson objective: Learners will build a main-idea sentence for a paragraph. The sentence will contain:

- The name of the main character
- The main thing that character did
- When and where the character did that main thing

Target paragraph: "In August, Clara went to the department store. She looked at clothing. She looked at sporting equipment. Then she recalled that she needed to fix her bike. So, she found a bike-repair kit and paid for it. Then she left the store."

Direction to students: *Read the objective and paragraph to yourselves. Then we'll work together to build a complete main-idea sentence.*

Teaching script: After all students have finished reading:

Who is the main character in the paragraph? (Response: Clara.) *So I will write "Clara" as the first part of the main-idea sentence.* (Write Clara on the chalkboard, leaving space to the left and right.)

Now tell me the main thing that Clara did. Don't tell where or when. Just tell what she did. (Idea: Bought a bike-repair kit.)

So for the next part of the main-idea sentence, I will write "bought a bike repair kit." (After the word Clara on the chalkboard, write bought a bike repair kit.)

That's a good main-idea sentence, but we can add more information. When did Clara buy the kit? (Idea: In August.)

I will write that information at the beginning of the sentence, followed by a comma. (Write In August, at the beginning of the sentence.)

Where did Clara buy the kit? (Idea: In the department store.)

I will write that information at the end of the sentence, followed by a period. (At the end of the sentence, write in the department store.)

Now I'll read the complete main-idea sentence: In August, Clara bought a bike-repair kit in the department store. That sentence tells the main thing the main character did. It also tells when and where she did it. It is the main idea sentence.

Source: Science Research Associates online.

As you can see in Table 8.6, these three types or variations of the direct instruction approach—Basic Practice, Explicit Teaching, and Active Teaching—are quite similar. This is understandable since the persons creating them were influenced by the same studies of effective teaching.

The Mastery Teaching Program   This variation of DI should not be confused with *Mastery Learning* presented in Chapter 4, has three major phases: *input,* where the teacher provides children with knowledge or skill through lecture or another means of presentation; *modeling,* where the teacher shows an example of what is expected as the end product of their work; and *checking for understanding,* where the teacher determines if the children "got it."

A Mastery Teaching lesson plan contains these seven parts:

1. Objectives, i.e., what students should know and be able to do
2. Standards, or level of performance, expected of learners
3. Anticipatory set, or the "hook" that will be used to grab learner attention
4. Teaching ("input," or what the teacher will do to facilitate learning; "modeling" of what will be the acceptable student end product, and "checking for understanding")
5. Guided practice and monitoring to find out if learning is taking place at the mastery-standards level

TABLE 8.6 Three Variations of Research-Based Direct Instruction

Basic Practice	Explicit Teaching	Active Teaching
• Introduce lesson	• Review previous work, check homework	• Review
• Develop lesson	• Introduce lesson	• Review, check homework
• Supervise practice	• Develop lesson	• Develop lesson
• Provide feedback, correction	• Check on understanding	• Check on understanding
• Provide independent practice	• Supervise practice	• Provide independent work in class
	• Provide feedback, correction	• Review
	• Provide independent practice	

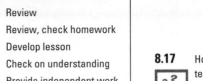

8.17 How do you feel about teaching in any of these three ways? Which do you prefer?

6. Closure to help students realize what they have mastered and how it may be applied

7. Independent practice or repetition of what has been learned to overcome forgetting (Hunter 1995, 2004).

A description of a Mastery Teaching lesson is available at the Wikibooks website.

The Direct Instructional System for Teaching and Learning (DISTAR) DISTAR is a powerful, yet controversial form of direct instruction that has gained most success with younger, lower socioeconomic children (Becker & Engelmann, 1989). See Spotlight on Research 8.4. It is controversial because teachers using it must follow predetermined, carefully scripted lesson plans. Consequently, and unfortunately, the lessons are referred to as "teacher proof," meaning that teachers cannot screw them up. The lessons draw heavily from the behavioral school of thought about learning, utilizing repetition and reinforcement (see Chapter 4). To learn more about commercially available DISTAR programs in several subjects go to the Online Learning Center: SRA. (See also Case 8.4.)

GOOD DIRECT INSTRUCTORS

As mentioned above, good direct instructors are effective teachers—they do what is necessary to maximize student academic learning. So, what are effective teachers like and what do they do? They are enthusiastic, warm and accepting, humorous, and credible (students trust them). They hold high expectations that students can learn, and are supportive, encouraging, businesslike, adaptable, flexible, and knowledgeable.

Briefly, this is what effective teachers do. They make sure they have students' attention, use instructional variety, use time well, maintain momentum when teaching, keep students interacting by utilizing good questioning technique, ensure orderly transition from one activity to another, are understandable, and make sure students are on-task and succeeding.

Good direct instructors make use of most of these qualities. Most notably, however, they *do not* employ much instructional variety. Everything is pretty much "by the book."

8.18 Which qualities of good direct instructors do you have? Which qualities would you like to gain or improve on?

GOOD DIRECT INSTRUCTION

Here are procedures that good direct instructors follow.

Preparation Proponents of direct instruction give little specific attention to lesson planning or preparation. This probably is because the study of effective teachers

www.mhhe.com/cruickshank6e

CHAPTER 8
Four More Instructional Alternatives:
Cooperative Learning, Discovery Learning,
Constructivism, and Direct Instruction
287

SPOTLIGHT ON RESEARCH 8.4
Findings on Research-Based Direct Instruction

Do students taught via direct instruction learn more? Since the variations are all based upon research on teaching—the effective teaching model—we would expect that teachers following Basic Practice, Explicit Teaching, and Active Teaching would be successful in bringing about students' academic achievement. Research seems to mostly support that expectation.

Orlich (2009) reports that research-based direct instruction "has been readily adapted for teaching the basics and for special education" (pp. 164–165). Relatedly, they note that it has been demonstrated to be effective. For example, they refer to Peterson (1979a, 1979b)

who reviewed a great number of studies that compare the use of traditional, direct teaching with more open, indirect, student-centered instruction. Peterson found students receiving direct instruction tended to perform better on achievement tests and slightly worse on tests of higher-order, abstract thinking involving creativity and problem solving.

Rosenshine (1987) reports similarly that on the basis of classroom studies, students taught with structured curricula using teacher-centered instruction generally do better than those taught by way of discovery learning, individualized instruction, or independent study approaches.

The Comprehensive School Reform Quality (CSRQ) Center (2006) reviewed the effectiveness of 22 widely used educational practices, including direct instruction. It reports that only two practices have moderately strong likelihood of increasing student academic achievement, direct instruction being one.

In the largest experiment to test K–12 math programs, the winners were *Math Expressions* and *Saxon Math*. Saxon is based on the explicit teaching approach while Math Expressions uses a combination of direct instruction with some emphasis on student thinking and reasoning (Viadero, 2009).

CASE 8.4
DISTAR in Action

A second-year Baltimore teacher, Matthew Carpenter, was observed and interviewed to see what the DISTAR program he used was like and how he felt about it.

Following one of the observations, the observer notes, "Mr. Carpenter's sixth graders . . . were working on their *reasoning* and *writing skills*. Their task: Take two sentences and make a new sentence from them that begins with the word 'No' and use the word 'only'. Mr. Carpenter then reads the two sentences. 'The wolves howled and ate at night' and 'The wolves did not eat.'

While his students are bent over their paper writing answers, he checks their work. (DISTAR theorists believe it's important to catch errors quickly before they are imprinted in learners' brains.)

Soon, Mr. Carpenter says, "The answer is . . . ?" Students shout in unison. "No, the wolves only howled at night."

Similar unison chanting of answers is audible from classrooms up and down the hall.

During an interview, Mr. Carpenter notes, "I like the structure (DISTAR provides). I think it's good for this group

of kids." (Ninety-six percent of Arundel School's students are considered poor in that they come from families qualifying for free school lunches.)

Source: Viadero (1999).

INVESTIGATING AND
SOLVING THE CASE

1. What principles of DISTAR are most obvious?

2. How would you teach sentence combining?

---

focuses on observing what they do in their classrooms when delivering instruction. However, it is probably true that effective teachers follow the preparation regimen that good presenters use—they establish the general purpose of the lesson, set specific learning objectives, collect and review subject matter and useful related materials, and plan the presentation.

Delivery Direct instruction usually seems to begin with a review of homework or some independent assignment. The review helps to determine the level of learners' understanding and accuracy. When either is low, reteaching is appropriate.

Following homework review and collection, the effective teacher ensures that learners are ready for the new material. That readiness may result from the homework review. If not, it is necessary to go over earlier related information or skills. When readiness is evident, the specific objectives of the lesson are communicated in terms of what the students are to know and to be able to do. The students are oriented to the lesson and its parts and to the way it will be conducted.

Now that the students are ready and aware of what is to be accomplished and how, the presentation is given. Instructional clarity is critical. The notion of clarity is fully developed in Chapter 11, and the behaviors characterizing clear teachers appear in Figure 11.6. These behaviors include a step-by-step presentation, use of examples and illustrations, cuing learners to important elements to notice and remember, and using numerous questions directed to all students in order to encourage participation and check understanding.

After the learners have achieved a good level of understanding, guided whole-class practice of the information or skill begins. The teacher provides exercises, and students respond to them aloud so that everyone is on the same page, so to speak, and the teacher is able to hear what students are thinking. The teacher acknowledges correct responses and reminds students specifically why their responses are right. Should misunderstandings and errors occur, the teacher reteaches, often using a different approach.

As soon as the teacher feels that learners are able to work on their own with a high level of accuracy, independent practice starts. At the outset, learners are informed that their work will be examined and that a high level of accuracy—for example, above 80 percent—is expected. After the work is assigned, the teacher monitors to help students stay on task and reduce errors. Practice continues until responses are both rapid and accurate, and learners are confident.

Closure In the closure stage, a direct instruction lesson fulfills two requirements. The first is the assignment of related homework. Assignments should be short, but regular. The second is that the teacher reminds students of the importance of the lesson's objectives and the need to be able to recall and use the newly acquired information or skill. The teacher plans dates and times for weekly and monthly reviews.

The principles and procedures of direct instruction fit closest to the behavioral school of thought (Chapter 4), which emphasizes reinforcement. At the same time, there are connections to the cognitive school, which affirms the need to review previously learned information and skills; limit the amount of new, difficult information presented; proceed in small steps; rehearse, elaborate, and summarize in student words and language; and over-learn.

The qualities of good direct instructors and direct instruction appear in Table 8.7. A sample lesson plan appears as **Lesson Plan 8.4** (on page 291).

WHEN DIRECT INSTRUCTION SHOULD BE USED

When the question of when direct instruction should be used is raised, the conclusion is that it is superior when the hoped-for result is to improve achievement in basic skills as measured by tests. It seems most valuable when teaching knowledge and explicit concepts and procedures—for example, teaching factual historical information (such as the chronology of the colonization of Africa), teaching grammatical concepts (what a sentence is), and teaching mathematical processes or procedures (how to solve an algebraic equation). In other words, use direct instruction when the content to be learned is well structured, clear, and unambiguous. It is also

TABLE 8.7 Qualities of Good Leaders of Research-Based Direct Instruction and of Good Direct Instruction

Good Leaders of Research-Based Direct Instruction Are . . .	Good Research-Based Direct Instruction
• Enthusiastic	*When preparing:*
• Warm, accepting	• Research on effective teaching hardly addresses what teachers do to prepare. We might assume they do the same things they would do when preparing a good presentation. (See Table 6.2.)
• Humorous	
• Supportive	
• Encouraging	*When delivering:*
• Businesslike	• Collect, review homework
• Adaptable-flexible	• Review earlier, related information
• Knowledgeable	• Communicate to learners what they are to know and be able to do
• Holders of high expectations for student success	• Present an overview or orientation of how the lesson will be conducted
• See also Table 6.2, Qualities of Good Presenters and Good Presentations	• Present information/skill to be learned
	• Proceed in small steps
	• Maintain a quick pace
	• Use many illustrations, examples
	• Encourage involvement of all students
	• Ask many questions to check for understanding
	• Repeat and elaborate on major points to notice, remember
	• Provide teacher-guided whole-class practice
	• Provide feedback and reteach to eliminate misunderstandings
	• Ensure that students can practice with at least 80 percent accuracy
	• Provide independent practice
	• Let students know the work will be examined
	• Monitor the work to keep students involved and to eliminate errors
	• Continue practice until learners are confident and their responses are both rapid and accurate
	When closing:
	• Assign short, regular, related homework
	• Establish when this information or skill will next be reviewed

felt that direct instruction is more suitable when the target material is arranged in a hierarchical or sequential manner. Finally, it is seen to be most useful during the first stages of learning unfamiliar material (Peterson, 1979a and others; Rosenshine, 2001; Berliner, 1982).

Peterson (1979a, 1982) addresses the related question, With whom should direct instruction be used? In response, she notes that this approach has been shown to be very effective for teaching younger, less academically ready learners. She also suggests that it may be the instructional alternative of choice when teaching children who need direction. Frequently, direct instruction is the method of choice when teaching low socioeconomic children.

LESSON PLAN 8.4

Abbreviated Direct Instruction Lesson: Roman Numerals

Curriculum tie-in: This lesson can be linked to the study of Roman civilization or the study of numerical systems.

OBJECTIVES

1. Learners will recognize the Roman numeral V and the rules used to create 4 and 6 from it.
   Specific objective: Learners will recognize that V = 5 and that placing I before V decreases its value by one while placing I after V increases its value by 1.

2. *Specific objective:* Learners will know and be able to use the Roman numerals for 1–6.

RESOURCES

1. Homework assignment: to locate objects containing Roman numerals that are on an assignment sheet (I, V, X, L, C, D, M).

METHODOLOGY

1. *Set induction.* "We will continue to think about the number system developed by the Romans. Yesterday I gave you an assignment sheet containing seven Roman numerals and asked you to find objects displaying some or all of them. What examples did you find?"

2. Inform learners of what they will learn and be able to do as a result of the lesson. "Today we will learn the Roman symbol for 5 and how the Romans used it to create the numbers 4 and 6. At the end of the lesson you will know the Roman numerals representing our numerals 1–6."

3. Begin the presentation proceeding in small steps, utilizing a quick pace, using as many examples as possible, involving all learners, checking for understanding, providing practice, and reteaching as necessary. An example follows.

4. "V represents our Arabic numeral 5. What does V stand for?
   Placing the Roman I (1) *after* V represents V + I. V + I then equals 6.
   What does VI represent?
   On your paper write the Roman numerals for 1, 5, 6.
   Placing the Roman I *before* V represents V – I. What does IV represent? Write that numeral on your paper.
   Now you know the Roman numerals for 1, 4, 5, and 6. What numerals don't you know from 1 through 6? Romans simply used two Is for II and three Is for 3. Write the Roman numerals for 1–6 on your paper.
   You have learned two rules Romans used when creating numerals: When a second numeral is placed after another it *increases* its value by that amount: when a second numeral is placed before another it *decreases* its value by that amount.
   (Student) go to the board and write the Roman numerals I–VI one under the other. (Student) go to the board and write the Arabic equivalents beside each Roman numeral.
   Which of the following are incorrect? IIII = 4, VI = 3, IV = 6?
   Go to the board and correct each."

ASSIGNMENT

1. Complete this test with 100 percent accuracy.
   1 written in Roman is _____
   5 written in Roman is _____
   IV written in Arabic is _____
   6 written in Roman is _____

2. Reteach as necessary.

CLOSURE

Review:
What is V?
How is V used to make 6?
How is V used to make 4?
What is the rule?
How are the following made: 2, 3, 7, 8?

LIMITATIONS OF DIRECT INSTRUCTION

Of course, direct instruction has its critics. Criticism includes that it restricts student autonomy. Even advocates acknowledge that the tight structure of lessons may stifle children and even teachers. The Direct Instructional System for Teaching and Learning (DISTAR) causes teachers to follow a script: teachers are told exactly what to say and do. Critics also warn that direct instruction does not promote achievement in creativity, abstract thinking, and problem solving or higher-level cognitive skills. Some feel it is not equal to other instructional alternatives when the goal is to improve cooperation, attitudes toward school, and, relatedly, school attendance. Finally, one study finds that by age 15, 46 percent of students receiving direct instruction were identified as having emotional problems (Gersten & Keating, 1987; Peterson, 1979b; Slavin, 1991; Stallings & Kaskowitz, 1975; Viadero, 1999). Spotlight on Research 8.4 reviews the findings on research-based direct instruction. Spotlight on Research 8.5 reviews similarly for learning theory-based direct instruction.

CHAPTER 8
Four More Instructional Alternatives:
Cooperative Learning, Discovery Learning,
Constructivism, and Direct Instruction

www.mhhe.com/cruickshank6e

291

Do students of teachers who use learning theory-based direct instruction learn more? We would presume so, but let's look at the research.

Research on the Mastery Teaching Program has not generally shown "that the students of teachers especially trained in this strategy have learned more than other students" (Slavin, 2008). Slavin suggests this may be because at some time all teachers have been exposed to and use learning theory and associated instructional maneuvers. Therefore, when it comes to learning theory, all teachers teach about the same way, anyway. However, Hunter, the developer of the Mastery Teaching Program,

feels that the reason her program has had limited success is that it has not been properly used.

What does research on DISTAR reveal? Much to the alarm of its critics, DISTAR has mostly been very effective in its purpose. Stallings and Stipek (1986) tell us that when low SES students spend four years (kindergarten through grade 3) in the Direct Instruction Follow-Through Model, they achieve close to national norms on achievement tests, performing much better than similar students who received other kinds of instruction. Meyer (1984) reports that students from an inner-city Brooklyn, New York, school that used DISTAR in

grades 1 through 3 were more likely to complete secondary school. Gersten and Keating (1987) also found positive long-term effects such as lowered dropout rates and increased proportions of students applying for college. Izumi's (2002) study of eight low-income California schools using direct instruction reveals that they did very well on the Academic Performance Test, scoring at least seven on the 10-point scale. Stallings and Stipek conclude, "One implication for elementary [teachers] is that a structured, carefully sequenced program for low-achieving children in the lower grades helps them to succeed academically" (p. 741).

8.19 What, to you, are the strengths and weaknesses of direct instruction?

A final caveat. One of the two forms of DI derives from the observation of teachers teaching reading and math to younger kids. These content areas are more structured—that is, they follow a more sequential, step-by-step learning process than other content areas such as social studies, art, and science. Direct instruction may not be the instructional alternative of choice for use in those content areas. Moreover, younger children may be more willing to be regimented.

SUMMARY ON DIRECT INSTRUCTION

Direct instruction is a label given to two related efforts to improve the academic learning of K–12 students. The first kind derives from observing *effective teachers* to see what they do to bring about consistently higher levels of student learning. There are three variations on this kind of direct instruction: Basic Practice, Explicit Teaching, and Active Teaching. Advocates who developed these variations believe that you should be educated and trained in direct instruction according to their particular model. Doing so, they say, should increase your ability to bring about student learning.

The second kind of direct instruction derives from learning theory—what we know and believe about how people learn. There are two popular variations: the Mastery Teaching Program and the Direct Instructional System for Teaching and Learning (DISTAR). Scholars who developed these forms believe that you should be educated and trained according to their model. Furthermore, they believe that after education and training, you will know how to use what is known about learning and, consequently, your students will benefit academically. The two kinds of direct instruction and program exemplars are illustrated in Figure 8.5.

Both kinds of direct instruction have the same purpose, which is to help students learn basic academic content. They also share common characteristics, including strong teacher direction, an academic orientation, high expectations for student achievement, student accountability and cooperation, a psychologically safe classroom atmosphere, and strict classroom rules and regulations.

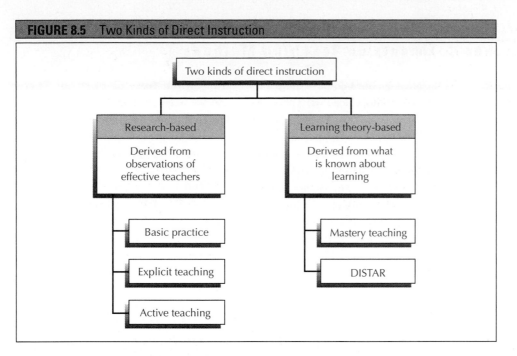

FIGURE 8.5 Two Kinds of Direct Instruction

Two kinds of direct instruction

Research-based — Derived from observations of effective teachers
- Basic practice
- Explicit teaching
- Active teaching

Learning theory-based — Derived from what is known about learning
- Mastery teaching
- DISTAR

Within the first kind of direct instruction, good instructors must have the qualities of *effective teachers,* which are elaborated in Chapter 10. These include enthusiasm, warmth, and humor. They must also be supportive and encouraging, businesslike, adaptable, and knowledgeable in their teaching area. Within the second kind of direct instruction, the requisite teacher qualities are not as clear.

Both kinds of DI require teachers to follow regimens mostly characterized by three words—practice, practice, practice. Effective teachers use many and varied kinds of practice, which is one of the major elements of learning.

For the most part, research findings support direct instruction, especially for low SES students in highly structured subjects such as reading and mathematics. (DISTAR has been extended for use in many subjects.)

8.20 What factors mentioned in Chapter 1 may affect your use of direct instruction?

Is There a Single Best Instructional Alternative?

In Chapters 7 and 8 you have learned about eight instructional alternatives: presentation, discussion, independent study, individualized instruction, cooperative learning, discovery learning, constructivism, and direct instruction. However, which is better?

According to experts, it all depends upon your purpose (Brophy, 2006a, 2006b; Cuban, 2009). "Sometimes a lecture is needed to propel students to the next level of understanding. The trick is 'sometimes'" (National Academy of Sciences, 1999). Experiential or hands-on learning is appropriate at other times. Experiential learning can be as ineffective as a dull presentation if it doesn't have a clearly defined purpose. "It's knowing when to use which [instructional alternative] based on the principles of learning" (Bransford, in Hoff, 1999).

Try Activity 8.10

Reviews of research report similar results "[That] instruction should be entirely 'student centered' or 'teacher directed' is not supported" (NMAP, 2008, p. xxii). Therefore, as a teacher you must be able to choose and use the most appropriate instructional alternative from the Wheel of Instructional Choice (Figure 7.5).

Does this conclusion sound similar to the one reached in the section at the end of Chapter 4 on learning, Is there a single best approach to student learning?

A student teacher quips about teaching method in **Case 8.5.**

www.mhhe.com/cruickshank6e

CHAPTER 8
Four More Instructional Alternatives:
Cooperative Learning, Discovery Learning,
Constructivism, and Direct Instruction
293

I hate the whole reasoning behind this smugness about "not lecturing" and "being creative" and "letting the students learn for themselves." It's like these people are saying, "All of our teachers thought they were *so great*, but *they* didn't have all the answers. They tried to imprison us in their mental universe, but we wouldn't let them, cuz we're rebels! And now we're stickin' it to the man by saying that we don't know any more than the kids do because we *all* have good thoughts!"

I don't ever think I would say to a class, "I know everything, I have all the answers." [Actually, on a bad/cocky day, I might.] But I *would* say, "I don't have all the answers, but I do have quite a few more than you do, since I went to college for four years, and then graduate school, to learn all of this stuff, whereas you are 13 and don't know Greece from your ass. Fortunately, I feel generous enough to want to share some knowledge with you here today, and every day for the rest of the year." This is what makes traditional teaching generous, and new teaching stingy. In new teaching, we say we don't know the answers, even though we do, thereby keeping the answers for ourselves while trying to make the students "figure out" or "find" or "discover" things that would be more efficiently and effectively transmitted from us to them. That's why we have teachers in the first place. Granted, many teachers *don't* know the answers to things, including "Why are you such a bad teacher?"

Source: *Oh, snap!* Blog online (2005).

INVESTIGATING AND
SOLVING THE CASE

1. What are your thoughts about teacher- versus-student-centered teaching?

Some Final Thoughts

Think of a teacher who helped you learn and enjoy learning. We assume that the teacher you target has a number of admirable personal and professional qualities and, further, that one of those qualities is the ability to use a wide range of instructional alternatives.

So that you may someday be thought of as an exceptional teacher, too, you have learned about eight teaching strategies, namely: presentation, discussion, independent study, individualized instruction, cooperative learning, discovery learning, constructivism, direct instruction. If you have had the opportunity to reflect on these practices and especially to try the end-of-chapter activities related to each method, then you have reached some degree of competence with them. Of course, practice makes perfect, and knowledge does not always equate with skill. To truly be skillful with any instructional alternative, you must work with it over time. In the months and years ahead, we hope you will find these two chapters particularly useful desk references as you strive to be the best teacher you can be.

8.21 How would you rank the eight instructional alternatives presented in Chapters 7 and 8? What accounts for your attraction to your top two choices? How does your ranking compare with your classmates'?

CHAPTER SUMMARY

- Cooperative learning describes instructional procedures that place learners in small work teams that are rewarded for what they collectively accomplish. The purpose of cooperative learning is to engender in students a collective caring, an "all for one, one for all" philosophy. Principal characteristics include small, heterogeneous teams and tasks that revolve around either mastering some knowledge or skill or participating in a group academic project. Cooperative learning draws on the cognitive, behavioral, and humanistic schools of thought, and its variations include STAD, TGT, TAI, Jigsaw, and CIRC.

- Good leaders of cooperative learning believe in its purpose; they are able to get students to work together, are competent presenters, effective organizers, and good work coordinators; and they are able to identify and help students and teams having difficulty.

- Good cooperative learning includes preparation, delivery, and closure. In STAD, preparation requires planning a good presentation, preparing the teams' assignments, and getting students ready to engage in teamwork. Delivery requires making a good presentation, setting team goals, preparing for teamwork, giving teams their assignment, quizzing students, and recognizing team accomplishments. Closure requires that students be reminded of what they have learned, that they relate new learning to earlier learning, and that students have the opportunity to use new learning.

- Cooperative learning has certain limitations. It requires higher-achieving students to assist low achievers and presumes high achievers are willing to do so. Additionally, since cooperative learning is a group activity, substantial teacher monitoring is necessary to keep teams on task.

- Discovery learning takes place when students are presented with experiences and are asked to derive their own meaning and understanding from them. Its purposes are (1) to provide students with the opportunity to think for themselves in order to figure something out, (2) to help students discover how knowledge is gained, and (3) to promote higher-order thinking skills such as analysis, synthesis, and evaluation.

- In discovery learning, the teacher is a catalyst who causes students to discover knowledge rather than spoon-feeding it to them. Teachers ask many, mostly higher-order questions: "Why?" "How come?" "What would happen?" and so forth. Good discovery-learning teachers believe in its purposes, tend to enjoy inquiry, are optimistic that students are inquiry oriented and capable of learning in this fashion, and hold high expectations of students; they are nurturing, thoughtful, patient, reflective, and accepting of students' ideas.

- Good discovery learning includes attention to preparation, delivery, and closure. Preparation includes determining the general purpose and specific objectives students are to accomplish, collecting useful materials, and planning lessons around inductive procedures. Delivery includes obtaining students' attention; presenting the baffling situation that requires investigation; promoting inquiry through use of observation, manipulation, analysis, and so forth; ensuring that learners know what to do; setting them free to inquire; monitoring; and, when necessary, guiding their inquiry and encouraging positive student interaction. Closure includes helping learners organize and define what they have found out and draw conclusions from it.

- Among the limitations of discovery learning are that not all things are amenable to classroom discovery, some discovery is too complex for K–12 student minds, and time constraints often limit the ability to explore.

- Research results on discovery learning are mixed and inconclusive. It seems a viable alternative that will enhance learning for some children while frustrating others.

- Constructivists want to maximize the likelihood that learners will understand and be able to use information. To do so, students must engage in active social or group learning (learning by doing and sharing); learning should be situated or occur in as realistic settings as possible; learners must

www.mhhe.com/cruickshank6e

CHAPTER 8
Four More Instructional Alternatives: Cooperative Learning, Discovery Learning, Constructivism, and Direct Instruction
295

bridge or relate new learning to what they already know or think they know; learners must interact with others and reflect on what they encounter; and teachers must provide scaffolding or help that enables students to learn successfully.

- A constructivist lesson has identifiable parts: purpose of the lesson (a challenge), establishing groups and group activities, bridging, question posing, exhibits, and reflection.

- Good leaders of constructivist lessons believe in teaching for understanding, engage students in active learning, want learners to draw their own conclusions and opinions, and are willing to provide all necessary assistance.

- Direct instruction is one of several terms used to describe the sequence of instructional events (1) that "effective" teachers have been observed to follow or (2) that teachers should follow if they want to utilize what is known about learning. Two major kinds of direct instruction are consistent with this definition. The first derives from observing effective teachers and includes three major subtypes: Basic Practice, Explicit Teaching, and Active Teaching. The second kind derives from analyzing and applying learning theory and has two major subtypes: the Mastery Teaching Program and DISTAR. The primary purpose of all these variations is to maximize learning of academic content or skills.

- Direct instruction teachers provide strong academic direction, have high expectations that students can and will learn, make students feel psychologically safe, urge them to cooperate, hold them accountable for their work, and closely monitor and control students' behavior. Good leaders of direct instruction are enthusiastic, warm and accepting, humorous, supportive, encouraging, businesslike, adaptable or flexible, and knowledgeable.

- Good direct instruction has three phases: preparation, delivery, and closure. The preparation that direct instruction teachers engage in is not clear. We can only assume it equates to preparing a good presentation. In DISTAR, preparation requires being well acquainted with the teacher's instructional manuals. Delivery requires some very major tasks including (for most variations) collection and review of previous work, reteaching when necessary, presentation of new material, teacher-guided practice and, finally, independent practice until 80 percent or higher proficiency is achieved.

- Generally, research on direct instruction is encouraging. All of its variations have been investigated; with the possible exception of the Mastery Teaching Program, they have proven to be more or less successful in increasing academic achievement in the basic skill areas such as reading and mathematics.

KEY TERMS

ISSUES

1. Some instructional alternatives foster competition, others cooperation. Which is preferable?

2. Some instructional alternatives depend upon whole-class instruction. Others depend upon the use of groups or independent work. Which is preferable?

3. Some instructional alternatives require teachers to teach directly. Others require a more indirect method: teachers draw things out of their students. Which is preferable?

4. Some instructional alternatives are more suitable to our personality and professional, job-related needs. Which alternatives are most attractive to you?

5. Some instructional alternatives meet different learners' needs. Which learner needs are the most important to you? To your classmates?

6. Given your responses to these questions, which instructional alternatives appeal most to you?

PROBLEMS.   Following are some problems related to topics covered in the chapter. What would you do in each circumstance?

Problem 1:   You try to initiate cooperative learning, but learners have been subjected mostly to competition for grades.

Problem 2:   You want to utilize discovery learning, but you find it difficult to get learners to think for themselves. They want you to tell them what they should know.

Problem 3:   Constructivism requires learners learn from personal experience. With so many tests students must pass and time so precious, you wonder when and how you can use this approach.

Problem 4:   Although you know that research supports use of direct instruction and you want to use it, you are troubled by what you feel are its restrictions on creative teaching.

THEORY INTO ACTION: ACTIVITIES FOR PRACTICE AND YOUR PORTFOLIO

ACTIVITY 8.1: Prepare a Cooperative Learning Lesson   Although a cooperative learning activity generally spans several class periods, one can be developed to fit a short period of time. Following the STAD procedure, plan a cooperative learning activity for use in class. Explain how you plan to present information, establish teams and charge them to master the material, give team members a quiz, determine scores, and provide recognition and reward.

Assessment: Did you follow the planning procedures for good presentations and good cooperative learning? (See Tables 7.2 and 8.2.)

ACTIVITY 8.2: Conduct a Cooperative Learning Activity   Deliver the lesson you prepared in Activity 8.1.

Assessment: To what extent did you actually follow the procedures for good presentations and good cooperative learning? (See Tables 7.2 and 8.2.) To what extent

www.mhhe.com/cruickshank6e

CHAPTER 8
Four More Instructional Alternatives:
Cooperative Learning, Discovery Learning,
Constructivism, and Direct Instruction
297

did you model the personal qualities of good facilitators of cooperative learning? (See Table 8.2.) How well do your peers feel you succeeded?

ACTIVITY 8.3: Observe Cooperative Learning It would be advantageous for you to see cooperative learning used in K–12 classrooms. Such observations would serve to confirm or deny what you have read and also help fix the concept in your long-term memory.

If you are assigned to a K–12 classroom, find out if and when your mentor teacher plans to use cooperative learning. If your mentor does not plan to do so, try to arrange a visit to a class where some sort of cooperative learning activities are in effect. If you cannot arrange to see this instructional alternative, perhaps your university instructor has a videotape on it. Videotapes are available from the Johns Hopkins Team Learning Project, Johns Hopkins University, 3505 N. Charles Street, Baltimore, MD 21218–7570, and from Teaching Inc., P.O. Box 788, Edmunds, WA 98020.

As you observe, record answers to these questions:

- Did the cooperative learning session have these identifying characteristics: heterogeneous groups, group cooperation, and group reward? How effective were these characteristics—did they work?
- What qualities of good cooperative learning were most obvious? (See Table 8.2 for ideas if STAD was the process used.)
- Did certain students seem to benefit more and others less? Why?
- What teacher and student needs seem to have been most fully met?

Additionally, talk with students about how they feel about cooperative learning and ask the teacher his or her perceptions of it.

ACTIVITY 8.4: Prepare a Discovery Lesson Using what you have learned about meaningful learning in general and about discovery learning in particular, prepare a discovery lesson that might be used with a group of your classmates. The lesson should be as brief as possible and should require your learners to discover some form of knowledge, either a concept, a fact, a generalization, a rule, or a law. (See Table 8.3 for ideas.)

Assessment: Did you follow the procedures for good discovery learning?

ACTIVITY 8.5: Deliver a Discovery Lesson Deliver your discovery lesson to a small group of your peers.

Assessment: Following the lesson, have your learners respond to these questions. To what extent did you:

- Challenge learners by presenting them with the need to find something out for themselves?
- Ensure that learners knew what they were to do?
- Provide them with useful resources if needed?
- Monitor and guide their activity and thinking?
- Encourage inductive processes: observation, organization, manipulation, and analysis?
- Encourage supportive peer interaction?
- Assist learners in phrasing their conclusions?
- Provide opportunities for learners to use their new knowledge?

ACTIVITY 8.6: Observe Discovery Learning Hopefully, you will be able to observe a discovery lesson. If you are assigned to a field experience, ask your mentor teacher if one is scheduled. Perhaps the teacher would conduct one just for you. Don't be afraid to ask. If a live discovery lesson is not available, perhaps your university instructor has captured one on videotape. In making your observation, whether real or recorded, answer the following questions:

- To what extent did the lesson possess the characteristics of discovery learning: the teacher acting as catalyst, students constructing their own knowledge, and the discovery revolving around mostly higher-order thought-provoking questions?
- What did the teacher do to prepare the lesson?
- What qualities of good discovery teaching were displayed by the teacher?
- What qualities of good discovery learning were most evident?
- In your opinion, what teacher and student needs did discovery learning seem to meet?
- Why do you believe that some students seemed to benefit more than others?

Interview students who seemed to benefit most and least. Ask them how they feel about discovery learning. Finally, ask the teachers how they like this instructional alternative and what they think are its advantages and disadvantages.

ACTIVITY 8.7: Prepare a Constructivist Lesson   Using what you have learned about meaningful learning in general and constructivism in particular, prepare a lesson that you can lead in this class. The lesson should be as brief as possible and require learners to maximize understanding of something using constructivist ideas. Ideas might include:

- A lesson in which learners think about and discuss the meanings or implications of good teaching.
- A lesson in which learners are asked to think about and discuss their understanding of constructivism or the relationship of constructivism and discovery learning.

Assessment: Did you follow the procedures for good constructivist teaching?

ACTIVITY 8.8: Deliver a Constructivist Lesson   Engage your peers in the constructivist lesson.
Assessment: Following the lesson have learners respond to these questions.
To what extent:

- Was the objective of the lesson to increase learner understanding?
- Was the lesson set or situated in reality or a close approximation of it?
- Were groups expected to think and share thinking?
- Were the learners expected to begin from what they already know or think they know?
- Were groups provided with questions that focus on improving understanding?
- Were learners expected and given opportunity to exhibit their understandings?
- Were learners expected to consider discrepancies between what they knew or thought they knew and changes in their perceptions and knowledge?

ACTIVITY 8.9: Observe Direct Instruction   A number of schools are attempting to put into practice what is known about effective schools, educational practices, and teaching. Many of those schools are the ones most likely to be implementing one or more of the direct instruction approaches you read about in this chapter.
If you are involved in a field experience, you may have the opportunity to observe one or more teachers using Basic Practice, Explicit Teaching, Active Teaching, the Mastery Teaching Program, or DISTAR. If not, perhaps your instructor has a videotape.

www.mhhe.com/cruickshank6e

CHAPTER 8
Four More Instructional Alternatives:
Cooperative Learning, Discovery Learning,
Constructivism, and Direct Instruction
299

As you observe, record answers to these questions:

- To what extent were the characteristics of direct instruction evident: the teacher providing strong academic direction, the teacher holding high expectations for student achievement, the students being held accountable for their work, the students expected to be cooperative, the students feeling psychologically safe, and the teacher controlling behavior?
- What qualities of a good leader of direct instruction were evident? (See Table 8.7.)
- To what extent was the teacher able to follow the regimen for good direct instruction? (See Table 8.7.)
- What teacher personality and professional needs did the instruction seem to meet?
- What student personality and educational needs did the instruction seem to meet?

Talk with the teacher about his or her feelings about direct instruction. Finally, ask a few diverse students whether they like to be taught this way.

ACTIVITY 8.10: Challenges

1. For each of the eight instructional alternatives presented in Chapters 7 and 8, describe in which school of thought about learning each seems to belong. Explain and justify your placement.
2. Describe something that can be best taught and learned using each one of the eight instructional alternatives.
3. Describe the kind of learner who might profit most from using each of the eight.
4. Describe the kind of teacher who might teach best using each of the eight.
5. Rank order the eight from most to least important to you and support the rankings.

REFERENCES

Anastasi, A., & Urbana, S. (1997). *Psychological testing*. Seventh Edition. Englewood Cliffs, NJ: Prentice Hall.

Augustine, D. K., Gruber, K. D., & Hansen, L. R. (1989/1990, December–January). Cooperation works. *Educational Leadership, 47*(4), 4–7.

Battistich, V., Solomon, D., & Delucci, K. (1993, September). Interaction processes and student outcomes in cooperative learning groups. *The Elementary School Journal, 94*(1), 19–32.

Becker, W., & Engelmann, S. (1989). *Analysis of achievement data on six cohorts of low income children from 20 school districts in the University of Oregon Direct Instruction Follow Through Model* (Technical Report #78-1). Eugene, OR: University of Oregon, Office of Education, Follow Through Project.

Benjamin, R. (1981). *Making schools work*. New York: Continuum.

Berliner, D. (1982). Issue: Should teachers be expected to learn and use direct instruction? *ASCD Update, 24*, 5.

Biemiller, A. (1993). Lake Wobegon revisited: On diversity and education. *Educational Researcher, 22*(9), 7–12.

Block, S. (2005, July). And the winner is . . . *American School Board Journal, 192*(7), 47.

Borman, G., Overman, L., & Brown, S. (2002). *Comprehensive school reform and student achievement*. Baltimore: Center for Research on the Education of Students Placed at Risk, John Hopkins University.

Brooks, J., & Brooks, M. (2002). *The case for constructivist classrooms*. Alexandria, VA: Association for

Supervision and Curriculum Development.

Brophy, J. (2006a). *Teaching*. Brussels, Belgium, International Academy of Education.

Brophy, J. (2006b, July). Graham Nuthall and social constructivist teaching. *Teaching and Teacher Education, 22*(5), 529–537.

Brophy, J., & Good, T. L. (1986). Teacher behavior and student achievement. In M. C. Wittrock (Ed.), *Handbook of research on teaching* (pp. 328–375). New York: Macmillan.

Bruner, J. S. (1961). The act of discovery. *Harvard Educational Review, 32*, 21–32.

Bruner, J. S. (2004). *The process of education*. Cambridge, MA: Harvard University Press.

CSRQ Center. (2006, November). Report on elementary school

comprehensive school reform models. Access: www.csrq.org

Cuban, L. (2009, April 29). Hugging the middle: Why good teaching ignores methodology. *Education Week, 28*(30), 30.

Dewey, J. (2005). *How we think.* New York: Barnes & Noble Books.

Ellson, D. (1986, October). Improving productivity in teaching. *Phi Delta Kappan, 68,* 111–124.

Fashella, O., & Slavin, R. (1997). Effective and replicable programs for students placed at-risk in elementary and middle schools. Paper prepared for the Office of Research and Development (Grant No. R1170-40005). Washington, DC: U.S. Department of Education.

Gagnon, G., & Collay, M. (2001). *Design for learning: Six elements in constructivist classrooms.* Thousand Oaks, CA: Corwin Press.

Gamoran (2009, August). *Tracking and Inequality.* Wisconsin Center for Educational Research. Madison, WI: University of Wisconsin.

Gersten, R., & Keating, T. (1987, March). Long-term benefits from direct instruction. *Educational Leadership, 44*(6), 28–31.

Good, T., & Brophy, J. (2007). *Looking into classrooms.* Ramsey, NJ: Allyn & Bacon.

Good, T., & Grouws, D. (1977). Teaching effects: A process-product study in fourth grade classrooms. *Journal of Teacher Education, 28,* 49–54.

Good, T. L., Grouws, D., & Ebmeier, H. (1983). *Active mathematics teaching.* White Plains, NY: Longman.

Good, T. L., Reys, B. J., Grouws, D. A., & Mulryan, C. M. (1989, December; 1990, January). Using work groups in mathematics instruction. *Educational Leadership, 47*(4), 56–62.

Hoff, D. J. (1999, January 13). NAS hoping to bridge divide on learning methods. *Education Week 18*(18), 9.

Hoffer, T. B. (1992, Fall). Middle school ability grouping and student achievement in science and mathematics. *Educational Evaluation and Policy Analysis, 14*(3), 205–227.

Hofwolt, C. A. (1984). Instructional strategies in the science classroom. In D. Holdzkom & P. Lutz (Eds.),

Research within reach: Science education (pp. 41–58). Washington, DC: National Science Teachers Association.

Hunter, M. (1995). Mastery teaching. In J. Block, S. Everson, & T. Guskey (Eds.), *School improvement programs* (pp. 181–204). New York: Scholastic Press.

Hunter, R. (2004). *Mastery teaching.* Thousand Oaks, CA: Sage Publications.

Hurley, E., Allen, B., & Boykin, W. (2009, April), Culture and the interaction of student ethnicity with reward structure in group learning. *Cognition and Instruction, 27*(2), 121–146.

Izumi, L. (2002). *They have overcome: High poverty, high performing schools in California.* San Francisco: Pacific Research Institute.

Johnson, D. W., & Johnson, R. T. (1989/1990, December/January). Social skills for successful group work. *Educational Leadership, 47*(4), 29–33.

Johnson, D. & Johnson, R. (2009, June–July). An educational success story: Social interdependence theory and cooperative learning. *Educational Researcher, 38*(5), 365–379.

Johnson, D. W., Johnson, R. T., & Holubec, E. J. (1998). *Cooperation in the classroom.* Revised Edition. Edina, MN: Interaction.

Johnson, D., Johnson, R., & Stanne, M. (2000). *Cooperative learning methods: A meta-analysis.* Minneapolis: University of Minnesota. Access: www.co-operation.org/pages/cl-methods.html

Johnson, D. W., Maruyama, G., Johnson, R., & Nelson, D. (1981). Effects of cooperative, competitive, and individualistic goal structures on achievement: A meta-analysis. *Psychological Bulletin, 89*(1), 47–62.

Joyce, B., Weil, M., & Callahan, E. (2008). *Models of teaching.* Boston: Allyn & Bacon.

Kauchak, D. P., & Eggen, P.D. (2006). *Learning and teaching: Research-based methods.* Boston: Allyn & Bacon.

King, L. H. (1993). High and low achievers' perceptions of cooperative learning in two small groups. *Elementary School Journal, 93*(4), 399–416.

Kirschner, P. A., Sweller, J., & Clark, R. E. (2006). Why minimal guidance during instruction does not work: An analysis of the failure of constructivist, discovery, problem-based, experiential, and inquiry-based teaching. *Educational Psychologist, 41*(2), 75–86.

Klahr, D., & Nigam, M. (2005, November). Equivalence of learning paths in early science instruction. *Psychological Science, 16*(11), 871–872.

Mayer, R. (2004, January). Should there be a 3 strike rule against pure discovery learning? *American Psychologist, 59*(1), 14–19.

McCown, R., (2001). *Educational psychology: A learning centered approach.* Boston: Allyn & Bacon.

Merwin, W. C. (1976). The inquiry method. In S. E. Goodman (Ed.), *Handbook on contemporary education.* New York: Bowker.

Meyer, L. A. (1984). Long-term academic effects of the Direct Instruction Project follow-through. *Elementary School Journal, 84,* 380–394.

Michaels, J. W. (1978). Classroom reward structures and academic performance. *Review of Educational Research, 47,* 87–98.

Msfrizzle (2006, January 21). *Life and simple machines.* Access: www.msfrizzle.blogspot.com/

Murphy, J., Weil, M., & McGreal, T. (1986). The basic practice model of instruction. *The Elementary School Journal, 87,* 83–95.

National Academy of Sciences. (1999). *How people learn: Brain, mind, experience, and school.* Washington, DC: National Academy Press.

National Mathematics Advisory Panel. (2008). *Foundations for success.* Washington, DC: U.S. Department of Education.

National Research Council. (2000). *Inquiry and the national science standards.* Washington, DC: National Academy Press.

Nuthall, G., & Snook, I. (1973). Contemporary models of teaching. In R. M. Travers (Ed.), *Second handbook of research on teaching* (pp. 47–76). Chicago: Rand McNally.

Oh, snap! Blog (2005, October 10). Baseball, anger toward Joe Buck

CHAPTER 8

Four More Instructional Alternatives:
Cooperative Learning, Discovery Learning,
Constructivism, and Direct Instruction

301

and other things. Access: at www
.blogger.com

Orlich, D. C. (2009). *Teaching strategies:
A guide to effective instruction.* Boston:
Houghton Mifflin.

Pavin, R. (1992, October). Benefits
of nongraded schools. *Educational
Leadership,* (2), 22–25.

Perkins, D. (1999, November). The
many faces of constructivism.
Educational Leadership, 57(3), 6–11.

Peterson, P. (1979a, October). Direct
instruction: Effective for what and
for whom? *Educational Leadership, 37,*
46–48.

Peterson, P. (1979b). Direct instruction
reconsidered. In P. Peterson &
H. Walberg (Eds.), *Research
on teaching: Concepts, findings,
and implications.* Berkeley, CA:
McCutchan.

Peterson, P. (1982). Issue: Should
teachers be expected to learn and
use direct instruction? *ASCD Update,
24,* 5.

Rosenshine, B. (1986). Synthesis of
research on explicit teaching.
Educational Leadership, 43(7),
60–69.

Rosenshine, B. (1987). Direct
instruction. In M. J. Dunkin (Ed.),
*The international encyclopedia of
teaching and teacher education*
(pp. 257–263). Oxford: Pergamon.

Rosenshine, B., & Meister, C. (1995).
Direct instruction. In L. Anderson
(Ed.), *International encyclopedia of
teaching and teacher education.* Second
Edition (pp. 143–148). Oxford:
Elsevier Science Ltd.

Rosenshine, B., & Stevens, R. (2001).
Teaching functions. In M. Wittrock
(Ed.), *Handbook of research on
teaching.* Third Edition (pp.
376–391). New York: Macmillan.

Runkel, P. J., & Schmuck, R. A. (1982).
Group processes. In H. E. Mitzel
(Ed.), *Encyclopedia of educational
research.* Fifth Edition (pp. 743–755).
New York: Free Press.

Science Research Associates (n.d.).
Direct Instruction. DeSoto, TX.
Access: www.SRA4Kids.com

Sharon, S., (1980). Cooperative
learning in small groups. *Review of
Educational Research, 50,* 241–271.

Sharon, S., & Sharon, Y. (1976).
Small group teaching. Englewood
Cliffs, NJ: Educational Technology
Publications.

Sharon, Y., & Sharon, S. (1989/1990
December–January). Group
investigation expands cooperative
learning. *Educational Leadership,
47*(4), 17–21.

Slavin, R. E. (1989/1990, December–
January). Here to stay or gone
tomorrow: Guest editorial.
Educational Leadership, 47(4), 3.

Slavin, R. E. (1991, February).
Synthesis of research on cooperative
learning. *Educational Leadership,
48*(5), 71–82.

Slavin, R. E. (1995). *Cooperative
learning: Theory, research, and practice.*
Boston: Allyn & Bacon.

Slavin, R. E. (1996, January). Research
on cooperative learning and
achievement: What we know, what
we need to know. *Contemporary
Educational Psychology, 21*(1),
43–69.

Slavin, R. E. (2008). *Educational
psychology.* Eighth Edition. Boston:
Allyn & Bacon.

Slavin, R. E., Karweit, N. L., & Madden,
N. A. (1989). *Effective programs for
students at risk.* Boston: Allyn &
Bacon.

Slavin, R., & Madden, N. (1989,
February). What works for
students at risk: A research
synthesis. *Educational Leadership,
46,* 4–13.

Stallings, J., & Kaskowitz, D. H. (1975,
April). A study of follow-through
implementation. Paper presented at
the annual meeting of the American
Education Research Association.
Washington, DC.

Stallings, J. A., & Stipek, D. (1986).
Research on early childhood
and elementary school teaching
programs. In M. D. Wittrock (Ed.),
Handbook of research on teaching.
Third Edition (pp. 727–753). New
York: Macmillan.

Strike, K. A. (1975). The logic of
learning by discovery. *Review of
Educational Research, 45,* 461–483.

Suchman, R. J. (1961). Inquiry
training: Builds skills for
autonomous discovery. *Merrill
Palmer Quarterly, 7,* 147–171.

Tamir, P. (1995). Discovery learning
and teaching. In L. Anderson (Ed.),
*International encyclopedia of teaching
and teacher education.* Second Edition
(pp. 149–155). Oxford: Elsevier
Science Ltd.

Viadero, D. (1999, March 17). A direct
challenge. *Education Week, 18*(27),
41–43.

Viadero, D. (2009, March 13). Study
gives edge to 2 math programs.
Education Week, 28(23), 1, 13.

Wallis, C. (1995, Spring). The learning
revolution. *Time, 145*(12), 49–51.

Walters, L. (2000, May/June). Putting
cooperative learning to the test
Harvard Education Letter. Access:
www.edletter.org/past/issues/
2000-mj/cooperative.shtml

Watson, B., & Konicek, R. (1990, May).
Teaching for conceptual change:
Confronting children's experience.
Phi Delta Kappan, 71, 680–685.

Webb, N. M. (1982). Student
interaction and learning in small
groups. *Review of Educational
Research, 52*(3), 421–445.

Wolk, S. (2008, October). School as
inquiry. *Phi Delta Kappan, 90*(2),
115–122.

Woolfolk, A. (2009). *Educational
psychology.* Upper Saddle River, NJ:
Pearson Publishers.

Evaluating Students' Learning

Conversation Starters

Is the assessment done in schools helpful or harmful for students?

This is a commonly asked question about contemporary education and, as you might guess, the answer depends largely on whom you talk to.

Those who believe assessment is not only valuable but critical for helping teachers and students be more successful argue that it is only by thoroughly understanding how well we are doing that we can make effective instructional decisions. If we don't know whether what we're doing is working, how would we know whether to change or continue it?

Those who feel that too much assessment takes place in schools often cite the large amounts of time and money that are invested in the process, particularly the costs associated with mandated standardized tests. They also often note that teachers' professional judgment is the most important indicator of how well both the teacher and her or his students are doing. How could a test provide all of the information that the classroom teacher can?

What do you believe is the best balance of assessment and teacher judgment?

State and federally mandated testing and rising expectation for data-based decision making are ubiquitous in education today. Teachers use a range of assessments to make decisions about how well their students are learning and how effective their instruction has been. These decisions, while often difficult, are important in helping teachers improve their performance and their students' learning (Green & Mantz, 2002; McMillan, 2001; Stiggins, 2006). They require teachers to measure student learning in one or more of several ways and to use that information to make judgments about the effectiveness of their instruction.

In this chapter, we examine ways teachers can accurately assess student learning to make decisions about how best to provide effective instruction for each student. We begin by defining assessment and underscoring its importance in effective teaching. Next, we examine several factors that influence the quality of assessments, and we look at the principal types of assessment. The next sections then deal respectively with standardized tests and testing and with teacher-made assessments and test construction. In the final section, we discuss systems for grading student performance and ways to effectively and fairly assign grades.

CHAPTER 9

Defining Classroom Assessment, Measurement, and Evaluation

When non-educators think of instructional assessment, they most often think of tests or projects administered to students at the end of instruction. However, good classroom assessment requires more than that. It requires teachers to continually gather accurate information about their students' progress across a range of sources, to synthesize that information, to make judgments about how well or how much each student has learned, and to adjust instruction accordingly.

Educational assessment serves at least two important purposes (Jung & Guskey, 2010). First, it provides information about the effectiveness of instruction. By gathering information before, during, and after instruction, teachers are able to plan and adapt instruction to better meet students' needs. Second, the information gained through assessment helps both students and teachers make more accurate determinations about what an individual student has or has not learned and why. Thus, teachers can reteach when necessary and avoid unnecessary repetition, and students can correct or modify misconceptions, errors, and inaccurate strategies.

Assessment is the process of collecting, synthesizing, and interpreting information to aid in decision making. This includes a wide range of activities from informal approaches, such as using questions within a lesson or watching students as they engage in small group discussions, to formal approaches, like projects or tests. Some of our assessments attempt to assign a numeric value to students' performances. When we do this, we are using **measurement.** For example, students' scores on a 20-item quiz represent measurement of how well the students understand the material.

Ultimately, the goal of our assessment or measurement is to make judgments about the "goodness" or quality of students' performances and, by extension, the effectiveness of our teaching. This process of using our assessment information to make this judgment is called **evaluation.** In order to make a decision about whether a student's performance is good, bad, acceptable, or unacceptable, we must compare this performance to some criterion or standard. Does a test score of 85 represent good, average, or poor performance? In making your decision, you might consider each student's score either in relation to some minimum score you have established or in relation to how well other students did. You may also consider other factors, not directly assessed, that might have affected the student's performance. Was the child feeling ill at the time? Did the child's performance improve from the last assessment, even if it did not meet the minimum acceptable level? Did you feel that the assessment was somehow unfair to the student?

While evaluation of student performance involves more than measurement, you must remember that the more you allow personal opinions or biases to influence how you interpret the results of assessment and to make judgments, the less accurate your assessments will be. Further, even if you attempt to be objective in interpreting information, both the methods you use to gather your information and the sources you use influence the accuracy of your evaluation. Let us now examine the factors more closely and then turn our attention to the various types of assessment.

9.1 What personal biases or opinions do you have that might influence your judgments of student performance?

Factors Influencing Assessment Quality

To use assessment effectively, teachers must consider several critical factors that influence the accuracy and usefulness of their assessments. They must select appropriate sources of information, they must ensure that their measurements and judgments are accurate, and they must determine how and why they will use the assessment. Further, because no single assessment is completely accurate, teachers must draw from across multiple sources. This process is called **triangulation.**

SOURCES OF INFORMATION

In Chapter 5, we introduced some sources of information, such as cumulative records, observations, and interviews, that allow teachers to get to know their students better. These and other information sources help teachers find out about students' strengths and weaknesses, likes and dislikes, and problems and successes. Teachers use this information to organize their classrooms and plan their curricula. In this chapter, we are most interested in sources of information that help determine what a student has learned and in what areas or ways the student may need more instruction. Although some of the more informal sources discussed in Chapter 5 can be used to assess academic achievement, teachers mostly gain this kind of information by analyzing students' work or through testing (Stiggins, 2000).

Students' Work   Obviously, a great deal of useful information about academic achievement is gained through assessing students' work. In contrast to merely examining the score a student obtains on a given piece of work, such as a homework assignment, teachers often want to know how a student arrived at an answer. For example, what process or method did the child employ, and how accurately did he or she employ it? By looking closely at the process the student used, the teacher can identify errors that prevent the student from completing the work accurately. Homework assignments, projects, worksheets, and even tests or quizzes can be designed so that teachers can observe and analyze students' work. When teachers do this, it is important that they give students feedback about their performance (see Chapter 11).

Tests or Projects   Both tests and projects require students to demonstrate how well they have learned targeted concepts and skills, and they allow teachers to describe their students' performance. Assessments, like other instructional activities, can also be structured so that students are encouraged to demonstrate how they solve problems or arrive at conclusions. Thus, tests and projects are rich sources of information. As with information from any source, however, the information they provide is useful only when it is accurate and unbiased.

Effective assessment requires that teachers collect and synthesize as much accurate information as possible from as many sources as possible (Ardovino, Hollingsworth, & Ybarra, 2000). Increasingly, teachers develop and use

"I see many of you anticipated a sneak quiz today."

assessment systems that incorporate multiple sources of data over time—for example, over the course of a unit or grading period. Often applying principles of backward design (see Chapter 6), assessment systems thoughtfully guide collection of data in ways that are linked across assessments and that are integrated with curriculum and instruction. By carefully coordinating these three elements, assessment information and instructional decisions are more likely to help students and teachers improve their performance.

ACCURACY OF INFORMATION

The data that teachers obtain about students and their progress is never completely accurate. For a variety of reasons, no single assessment is ever totally free of bias or error. In fact, some of the information sources just noted are easily identified as subject to inaccuracy. For example, opinions from teachers or parents are likely to be somewhat inaccurate because they are highly subjective. Likewise, teachers' observations of their students are inevitably selective and incomplete; they are influenced by personal values and, consequently, are open to error and bias. Thus, teachers must take care to identify potential biases or errors when gathering and using information from these and other sources.

Even structured assessments like tests or performances are subject to error. No one assessment can precisely measure a given student's knowledge or achievement. First of all, tests are selective. They normally measure only part of what a teacher attempts to teach. Also, they do not test for knowledge that a student may have acquired from other sources such as books, friends, or other teachers. Furthermore, the student's internal condition at the time of testing can influence results. Perhaps the student was tired or ill when taking the test. Or perhaps the test emphasizes material that the student happened to review just before taking the test. In each case, the score obtained is not a full or accurate measure of the student's total knowledge on the subject. It is for this reason that assessment systems incorporate several coordinated assessments over time.

In addition to using multiple sources of data, a teacher must consider the accuracy of information gained from tests, projects, or other sources to gauge student performance. This includes asking: (1) Does the information provided by the assessment allow reasonable conclusions to be drawn about what the student has learned (*validity*)? and (2) Does the assessment provide consistent measurements (*reliability*)? These two factors are often discussed as they relate to tests, but they are equally important in judging information collected from any assessment (Wiggins, 1998).

Validity   **Validity** refers to the extent to which a particular assessment provides information that allows accurate and meaningful conclusions to be drawn. Thus, validity is always a function of the match between the purposes or uses of an assessment, the information it provides, and the claims that we make on the basis of this information. Each of these three elements makes an important contribution to the validity of an assessment, so it will be useful to examine each of them.

The first element of validity is that the assessment measures what it is intended to measure. Webb (1999) uses the term *alignment* to refer to the match between what is taught and how it is taught with what is assessed and how this is done. A valid or aligned assessment measures the content or skills that were the focus of instruction as fully and thoroughly as possible. A valid assessment is matched with curriculum and instruction in: (1) the breadth or range of concepts or skills they include; (2) the depth or level of detail at which students are engaged; (3) the emphasis placed on particular concepts, ideas, or skills; and (4) the cognitive level or complexity that is expected, often in terms of Bloom's taxonomy.

Validity also refers to the extent to which conclusions drawn from the results of an assessment are appropriate, given the assessment itself and the original purposes for which it was intended. If our intention, drawn from our objectives or standards, is to determine students' mastery of a set of basic terms in science, and our assessment provides information on this, validity would require that we use this information only to discuss students' mastery of concepts. If we were to draw conclusions about a student's scientific ability on the basis of this vocabulary assessment, our use of the results would not be valid.

Perhaps an extended example would be useful. Let's suppose that you teach a three-week unit on African-American writers of the late nineteenth and twentieth centuries. Your objectives focus on students' awareness of 10 major authors and their most important works (knowledge level) and students' ability to examine a work and appropriately discuss ways in which the work reflects both African themes or motifs and the social conditions of the time in which it was written (analysis). You decide to assess these objectives by having students develop short multimedia presentations on authors of their choice. If students' scores on this assessment were accurate measures of their mastery of the objectives at the levels and depth that were expected, and if your conclusions were limited to each student's mastery of these objectives, the assessment would be highly valid. If, however, students' scores reflected their differing skill in using technology (which was not one of your objectives) or their access to technology necessary to develop the presentations, then the assessment is less valid.

To summarize, validity is the accuracy with which assessment information is collected and used. It thus gives you information about your students' learning and the success of your instruction. Validity is not either-or, but rather a matter of degree, so you must decide whether a given assessment is *sufficiently* valid for your purposes. In later sections, we discuss the ways in which you can make your assessments more valid.

Reliability   In addition to measuring what you want it to measure, you hope that your assessment provides you with *consistent* measures of your students' learning. This consistency is referred to as *reliability*. Specifically, reliability means that an assessment will yield nearly the same scores if the individuals were to engage in it repeatedly. As with validity, no assessment can be expected to provide exactly the same measurements every time, so reliability, like validity, must be thought of as a matter of degree.

An assessment that lacks reliability produces results that do not accurately reflect students' understanding or ability due to some error in the assessment itself. Sometimes, in an attempt to be helpful, teachers actually reduce the reliability of assessments. For example, when you provide additional clarification or guidance

9.2

Did you ever feel that a teacher had made an inaccurate assessment of your performance? Why do you feel the assessment was inaccurate?

about an assessment task to some students but not others, you have reduced the reliability of the assessment across students, and, at least to some extent, their performances may be different.

Unreliable assessments lead us to draw inaccurate conclusions about student learning. If they have engaged in a flawed assessment that produces unreliable results, students may appear to have made little academic progress when, in fact, they may have learned quite a lot. Reliability is difficult to assess. Manufacturers of commercially available tests usually provide statistical indications of the reliability of their tests called **reliability coefficients.** These coefficients range from .00 to 1.00, with zero representing no reliability and 1.00 indicating perfect reliability. Generally, reliability coefficients above .85 are considered acceptable. Although you may be unable to compute the reliability coefficient of your own assessments, you can improve their reliability by formalizing and structuring your assessments and by being certain to score objectively and consistently. Guidelines for constructing reliable tests and other assessments appear in a later section.

Students with Special Needs   Before leaving the topic of assessment accuracy, we should take a moment to discuss the ways in which assessment can appropriately be modified or accommodated. Most states currently require that all students, even those with special needs or who are not fully proficient in English, participate in mandated testing. Because the stakes of these tests are so high for both students and teachers, it is important that you understand how changes to the context or processes of an assessment may impact both your students' performance and your own professional credibility.

The term **accommodations** refers to adaptations in the testing environment that change only the manner in which students participate in the assessment. Accommodations may take the form of providing Braille versions of a written test for visually impaired students, allowing a learning disabled student more time to take the test, providing a scribe to record answers for a student with a disability that precludes writing, having the mathematics portion of a test read to a student in her or his native language, or others. Notice, however, that these adaptations do not change the intellectual task the student is expected to perform. Accommodations allow students to demonstrate the same understanding or content-based abilities as all other students, but adapt the assessment context to accommodate the students' special needs.

In contrast, when an assessment is adapted in ways that change the intellectual task or cognitive level being assessed, **modifications** are being made. Often modifications adapt the breadth, depth, or complexity of content that the student is expected to master in order to allow the student to be successful. Two things are important to remember. First, modifications produce assessment results that represent something very different than those obtained for other students. To compare the results a student obtained from a modified assessment with those of a student whose assessment was not modified would be *invalid*. Second, some adaptations reflect accommodations in one situation, but modifications in another. For example, reading the mathematics portion of a test to a student who is not proficient in English is acceptable—the student still is being assessed on mathematics ability. However, reading the language arts portion of the same test would not be acceptable because the test is no longer measuring the student's ability in language arts.

TYPES OF ASSESSMENT: FORMATIVE VERSUS SUMMATIVE

We have seen that instructional assessments use information from a variety of sources and that this information can have various degrees of accuracy. Instructional assessments also vary in terms of their use. Typically, we think of assessment as occurring after instruction with the results used to determine students' grades. However, in an argument only scholars could love, Scriven (1967) and Cronbach (1963) were among the first to recognize that assessment conducted only *after* instruction is completed is not very useful in improving instruction or learning. Although necessary to assign grades, postinstructional assessment does not help the teacher or the student correct deficiencies. Equally important is assessment conducted *during* instruction. This type of assessment can be used to adapt instruction to meet the needs of the student while learning is taking place.

The terms Scriven introduced nearly half a century ago are still used to describe these different types of assessment. **Formative assessment** refers to assessment conducted during the course of instruction. Such assessment provides feedback while it is still possible to influence the instructional and learning process. Although student performance may be graded during formative assessment, the primary purpose is to provide feedback that can be used to plan or alter instruction. Formative assessment enables the teacher to form effective instruction and thereby improve students' performance. Formative assessment consists of both informal teacher observations and examples of student work, including responses to teachers' questions or any work students might complete within a larger unit of instruction. The feedback provided through formative assessment allows the teacher to adjust instruction and improve students' performance before a final assessment of learning is conducted.

Summative assessment is the term used to describe assessment conducted *after* instruction is completed. This type of assessment is used to make final judgments about a student's learning. Its primary purpose is not to adapt instruction or to remedy learning deficiencies; rather, it attempts to *summarize* a student's achievement or progress, generally in the form of a grade or score. Summative assessment generally involves information gathered from examinations or other projects due at the end of the term. In many cases, formative assessment of similar but less encompassing student work has taken place prior to this final assessment.

Effective teachers use both formative and summative assessments. However, formative assessments conducted and then communicated to students through a variety of formal and informal methods are most closely related to improved learning (Black & William, 1998; Guskey & Bailey, 2001). Table 9.1 provides a brief comparison of formative and summative evaluation.

Standardized Testing and Standard Scores

You may remember from Chapter 5 that a common type of assessment in schools is **standardized testing.** Calls for greater accountability for students' learning and more rigorous standards have led nearly all western countries to require students to pass standardized tests at several grade levels. Further emphasizing the importance of these tests in the early part of this century has been federal legislation (see Spotlight on Research 9.1) that required states to use results from these assessments to award funding, judge the quality of schools and teachers,

TABLE 9.1   Characteristics of Formative and Summative Assessments

	Formative	Summative
Purpose	To monitor and guide a learning process while it is still in progress	To judge the success of a learning process at its completion
Time of assessment	During the process	At the end of the process
Type of assessment technique	Informal observation, quizzes, homework, pupils' questions, worksheets	Formal tests, projects, term papers
Use of assessment information	Improve and change a process while it is still going on	Judge the overall success of a process; grade, place, and promote

Source: P. Airasian. (2005). *Classroom assessment,* 4th ed. New York: McGraw-Hill.

SPOTLIGHT ON RESEARCH 9.1
What Is "High-Stakes Testing"?

"More is riding on test performance than ever before. In response to widespread public demand, states are implementing new accountability systems that hold schools, teachers, and students responsible for demonstrating acceptable levels of student achievement . . . Centrally featured in these new systems are 'high-stakes' tests" (WestEd Policy Brief, 2000, p. 1).

As interested citizens and parents, we have all frequently heard of what are called "high-stakes" tests. Nearly every issue of professional journals in education has one or more articles that discuss issues associated with the use of formalized, mandated tests by which students and educators are judged. However, there is considerable misunderstanding about so-called "high-stakes" testing, even among educators.

The term "high-stakes" is often associated with nearly any type of standardized achievement test that is administered in schools today, but not all of these tests are, in fact, "high-stakes." What, then, is a "high-stakes" test?

According to the American Educational Research Association, "high-stakes" refers to any test that carries "serious consequences for students or for educators" (AERA, 2004). For students, these tests are used to identify those in need of remediation or special programs, to make decisions about whether or not a particular student will be passed on to the next grade (or retained), and even whether or not students will receive a high school diploma. For example, at least 27 states currently base students' promotion, graduation, or both on their performance on a mandated achievement test. Students whose performance does not meet required

levels are provided with remediation and generally are allowed to take the test one or more additional times. However, if their performance continues to fall short of the requirements, they may be retained, not allowed to graduate, or provided with a "certificate of attendance" rather than a high school diploma.

Similarly, students' performance on these tests has increasingly been used to make decisions about the performance of teachers and schools. Many states have based funding to schools or school districts on the performance of their students on these tests and provide sanctions for schools where students perform worse than expected or rewards for schools where students perform better than expected. The federal No Child Left Behind Act and a small number of states have even included processes that allow parents whose children attend poorly performing schools, as measured by mandated achievement tests, to move their children into other public schools or into private schools with funds provided by the state or federal government. More recently, some schools have begun basing teacher salaries or other incentives on their students' performance on achievement tests. In early 2004, the association representing teachers in Denver public schools voted to implement a system of merit pay that would tie salary increases to students' achievement for most teachers.

The benefits and drawbacks of "high-stakes" testing are among the most debated educational issues today. However, Professor Daniel Koretz of the Harvard University Graduate School of Education has noted that, "The current emphasis on high-stakes testing, which is nearly universal in the policy world, is

really not new . . . it dates back at least twenty-five years or more" (Koretz, 2002). Professor Koretz suggests that, whether or not it was justified, concern about the performance of students in U.S. public schools grew dramatically from the late 1960s to the mid-1980s. In the late 1980s and through the 1990s, most states implemented higher or more rigorous curricular requirements for high school graduation and programs of statewide testing of student achievement for accountability purposes. The current widespread use of achievement testing and the stiffer consequences associated with their results represent a continuation of these trends.

Many professional education organizations have expressed concern about "high-stakes" testing, and some have expressly opposed it. For example, the National Council of Teachers of Mathematics' position is that "far-reaching and critical educational decisions should be made only on the basis of multiple measures" (NCTM, 2004). The International Reading Association goes even further stating that the organization "strongly opposes high-stakes testing" (International Reading Association, 2004). In contrast, policy makers and a majority of citizens believe that such tests are valuable and should be continued.

In the end, it is generally agreed that the use of tests to measure student learning and the use of scores from these tests to judge the amount of student learning and the effectiveness of teachers or schools will continue for the foreseeable future. Professor Koretz states, "Accountability systems are going to stick around, and tests are clearly going to be a big part of them."

Source: Koretz (2002).

and even support families in moving from low-performing public schools to private schools. Because these tests are often used to make decisions with extremely important consequences for students and teachers, they are often referred to as "high-stakes" tests.

The results of standardized tests represent the most common method of evaluating teachers, schools, and students (Baker, 2007; Laitsch, 2006). Nearly two decades ago it was estimated that 127 million standardized tests were administered to students in the United States each year at an annual cost of nearly $900 million (Willis, 1990). Since then, the number of such tests has increased dramatically, and some have estimated the cost of these tests to be as much as $22 billion (Phelps, 2000).

Administering and interpreting the results of standardized tests have become critical tasks for every teacher. As a result, we now turn our attention to this form of assessment. We will examine the standardized testing process and discuss how the scores from such tests are reported and used.

THE STANDARDIZED TESTING PROCESS

Standardized tests get their name because they are administered and scored in consistent, uniform ways. Any student taking a nationally standardized test will take the test under roughly the same conditions as any other student, no matter where or when the test is administered. This uniformity includes all controllable factors that might influence a student's performance on the test: the materials used, the time limits, oral instructions, preliminary demonstrations, policies for handling questions from students, and any other detail believed to affect test performance.

9.3 What standardized tests have you taken?

For example, when you took the SAT or ACT, you completed the test under the same conditions as all other students who took the exam. You were given the same instructions, the test booklet and scoring sheets or computer interface were the same, the questions you answered were of equivalent difficulty and type, the equipment you were allowed to use was the same (pencils, calculators, and so on), you had the same amount of time to complete each section, and your scores were reported in the same ways. As a result, your performance can be compared with that of all other students who took the exam, even if they took it at another time or in another place. This ability to make comparisons across large groups of pupils is the greatest benefit of standardized tests.

Standardized tests offer several additional benefits. They are efficient in measuring a wide range of student learning relatively quickly and inexpensively. They are fairly and objectively scored. They tend to be more reliable than teacher-made tests, and they can be developed to assess higher-order thinking. In spite of these benefits, standardized tests are often criticized for emphasizing low-level basic skills and for cultural, racial, and gender bias (Isaac & Michael, 1997; Wiggins, 1998). The harshest criticisms of standardized tests arise when the tests are misused or their results misinterpreted (Popham, 2004).

In addition to preparing your students to take standardized tests, you will also be expected to administer these tests. When administering a standardized test, it is important that you follow the directions provided exactly (Hanna & Dettmer, 2004). Failure to do so makes the results of the test less accurate and may put your students at a disadvantage. A major responsibility when administering the test is to allow all students an equal opportunity to do well. Thus, you must ensure that each student has the necessary materials, desk space, and time. Further, you should carefully read the instructions using a calm, clear, relatively slow speaking voice that all students in the room can hear. Voice inflection, tone, and facial expression should reinforce the instructions. You must also monitor students as they complete the examination, making sure that students begin and end at the appropriate times and do not cheat. Each standardized test will provide instructions for administering the exam, and you are well advised to follow them.

Try Activity 9.3

The best way to help your students do well on standardized tests is to ensure that you give them opportunities to learn the concepts or ideas that will be on the test (Carr & Harris, 2001; Schmoker & Marzano, 2003). While it is not always possible to know exactly what a standardized test will include, many state-mandated tests are designed directly to measure students' mastery of specified state curriculum standards. By incorporating these into your instruction, you give students the opportunity to master them. In addition to guiding your students in mastering the content to be tested, you can further improve their performance on standardized tests by helping them develop good test-taking skills or **test sophistication** (Baker, 2007; McMillan, 2001; Walker-Wilson, 2002). For example, before students take a standardized test, provide them with opportunities to respond to questions of similar types and under similar conditions. You may also wish to give students suggestions about when or if to guess at the correct answer and how to manage their time. Such guidance helps students feel more comfortable and confident when taking the test and—especially for disadvantaged students—can substantially improve their test performance (McMillan, 2001).

INTERPRETING STANDARDIZED TEST RESULTS

As use and importance of standardized tests has increased over the past 20 years, so too has the responsibility of the teacher to understand and use their results. In this section, we examine the various ways of reporting standardized test scores. Knowing this, you can then use this information to evaluate your students' progress and improve your own teaching.

Criterion- versus Norm-Referenced Scores   To interpret test scores, you must compare a particular score to some standard. The two most widely used standards are (1) the scores of other students or (2) an established, fixed criterion. When students' scores are compared to one another, a **norm-referenced** approach is being used. In this approach, the number of items a student answered correctly or incorrectly (called *raw score*) is less important than how the child's performance compares to other students who took the test. Norm-referenced test scores provide little information about what specific learning a student has gained or in what areas the student may need remediation. What they do show is how well the student's achievement compares with other students in the class, school, district, state, or nation who have taken the test. This comparison group is called a norming sample. Because comparisons of all students who took the test are possible, even if the students were

"It's exam week, and they're not in a good mood. Let's be careful out there."

in different schools or different parts of the country, schools or state agencies often use the results of norm-referenced testing to make policy decisions.

When you compare students' raw scores to an established standard or criterion, you are using a **criterion-referenced** approach. In this approach, the number of items answered correctly or incorrectly is used to determine whether a student has mastered specific learning objectives. When a student's score is lower than the established criterion, the testers believe that the student has not sufficiently mastered the objectives. The results of criterion-referenced testing provide more detailed information about the specific learning the student has gained and the particular areas in which the student needs more work. Thus, criterion-referenced test results can be of tremendous benefit in evaluating, planning, or adapting classroom instruction. However, they give little information about how well your students' performance compares with that of other students. A comparison of norm-referenced and criterion-referenced tests appears in Table 9.2.

TYPES OF SCORES FROM STANDARDIZED TESTS

The results of standardized tests are reported in a variety of ways, including as both criterion-referenced and norm-referenced scores. In fact, most test reports provide several types of scores for each student on the same section or sections of the test. Because these scores are often confusing and because teachers are increasingly expected both to understand and communicate them to parents, it is critical that we devote some of this chapter to explaining the most common types of scores from standardized tests.

In order to understand, communicate, and use the information provided by standardized tests, we must first understand (1) the various types of scores that can be reported and (2) what they mean in terms of student performance. Students' performance on tests may be reported as *standard scores* like z-scores and T scores, which are often discussed in education textbooks. However, most standardized tests now report students' performance in terms of raw score, percentile ranks (PR), Normal Curve Equivalent scores (NCE), stanine scores, and grade equivalent scores. In the sections that follow, we will discuss what these scores mean using the example test report presented in Figure 9.1.

Raw score is the number of test items or points that a student obtained on a particular section of the test. Just like the raw score that a student may obtain on a classroom quiz or paper, for example 8 out of a possible 10, this number can only be interpreted if we have additional information. In the example in Figure 9.1, raw score is reported in the first column (RS). As you can see, two numbers are presented for each portion of the test and are separated by a slash. The first number tells us how many items the student completed successfully and the second number indicates the total number of items possible. In this example, our student accurately completed 11 of 17 items in the area of Reading Comprehension, 9 of 15 items in Vocabulary, and 12 out of 18 in Mathematics. The next column (MCL) uses this information to indicate whether the student met the established

TABLE 9.2 Comparison of Norm-Referenced and Criterion-Referenced Tests	
Norm-Referenced Test	**Criterion-Referenced Test**
Reports the student's performance in relation to other students who took the test	Reports the student's performance in relation to a fixed, usually predetermined standard
Provides information about general learning and achievement	Provides information about specific learning and mastery of particular objectives
Is useful in making policy decisions at the national, state, and local levels	Is useful in designing the most appropriate instruction for individual students

FIGURE 9.1　Individual Student Test Report

Test Date:　04/17/10
Norms Date:　2005

School:　Metropolitan Community
District:　Metropolis County

Form: A　Level: 14

Student Record Sheet
Student Name:　BERTRAND,　Adrian　L.
Birthdate:　05/20/01
Grade:　4.7
Teacher:　Smith, T.

				SCORES				
	RS	MCL	DP	SP	NP	NCE	GE	ST
Reading Comprehension	11/17		70	63	52	61	4.5	5
Vocabulary	9/15		63	51	50	50	4.5	5
Mathematics	12/18		89	81	77	66	4.7	6
COMPOSITE	32/50		74	65	60	55	4.4	5
Science	15/18	*	92	85	79	67	4.8	7
Social Studies	11/15	*	79	74	72	62	4.7	6

minimum competency level of 75 percent. As such, this column represents a criterion-referenced method of interpreting the student's performance on each section of the test.

Another common form of standard score is **percentile rank (PR).** When you received the results of your ACT or SAT, they were likely reported as percentile rank scores. A percentile rank score indicates what percentage of people taking the test scored at or below a given raw score. Thus, a percentile rank of 50 indicates that a student's raw score was the same as the mean, that her score was equal to or better than 50 percent of the people in the original norming sample. Test reports often include percentile rank scores based upon multiple norming groups (e.g., all students in the school, in the district, in the state, or in the nation). As a result, interpretation of these scores requires that we know and understand the comparison or norming group on which they are based.

Our example above may help make this clearer. The third, fourth, and fifth columns report our student's performance in terms of percentile rank. The third column (DP meaning District Percentile) uses other students in our district as the norming group, the fourth column (SP for State Percentile) uses students in our state, and the fifth column (NP) uses a national norming group. Remember, however, that each of these percentile rank scores is a way to interpret our student's raw score on each section of the test. In the example test report in Figure 9.1, DP reports a percentile rank of 70 in Reading Comprehension based on other students in our district, SP indicates that a raw score of 11 is a percentile rank of 63 when compared with other students in our state, and NP reports that this same raw score reflects a percentile rank of 52 based on the national norming group. While each of these scores is based on the student's raw score of 11 in Reading Comprehension, they differ because this raw score is compared to the performance of three different groups. A raw score of 11 in Reading Comprehension is as good as or better than 70 percent of the students in our district, as good as or better than 63 percent of students in our state, and as good as or better than 52 percent of students nationwide. Which of these percentile rank scores is most useful? It depends on what the information is to be used for, a question that we will leave for another time. For now, it is enough to understand what PR scores mean.

Normal Curve Equivalent (NCE) scores look very much like percentile rank scores, but they are easier to use when doing calculations with students' test scores. As a result, many district personnel (like school counselors or administrators) prefer to rely on these scores. Like percentile rank, NCE scores have a mean of 50. However, NCE scores use an equal interval scale of 21.06 percentile points for each standard deviation. Thus, as a student's score moves farther from the mean, NCE and PR scores begin to vary considerably. In the Figure 9.1 example, our student's performance in Reading Comprehension is reported as an NCE of 61 (based upon the national norming group).

Stanine scores are commonly used to report the results of standardized tests in education. Stanine gets its name from the scale it applies to standard scores. In this scale, 5 is the midpoint, or mean, and the entire scale contains nine values. Hence, it is a "standard nine," or "stanine" scale. Using our example, our student's raw score of 12 in mathematics represents a stanine score of 6. In this example, the stanine score is based upon the national norming group.

Grade equivalent (GE) scores are easily interpretable and particularly common in education. Grade equivalent scores compare a student's performance with the scores of other students of varying grade levels who took the same test. For example, if a student's raw score is similar to that obtained by seventh graders who took the test, the grade equivalent score would be 7. Decimal places are used to indicate months of the academic year, with 1 referring to the first month of the academic year and 9 typically referring to the last. Thus, our student's GE score of 4.8 on the science portion of the test means that the raw score of 15 was roughly equal to that of fourth-grade students in the eighth month of the school year (approximately April). The scale for grade equivalent scores is created by administering the test to large numbers of students at various grade levels and computing the distribution of scores for students at each month of each grade.

It is important to note that the students at various grade levels all take the *same* test. If the test is intended for students in the fourth grade, all students in the norming sample take this fourth-grade test, *not* a more or less advanced version. In this example, if our fourth-grade student had achieved a GE score of 9.1, his score on this fourth-grade test was roughly equal to that of students in the first month of ninth grade. This score would indicate only that our fourth grader had mastered the fourth-grade material as well as the typical ninth grader. It does *not* mean that the fourth-grade student is capable of doing ninth-grade work.

Remember that no test is completely accurate in measuring a student's knowledge or ability. Some error is always present. Because of this, many test manufacturers now report student performance not as a single score, but as a range of scores that the student would likely obtain if he or she took the test several times. This **score band** includes the student's actual score (usually at the middle of the band) and indicates how much above and below that score the student might have performed. Although less precise than other types of scores, score bands are a useful way to use the results of standardized tests. They prevent us from attempting to make very fine judgments between students whose scores did not differ much.

Try Activity 9.1

SUMMARY OF STANDARDIZED TESTING

Standardized tests have become extremely important in the lives of both teachers and students. They are legitimately called "high-stakes." It is critical that you be aware of how best to help your students perform well on these tests, and you must understand and be able to use the results that they provide.

Teacher-Made Assessments

Standardized tests are increasingly important in determining educational policy at the national, state, and district levels. However, the most common form of classroom assessment remains the teacher-developed assessment (Brookhart, 2004). It has been estimated that teachers spend nearly one-third of their time in developing and administering assessment activities (Green and Mantz, 2002). (See Highlight 9.1.) Well-made teacher-constructed assessments have several advantages over standardized tests. First, since the classroom teacher develops them, they can be keyed to the specific content and objectives that teacher has taught rather than to general content "most" teachers teach at that grade level. Second, teacher-made assessments are far less expensive than commercially produced tests. Third, when they are well-constructed around the instructional objectives, teacher-developed assessments provide more detailed and specific information on how well students have mastered the course content. However, in spite of these advantages, teacher-made assessments are often poorly constructed and thus often provide inaccurate information. Even advocates of teacher-developed assessments concede that many teacher-made assessments are much worse than the standardized tests students take (Green & Mantz, 2002; Smith, 2009; Stiggins, 2006).

Because teacher-made assessments are so common and potentially valuable, we now engage in an extended discussion of how best to develop and use the two primary types of teacher-made tests: pencil-and-paper tests and observational or performance assessment. After defining and describing each type of assessment, we will discuss the specific strengths and weaknesses, note considerations in selecting or developing appropriate instruments, and suggest methods of scoring.

PENCIL-AND-PAPER TESTS

The most recognizable and traditional type of teacher-made assessment is the pencil-and-paper test. Each of us has spent countless hours frantically writing our responses to essay questions or using our pencils to fill in the dots on a scoring sheet. And, perhaps just as often, we have spent time after the exam thinking about how unclear some of the questions were or wondering why the instructor asked so many questions about one aspect of the content while totally neglecting other aspects. In each case, we were prevented from giving a true account of how much we had learned because of a poorly developed test. It is your ethical responsibility as a teacher to make sure that your students have the opportunity to make a valid showing of how much they have learned.

Pencil-and-paper tests most often use items of two types. One type requires students to select a correct response from a list of possible answers called **selected response items.** Multiple-choice, true-false, matching, and completion items are all selected response types. The other type of item requires students to develop or create a response in their own words. These are called **created response items.** Essay or short-answer questions are examples of created response items.

Each item type possesses advantages and disadvantages depending on the ease or difficulty of construction and scoring. In other words, one type of item is easier to write but more difficult to score, while the other is just the opposite. Many people believe that one item type is inherently better than another, for example, that essay items are more valuable than multiple choice. Bart (2009) writes,

> If you think multiple choice tests are only good to assess how well students memorized facts, it may be time to rethink your testing strategy. Although they are not appropriate for every situation, when properly developed, multiple choice tests can be used to assess higher levels of thinking, including application and analysis.

Thus, we should know about and be able to use items of each type when appropriate.

According to Green and Mantz (2002), most teachers do not use assessment strategies in their classrooms that are likely to improve instruction or student learning. Their own work suggests that teachers feel comfortable using informal, formative types of assessment with their students. Observing students while they work in groups and asking guiding questions are the most commonly used strategies. Teachers feel that these approaches allow them to provide students with feedback for improving their performance. In contrast, teachers indicated that they were not comfortable developing their own formal assessments to gauge students' learning nor were they confident that they understood how to use assessment results to improve their own practice.

Green and Mantz suggest that a focus of teacher preparation in recent years has been on incorporating formative and informal assessment approaches into classroom instruction. They believe this focus has been successful in promoting the use of these strategies. However, they express concern that, in an era of increasing accountability, the assessment strategies that teachers use "may not be sufficient to prepare teachers to assess student learning effectively" (p. 6).

Source: Green & Mantz (2002).

Created Response Items   Created response items require students to compose an answer, generally in their own words, rather than select the appropriate answer from a list. Created response items can require students to generate anything from a short sentence to a multiple-page essay. Well-written created response items can allow students to demonstrate learning at all cognitive levels—from recall through evaluation. They can push students to organize or reorganize ideas and concepts, apply content in unique ways, and solve problems. Poorly written created response items may discourage creativity, confuse and frustrate students, and result in unfair and inaccurate judgments about students' progress.

Created response items possess several advantages. First, they are easy to write—much easier, in fact, than selected response items. This is especially true when the teacher is attempting to assess higher-level cognitive processes. Thus, created response items require less time to construct. Second, because students must organize and express their answers in their own words, created response items allow teachers to assess students' ability to communicate ideas. Third, they reduce the likelihood that students will simply guess the correct answer.

Created response items also have disadvantages. Although they can be constructed rather easily and quickly, they are extremely time-consuming to score. Imagine, for instance, the high school teacher who administers a five-item essay exam to four classes, each with thirty students. If the response to each item was only one-half page, this teacher would have to read 300 pages of students' responses! Providing prompt and detailed feedback to students about their performance on this exam would be a daunting prospect.

Another disadvantage of created response items is that they limit the amount of content the test can cover. Because students must be allowed sufficient time to think about the item, compose an answer, and put it on paper, the test can include only a few items. Thus, a test consisting entirely of created response items cannot possibly assess all that has been taught or learned. In essence, the validity of the test is reduced because it does not cover all important aspects of the content.

The final and most troubling disadvantage of created response tests is that they are difficult to score reliably. Created response items require teachers to make judgments about the quality of students' responses. Several factors can bias these judgments and result in unfair scoring. For example, the quality or legibility of the students' handwriting, grammar, writing style, or length of response have long been known to influence the score that teachers assign to created responses (Stanley, 1958). This may be a particular problem for young students or for students with limited English proficiency. In addition, teachers' opinions and expectations of students can lead them to score responses unfairly. For instance, a student who has contributed to class discussions and seems motivated and interested is likely to receive a higher score than another student who is perceived as uninterested and unmotivated but makes the same response.

Created response items can be written as **restricted response** or **extended response items.** Restricted response items set explicit parameters within which students are to respond. Such items may restrict the topic or topics to be included or the length or space devoted to the response, and they often make specific suggestions about aspects of the content the response should address. Restricted response items do not allow students as much flexibility or creativity in responding. However, because they reduce variability in the style, length, and topics of students' responses, they are generally more reliable and fair than extended response items.

Extended response items often do not place any restrictions on students' responses. As a result, they allow much greater creativity and flexibility in creating the response. Students can write as much or as little as they wish and can include all aspects of the content they deem necessary. Extended response items give us a better picture of how well students can communicate and approach problems creatively, but they are more open to biased and unfair scoring. As a result, you should use restricted response items in most situations. Examples of restricted and extended items are shown in Figure 9.2.

Once you have decided that your instructional objectives can best be assessed through created response items, you can do several things to improve the validity, reliability, and thus the accuracy of your test. Your goal should be to create assessment instruments that provide accurate measures of how well each student has mastered all the objectives. The test should be representative of the breadth, depth, and emphases of the objectives and should require students to perform or respond at cognitive levels matching your objectives. If you have written clear and complete instructional objectives, constructing a created response test is a relatively easy procedure. Just follow these guidelines.

- First, consider which objectives are most important to your assessment. As noted earlier, created response items take students longer to complete, so you may be unable to assess all objectives. In that event, you should select those most critical to students' mastery of the material, those that were most emphasized in instruction, or those that are broad enough to encompass other objectives. However, you must be realistic in determining how many created response items students can handle. All students should be able to answer all questions in the time allowed.

- Second, write restricted response items that cover all of your objectives. Always be sure the items reflect the verbs from your objectives (compare, contrast, list, and so on) and provide specific information about the length, components,

"I didn't understand half of what you wrote—I like that in a thesis."

FIGURE 9.2   Created Response Items: Restricted versus Extended Response

Restricted Response

List, describe, and present an example of each of three literary devices Poe uses to set the mood in the introductory paragraph of *The Fall of the House of Usher*. Use no more than five complete sentences.

Extended Response

Discuss and provide examples of the literary devices Poe uses to set the mood in the introductory paragraph of *The Fall of the House of Usher*.

---

and style to be used. It is also a good idea to indicate whether spelling or grammar will be considered, whether an outline is acceptable, and how much weight you will apply to each element of the response.

- Third, after writing the items, it is a good idea to immediately compose a complete model response that can serve as your guide in scoring students' responses. Make a note about the time it took you to construct each answer, and use this to determine how much time students will need to answer the item. (Remember, it will take students much longer to think about, create, and write their answers.) Then, after making sure that your response provides a satisfactory answer, identify and list the characteristics or components that make it exemplary.

- Fourth, try to select several items requiring relatively short answers rather than a few questions requiring extensive answers. This allows you to assess more of your objectives (improving the validity of the test) and gives students a better opportunity to accurately demonstrate what they know (better reliability). It is also wise to construct the test in such a way that all students are expected to answer all items.

Before duplicating the test, write instructions for completing the test that include guidelines for composing and writing each response, information about how you will score the items, and the weight you will give each item. When appropriate, suggest the amount of time students should spend on each item as well. Then carefully proofread the test, perhaps asking a colleague to read through it for clarity and to ensure that your time frame is reasonable.

As noted earlier, a major weakness of created response tests is that they are difficult to score reliably and objectively. Using restricted rather than extended response items helps by more clearly defining the range of information and detail that students should include in their responses. In addition, judging each student's response against the components and characteristics you identified in your model response makes scoring more consistent and objective. Guidelines for improving your scoring of created response items follow.

- First, attempt to score the tests without knowing which student made the response you are reading. You might have students put their names only on the last page of the test, assign each student a code to use in place of their name, or cover the students' names until you have scored all items.

- Second, score only one item at a time for all papers. This allows you to more consistently apply the same criteria to all students' responses. It also reduces the likelihood that you will allow your opinion of an early answer to influence your scoring of one you read later.

- Third, don't score all papers at once. Scoring essay examinations takes a great deal of time and energy. If you become fatigued, you are less likely to be objective and accurate in your scoring. It is best to score all students' responses to one particular item, then move to another item, and so on until you begin to feel tired. Do not attempt a marathon session in which you sit for hours in order to "get through" a stack of papers.

- Fourth, after scoring all responses, reread all or a random sample of the papers to ensure that you have scored them accurately. It is often a good idea to organize the papers into high, moderate, and low scores and then to reread some papers in each category to check your scoring.

- Fifth, when necessary, adjust your scoring to reflect poor teaching. When no student is able to respond to an item with reasonable accuracy, you may wish to eliminate the item or reconsider the criteria you used to score it.

Created response items serve a useful purpose in classroom assessment. Because they are easy to construct, they are less time-intensive up front. They are also easier

Try Activity 9.2

to adapt to higher-order cognitive processes. However, they are extremely time-intensive to score and highly susceptible to scoring bias. These characteristics have led some to suggest that created response items, in spite of their intuitive appeal, are appropriate only when selected response items *cannot* be used. Table 9.3 briefly summarizes the guidelines for writing and scoring created response items.

Selected Response Items Selected response items require students to select the most appropriate answer from a list of alternatives or to complete the item with a single, short answer (usually a word or short phrase). Students are not asked to compose a new or unique response, as in created response items. As noted earlier, many people believe that selected response items are not effective in assessing students' higher-order cognitive skills. However, such items, when written carefully, can be as effective as any other item in encouraging students to use high-level thinking skills. One way to do this is to write items that require students to identify metaphors or to answer questions about an extended, detailed scenario or problem.

Selected response items possess many advantages. Probably the most important is that they are less subject to scoring bias—the student either does or does not select the appropriate alternative. Reliability and fairness are increased because scores are not based upon the judgment of the scorer. Also, since selected response items take less time for students to complete, they allow the teacher to assess more content and objectives. As a result, tests that use these items tend to be more valid. Scoring is easy, quick, and less subject to bias. Because they do not require students to compose an answer, selected response items measure students' mastery of the content rather than their ability to write or communicate effectively.

On the other hand, selected response items are difficult and time-consuming to write. They are much more time-intensive up front than created response items are. A major weakness of selected response items is the difficulty of constructing items that encourage students to apply higher-order cognitive skills. While such items can be written, they usually take considerable thought. As a result, selected response items often emphasize lower-order thinking.

There are four types of selected response items: multiple-choice, matching, true-false, and completion. In the following sections we will examine the construction, uses, and scoring of selected response items.

Most of us have taken innumerable **multiple-choice** tests during our schooling. Nearly all standardized tests use them, as do many teacher-made tests. Multiple-choice items consist of two parts: a **stem** which presents a problem or asks a question, and several **alternative responses.** Students are expected to select the alternative

---

TABLE 9.3 Guidelines for Writing and Scoring Created Response Items

Writing Items	Scoring Items
1. Key all test items to your instructional objectives.	1. Compose a model response immediately after writing each item.
2. Select the most important objectives, and write at least one item for each.	2. Identify components that make your response exemplary.
3. Begin each item with the verb from your objective.	3. Score all student responses against the model.
4. Write restricted rather than extended response items.	4. Score items without knowing which student constructed them.
5. Include as many items as students can reasonably complete.	5. Score only one item at a time for all papers.
6. Indicate whether spelling and grammar will be considered in scoring.	6. Avoid becoming fatigued.
7. Proofread carefully before duplicating.	7. Review a sample of the tests to check the accuracy of your scoring.

that offers the best solution to the problem or that best answers the question the stem presents.

Multiple-choice items possess several strengths. They are probably the most versatile selected response item in that they can be used to evaluate learning in any content area and at all cognitive levels. Because each item takes relatively little time for students to complete, multiple-choice questions allow teachers to evaluate more instructional objectives than created response items. Similarly, multiple-choice items allow teachers to make fine discriminations in the depth and breadth of students' understanding. In contrast to created response items, multiple-choice items can be easily and reliably scored.

There are two primary disadvantages in using multiple-choice items. The greatest disadvantage is that they are difficult and time-consuming to construct, particularly when writing items to assess learning at the higher levels of thinking. High-level items require teachers to process the information at the more advanced levels, then create a problem or question that is likely to elicit similar processing in students, and finally to generate several *realistic* alternative responses, each requiring high-level thinking. A second disadvantage is that, unlike created response tests, multiple-choice tests do not allow us to evaluate how well students are able to communicate their understanding. Students merely select a response.

There are several things you can do to improve the validity and reliability of your multiple-choice tests. As with any test, you should write your multiple-choice items during the planning process to match your instructional objectives. Using your objectives or instructional plan as your guide, you then determine roughly the number of items to devote to each part of the content. You now have a rough test plan and are ready to begin writing or selecting individual test items.

The process of writing multiple-choice items begins with the stem. It must be clearly written in simple language, and it should ask a question or present a problem—not just make an incomplete statement. The stem should be clear enough that the respondent could generate the most appropriate answer even if the alternative responses were not presented. Be certain that each stem presents a new problem and that neither the stem nor alternative responses provide clues to other items. It is also wise to avoid using negative questions or statements in the stem or alternative responses.

For example, the stem, "The American Revolution could not have been won if the British military had not . . ." is confusing. It includes too many negatives and does not ask a question. A better way to write this stem would be, "Which of the following errors the British military made was critical to the outcome of the American Revolution?" This stem avoids negatives, presents a complete question, and uses clearer wording.

After writing the stem, you construct three to five reasonable alternative responses, writing the correct response first and then the others. It is not necessary to include an equal number of alternatives for every item. To reduce the likelihood that students can guess the correct answer, each alternative should present a reasonable answer to the problem presented in the stem, but only one should be most defensible. Avoid responses that are unreasonable and avoid using "none of the above" or "all of the above" since they encourage guessing. Be certain that neither the stem nor the responses provide grammatical clues to the correct response or to other items. This is most often a problem when the stem is an incomplete statement. For example, the stem might be, "George Washington was a . . .". In this example, the correct response must begin with a consonant to be grammatically correct. The response, "affluent land owner" would probably not be the correct answer because it doesn't complete the statement grammatically.

Finally, each alternative should be roughly the same length (in poorly constructed items the longest response is often the most appropriate). Figure 9.3 summarizes the guidelines for writing effective multiple-choice items.

FIGURE 9.3 Guidelines for Writing Multiple-Choice Items

1. Write the stem so that it presents a complete question or problem. Avoid stems that are incomplete statements.

2. The stem should be sufficiently clear that the learner could generate the correct answer even if it were not provided.

3. Avoid using negative questions or statements in the stem or responses.

4. Avoid placing grammatical cues that suggest the correct alternative in the stem.

5. Write the correct response first, then generate between two and four reasonable alternatives.

6. Write alternative responses of roughly equal length.

7. Avoid using "none of the above" or "all of the above."

8. To assess higher-order thinking, write items that require students to identify metaphors or to answer questions about an extended, detailed scenario or problem.

9. Avoid establishing a pattern of responses.

10. Proofread all items carefully.

11. Place the entire item (stem and all alternatives) on the same page.

Matching items can be thought of as a series of multiple-choice items with all stems using the same list of alternative responses. Matching items present a list of stems, often called *descriptors,* in the left column, and a slightly longer list of alternatives in the right column. Students are to select for each stem the most closely related or appropriate alternative. Matching items are effective in assessing students' ability to identify relationships between words, terms, or factors. Thus, they are most useful in measuring learning at the knowledge and comprehension levels. Matching items can require students to match terms or words with definitions, short questions with answers, symbols with proper names, descriptive phrases with other phrases, causes with effects, principles with situations in which they apply, and parts or pictorial units with names.

Matching items are less versatile than multiple-choice but more effective than true-false or short-answer items. They are easy to construct and score. Because students can complete them quickly, a large number of items can be used and, thus, more of the objectives assessed. The most significant disadvantages of matching items are related to the low level of thinking they require. Matching items encourage memorization and recall rather than understanding, and they tend to focus on trivial material.

As with other types of items, it is best to write matching items during the planning stage. As a general rule, a series of matching items should include between 10 and 12 stems dealing with a clearly related set of ideas or concepts. When items deal with obviously different topics, students can more easily guess the correct answer to any one stem because some alternatives could not apply. The stem should be the longer of the two-item parts, it should be numbered, and it should appear in the left column. Alternative responses should be shorter in length, lettered, and appear in the right column. The list of alternatives should contain about 25 percent (two or three) more items than the list of stems, and the instructions should specify whether alternatives can be used more than once. As with multiple-choice items, each alternative in the list should present a plausible answer to the stem. The entire series of matching items, including the stems and alternatives, should appear on a single page so that students need not go back and forth between pages. Lastly, clear instructions should be given about how to record answers. Generally, space should be provided so that students can record their answers in blanks to the left of each numbered stem. Figure 9.4 depicts an abbreviated series of both good and poor matching items.

True-false items ask students to indicate whether a statement is true or false. Because the response options are limited to one of two choices, these items are sometimes called *alternative choice.*

FIGURE 9.4   Examples of Poor and Good Matching Items

Poor Matching Series

For each numbered item on the left, write the letter of the most appropriate description from the column on the right.

_____ 1. Abraham Lincoln		a. A cemetery in Pennsylvania
_____ 2. Jefferson Davis		b. Where slaves were traded
_____ 3. Gettysburg		c. President of the Confederacy
_____ 4. John Wilkes Booth		d. President of the U.S.
_____ 5. Slave auction		e. Assassinated Lincoln

Good Matching Series

For each numbered description in the left column, write the letter that corresponds to the most appropriately described individual from the right column. Each individual may be described more than once.

_____ 1. President of the Confederacy		a. Abraham Lincoln
_____ 2. Assassinated Lincoln		b. John Wilkes Booth
_____ 3. Confederate General		c. Ulysses S. Grant
_____ 4. Killed at Bull Run		d. Robert E. Lee
_____ 5. Union General		e. Jefferson Davis
		f. James Madison

Alternative-choice items appear often in teacher-made tests. They are easy to construct and score, but they are not very reliable or versatile. They allow the teacher to assess whether students have learned large amounts of material, but they encourage guessing and memorization rather than understanding. Most items of this type are written at the knowledge level, in part because few high-level statements are definitively true or false.

When alternative-choice items are deemed the most effective way to evaluate students' knowledge- or recall-level learning, the guidelines in Figure 9.5 can improve their quality.

Alternative-choice items are efficient only when assessing student recall of large amounts of content. However, to make true-false items more versatile, some have suggested requiring students to correct false statements or to explain their answers. When these tasks are required, the item more closely resembles a completion or created response item and may push students beyond mere recall.

Completion items require students to supply missing words from a statement or write a short phrase that answers a question posed in a stem. These items may present statements with critical words or phrases deleted and symbolized by blanks, or they may ask simple questions. Although they do not present a list of alternative responses as other selected response items do, neither do they require students to create unique responses.

Completion items are particularly useful with young children who may be able to write but cannot easily create extended responses. Completion items are easier to construct than other forms of selected response items because they do not require you to develop plausible alternative responses. Like other selected response items, they require little response time and thus can be used to assess a large amount of content. Further, because responses are not provided, students don't guess as much. On the other hand, these items typically focus only on recall of specific names or facts. They are also difficult to score objectively. For example, a student may not have provided the expected response because she could not remember the specific

FIGURE 9.5   Guidelines for Writing Alternative-Choice Test Items

1. Write each item as a true statement, and then change some to make them false.

2. False statements should be false because of substantive information rather than trivialities.

3. Keep all items the same length (false items are often shorter than true).

4. Avoid direct quotes from the textbook or lecture notes. Quotation items are nearly always recall level.

5. Avoid using negative statements. Negative statements are more difficult to write clearly.

6. Be careful of specific determiners ("always," "never," and so on). Since few things are "always" or "never" true, a testwise student will guess "false." Likewise, avoid indefinites ("sometimes," "often," and so forth). Since most things happen only some or most of the time, testwise students will guess "true."

7. Limit each statement to one main idea or point. Including too much information in one item will only confuse students.

8. When possible, include the crucial information near the end of the statement to help make the stem clearer.

9. Be certain that each statement is genuinely true or false.

10. Include approximately an equal number of true and false items.

11. Avoid a pattern of responses (for example, alternating true and false).

---

term or name, but she did provide a description of the person whose name she could not remember. Is this a correct or an incorrect response?

Completion items are most appropriate for assessing young learners or knowledge-level instructional objectives. Figure 9.6 provides guidelines for writing effective completion items.

Packaging the Test   As noted earlier, the most effective assessments are planned early in the instructional process. Regardless of the type of test items used, it is wise to develop your test items either while planning (shortly after developing instructional objectives) or as you conduct instruction (to match the instructional methods and emphases). In developing a pencil-and-paper test, validity and reliability are primary considerations. You want to ensure that the test accurately measures the breadth, depth, and levels of students' learning. Thus, you should attempt to ensure validity—the closest possible match between your objectives or topical coverage and the assessment.

One way to improve validity is through the use of a **test blueprint.** A test blueprint is a matrix that depicts the relationship between instructional objectives or topics covered, cognitive levels, and items on a test. An example of a test blueprint appears

---

FIGURE 9.6   Guidelines for Writing Completion Items

1. Provide clear instructions regarding the use of synonyms, spelling, and so on.

2. Be certain that only one correct answer is possible.

3. Avoid using direct quotes from the textbook or class notes.

4. When including blanks, try to use no more than one. Multiple blanks in a statement make it less clear.

5. Require only a single word or brief, definitive phrase rather than an extended response.

6. Direct questions generally are clearer than incomplete statements.

7. Be certain each statement is factually correct.

8. Omit only key words or phrases, not trivial information.

9. When using blanks, place the blank at or near the end of the statement to make the statement clearer.

10. When the response is to be numeric, include in the statement the units in which the student is to express the response.

in Table 9.4. As you can see, the topics of instruction are listed in the left column. Across the top are each of the six levels of Bloom's taxonomy of cognitive objectives. The far-right column indicates the total number of test items for each objective, and the bottom row indicates the total number of test items at each cognitive level.

When building a test, you first determine the total number of items you wish to include and put this number in the bottom row of the far-right column. Then you determine how many items will address each topic and indicate this in the right column. This judgment should be based on the importance of the topic and on the emphasis you placed on it during instruction. For each topic, you then decide how many questions to ask at each cognitive level and indicate this in the appropriate columns. You can include some test items at cognitive levels *lower* than the instructional objective (because the higher levels require students to use lower-order skills), but it is not appropriate to include items that require higher levels of thinking than your instruction directly promoted. After completing the test blueprint, you "build" the test to include the number and types of items identified in the blueprint. If you have developed a number of potential test items as you planned or conducted instruction, you construct the test simply by selecting the best of these items.

In the example provided (Table 9.4), the teacher wishes to construct a 25-item test that assesses students' learning in five topical areas of a unit on dinosaurs. The blueprint indicates that the greatest instructional emphasis was placed on helping students learn the names of dinosaurs, because 10 items, or 40 percent, of the test, relate to this topic. Slightly less emphasis is placed on the causes of extinction (six items), while roughly equal emphasis is placed on physical characteristics, herbivores, and carnivores (three items each). The blueprint also suggests that students will be expected only to recall the names of dinosaurs, perhaps through true-false or completion items. But some higher-level thinking will be required of students on the other topics, probably through multiple-choice or matching items.

In addition to using the test blueprint, you can do several other things to improve the quality of your tests. Figure 9.7 lists all the suggestions.

Administering the Test   After constructing the test, you can improve the accuracy of your assessment by providing students with as much information as possible about the nature of the test and by following preset testing procedures. Students should know well in advance when a test will be administered, what material will be covered, what types of items will be included, and how the test will be scored. This allows them to better prepare. In addition, it is a good idea to establish a set of procedures for test taking and then to follow them consistently. These procedures would include information about what materials are required for tests, whether the teacher will answer questions during the test, what students are to do when they have completed the test, and so on. Establishing these procedures provides continuity for students and allows them to concentrate on the test rather than to have to remember a new set of expectations each time. Remember also to develop accommodations or modifications that may be necessary to allow each student the

9.5   Do you prefer to take created response or selected response tests? Why? How might this influence the way you test your own students?

TABLE 9.4	Test Blueprint for Unit on Dinosaurs						
Topic	**Recall**	**Comprehension**	**Application**	**Analysis**	**Synthesis**	**Evaluation**	**Totals**
Names of dinosaurs	10 (40%)						10 (40%)
Physical characteristics		3 (12%)					3 (12%)
Carnivores	1 (4%)		2 (8%)				3 (12%)
Herbivores	1 (4%)		2 (8%)				3 (12%)
Extinction	2 (8%)	3 (12%)	1 (4%)				6 (24%)
Totals	14 (56%)	6 (24%)	5 (20%)				25 (100%)

FIGURE 9.7 General Suggestions for Test Construction

1. Use a test blueprint to improve the validity of the test.

2. Write several more items than you will use. Then select the items that best fit your test blueprint.

3. Include some questions that all students can answer correctly.

4. Use only two or three item types in each test. Use only one type for young learners. Using several types of questions in a single test can be confusing to students.

5. Be certain to include clear and thorough instructions on the test. These should inform students about recording their answers, scoring, weighting of items, and so forth.

6. Organize all test items of similar type together. For example, keep multiple-choice items separate from completion items.

7. Properly space items to improve clarity. More space should be provided between items than between stems and responses. Created response items must allow sufficient space for students' answers.

8. Include as many items as possible to enhance reliability, but be realistic about the number of items students can complete. Remember that created response items take much longer to complete than selected response items.

9. Keep all parts of each item on the same page. In other words, ensure that each stem and its alternative responses appear on the same page.

10. Check to ensure that there is no predictable pattern of correct responses.

11. Provide space for pertinent information (name, date, course or course number, and so on).

12. *Proofread the test!* Check for clarity of directions, grammatical accuracy (especially among distractor alternatives), typographical errors, spelling, and format.

opportunity to accurately demonstrate her or his learning. Figure 9.8 lists several suggestions for administering classroom tests.

OBSERVATIONAL, PERFORMANCE, AND AUTHENTIC ASSESSMENT

Sometimes students' learning is not easily measured by pencil-and-paper tests. When the instructional objectives require students to produce a product, follow a set of procedures, or perform a physical task, the most effective form of assessment involves

FIGURE 9.8 Guidelines for Administering Classroom Tests

1. Establish test-taking procedures, teach them to students, and then follow them consistently. For example, students should know whether questions will be answered after they begin the test, what to do when they are finished with the test, and so on.

2. Allow sufficient time for all students to complete all parts of the test. Don't let time keep some students from doing as well as they could.

3. Organize the physical setting before students enter the room to begin the test.

4. Before handing out the test, be certain that all students have the necessary equipment or materials to complete the test.

5. Have any necessary accommodations or modifications prepared and in place prior to the beginning of the test.

6. Explain or review test procedures or rules (for example, what to do when finished with the test) before handing out the test.

7. Control distribution of the test so that no student receives the test much sooner than others. It is wise to have students wait to begin reading or working on the test until your signal.

8. Note corrections before students begin.

9. Avoid discussion of the test or items after students have begun. If you must provide additional information or guidance about the test or an item to any student, announce this information to all students.

10. Monitor test behavior throughout the testing period.

"Dad, I got an A+ on my science project!"

observing and *evaluating* the quality of their product, procedure, or performance. For example, an art teacher might evaluate the quality of students' projects, a speech teacher might assess students' ability to make speeches of various kinds, a foreign language teacher might evaluate students' ability to speak fluently in the language, a science teacher might evaluate how well students follow a set of procedures for conducting an experiment, or a language arts teacher might evaluate students' ability to write creatively.

Pencil-and-paper tests require learners to perform a *cognitive* task and then to record an answer that indicates the result. Performance assessments require students to demonstrate learning by *performing tasks* or *producing products* that the teacher can observe and evaluate. As a result, performance assessments are often believed to be more authentic or realistic than traditional forms of testing. In addition, such authentic assessment is often more formative in nature and, as a result, is more conducive to changes in instruction (Bol & Stephenson, 1998). Thus, many educators believe that such *authentic assessment* should replace many pencil-and-paper assessments (Haertel, 1999; Wiggins, 1998).

As with all forms of assessment, a primary concern in authentic assessment is the accuracy of the information gathered. Although teachers observe students' performances or products in informal ways throughout the learning process, such informal observations occur spontaneously. By contrast, to make authentic assessment or performance assessment most fair and useful, teachers carefully plan formal observation and evaluation based upon well-defined criteria, permitting the teacher to make accurate judgments about performances or products (Arter & McTighe, 2001; Wiggins, 1998). This provides greater validity and reliability. Conducting formal evaluation of student performances or products using written checklists, rating scales, or rubrics is a common way to increase the validity and reliability of performance assessment.

Checklists   A checklist is a written instrument that lists the specific elements deemed necessary for desirable performance. The teacher observes students' performance or products and then marks whether or not each element was present. The overall performance is judged according to the extent to which it included all necessary elements. For example, a music teacher might assess students on their ability to play three scales. An example of the checklist for this performance appears in Figure 9.9.

An advantage of checklists is that they can help the teacher and student focus on the most important aspects of a performance. Although the total task may be complex, the checklist can help the student see what things must be done to perform the task. Similarly, the checklist provides specific feedback about elements of the

FIGURE 9.9 Checklist for Scale Performance

Criterion	B♭	F	G
1. Correct notes	_____	_____	_____
2. Good tone quality	_____	_____	_____
3. Consistent rhythm and tempo	_____	_____	_____
4. Proper instrument position	_____	_____	_____
5. Proper posture	_____	_____	_____
6. Good breath control	_____	_____	_____

student's performance that are or are not present. Thus, the student and teacher know precisely what the student needs to improve.

The primary disadvantage of checklists is that the quality of each specific element is not evaluated. The checklist allows the teacher to record only whether the element was present, not how well the element was performed. For instance, in Figure 9.9, the teacher records whether the student used proper instrument position while playing each scale. However, although some students may have better instrument position than others, the checklist does not provide for differentiation or assessment of quality. Another difficulty in using checklists lies in making a judgment about the overall performance. Is each element on the checklist absolutely necessary for effective performance? If so, students must be expected to demonstrate every checklist element in the performance. In some cases, however, there are likely to be some elements that are desirable but not absolutely necessary. In these cases, how many of the elements must be demonstrated for a student's performance to be acceptable? These questions are difficult to address.

Rating Scales   A rating scale is much like a checklist in that it lists the specific elements of desirable performance. However, rating scales allow the teacher to make a judgment about the quality of each element. Rating scales assess not just whether an element was present, but also how well or accurately it was performed. As a result, rating scales possess the strengths of checklists with fewer of the disadvantages.

Three types of rating scales are commonly used in the classroom (see Figure 9.10). In *numeric* rating scales, a number indicates the quality of performance. A higher number generally reflects greater quality. *Graphic* scales require the observer to place a mark along a continuum indicating performance quality. *Descriptive* scales rate performance on a continuum that includes terms that describe various levels of quality.

Arriving at a grade or overall judgment about a student's performance is somewhat easier using rating scales than using checklists. The teacher makes such judgments by summarizing across the ratings of the specific elements. Typically, summarization produces a single number representing a measure of the overall quality of the performance. Numeric scales are particularly easy to summarize either by adding the item ratings or by computing the mean rating. Graphic and descriptive scales can be summarized numerically by assigning a number to each graphic or descriptive item rating and then proceeding as you would with numeric scale data. It is sometimes useful to summarize the student's performance more descriptively, particularly when graphic or descriptive scales are used. In such cases, the descriptors for each performance element can be combined into a single global scale and an overall rating assigned based upon total performance.

Rubrics   A rubric is a matrix or table that expands on the detail included in descriptive rating scales, the specificity of checklists, and the ease of synthesis of numeric rating scales. Rubrics can be designed as analytic or holistic. In *analytic* rubrics, each column represents a particular aspect of performance to be evaluated, and each row conveys descriptions of the characteristics of each element at varying levels of

FIGURE 9.10 Rating Scales for Scale Performance

Numeric Rating Scale
Circle the number representing the quality of the student's performance (1 = unsatisfactory, 2 = poor, 3 = average, 4 = good, 5 = excellent).

Criterion		Rating			
1. Student plays correct notes.	1	2	3	4	5
2. Student uses good tone quality.	1	2	3	4	5
3. Rhythm and tempo are consistent.	1	2	3	4	5
4. Proper instrument position is used.	1	2	3	4	5
5. Proper posture is evident.	1	2	3	4	5
6. Student uses good breath control.	1	2	3	4	5

Graphic Rating Scale
Place a check on each scale to represent the quality of the student's performance.

Criterion	Rating
1. Student plays correct notes.	Poor — Fair — Good — Superior
2. Student uses good tone quality.	Poor — Fair — Good — Superior
3. Rhythm and tempo are consistent.	Poor — Fair — Good — Superior
4. Proper instrument position is used.	Poor — Fair — Good — Superior
5. Proper posture is evident.	Poor — Fair — Good — Superior
6. Student uses good breath control.	Poor — Fair — Good — Superior

Descriptive Rating Scale

Criterion	Rating		
1. Student plays correct notes.	Some notes; some in tune	All notes; most in tune	All notes; all in tune
2. Good tone quality is used.	Unclear, fuzzy, soft	Clear, but soft and weak	Clear, strong, and loud

mastery. Usually, the rubric presents a numeric scale or score associated with performance at each level for each element (Wiggins, 1998).

Figure 9.11 depicts an analytic rubric for evaluating students' writing. The four columns indicate the four aspects of students' writing we wish to evaluate (grammar, spelling, punctuation, and capitalization). For each of these aspects of writing there are four rows, each describing a level of performance. Also, notice the numbers that appear at the top of the columns and to the left of the rows, indicating the total possible score for each aspect and the range of scores associated with varying performance levels within each row. On the basis of these numbers, we can see that the writing assignment is worth a total of 40 points and that each of the four elements is of equal value (that is, they each contribute one-fourth of a student's total score on this assignment). While this rubric allows for some teacher flexibility within each row by applying a range (for example, 8–10 for exemplary) at each level, these ranges are not necessary in a rubric.

An *holistic* rubric is also designed to guide students in developing or evaluating their work and to assist teachers in making their evaluations of student work more accurate. Like analytic rubrics, holistic rubrics contain descriptive language to establish the particular characteristics and levels of quality that are being evaluated. However, rather than scoring these elements independently or separately, as an analytic rubric does, an holistic rubric provides only a single score or judgment of the work as a whole.

Using a rubric, the teacher can more easily and more consistently assign scores to students' work. Importantly, students can also use the rubric to evaluate their own or others' work and to provide more meaningful feedback. The rubric helps

FIGURE 9.11 Rubric for Evaluating Students' Writing

	Grammar 10 points	Spelling 10 points	Punctuation 10 points	Capitalization 10 points
Exemplary 8–10 points	• All sentences are complete thoughts. • All verbs match their subjects. • All pronouns are used appropriately. • No conjunctions are used at the beginnings of sentences.	• Every word is spelled correctly. • Every word is written legibly.	• Each sentence ends with appropriate punctuation. • Commas are used appropriately throughout. • Apostrophes are used correctly to represent plural and singular possessives.	• Each sentence begins with a capital letter. • All proper nouns are capitalized.
Good 5–7 points	• All sentences are complete thoughts. • Most verbs match their subjects. • All pronouns are used appropriately. • Few conjunctions are used at the beginning of sentences.	• Most words are spelled correctly. • Every word is written legibly.	• Most sentences end with appropriate punctuation. • Commas are used appropriately throughout. • Apostrophes are used to represent most possessives.	• Most sentences begin with a capital letter. • Most proper nouns are capitalized.
Fair 2–4 points	• Some sentences are complete thoughts. • Some verbs match their subjects. • Some pronouns are used appropriately. • Some conjunctions are used at the beginnings of sentences.	• Most words are spelled correctly. • Most words are written legibly.	• Some sentences end with appropriate punctuation. • Some commas are used appropriately. • Few apostrophes are used to represent possessives.	• Some sentences begin with a capital letter. • Some proper nouns are capitalized.
Poor 0–1 points	• Few or no sentences are complete thoughts. • Few or no verbs match their subjects. OR • No attempt was made.	• Few words are spelled correctly. • Few words are written legibly. OR • No attempt was made.	• Few sentences end with appropriate punctuation. • Few commas are used appropriately. OR • No attempt was made.	• Few sentences begin with a capital letter. • No proper nouns are capitalized. OR • No attempt was made.

both the teacher and the student focus attention on the aspects of the writing considered most important.

Rating scales, checklists, and rubrics are effective ways to improve the accuracy of your assessment when judging students' performances, products, or projects (Ardovino, Hollingsworth, & Ybarra, 2000; Oosterhof, 2003). They are most accurate when they meet four conditions. First, the specific elements that constitute effective performance or an acceptable product must be identified, delineated, and made known to the learners. Second, each specific element must be observable and described thoroughly in clear terms. Third, the setting or context in which the performance or product will be judged must be specified. And fourth, performance is evaluated using predetermined scoring or rating procedures.

Portfolio Assessment Portfolio assessment is a particular type of performance assessment and is among popular alternatives to traditional testing (Daniels, 1999; Wiggins, 1998). Even advocates of alternative assessment acknowledge that the validity and reliability of portfolios can be problematic, but they claim well-designed portfolios offer an excellent and supportive approach to student assessment (Wiggins, 1998).

A *portfolio* is a collection of student work that is intended to demonstrate accomplishment. The individual pieces that are included can be selected to reflect a student's growth or development over time, competence level or ability in academic performances, or ability to analyze or evaluate one's own work (Wiggins, 1998). In portfolio assessment, the student and teacher identify several samples of work based upon the purpose of the portfolio. These samples can include a variety of products, including papers, projects, quizzes, homework, journals, and even tests. You might also choose to include video- or audiotapes of student performances. In addition to these samples of students' work, the portfolio might also include evaluations of the work by the student, by other students, and by the teacher. Thus, the portfolio is a collection of student work that provides detailed and descriptive information about how well the student is doing or how much she or he has improved.

Portfolio assessment goes beyond merely collecting students' work. As an assessment tool, portfolio assessment uses the collection of student work (the portfolio) as the medium for evaluating student performance. Like any performance assessment, it is critical that we clearly understand what the portfolio is intended to do, what kinds of work are most likely to help us evaluate the students' performance in meaningful ways and thus should be included, and on what basis we will make judgments about quality. For example, if we want to use portfolio assessment to help us make judgments about our students' ability to write effectively, we must be certain that the types of written work students include give each student the opportunity to demonstrate the range of skills we are expecting, that we have clearly established criteria with which to make our judgments fairly and consistently, and that students understand how and why the portfolio is to be used.

Grading and Assigning Grades

In most cases, the final step in our classroom assessment is assigning each student a grade. Grades represent a simple way to summarize students' performance or learning over time and across a variety of experiences. Thus, while assessment involves both summative and formative techniques, grading is typically a summative process. Ultimately, you must synthesize the information you have about a student's learning or progress, make a judgment about the quality of the progress, and assign a grade that you believe accurately and fairly represents this judgment.

Grading is an important, though often intimidating, part of teaching. Many teachers report anxiety and dread about determining and reporting students' grades (Airasian, 2005; Guskey & Bailey, 2001; Hasiotis 2006). Some of this anxiety is due to the importance parents, students, and school officials place on grades as the primary source of information about the student's progress. Assigning grades is also difficult because it forces teachers to move from the role of facilitator of learning to that of objective observer and judge (Marzano, 2000). Finally, grading is often intimidating to teachers because many teachers do not feel sufficiently prepared to meet this challenge (Green & Mantz, 2002; Jung & Guskey, 2010). (See Case 9.1.)

9.6 Why do you suppose some teachers dislike assigning grades? How do you feel about this aspect of your professional responsibilities?

In spite of the difficulty and anxiety associated with grading, grades are used for several reasons (Airasian, 2005; Marzano, 2000). *Administratively,* grades are used to make decisions about which classes students should take, how well they are progressing, and whether they should be advanced to the next grade or graduated. *Informationally,* grades tell parents, students, and school officials how well students are learning and progressing. For some students, grades serve a *motivational* purpose, pushing them to work harder. For all these reasons, it is a teacher's responsibility to select and implement a grading system that is accurate, fair, consistent, and supportable.

In selecting and implementing a grading system, four factors must be considered. First, what standards or objectives were you and your students focusing on? Second,

"My Test Must Have Been Bad"

Mr. Terry Collins had just finished grading his students' most recent essay exams for each of his four American History classes. His classes were large this year, from 32 in his third period class to 38 in his last period class, and each student had answered three essay questions. Terry was exhausted but relieved that the papers were finally done.

As he recorded grades in his online gradebook, he realized that the scores he had given his two best students were lower than he would have expected. In fact, even though both of these students routinely got As on their work in his classes, one had received a B and the other a B– on this exam. Even more surprising, several students who usually did only average work had scored better on the exam than these students. Terry believed that something must have been wrong with the questions themselves or with the way in which he had scored the exams.

Because these scores seemed so out of character, Terry decided that it wouldn't be fair to students to weight the scores on this exam as heavily as those on other exams for the term. His solution was to add five "bonus" points to every students' exam score. Doing this raised the scores of his two talented students to at least an A–, which he felt was more fair to them. For three other students, this meant that their scores were higher than the total number of points on the exam, but he felt that because they would get As anyway, this was not a problem.

INVESTIGATING AND SOLVING THE CASE

1. What other potential causes for the low scores of the two students did Terry fail to consider?
2. How would you have dealt with what appeared to be unusually low scores for these students?
3. What are some of the problems that Terry's solution might have created in terms of validity or fairness?

---

what assignments, performances, or projects should you consider in the grade? Third, what standard will you use to make judgments about the quality of the students' performance? And, fourth, how will you synthesize information from several assignments or sources into a single grade? Let's look at each of these factors.

WHAT SHOULD YOU CONSIDER WHEN ASSIGNING A GRADE?

The grade that you assign represents a summary of how well the student performed across several tasks or situations and using some established set of criteria. Jung and Guskey (2010) suggest that the most effective grading systems make clear distinctions between three types of criteria. *Product criteria* make judgments about what students know and can do at a particular point in time. *Process criteria* focus judgments on students' behavior and actions as they have progressed to their current level. *Progress criteria* focus on the extent to which the student has demonstrated growth or gain over time.

Your assignment of grades should be based on information from multiple sources that were intentionally selected and designed, perhaps as part of your assessment system. The more sources of information, the more accurate your "picture" of the student's progress will be. Common information sources include tests, quizzes, homework, performances, portfolios, and projects. By including information from several of these sources, you are better able to judge the quality or extent of a student's progress.

Some teachers also consider attendance records or informal observations of a student's behavior, attitude, participation, motivation, or effort. However, it is generally best to include in the grade only factors that directly reflect a student's achievement (Airasian, 2005; Marzano, 2000; Stiggins, 1997). When the grading system combines achievement with other less clearly defined factors, such as motivation or attitude, grades can become inconsistent and less informative. To address this problem, some grading systems assign each student multiple grades: one may reflect achievement, while a second is a judgment about motivational or behavioral factors, and a third might reflect growth. When only one grade can be assigned, it should indicate only the student's achievement. Information about other factors can be conveyed through written notes or conferences with the student or the student's parents.

While it is desirable to include information from as many sources as possible, teachers must be realistic about the number of assignments they can evaluate and record. Certainly it is realistic to include all test scores in the grade as well as scores from all major products, projects, or performances the students completed during the grading term. However, you may need to be selective about how many other assignments to include. For example, if you have daily quizzes or daily homework assignments, it may be unreasonable to include every quiz or homework score in the final grade. Each teacher must decide how many of these factors to consider in the students' final grades.

WHAT STANDARD SHOULD YOU USE?

As noted earlier, grading requires that you make judgments about the quality of students' progress or learning. The information obtained from the sources we have discussed does not tell you whether a student has performed well. You make that determination by comparing students' performance to some standard or criterion. The three most commonly used standards are (1) the performance of other students, (2) a predetermined fixed criterion of performance, or (3) each student's earlier performances.

Comparison with Other Students   You may recall from our explanation of test scores that when a given score is reported as a comparison with other students' scores, it is a *norm-referenced assessment.* We use the same term to describe grades that compare a student's performance with that of other students. When we talk of teachers who "grade on the curve," we mean that the teacher is using a norm-referenced grading system. In this system, the grade a particular student receives depends upon how well the other students in the class performed. If the student did better than most other students, the grade will be high; if the student did more poorly than most other students, the grade will be low.

Norm-referenced grading systems typically take one of two forms. In a *fixed percentage system,* the grading scale defines what percentages of the class will get particular grades. Generally, the scale is constructed so that most students get Cs, somewhat fewer get Bs and Ds, and the fewest number of students get As and Fs. For example, in the fixed percentage scale that follows, 10 percent of the students would receive an A, 10 percent an F, 20 percent a B, 20 percent a D, and 40 percent a C. Thus, using the sample test scores depicted in Figure 9.12, Bill would get an A; Mary and Joan a B; Karen, Kevin, Pam, and Paul would get Cs; Elizabeth and Kaya Ds; and Kip an F. This is true even though the difference between Bill and Kip is only 10 points and in spite of the fact that the highest score was only 85 out of 100.

Grade	Percentage
A	10%
B	20%
C	40%
D	20%
F	10%

As you can see, in this type of grading system, grades are only an indication of how well the student performed *compared with other students,* not of how high or low they scored. If all students performed well, those who performed even slightly less well would receive lower grades. Thus, an A on one assignment does not equal an A on another.

"I don't know why you're so surprised by his poor grades. Every day you asked him what he did at school, and every day he answered, 'Nothing.'"

FIGURE 9.12 Sample Raw Scores on a 100-Point Test

Student	Score
Bill	85
Mary	83
Joan	83
Karen	82
Kevin	82
Pam	81
Paul	78
Elizabeth	76
Kaya	76
Kip	75

More common is a *flexible distribution system.* In this system, students' grades are still based upon comparison with other students, but the percentages of students who will receive each grade are not predetermined. Instead, the percentages are adjusted to reflect situations where all students do well or all students do poorly. Unlike the fixed percentage scale, the flexible scale can be adjusted so that no students receive any particular grade. In the set of scores depicted in Figure 9.12, all the students performed at roughly the same level. None of them appears to have done particularly well, and none particularly poorly. You might elect to adjust the scale so that no students receive an A, D, or F. Thus, you might award Bs to students with scores from 81 to 85, and Cs to students with scores from 76 to 78.

Norm-referenced grading systems are commonly used. However, the effects of this form of grading are predominately negative, particularly for less able students. Norm-referenced grading reduces students' motivation, increases anxiety, promotes negative interactions among students, diminishes students' study habits, and reduces learning (Marzano, 2000). Additionally, grades based upon this system are difficult to interpret because they do not provide an accurate indication of subject mastery (Airasian, 2005). For these reasons, it is wise to avoid using this system.

Comparison with a Predetermined Criterion The most common method for reporting grades is on the basis of the extent to which a student has demonstrated mastery of specific state or local curriculum standards. These grading systems are *criterion-referenced* assessments. In this type of system, a student's grade in no way depends upon the performance of other students. Instead, the grade is based upon the extent to which the performance demonstrates mastery. Often, this means the proportion of points earned (for example, on a test or other assessment) out of the total number possible. If a student gets most of the possible points, the grade is high; if the student gets fewer of the possible points, the grade is lower. The teacher determines the proportions associated with particular grades in advance and compares each student's performance with this scale. A common criterion-referenced grading scale follows:

Percentage	Grade
92–100	A
84–91	B
76–83	C
65–75	D
00–64	F

Let's use the test scores in Figure 9.12 to see what grades we would assign using this criterion-referenced system. In this example, no students would receive an A, Bill would receive a B, most students would receive a C, and Kip would receive a D. As you can see, using a criterion-referenced scale, any student could receive *any* grade.

The criterion-referenced system is intended to measure students' learning against an objective criterion rather than against the performances of other students. Thus, grades assigned using this system are more likely to be accurate indicators of students' achievement (Airasian, 2005; Brookhart, 2004). A primary advantage of this system is that the meaning of particular grades is clearer. An A or "Met standard" represents a given level of performance regardless of the situation or the ability of other students in the class. Although determinations about the scale may be subjective, grades assigned using a criterion-referenced system are considered less subject to bias. For these reasons, the criterion-referenced system is generally the most appropriate system for assigning grades.

Comparison with the Student's Earlier Performances　Norm-referenced and criterion-referenced grading systems assign grades by comparing a student's performance with an external standard. However, these systems do not account for differences in students' abilities or background knowledge or growth. A student who has little aptitude or background in a subject is graded using the same standard as a student who finds the subject very easy or who is very experienced. Thus, some teachers believe that a **self-referenced grading system** that focuses on student growth and improvement is more desirable. In a self-referenced system, grades are determined by comparing a student's current performance with past performance. In other words, the grade is based upon individual improvement or growth. A student who improves a great deal will receive a high grade; a student who improves only slightly will receive a lower grade.

Self-referenced systems predetermine how much improvement is necessary for a student to receive a particular grade. As with criterion-referenced scales, differing amounts of improvement are associated with different grades. The scale below depicts a self-referenced scale for assigning grades based on improvement.

Points Improved	Grades
Perfect score	A
12 or more	A
9–11	B
4–8	C
1–3	D
No improvement or decline	F

Self-referenced scales typically include allowances for students who are already performing at high rates. This is done to avoid penalizing students for doing well. For example, a student who received 98 out of 100 on the previous performance could improve no more than 2 points, earning a D on the scale. However, in the scale, a student could still earn an A if he or she receives a perfect score on the current performance. In spite of this allowance, self-referenced scales are biased against students who do very well in early performances. It is more difficult to improve or maintain performance that is already nearly perfect than to improve very weak performance. Although self-referenced grading systems avoid the competition or rigidity of norm- and criterion-referenced systems, the grades assigned in self-referenced systems do not reflect the level of a student's mastery or ability in the subject. An A may mean near-perfect mastery or only limited mastery from a student who performed very poorly at first. In spite of its intuitive appeal, self-referenced grading

Try Activity 9.4

systems probably should be avoided in most circumstances. Table 9.5 compares the three types of grading systems.

HOW WILL ASSESSMENT INFORMATION BE SYNTHESIZED?

In assigning grades that represent an overall judgment about a student's performance, several types of performance (tests, quizzes, homework, projects, and so on) must eventually be combined into a single letter, number, or symbol. After determining which performances to grade, you must then determine how to grade each one. Finally, you must combine the grades from the selected performances and arrive at a single grade that reflects overall learning. A variety of computer programs are available that use information provided by the teacher to store and then synthesize individual student performances. However, because these programs require the teacher to determine how selected performances should be included in the final grade, it is important to understand the factors that must be considered.

As you prepare to synthesize selected performance scores, remember that the scores reflect different content, objectives, and levels of importance. Not all scores or grades are of equal value. For example, Figure 9.13 presents performance grades for five students. As you can see, the teacher recorded information about students' performance on two tests, two homework assignments, a quiz, and a project. If we were to look only at the grades, each would be considered of equal importance or weight. Bill's grade of A on the first test receives no more weight than Karen's A

9.7 Which grading system do you prefer as a student? Why? Which do you as a teacher believe is most desirable?

TABLE 9.5 Comparison of Norm-Referenced, Criterion-Referenced, and Self-Referenced Grading Systems

	Norm-Referenced System	Criterion-Referenced System	Self-Referenced System
What comparison is made?	Pupil to other pupils	Pupil to predefined criteria	Pupil to pupil's earlier performance
Method of comparison	Grading curve; percent of pupils who can get each grade	Standard of performance; scores pupils must achieve to get a given grade	Standard of improvement; amount of improvement pupils must exhibit to get a given grade
What the grade describes	Pupil's performance compared to others in the class	Pupil's percentage of mastery of course objectives	Pupil's improvement from earlier performance(s)
Availability of a particular grade	Limited by grading curve	No limit on grade availability	No limit on grade availability

FIGURE 9.13 Sample Term Grades (Numeric Conversion)

Student's Name	HMK 1	HMK 2	Quiz	Test 1	Test 2	Project
Adams, Bill	✓ (3)	+ (5)	B (4)	A (5)	A (5)	A (5)
Darby, Joan	✓ (3)	✓ (3)	B (4)	C (3)	B (4)	A (5)
Evans, Karen	+ (5)	✓ (3)	A (5)	B (4)	B (4)	B (4)
Stone, Elizabeth	+ (5)	✓ (3)	A (5)	B (4)	B (4)	A (5)
Thompson, Kaya	− (1)	✓ (3)	D (2)	C (3)	B (4)	C (3)

on the quiz. However, you probably want the test scores and project to carry more weight than the homework or quiz scores.

Synthesizing grades is easier if you establish a grading system that reports all grades in the same fashion, for example, as letters, scores, checks, or pluses. However, some teachers elect to use different symbols for different types of assignments. In Figure 9.13 homework grades are reported as checks, pluses, or minuses; while tests, quizzes, and projects are reported as letter grades. In this case, you must convert each of these different symbols to a single scale. You could do this by converting all symbols to numbers. Using the information in Figure 9.13, you could convert the homework grades to numbers by awarding 5 points for a plus, 3 for a check, and 1 for a minus. Similarly, you could convert letter grades by assigning 5 points for an A, 4 for a B, 3 for a C, 2 for a D, and 1 for an F. Now, all the information is in numeric form and can be synthesized mathematically, typically by computing the average of the scores. However, before doing so, you must decide how important each number or grade is in the overall summary. For example, the project is probably most important, the tests next, and the homework and quizzes less so.

Most teachers weight individual performance grades just prior to synthesizing them. To do this, they multiply each individual performance score by a weight that reflects its importance. Using the converted (numeric) information in Figure 9.13, each individual test score could be multiplied by 2 and the project score by 3. The resulting weighted numeric scores appear in Figure 9.14. You could now use these weighted or adjusted scores in your synthesis.

When all scores have been converted to the same, usually numeric, scale and weighted to reflect differing levels of importance, you are ready to synthesize them into a single grade.

To do this, add the weighted individual performance scores. Then divide this total by the *weighted* number of performances. In our example, the original number of performances was 5, but we multiplied some of these in order to weight them. The *weighted* number of performances is 10 because the tests each count as 2 performances and the project counts as 3.

Try Activity 9.5

Homework 1	= 1
Homework 2	= 1
Quiz	= 1
Test 1 ($\times$ 2)	= 2
Test 2 ($\times$ 2)	= 2
Project ($\times$ 3)	= 3
Weighted total	=10

FIGURE 9.14 Sample Term Grades as Weighted Numeric Scores

Student's Name	HMK 1	HMK 2	Quiz	Test 1	Test 2	Project	Average Grade
Adams, Bill	3	5	4	10	10	15	4.7-(A)
Darby, Joan	3	3	4	6	8	15	3.9-(B)
Evans, Karen	5	3	5	8	8	12	4.1-(B)
Stone, Elizabeth	5	3	5	8	8	15	4.4-(B)
Thompson, Kaya	1	3	2	6	8	9	2.9-(C)

Students' grades are determined by comparing their weighted averages to the 5-point scale we originally used to convert symbols and letters to numbers. Figure 9.14 depicts the weighted averages and grade for each of the five students.

Grading is an anxiety-producing but important part of teaching. It is often the final result of your overall assessment program. When well planned and accurately implemented, grading is a fair, accurate, and supportable process that can provide valid information about students' learning and performance.

Try Activity 9.6

TECHNOLOGY IN ASSESSMENT AND GRADING

As in nearly every other aspect of life today, computers and technology have come to be used more and more frequently by teachers in the process of assessing students, maintaining information, analyzing information, and computing grades. Undoubtedly, the use of word processing software for developing assessment materials, like tests or rubrics, has made the task of revising and improving these materials much easier and faster. Further, commercially available computer "gradebooks" make the task of synthesizing assessment information much easier and more reliable. However, the application of technology to assessment and grading can include a wide range of activities.

Hanna and Dettmer (2004) note 13 categories in which computer technology is used by teachers to enhance their assessment. In addition to uses like those mentioned above, Hanna and Dettmer specify such uses as developing personal test-bank files, using optical scanning and recording of tests, computer-based testing, and electronic portfolios. Across these areas, and despite the ease with which many available programs can be used, it remains important that we, as teachers, make wise decisions about the information that will be input. As the old adage about computing goes, "garbage in = garbage out."

Some Final Thoughts

An important part of effective teaching is assessing students' learning. Doing so helps teachers determine not only how well or how much students have learned, but also how effective their own instruction has been. Accurate evaluation requires that teachers gather valid, reliable information from diverse sources and then make judgments based on that information. Tests, both standardized and teacher-made, are the most recognized source of assessment information, but most teachers use a variety of other sources, both formal and informal. Their ultimate goal is to make fair, consistent, and valid judgments which give meaningful feedback to students, parents, themselves, and other education professionals.

CHAPTER SUMMARY

SUPPLEMENTAL RESOURCES

Go to the text's Online Learning Center at www.mhhe.com/cruickshank6e to access the chapter's **study tools** including web links, practice for Praxis™ case studies, and video clips.

- The process of collecting, synthesizing, and interpreting information to aid in decision making is called *assessment*. The process of describing students' performance in terms of a number or score is referred to as *measurement*. *Tests* are the most commonly used measurement instruments. The process of making a qualitative judgment (good or bad performance) based on assessment information is referred to as *evaluation*.

- The effectiveness of an assessment depends upon the sources used to gain information and the accuracy of the information. Formal sources of information such as tests, quizzes, homework, projects, or performances are more teacher-controlled and can be repeated as needed. Informal sources such as teacher observations of spontaneous student behavior; conversations with students, parents, or other

- teachers; or access to students' logs and diaries can also be valuable but are more prone to subjective bias and error.

- The accuracy of assessment information depends upon its validity and reliability. *Validity* is the term used to describe the degree to which a test or other data source measures what it is supposed to measure. A valid assessment of student learning (1) measures understanding or mastery of all the important content or skills that were taught and nothing more; (2) assesses them in the same ways and at the same levels as they were taught; and (3) maintains the same content emphasis as the instruction.

- *Reliability* refers to the consistency with which an assessment source, such as a test, yields nearly the same scores for anyone who might take the test repeatedly. The primary way to improve reliability is to obtain information from as many valid sources as possible. Although reliability is often difficult to assess, test manufacturers typically provide information about the reliability of their tests.

- Assessment can be conducted either during instruction or at the conclusion of instruction. Formative assessment is conducted during the instructional process and is used primarily to help improve student and teacher performance. Summative assessment is conducted at the conclusion of instruction and is used primarily to make final judgments about a student's learning. Effective teachers make use of both types of assessment to improve their teaching and make good instructional decisions.

- Standardized testing has become increasingly common in U.S. public schools in recent years, and the results of these tests are often used to make policy decisions at the national, state, and local levels. Standardized tests get their name because they are administered and scored in consistent, uniform ways. They typically control the materials students may use, limit the time they can take, provide the instructions, and control any other details believed to affect test performance. Although standardized tests are effective in measuring a wide range of learning, are scored objectively and fairly, and can be designed to assess higher-level thinking, their results are often misinterpreted and misused. Teachers can help their students perform better on standardized tests by giving them experience in taking similar kinds of tests and by offering suggestions about when to guess and how to manage time.

- The results of standardized tests are commonly reported in one or more of the following ways.
  1. Students' test scores can be reported as a raw score, in relation to the scores of other students, or in relation to some predetermined criterion or standard.
  2. Raw score is the number of items answered correctly. It tells us little about what or how much the student has learned.
  3. A criterion-referenced score compares the student's raw score with an established standard of mastery and provides detailed information about the specific objectives a student has mastered.
  4. A norm-referenced score compares the student's raw score with the performances of other students who took the test (usually reported as standard scores).

- Standardized test scores are reported in a variety of forms. Some test reports include students' raw or obtained scores. However, nearly all standardized tests report normal curve equivalent (NCE), percentile rank, stanine, and grade equivalent scores for students. In addition, many test publishers also provide score bands, ranges within which the most accurate measure of a student's performance would likely fall.

- The most common form of classroom assessment is developed by the teacher. When properly constructed, such assessments can be more cost-effective and valid than standardized or commercially produced tests because they reflect the instruction a teacher actually provided to a specific group of students rather than some national norm. Teacher-made pencil-and-paper tests use two types of test items: created response items and selected response items. Created response test items, which require students to compose an answer in their own words, are relatively easy to write. These items not only assess students' understanding but also their ability to communicate. However, they are also time-consuming to score and are difficult to score reliably and objectively. Restricted response items make the parameters (expected length and coverage) of students' answers explicit. Extended response items do not impose parameters and thus allow students to be more creative.

- Selected response items, which require students to select the most appropriate answer from a list of alternatives, are easier to score objectively and typically allow the tester to assess a greater range of content. However, these items require more time to write and often elicit only lower-level thinking. Selected response items include multiple-choice, matching, true-false, and completion items.

- Observational, performance, and authentic assessments require students to apply learning by performing physical tasks or producing concrete products for observation and evaluation. Because students are actually applying their learning to solving real problems, the term *authentic assessment* is often used to refer to this type of assessment.

- Formal observation and performance evaluation are most accurate when they are based upon well-defined criteria. Checklists, rating scales, and rubrics are the most common instruments teachers use to guide observational assessment. They each list the specific elements deemed necessary to desirable performance. While checklists allow the observer only to indicate whether or not an element was present, rating scales allow the observer to make a judgment about the quality of each element presented. Rubrics tend to expand and improve upon these by providing greater detail and description of performance levels.

- In portfolio assessment, samples of each student's work are collected to see progress or development over time. Portfolios might include tests, quizzes, papers, and other student projects, as well as evaluation of the products and portfolio by the teacher, the student, or the students' peers. A critical feature of portfolio assessment is the learner's involvement in collecting and evaluating the work samples.

- Grading is an attempt to summarize students' performance or learning across a variety of experiences and over an extended time period. In spite of the anxiety many teachers experience in assigning grades, the grades serve several important administrative, informational, and motivational purposes. Although grades should be based on as many different sources of information as possible, teachers should not become unrealistic about how many student performances they can include in their grading system.

- Although factors such as behavior or attitude can be considered when assigning grades, it is best to limit grades to students' academic achievement. When grades are based upon factors other than achievement, they are less informative. To overcome this limitation, some grading systems allow the teacher to assign each student a grade for achievement and a grade for behavior or attitude.

- Teachers can also assign grades by comparing students' performances to one another, to a fixed standard, or to previous performance. Norm-referenced grading systems compare each student's performance to the scores of other students.

  1. In a fixed percentage system, the percentage of students who will receive each grade is predetermined. Most students in this system get Cs.
  2. In a flexible distribution scale, the percentage of students who will receive each grade is adjusted to reflect situations where all students do well or all students do poorly.

3. Research has shown that norm-referenced grading systems promote several negative consequences, including competition, anxiety, and reduced learning.

- Criterion-referenced grading systems assign grades by comparing students' performance with a predetermined standard that shows how well each student has mastered the targeted objectives or content.

- Self-referenced grading systems compare each student's current performance with his or her previous performance. Many believe this system is more equitable for students of lower ability who fare poorly when compared to other students.

- Ultimately, teachers must synthesize several sources of information in order to assign a single grade that reflects students' overall performance. The process of synthesizing is easier if all grades are recorded in a similar fashion, for example, as letters or numbers. However, when different types of grades have been used, all must be converted to the same, usually numeric, scale.

- To develop an overall course grade, each assignment grade must be weighted to reflect its relative importance within the course.

- The most common way to synthesize assignment grades is to (1) convert them all to numbers, (2) compute the arithmetic mean or average, and (3) convert this numeric average into a letter grade.

KEY TERMS

Assessment, 304
Measurement, 304
Evaluation, 304
Triangulation, 305
Assessment system, 306
Validity, 307
Reliability coefficients, 308
Accommodations, 308
Modifications, 308
Formative assessment, 309
Summative assessment, 309
Standardized testing, 309

Test sophistication, 312
Norm-referenced, 312
Criterion-referenced, 313
Raw score, 313
Percentile rank (PR), 314
Normal curve equivalent (NCE) scores, 315
Stanine scores, 315
Grade equivalent (GE) scores, 315
Score band, 315
Selected response items, 316

Created response items, 316
Restricted response or extended response items, 318
Multiple-choice, 320
Stem, 320
Alternative responses, 320
Matching items, 322
True-false items, 322
Completion items, 323
Test blueprint, 324
Self-referenced grading system, 335

ISSUES AND PROBLEMS FOR DISCUSSION

ISSUE

1. "My school has been on academic probation for three years now. We lost about 20 percent of our students because we were forced by the state to give parents the option of transferring to another school in the district, and this past year we had to begin offering free afterschool tutoring to all students who were not working at grade level. If our students don't do better on the state's test this spring, the district will close our school and send teachers and students to other schools in the district next year. I feel like I'm doing everything I can, but a lot of my students come from poor families and they just never seem to do well enough to pass."

2. "Our district has implemented common assessments in each core subject at each grade level. Many of these are performance assessments that are scored using a rubric. When we compared scores on one of these recently, one teacher's scores were quite a bit higher for her students than those of anyone else. She says that

she spent a lot of time on this unit and that she isn't surprised by the difference in scores, but the rest of us worry that that she isn't using the rubric in the same ways we are. Since these scores are kept by the district, we're afraid it will look like our students don't do as well."

PROBLEMS Teachers made the following comments or described the following incidents. What do you think about each, or how would you deal with it?

Problem 1: "Notices were just sent home to families of students who had not passed the state-mandated testing this spring and who were going to have to go to summer school for remediation. I got a call this morning from a mother whose daughter failed the mathematics portion of the state test and is going to be required to take summer school. The mother is really, really angry because her daughter has made Bs and Cs in math all year long and she doesn't understand how she could not have passed the test. I looked at her test scores and she actually failed by a long way. Making it all worse, we only have three days left in the school year and the daughter is going to get a B− in math for the last grading period. Mom has scheduled a meeting with the principal and me after school today, and I'm pretty nervous about it."

Problem 2: "I told my students at the beginning of the year that each grading period they could drop their two lowest scores before I assigned period grades. Now, with two more units remaining in the grading period, several students realize that they can earn a good grade without doing anything for these last three weeks. I'm not sure what to do. These units are important, and I want them to be responsible for the material."

THEORY INTO ACTION: ACTIVITIES FOR PRACTICE AND YOUR PORTFOLIO

ACTIVITY 9.1: Interpreting Standard Test Scores Explain what each of the following scores would tell us about the student's performance.

1. A raw score of 21/25
2. A percentile rank of 32
3. A score band ranging from the 55th to 63rd percentiles
4. An NCE score of 37
5. A stanine score of 8
6. A grade equivalent score of 6.3

ACTIVITY 9.2: Writing Created Response Items Write a broad instructional objective from your subject area. Develop an extended response item that assesses students' mastery of the objective, and write a model response. Next, rewrite the item as a restricted response item using your model response as a guide.

ACTIVITY 9.3: Writing Selected Response Items Using the instructional objective you developed in Activity 9.2, write at least three selected response items that you could use to assess students' mastery of all or part of the objective. Now, write a single multiple-choice item that requires students to at least synthesize information related to the objective in order to answer.

ACTIVITY 9.4: Developing a Scoring Rubric
Identify a performance task that would allow you to assess students' mastery of some aspect of your subject area. Next, develop a set of procedures or guidelines that help students understand what they are to do, under what circumstances they

will do it, and how they will be evaluated. Finally, develop a detailed rubric by which students' performance of the task could be scored. Have a classmate read through your task guidelines and rubric to make sure they are clear.

ACTIVITY 9.5: Developing a Grading System
Develop a reasonable grading system for a course you are likely to teach. Include and justify a variety of sources of information, the way each source will be graded or scored, the weight you will apply to each, and the standard you will use to assign grades.

ACTIVITY 9.6: Synthesizing Assessment Information
Using the grading system you developed in Activity 9.4, randomly assign grades or scores for each assignment to 10 imaginary students. Based upon the system you have chosen, synthesize this information and assign a letter grade to each student. You should be able to clearly explain how and why each student is receiving the assigned grade.

REFERENCES

AERA (2004). *Position statement concerning high stakes testing in preK–12 education*. Available at www.aera.net/about/policy/stakes.htm (Accessed 11/19/04).

Airasian, P. (2005). *Classroom assessment*. Fourth Edition. New York: McGraw-Hill.

Ardovino, J., Hollingsworth, J., & Ybarra, S. (2000). *Multiple measures: Accurate ways to assess student achievement*. Thousand Oaks, CA: Corwin.

Arter, J., & McTighe, J. (2001). *Scoring rubrics in the classroom: Using performance criteria for assessing and improving student performance*. London: Corwin Press.

Au, W. W. (2009). High-stakes testing and discursive control: The triple bind for non-standard student identities. *Multicultural Perspectives, 11*(2), 65–71.

Baker, E. L. (2007). The end(s) of testing. *Educational Researcher, 36*(6) 309–317.

Bart, M. (2009, January 14). Rethinking multiple choice tests for assessing student learning. *Faculty Focus*. Retrieved from http://www.facultyfocus.com/articles/educational-assessment/rethinking-multiple-choice-for-assessing-student-learning/

Black, T., & William, D. (1998). Inside the black box: Raising standards through classroom assessment. *Phi Delta Kappan, 80*(2), 154–157.

Bol, L., & Stephenson, P. (1998). Influence of experience, grade level, and subject area on teachers' assessment practices. *Journal of Educational Research, 91*(6), 323–331.

Brookhart, S. (2004). *Grading*. Columbus, OH: Pearson.

Carr, J., & Harris, D. (2001). *Succeeding with standards: Linking curriculum, assessment, and action planning*. Washington, DC: Association for Supervision and Curriculum Development.

Cronbach, L. (1963). Evaluation for course improvement, *Teachers College Record, 64*(8), 231–248.

Daniels, V. (1999). The assessment maze: Making instructional decisions about alternative assessment for students. *Preventing School Failure, 43*(4), 171–178.

Eisner, E. (1999). The uses and limits of performance assessment. *Phi Delta Kappan, 80*(9), 658–660.

Green, S., & Mantz, M. (2002). *Classroom assessment practice: Examining impact on student learning*. Paper presented at the Annual Meeting of the American Educational Research Association. New Orleans, LA.

Guskey, T., & Bailey, J. (2001). *Developing grading and reporting systems for student learning*. London: Corwin Press.

Haertel, E. (1999). Performance assessment and education reform. *Phi Delta Kappan, 80*(9), 662–667.

Hanna, G., & Dettmer, P. (2004). *Assessment for effective teaching: Using context-adaptive planning*. Boston, MA: Pearson.

Harvard University Graduate School of Education (2002). *High-stakes testing: Where we've been and where we are*. Available at http://gseweb.harvard.edu/news/features/koretz03212002.html. (Accessed 11/19/04).

Hasiotis, D. (2006). *All in a day's work: What standing in the way of teacher effectiveness?* Unpublished research report. New York: Common Good.

International Reading Association (2004). *Position statement: High-stakes assessments in reading*. Available at www.reading.org/resources/issues/positions_high_stakes.html (Accessed 11/19/04).

Isaac, S., & Michael, W. (1997). *Handbook in research and evaluation*. (3rd ed.). San Diego, CA: Educational and Industrial Testing Services.

Jung, L. A., & Guskey, T. R. (2010, February). Grading exceptional learners. *Educational Leadership*, 31–35.

Koretz, D. (2002, October). No Child Left Behind?: A faculty response to President Bush's education bill.

HGSE News. Retrieved January 10, 2008, from www.gse.harvard.edu/news/features/koretz10012002.html

Laitsch, D. (2006). *Assessment, high stakes, and alternative visions: Appropriate use of the right tools to leverage improvement*. Unpublished research report. Tempe, AZ: Education Policy Research Unit, Arizona State University. (Accessed on June 7, 2007 at http://epsl.ase.edu/epru/documents/EPSL-0611-222-EPRU.pdf).

Marzano, R. (2000). *Transforming classroom grading*. Alexandria, VA: Association for Supervision and Curriculum Development.

McMillan, J. (2001). *Essential assessment concepts for teachers and administrators*. London: Corwin Press.

Mertler, C. (1999). Assessing student performance: A descriptive study of the classroom assessment practices of Ohio teachers. *Education, 120*(2), 285–297.

NCTM (2004). *Position statement on high-stakes testing*. Available at www.nctm.org/about/position_statements/highstakes.htm (Accessed 11/19/04).

Oosterhof, A. (2003). *Developing and using classroom assessments*. Third Edition. Upper Saddle River, NJ: Pearson.

Phelps, R. (2000). Estimating the cost of standardized student testing in the United States. *Journal of Education Finance, 25,* 343–380.

Popham, W. (2004). *Classroom assessment: What teachers need to know*. Boston, MA: Pearson.

Schmoker, M., & Marzano, R. (2003). Realizing the promise of standards-based education. In A. Ornstein et al. (Eds.), *Contemporary issues in curriculum*. Third edition. Boston, MA: Pearson.

Scriven, M. (1967). The methodology of evaluation. In R. W. Stake (Ed.), *Perspectives on curriculum evaluation. AERA Monograph Series on Curriculum Evaluation, no. 1* (pp. 39–83). Chicago: Rand McNally.

Smith, K. (2009, November). From test takers to test makers. *Educational Leadership,* 26–30.

Stanley, J. (1958, April). ABCs of test construction. *NEA Journal,* 224–229.

Stiggins, R. (1999). Are you assessment literate? *High School Magazine, 6*(5), 20–23.

Stiggins, R. J. (2000). *Classroom assessment: A history of neglect, a future of immense potential*. Paper presented at the Annual Meeting of the American Educational Research Association.

Stiggins, R. (2006). Assessment for learning: A key to motivation and achievement, *Phi Delta Kappa Edge, 2*(2), 1–19.

Walker-Wilson, L. (2002). *Better instruction through assessment: What your students are trying to tell you*. Larchmont, NY: Eye on Education.

Webb, N. (1999). *Alignment of science and mathematics standards and assessments in four states*. Research Monograph No. 18, National Institute for Science Education. Madison, Wisconsin: University of Wisconsin.

WestEd (2000). *The high stakes of high-stakes testing*. San Francisco, CA: WestEd.

Wiggins, G., (1998). *Educative assessment: Developing assessments to inform and improve student performance*. San Francisco, CA: Jossey-Bass.

Willis, S. (September, 1990). Transforming the test: Experts press for new forms of student assessment. *ASCD Update,* 3–6.

The Effective Teacher

PART THREE

3

The role of the classroom teacher is critical. The teacher is, after all, the point of contact between the educational system and the pupil: the impact of any educational program or innovation on the pupil operates through the pupil's teachers. Thus, maximizing teacher effectiveness is a major goal of education (Medley, 1986, p. 4).

In fact, Cruickshank and Haefele (2001) described 10 kinds of good teachers (see Table P3-1). Every teacher draws upon each of these areas, though we are all better in some than in others. As you progress in your teaching career you will develop qualities across the 10 kinds of good teaching. However, while all teachers make some difference in their students' lives, some teachers consistently have a greater and more positive influence than others. They seem to relate to students better and to be more successful in helping their students gain meaningfully from their instruction.

In *The Act of Teaching*, we have from the first edition chosen to focus our attention on what Cruickshank and Haefele call the *effective teacher*. As we prepare this most recent edition of the textbook, the extent to which teachers and principals are held directly accountable for producing measurable student learning is greater than ever. Beginning with *A Nation at Risk* in 1983, federal and state education policy has increasingly emphasized the use of standardized tests to make judgments about the quality of teachers and schools. Throughout the early part of this century, the No Child Left Behind Act (NCLB) dramatically increased the consequences of poor academic performance, not only for students but for teachers and schools.

At the time of this writing, the Obama administration is further reinforcing the principles of standards-based curriculum and the use of student achievement data as measurements of success. Through the largest single federal investment in education in history, Race to the Top,

TABLE P3-1 Good Teachers, Plural

Ideal teachers meet subjective standards set by school principals, supervisors, and education professors.

Analytic teachers use observation techniques (e.g., Flanders Interaction Analysis) to record the extent to which they are meeting their instructional intentions.

Effective teachers bring about higher student achievement.

Dutiful teachers perform their assigned teaching duties well.

Competent teachers pass tests (e.g., NBPTS, Praxis) that indicate they possess requisite teacher attributes.

Expert teachers have extensive and accessible professional knowledge and can do more in less time.

Reflective teachers examine the art and science of teaching to become more thoughtful and skillful practitioners.

Satisfying teachers please students, parents-caregivers, colleagues, and/or supervisors.

Diversity-responsive teachers are sensitive to the needs of learners who are different.

Respected teachers possess and demonstrate qualities regarded as virtues.

the U.S. Department of Education stipulates that measurable student learning is the primary criterion by which the quality of schools will be judged. This is not new, and it represents a continuation of principles implemented in earlier decades at the state level and through NCLB at the federal level. However, Race to the Top extends the use of measures of student learning by requiring that teacher evaluation and compensation be based largely on teachers' ability to produce student achievement growth, often referred to as "value-added."

There are many details to be negotiated as Race to the Top and other state and federal initiatives are developed and implemented. However, the formal expectation for educators and schools to demonstrate their impact on students' learning is likely to become more intense. As Elmore (2000) has noted, educators and policymakers "are still left with the problem of how to account for the public expenditures they are receiving" (p. 10). Thus, it is important for every teacher to understand and be able to use what research tells us about how to facilitate students' academic performance. It should be noted that research suggests that many of the skills and attributes that teachers use to promote students' learning also encourage the development of other valuable outcomes, like self-esteem, persistence, and self-confidence (Wayne & Youngs, 2003).

In this section of the text, The Effective Teacher, we examine the skills, attributes, and behaviors of the *effective teacher*. What exactly is an "effective" teacher? What makes one teacher more effective than another, and what can be done to improve effectiveness? The next five chapters are devoted to answering these questions. In Chapter 10, Personal Attributes and Characteristics of Effective Teachers, we describe research on teaching and then examine the personal attributes or characteristics associated with effective teachers. In Chapter 11, Professional Skills and Abilities of Effective Teachers, we focus on the professional skills effective teachers use to maximize their students' learning. In Chapter 12, Classroom Management Skills of Effective Teachers, we discuss the organizational and managerial strategies effective teachers use to maintain a positive learning environment. Chapter 13, Problem-Solving Skills of Effective Teachers, explains how effective teachers solve classroom problems. Finally, Chapter 14, Reflective Skills of Effective Teachers, describes how effective teachers consider and solve classroom problems or issues.

Personal Attributes and Characteristics of Effective Teachers

CHAPTER 10

Research on Teaching
    Defining Effective Teaching
    The Search for Effective Teachers
Effective Teachers: Personal Attributes and Characteristics
Motivating Personality
    Enthusiasm
    Warmth and Humor
    Credibility
Orientation Toward Success
    High Expectations for Success
    Encouraging and Supportive
Professional Demeanor
    Businesslike
    Goal-Oriented
    Serious
    Deliberate
    Organized
    Adaptable/Flexible
    Knowledgeable
Some Final Thoughts

Conversation Starters

What kind of teachers do our children need?

Part of the thrill of teaching is the awareness of knowing that our professional activity will have lifelong impacts for our students. However, the kind of teacher children need to fully reach their potential and to lead productive lives is often debated. Certainly we need teachers who focus their own effort and their students' attention on the work of schools: mastering academic content, nurturing appropriate values, and developing worthwhile skills. But we also need teachers who care about and understand children, who convey to their students that they are valued, and who make students feel safe.

How will you balance these two professional roles?

347

In this chapter we examine the personal attributes or characteristics of teachers whose instruction seems most successful. Our emphasis is on an examination of those personal attributes of a teacher that seem most closely connected to students' learning. Before discussing specific personal attributes, we will examine how researchers have studied effective teachers and defined effective teaching. Then, we will look at eight attributes characteristic of effective teachers; they are

1. Enthusiastic.
2. Warm and humorous.
3. Credible.
4. Holding high expectations for success.
5. Encouraging and supportive.
6. Businesslike.
7. Adaptable/flexible.
8. Knowledgeable.

Research on Teaching

To understand the importance of teachers' characteristics and the behaviors associated with effective teaching, it will be helpful if we first determine what the term *effective teaching* means and how effective teachers can be identified.

DEFINING EFFECTIVE TEACHING

10.1 Why do you think each of us has unique ideas about what good teaching is? What clues does Chapter 7, on instructional alternatives, offer?

As we noted earlier, there are many ways to define good teaching. Columnist William Raspberry (1993) probably expresses the feelings of many of us when he suggests that good teachers are caring; supportive; concerned about the welfare of students; knowledgeable about their subject; able to get along with parents, administrators and colleagues; and genuinely excited about what they do. However, despite the value of these characteristics, they overlook the fundamental fact that teachers are expected to help students learn. Cruickshank and Haefele refer to this type of good teacher as the *effective teacher.*

The effective teacher—one who is able to help students learn more in ways that can be measured—is reflected in the large number of state and federal accountability programs. High-stakes testing for student promotion or graduation and consideration of student performance on these tests in establishing salaries of teachers and administrators are increasingly common throughout the U.S. One of the broadest and most consequential programs focused on effective teaching was the federal No Child Left Behind Act (NCLB). Through NCLB, schools whose students consistently failed to perform at desired levels were subject to a range of penalties (see Highlight 10.1 for a description of NCLB). Although the Obama administration is likely to make major changes to this legislation, the focus on measuring the effectiveness of teachers and schools is likely to continue.

Clearly, teachers are now held accountable for their *effectiveness* in helping students learn content. But, what do teachers do that makes them more or less effective? This question has been the focus of research for many, many years. In fact, for over a century, educational researchers have attempted to identify effective teachers. Early research defined effective teachers as those who received high ratings from their superiors. This research attempted to link administrative ratings with such traits as teachers' buoyancy, cooperativeness, dependability, emotional stability, expressiveness, forcefulness, judgment, mental alertness, personal magnetism, physical drive, and ethical behavior.

Although this type of research continued until the mid-1960s, the results were discouraging. None of these personality traits were consistently tied to the rating

The No Child Left Behind Act of 2001, often referred to as NCLB, represented legislative reauthorization of the Elementary and Secondary Education Act of 1965. Through a variety of measures, No Child Left Behind specified that all children would be achieving at grade level by the year 2014. Unlike previous federal legislation, which tended to emphasize and support particular programs or approaches for dealing with disadvantaged students, NCLB directly tied federal aid for schools to students' academic performance and imposed specific requirements on states to deal with schools in which students consistently performed at low levels.

NCLB was complex and included a number of requirements and consequences for states, districts, and schools associated with student academic performance. Among these were increased standards for the preparation and assignment of teachers, greater state and district flexibility in using federal education funds, and an emphasis on "scientifically-based research." However, the aspects of the legislation that most directly impacted on teachers and schools were those associated with accountability.

In order to maintain federal aid, each state was required to ensure that every student made Adequate Yearly Progress (AYP) in reading and mathematics. This required that states establish levels of grade-appropriate proficiency in reading and mathematics, that all students in grades three through eight were tested annually in these subjects, and student performance was reported by schools and districts for all students and for those in particular subgroups of students (based on poverty, race, ethnicity, disability, and limited English proficiency). A school or district was considered to be "in need of improvement" when one or more student subgroups failed to meet the state-established proficiency level for two consecutive years. Schools deemed "in need of improvement" were subject to a series of corrective measures that range over time from special assistance and restructuring of staff to takeover by the state or management by private firms.

In addition to the school or district-wide consequences of failure to make Adequate Yearly Progress, No Child Left Behind also stipulated that individual families in these schools be allowed expanded choice of their children's schools. For a family whose children attended a school deemed "in need of improvement," they were to be allowed to select another school within their district that they believed might better serve their children. Further, if these children attended schools that received Title I federal education funding, federal funds could be used to secure additional or supplemental education services from either the public or private sectors.

Across its components, NCLB represented an extremely broad and direct federal involvement in education. The legislation has been the subject of substantial criticism from a range of educators since it was first introduced. The impact of these criticisms has already been seen as federal education officials have adapted some of the more stringent aspects of the legislation to allow greater flexibility for states and schools. Over time, it is reasonable to expect that additional adaptations will be made to NCLB. However, the focus of federal education policy on student academic performance is unlikely to change in the near term.

Source: See the U.S. Department of Education—No Child Left Behind and Council of Chief State School Officers websites for more information.

---

levels teachers received. Many scholars concluded at that point that little could be determined about what made teachers effective.

Fortunately, several events during the 1960s prompted valuable and productive research into the definition and nature of effective teaching. Among the most powerful catalysts for more productive research was the *Equality of Educational Opportunity* study (Coleman, Campbell, Wood, Weinfeld, & York, 1966). This study was commissioned by the United States Department of Health, Education, and Welfare to examine the differences between schooling opportunities and resultant learning outcomes for white and black children.

Coleman, the major investigator, and his colleagues found that students attending some schools did indeed achieve more than students attending others. However, when he investigated why this was true, he found that differences in pupils' achievement among schools was associated largely with one factor—the socioeconomic status (SES) of the pupils. What was even more surprising and

 Web Links
U.S. Department of Education—No Child Left Behind

Council of Chief State School Officers

disappointing to many educators was Coleman's finding that the usual factors thought to contribute to school achievement, such as class size, textbook quality, the school facility, and teachers' experience, had little impact on student learning. Reanalysis of Coleman's findings and numerous studies since (Chall, 2000; Hanushek, 1997; Walshaw & Anthony, 2008) continue to suggest that SES is clearly related to students' achievement.

Needless to say, educators were extremely disturbed by the news that most of students' school achievement was determined by their SES rather than the school they attended or the teachers they experienced. These reports prompted renewed interest in defining and describing effective teaching. Many educators reasoned that since schools and teachers seemed to have limited influence, it was important to learn how to make the most of that influence. Thus, educational researchers sought to identify the characteristics of teachers and schools that seemed to be making the most difference for their students. Thus was born a second and highly productive era of research on effective teaching. In this second era of research, researchers identified effective teachers not according to supervisor ratings but according to their ability to help students gain the most from instruction.

THE SEARCH FOR EFFECTIVE TEACHERS

10.2 How would you feel if you were told that you would be hired, fired, promoted, or receive salary increases based on your students' performance on a standardized test? Would it change your approach to teaching? If so, how?

Shortly after publication of the Coleman report, educators began to investigate teachers' behaviors and attributes that seemed linked to greater learning. Guided by the notion that students' learning was, in part, the result of these attributes and behaviors, educational investigators began identifying teachers who were consistently able to produce high levels of learning. Often, though not always, the researchers measured learning by performance on standardized achievement tests. Then the investigators observed these teachers to determine whether they possessed common characteristics or teaching behaviors that might explain their students' success. Thus, in this era, research considered a teacher who produced more learning than others teaching similar students to be an effective teacher.

Even though many of the original studies were done several years ago, research over the past five decades has continued to support and clarify teacher behaviors and attributes associated with greater student learning. Importantly, these behaviors also are linked to other desirable outcomes for students, such as increased satisfaction and better attitudes toward school, better self-concept, and higher graduation rates (Walberg & Paik, 2000; Wenglinsky, 2000). One of the most exciting things about these findings is that they are not just theory; they reflect what living, breathing teachers do. By being aware of these attributes and developing these skills, you can help your students be even more successful.

Effective Teachers: Personal Attributes and Characteristics

Although *teachers' personal attributes* are expressed through behavior, they are primarily personality traits that all individuals possess and exhibit to varying degrees. For example, some teachers naturally display greater enthusiasm than others through their speech and actions. This may be the result of greater enthusiasm for their work or simply differences in personality that limit or enhance their expression of enthusiasm. Some personal attributes, like enthusiasm or warmth, are difficult to acquire or to enhance because they are so firmly rooted in our personalities. Others, such as a professional businesslike demeanor, are somewhat easier to acquire and modify. By becoming more aware of personal attributes that research shows are common among successful teachers and by matching them against your own natural tendencies, you will be able to begin building your own unique teaching persona—one that will maximize your ability to make positive connections with your students.

The remainder of this chapter will deal with eight personal attributes identified by research as common among effective teachers. To guide our discussion, we have organized these attributes under three broad headings: motivating personality, orientation toward success, and professional demeanor. *Motivating personality* includes the attributes enthusiasm, variety, and warmth and humor. These attributes help get and keep students involved and interested in learning. *Orientation toward success* means teachers believe in their own and their students' abilities to be successful. Attributes like expecting success and being encouraging and supportive of students convey this orientation. *Professional demeanor* means that the teacher is focused on helping students learn. Effective teachers are professionally knowledgeable and businesslike; students see them as credible and worthy of trust. As you will see, these three groups of attributes are highly interrelated. For example, being prepared for class conveys confidence, builds credibility, makes the atmosphere of the classroom more businesslike, and enables teachers to more easily adapt their instruction to students' needs.

The following pages will examine these attributes in some depth. First, we will present a definition or description of each, followed by an examination of the research that supports its importance. Finally, we will discuss the specific behaviors that characterize each attribute. As you read these sections, remember that these attributes have been linked to increased student learning. Consider the extent to which you naturally possess and demonstrate each one and ways in which you might employ them more effectively with your students.

Motivating Personality

Effective teachers possess a motivating, stimulating personality. They seem to enjoy what they are doing, they are supportive of students, and they are believable and easy to trust (Brophy, n.d.; Grouws & Cebulla, 2000; Peart & Campbell, 1999; Young, Whitley, & Helton, 1998). In this section, we discuss three particular attributes that are characteristic of teachers with motivating personalities: enthusiasm, warmth and humor, and credibility.

ENTHUSIASM

One of the teacher attributes most closely linked to desirable student outcomes is enthusiasm. Enthusiastic teachers convey to students that they are confident and enjoy what they are doing, that they trust and respect students, and that the subject they teach is valuable and enjoyable (Ellis, 2001). Enthusiastic teaching helps students persist at tasks, motivates them, and leads to increased learning and satisfaction (Denight & Gall, 1989; Huebner 2010; Patrick, Hisley, & Kempler, 2000).

Although enthusiasm is difficult to define, Good and Brophy (2000) suggest that a teacher's enthusiasm has two important dimensions: interest and involvement with the subject matter, and vigor and physical dynamism. Enthusiastic teachers often are described as dynamic, stimulating, energetic, and expressive. Their behavior suggests they are committed to students and to their subject.

People convey enthusiasm through variety in speech, gestures, and facial expressions. As they teach, enthusiastic teachers move around the room, front to back as well as side to side. They are animated and gesture with their hands, arms, head, and shoulders to reinforce or emphasize their points. They make eye contact with all students, encourage all students to participate, and solicit and use input from all students. Enthusiastic teachers maintain a brisk lesson pace while allowing and adjusting for students' understanding. They promote interest by varying the speed, pitch, and inflection of their voices, and they use pauses to reinforce points and add variety. Their changes in facial expression (for example, eyes widening or narrowing, smiling or frowning) are frequent and positive and further reinforce what they say.

10.3 Do you think it would be better to feel enthusiastic but be unable to convey it to students, or to lack enthusiasm but be able to act enthusiastic? Why?

10.4 Is there something you may have to teach that you feel unenthusiastic about? How will you deal with it?

Try Activity 10.1

Maintaining such a dramatic, animated presence from 8:15 A.M. until 3:00 P.M. is a difficult, perhaps impossible task. Fortunately, constant enthusiasm is not necessary. In fact, like other factors, levels of animation are most effective when they vary. A teacher who never ceased moving, always using broad gestures and smiling, would soon become routine or even annoying. Nonetheless, remember this advice: While teachers often expect students to be interested in *what* they say, students more often react to *how enthusiastically* it is said (Denight & Gall, 1989).

Remember, you are only enthusiastic if your students perceive you to be. In other words, just feeling enthusiastic about your students and your subject does not ensure that your students will see you as enthusiastic. What behaviors do students perceive as teachers' enthusiasm? Table 10.1 presents teacher behaviors that students use to differentiate between enthusiastic and unenthusiastic teachers. Note that none of these behaviors alone conveys enthusiasm. Rather, they collectively lead students to perceive the teacher as enthusiastic.

WARMTH AND HUMOR

Whether you realize it or not, as the adult authority in the classroom, you will set the tone, define roles, establish parameters, and promote patterns of interpersonal relationship among your students. These characteristics are particularly important when working with minority students and those from poverty backgrounds (Quindlen, 2002). Teacher warmth and humor are important factors in promoting a supportive, relaxed, satisfying, and educationally productive environment for your students (McDermott & Rothenberg, 2000). By contributing to a safe and productive environment, warmth and humor indirectly promote learning. In Chapter 12 we will also see that a supportive classroom climate reduces students' misbehavior.

While most people watching various teachers could probably agree on whether they conveyed warmth and humor, it is difficult to explain precisely what constitutes warm behavior or a good sense of humor. However, the two attributes are related.

"If I smile for the yearbook picture, no one will recognize me."

TABLE 10.1 Teachers' Enthusiasm	
Enthusiastic Teachers . . .	**Unenthusiastic Teachers . . .**
• Appear confident and friendly	• Appear anxious or defensive
• Establish and convey the relevance of the subject to their students	• Are mechanistic, go through the motions without relating the lesson to the students' interests or needs
• Use broad, animated gestures to emphasize or reinforce points	• Often stand or sit in one spot throughout the lesson
• Are creative and varied in their instructional approach	• Use only one or two instructional alternatives
• Are engaged and dramatic when they teach	• Are disinterested and disengaged
• Maintain eye contact with all students	• Avoid eye contact with students
• Use varied pitch, volume, inflection, and pauses to make vocal delivery more interesting	• Speak in a monotone
• Are patient	• Are impatient
• Are insistent that students successfully complete tasks	• Give up quickly when students do not easily arrive at the correct response
• Are aware of and quickly deal with off-task behavior	• Ignore students' off-task behavior
• Maintain a quick lesson pace	• Use time inefficiently; stall
• Have a sense of humor; can laugh at themselves	• Are frequently critical
• Use movement to maintain interest and attention	• Seldom move from the front of the room

Source: Adapted from V. Carusso (1982). Teacher enthusiasm: Behaviors reported by teachers and students. Paper presented at the annual meeting of the American Educational Research Association. New York, NY.

Warmth　A teacher manifests warmth through positive, supportive interpersonal relationships with students (Goleman, 1998; Peart & Campbell, 1999). It is important that you allow students to get a sense of your personality. Students often say that good teachers "are real people." Positive classroom relationships are fostered when you are friendly, maintain a positive attitude, demonstrate interest in your students as individuals, appear to be open and willing to "work things out" with students, and work hard to help them succeed academically. On the other hand, you reduce warmth and injure classroom relationships when students perceive you as unfair, when you are overly judgmental or inflexible, or when you discourage student-teacher interactions.

Specifically, then, what can you do to convey warmth to your students? Many of the teacher behaviors that convey enthusiasm also convey warmth. **Figure 10.1** lists suggestions to help you promote a sense of warmth with your students.

Humor　An appropriate sense of humor is one of the characteristics students frequently note in the teachers they enjoy (Brophy, n.d.; McDermott & Rothenberg, 2000). These teachers make learning fun. Humor can defuse tension, communicate the teacher's security and confidence, promote trust, and reduce discipline problems.

Effective use of humor has both a spontaneous and a deliberate, or planned, dimension. We convey a sense of humor through our ability to laugh when something funny occurs. During the course of a typical school day, any number of humorous events or accidents occur. Don't be afraid to laugh at these things. You must especially learn to laugh at yourself. All teachers make mistakes. They trip over the cord to the computer and drop stacks of papers as they rush to hand them back. Laugh at these events! Keep them in perspective, and don't take yourself too seriously. On the other hand, avoid sarcasm or cynicism, and be extremely careful about teasing students. Sarcasm and cynicism often send a message of indifference, disinterest, or dislike. And, although some students may respond positively to teasing by the teacher, many may respond negatively by assuming the role of "class clown" or, perhaps more serious, by feeling hurt or embarrassed. Be yourself, be a real person, but remain aware that you set an example for acceptable classroom behavior that students will tend to follow.

While much classroom humor is spontaneous, effective use of humor in the classroom also has a deliberate dimension. Plan lessons that incorporate or point out amusing aspects of the topic. This should go beyond using cartoons and jokes to more substantive aspects of the lesson. For example, a middle school English teacher might use humor to initiate a unit on Edgar Allen Poe's work by humorously

10.5　Do you feel comfortable laughing at yourself in front of people? Why or why not?

FIGURE 10.1　Conveying Warmth

1. Greet students by name at the door. Comment on their personal achievements outside your classroom or other aspects of their personal lives.

2. Smile frequently.

3. Be yourself. Convey your personality, likes, dislikes, even opinions.

4. Use nonthreatening physical proximity to students. Moving closer to students can be used to convey a sense of trust and openness.

5. Encourage students to approach you and to be open with you. Keep most in-class interactions on academic topics, but express interest and willingness to talk with students about nonacademic concerns outside of class.

6. Draw out students' opinions, feelings, and ideas, and actively incorporate these into your instruction.

7. Provide remediation and time for all students to master the material and to be successful.

8. While conveying genuine interest, concern, and acceptance of all students, avoid becoming "one of the students" by lowering expectations or joining them socially. This is especially true for new teachers who may be close in age to their students.

drawing attention to his eccentric life and work. The teacher could appear in dark, drab clothes like those Poe might have worn, perhaps with a black plastic bird (a raven) on his shoulder. He could play the role of Poe, exaggerating demented or paranoid speech and mannerisms, to introduce Poe's work in the context of his life. The teacher might talk as Poe would have about the difficulties of his life and writing, introducing the works to be studied in class. The intentional, structured combination of humor and content would make the lesson more memorable and the teaching more effective.

Warmth and humor are means to desirable ends, not ends in themselves. Used in moderation, they help create a relaxed, comfortable, engaging environment in which students can learn. However, teachers who place too much emphasis on warmth and humor actually reduce learning (Chall, 2000). Thus, warmth and humor are best used naturally and sparingly.

CREDIBILITY

10.6 What factors do you use to determine the credibility of your teachers?

Effective teachers appear to students to be credible and worthy of trust (Good & Brophy, 2000; Thweatt & McCroskey, 1998). Once again, it is important to point out that your credibility exists in the eyes of the beholders, your students. Regardless of a teacher's knowledge, experience, education level, or position—all elements that might be expected to enhance your credibility—you are credible only when your students believe you are. In the early grades, teachers, as adult authority figures, have some degree of built-in believability with students. However, as students become more mature, they are less likely to assume that teachers are automatically credible. As university students, you continually make judgments about the credibility and trustworthiness of your instructors. These judgments determine, at least in part, the perceived effectiveness of each instructor.

10.7 Have you ever had a teacher who betrayed your trust? What happened? How did it make you feel toward the teacher?

What can you do to establish yourself as credible and trustworthy? Three elements seem important: your credentials, the messages you send to students, and your behavior (Thweatt & McCroskey, 1998). Your credentials are most likely to influence the perceptions of young students who are relatively knowledgeable about the subject or who are highly motivated to succeed. However, even under these conditions, your credentials are only helpful if students are aware of them. The content of the messages you deliver also impacts your credibility. When you are able to demonstrate to students how the topics you present are related to their interests and needs, they view you as more credible. For today's student, your ability to use technology to teach and to communicate are also important for credibility (Henderson, 2010). Most important, however, is your behavior. Credibility and trust are the result of being open, honest, and equitable in your dealings with students, and of openly soliciting and accepting students' comments or criticisms, of defining your expectations and the relevance of the subject, of communicating clearly, and of demonstrating interest and concern for your students' success. As you can see, credibility and trust must be earned.

Orientation Toward Success

Effective teachers are positive people. They generally believe in their students' abilities to learn and in their own ability to help students be successful (Elmore, 2000). Importantly, they seem able to communicate a positive attitude and to develop this in their students. Specifically, effective teachers have high expectations of success and are encouraging and supportive of students.

HIGH EXPECTATIONS FOR SUCCESS

Effective teachers hold high expectations of success for themselves and their students. They genuinely believe all students can master the content and that they themselves have the ability to help all students learn. It would appear that teachers' expectations

sources and materials (old textbooks, magazines, videotapes, computer programs, and so on). You should also be sure to give these students the attention they need in order to succeed. This attention should include both your own time and opportunities for group work and peer tutoring. When you devote time to helping students understand the material, you convey a positive message both about your expectations and about the importance of the material.

When most teachers think about expectations for success, they generally think of teachers' expectations for students. However, the most effective teachers also maintain high expectations for themselves as well. Their own high personal standards motivate them to be well-prepared for class, use class time efficiently, and provide substantive feedback to students. They exhibit thorough knowledge of their subject; convey confidence and calm; dress, act, and speak professionally; and intentionally work to improve their own professional ability.

Try Activity 10.2

As we have discussed, you will most often convey your expectations indirectly, through your actions rather than your words. How, then, can you convey high expectations to students? Table 10.2 contrasts the behaviors of teachers who hold high expectations of students with those of teachers who hold low expectations.

ENCOURAGING AND SUPPORTIVE

Effective teachers are encouraging and supportive of students, addressing students' needs to belong, to be liked, and to be successful (Hoy, Tarter, & Hoy, 2006). Ornstein and Lasley (2000) define teachers who are encouraging as those who respect and genuinely believe in students' abilities. They help students feel accepted as individuals, and they recognize effort and potential, not merely correct answers. Thus, encouragement relates to other important attributes like warmth,

10.10 Do you believe you can help all students learn? Explain.

TABLE 10.2 Teachers' Behaviors That Convey High or Low Expectations of Students and Themselves	
Teachers with High Expectations . . .	**Teachers with Low Expectations . . .**
• Clearly inform students of the lesson objectives	• Do not convey the objectives or convey unclear objectives
• Provide extended, organized, well-paced explanations	• Provide explanations that are incomplete and often unclear
• Clearly relate lesson content to student interests	• Make few attempts to relate lesson content to student interests
• Set reasonable standards and modify them frequently	• Set standards that are too high or low and are too rigid
• Plan for and provide remediation when necessary	• Do not provide remediation
• Maintain consistent discipline and task direction	• Do not maintain consistent discipline or task direction
• Solicit and incorporate input from students they instruct	• Discourage or ignore student input
• Frequently smile, nod, and maintain eye contact	• Convey less attention in academic situations
• Call upon all students frequently and equitably to respond	• Seldom and inequitably call on students to respond
• Use wait time to allow students to consider before responding	• Allow students little or no wait time as they attempt to respond
• Help students modify incorrect or inadequate responses	• Frequently provide praise for incorrect or inadequate responses
• Use criticism infrequently	• Frequently criticize students' performance
• Provide extensive, frequent, and specific feedback	• Provide infrequent and vague feedback
• Seldom interrupt students while they are working	• Often interrupt students while they are working

enthusiasm, and expectations for success. Through encouragement and support, you can help students meet your expectations for success even when they experience some difficulty along the way.

Encouragement is particularly important when students are most likely to experience reluctance and difficulty. This occurs in the early stages of learning a new task or concept, in low-achieving students, and for minority and female students (O'Halloran, 1995; Walshaw & Anthony, 2008; Weiss & Pasley, 2004). Encouragement can motivate students to attempt tasks they may be reluctant to start and to continue working when they are struggling or becoming frustrated.

How can you encourage students without being condescending? First, a classroom environment that is supportive, safe, and open will promote students' willingness to begin new or unfamiliar tasks. Students must feel that the tasks you assign are realistic and important, that you will help them succeed, and that they can approach you for assistance if needed. Figure 10.2 lists some ways to demonstrate your encouragement and support.

When students have begun a task but are becoming frustrated and are ready to give up, it is important to help them continue. Words of encouragement such as, "You can do it," "What you've done so far is good. What *could* we do next?" "I understand how frustrating this is, but I know that you can do it," "Let's try the next step together," "Don't give up, you're getting there," or "I *know* you can do it" indicate to students that you are aware of and sympathetic to their struggles but that you are confident they can work through the task successfully. It is important in this situation that you help the students successfully complete the next step in the process with as little direction as possible. Ask questions or point out factors that help the students discover what they need to do next rather than simply give the students the right answer. By helping students work through problems mostly on their own, you build their confidence.

10.11 Do you believe all students can be academically successful in your classroom? Why or why not?

Professional Demeanor

Attributes under this heading may be the easiest for you to modify. Effective teachers, while being motivating and positive, also establish and maintain a professional demeanor. They are businesslike and task-oriented, yet flexible and adaptable when necessary to help students be successful. They are knowledgeable not just of the subjects they teach, but also of **pedagogy** and students.

BUSINESSLIKE

A common characteristic of effective teachers is a task-oriented, businesslike classroom demeanor (Brophy, 1998; McDermott & Rothenberg, 2000; Meichenbaum & Biemiller, 1998; Schmoker & Marzano, 2003). When you first hear effective teachers described in this way, you may imagine a cold-hearted, unsmiling taskmaster who

---

FIGURE 10.2   How to Demonstrate Encouragement and Support for Your Students

1. Use positive comments about students' abilities rather than negative comments about their performance.
2. Be aware of and note improvement, not just perfection.
3. Help students learn to work through their own problems and evaluate their own work.
4. Be optimistic, positive, and cheerful.
5. Demonstrate good, active listening when students are speaking (focus your attention on the student, nod, and so on).
6. Provide several alternative routes to task completion and allow students some degree of choice.

uses an "iron hand" to force students to do nothing but work seriously on boring, quiet tasks. However, this is not the case at all. In fact, students often perceive businesslike teachers to exhibit greater warmth and concern than other teachers (Chall, 2000; Hoffman, 2001).

The business of the classroom is learning. A businesslike teacher is one who emphasizes and focuses classroom activities on tasks most likely to help students learn. He directs his own behavior and his students' behavior toward the successful and efficient attainment of meaningful, clearly defined learning outcomes. If the teacher does this, learning is likely to improve and the teacher can be considered successful—that is, effective. If the teacher spends too much energy and time on tasks or activities not likely to improve students' learning, the teacher will be unsuccessful.

An analogy may help demonstrate this idea. Imagine for a moment a young boy who has suffered life-threatening injuries in a serious automobile accident. His family accompanies him to the hospital. The physician meets the patient and his distraught family at the emergency room door. She acknowledges the family and immediately begins to determine the nature of the boy's condition. The family is directed to wait in the emergency room lobby, feeling anxious and alone. When the little boy's condition is stabilized, the physician briefly speaks to the child's family. She then instructs a nurse to stay with the family for a few minutes, excuses herself, and immediately begins treating another emergency admission. The physician's behavior toward the family seems somewhat cold, but she has saved the little boy's life.

Now let us assume for a moment that rather than beginning immediately to treat the young boy, the doctor, feeling tremendous sympathy for his family, spends several minutes consoling them. The physician instructs an aide to keep the child comfortable while she remains to talk with the boy's family, build rapport with them, and console them. After several minutes they feel somewhat better, and the physician leaves them to attend to the child. Unfortunately, during this time the little boy's condition has worsened. Although we might consider the physician a caring person, we would probably not consider her an effective physician.

Exaggerated though the analogy may be, it makes the point that the effective physician is the one who most effectively conducts the "business" of medicine. The best doctor would save lives *and* exhibit warmth and caring. However, we would expect a physician to focus on the primary business of the profession. Thus, sympathy and caring are important but not sufficient for effective doctoring . . . *or* for effective teaching.

There appear to be four aspects of businesslike teacher behavior. A businesslike teacher is goal-oriented, serious, deliberate, and organized.

GOAL-ORIENTED

Businesslike teachers focus their efforts on helping students achieve learning goals, often based on state and local standards. In the chapter on planning instruction, we discussed the importance of establishing the desired outcomes of instruction and of basing our instruction on these objectives. Businesslike teachers establish clear, realistic, specific objectives and communicate these to students. They plan and conduct instruction in ways that efficiently and systematically move students toward the objectives. They actively seek input from students about the reasonableness of the objectives and about problems the students may be having, and they use this information to modify their instruction when necessary. They optimize activities and time devoted directly to helping students reach the established goals and minimize approaches, comments, questions, or behaviors that are not directed toward the goals.

SERIOUS

Businesslike teachers value learning and model this to students through their words and actions. This does not mean that they do not use humor, but their humor is natural and without cynicism or sarcasm. These teachers convey seriousness of

10.12 How can you convey warmth and encouragement to students while also being businesslike?

10.13 Are you naturally a goal-oriented person? If so, how would you use this trait in your classroom? If not, how might you monitor yourself to get better at this in your classroom?

purpose through earnest and genuine expressions indicating the value of the tasks at hand, reasonable expectations, guidance in task execution, and efficient use of time. The teacher treats the subject seriously, maintains a professional and confident image, and uses appropriate verbal and nonverbal behaviors.

DELIBERATE

Also important is a businesslike teacher's ability to establish and maintain a sense of purpose throughout each lesson. Careful planning of instruction allows such teachers to be concise, thorough, and exact in conducting instruction. Businesslike teachers organize instructional activities or tasks in logical sequences, including a clear introduction, presentation, and closure. This type of teacher deliberately conducts instruction in ways that devote equal attention to all students.

Although deliberateness requires systematic planning and implementation of instruction directed toward specific goals, it does not mean that the teacher is inflexible. When the teacher becomes aware that students do not understand or that the planned instructional activities are not working effectively, the activities are adapted. Teachers must adapt as quickly as possible, but not without careful consideration of the learning objectives. In other words, they might ask why the planned activity is not helping students reach the goals, what alternative activities might help, and which alternative can immediately be implemented? Even when teachers deviate from planned instruction, they should remain focused on the original learning goals.

ORGANIZED

Businesslike teachers organize the classroom and instruction based upon the established goals. Furniture, resources, materials, equipment, and activities are organized to minimize disruptions. Teachers use available personnel, such as aides or parent volunteers, to promote desirable learning outcomes rather than to reduce their workload. Even classroom management and discipline procedures are intended to promote the established goals.

Generally, then, a businesslike teacher is openly focused upon the business of promoting students' learning. Guided by clearly established goals and objectives, the teacher plans for, implements, and adapts whatever instruction will most efficiently help students reach learning objectives. Although many distractions may arise, the teacher minimizes activities or time not directed toward reaching the objectives. Remember that this businesslike focus can be maintained without sacrificing genuine warmth and caring for students. Table 10.3 contrasts the behaviors of teachers who are businesslike with those of teachers who are not.

ADAPTABLE/FLEXIBLE

A supervising teacher once told her student teacher, "No matter what you plan for, something else will happen." Teaching may not be quite that unpredictable, but certainly the most effective teachers are prepared for and able to adapt to a variety of circumstances (Heritage, Kim, Vendlinski, & Herman 2009; McDermott & Rothenberg, 2000). As you have probably noticed from your years of experience as a student, an effective teacher must be flexible and adaptable.

In the next chapter, we will discuss the importance of systematically building variety into your instruction and instructional activities. However, for now, let us focus on the ability to react appropriately and relatively quickly to changing classroom circumstances.

Flexibility and adaptability in this sense requires that you be *aware* of the need for change and be *able* to adapt to those changes. As you work with students, you must consciously monitor the effectiveness of the activities you and your students

10.14 Do you feel you can be flexible and adaptable when you teach? How could thorough planning help make you *more* flexible during the lesson?

TABLE 10.3　Teachers' Businesslike and Nonbusinesslike Behavior

Businesslike Teachers . . .	Nonbusinesslike Teachers . . .
• Establish clear academic goals and objectives	• Fail to establish academic learning goals
• Communicate the goals and objectives to students	• Do not communicate the goals and objectives to students
• Plan lessons directed at helping students reach the objectives	• Do not plan sufficiently or direct instruction toward objectives
• Seek input from students about the reasonableness of goals	• Disregard or fail to solicit students' input about the reasonableness of goals
• Emphasize activities and time devoted to academics	• Emphasize nonacademic activities and use time inefficiently
• Treat the subject seriously and respectfully	• Are sarcastic or make light of the subject
• Maintain a professional image	• Seem to be "one of the kids"
• Involve all students in the instructional activities	• Neglect some students while focusing mainly on good students
• Organize the room and equipment to minimize disruptions	• Fail to carefully organize the physical setting
• Use aides or volunteers to provide additional academic attention for students	• Use aides or volunteers primarily to deal with administrative tasks

are engaged in. Through a variety of verbal and nonverbal cues, you can ascertain, or "read," the need for adapting or flexing. Nonverbally, students may appear puzzled, confused, frustrated, or bored. Verbally, they may appear unable or unwilling to respond accurately to your questions, to complete assigned tasks, or to ask meaningful questions. In each case, you must first be aware that a problem exists and then be willing to adapt your goals and instruction as needed. In short, you should avoid a tendency to stick with your lesson plan if it is not working. Next, you must determine potential alternatives that will help you reach the established objectives, select an alternative, and implement it, often in a matter of a few seconds. Chapter 11 will present specific skills that will help you read and adapt your instruction.

Figure 10.3 notes characteristics of the flexible, adaptable teacher. Notice that some of these suggestions are directed at planning developmentally appropriate instruction to reduce the need for subsequent changes. Still, as noted in Chapter 6 on planning, even the best plans often need some adjustments to fit individual students and classes.

The ability to recognize the need for change and to adapt instruction accordingly is probably the most difficult task for beginning teachers. However, with time and a conscious attempt to develop a varied teaching repertoire, you can improve your ability to adapt your instructional approach, even during the lesson!

FIGURE 10.3　Enhancing Flexibility and Adaptability

1. Clearly define goals, objectives, or intentions and make them known to students.

2. When planning instruction, consider students' characteristics, attributes, preferences, and interests.

3. Plan instruction that is interesting to the students and is directed toward the intended learning outcomes.

4. While implementing the planned instruction, systematically and continually monitor students' verbal and nonverbal behavior to determine the appropriateness of your instruction (for example, puzzled or frustrated looks, inability to answer questions or to complete tasks, and student questions or comments that indicate a lack of understanding).

5. When the planned instruction appears to be inappropriate, attempt to determine why and to identify alternatives.

6. When necessary, implement an alternative and again monitor its effectiveness.

The relationship between what teachers know and how much their students learn has always been debated. Many proposals to reform education have emphasized the importance of teachers' content knowledge. In fact, some proposals have suggested that content knowledge and supervised apprenticeships may be all that are necessary for the preparation of teachers.

Wayne and Youngs (2003) conducted an extensive review of research on this topic in order to attempt to address the issue. They identified 21 studies that met their criteria for inclusion and that examined the relationship between measures of teachers' college preparation and their students' learning. Among their findings they report:

- In general, there are positive relationships between some measures of teachers' preparation and their students' learning.
- Teachers' ratings by their college instructors during their preservice preparation are associated with higher student learning.
- Teachers' scores on licensure and other certification tests are positively associated with greater student learning.
- With the exception of mathematics, the number or type of degrees held by the teacher, amount or type of coursework, or whether or not the teacher was certified are not found to be related to students' learning.

Source: Wayne & Youngs (2003).

"For that you went to college?"

10.15 Which of the three types of knowledge Porter and Brophy (1988) defined do you feel you most possess? Which do you feel you least possess?

KNOWLEDGEABLE

Brief mention should be made of the role of subject matter knowledge in effective teaching. Knowledge of the subjects they teach seems intuitively to be an important attribute of effective teachers. Certainly it is reasonable to believe that good teachers know their subjects well. However, there is little agreement regarding *how much* knowledge a teacher must have to teach well (Glass, 2002). We have all experienced teachers who were obviously quite knowledgeable about the subject they taught but unable to help students learn it, as well as teachers who effectively facilitate learning with substantial but not overly extensive knowledge of the subject.

Although this attribute has been frequently studied, research findings are mixed on the direct importance of teachers' subject knowledge in promoting students' learning (Rivkin, Hanushek, & Kain, 2000; Wayne & Youngs, 2003; Wenglinsky, 2000). However, research seems consistently to indicate that knowledge of the subject is important but not sufficient for effective teaching (Graeber, 1999; Heritage, Kim, Vendlinski, & Herman, 2009; Peart & Campbell, 1999; Public Agenda, 2004). The most effective teachers combine content knowledge with knowledge of teaching (that is, pedagogy) and with knowledge of students. Collectively, this unique professional wisdom is sometimes referred to as pedagogical content knowledge (Shulman, 1986). Knowledge of the subject and of learners helps make the teacher more aware of the misconceptions students are likely to have or to develop about the subject. Knowledge of pedagogy and of learners allows the teacher to select and implement instructional alternatives that can best address students' misconceptions. Thus, effective teachers are knowledgeable about their subject and how best to help the individual students in their classes come to understand it appropriately (see **Spotlight on Research 10.1**).

Some Final Thoughts

In this chapter we have discussed eight teacher attributes or characteristics that help students learn more effectively. We learned that effective teachers are positive and confident about their own and their students' success, are supportive and encouraging of students, and are professional in their demeanor. We also saw that these teachers primarily convey these attributes through behavior and that speech is sometimes at odds with how a teacher really feels. It is important to remember that these attributes and the specific behaviors that seem to communicate them to students are interrelated. When one is modified, the other also changes. Though teachers' attributes are difficult to change, teachers should be aware of how various attributes impact on students and should work to enhance those that have positive effects.

CHAPTER SUMMARY

- There are many types of good teaching, each of which has particular strengths or advantages. As a result, it is difficult to define exactly what constitutes the most effective type of teaching. In fact, while research on effective teaching has been conducted for over a century, until the last half of the twentieth century, many believed that effective teaching could not be described or taught.

- Civil rights developments during the 1960s prompted an era of research on effective teaching. The *Equality of Educational Opportunity* study, by Coleman and his associates, spurred increased interest in identifying and describing effective teaching. Coleman found that teaching and schools made little difference in students' achievement. The greatest single contributor to academic success was the student's SES and family background.

- Researchers in this era began to define effective teachers as those who helped their students learn more than other teachers with similar students. These researchers observed the classrooms and classroom behaviors of effective teachers and found that they shared several common attributes and abilities that tended to increase students' learning and satisfaction with teaching and to enhance students' self-concept.

- Personal attributes are primarily inherent personality traits that everyone possesses and exhibits to varying degrees. Attributes are expressed through verbal and nonverbal behavior, and some, like warmth, are difficult to change because they are so much a part of our personalities. Other attributes, such as businesslike demeanor or flexibility, can be modified through awareness.

- Effective teachers' personal attributes can be organized around three broad characteristics: motivating personality, orientation toward success, and professional demeanor.

- At least three specific attributes are associated with teachers who possess a motivating personality: enthusiasm for their students and their subject matter, warmth and humor, and credibility and trustworthiness.

- Teachers' enthusiasm promotes learning by helping to motivate students, by keeping them persistent at tasks, and by helping them feel more satisfied with the teaching. Enthusiastic teachers vary their voices, gestures, and expressions; they move around the room from front to back and side to side; and they maintain a quick lesson pace involving high levels of interaction with students.

- Warmth and humor seem mostly to influence students' learning indirectly by promoting an environment that makes students feel free and motivated to participate. Teachers convey warmth by being "real" people, by demonstrating concern for students' success, and by being open. Humor can be spontaneous or planned. Teachers should be able to laugh at themselves and their mistakes; they should avoid using sarcasm or teasing students. However, warmth and humor, if overemphasized, actually reduce classroom learning, so they are best used naturally and sparingly.

- Credibility and trustworthiness create a relaxed, supportive environment where students trust the teacher to help them succeed. Teachers develop credibility and trust through open, honest teacher-student interaction, not through a teacher's position or credentials; and these qualities exist only if students perceive them.

- Effective teachers are positive people, oriented toward and optimistic about their own and their students' success. Specifically, effective teachers have high expectations for success and are encouraging and supportive of students. They believe in their own ability to help every student learn successfully. Expectations appear to influence teachers' behavior toward students, which in turn affects learning. When teachers expect certain students to fail, they tend to reduce the amount of time and attention devoted to those students, thus increasing the likelihood the students will be unsuccessful. Even more critical than inaccurate initial expectations is the failure to modify those expectations when necessary.

- A good rule of thumb for teachers is to ensure that every student is successful most of the time. Students with low academic self-concepts should be successful almost every time, until their confidence improves. Students with strong academic self-concepts should also be successful most of the time, but not quite so often. Remediation, that is, providing reteaching when a student doesn't master the content, is a good way to convey high expectations and to promote success.

- Effective teachers are encouraging and supportive of students and convey a sense of genuine respect for them and for their individual abilities. Encouragement and support are most important when students are reluctant to begin new tasks or when they experience difficulty and frustration. Teachers demonstrate encouragement and support by avoiding negative comments, by noting improvement—not just perfection—and by helping students reach realistic goals.

- Effective teachers exhibit a professional but flexible demeanor in the classroom. Businesslike behavior; the ability to be flexible and adaptable when necessary; and thorough understanding of subject, pedagogy, and learners all enhance professional demeanor.

- Businesslike teachers focus on promoting learning in a variety of ways. They direct classroom activities toward helping students reach the established goals and objectives. They establish the importance and seriousness of the subject and of the goals and convey this importance to students. Instruction and instructional activities are deliberate and carefully planned to allow the teacher to be concise, thorough, and efficient. The classroom and classroom activities are organized to help students reach the desired goals.

- A professional demeanor also includes the ability to calmly and effectively adapt to changing classroom circumstances. This includes the ability to "read" what is happening in the classroom: the level of students' understanding and motivation, changes in the classroom environment, and problems with instruction. When problems arise, teachers must "flex" or adapt their instruction to more effectively reach the established goals.

- Teachers who exhibit a professional demeanor are also knowledgeable of their subject, pedagogy, and students. Knowledge of the subject is most useful when it is integrated with knowledge of pedagogy and knowledge of learners. Only then can teachers select, plan, and implement the most effective instruction.

KEY TERMS

Self-fulfilling prophecy, 355　　　Sustained expectations, 355　　　Pedagogy, 358

PART THREE
The Effective Teacher
364

www.mhhe.com/cruickshank6e

ISSUES

1. How can you balance a high level of challenge for students while also being supportive and helping them develop confidence?

2. The standards that your students are required to master do not reflect what you believe to be the most important things for your students to learn. How will you deal with this? What are the possible consequences for you and for your students?

PROBLEMS   Teachers commented on the following incidents or problems. Would you have anticipated these situations? What would you do in each situation?

Problem 1:   "A student returned with a cast on his lower left arm. Giving him the usual sympathy and understanding was not enough. During class he did many things to draw attention to himself. I was quite irritated at the end of class and had to struggle with myself to keep my temper and irritation under control. He is a very immature student and this demonstrated his immaturity again."

Problem 2:   "I have one little boy who copies even when he knows the correct answer. I'm trying to build his self-confidence; but, he continues to look on others' papers. When I move him away from the rest of the class, his work is very good. He seems to need reassurance by looking at others' work."

THEORY INTO ACTION: ACTIVITIES FOR PRACTICE AND YOUR PORTFOLIO

ACTIVITY 10.1: Observing Enthusiasm in the Classroom   During your next visit to a classroom, take the time to observe the teacher's level of enthusiasm. Use the behaviors in Table 10.1 as a guide. Did the teacher demonstrate these behaviors? How enthusiastic did the teacher appear to you? If you have an opportunity, ask students how enthusiastic they believe their teacher to be. Do their perceptions match your own? Why or why not?

ACTIVITY 10.2: Maintaining Positive Expectations   If you have friends who are currently student teaching or are in their first year of teaching, arrange to speak with them about maintaining positive expectations. What do they find most difficult? Do they feel they have high expectations for all students? Do they seem to hold high expectations for themselves? What do they do to avoid becoming pessimistic or lowering their expectations too far? What advice might they offer to help you maintain positive expectations?

REFERENCES

Brophy, J. (n.d.). *Teaching*. Brussels: International Bureau of Education.

Brophy, J. (1998). *Motivating students to learn*. Boston: McGraw-Hill.

Chall, J. (2000). *The academic achievement challenge: What really works in the classroom?* New York: Guilford Press.

Coleman, J., Campbell, J., Wood, A., Weinfeld, F., & York, R. (1966). *Equality of educational opportunity*. Washington, DC: U.S. Department of Health, Education, and Welfare, Office of Education.

Cruickshank, D., & Haefele, D. (2001). Good teachers, plural. *Educational Leadership, 58*(5), 26–30.

Denight, J., & Gall, M. (1989). *Effects of enthusiasm training on teachers and students at the high school level*. Paper presented at the annual meeting of the American Educational Research Association. San Francisco, CA.

Ellis, A. (2001). *Teaching, learning, and assessment together: The reflective classroom*. Larchmont, NY: Eye on Education.

Elmore, R. (2000). *Building a new structure for school leadership*.

Washington, DC: The Albert Shanker Institute.

Gill, S., & Reynolds, A. (1999). Educational expectations and school achievement of urban African American children. *Journal of School Psychology, 37,* 403–424.

Glass, G. (2002). Teacher characteristics. In A. Molnar (Ed.), *School reform proposals: The research evidence* (EPSL–0201–101–EPRU). Tempe: Arizona State University, Education Policy Research Unit.

Goleman, D. (1998). *Working with emotional intelligence.* London: Bloomsbury.

Good, T., & Brophy, J. (2000). *Looking in classrooms.* Eighth Edition. New York: Addison-Wesley Longman.

Graeber, A. (1999). Forms of knowing mathematics: What preservice teachers should learn. *Educational Studies in Mathematics, 38,* 189–208.

Grouws, D., & Cebulla, K. (2000). *Improving student achievement in mathematics.* Brussels: International Bureau of Education.

Hanushek, E. (1997). Assessing the effects of school resources on student performance: An update. *Educational Evaluation and Policy Analysis, 19,* 141–164.

Henderson, J. (2010). Forming assessment through technology. *Education Update, 52*(2), 1, 4–5.

Heritage, M., Kim, J., Vendlinski, T., & Herman, J. (2009). From evidence to action: A seamless process in formative assessment? *Educational Measurement and Practice, 28*(3), 24–31.

Hoffman, N. (2001, March 28). Toughness and caring. *Education Week, 20*(28), 40, 42.

Hoy, W. K., Tarter, C. J., & Hoy, A. W. (2006). Academic optimism of schools: A force for student achievement. *American Educational Research Journal, 43*(3), 425–446.

Huebner, T. A. (2010, February). Differentiated Instruction. *Educational Leadership,* 79–81.

Kaufman, K., & Aloma, R. (1997). Orchestrating classroom complexity: Interviews with inner city educators. *The High School Journal, 80,* 218–226.

Kolb, K., & Jussim, L. (1994). Teacher expectations and underachieving gifted students. *Roper Review, 17,* 26–30.

McDermott, P., & Rothenberg, J. (2000). *The characteristics of effective teachers in high poverty schools: Triangulating our data.* Paper presented at the annual meeting of the American Educational Research Association. New Orleans, LA. (ERIC Document Reproduction Service ED 442 887). Educational Research Association, New Orleans.

Medley, D. (1986). Teacher effectiveness. In H. Mitzel (Ed.), *The encyclopedia of educational research* (pp. 1894–1903). New York: Macmillan.

Meichenbaum, D., & Biemiller, A. (1998). *Nurturing independent learners: Helping students take charge of their learning.* Cambridge, MA: Brookline.

Obiakor, F. (1999). Teacher expectations of minority exceptional learners: Impact on "accuracy" of self-concepts. *Exceptional Children, 66*(1), 39–53.

O'Halloran, C. (1995). Mexican American female students who were successful in high school science courses. *Equity and Excellence in Education, 28,* 57–64.

Ornstein, A., & Lasley, T. (2000). *Strategies for effective teaching.* New York: McGraw-Hill.

Patrick, B., Hisley, J., & Kempler, T. (2000). "What's everyone so excited about?" The effects of teacher enthusiasm on student intrinsic motivation and vitality. *The Journal of Experimental Education, 68,* 217–236.

Peart, N., & Campbell, F. (1999). At-risk students' perceptions of teacher effectiveness. *Journal for a Just and Caring Education, 5,* 269–283.

Public Agenda. (2004). *A sense of calling: Who teaches and why.* Available at www.publicagenda.org/specials/ teachers/teachers.htm (Accessed on 11/19/04).

Quindlen, T. (2002). Reaching minority students: Strategies for closing the achievement gap. *Education Update, 44*(5), 1, 6–8.

Raspberry, W. (1993, September 27). Children will learn if they're properly taught. *Columbus Dispatch,* p. 9.

Rivkin, S., Hanushek, E., & Kain, J. (2000). *Teachers, schools and academic achievement.* Unpublished research report.

Schmoker, M., & Marzano, R. (2003). Reaching the promise of standards-based education. In A. Ornstein and others (Eds.), *Contemporary issues in curriculum.* Third Edition. Boston, MA: Pearson.

Shulman, L. (1986). Those who understand: A conception of teacher knowledge. *American Educator, 10,* 9–15, 43–44.

Thweatt, K., & McCroskey, J. (1998). The impact of teacher immediacy and misbehaviors on teacher credibility. *Communication Education, 47,* 348–358.

Walberg, H. (1991). Productive teaching and instruction: Assessing the knowledge base. *Phi Delta Kappan, 71*(6), 470–478.

Walberg, H., & Paik, S. (2000). *Effective educational practices.* Brussels: International Bureau of Education.

Walshaw, M., & Anthony, G. (2008). The teacher's role in classroom discourse: A review of recent research into mathematics classrooms. *Review of Educational Research, 78*(3), 516–552.

Wayne, A., & Youngs, P. (2003). Teacher characteristics and student achievement gain: A review. *Review of Educational Research, 73*(1), 89–122.

Weiss, I., and Pasley, J. (2004). What is high-quality instruction? *Educational Leadership, 61*(4), 24–28.

Wenglinsky, H. (2000). *How teaching matters: Bringing the classroom back into discussion of teacher quality.* Princeton, NJ: Educational Testing Service.

Wolfe, P. (1998). Revisiting effective teaching. *Educational Leadership, 53*(3), 61–64.

Young, B., Whitley, M., & Helton, C. (1998). *Students' perceptions of characteristics of effective teachers.* Paper presented at the annual meeting of the American Educational Research Association. New Orleans, LA. (ERIC Document Reproduction Services ED 426 962).

Professional Skills and Abilities of Effective Teachers

Focusing and Engaging Students' Attention
- Establishing Set
- Using Variety

Using Instructional Time Efficiently
- Optimizing Time

Conducting Interactive Instruction
- Using Questions
- Providing Clear Instruction
- Monitoring Students' Progress
- Providing Feedback and Reinforcement

Some Final Thoughts

Conversation Starters

What is it that teachers really must know or be able to do?

Teachers assume a wide range of roles, from nurturer, and even caretaker, to context expert and academic leader. Some people believe that good teachers are "born" not made. They possess the natural ability to teach and primarily just need help to master the content they will teach. Other people believe that good teachers are, in fact, "made" not born. In this view, good teachers must be helped to develop not only their understanding of content, but also develop their professional skill in helping students learn.
Do you believe teaching is something that is learned or something that is a result of natural ability?

The *personal* attributes of teachers discussed in Chapter 10 are vital in establishing an environment that supports students and encourages them to learn. Although teachers can modify these attributes through awareness and determination, they are often difficult to change substantially. In contrast, teachers can acquire and use a variety of *professional* skills that research shows can have a profound impact on students' learning. In fact, these skills may be among the most critical factors in determining a teacher's effectiveness (Rosenshine, 2002; Wang, Haertel, & Walberg, 1993–94; Wenglinsky, 2000). Across these skills, effective teachers engage students in meaningful interactions with content and ideas (Walshaw & Anthony, 2008). Importantly, they are of the greatest benefit to students with special needs (Banikowski, 1999; Winter, 2001). This chapter focuses on the following seven teaching skills, all important in helping students learn:

1. Establishing set.
2. Using variety.
3. Optimizing instructional time.
4. Using questions.
5. Providing clear instruction.
6. Monitoring students' progress.
7. Providing feedback and reinforcement.

To guide our discussion of these teaching skills, we will organize them into four broad areas of classroom instruction. First, we will discuss how teachers engage and maintain students' attention; second, how teachers optimize instructional time; third, how teachers go about interactive instruction; and fourth, how teachers use feedback and reinforcement.

As you read this chapter, remember that these are skills that effective teachers use consistently and proficiently. The better you are at incorporating them into your teaching style, the more your students will gain from instruction since research has linked them to students' learning. Further, it has been shown that any teacher can learn to use these skills more effectively to increase learning in his or her classroom (Joyce & Weil, 2000; Meichenbaum & Biemiller, 1998; Walberg & Paik, 2000). Consequently, we have incorporated practice exercises that will help you acquire these behaviors into Units 1, 2, and 3 of the Practice Teaching Manual.

Focusing and Engaging Students' Attention

Effective teachers are able to get students' attention at the beginning of a lesson and to hold their attention throughout the lesson (Lunenburg, 1998). To accomplish this, teachers must be skilled in establishing set (providing a context for the lesson and instruction) and in using variety.

ESTABLISHING SET

Students learn more when teachers begin their lessons by **establishing set,** that is, by providing a context for the lesson and the instruction. This is variously referred to as **set induction,** providing advance organizers, or lesson entry. Whatever the label, you may recall from Chapter 6 that a teacher uses this skill at the beginning of an instructional segment and generally intends it to do one or more of the following:

1. Capture students' attention or provide them with a framework for the lesson.
2. Help students relate new material or information to what they have previously learned.
3. Determine students' entry-level knowledge prior to introducing new content.

When our purpose is to engage students' attention in a new instructional activity, we are establishing **orientation set.** This type of set may vary from a few minutes at the beginning of a single lesson to a full class period at the beginning of a new unit of study. When the primary goal of a set is to help students understand how the new material relates to what they learned previously, we are using **transition set.** This might include a brief review of previous lessons, a discussion to focus students on what they already know about a topic, or a single sentence that shows the relationship to previous material (that is, "Yesterday we learned two causes of the Civil War. Would someone name them for me?" . . . "Today we'll learn two more reasons . . ."). We use **evaluative set** to establish what students already know about a topic. The teacher might ask students questions about the topic or give a short quiz or pretest to make judgments about how best to teach the lesson.

The notion of establishing set before introducing students to new material relates closely to cognitivist approaches to learning and to what is often called "brain-based teaching" (Banikowski, 1999; Lock & Prigge, 2002), particularly reception learning (see Chapter 4). Researchers note that learning increases and becomes more efficient when new material is related to previously learned material. Meichenbaum and Biemiller (1998) and Brophy (n.d.) both report that students' achievement and long-term retention is greater when teachers deliberately establish set. Generally, establishing set seems to help students learn more by focusing their attention, improving their ability to self-monitor their understanding, and increasing the likelihood that new information is linked to existing knowledge or schema (Eby, 2001).

To be effective, information or activities used to establish set must be (1) at a higher level of abstraction or broader in scope than the content to be learned in order to encompass the specific concepts of the lesson and (2) related directly to students' prior knowledge (Rosenshine, 2002). Thus, the early minutes of a lesson may be used to promote several goals and are critical to establishing a tone and instructional pattern that allow students to learn.

The beginning of the lesson should accomplish four goals. First, it should be more than a simple, dry introduction, an overview of the material, or a statement like "Open your math books to page 79." Establishing an effective set requires a configuration of several general characteristics (Arends, 2001). First, the topic should be introduced in a way that makes it novel, interesting, or relevant to students. Often teachers begin a lesson by performing a demonstration with a surprising or unexpected outcome in order to stimulate curiosity about the topic of the lesson. For example, one of the authors can still remember the beginning of a lesson on how we learn. The teacher began by having each of two mice begin at one end of a maze at the other end of which was cheese. One mouse (which had worked in the maze several times before) ran immediately through the maze to the cheese and the second (which had never been in the maze) tried various paths without success.

A second goal of the beginning of the lesson is to establish an interactive climate and tone. It is important that teachers immediately involve students in responding to questions or in thinking and talking about the topic. In the previous example, the teacher asked her students what they thought would happen before placing each mouse in the maze. After students witnessed each mouse, the teacher asked them to describe what they saw, what they believed explained what they had seen, and gradually guided them to the topic of the lesson.

A third objective of the lesson introduction is to direct students' attention to important aspects of the content or communicate the lesson objectives. Sometimes teachers will put a topical outline on the board to highlight important aspects of the lesson. Sometimes they use a demonstration, note the major reasons behind the events in the demonstration, and explain how the lesson will focus on these reasons. For example, after asking students to explain what they observed and to speculate about its causes, the teacher might use students' responses to note that

11.1 What is the most memorable lesson entry you've ever experienced? Did it help you learn more?

Try Activities 11.1 and 11.2

one of the mice had learned how to get to the cheese, that several learning theorists had attempted to explain how this took place, and that by the end of the class they would be able to explain the behavior of the mice from two of these.

Fourth, the entry should link today's lesson with what students already know. "Remember yesterday we talked about . . . ? How might that explain what we saw in the demonstration? . . . Well, today we're going to talk about . . ." Figure 11.1 presents some specific ways of establishing an effective set for your lessons.

USING VARIETY

11.2 What kinds of variety have your own teachers used? How effective were they for you?

Educators have long known that variety increases students' motivation and learning, and researchers have supported this belief. Effective teachers use variety in virtually every aspect of their classroom behavior including nonverbal behavior, instructional approaches, classroom organization, questioning, types of assessment, and gestures. Differentiated instruction is an approach that is specifically intended to allow variety and student-based strategies (Huebner, 2010; see Highlight 11.1). We have all experienced teachers who taught every lesson for the entire year in the same way, with the same activities arranged in the same order, using the same, monotonous voice patterns and few gestures. This lack of variety in instructional patterns can negatively affect learning. Imagine a teacher (perhaps you can even remember one) who responded to every student's answer or contribution with, "Exactly!" The first few times you witness a student receiving this response, it seems enthusiastic and encouraging. However, eventually, even if every student's answer is correct, "Exactly!" is no longer effective and may, in fact, become annoying. The same holds true for many other teacher behaviors.

Rosenshine and Furst (1971) identified variety as the second strongest predictor of teachers' effectiveness. However, variety probably does not directly improve learning. Instead, it has a positive effect on students' attention and involvement, thus making students more receptive to learning. Teachers who use variety not only prevent students from becoming bored, they also keep them interested and actively involved in the lesson. A teacher's knack for variety fosters interest and engagement on the part of students; this in turn leads to increased learning (Hidi & Harackiewicz, 2000; Doyle, 1986).

Researchers have identified specific ways teachers can introduce variety into their classrooms (Ellis, 2001; Huebner, 2010; Lock & Prigge, 2002). Their suggestions can be organized into two major categories: variation in instructional activities and materials, and variation in teacher-student interaction.

Instructional Activities and Materials   As we discussed earlier, one way of establishing effective set in your lessons is to pique students' interest by presenting novel situations or problems. In addition, teachers can vary their instruction by using a variety of instructional alternatives: cooperative learning, discussion, seat work,

---

FIGURE 11.1   Establishing Set

1. Review previous material.
2. Ask a curiosity-provoking question or pique students' interest by using a unique problem or scenario.
3. Provide an overview of the major points or topics of the lesson.
4. Demonstrate the concept or ideas of the lesson.
5. Provide a visual schema that depicts the relationship of various aspects or concepts of the lesson.
6. Provide a problem (orally, visually, or by some other means) to engage students in processing the concepts to be learned.
7. Convey interest, enthusiasm, and curiosity about the topic.
8. Inform students of the objectives or goals of the lesson, and point out its relevance to their lives.

Classrooms today are strongly guided by state curriculum standards for what students should know and be able to do. These standards are intended to ensure that every student is given the opportunity to master a set of agreed upon academic content and cognitive skills. However, despite this focus on common curriculum for all students, schools include a more diverse population of students than at any time in our country's history. This puts today's teachers in an interesting situation as they try to balance the expectation that all students will master similar standards against the reality that each student has her or his own interests, abilities, and approaches to learning. As Hill (2009) notes, "We know that not all students are alike, yet they are often faced with participating in a 'one-size-fits-all' lesson despite their individual knowledge and skills."

Differentiated instruction is intended to provide a framework through which teachers can provide instruction that is tailored to individual student needs and abilities, while also focusing on common and accepted standards or objectives for all students.

According to Hall (2002), differentiated instruction is

> . . . a process to approach teaching and learning for all students of differing abilities in the same class. The intent is to maximize each student's growth and individual success by meeting each student where he or she is . . . rather than expecting students to modify themselves for the curriculum.

A key to the effectiveness of differentiated instruction is a set of clearly defined learning objectives or standards. It is critical that you know exactly what it is your students are going to be expected to know or be able to do upon completion of the instruction. State or district standards, as well as teacher developed learning objectives, provide a good basis for differentiated instruction. All instructional activities are designed to ensure students successfully master these standards, but that they are allowed to reach mastery in one of several different ways.

Differentiation can take place in a number of ways. Tomlinson and Strickland (2005) suggest that teachers generally vary instruction for differing student needs by adapting the content to which students are exposed, the process by which students engage with the content, or the student product or performance that is used to demonstrate mastery. Hall (2009) adds that differentiation can be based on allowing flexibility of the pace at which students are expected to achieve mastery, the depth of knowledge or understanding students are expected to achieve, or the differing interests students have. Across these, the fundamental characteristic of differentiated instruction is that instruction and instructional approaches are, to the fullest extent possible, tailored to best match students' interests, prior knowledge, and learning preferences.

When concrete standards or learning objectives are established, the first step in differentiating instruction is to gather data on the students prior to providing instruction. The goal is to obtain evidence about their current understanding or mastery of a topic, their interests, and the ways in which they prefer to learn. Data may be gleaned from formal measures, like previous achievement tests, teacher-developed pretests, or learning style inventories; or from more informal sources such as conversations with students, information from previous teachers, or observation as students work on particular learning tasks. These data are then used to make decisions or to develop alternatives that allow students to engage with the content in ways that fit with their current level of understanding, the ways and pace at which they prefer to learn, and ways that draw upon their interests.

Hall presents examples of instructional approaches that allow a teacher to differentiate instruction to better meet students' needs. These include the following:

- **Tiered Assignments:** Multiple tasks that deal with the same topic/standard but that allow students to work at the cognitive level that best matches their current ability.
- **Compacting:** Instruction and instructional activities that eliminate aspects that students have already mastered.
- **Learning Contracts:** Agreements in which the teacher stipulates what is to be learned and any required activities or products, and the student stipulates the ways in which she or he will complete the instructional task.
- **Flexible Grouping:** Forming small instructional groups that consist of students at similar levels of understanding, with similar interests, or with similar learning preferences and reforming these groups frequently to ensure they reflect students' changing understanding and different content.
- **Independent Study Projects:** Student-developed activities and products that they believe will best help them master the appropriate standards or objectives, within parameters established by the teacher.

Differentiated instruction is widely used and is increasing in use as state and national accountability programs focus

(continued)

attention on achievement for all students, regardless of their differences. According to Huebner (2010), "a growing body of research shows positive results for full implementation of differentiated instruction in mixed-ability classrooms"

(p. 79). As such, it offers a strategy that the skillful teacher can use to further help students toward academic success.

In today's standards-based classrooms, focused on helping each student learn in ways that are most effective and that help

her or him achieve success, differentiated instruction is a commonly used strategy.

Differentiated instruction integrates several basic practices that are supported by research in a range of areas.

---

direct instruction, inquiry learning, and so on (see Chapters 7 and 8). Ideally, every lesson should allow students to experience the content through several senses. You might tell students about certain ideas or have them read about them; ask them to conduct an experiment or activity in which they manipulate materials and can see, feel, hear, taste, or even smell the results of their manipulations; then organize them into small groups to write a summary of their observations.

Interacting with Students   In addition to introducing students to content in a variety of ways, Grouws and Cebulla (2000) emphasize the importance of varying the ways teachers interact with students. Even having students work independently in small groups can become monotonous if used without variation. Ensuring that there are multiple and different steps to the groups' tasks, interjecting questions or encouraging comments, and breaking up the task with some whole class conversation or discussion of groups' progress will help keep students involved.

Teachers should also vary the ways in which they reinforce or praise students for desirable performance or inform them about their progress. Smiling at students, maintaining eye contact, moving closer, laughing, and gesturing toward students often can be reinforcing and convey support and interest. More explicitly, you can give students rewards for desirable performance. Verbal praise, recognition of outstanding work, free time, or tokens are examples. Researchers note that, just as a single instructional alternative eventually becomes monotonous and ineffective, so too does a single form of reward. Likewise, teachers can and should provide

11.3   Why do you think it is so easy for teachers to "get in a rut" rather than use variety? What will you do to make sure that you continually incorporate variety?

"Go to kindergarten, finger-paint, have quiet time, play with building blocks, eat lunch, listen to a story, take a nap, color, go home from kindergarten—day after day, week after week. I'm 5, and I'm in a rut."

students with information about their performance in a variety of forms—not just in written comments or grades on students' papers. Verbal information from the teacher, peers, and group are important ways of accomplishing this. We will discuss reinforcement and feedback in detail later in this chapter.

Try Activity 11.3

Using Instructional Time Efficiently

The most effective teachers learn to optimize the time available for instruction. It's only reasonable that students learn more when they spend more time engaged in learning activities. Three factors contribute to more efficient use of instructional time: (1) time on task, (2) maintaining momentum, and (3) smooth transitions.

OPTIMIZING TIME

Research has shown that **time on task** is consistently related to increased learning. When teachers and students spend more time actively engaged in academic tasks, students learn more (Brush, 1997; Glatthorn, 2000; Good & Brophy, 2000; Grouws & Cebulla, 2000; Marzano, 2002; Schmidt et al., 2001; Yair, 2000). Interestingly, however, only a small percentage of available instructional time is actually used for meaningful instruction (Bracey, 2001; Glass, 2002). An examination of the reasons for this can show where time is lost and how to maximize the use of available time.

It is useful to think of instructional time in terms of four levels, somewhat like the target in Figure 11.2. At each level, less time is used for instruction than is available. For example, at the broadest level is **mandated time;** that is, the formal time scheduled for school or academic activities. The length of the school year, day, and periods determine the maximum time available for instructional activities. Teachers are compelled to work within the constraints and schedules established by their state, school district, and school. Schools in most states schedule approximately 185 school days; the typical school day is about 7 1/2 hours in length; and the typical high school period is about 50 minutes. It should be noted, however, that there

FIGURE 11.2 The Relationships among the Four Levels of Instructional Time

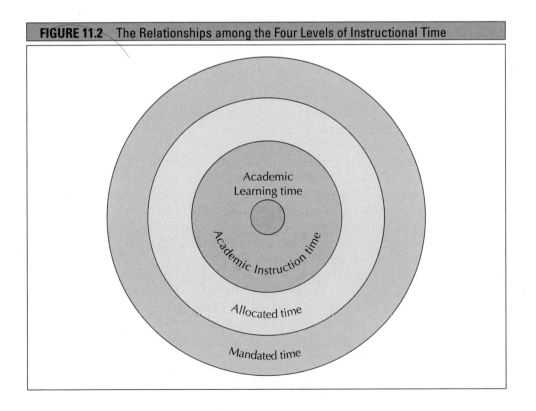

Academic Learning time

Academic Instruction time

Allocated time

Mandated time

CHAPTER 11
Professional Skills and Abilities
of Effective Teachers

is much disparity even in amounts of mandated time. In fact, Harnischfeger and Wiley (in Jeynes, 2003) found a difference of 45 minutes in the length of the school day for second graders *within the same school district!* In this school district, as in many others, the maximum available time for school-related activities is much greater for some students than for others.

Obviously, not every minute of mandated time is used for instruction. Some time is scheduled for lunch, moving from class to class, recess, homeroom, and other noninstructional activities. Thus, only a portion of mandated time is actually allocated to instruction.

Allocated time is the amount of mandated time intended or scheduled for academic activities. Research indicates that less than 75 percent of mandated time is allocated to academic tasks. Nonacademic activities (that is, convocations, field trips, pep rallies, special programs or speakers, and so on) and formal transitions (that is, passing periods, restroom breaks) take over 25 percent of mandated time. Based upon several studies, it would appear that only about seven of every 10 mandated days is actually available for academic or instructional purposes. The remaining three days are consumed by the nonacademic activities cited above (Bracey, 2001; Glass, 2002; Smith, 2000).

The next circle in Figure 11.2 represents the amount of allocated time during which the teacher is actually conducting instructional activities. This is called **academic instruction time.** Just as allocated time is always less than mandated time, the amount of time spent in academic instruction is always less than is allocated. Less than 60 percent of allocated time in elementary schools and less than 45 percent of allocated time in high schools is spent in academic instruction. While allocated and mandated time are often beyond the control of teachers, maximizing the amount of allocated time spent in academic instruction is their responsibility (Clare, Jenson, & Kehle, 2000; Smith, 2000).

Most teachers do not realize how much class time they spend in noninstructional tasks and activities. For example, although a seventh-grade social studies teacher may have 50 minutes of allocated time five days a week, not all of the 250 minutes allocated to instruction will be devoted to it. Some time will be spent socializing, organizing or preparing instructional materials, giving directions, or intervening in discipline problems. Additional time will be lost to absenteeism, administrative requests, and other disruptions. Using Doyle's data, of the 250 minutes allocated over five days, fewer than 145 minutes will be spent in academic activities.

Returning again to Figure 11.2, let's now examine the smallest but most critical circle. This inner circle represents the amount of academic instruction time during which students are *actively* and *successfully* engaged in learning and is referred to as **academic learning time (ALT),** or engaged time. Two factors are considered in determining academic learning time. First is the amount of time a given student is actively engaged in the instruction/learning process. Rather than daydreaming, doodling, or misbehaving, the student is attentive to the learning activity. This attention may be overt, such as answering a question, participating in a discussion, solving pencil-and-paper problems, manipulating concrete materials in an experiment, or talking to another student about the instructional task. It may also be less obvious, as when students are actively thinking about the academic task even if they do not exhibit any outward signs of engagement.

The second factor considered in ALT is a student's success at the activity. If a student is actively engaged in completing an academic activity incorrectly, she may actually be practicing and learning an incorrect process. For academic instruction time to be considered "engaged," or academic learning time, *given learners must be actively engaged in meaningful academic tasks at which they are mostly successful.*

Even though teachers may be conducting instruction, it is unlikely that every student will be engaged in the activity at any given time. In fact, no individual student is likely to be engaged 100 percent of the time. Thus, more time is lost.

11.4 Have you experienced teachers who seemed not to use time efficiently? What did they do? Do you think they realized how they used time? Why or why not?

"They never quit, do they?"

Borich (2004) suggests that an effective teacher probably maintains an academic engagement rate of 80 to 95 percent. However, Yair (2000) indicates that in most classrooms, students spend about 30 percent of instructional time engaged in academic activity under the supervision of a teacher or aide. Students with special learning needs are likely to be engaged at even lower levels without direct attention by the teacher (Winter, 2001). If we consider these data in terms of our middle school social studies example, of the 145 minutes per week when the teacher was providing instruction, the typical student would be *engaged* for only about 50 minutes.

An examination of the tremendous loss of time between mandated and engaged time shows how critical it is for teachers to take full advantage of the time they have. As previously noted, while state and school officials generally set mandated or allocated time, teachers can increase their students' academic learning time through the skillful application of professional teaching skills.

One way to guard against loss of academic learning time is to be aware of potential detractors. At the district level, time is frequently lost to snow days, weather delays, and teachers' strikes. At the school level, fire drills, convocations, trips, passing periods, lunch, recess, and homeroom periods reduce time. At the classroom level, time is lost by starting class late or ending early, by providing unmonitored study time, by spending too much time on administrative tasks, by using films, computers, or games excessively, by spending too much time on discipline problems, by failing to monitor or making too many transitions, or by straying from the lesson at hand.

Try Activity 11.4

How can teachers improve their use of time? First, they should deliberately attempt to use most of the available time for instruction rather than other tasks. Begin and end each lesson on time. Have materials, equipment, and activities planned and ready so that you can begin as soon as the period begins. Establish and enforce rules requiring students to be on time and to be prepared for class. To avoid wasting time at the end of the lesson, plan more instruction than you think you will need. If you finish early, spend the remaining time reviewing with students rather than having them do individual seat work or giving them "free time." If individual seat work is assigned, monitor students to be sure they are engaged in the learning task. It is also helpful to use and enforce a signal that indicates to students that they may begin putting away their materials at the end of the lesson or period. This allows you to keep students involved for the maximum amount of time and prevents the problem created when students close their books or stand to leave while you are attempting to finish the lesson. Make sure, however, that you allow students sufficient time to put away materials before leaving the room or moving to another activity.

11.5 Are you good at managing your time? Do you think you will be better or worse at managing classroom time? How will you know?

Establishing and maintaining rules and procedures for routine activities can also provide more time for instruction by reducing the amount of time needed for giving directions. Chapter 12 provides detailed information about rules and procedures. Briefly, though, you should teach and enforce procedures for obtaining or returning materials and equipment, checking homework, making up missed work, and completing group or individual seat work. Similarly, when you must give directions, explain the tasks and procedures clearly and completely. Check for understanding of these procedures, answer students' questions, and give them feedback *before* telling them to begin.

Another important factor in increasing students' engagement is to create and maintain a highly interactive instructional pattern. Use a variety of instructional behaviors and alternatives. Make assignments interesting, relevant, and at a level that allows most students to complete them successfully without your guidance. Spend the majority of your classroom time in teacher-directed activities where you can more carefully monitor students' engagement. Randomly circulate around the room, especially when students are working in small groups or at individual seat work. Reinforce students verbally and nonverbally for remaining on task, and quickly redirect off-task behavior.

11.6

How well are you able to monitor several activities or tasks at once? How might this affect your classroom?

Maintaining Momentum   The concept of momentum is related to the effective use of time. Momentum refers to the flow of activities and to the pace of teaching and learning maintained in the classroom. The most effective teachers maintain a smooth, relatively rapid instructional pace. Their classroom activities are orderly, and changes occur easily without disrupting the instructional flow since these teachers have established effective routines and follow them. The speed at which they conduct instructional activities, while brisk, matches the difficulty of the content and the students' abilities.

Your skill in maintaining momentum is important when considered in light of the research on time. Your goal should be to maximize your students' engagement, to help them work through relevant materials and activities as quickly and as successfully as they can. By adapting the pace of your instruction to students' abilities and success and by working to maintain a smooth flow of classroom activities with few disruptions and little "down time," you help students learn more.

It is easier to maintain momentum in teacher-guided instructional activities than during seat work or small-group work (Brush, 1997; Grouws & Cebulla, 2000; Leather, 2000). Teacher-guided instruction allows the teacher greater control of the pace and flow of the lesson, whereas small-group or individual seat work relies heavily on students' motivation to maintain momentum.

You must consider how best to maintain momentum when planning and implementing instruction. The pace of instruction must be adapted to the difficulty or complexity of required tasks and to each student's ability or confidence. For example, you must plan for and use a slower pace early in the learning process or when the task requires higher-order thinking skills. For lower-order tasks such as rote practice or recitation, a quicker pace is more appropriate. Further, the pace should vary in your long-term plans, including your weekly and monthly reviews.

Effective teachers must learn to monitor and deal with concurrent classroom activities. While working with a small reading group in the back of the room, they must also be aware of and keep students working at their desks in the front of the room, at computers, or on projects. Momentum is enhanced when teachers organize their classrooms to minimize disruptions and time lost to giving directions or reexplaining. Rules and procedures that enable students to complete tasks on their own help reduce disruptions. Teachers must also be careful to avoid getting "bogged down" in unimportant or minor aspects of the topic, digressing from the topic at hand, or spending too much time with a single student or group of students.

Making Smooth Transitions   Instructional transitions are "points in instructional interactions when contexts change" (Doyle, 1986, p. 406). Instructional transitions require that teachers refocus students' attention on changes in the direction of a discussion or lesson. Transitions occur when you change the topic, its focus, or the activity at hand. Major transitions take place between class meetings or lessons (the time from the end of one class to the beginning of the next class), between lessons in the same room (particularly in elementary classrooms), and between different instructional activities within the same lesson (changing from lecture to lab work). Because major transitions often involve changes in equipment or location, they take more time, and when poorly planned, they are a major contributor to classroom disruption. We will discuss major transitions and how to deal with them more fully in Chapter 12.

Minor transitions occur within a lesson when the speaker moves from one aspect of the topic to another, when the speaker pauses, or when the speaker changes (a new speaker begins). These minor transitions are necessary and desirable because they help learners organize their thinking by signaling the move from one topic or aspect of the topic to another. They also allow more people to contribute to the discussion or lesson.

Transitions, particularly minor transitions, are frequent occurrences in classrooms and largely determine the smoothness and momentum of the lesson.

11.7

How might you monitor your use of instructional time?

Poor transitions can greatly detract from effective use of instructional time. As a result, teachers should work to ensure that their transitions are few in number and that they are as well-organized and as brief as possible. Problems result when transitions are not well-structured, when students do not want to stop what they are doing or have not had sufficient time to complete the assigned task, or when the next instructional segment is delayed for some reason (Brown & Brown, 1999).

To make your instructional transitions smoother, you should practice the following routine. First, plan for the transitions. When preparing your lessons, you can predict points where changes in focus or activity will occur or when waiting is inevitable. You should determine what materials and procedures you will need to begin the next segment as quickly as possible and what both you and your students should do during the transition. An important part of planning for transitions is having all materials and equipment prepared, readily available, and in working order. Also, you can routinize daily or frequent transitions through patterns or procedures. For example, students can be taught what they are to do when they finish a test early, while you take roll, or when they move from one area of the room to another. Establishing these patterns saves time that might otherwise be spent giving directions and allows students to engage in constructive activities rather than just sit and wait. Figure 11.3 lists specific steps you can take to optimize your use of time.

Conducting Interactive Instruction

Effective teachers are able to conduct instruction that keeps students actively involved in the lesson. In addition to establishing set and using variety to keep students motivated, the best teachers are skilled in questioning, in guiding students to a clear understanding of the content, and in monitoring understanding.

USING QUESTIONS

The most effective teachers establish and maintain highly interactive classrooms—classrooms characterized by student-student and teacher-student dialogue on content rather than simply teacher talk (Lock & Prigge, 2002; Marzano, 2002). Integral to this type of classroom is the teacher's ability to use questions effectively. Questions are a fundamental strategy through which teachers help students process ideas or concepts. Walshaw and Anthony (2008), note that questions enable teachers to "engage students in thoughtful and sustained discourse that can make a

---

FIGURE 11.3 Optimizing Instructional Time

1. Have materials and equipment ready prior to class.
2. Begin on time.
3. Establish and enforce rules for entering the classroom and beginning class.
4. Establish and enforce procedures for routine tasks and transitions, like turning in work and obtaining or putting away equipment, so that students can do these chores without your direction.
5. Plan more instructional material than you think you will need.
6. Maintain a relatively brisk instructional pace, varying the pace as needed to accommodate learners and match the difficulty of the content.
7. If you finish your planned lesson early, use the remaining time to review with students. Avoid giving students "free time" or individual seat work.
8. Establish a signal that informs students when they are to begin putting away their materials or when they are dismissed.
9. Maintain a highly interactive instructional pattern. Question all students, move frequently, use variety, and convey enthusiasm to help keep students actively engaged.

difference to learning when the discourse is centered on powerful ideas" (p. 516). This interface in interactive teaching is critical because it shifts the focus from the teacher to the students. Importantly, technology offers the teacher additional tools that can engage more students in these interactions (Henderson, 2010).

Effective questions require students *to actively process information and compose an answer.* Good questions increase students' engagement, raise the level of thought, help students organize their thoughts, guide students more successfully through academic tasks, and allow the teacher to monitor understanding and provide feedback. In spite of the obvious value of good questions, it appears that teachers seldom use questions as effectively as they could (Ornstein & Lasley, 2000). Most teachers' questioning patterns include giving information that is unnecessary or confusing, posing more than one question at a time, or failing to specify the nature of the expected answer (Traver, 1998). What, then, do we know about good questions and questioning patterns?

Questions comprise about one-third of the classroom interactions between teachers and students, and educational research has shown that effective questioning directly and indirectly influences the amount, level, and type of learning. Good and Brophy (2000) reviewed research on questioning and concluded that students learn more when teachers ask frequent questions and include a variety of questions in their lessons. Further, research on questioning suggests that teachers' use of higher-order questions promotes students' higher-order thinking (Walshaw & Anthony, 2008). Good and Brophy (2000) conclude that questions are important because the more frequently students interact with the teacher and their peers about the subject, the more they learn. The following discussion organizes what researchers know about questioning into three areas: asking questions, obtaining answers, and following up questions or reacting to student responses. (See Spotlight on Research 11.1.)

How to Ask Questions If teachers want their questioning to be effective, they must be sure to phrase questions clearly and concisely. Too often, teachers ask questions that are almost impossible for students to answer accurately. They fail to make clear what it is they want to know of students or how they want them to answer. Clear questions use natural, unambiguous language appropriate to the level of the students. They are also concise, including only the words, terms, and information students need in order to answer the questions. They convey the specific points students should attend to, but they do not include unnecessary words or parenthetical expressions. Finally, they are directed toward academic content or the objectives of the lesson.

To be effective, questions should require students to *process* or think about what they are learning and to *compose* an answer. This means teachers should avoid asking rhetorical questions or questions that have only one answer. Closed-response questions, which can be answered with a simple yes-no or true-false response, allow students to guess at the answer without processing the content. Even when students do process what they have learned in order to answer a closed-response question, they can still *select* a response rather than *compose* one. It is easy to reword closed-response questions to require students to create more thoughtful, detailed responses.

Rhetorical questions, that is, questions asked for effect rather than to generate students' responses, are problematic because they can, over time, inhibit students' responses. Students become unsure whether a question is merely rhetorical or whether they are supposed to respond. For similar reasons, teachers should avoid including the answer within the question or answering a question themselves.

In addition, teachers should take care to ask only one question at a time. Many times teachers ask multiple questions without realizing it. While asking a question, they think of another aspect of the content they also want to address. As a result, it

11.8 When you teach, do you ask lots of questions? Do you ever get nervous about asking questions when you're in front of a group? Why?

11.9 Teachers ask mostly lower-order questions in their classes. Why do you think this might be?

Research on effective teaching requires that researchers spend huge amounts of time in classrooms, observing and talking with teachers and students. An example of this approach is a study by Weiss and her colleagues in which 364 science and mathematics lessons were observed to determine the extent to which teachers applied effective instructional practices.

The researchers note that a majority of the classes they observed throughout the U.S. fell "very short of the ideal of providing high-quality mathematics and science education for all students" (p. 25). In fact, while only 15 percent of the lessons were rated as being of high quality, nearly 60 percent were rated as low quality. However, the researchers did find some things to be characteristic of classrooms in which teaching quality was rated highly:

- Lessons reflected a high level of student engagement with the content. This engagement was encouraged by using real world examples, building on students' prior knowledge, and including a variety of experiences in each lesson.
- The classroom environment was respectful of students and encouraged them to participate but also challenged them to think deeply about the content.
- All students were actively encouraged to participate throughout the lesson. Teachers consciously worked to engage every student and, when necessary, adapted particular activities to best match students' abilities.
- Teachers used questions to monitor students' understanding and to promote their thinking about the content in meaningful and new ways. Low-level, short answer questions were uncommon.
- Teachers worked intentionally and directly to help students make sense of the content. As students were engaged in activities that exposed them to the content and to begin building their own understanding, teachers used explanations, questions, and other techniques at appropriate times to ensure that students were making appropriate connections among concepts or ideas.

Source: Weiss & Pasley (2004).

---

may not be clear whether one answer is expected for all the questions or whether a different answer is expected to each question. Similarly, students probably are confused when their teacher asks a question and then immediately rephrases it. This creates two problems. First, students' thinking about the original question is interrupted and, second, the rephrasing is often sufficiently different from the original to make the students wonder if it is a separate question.

An additional consideration in formulating and asking questions is the *type of question* or level of thought required of the students. Questions can be of several types or levels and are intended for a variety of purposes. Questions may be lower- or higher-order, convergent or divergent, narrow or broad, and content or process.

The lower- and higher-order delineations refer to the level of thought required in order to answer the question. Bloom's taxonomy, discussed in Chapter 6, is the most frequently used system for organizing questions along this hierarchy. Lower-order questions require students to respond at the knowledge, comprehension, and sometimes application levels of the taxonomy. Students can generally answer these questions using existing knowledge, either by recalling and then restating them, by rephrasing them, or by performing a task. Higher-order questions require the cognitive skills of analysis, synthesis, or evaluation and thus require more complex and original thinking.

Questions can also be categorized as convergent or divergent—labels that refer to the direction of thought required to reach an answer. In answering convergent questions, students' thought processes proceed from broad or general to narrow or specific. These questions require one or a small number of correct responses. Factual questions asking who, what, when, or where as well as closed-response (yes-no) questions are examples of convergent questions. These questions are most appropriate for helping to reinforce specific, important aspects of the content.

Try Activity 11.5

Divergent questions require thinking that moves from the narrow or specific to the broad or general. They require students to identify or generate several potential answers—any of which might be accurate. The difference between convergent and divergent questions is easy to see in mathematics instruction. Suppose students are presented with the numeric statement 7×9. A convergent question might be "What is seven times nine?" Students are expected to arrive at the one correct answer. This example is also a lower-order question. However, the same numeric statement (7×9) might also serve as the basis for a divergent question like "How many different ways could you determine what seven times nine is?" To answer this question, students might use simple addition, commutative property, combinations of mathematical principles, manipulative solutions, or other creative methods to generate answers to the question. Rather than focus on the single correct answer, as in the convergent question, students must expand on or diverge from the initial facts to generate the answer.

11.10 Could a teacher use so many questions that students learned less? Why or why not?

Questions may also emphasize *content* or *process*. Content questions deal directly with the information being learned and make up about 80 percent of the questions teachers ask (Borich, 2004). The question and the expected answer are drawn directly from the content of instruction, and the teacher generally has a "correct" answer in mind. Content questions are often associated with lower-order cognitive processes. However, because they focus students' attention on important aspects of the content, they have been found to improve students' achievement (Borich, 2004). On the other hand, teachers use process questions to stimulate students' thinking. Although these questions deal with content, they place less emphasis on the "correctness" of answers and more on pushing students to think about the content in different, creative, or complex ways (Walshaw & Anthony, 2008). Thus, process questions are generally higher-order and divergent. These questions are used much less often than content questions and are less closely related to achievement. However, they do appear to promote students' abilities to think at higher levels and to solve problems (Blythe, Allen, & Powell, 1999; LeNoir, 1993).

Several common recommendations for improvement apply to each of these types of questions. First, just as in other aspects of instruction, you should use a variety of question types. Although most teachers rely heavily on lower-order, convergent questions, the importance of developing students' thinking and problem-solving abilities requires that you deliberately incorporate process, higher-order, and divergent questions into your lessons. Second, you should match the type and level of questions you ask to your objectives and your students. When teaching toward lower-order objectives, lower-order questions make sense. When your objectives include higher-order processes or when you want to promote students' critical thinking, you must integrate higher-order, divergent, and process questions into your lessons.

To ensure good phrasing and appropriate types of questions, you should consider your questions and questioning patterns when planning your lessons. After all, good class discussion and interaction don't just happen. Some questions emerge spontaneously from the lesson as a result of students' comments or questions. These you cannot plan in advance. However, you can write many of the critical questions into your lesson plan. There are at least four important reasons for doing this.

First, integrating planned questions into your lessons increases the likelihood that you will conduct an interactive lesson. Second, when you prepare questions in advance, you are more likely to focus them on the major objectives of the lesson. If you rely totally on spontaneous questions, you can easily get side-tracked and ask too many questions on one aspect of the lesson while neglecting others. Third, including some pivotal questions in the lesson plan makes it more likely that you will ask a variety of questions at a variety of levels. Divergent, higher-order, and process questions are more difficult to develop than are convergent, lower-order, and content questions. That may partly explain why teachers use them less often (Glickman, 2002). Preparing some of these questions in advance, even if you don't use them all, directs your attention toward more advanced levels of thinking. Fourth, writing pivotal questions in advance makes it more likely that you will phrase the questions clearly and concisely.

Obtaining Good Answers   After teachers have developed and phrased their questions, they must get students to respond to them. As mentioned, asking clear and varied types of questions at a variety of levels promotes students' participation. Research also suggests that soliciting answers in certain ways can enhance the effectiveness of questions and the quality and quantity of students' responses. It is particularly important that teachers use wait time and that all students participate.

Wait time refers to the pauses that effective teachers use when they solicit and react to students' responses. Rowe's (1987) work has served as the basis for most subsequent research on wait time. The early research of Rowe and others focused on the importance of asking a question, pausing, and then calling on a student to respond. Investigators have determined that in addition to pausing after the question is asked, it is also important to pause before reacting to the student's answer or calling on a second student to respond (Hill, Rowan, & Ball, 2005). Thus, wait time includes (1) the pause between the teacher's question and the student's response and (2) the pause between a student's response and the teacher's reaction. Figure 11.4 depicts this sequence.

Most teachers pause for less than one second before calling on a student to respond. In contrast, the most effective teachers include pauses of from three to five seconds after asking a question and before reacting to a student's response. Research on wait time has found that those three- to five-second pauses produce the following desirable and important outcomes: students' responses are longer and more thorough, the cognitive level of students' responses is higher (for example, they display more analysis, synthesis, and evaluation), students volunteer more information to support their responses, and students' confidence in their responses is greater. In addition, more students respond to questions, particularly those labeled as "slow." Finally, positive interactions among students and between students and the teacher increase, as do the number of relevant questions students ask (Grouws & Cebulla, 2000; Rowe, 1987; Tobin, 1987; Traver, 1998; Walberg, 2003).

11.11   Why might you feel that the pause you use after a question is longer than it really is?

FIGURE 11.4   Sequence of Teachers' Questioning

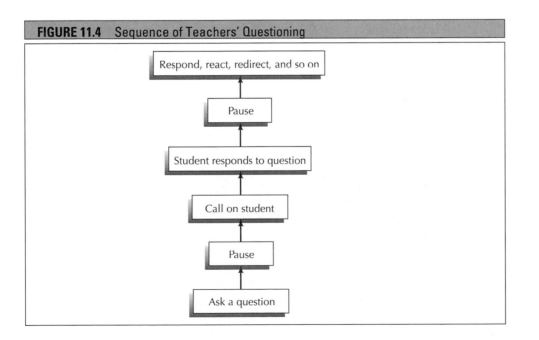

Respond, react, redirect, and so on

Pause

Student responds to question

Call on student

Pause

Ask a question

Increasing wait time seems a simple thing to do, but, especially for beginning teachers, it often proves difficult. A pause of five seconds can seem like an eternity when you are insecure about the effectiveness of your instruction or unsure whether anyone will answer your questions! Still, as you learn to incorporate these pauses, they become easier, and they give all students increased time to think and participate.

You can do several things to make your use of wait time more effective. First, you should adopt a policy restraining students from shouting out their answers. Allowing callouts prevents you from controlling the length of the pause after your question and reduces wait time. After asking a question, count to five in your head while scanning the room, then call on a student to answer. Do not repeat, rephrase, or add to the question until at least several seconds have passed. Doing so interrupts students' thinking and may interfere with their ability to respond. When students respond, it is important you do not interrupt before they have completed their answers, even if they are absolutely correct. When they are finished answering, pause, use a few seconds to think about their answers, allow other students to think about the answer, and consider how best to react or follow up.

The use of wait time must be balanced against the brisk pace needed to maintain the momentum of a lesson. Specifically, teachers should match wait time with the level or difficulty of the question asked. Lower-order, convergent questions generally require shorter pauses than higher-order, divergent, and process questions. Vary wait time to accommodate the students' need to process the question, generate an answer, or consider the response of another student.

The second factor to consider during the response phase of questioning is how to maximize student participation. Students' learning and affect are related to the number of opportunities students have to participate in the lesson and to respond to questions. Thus, a goal of your questioning should be to ensure that all students have an equal opportunity to respond successfully. Questioning can help you monitor understanding, keep students engaged, and serve as a measure of the success of your instruction, but it is imperative that you ask *all* students to respond to your questions. This is especially difficult but important in a class with diverse abilities or cultural backgrounds.

Mastering the effective use of wait time will increase participation in your questioning. However, most teachers still call primarily on volunteers to respond

"Say your car gets 23 miles per gallon at 55 miles per hour and your fuel tank holds 16 gallons. If gas costs 86¢ per gallon and you know the capitals of all 50 states, how much will it cost to drive to the capital of Nebraska?"

to questions. This practice results in an unfair distribution of questions and unequal opportunities to respond. Effective questioning requires that you call on all students, especially nonvolunteers. A good practice is to ask a question, pause to allow all students to think about the question and develop a response, and then select a student to respond. To ensure an equitable distribution of questions, it can be helpful to use a pattern in selecting students to answer. For example, you might write each student's name on a note card and then randomly select from the students' cards for participation. Using a pattern enables you to know which students have already been asked to respond. To keep all students alert, even when they have already answered a question, it is a good idea to vary your pattern and to call randomly on students to make follow-up responses.

Incorporating wait time and equitably distributing the opportunity to respond work together to improve the effectiveness of your questioning. Wait time allows more students the opportunity to process an answer. While some students can do this relatively quickly (usually those who volunteer most frequently), others require more time to arrive at an answer. Thus, wait time increases the number of students who can respond accurately to the question. Calling on all students, even when they do not volunteer, maintains students' engagement. It allows all students some opportunity to interact with you and to be successful and provides you with a more complete assessment of how well students understand the material. (See Case 11.1.)

Following Up Students' Responses After a student has responded to your question, you must respond or react to the reply. This phase of the questioning process is called follow-up. Your follow-up behavior will either encourage or discourage thoughtful, successful participation in your lessons and, thus, the long-term success of your instruction (Burns, 2010; Latham, 1997; Walshaw & Anthony, 2008).

The most frequent though ineffective teacher's reaction is "OK" or "uh-huh" (Sadker & Sadker, 2001). Instead of such routinized and meaningless responses, you should attempt to clarify, synthesize, expand, modify, raise the level of, or evaluate students' responses. The effective use of follow-up is based upon the accuracy and confidence of the students' responses (Good, 1988; Hidi & Harackiewicz, 2000; Sternberg, 1994). They can range from correct and confident to wrong and careless. Research suggests the following responses and reactions:

1. When a student responds correctly and confidently, accept and acknowledge the response and move on. Do not overpraise.
2. When a student responds correctly but hesitantly, provide feedback to the student or use additional questions that encourage the student to determine why the response is correct. Before moving on, be certain the student understands why the answer was correct.
3. When a student responds confidently but incorrectly, reinforce the initial effort, then use additional questions to help the student arrive at the correct answer. Avoid giving the student the answer or calling on another student to respond. You may give reinforcement for participation and effort, but there should be no confusion regarding the fact that you are reinforcing participation, not accuracy.
4. When a student responds incorrectly and carelessly, provide the correct response and move on. You should never avoid following up or correcting an incorrect answer.

Generally then, follow-up is used any time the student fails to respond accurately and/or confidently. These follow-ups can be divided into four types: providing the correct answer, probing, redirecting, or rephrasing. Providing the correct answer is advisable only when a student has responded carelessly and incorrectly. The remaining three follow-up methods deserve discussion.

11.12 Does it make you feel uncomfortable when a teacher calls on you to respond when you haven't volunteered? Why or why not? Could the teacher help you feel better about it?

11.13 Teachers often just give students the correct answer after an incorrect response. Why?

CHAPTER 11
Professional Skills and Abilities
of Effective Teachers

Five times every day, Betty Gillrush teaches the same sixth-grade science lesson—the same lesson in the same way.

It's review day, and Betty has her lesson plan all laid out. Ten minutes of review and 40 minutes of worksheets while she catches up her grade book.

Today's "short-shot" question (every teacher in the district must have one each day) is written on the board: "(Blank) (blank) is the main source of drinking water."

Betty's students have been studying water supply and pollution all week, but nobody seems to remember the answer to the short-shot.

"Now, you remember we talked about this yesterday. What are the sources of drinking water?" A few students offer suggestions. "Rain," one says. "The ocean," says another.

"No, we don't usually get our drinking water from the ocean because we have to take the salt out first," Betty replies in a sing-song, patronizing tone.

"How did salt get into the ocean?" asks a girl sitting in the front row.

"When water flows over the land, it dissolves some things called salts, not salt, and they get into the ocean. Now, who knows the answer to the short-shot? It's *groundwater*. Remember from yesterday? Groundwater is the main source of drinking water. And what is groundwater?"

"It's laying on the ground!" says a boy who's been fidgeting in his seat.

The tone of her voice is not angry or mean, but exasperated. "No, groundwater is the water that's under the ground that we get from wells and springs. Remember?"

Betty Gillrush launches into a rapid review of the previous week's lessons. She discusses groundwater pollution, landfills, thermal pollution, and the heavily polluted creek that runs behind the school. The entire time she stands in front of the class, book in hand, calling on a few of the students who raise their hands, mostly sitting in the front of the room. Others are ignored.

Fifteen minutes into the period Betty hands out the worksheets, which ask review questions about the material she's just reviewed. "You can use your books to find the answers to these questions," she says. Several students raise their hands to say they don't have books. She searches around for extra copies and batches several students together. A few students begin a lethargic search for information they can use to fill in the worksheet blanks. Others stare into space.

Betty begins to work at her desk in the back of the room, returning to student tables from time to time to answer questions. The students are having trouble finding a particular worksheet answer from the book. She urges some students to figure it out, but whispers the answer to others.

As the class period draws to a close, Betty Gillrush returns to the front of her classroom. "One more time now," she says. "Let's look at our short-shot. What is the main source of drinking water, class?"

The students stare back at her with blank expressions.

"You remember," she urges them. "It's *groundwater*. Remember?"

The students begin to gather their belongings in anticipation of the bell. In her best class-control voice, Betty Gillrush declares, "I've been concerned about what's been going on in here lately, but you all did very well today. Keep it up!"

Source: MiddleWeb online.

INVESTIGATING AND SOLVING THE CASE

1. In what ways does Betty's lesson reflect her attempts to demonstrate or use effective teaching skills?
2. There are many ways in which Betty seems to fail to apply effective teaching skills. What are some of these?
3. Why do you suppose even good teachers have lessons that sometimes go like Betty's does?
4. If you were in Betty's position, what things would you have attempted to do differently?

Probing means asking additional questions of the responding student to help expand or raise the level of the response (Burns, 2010). Probing questions are often intended to focus attention on important aspects of the question that enable the student to improve the response (see Figure 11.5). In this case, probing should include convergent questions phrased in simple but not condescending terms. Frequently, more than one question is needed to address particular aspects of the original question or response and to guide the student toward a more correct or complete answer.

FIGURE 11.5 Examples of Follow-up Questioning Techniques

Probing (to raise the level of a student's response)

Teacher:	"Why might President Ford have pardoned former President Nixon?" (Pause) "David?"
David:	"To prevent embarrassment of the Republican party."
Teacher:	"Can you explain how the pardon might prevent embarrassment?"
David:	"Well, if the investigation had continued, they might have found that there were a lot of other people, mostly Republicans, who were involved."
Teacher:	"Why do you think that might be true?"
David:	"Hmmm. Well, because since then some others have admitted being involved or named people who were."
Teacher:	"OK, so let's say President Ford doesn't pardon Nixon and all of this is revealed, what do you think would be the result?"

Probing (to help a student answer correctly)

Teacher:	"Ball, bed, bug, baby. These are all words that begin with the *b* sound. What are some other words that begin with the *b* sound?" (Pause) "Danielle?"
Danielle:	(Silence)
Teacher:	"Okay, does Danielle start with a *b* sound?"
Danielle:	"No, it's a *d*."
Teacher:	"Right. What about Brittany? Does Brittany start with a *b* sound?"
Danielle:	"Yeah!"
Teacher:	"Okay, Danielle. Think of the sound. What words do you know that start with that sound?"
Danielle:	(Pause) "Bunny!"
Teacher:	"Right! Bunny!"

Redirecting (after an incorrect response)

Teacher:	"What was the name of the Watergate special prosecutor?" (Pause) "Trevor?"
Trevor:	"Strom Thurmond?"
Teacher:	"No. Thurmond is a senator. What was the name of the special prosecutor?" (Pause) "Steve?"
Steve:	"Archibald Cox."
Teacher:	"Yes."

Rephrasing (to clarify a question)

Teacher:	"Why did Gerald Ford pardon Richard Nixon?" (Pause) (No student responses) "What was the reason Ford gave for the pardon in the speech we just watched?" (Pause) "Kassandra?"
Kassandra:	"He said he thought the country needed to put the issue behind us and move on."

Probing can also be used to raise the level of a student's response. As noted earlier, teachers generally ask convergent, content questions at the lower cognitive levels. Further, most students respond with lower-order, convergent answers, even when the teacher has asked a higher-order or divergent question (Sternberg, 1994). Probing can be used after such a response to prompt the student to use higher-order processes. Simple ways of doing this include asking students to explain why they responded as they did, to provide an example that supports their answer, or to describe how their response would change if a particular aspect of the original question had been different.

Redirecting is another way of following up an incorrect response. When redirecting, the teacher asks another student to answer the same question (see Figure 11.5). This method of follow-up is highly effective with students whose academic self-concepts are strong. It appears that students who are academically confident are challenged by this technique and motivated to work harder. However, redirecting is not effective with students whose academic self-concepts are weak. In fact, redirecting following an insecure student's incorrect response is likely to reduce the student's self-concept, motivation, participation, and learning.

Rephrasing simply means restating the same question in different terms. When students fail to respond to a teacher's question, it is often due to poor phrasing of the initial question. Thus, rewording the question may make it clearer, simpler, or focus students' attention on critical aspects (see Figure 11.5). Rephrasing generally is not an effective follow-up technique and should be avoided. A better technique is to elicit some type of response, then use probing questions to help the student arrive at a correct response. While all teachers occasionally ask poorly stated questions, careful consideration of questions during planning, monitoring their effectiveness during instruction, and questioning with confidence will eventually reduce the need for rephrasing.

Try Activity 11.6

To summarize, questioning is a vital aspect of effective, interactive teaching. It promotes a number of desirable outcomes and can be used for several purposes. Table 11.1 provides an overview of correct and incorrect questioning techniques.

PROVIDING CLEAR INSTRUCTION

Throughout this chapter we have focused on teachers' attributes and behaviors that appear to directly or indirectly promote greater learning, achievement, and motivation. Each characteristic or behavior is grounded in research. We now turn our attention to a complex teaching skill that may contribute more to teacher effectiveness than any other.

Instructional clarity has been the focus of much research ever since Rosenshine and Furst (1971) identified it as the "most promising teacher variable related to student achievement" (p. 107). **Instructional clarity** refers to the teacher's ability to provide instruction that helps *students come to a clear and accurate understanding of important concepts or ideas.* Thus, clarity is something students achieve, not something the teacher does. However, research has identified specific teacher behaviors that students say help them achieve this clarity of understanding. For students with learning disabilities, the clarity of the teacher is of critical importance (Banikowski, 1999; Winter, 2001).

According to students, clear teachers emphasize important points by repeating them, writing them on the board or in presentations, pausing after stating them, and reviewing them. They monitor students' clarity of understanding by asking questions and providing students with activities and experiences that allow them

TABLE 11.1 The Do's and Don'ts of Effective Questioning	
Do	**Don't**
1. Match questions to the objectives and use a variety of question levels and types.	1. Emphasize only lower-order or convergent questions.
2. Ask lots of questions throughout the lesson.	2. Use questions mainly to review at the end of the lesson.
3. Ask a question, pause, and then call on a student by name to respond.	3. Allow callouts or fail to include pauses after your questions.
4. Ensure that all students get equal opportunities to successfully answer questions.	4. Rely on volunteers.
5. Follow up lower-order, inaccurate, and incomplete answers.	5. Overlook or allow to go uncorrected inappropriate or incomplete answers.
6. Write questions, especially critical questions, into your lesson plan.	6. Rely solely on your ability to generate spontaneous questions during interaction.
7. Keep questions clear, brief, and to the point.	7. Use long questions or ask multiple questions simultaneously.
8. Ask questions to keep students engaged.	8. Ask questions as a punitive, disciplinary tool.
9. Write the objectives and summary of the lesson as questions.	9. Devise questions only on major points.
10. Match nonverbal behavior with the questions you ask.	10. Convey disinterest in asking questions or in students' responses.

to apply their knowledge. When students do not understand, clear teachers repeat, review, or rephrase important points. Not surprisingly, teachers who most often and most proficiently use these behaviors to help students understand are associated with significantly greater student learning and satisfaction than teachers who do not (Chesebro & McCroskey, 2001; Hativa, 1998).

The teachers' behaviors that make instruction clear apply not only to the ability to explain content clearly, but also to the ability to structure presentations. Importantly, this lesson-structuring problem applies to both teacher-directed and student-directed instruction (Heritage, Kim, Vendlinski, & Herman, 2009; Rosenshine, 2002). These specific behaviors involve (1) preparing and entering the lesson, (2) introducing and emphasizing content, (3) elaborating on important ideas or concepts, and (4) monitoring students' understanding and remediating when students fail to understand. The following discussion of teacher clarity will be organized around these four topics.

Preparing and Entering the Lesson   Clear instruction is logically organized and is conducted in a way that helps students see the relationships between major concepts or ideas. Accordingly, clear teachers organize their lesson content and activities logically, inform students of the objectives of the lesson, and introduce the content or activities step by step. During planning, these teachers determine the most logical way to introduce content based upon their students' abilities, previous learning, interests, and the natural structure of the content. Chapter 6 explained some of the ways this can be done (for example, chronologically). For logical organization to make instruction clearer, the organization must be obvious and logical *to students*.

At the beginning of the lesson, teachers should inform students of the lesson objectives. As noted in our discussion of establishing set, teachers should provide an overview of the lesson to help students establish a mental framework for the concepts or activities and to enable them to monitor their own understanding. Students find instruction clearer when the teacher gives it step by step. In other words, teachers should provide instruction and instructional activities in a way that helps students understand the relationship between the concepts. Doing so helps students incorporate the new learning with previous learning more accurately.

Introducing and Emphasizing Important Points   Beyond planning and organizing, clear instruction focuses students' attention on important aspects of the instruction. A common way to do this is to write the major points on the board and/or have students record them. It is important, however, that you monitor your use of the board to ensure that you do not overuse it for minor or unimportant points. Students will perceive things you write on the board as important. Consequently, if you fill the board with minor points or fail to put some or all of the major points on the board, the effectiveness of this technique is reduced.

Another way to reinforce important aspects of the lesson is to point them out through verbal structuring or cuing. Enumerating important points helps structure them. For example, "The first point we will discuss is . . ." "Second, . . ." and "Finally, . . ." enables students to organize their thoughts and the content. Likewise, comments such as, "It is important for you to remember this" or "Listen carefully because this is an important point" alert students to pay close attention to what you are about to say. Repeating important points also cues students. You might combine these reinforcers into a pattern in which you state a point, pause or write it on the board, and then repeat it. To provide even more reinforcement, you could note that this is an important point, state it, write it on the board, and then repeat it.

Finally, you reinforce major points when you review or summarize them. In Chapter 6 we applied the term *closure* to this element of the lesson. Upon completing the lesson or important segments of the lesson (immediately preceding a transition), you should summarize or have students summarize the major ideas of

11.14   Have you ever had a teacher who was obviously knowledgeable, but not clear in helping you understand? How did you feel? Did the teacher realize the problem?

the lesson segment. This serves to repeat major points, further identify them as important, help achieve closure, and prepare students for a smooth transition to the next segment.

Elaborating on Important Ideas or Concepts   In addition to identifying and reinforcing major points for students, you can deepen their understanding of the content by providing examples, explanations, and elaborations. Examples and nonexamples (items that do *not* fit the concept) that illustrate the major points can be vital to students' understanding. Examples can be verbal, written, pictorial, or concrete depending upon the content and the level of the learners. For instance, if learners are familiar with ants, merely noting that ants are an example of an insect may be sufficient. They do not need to see an ant for the example to be useful. However, if you were to use a potentially unfamiliar example of an insect, such as a walking stick, a concrete or pictorial example might be necessary. Further, you would need to make clear how or why the example relates to the concept—in this case, what characteristics classify a creature as an insect. Adding nonexamples, such as a scorpion, would further clarify the concept.

Relatedly, clear instruction helps students see how things are similar or different. You can describe, demonstrate, explain, or show students how two ideas, concepts, examples, or ways of doing things are alike and how they differ. Again, this type of instructional behavior helps students assimilate new information more accurately. When the lesson involves learning a task or skill, it is important that you demonstrate the task and, while doing so, explain what you are doing and why. For example, if you were helping students learn to draw circles with a compass, you might place the pointer and explain why you put it there; explain that the pointer must be kept securely in place with one hand, and show them how to do so; place the marker end of the compass solidly on the paper; and then demonstrate and explain how to turn the compass, ensuring that the mark is complete.

Students also note that clear teachers explain unfamiliar words, whereas unclear teachers often fail to do so. A good rule of thumb is to assume that all new terms are unfamiliar to students and explain or define them *before* using them in the lesson. Finally, students' understanding is enhanced when you briefly pause after introducing something important. Just as wait time allows students to think about a question, pausing after introducing an important point allows students to think about it. It also signals the importance of the ideas.

Ensuring Students' Understanding   The final aspect of instructional clarity involves monitoring and correcting students' understanding by providing opportunities for students to apply the concepts or ideas. Critical to this is your ability to use frequent questions at a variety of levels. In addition to asking questions that assess students' understanding, you should build time for student-generated questions into the lesson. Often, if you have established an open and interactive climate, simply including a long pause after a lesson segment will prompt students who do not understand to ask for clarification. You may also call for students' questions by asking "Are there any questions?" However, in such a general call for questions, extended wait time is critical. Many students will have to think through the content to determine whether they need to ask questions, some will need time to formulate the question they want to ask, and some will need time to work up the courage to ask. Thus, after inviting questions, it would not be inappropriate to pause for as long as five to ten seconds while scanning the room. A better alternative would be to ask for specific questions, such as "What questions do you have about the three points we just discussed?" and then follow up to see how well students understand.

In addition to allowing time for questions, you should include activities that allow your students to apply or use their new understanding, then closely monitor their performance and provide corrective feedback as needed. In Chapter 6 this

11.15   As a learner, how do you reinforce your own learning? How do you identify what is important? How do you link it with what you already know?

Try Activity 11.7

was described as providing guided practice. You can have students work individually at their seats, in small groups, or at the board with the entire class contributing. When a student cannot answer a question, cannot accurately apply the concepts to the examples, or asks a question indicating misunderstanding, it is important that you correct the misunderstanding. Several of the earlier mentioned behaviors, like repeating things, rephrasing, probing, or providing additional examples and further explanation, may help clear up confusion.

To summarize, instructional clarity refers to a broad and important set of teachers' behaviors. The major focus of clarity is on helping students understand what you have taught. Remember, clarity is something the student, not the teacher, achieves. However, by learning to use behaviors that make instruction clearer to students, you can greatly improve the effectiveness of your teaching. Figure 11.6 summarizes 10 specific behaviors related to clear instruction.

MONITORING STUDENTS' PROGRESS

Effective teachers are adept at monitoring students' understanding, not just their behavior (Marzano, 2002; Walberg, 2003). They carefully and continually assess students' performance and progress and check for understanding in a variety of ways. If students seem to lack understanding, it cues effective teachers to review and possibly adapt their instruction. Monitoring also conveys teachers' interest in their students' progress and task orientation. If the teacher has established an interactive environment in which students participate freely by asking and answering questions, many opportunities will be available for monitoring understanding.

As noted earlier, monitoring is an important element of instructional clarity. It is also closely tied to the effective use of instructional time and to effective feedback, each of which has been found to influence students' learning.

Monitoring is especially critical in the early stages of learning when misunderstandings or lack of background knowledge are most likely to affect students. Monitoring during this time allows teachers to correct students before they learn and habituate improper patterns of thinking or behavior. As we will discuss in detail later, it also allows teachers to provide feedback to help students understand why their performance is correct.

You can monitor student understanding in numerous formal and informal ways. Tests, quizzes, homework, and projects are examples of formal monitoring. Although formal monitoring is important, particularly in determining grades,

---

FIGURE 11.6   Behaviors That Characterize Clear Teachers

1. The lesson is planned and implemented in an organized manner.

2. Students are informed of the lesson objectives in advance.

3. The lesson is conducted step by step.

4. The teacher draws students' attention to new or important points by writing them on the board, by repeating them, by reviewing them at appropriate points in the lesson, and by incorporating deliberate pauses that allow time for processing and reflection.

5. The teacher presents and works examples that explain and support the concept or ideas being taught.

6. The teacher explains unfamiliar words before using them in the lesson and points out similarities and differences between ideas.

7. The teacher asks students lots of questions and gives application exercises to find out if students understand the content.

8. The teacher carefully monitors students' work for understanding.

9. The teacher encourages and allows time for students to ask questions.

10. When students do not understand, the teacher repeats main points, presents additional examples or explanation, or elaborates until the students achieve clear understanding.

---

informal monitoring is more frequent and immediate, and it can impact more directly on instructional behavior and learning. Good teachers are constantly aware, or "withit" (Kounin, 1970). They ask questions of all students, provide a supportive, open environment in which students feel free to ask questions or clarify misunderstandings, and watch for verbal and nonverbal indications that students do not understand.

11.16 Did you ever feel as if a teacher were "clueless" about your lack of understanding? How did it make you feel? Why did the teacher seem to remain unaware?

Specifically, you can improve your ability to monitor students' understanding in several ways. Establish set and use advance organizers at the beginnings of lessons to help students understand the task and monitor their own progress. Get to know students and call on them by name. Move around the room to monitor attention and stay in closer proximity to all students. Maximize interactive, whole-group instruction and minimize small-group or individual work, especially when no additional adult help is available. Use good questioning techniques: Call on all students—not just those who raise their hands; ask questions at a variety of cognitive levels; and allow wait time. Maintain eye contact with all students by scanning the room for both understanding and misbehavior. Convey openness and availability for help. Spend very little time sitting at your desk, even when students are engaged in individual seat work. Instead, move around, scan, avoid turning your back to the class, and be careful not to spend too much time with any one student or group of students. As you will see in Chapter 12, these behaviors are also characteristics of teachers who are effective classroom managers.

PROVIDING FEEDBACK AND REINFORCEMENT

During the instructional process, effective teachers frequently provide students with information about their academic performance (Walberg, 2003). They most commonly do this through feedback and reinforcement. Although similar, feedback and reinforcement are not the same. Reinforcement is meant to improve students' motivation, while feedback is intended to inform students about the accuracy of their performance. In order to use these skills effectively, teachers must understand each of them and how to apply them.

Both reinforcement and feedback are ways of responding to students' performance. They are skills that teachers employ after a student has done something—for example, answered a question, contributed to a discussion, turned in homework, or completed a project. In a classroom where the teacher has established an interactive tone, opportunities for teachers to provide feedback and reinforcement arise naturally and almost constantly. Research indicates that about one-third of classroom interactions are teachers' responding behaviors. Thus, a teacher's ability to respond appropriately can greatly influence students' performance and motivation.

Feedback   Feedback (sometimes called *knowledge of results,* or *KR*) is primarily intended to (1) inform students about the quality and accuracy of their performance and (2) help them learn how to monitor and improve their own learning. For example, teachers use feedback on students' papers to inform them of how well they did in comparison to some standard, what could be improved, and how to improve. The information teachers provide through feedback relates directly to the quality or accuracy of the student's academic performance (Glickman, 2002; Walberg, 2003).

For some students, feedback can also provide reinforcement by helping them feel more secure in their ability to complete the task successfully. However, feedback is not always reinforcing, nor is it intended to be.

Teachers must be able to use both feedback and reinforcement effectively. However, skill in providing feedback is more important in helping students learn than ability to provide reinforcement, particularly praise (Chall, 2002). While feedback helps the learner to accurately understand and successfully complete necessary tasks, it does not necessarily reinforce or reward the student's performance.

Effective feedback includes information about (1) the *criteria* used to evaluate performance, (2) how the *student's performance relates* to the standard, and (3) specifically how the performance can or should be *improved* (Behets, 1997; Chesebro & McCroskey, 2001; Shute, 2010). Most people think of feedback as verbal or written comments from the teacher. However, students often learn about the adequacy of their performance simply by observing or comparing their own performance with some standard. Thus, while students can learn from feedback provided by the teacher or peers, they can also learn by examining their performance using rubrics, peer evaluation and feedback, self-reflection, or other methods. The immediate goal of feedback is to improve students' understanding and performance. A long-range goal is to enable learners to judge for themselves the adequacy of their own work or performance.

Several principles can make teachers' feedback more effective:

11.17 What kind of feedback have you found most useful from your own teachers? What was it that made this effective?

1. Provide feedback as frequently as possible—every day for every student, if possible. It is important that you plan and maintain a highly interactive environment providing a variety of opportunities for students to practice or perform, and that you monitor and provide feedback on these performances.

2. Provide feedback as soon after performance as possible. For example, return papers quickly, try to grade immediately following performance, and provide verbal feedback while monitoring students' practice.

3. Make your feedback specific rather than general. For example, use students' names and comment specifically on their performance instead of simply saying "good job" or writing "weak here."

4. Focus feedback on the *quality* of the student's performance, not on his or her intentions or motivations. Good feedback can convey confidence in a student's ability without giving the impression that incomplete or inaccurate work is acceptable and without appearing cold and impersonal. One way to do this is to include feedback on the process (how to do it better) along with the adequacy of the performance.

5. Design and use feedback that teaches students how to gauge their own progress and performance. Gradually allow students to assume more and more responsibility for assessing their progress. Allow them to score their own or each other's papers and provide mutual feedback, to engage in peer editing as a part of the writing process, to watch or listen to recordings of their performances, and so on.

Reinforcement Reinforcement is intended to strengthen and increase the frequency of a desirable behavior or response, usually by providing some type of reward. Reinforcement lets students know when they have done something well in the hope that they will do it again or with greater frequency. When a normally quiet student voluntarily responds to a question, you might attempt to reinforce him, perhaps through a smile or gesture, in the hope that he will contribute more often in the future. Your focus should be on rewarding the student for his participation (that is, his behavior), not necessarily on the accuracy of his response. Chapter 12 will discuss this type of reinforcement further.

In contrast to feedback, which is directed toward improving the quality of students' performance, reinforcement is directed toward increasing motivation. Often reinforcement is provided through verbal praise, but it can take many forms. Repeating or paraphrasing a student's comment or answer or including it in your discussion can be reinforcing. Nonverbal expressions like nods or smiles, eye contact, gestures, or proximity may also reinforce students. More tangibly, reinforcement can take the form of free time, candy, tokens, or other rewards.

Reinforcement, particularly in the form of praise or rewards, is only marginally effective in increasing learning (Chall, 2002; Dweck, 2008). In fact, the relationship between learning and the use of praise seems to be curvilinear. That is, increasing the use of praise will help students learn more only up to a point. After that, increased praise will probably diminish learning. One reason for this may be that praise and other rewards are reinforcing only if the student perceives them to be. If the reward is embarrassing or of no interest to the student, the reward is likely to diminish rather than increase learning (Kennedy, 1997). A second problem with praise and reinforcement is that teachers often unknowingly reinforce the wrong behavior (Callahan, Clark, & Kellough, 2002). For example, to get an unsuccessful student to contribute more often to class discussions, teachers may praise an incorrect or inappropriate contribution rather than the behavior of participating. The result may be that the student does contribute more often, but also learns inaccurate content.

Because reinforcement focuses on students' motivation and self-concept, it is most important early in the learning process and with low-achieving students. Reinforcement is most likely to be successful (1) when it specifically identifies the behavior or performance being rewarded, (2) when it is contingent upon desired behavior or performance (it is not offered when students respond or behave incorrectly), and (3) when it is believable. Criticism (the opposite of praise) can be effective with high-achieving students when used in moderation. Generally, however, it is not effective in promoting learning, and it often is counterproductive, diminishing students' self-concept and motivation (Chall, 2002).

Although a powerful tool, reinforcement should be used sparingly and with caution. Brophy (1998) notes that teachers should try structuring the classroom in order to elicit good student performances in the first place rather than on reinforcing good performance after it has been elicited. Teachers should provide heavy reinforcement and feedback to all students early in the learning process and to low-achieving students throughout. Especially with older students, reinforcement and praise should be low-key, private, and specific to the student's performance.

Reinforcement can and should focus on both motivation and outcome. However, it should be keyed to desirable performance, and the teacher should make clear the specific behavior being reinforced. Although some students should be rewarded for participation even if the response is incorrect, make clear that the reward is for *participation,* not incorrect *performance.* When offering reinforcement or praise, be certain to match verbal and nonverbal behavior. That is, don't tell a student she did a nice job with a scowl on your face! Closely monitor the effectiveness of your reinforcement of each student. Remember, although you may intend your actions to be reinforcing, the student may not perceive them that way. Finally, allow yourself to be somewhat spontaneous with your use of praise; it is more sincere.

11.18 Why do you think teachers emphasize reinforcement and neglect adequate feedback?

Some Final Thoughts

Running through all the specific behaviors discussed in Chapters 10 and 11 is the notion of providing students with instruction that will maximize their learning and their motivation to learn. Establishing set helps students focus. Momentum, variety, and enthusiasm maintain students' interest and engagement. Questions, when used well, help students process the lesson content in order to better understand it. Thus, although we have emphasized teachers' personal attributes and professional behavior, we must always remember that these are merely efficient means to desirable ends. They are not ends in themselves. For example, questions are not used for their own sake, but to help students learn more and better. However, much evidence indicates that these attributes and behaviors are critical in maximizing learning and motivation. They are the foundation upon which instructional alternatives and classroom management strategies are built. The better you are able to use them, the more effective your use of any instructional method, alternative, or strategy will be.

11.19 What can you do now to help ensure that you will make use of what is known about effective teaching in your own classroom?

- Effective teachers possess a repertoire of professional skills that enable them to help students learn more. These professional skills are more open to improvement than personal attributes are. They can be organized around four aspects of instruction: engaging and maintaining students' attention, optimizing the use of instructional time, promoting meaningful teacher-student interaction, and providing effective feedback and reinforcement.

- Skilled teachers engage students' attention and maintain their interest and motivation by establishing set at the beginning of the lesson and incorporating variety in their lessons.

- There are three major types of set. Orientation set engages students in a new instructional activity. Transition set helps students see the relationship between past and present learning. Evaluative set establishes what students may already know about a topic.

- The beginning of a lesson is critical because it establishes a climate or tone for the lesson. The beginning of the lesson should engage students' interest through an interesting or provocative problem; should establish an interactive climate that encourages students to participate; should make students aware early in the lesson of the major topics, objectives, or tasks for the lesson; and should make clear the relationship between the current lesson and previous lessons.

- An effective teacher uses variety in nonverbal behavior, instructional approaches, types of assessment, and a host of other areas. Variability, which Rosenshine and Furst (1971) found to be closely related to students' learning, probably increases learning by helping students remain more interested and engaged.

- The most effective teachers maximize the time available for instruction. The three factors most closely related to the efficient use of instructional time are time on task, momentum, and smooth transitions.

- *Time on task* is a broad term that refers to the amount of time students are actively engaged in academic tasks. Generally, the more time students spend actively engaged in academic tasks, the more they learn. However, only a small percentage of available time is actually used for academic tasks.

- Instructional time can be organized around four levels. Mandated time is the formal time scheduled for school or academic activities: for example, the length of the school year, day, or period. Allocated time is the amount of mandated time intended solely for academic activities. It excludes such things as passing or lunch periods. Academic instruction time is the amount of allocated time during which the teacher is conducting instructional activities. This is time left after taking attendance, giving directions, and so on. Academic learning time is the amount of time a given student spends actively engaged in academic tasks she is mostly successful at doing. This eliminates the part of academic learning time when the student may not be paying attention or may be inaccurately learning the content.

- From mandated to academic learning time, much opportunity for learning is lost. Effective teachers maximize students' engagement by beginning and ending on time, minimizing time spent giving directions, establishing rules and procedures that minimize disruptions, and actively monitoring students' engagement. They also create a highly interactive and varied environment that gets students' attention and holds it throughout the lesson.

- Momentum refers to the flow and pace of classroom activities. Maintaining momentum helps maximize academic learning time by maintaining a brisk instructional pace that still allows students to be successful. Momentum must be adapted to students' needs and to the difficulty or complexity of the required

SUPPLEMENTAL RESOURCES

Go to the text's Online Learning Center at www.mhhe.com/cruickshank6e to access the chapter's **study tools** including web links, practice for Praxis™ case studies, and video clips.

tasks. Generally, teacher-directed instruction allows greater control of momentum and instructional time.

- Instructional time is enhanced when teachers plan for and implement smooth transitions. Transitions are points where students' attention is refocused to new topics or activities.

- Teachers should work to minimize the number and length of transitions and to make them as organized as possible. They should develop routines and procedures for frequently occurring transitions, should inform students about what they are to do ahead of time, and should monitor the transition.

- Effective teachers keep students involved in their lessons through questioning, instructional clarity, and monitoring of understanding.

- Questioning involves not only asking good questions but also knowing how to obtain answers and how to react to students' responses. The most effective questions require students to process information and formulate a correct answer. Closed-response questions should be avoided or minimized. Questions should be phrased clearly and concisely in direct, natural, unambiguous language and should vary in form and in cognitive level depending upon the objectives of the lesson. Teachers ask more and better questions when they include them in their lesson planning. Teachers can enhance the effectiveness of their questioning by using wait time and maximizing student participation. Wait time refers to the pauses teachers place between the question and a student's response and between a student's response and the teacher's reaction. Ideal wait time appears to be between three and five seconds, and allows students to think about the question or response.

- We should address questions to all students, not just volunteers. This keeps the class alert, allows everyone to participate, and permits the teacher to better monitor the success of instruction.

- After a student responds to a question, the teacher's reaction is critical. Possible responses include probing, redirecting, rephrasing, or giving the student the answer. Probing means asking the student additional questions to expand or raise the level or accuracy of the response. Redirecting involves asking another student to answer the same question. This should generally be avoided. Rephrasing means rewording the original question to make it clearer. Generally, this should be done only after the student has unsuccessfully attempted to respond.

- Teachers whom students find most enjoyable and helpful provide instruction that leads them to a clear understanding of the material. Instructional clarity is achieved through logical organization, identifying and reinforcing main points, using good examples to elaborate, and monitoring and correcting.

- Clear teachers use logical organization by informing students of the lesson objectives early in the lesson and presenting the content so that students can see the relationships between concepts or ideas.

- Clear teachers help students identify and reinforce important aspects of the lesson by noting and repeating major points and writing them on the board. Reviews and summaries are included throughout the lesson to help reinforce major points and draw broader conclusions.

- Clear teachers elaborate on important ideas and concepts using concrete, verbal, or written examples and by explicitly showing how ideas, concepts, and tasks are similar to and different from one another.

- Clear teachers monitor and quickly correct students' misunderstandings by asking questions and assigning application exercises throughout the lesson to monitor understanding and to allow students to clarify their own misconceptions.

- Effective teachers carefully and continually assess students' understanding through good questioning and by establishing an open, interactive classroom climate in which students are more likely to ask for help.

- Effective teachers provide students with frequent feedback and reinforcement for their academic performance. Although reinforcement and feedback are both means of responding to student performance, they are designed to achieve different ends.
- Feedback is primarily informational and is intended to help students improve their performance. It is probably more important than reinforcement in promoting learning.
- The most useful feedback includes the standard performance was judged against, how the student's performance compares with that standard, and specifically how the performance can be improved. Feedback should be provided frequently, as soon after performance as possible, and should focus on the quality of performance rather than the student's intentions or effort.
- Reinforcement is intended to strengthen or promote desirable behavior by providing some type of reward. Reinforcement is directed toward motivating students. Thus, it is most useful at points where students are most likely to become frustrated and give up (for example, early in the process of learning a task or at any time with less able students).
- Reinforcement in the form of verbal praise is only marginally effective. The most effective reinforcement is specific to the behavior being rewarded, contingent upon the desired behavior or performance, and believable or genuine.

KEY TERMS

Establishing set, 368	Time on task, 373	Probing, 384
Set induction, 368	Mandated time, 373	Redirecting, 385
Orientation set, 369	Allocated time, 374	Rephrasing, 385
Transition set, 369	Academic instruction time, 374	Instructional clarity, 386
Evaluative set, 369	Academic learning time (ALT), 374	Feedback, 390

ISSUES AND PROBLEMS FOR DISCUSSION

ISSUES

1. "I think it is difficult to meet with three reading groups all working at different levels in the 60 minutes allotted to reading. I find myself neglecting the top group. Also, I don't like giving the groups busywork since it is wasted time for everyone, including the grader. How do others deal with this?"

PROBLEMS The following are problems and concerns teachers have expressed. How do you feel about them? What would you do in each teacher's place?

Problem 1: "Today I spent all afternoon on one lesson. I spent from 12:30 to 1:15 and again from 1:30 to 2:15 on math. They were all 'higher than kites' and it was probably due to Halloween. I caught about five kids writing notes instead of paying attention. When I checked to see if they knew what they were doing, they didn't!"

Problem 2: "We have a good program called 'Book It' to encourage reading. My main concern today is providing my first-grade 'Book It' students with adequate time for oral book reports without neglecting the rest of the class."

Problem 3: "What concerns me is the way so many of my students won't listen to directions. I gave a math assignment and had about 10 kids that didn't know what to do. The lack of inner discipline I see in many students worries me."

Problem 4: "Today's class was disrupted by constant talking. Every time the group was given a new direction or activity, they began talking. I had to remind them more than once to remain quiet."

THEORY INTO ACTION: ACTIVITIES FOR PRACTICE AND YOUR PORTFOLIO

You have learned about the importance of developing several professional skills to improve your instruction. The following exercises will help you apply your understanding.

ACTIVITY 11.1: Planning to Establish Set   Develop a lesson plan for a 10-minute lesson segment in which you will establish at least one of the three types of set. Then, ask a classmate to evaluate the plan using the guidelines in Figure 11.1.

ACTIVITY 11.2: Establishing Set in the Classroom   Conduct an observation of a teacher, focusing on the teacher's use of set induction. Did the teacher establish set? How long did the set take? Which type or types were used? To what extent did the teacher include the four general aspects of effective set? What, if anything, could be done to establish set more effectively?

ACTIVITY 11.3: Variety in College Instruction   Think about one of your current courses. Keep a running list or journal of the forms of variety the instructor uses over a two-week period. Then, label each type of variation as "variety of instructional materials" or "techniques" or "interaction." Which type of variety is used most often? How effective is the instructor's use of variety? List some specific ways in which the teacher could enhance variety.

ACTIVITY 11.4: Observing and Recording Instructional Time   Make two detailed observations of the use of time during teacher-directed lessons. You will need a stopwatch or watch with a second hand. In the first observation, record the amount of time the teacher devotes to academic tasks (for example, providing instruction, answering content questions, and so forth) and the amount of time devoted to noninstructional tasks (taking attendance, correcting behavior, giving directions). What proportion of the time was devoted to instructional tasks? To noninstructional tasks? What might the teacher do to increase the amount of instructional time?

In a second lesson, use this same procedure to assess the academic learning time of one student. At the beginning of the lesson, select a student to observe. Record the amount of time the student appears to be engaged in academic tasks and compare this with the total length of the lesson. What percentage of the time was the student engaged? Were there particular activities that seemed more or less engaging to the student? What did the student do when not engaged? Do you believe this student is typical of the other students in the classroom?

ACTIVITY 11.5: Asking Clear Questions   Rewrite each of the following questions to make them more effective.

1. "What did we say was the capital of Russia?"
2. "True or false? 6×8 is the same as 8×6."
3. "What is the importance of the Eighteenth Amendment to the Constitution? Today we're going to talk about that."

4. "David, you weren't paying attention. What did Aaron just say?"

5. "What could possibly justify the enormous loss of human life during the Vietnam War?"

6. "Can anyone tell me who wrote *A Christmas Carol?*"

ACTIVITY 11.6: Planning for Effective Questioning Generate a list of questions you might use if you were teaching a lesson on American holidays. Attempt to include questions of each type and level. For example, generate lower- and higher-order questions, convergent and divergent questions, process and content questions, and so on.

ACTIVITY 11.7: Planning for Giving Clear Instructions Develop a plan for a short lesson following the suggestions for instructional planning in Chapter 6. Then make notations to help you improve the clarity of the lesson. For example, underline or highlight specific information you will write on the board, indicate points where you will review and summarize, and include questions you will ask to monitor students' understanding.

REFERENCES

Arends, R. (2001). *Learning to teach.* Fifth Edition. New York: McGraw-Hill.

Banikowski, A. (1999). Strategies to enhance memory based on brain-research, *Focus on Exceptional Children, 32*(2), 1–16.

Behets, D. (1997). Comparison of more and less effective teaching behaviors in secondary physical education. *Teacher and Teacher Education, 13,* 215–224.

Blythe, T., Allen, D., & Powell, B. (1999). *Looking together at student work: A window into the classroom* (videotape). New York: Teachers College Press.

Borich, G. (2004). *Effective teaching methods.* Fifth Edition. Upper Saddle River, NJ: Pearson.

Bracey, G. (2001). At the beep, pay attention. *Phi Delta Kappan, 82,* 555–556.

Brophy, J. (n.d.). *Teaching.* Brussels: International Bureau of Education.

Brophy, J. (1981). Teacher praise: A functional analysis. *Review of Educational Research, 51*(1), 5–32.

Brophy, J. (1998). *Motivating students to learn.* Boston: McGraw-Hill.

Brophy, J., & Good, T. (1986). Teacher behavior and student achievement. In M. Wittrock (Ed.), *The handbook of research on teaching* (pp. 328–375). New York: Macmillan.

Brown, S., & Brown, D. (1999). Making the most of a 30-minute class. *Strategies, 13*(2), 33–36.

Bruer, T. (1997). Education and the brain: A bridge too far. *Educational Researcher, 26*(8), 4–16.

Bruer, T. (1999). *The brain and education: Misconceptions and misinterpretations.* Paper presented at the annual meeting of the American Educational Research Association. Montreal, Quebec.

Brush, T. (1997). The effects of group composition on achievement and time on task for students completing ILS activities in cooperative pairs. *Journal of Research on Computing in Education, 30,* 2–17.

Burns, M. (2010, February). Snapshots of student misunderstanding. *Educational Leadership,* 18–22.

Callahan, J., Clark, L., & Kellough, R. (2002). *Teaching in the middle and secondary schools.* Seventh Edition. New York: Prentice Hall.

Chall, J. (2002). *The academic achievement challenge: What really works in the classroom?* New York: Guilford Press.

Chesebro, J., & McCroskey, J. (2001). The relationship of teacher clarity and immediacy with student state receiver apprehension, affect, and cognitive learning. *Communication Education, 50*(1), 59–68.

Clare, S., Jenson, W., & Kehle, T. (2000). Self-modeling as a treatment for increasing on-task behavior. *Psychology in the Schools, 37,* 517–522.

Doyle, W. (1986). Classroom organization and management. In M. C. Wittrock (Ed.), *The handbook of research on teaching* (pp. 392–431). New York: Macmillan.

Dweck, C. (2008). The perils and promises of praise. *Educational Leadership, 65*(2), 34–39.

Eby, J. (2001). *Reflective planning, teaching, and evaluation for the elementary school.* New York: Prentice Hall.

Ellis, A. (2001). *Teaching, learning, and assessment together: The reflective classroom.* Larchmont, NY: Eye on Education.

Glass, G. (2002). Time for school: Its duration and allocation. In A. Molnar (Ed.), *School reform proposals: The research evidence* (EPSL–0201–101–EPRU). Tempe: Arizona State University, Education Policy Research Unit.

Glatthorn, A. (2000). *The principal as curriculum leader: Shaping what is taught and tested.* Thousand Oaks, CA: Sage Publications.

Glickman, C. (2002). *Leadership for learning: How to help teachers succeed.* Alexandria, VA: Association for Supervision and Curriculum Development.

Good, T., & Brophy, J. (2000). *Looking in classrooms.* Eighth Edition. New York: Addison-Wesley Longman.

Grouws, D., & Cebulla, K. (2000). *Improving student achievement in mathematics.* Brussels: International Bureau of Education.

Hall B. (2009). Differentiated instruction: Reaching all students. *Research into Practice*. Retrieved from http://pearsonschoolapps.com/live/assets/200932/PHMath2011_BasiaHall_24382.pdf

Hativa, N. (1998). Lack of clarity in university teaching: A case study. *Higher Education, 36*, 353–381.

Henderson, J. (2010). Forming assessment through technology. *Education Update, 52*(2), 1, 4–5.

Heritage, M., Kim, J., Vendlinski, T., & Herman, J. (2009). From evidence to action: A seamless process in formative assessment? *Educational Measurement and Practice, 28*(3), 24–31.

Hidi, S., & Harackiewicz, J. M. (2000). Motivating the academically unmotivated: A critical issue for the 21st century. *Review of Educational Research, 70*(2), 151–179.

Hill, H., Rowan, B., & Ball, D. (2005). Effects of teachers' mathematical knowledge for teaching on student achievement. *American Educational Research Journal, 42*, 371–406.

Huebner, T. A. (2010, February). Differentiated Instruction. *Educational Leadership, 79–81*.

Jeynes, W. (2003). *Religion, education, and academic success*. Charlotte, NC: Information Age Publishing.

Joyce, B., & Weil, M. (2000). *Models of teaching*. Sixth Edition. Needham Heights, MA: Allyn & Bacon.

Karweit, N. (1984). Time-on-task reconsidered: Synthesis of research on time-on-task. *Educational Leadership, 32–35*.

Kennedy E. (1997). A study of students' fears of seeking academic help from teachers. *Journal of Classroom Interaction, 32*, 11–17.

Kounin, J. (1970). Observing and delineating technique of managing behavior in classrooms. *Journal of Research and Development in Education, 4*(1), 62–72.

Latham, A. (1997). Asking students the right questions. *Educational Leadership, 54*, 84–85.

Leather, R. (2000). Concentration skills. *Child Education, 77*(12), 40–41.

LeNoir, W. (1993). Teacher questions and schema activation. *The Clearinghouse, 66*, 349–352.

Lock, R., & Prigge, D. (2002). Promote brain-based teaching and learning, *Intervention and School Clinic, 37*(4), 237–241.

Lunenburg, F. (1998). Techniques in the supervision of teachers: Preservice and inservice applications. *Education, 118*, 521–525.

Marzano, J. (2002). *Qualities of effective teaching*. Alexandria, VA: Association for Supervision and Curriculum Development.

Meichenbaum, D., & Biemiller, A. (1998). *Nurturing independent learners: Helping students take charge of their learning*. Cambridge, MA: Brookline.

Metcalf, K. (1991). Improving problem-solving instruction using research of instructional clarity. *Issues and Trends in Education, 1*, 6–12.

Metcalf, K., & Cruickshank, D. (1991). Can teachers be trained to be more clear? *Journal of Educational Research, 85*, 107–116.

MiddleWeb online. Access: www.middleweb.com/Tradtch.html .Accessed 01/03/2008.

Monk, D., & Walberg, H. (1991). *Improving educational productivity*. Greenwich, CN: Information Age Publishing.

Ornstein, A., & Lasley, T. (2000). *Strategies for effective teaching*. New York: McGraw-Hill.

Rosenshine, B. (2002). Converging findings on classroom instruction. In A. Molnar (Ed.), *School reform proposals: The research evidence* (EPSL–0201–101–EPRU). Tempe: Arizona State University, Education Policy Research Unit.

Rosenshine, B., & Furst, N. (1971). Research on teacher performance criteria. In B. Smith (Ed.), *Research in teacher education* (pp. 37–72). Englewood Cliffs, NJ: Prentice Hall.

Rowe, M. (1987). Wait time: Slowing down may be a way of speeding up. *American Educator, 11*(1), 38–43, 47.

Sadker, M., & Sadker, D. (2001). Questioning skills. In J. Cooper (Ed.), *Classroom teaching skills* (pp. 143–180). Boston: Houghton Mifflin.

Schmidt, W., McKnight, C. C., Houang, R. T., Wang, H.-C., Wiley, D., Cogan, L. S., & Wolfe, R. G. (2001). *Why schools matter: A cross-national comparison of curriculum and learning*. San Francisco: Jossey-Bass.

Shute, V. J. (2010). Focus on formative feedback. *Review of Educational Research, 78*(1), 153–190.

Smith, B. (2000). Quantity matters: Annual instructional time in an urban school system. *Educational Administration Quarterly, 36*, 652–682.

Sternberg, R. (1994) Answering questions and questioning answers: Guiding children to intellectual excellence. *Phi Delta Kappan, 76*, 135–136.

Tobin, K. (1987). The role of wait time in higher cognitive learning. *Review of Educational Research, 56*, 69–95.

Tomlinson, C. A., & Strickland, C. A. (2005). *Differentiation in practice. A resource guide for differentiating curriculum*. Alexandria, VA: Association for Supervision and Development.

Traver, R. (1998). What is a good guiding question? *Educational Leadership, 55*(6), 70–73.

Walberg, H. (1990). Productive teaching and instruction: Assessing the knowledge base. *Phi Delta Kappan, 71*(6), 470–478.

Walberg, H. (2003). Productive teachers: Assessing the knowledge base. In A. Ornstein, L. Behor-Horenstein, & E. Pajak (Eds.), *Contemporary issues in curriculum*. Boston, MA: Allyn & Bacon.

Walberg, H., & Paik, S. (2000). *Effective educational practices*. Brussels: International Bureau of Education.

Walshaw, M., & Anthony, G. (2008). The teacher's role in classroom discourse: A review of recent research into mathematics classrooms. *Review of Educational Research, 78*(3), 516–552.

Wang, M., Haertel, G., & Walberg, H. (1993–94). What helps students learn? *Educational Leadership, 51*(4), 74–79.

Weiss, R., & Pasley, J. (2004). What is high-quality instruction? *Educational Leadership, 61*(5), 24–28.

Wenglinsky, H. (2000). *How teaching matters: Bringing the classroom back into discussions of teacher quality*. Princeton, NJ: Educational Testing Service.

Winter, C. (2001). *Brain based teaching: Fad or promising teaching method*. Unpublished paper. University Park, IL: Governors State University (ERIC Document Reproduction Service ED 455 218).

Yair, G. (2000). Not just about time: Instructional practices and productive time in school. *Educational Administration Quarterly, 36*, 485–512.

Zahorik, J. (1987). The effects of planning on teaching. *The Elementary School Journal, 71*, 143–151.

Classroom Management Skills of Effective Teachers

Conversation Starters

What effect does an individual teacher have on a class—would a teacher swap make a difference?

Take one class of well-behaved, on-task students and another classs in which students appear rowdy and out of control. Swap the teachers for two weeks.

Would the students' behavior and learning change? If so, how and why? What is the key to having a class of well-behaved students focused on learning?

"I feel ready to teach, but what do I do if I can't get the students to settle down and listen to me?"

The anxiety this student teacher expresses reminds us that a common, persistent problem among teachers, and perhaps the greatest fear of new teachers, is classroom management. Indeed, a survey conducted by the U.S. Department of Education revealed that less than 20 percent of first-year teachers felt well prepared to deal with classroom management and discipline (Phi Delta Kappa International, 2006). While the characteristics of an effective classroom manager are somewhat obvious, you might wonder how you become an effective classroom manager. Are effective classroom managers born or made?

Fortunately, effective classroom managers are made. According to Marzano, Marzano, & Pickering (2003), good classroom managers are simply teachers who understand and use specific techniques—research-based techniques that direct their behavior which, in turn, changes the behavior of students and leads to higher student engagement and achievement. In fact, research suggests that it is relatively easy to become a skilled classroom manager. Even minimal training, such as reading this chapter and receiving minimal instruction, can significantly improve your management skills (Emmer, Sanford, Clements, & Martin, 1982; Emmer, Sanford, Evertson, Clements, & Martin, 1981).

Teachers who manage their classrooms effectively have a plan. You should begin developing a classroom management plan at once. Your plan should include four parts. First, you must anticipate and decide how to *prevent management problems* from occurring. Second, you should decide how to *monitor students' behavior* in order to maintain a good learning environment. Third, you should plan how to *react when students misbehave* in your classroom. Finally, you need to determine how to *reestablish the learning environment* when misbehavior disrupts your classroom community. This chapter is organized to help you develop specific management strategies in each of these four areas.

What Is Classroom Management?

Traditionally, classroom management has been focused on how teachers react *after* students misbehave. The emphasis was on **discipline,** or the specific actions teachers or others take in response to a student who disobeys a reasonable classroom or school rule (Wolfgang & Kelsay, 1995). Some teachers spend as much as 80 percent of their time and effort trying to control student behavior (Englander, 1986).

Surprisingly, this approach does not seem to work. Teachers who are obsessed with disciplining students or who neglect instructional preparation in favor of total control tend to end up with *more* control problems than teachers who are well prepared and who focus their efforts on helping students achieve academically (Brophy & Evertson, 2000). This may be because teachers, especially novices, frequently believe learning cannot take place until the classroom is organized and the students are under control. They focus their time and energy on controlling students rather than on teaching-learning processes (Anderson, 1991; Dollard, 1996).

Research suggests that these control-oriented teachers may be trying too hard and teaching too little. That is, they are not presenting the clear, uninterrupted, brisk-paced lessons essential to students' involvement and learning. Every research study attempting to link learning with some classroom influence shows that effective management skills are positively related to students' achievement. That is, when students spend more time engaged in learning tasks and correspondingly less time engaged in nonacademic behaviors, they learn more. In short, academic engagement is inversely related to students' misbehavior (Hawley & Rosenholtz, 1984).

In the 1970s, research by Kounin shifted attention from reactive disciplinary strategies to **proactive,** or preventive, views of classroom management. Effective

12.1 What characteristics have you observed in effective classroom managers?

12.2 What are your greatest fears about classroom management?

proactive management includes establishing clear rules and predictable routines, monitoring behavior, consistently enforcing rules, and anticipating behavior problems and responding immediately (McGinnis, Frederick, & Edwards, 1995). It is clear that the most effective classroom managers are those who anticipate events or situations that precede academic or behavioral problems and act to prevent problems from arising in the first place (DiGiulio, 2007; Kern & Clemens, 2007). Kounin's work reminds teachers that although they must be able to discipline students when necessary, effective instruction must be the first priority. Indeed, proactive or **antecedent strategies** reduce disruptive behavior by at least 75 percent (Jones & Jones, 2009). Doyle (1983) found that the curriculum and daily academic work are an integral part of classroom management because they can motivate students, engage them in challenging activities and thinking, and prevent them from drifting into misbehavior. Effective classroom managers, then, strive to elicit students' cooperation and involve them in high-interest activities, thus preventing potential discipline problems.

For today's classrooms, a comprehensive management plan should include both proactive (preventive) and reactive (disciplinary) management strategies. **Classroom management,** then, can be defined as the provisions and procedures necessary to create and maintain a classroom community in which teaching and learning can occur. This means that when you plan your classroom management strategies you need to consider the sort of classroom environment you want and the rules and routines necessary to establish this learning community. Further, you must learn how to hold students accountable for following classroom procedures and how to reinforce and reward students for doing so. Finally, you need to plan how you will intervene when misbehavior does occur.

12.3 How, if at all, have you changed your mind about classroom control?

Preventing Management Problems

The transition from the world of preservice education to the real world of teaching is problematic and traumatic. Why? Because preservice teachers like you rarely see practicing teachers take an empty classroom, multitudes of raw materials, a designated group of students, and school goals and organize them into a dynamic, safe, cooperative learning community. Think about the classroom observation experiences you have had thus far. Most education students observe and practice in classrooms that are already well-established. As a result, the issue of how to set up a classroom with a positive learning environment is generally overlooked in teacher preparation programs.

Fortunately, even if you have not observed a teacher establishing a positive learning environment, you do not have to depend on your intuition or on trial and error when you attempt to set up your own classroom. Research over the past three decades tells us exactly what effective classroom managers do to prevent management problems and to establish classrooms where teaching and learning occur. Effective teachers begin early in the school year to systematically implement a carefully developed plan. They thoughtfully establish the physical and psychological environments in their classrooms. Further, they plan and implement classroom routines to make the classroom a more predictable place. Let's focus in more detail on these aspects of preventive management.

ESTABLISHING THE PHYSICAL AND PSYCHOLOGICAL ENVIRONMENTS

The classroom environment has a powerful impact on students' behavior, learning, and motivation. Years ago, Lewin and his associates showed that the interaction between one's needs and the surrounding environmental conditions is a key factor in explaining an individual's behavior (Lewin, Lippitt, & White, 1939).

Teachers can manipulate two elements of the classroom environment to increase learning and improve behavior. The **physical environment** consists of those aspects of the classroom that are independent of the people who inhabit it. The shape and size of the room, the seating arrangement, and the location and availability of equipment and materials are major aspects of the physical environment. Because these are concrete and observable, most of the students in a classroom would describe the physical environment in the same way.

In contrast, the **psychological environment** exists only in the minds of those who occupy the classroom. As a result, the students and teacher may experience and describe the psychological environment in different ways. The psychological environment is sometimes referred to as the classroom **climate.** It includes the emotional tone of the classroom and the comfort level students feel with the teacher, learning tasks, and one another as a social group (Eggen & Kauchak, 2009; Walberg, 1987).

OLC Web Link
Busy Teachers' Café

Planning the Physical Environment   Effective classroom management starts with decisions about the physical environment in the classroom, or classroom design. Ideally, the design reflects a learning community where work flows throughout the classroom, where materials are readily available, and where the logical organization of the classroom enables students to feel safe and to maximize learning. Traditional classrooms are designed around a "chalk and talk" view of learning, with students seated in rows that require them to focus on the teacher and chalkboard, reinforcing the notion that the teacher is the main source of knowledge and largely responsible for students' learning. Increasingly, teachers are viewed as the "guide on the side" or as learning coaches, with students held responsible for their own learning. This dramatically impacts the design of the physical environment by requiring places for students to learn from each other and to readily access computers and learning resources (Cookson, 2006). In either case, how you arrange your classroom and your students' places within it has important management considerations.

We know that the physical environment influences students' behavior and learning. As presented in Chapter 4, Maslow identified a hierarchy of the needs that motivate human behavior and learning (Maslow & Laury, 1998). Maslow's work suggests that everyone, students and teachers alike, has a basic need to feel safe and secure in their surroundings. They also need to feel valued as members of a social group or learning community and to be challenged by new and engaging experiences. Student misbehavior is often a result of their efforts to meet these basic needs. For example, a student seated close to a computer station used by students doing group projects may feel threatened when classmates congregate there. She may verbally or physically lash out at the students to keep them out of "her" space. Thoughtful classroom design can minimize or eliminate this and many other classroom problems.

12.4   Where do you prefer to sit in a classroom? Why?

Seating Patterns   One of the most obvious aspects of the physical environment is the seating arrangement. Students need to know that the classroom is a safe, comfortable place for positive social and academic experiences. They need enough space to move freely and to work at their desks or in small groups without distractions.

As you plan, remember that seating arrangement impacts student behavior and academic achievement (Pace & Price, 2005). How do students interact when they are seated in traditional rows? They tend to be focused on instruction and to persist at independent learning tasks since it is difficult for them to interact with each other (Wheldall, Morris, Vaughan, & Ng, 1981). In contrast, students seated face to face around tables interact more frequently with their peers. Sitting around a table seems to influence the development of student leadership abilities. Weinstein (1987) found that when students are assigned to sit at tables with two on one side and three on the other, twice as many leaders emerge from the side where only two students sat, perhaps because these students could influence more people. In a circular seating arrangement, students are most likely to speak to those seated directly across from them. They rarely speak to persons seated beside them. This suggests that teachers can influence the flow of discussion by purposefully seating students. For example, when a quiet student sits opposite the leader, chances are that the quiet student will participate more than usual. Conversely, placing an overly vocal student next to the leader should prevent that student from dominating the discussion.

Seating arrangement also affects the interactions between students and the teacher. Students seated in the front and down the middle of a traditional classroom define a triangular area in which most interaction occurs called the **action zone** (Figure 12.1). Teachers are physically closer to and interact more frequently and more positively with students seated in the action zone. These students tend to participate more, work more persistently, and hold more positive attitudes toward the class. Students seated outside of this zone and farther from the teacher attain lower levels of achievement and hold less positive attitudes toward learning (Adams & Biddle, 1970). Research suggests that students who choose seats outside the action zone tend to have lower self-esteem, to doubt their academic ability, and to feel threatened by the classroom environment or the teacher. Seated along the periphery of the classroom, these students are less engaged with the teacher and the lesson and are more easily distracted. They also interact with each other more than students seated at the front (Granstrom, 1996). This leads to increased failure, which reinforces their self-doubt and low self-esteem (Dykman & Reis, 1979).

In Chapter 11, we discussed the importance of an interactive classroom to learning. When students are involved and interacting in the classroom, they feel a sense of belonging and, because they are engaged, they are less likely to misbehave. This suggests that teachers should consider the student-teacher action zone when arranging students. While allowing students to select their own seats, especially at the secondary level, has some psychological benefits, it may be advisable

---

FIGURE 12.1 Action Zone in the Classroom

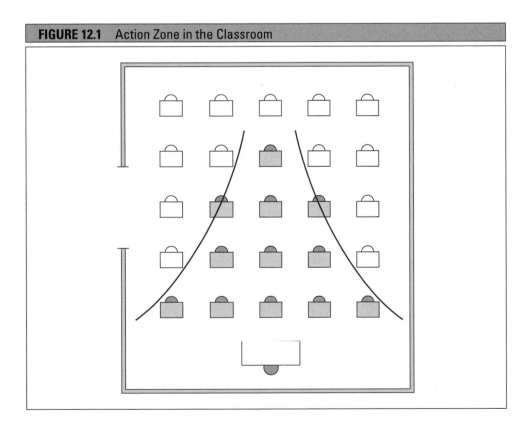

to gradually move students with academic or behavioral problems into the action zone to increase their academic engagement. Relatedly, teachers should be sure to call on students seated on the edges of the classroom, especially non-volunteers. The location of the action zone can be changed by the way a teacher instructs and monitors students. Because the action zone is defined in terms of the teacher's position in the classroom, it can be redefined by relocating the teacher's desk or teaching station, or by circulating to all parts of the room while delivering instruction.

No single seating arrangement is ideal for all classes, learning situations, or individuals. Generally, seating in rows works best to maximize on-task behavior during independent work. Rows are also most beneficial for special needs students in inclusive classrooms. Researchers found that sitting in rows doubled the on-task behavior and decreased the disruption rate by two-thirds for students with behavioral disorders and learning disabilities (Wheldall et. al., 1981; Wheldall & Lam, 1987). Dunn (2001) found that the best arrangement has wide walkways so that the teacher can easily move among students. Moving around the classroom during instruction makes it possible to monitor all students more closely and to interact with them more equitably. One teacher describes her movement around the classroom as "talking and stalking" to keep students engaged in learning. The North Carolina Teachers' Network website shows you how to arrange the classroom for the various instructional approaches discussed in Chapters 7 and 8. Click on "New Teacher Support" for diagrams.

Rather than constantly changing the arrangement of student seats, some teachers use a "home base formation" that serves as a semipermanent arrangement. This formation should be suitable for many teaching situations and easily moved into alternative formations as needed. Borich (2006) suggests traditional rows as the home base formation because this arrangement conveys a businesslike appearance, is easily monitored, and can be reorganized quickly into small groups, circles, or other formations for increased interaction among students. Weinstein and Mignano (2010) agree that novice teachers should seat students in rows until they feel confident in their management abilities. However, the arrangement may be modified later based on students' characteristics and the type of learning community the teacher wants to establish.

Equipment and Materials   Where and how you store supplies and equipment will affect their accessibility. Providing students ready access to reference books, computers, and supplies will reduce the number of times you need to handle supplies or give instructions. Students should have access to resources and supplies without reaching across other students' desks or crowding their chairs. Equipment should also accommodate the physical needs of students. For example, teachers should provide appropriate scissors and desks for left-handed students and wheelchair accessible laboratory equipment when needed. Realizing that ADHD students may need to move around, one teacher allowed an ADHD student to sit in a chair that was on wheels and swiveled. The student could spin and fidget but had to stay at his desk and on task, not disturbing others or the lesson.

Organize your classroom to prevent lines and bottlenecks around storage areas, reference shelves, and computer workstations. Have a clear plan that allows sufficient time to clean up after labs or activities. When several students are waiting or pushing to return supplies, inappropriate behavior is bound to erupt.

Room Arrangement   Research attests to the impact of room arrangement on students' behavior and learning. It suggests that an attractive, well-organized environment leads to more positive attitudes, better grades, and more receptive students. Further, students persist longer at tasks, participate more in discussions, and feel closer to the group in pleasantly arranged classrooms. Conversely, unattractive

Web Link
North Carolina Teachers'
Network

Try Activity 12.1

Web Link
Classroom Setup Tool

classrooms have been linked to frequent absenteeism, discomfort, fatigue, and complaints from both parents and students (Sommer & Olsen, 1980; Wang, Haertel, & Walberg, 1993–94). A pleasant and comfortable physical environment is especially important to students with low self-esteem or with a history of school failure; that is, students who are at risk of failing or leaving school (Raviv, Raviv, & Reisel, 1990).

Today, teachers have more physical space to arrange and manage. In 1970, an average elementary school provided 62 square feet for each student. By 1995, each pupil had 111 square feet—a 79 percent increase (White, 1996)! Today's technology-enriched classrooms require 15 to 20 square feet of additional classroom space per computer workstation. Middle and high schools have grown similarly. Regardless of whether your actual classroom space is larger, it will be more complex. Regular classrooms are being outfitted to accommodate physically challenged students and rewired to incorporate new technology into everyday instruction. Distractions and congestion can be minimized in these complex classrooms by arranging furniture in a way that orients students toward the primary sources of information yet also gives them access to resources and activities without disturbing others. For example, if you do choose to seat students in groups or around tables, be sure all students can see the teaching center of the room without looking around other students, turning their chairs, or uncomfortably twisting their bodies. The teacher should also have an unrestricted view of all students and access to projection equipment and the board.

When arranging the physical environment, it is also important to consider the types of instructional activities that will occur in the classroom. Use open space or furniture to establish activity boundaries or to separate incompatible activities. For example, you might use low bookcases to separate group work or activity centers from seatwork areas. Dividers like these should be high enough to provide an undisturbed work space for students in that area but low enough for you to see students in all parts of the room. Also, be sure to provide open lanes for movement between frequently used activity areas, such as between students' desks and the computer station or the printer. You will also need to determine where to direct student traffic to avoid distractions and congestion where students are working. Figures 12.2 and 12.3 (on page 409) contrast good and poor classroom arrangements. What advantages and problems do you see with each arrangement?

Planning the Psychological Environment   We can think of the psychological environment as the climate or atmosphere of the class that potentially influences what students learn. A positive learning environment promotes cooperative working relationships and helps prevent discipline problems (Cookson, 2006). Three aspects of the psychological environment are consistently linked with students' learning: emotional affect, or tone; task orientation; and organization (Wang, Haertel, & Walberg, 1993–94).

Tone   An **inviting classroom** is an appealing, positive place that provides a sense of physical and emotional safety for students and the teacher. That is, it has a positive tone. Maslow's hierarchy of needs (Maslow & Laury, 1998) outlines what motivates and influences human behavior and helps us understand why an inviting classroom is so important (Figure 12.4 also on page 409). Maslow described the most basic human need as that for safety and security, followed by a need for acceptance or esteem and recognition. Only when these needs have been met is it possible to fulfill the human need for aesthetic pleasure and mental challenges. This suggests that students are most able to learn and to behave appropriately when they feel safe, secure, and accepted.

How can you create a classroom where students feel psychologically and emotionally safe? Such a classroom is characterized by three qualities: it is attractive, it encourages prosocial development, and it exhibits ownership.

12.5   Recall a classroom that you think had a good physical environment. What was it like?

12.6   What classroom characteristics make you feel energized and ready to learn?

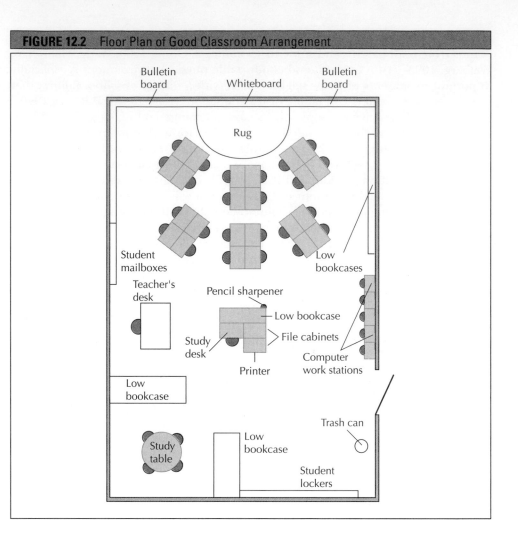

FIGURE 12.2   Floor Plan of Good Classroom Arrangement

12.7 Do the needs of today's students differ from those of students when you were in school? How could this influence your classroom environment?

Effective teachers use color, light, temperature, and displays to create an attractive classroom tone where students feel safe and comfortable (Cookson, 2006; Intrator, 2004). For example, to offset the cold impression that wood or linoleum floors, Formica desks, fluorescent lights, and plaster or concrete walls convey, you could use soft, textured bulletin board coverings, plants, family photographs, a rocking chair with a seat cushion, and movie posters. Conveying a sense of softness and safety is especially important for young children. Use light, texture, and color in a coherent, orderly way and in moderation. Overuse may overstimulate students, tiring them emotionally and distracting them from learning.

Even if you share a classroom with other teachers you can create a sense of softness and psychological safety. One teacher carried a small vase of flowers from room to room to soften the mood in any classroom in which she taught her English classes. Carrying a colorful, textured book bag or a personalized coffee mug or wearing colorful neckties or accessories conveys a sense of softness to students. Your worksheets and handouts add to the positive tone if they are duplicated on colored paper, contain pictures or cartoons, and are neat and uncluttered.

Traditional classrooms are often described as lonely, isolated, silent, competitive, and lacking in spontaneity and interaction (Lyman & Foyle, 1990); especially by low-achieving and minority students. Further, Goodlad (1984) described classrooms as having a "flat, neutral emotional ambiance [where] . . . boredom is a disease of epidemic proportion" (p. 9). In contrast, inviting classrooms are communities of learners that demonstrate trust and mutual respect between

FIGURE 12.3   Floor Plan of Poor Classroom Arrangement

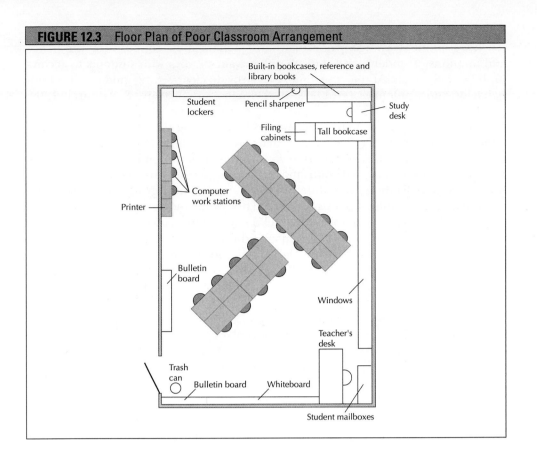

teacher and students, academic rigor, cooperative relationships among students, and a sense of student satisfaction (Bartolomé, 1996; Canter, 1996; Cookson, 2006).

You as the teacher are a key in establishing this inviting classroom community. Research shows that many disciplinary problems can be prevented with better teacher-student relationships (Sheets & Gay, 1996). But this doesn't mean trying to be a friend to students, even at the high school level. Wubbels and his colleagues

FIGURE 12.4   Hierarchy of Human Needs

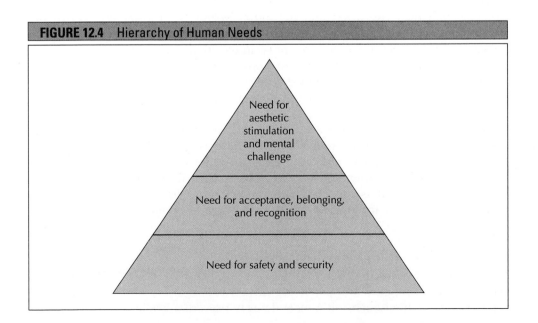

studied the dynamics of teacher-student relationships and found that optimum teacher-student relationships occur when teachers show concern for the needs and opinions of students and show that they want to work with students to accomplish learning goals. At the same time, they provide clear, strong guidance for both behavior and academics (Wubbels, Brekelmans, vanTartwijk, & Admiral, 1999; Wubbels & Levy, 1993).

12.8 How can a teacher show respect for students? What shows a lack of respect for students?

You can build relationships with students by modeling the trust and respect you want from them. Canter (1996) stresses that you should listen to your students, make eye contact with them, and give them your complete attention during interactions. You should speak respectfully with students and be aware of words and actions that students, especially those from different cultural and ethnic groups, consider disrespectful. Further, Canter suggests getting to know your students as individuals. Greet them at the door by name and with a hello and a smile. Acknowledge their birthdays and other events in their lives and attend their sports events, recitals, and concerts. This shows students that you care about and support them both in and out of the classroom. When students feel that their teachers care about them, they are more intrinsically motivated to learn and to assume responsibilities in the classroom (Grolnick, Ryan, & Deci, 1991).

Freiberg (1996) observed that too often classroom relationships based on trust and support in the elementary grades are replaced by classrooms that emphasize compliance and obedience in later grades, especially in urban schools. Without a cooperative, supportive psychological environment, students tend to pass through school without active involvement, commitment, or a sense of belonging and tend to achieve little (Intrator, 2004). In contrast, inviting classroom communities exhibit ownership. Recall that Maslow suggested that a feeling of belonging and recognition of achievement are basic human needs. Students sense ownership when they participate in activities that increase status, visibility, recognition, and group cohesiveness. Cover classroom walls with students' work. Let students create signs and exhibits. Feature student information and newspaper clippings. This psychological environment encourages prosocial development in students.

12.9 What qualities do you have that will enable you to establish an inviting learning community? What skills do you need to acquire?

Task Orientation A classroom with a positive psychological environment is a busy, task-oriented place. In task-oriented classrooms, students perceive there are definite learning goals to pursue and believe they will be held accountable for reaching those goals. The assigned work is matched to students' instructional levels and students can choose among activities to show that they have accomplished the learning objectives (Kern & Clemens, 2007). Relatedly, they spend most of the classroom time working toward those learning goals. Even during free time, the classroom environment should encourage intellectual exploration. For example, learning centers displaying enrichment books and motivational posters add to a task-oriented environment. Computers that are turned on and ready for use, rather than shut down and buried under books, also encourage learning and exploration.

Try Activity 12.2

Organization As we have seen, a classroom with a positive psychological environment is also organized in a predictable way. Clear, concise, concrete expectations outline appropriate behavior and learning. Routines provide structure by establishing when the computers can be used, how to turn in papers for grading, and how to gain the teacher's attention. Teachers who are effective managers organize their classrooms with appropriate rules and routines. This is the focus of our next section.

ESTABLISHING CLASSROOM RULES AND ROUTINES

Effective classroom management is proactive. As we have seen, by thoughtfully establishing the physical and psychological environments in your classroom, you can prevent much misbehavior. A second way to prevent misbehavior is to organize the procedures and movement in the classroom. In a well-organized classroom, students clearly understand how to behave responsibly and are guided toward pro-social behaviors by the predictable structure of the classroom. Thus, you can prevent misbehavior in your classroom and establish a learning environment by developing rules and implementing routines that create order, structure, and a sense of community. Classroom **rules** are explicit statements that present behavior expectations and that help to establish a predictable learning environment (Grossman, 2004; Kerr & Nelson, 2006). Classroom **routines** are established procedures that direct and coordinate how students move and how events occur. Thoughtfully developed rules and routines encourage students to accept responsibility for their own behavior.

Research shows that academic achievement for students at all levels is significantly higher in classrooms where rules and routines are implemented. Further, it shows that rules and procedures at home have a profound impact on student learning and student behavior in school (Marzano, Marzano, & Pickering, 2003). Today's classrooms are unpredictable and complex because of increased student diversity, increased accountability for teachers, and shifting societal norms (see Chapters 2 and 3). This complexity complicates learning for many students, especially those with learning, language, or social challenges. Jackson (1990) contends that many students fail at school not because they lack intelligence, but because they are unable to decipher or understand classroom procedures which may vary greatly from the routines at home. This suggests the need for well-articulated rules and routines that are negotiated with students to make the classroom less complex and to maximize student learning.

Teachers also benefit from rules and routines. A predictable classroom is less stressful for the teacher. Certain routines, such as taking attendance and collecting papers, become automatic, predictable classroom events and enable teachers to use class time more effectively. Routines help ensure that needed materials are available and that students know how to go about their learning activities. Routines make lessons smoother and more effective by reducing interruptions for questions such as, "Can I use the computer now?" or "Where should I put my homework?" Further, 61 percent of teachers surveyed strongly agreed that strictly enforcing rules and routines can create the right tone and prevent more serious problems (Wooden, 2004).

Given the benefits of classroom rules and routines for both students and teachers, it is important to consider how to establish them. Indeed, in well-organized and managed classrooms, teachers spend at least as much time early in the year planning and establishing classroom rules and routines as they do on content instruction (Emmer, Evertson, & Anderson, 1980).

Developing Classroom Rules   Too often, teachers develop rules and assume that appropriate student behavior will follow. But rules alone, without a management plan that includes classroom routines, individual responsibilities, and a discipline strategy, have a marginal effect on behavior (McGinnis, Frederick, & Edwards, 1995).

Researchers provide guidelines for establishing effective classroom rules. The general consensus is that four to five rules is the maximum number that students can easily recall, although this number may need to be expanded or reduced based on grade level (Gable, Hester, Rock, & Hughes, 2009; Kern & Clemens, 2007). Rules should convey exactly what type of behavior is expected in observable, measurable terms. The wording of the rules should be simple and specific enough to avoid alternative interpretations. It is also best to state rules positively and to explain the desired behavior. For example, "keep your eyes on the teacher" is better than "no looking around." Finally, rules should be posted in a prominent place for all to see. Using pictures to illustrate rules helps young children, those with visual learning styles, and students with reading or language difficulties.

12.10   Think about a typical day. What routines do you follow to organize your life and make it less complex?

12.11   What problems have you observed because teachers haven't developed or communicated routines?

Try Activity 12.3

 Web Link
Teaching Resources by Laura Candler

CHAPTER 12
Classroom Management Skills of Effective Teachers

Web Link
Education World

Should students have a voice in developing classroom rules? Research suggests that the most effective classroom managers engage students in the design of rules and routines (Kern & Clemens, 2007; Marzano, Marzano, & Pickering, 2003; McGinnis, Frederick, & Edwards, 1995). The Education World website provides activities for involving students in creating classroom rules. Marzano and his colleagues suggest starting with a discussion about rules and expectations for behavior in real life, such as how the rules that guide behavior while having dinner at home with guests do not apply when you're lunching at McDonald's with friends. A discussion of how expectations define appropriate behavior and the importance of rules in various social situations leads nicely to a discussion of classroom rules. Present a basic framework of rules that you have already developed, explaining and providing examples of each one. Incorporate student input that emerges from the discussion and with which all parties agree, keeping in mind that you, the teacher, should have the final word in the deliberations. As we have seen, an effective, inviting classroom is built on a foundation of trust and respect. The discussion about rules should communicate that students' perspectives and input are an essential part of establishing the learning community.

Web Link

Scholastic Teaching
Resources

Developing Classroom Routines   Routines or procedures provide the infrastructure that guides daily life in classrooms and supports rules and expectations. Routines lead to a more predictable, less confusing classroom environment so students are more likely to be engaged in learning and less likely to display problem behavior. Effective managers establish four types of routines in their classrooms: management, activity, instructional, and executive planning routines (Leinhardt, Weldman, & Hammond, 1987; Yinger, 1979). For each one, the teacher must predetermine to whom the routine applies, when it applies, and what procedures or steps are involved.

Management Routines   **Management routines** involve nonacademic matters such as distributing and collecting materials and papers, leaving and entering the room, making transitions between activities and classes, cleaning the room, and taking attendance. Highlight 12.1 provides an example of management routines using technology in a classroom. Because they communicate expectations for behavior, management routines are the nuts and bolts of a smoothly functioning classroom.

Many management routines are related to classroom transitions such as entering and leaving the room. Transitions are frequent classroom events. Doyle (1986) observed about 31 major transitions each day in most elementary classrooms, and Steele (1988) found that transitions in secondary classrooms occur three or four times per hour. While effective classroom managers conduct transitions in approximately 30 seconds, less effective teachers require up to nine minutes (Steele, 1988). As we learned in Chapter 11, poorly conducted transitions are disruptive, waste instructional time, and encourage misbehavior.

How can you conduct quick and orderly transitions in your classroom? *First, you must signal the students that a transition is about to begin.* The signal may be verbal or nonverbal. Some teachers, for example, use a phrase such as "Attention, please" to attract students' attention before beginning the transition. Elementary teachers often use nonverbal cues such as dimming the lights or raising their hand. Songs or clapping sequences are especially effective with primary students. A clapping sequence requires students to stop what they are doing, put all supplies down, and clap their hands while they focus their attention on the teacher. Another teacher's approach is more dramatic. He calls out "Funny face," and students freeze with any funny expression on their face, as long as their mouth is closed. He calls, "Superman," and students freeze in place, puff out their chests, and put their hands on their hips. The nature of the signal is less important than what it does. That is, students must be taught to respond with full attention to the teacher as soon as the

12.12   How have you seen teachers focus students' attention?

Teachers are the gateway to technology use by students. In his study of how routine use of technology affects teaching and learning, Cuban (2001) noted that technology increases the complexity of classrooms. Technology raises issues of managing resources and students. Below, experienced teachers share their management tips for one-computer classrooms, where management issues are especially acute.

Managing Resources

- Locate the computer where students have easy access and enough room for small group work. Keep the computer away from direct sunlight, water, magnets, and chalk dust. Be sure you can see the computer so that you can supervise its use from anywhere in the classroom.

- Require students to use headphones when working with programs that have sound. To prevent head lice outbreaks, have students bring their own headphones and store them in large freezer zip lock bags with students' names on them.

- Provide students with a thumb drive to save their work. Teach students to back up their work on the hard drive. Whenever students save a file, give them the exact name to use when saving the file in case it is saved in the wrong location.

Managing Students with Routines

- "I have one computer for 26 students in my fourth-grade class. One thing I have found successful is to provide a question of the day about the particular history topic that I am teaching. I bookmark a website in the morning. I leave a small notepad and pencil near the computer. I also put a Popsicle stick on each student's desk with his or her number. When they have answered the question at the computer, they leave their stick in a cup by the computer. This way I can tell who still needs to go back to the computer. At the end of the day, we pull names to find out who answered the question correctly."

- "Many of my learning centers in my eighth-grade classroom require research. Not all of the students have access to a computer at home. I have found it very useful to have sites ready for them to use for their research. I have bookmarked them in the past, but the students did not know the best sites to go to for their particular research needs. I also ended up with so many sites bookmarked that it became difficult to find the one they wanted. I have now created a notebook with the first page from the sites I have found useful. This allows the students to preview the material that will be found on the site. This cuts down on the amount of time the students need to be at the computer randomly surfing, and they go directly to a useful site and conduct their research. We update the notebook as we discover useful sites."

- "Many of my high school English students are more tech savvy than I am, so I use them as 'trained experts' to help their classmates. Interested students prepare a resume showing their computer skills (keyboarding, hardware, software programs, printing, scanning, editing). I appoint and schedule 'experts' based on these resumes. I 'train' them so that they know the difference between helping their classmates and doing their work for them! Experts' names and skills are posted near the computer so students know who to consult for specific help. As students gain computer skills, they update their resumes and may be approved to assist in additional areas. This gives students experience with developing and updating a resume and frees me up to help students with developing concepts, planning, and revising instead of being tied to the computer."

signal is given. Never proceed with the transition until all students have responded to the cue and are attending to you.

Second, give clear directions about what students are to do. When students are first learning the transition routine, it is important to break the transition down into a few simple steps. Reinforce understanding by writing directions on the whiteboard or by asking students to repeat them. With younger students or students with limited English proficiency, it is especially important to demonstrate each step of the directions and to check for understanding. You might, for example, ask everyone to point to where they are to put the glue when they clean up and then to point to where they are to put their finished projects. If you are breaking the class into small groups, ask the students to point to where their group will meet. Never allow students to begin moving until all students have convinced you that they know exactly what they are to do next. This is as important for secondary students as it is for younger students.

Third, signal students to make the transition. Perhaps the most difficult aspect of classroom transitions is monitoring students who are in different stages of carrying out the directions. Monitoring is much easier if all students make the transition at once. That is, part of the class should not be finishing the last step of a laboratory experiment while others are cleaning up and still others are assembled in the front of the room awaiting the class discussion. This requires that you manage *three* different groups of students at one time. Some students will inevitably make the transition more quickly than others; therefore, it is important that you monitor all stages of the transition. Circulate around the room, encouraging the slower students and letting everyone know that you are aware of what is going on throughout the room. Use statements like, "Thanks for doing such a thorough job of cleaning up, Sam. Now you're ready to move to the front of the room," or "I see that four people are already cleaned up and waiting quietly in their seats for the discussion to begin."

As with rules, you must teach your students classroom routines rather than just announcing or posting them. One teacher has a large flip chart inside his classroom door with laminated pages. Each page lists the routines for the major transitions that occur such as going to the library or to an assembly. Before major transitions, he asks a student to flip to the appropriate page and review the procedure with the class. Occasionally, after a transition, the teacher flips to the appropriate page and asks students to evaluate how well they did (Marzano, Marzano, & Pickering, 2003). Once students learn the directions and your expectations during transitions, these become management routines that save instructional time and reduce the stress on both you and your students. Because students know what they are to do, they are less likely to misbehave.

Activity Routines   Generally when teachers think about a school day or class period, they think of it as made up of many different kinds of activities. For example, an elementary teacher may conceptualize the morning as including attendance and announcements, sharing time, silent reading, whole-class reading time, and then recess. A secondary physical education teacher may think about a period as attendance, warm-up, fitness walk or run, skill instruction, then wrap up or closure. Activities are the basic structural units of the classroom. Effective teachers establish **activity routines** that spell out how each kind of activity will be conducted. This is especially important for inclusion students or students who have been schooled in another country. If they were used to rote learning, they will need clear directions and encouragement to participate in student-centered activities and to develop new ways of learning.

Activity routines require planning the location, duration, and participants. Further, activity routines specify the content, structure, and sequence of the activity and let students know what materials are needed. Activity routines also provide important guidelines for appropriate student behavior and interactions. They establish acceptable ways for the students and teacher to gain each others' attention and apprise students of when it is acceptable to interact with one another.

One primary grade teacher, for example, sits in a rocking chair with her students seated around her on a rug while she reads to them. This "rug time" is an established activity with routines. When the teacher announces that it is rug time, students know to get up from their desks, push in their chairs, and quietly walk to the rug area, taking nothing with them. At the rug area, students know they are free to choose where they will sit but must avoid crowding other students or sitting near someone who might distract them. Although they do not need to raise their hands to talk, students may not interrupt the teacher or their classmates while they are talking. At the end of the story, students know that rug time is over and they return to their desks in an orderly fashion. The students in this class follow the rug time routines automatically without being reminded of how to behave, where to sit, and so forth. This teacher has a well-established activity routine!

One secondary English teacher has activity routines to hold students accountable for their assignments and seatwork. She posts a weekly chart listing the daily assignments and how many points each is worth. Students keep a copy of the chart in their notebooks and record the number of points they earn. The chart also tells students what materials and books to bring to class each day. When students are absent, they are responsible for checking the list to find out about missed assignments, talking with the teacher the first day they return to class, and completing the assignments and placing them in a special folder within two days. Any papers returned during their absence can be picked up in another folder.

Instructional Routines **Instructional routines** establish what the teacher will do while teaching. For example, when one mathematics teacher is about to begin teaching a new concept, he sets up the teaching station by pulling down the projection screen and focusing the overhead projector. His overhead transparencies are in a three-ring binder, so he turns to the appropriate lesson and pulls out the sequenced transparencies for that lesson. Immediately following the lesson, he washes and returns the transparencies to the notebook. The handouts he needs for class are stacked next to the overhead projector in the order in which they will be distributed. Routine use of the overhead projector, transparencies, and handouts are the backbone of this teacher's instructional routine.

Instructional routines such as this correlate with the teacher's strategies or style, making the teaching more predictable and efficient. As a teacher, you should establish routine ways of giving directions, demonstrating, instructing, monitoring, reviewing, and questioning students. Such routines are especially helpful for young students and for those with limited English proficiency or limited attention spans. In these situations, directions should be precise, specific, direct, and issued one at a time.

Let's examine the instructional routine one kindergarten teacher uses for giving directions in a bilingual classroom. When giving directions for completing one activity, the teacher clearly outlines the three things the students need to do: color the picture of the astronaut, cut it out, and paste it somewhere on the class moonscape mural. As she describes what to color, she prints the key word "color" on the chalkboard and draws a crayon after the word. She then quickly models how to color the astronaut. The teacher repeats this procedure for the next two directions in the sequence, cutting and pasting. After she has told and shown the students what they are expected to do, she checks their understanding of the directions by asking individual students to remind the class of the first, second, and third things they are to do. By the time the children begin the activity, the teacher is certain that they all heard, saw, and understood the tasks. Her predictable approach to giving directions is especially important for her students with limited English skills.

Executive Planning Routines **Executive planning routines** include establishing how, when, and where you will complete your teaching tasks—for example, how and when you will plan for instruction, correct papers, use your preparation time at school, and fulfill clerical responsibilities such as filling out attendance reports and grade cards. Establishing these routines helps you manage time more effectively so that you can balance your professional and personal responsibilities.

Some teachers involve students in executive planning routines. A secondary math teacher, for example, has students check their own homework with red pen or pencil. Another teacher has students trade papers to check. Both teachers collect

12.13 What personal responsibilities will affect your professional life as a teacher? What executive planning routines will you need to implement to balance these demands on your time?

Web Links

North Carolina's SERVE
Center

North Carolina Teachers'
Network

Jefferson County Schools

papers afterward to record grades and are careful to return all papers by the end of class on Friday. While involving students in various routines saves time, you will need to consider the merits versus the risks of these systems.

Because executive planning routines are so personal, they vary tremendously from teacher to teacher. To establish your own routines, talk with expert teachers about how they manage their time and balance their many roles. The National Education Association website provides a wealth of tips from teachers to help you get organized, manage your classroom, manage technology, and effectively develop your own routines. Other websites provide help with setting up a grade book using a spreadsheet (see the SERVE Center webpage) or setting up student files (see the North Carolina Teachers' Network webpage for New Teacher Support on getting organized). Others provide sample forms, letters, logs, and certificates that can help you with your management plan (see the Jefferson County Schools [Tennessee] website or websites listed on the North Carolina Teachers' Network webpage).

Try Activity 12.4

STARTING THE SCHOOL YEAR

Student learning is directly related to classroom management that is established during the first week of school (Wong & Wong, 2001). Developing and presenting clear rules and routines for student behavior is arguably the single most important management strategy because they clearly communicate your expectations to students (Kern & Clemens, 2007). You must implement your management plan and gain student cooperation early in the school year and then maintain it throughout the year. Following are guidelines for preventing classroom problems based on researchers' observations of well-managed elementary and secondary classrooms (Emmer, Evertson, & Worsham, 2008; Evertson & Emmer, 2008; Good & Brophy, 2007).

Begin to Establish Routines on the First Day of Class   Sterling (2009) points out that what you do the first day of class counts, but what you do the first ten minutes counts even more! The first time they meet with students, effective classroom managers clearly demonstrate that they have thought about routines and procedures, they negotiate these with students, and they begin to implement them immediately. As previously discussed, you should plan the way you will arrange your classroom space, furniture, and equipment and procedures for their use. To prevent overburdening the students, your first meetings with the class should focus on routines that address students' concerns: guidelines for interacting with others; procedures for meeting basic needs such as using the restroom and drinking fountain; your expectations as their teacher.

Clearly Communicate and Model Classroom Routines   Simply announcing or posting classroom routines and rules will not establish a well-managed classroom. Researchers found that effective managers devote a large amount of time during the first days of school to *teaching* the routines. In fact, effective elementary teachers spend more time during the first days of school teaching about rules and routines than academics (Leinhardt, Weldman, & Hammond, 1987). They follow up this initial instruction with about three weeks of reviewing and remediating the routines (Emmer, Evertson, & Anderson, 1980). Of course, secondary students more familiar with school routines would not need such a prolonged emphasis on routines, but they do need to know what you expect.

How do you teach routines and rules? First, you must clearly communicate and model them. Further, you should help students understand *why* the routines are necessary. Especially with secondary students, a discussion about how rules and routines benefit the students, teacher, and the class as a whole is important. Finally, provide situations in which the students can practice the routines and give immediate, specific feedback on their performance and cooperation.

Be Sure Students Feel Good about the Classroom Arrangement and Routines   If students feel comfortable with the classroom arrangement and the availability of supplies, they are more likely to use them carefully and quietly. Similarly, if they feel that the rules and routines are realistic, attainable, and fair, they are more likely to follow them.

You can help ensure that students feel comfortable and successful by providing situations in which they can practice using classroom resources and following routines. Then observe. If an arrangement or routine seems awkward or unnatural for students or if it just doesn't work, discuss with students more appropriate ways of doing things. Once you and the students have agreed upon a set of rules and routines, it is a good idea to limit instruction to whole-class teaching rather than breaking down into small groups. This will give you time to observe how well the routines fit the class. It will also ensure that all students have mastered the routines before they are placed in small-group or individualized situations that are more difficult for you to manage.

Communicate That You Are Prepared and Competent   Your teaching behaviors should always communicate to students that you are well-prepared and capable of instructing and managing. This doesn't mean that you will be a perfect teacher and classroom manager, but it does mean that you will be predictable. That is, students will know what is expected of them as members of a learning community and the consequences of disrupting that community. This predictability establishes an environment in which you are able to teach, students are able to learn, and misbehavior is less likely to occur.

Hold Students Responsible for Following Routines and Rules   Early in the year, effective classroom managers remind students of appropriate procedures prior to an activity and correct them if they follow routines improperly. Such frequent feedback is essential to learning both the classroom routines and expectations for students' behavior.

Monitoring Students' Behavior

Even when students have settled into the classroom and have learned the routines and procedures, your management work is not done! Observations of effective classroom managers show us that such teachers monitor students' behavior throughout the year especially around holidays and other events that may excite or distract students. Even the best learning environment can deteriorate if it is not maintained. Monitoring enables you to signal students when they are drifting into inappropriate behavior and to redirect their attention to instruction, thus preventing more serious misbehavior.

HOLDING STUDENTS ACCOUNTABLE

Unfortunately, students are sometimes reluctant to take responsibility for their behavior and learning. As a result, teachers must be alert to follow through and reinforce the classroom norms and responsibilities established early in the year. Teachers need to develop creative and constructive procedures not only to hold students accountable for their learning and behavior, but also to help them take responsibility for maintaining a learning community.

In a classic study involving years of classroom observations, Kounin (1977, 1983) described strategies effective classroom managers use to monitor students and to hold them accountable for their behavior and learning throughout the school year (**Figure 12.5**). While his terms may be awkward, the management skills he describes are timeless.

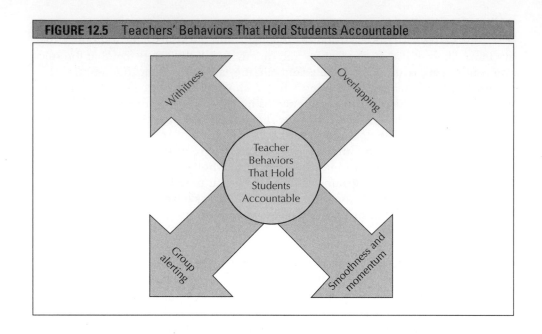

FIGURE 12.5 Teachers' Behaviors That Hold Students Accountable

Withitness

Overlapping

Teacher Behaviors That Hold Students Accountable

Group alerting

Smoothness and momentum

Withitness   Effective managers monitor classrooms using **withitness;** that is, they are aware of students' behavior in all corners of the classroom at all times. Such teachers seem to have eyes in the backs of their heads! How can you communicate to your class that you are "withit"? For one thing, try not to turn your back to the class when you are writing on the whiteboard. Instead, stand at an angle to the board so that you can easily glance over your shoulder to observe students' behavior. Similarly, when working with individual students, remain standing and periodically scan the entire classroom. Establish eye contact with students who seem to have questions or who you sense may begin to act inappropriately. Withit teachers detect inappropriate behavior early and deal with it quickly. They know who started the problem and do not depend on students to tell them what happened. Nor do they scold the wrong student. Withit teachers not only prevent classroom problems, they also produce greater student achievement (Anderson, Evertson, & Brophy, 1979; Brophy & Evertson, 2000). In fact, withitness is the most effective teacher skill at reducing disruptive behavior (Marzano, Marzano, & Pickering, 2003).

Overlapping   Effective classroom managers are also able to monitor more than one classroom activity at a time, an ability called **overlapping.** Overlapping is especially important when students are involved in collaborative work. Teachers who overlap can, for example, instruct a small group of students while keeping the remaining students on task. Suppose that you are working with a group of five students on math problems while the rest of the class is working on a review exercise. As you scan the classroom, you notice that a group in the back corner has stopped working and started talking. Using overlapping, you could ask your group to try the next problem on their own. You then establish eye contact with the misbehaving students to signal them to get back to work. Or you could walk back to them to determine whether they have a question and to redirect their attention to the review exercise. By the time the students in your group finish working the next problem, you would be back to continue your instruction.

Smoothness and Momentum   **Smoothness** and **momentum** are strategies for pacing the lesson. We know that instruction delivered at a brisk pace results in higher levels of on-task behavior and student engagement (Kern & Clemens, 2007). In a well-paced lesson, there is more opportunity for students to respond, to gain feedback, and to stay focused. In Chapter 11, we discussed how effective teachers use cues—for example, verbally identifying the first, second, and third points in the lesson—to help students focus and proceed smoothly and quickly through the lesson. In addition, effective teachers who demonstrate smoothness focus on the subject at hand rather than attending to irrelevant or intrusive details; they do not interrupt students engaged in learning activities; and they follow through rather than leaving activities "hanging in mid-air." Have you ever been interrupted when taking a test by a teacher announcing a correction of a typographical error? Have you ever had a teacher lapse into telling a personal story during a lesson? Those teachers were not demonstrating smoothness.

Momentum concerns a teacher's ability to avoid behaviors that slow down the pace of the lesson. Such behaviors include overdwelling on students' behavior or on a minor point in the lesson and dealing with students individually rather than as a group. A teacher exhibiting good momentum, for example, gives clear directions regarding an assignment to the entire class, then checks for understanding of those directions. A teacher lacking momentum fails to give clear directions and so must respond to students individually when they question the details or directions of the assignment. While students are waiting for the teacher to answer their questions, they can easily drift off task.

Group Alerting   You can also monitor students' behavior and hold them accountable for learning by using **group alerting.** As discussed in Chapter 11, you can keep everyone's attention by calling on nonvolunteers as well as volunteers and by using various questioning strategies to keep students in suspense about who will be called on to recite.

You can also keep students alert by asking or reminding them of what they should be doing, by having them repeat rules and routines they should be following, and by calling attention to appropriate behavior. General comments such as "I'm still waiting for everyone to put their pencils down and look up here" or "I see that two people need to stop whispering and turn to page 572 and follow along" will alert students regarding their behavior.

Controlling the time available for a task also keeps students engaged in learning activities. When allocating time to group activities and independent work, be sure to give students just enough time to complete the task. Too little time will cause concern, stress, frustration, and perhaps inappropriate behavior. Too much time may allow students to drift into casual conversation or other interfering behaviors. Cuing or reminding students about the time helps them to be accountable for their behavior. Statements such as "We'll begin cleaning up in five minutes, so you should be finishing the last step of your experiment" should prod students who are off task toward more appropriate behavior.

Likewise, using **proximity** or adjusting the amount of space between you and your students can influence their behavior and keep them alert. Moving toward off-task students raises their awareness of your presence and helps them refocus attention on the learning activity. If the inappropriate behavior persists, it may be necessary to pause next to the students until they adjust their behavior and reenter the lesson (Gunter, Shores, Jack, Rasmussen, & Flowers, 1995). Think about how you feel when a teacher stands near your desk. Your level of concern can become so elevated that your palms sweat, you are distracted, and learning is actually inhibited. So use proximity for monitoring behavior rather than for intimidation.

Finally, the visibility of the teacher and availability of materials in the classroom also hold students accountable and alerts them to stay on task. Circulate randomly around the classroom during independent seat work or small-group projects. Students need to see that you are available to answer questions and to redirect their attention. Similarly, supplies and materials that students need should be visible and accessible. This removes one excuse for not engaging in the learning activity.

Try Activity 12.5

REWARDING AND REINFORCING STUDENTS

A second key to maintaining a learning environment is to reinforce responsible behavior. We talked about feedback and reinforcement in Chapter 11, but it is such an important part of your comprehensive management plan that we want to revisit it. According to **reinforcement theory,** which is based on operant conditioning (discussed in Chapter 4), behavior that is rewarded is strengthened and therefore likely to be repeated. Conversely, behavior that is not somehow reinforced will eventually diminish. Early psychologists like Thorndike and Skinner recognized the importance of **positive reinforcement;** that is, providing something that an individual needs, values, or desires as perhaps the most effective means of encouraging prosocial behaviors (Goetz, Alexander, & Ash, 1996). The use of reinforcement theory has evolved. Whereas reward systems once emphasized controlling students, they now focus on helping students to take responsibility and to learn self-control. Reward systems have also shifted their focus from inhibiting misbehavior to rewarding positive academic performance and social choices (Brophy, 1983; Evertson & Harris, 1992). Correctly implemented, reinforcements and rewards provide a systematic and humanistic approach to guiding students away from misbehavior and toward independent self-control which is essential for a learning environment.

Unfortunately, because teachers are consumed with other classroom events, many appropriate things students do go unnoticed and unrewarded in today's busy classrooms. By monitoring behavior and acknowledging students who behave responsibly, teachers reinforce the importance of such behavior. Similarly, many teachers unintentionally reinforce and thus encourage undesirable behaviors. For example, researchers who studied student out-of-seat behavior observed that the more frequently teachers corrected students by asking them to sit down, the more students got out of their seats! Inadvertently, the teachers were giving students the attention they were seeking only when they got out of their seats, thus encouraging the unwanted behavior.

Applying Reinforcement Theory   Although using reinforcement to maintain a learning environment sounds easy, it can be difficult. First, the teacher's delivery is vital in determining a reinforcement's effectiveness. As we learned in Chapter 11, reinforcers must be given immediately after the desirable behavior, not hours, days, or weeks later. Otherwise, the effect of the reinforcer is dramatically reduced. Further, in order to effectively influence students' behavior, the reinforcement must be accompanied by specific feedback on the student's behavior. At the elementary level, the most powerful reinforcers identify both the individual who is behaving appropriately and the appropriate behavior. For example, it is relatively ineffective to tell Cindy, an impulsive student, that you appreciated how good she was in class today. She does not know what she did right, so she cannot repeat that behavior tomorrow. Further, the reinforcement was too far removed from her appropriate behavior. Instead, tell her five times during the day that you notice she is raising her hand before speaking in class, a real improvement. Point out how this appropriate behavior helps both her and her classmates to learn. This specific, immediate feedback encourages her to control herself and to take responsibility for raising her hand in the future.

Second, it is essential to remember that students respond differently to different kinds of reinforcers. In other words, what is rewarding to one student may not be rewarding to others. For example, some students thrive on praise, while others cringe upon receiving public recognition. At least in part, this varied response is linked to cultural and socioeconomic differences among students. For example, De Laque and Sommer (2000) found that students rooted in some Asian cultures preferred reinforcement and feedback that was indirect and focused on group rather

Web Link
Tips/Classroom Management/
Rewards

than individual efforts. In contrast, students with European roots preferred direct, individual feedback especially related to effort and actively solicited this reinforcement from the teacher!

Sometimes what is reinforcing to students surprises teachers. For example, in one kindergarten class the teachers used stickers to reward students for following the class routines. To the students, however, the stickers themselves were not sufficient reinforcement. The real reward was in being allowed to wear the stickers on their faces throughout the day! In another situation, a middle school awarded points to students for appropriate behavior. Students could redeem 1,000 points for lunch with the principal at a fast-food restaurant nearby. Teachers soon found that this was not an appropriate reinforcer; while the students wanted the principal to take them to lunch, they wanted to keep it short. They wanted to get back to school early enough to play basketball with their friends during the lunch break!

An effective teacher is aware of the types of reinforcers learners need and want. Four types of reinforcers are commonly used in classrooms: social, activity, tangible, and negative reinforcers (Goetz, Alexander, & Ash, 1996; Hunter, 1990; Kazdin, 2001). **Social reinforcers** send a positive message to the student from the teacher, a message of approval. Verbal praise, smiles, time spent with students, and appropriate physical contact are social reinforcers that are easy to give. These are often the most powerful reinforcers. However, while these are effective in monitoring students' behavior and maintaining a learning environment, they may not be strong enough to eliminate misbehavior in some situations.

When dealing with older students, verbal reinforcers should focus on benefits for the student rather than on the teacher's approval (Hunter, 1990). Whereas primary grade students and, often, students with academic or behavioral challenges, are delighted that their behavior pleases the teacher, some older students may not care about the teacher's approval or about maintaining a learning environment. While a statement such as "I like the way Max is getting right to work on his math problems" may effectively encourage a primary student, it is important to show the benefit of that appropriate behavior to Max if he is an older student. Try saying, "Max, you've gotten right to work on your math problems! That means you'll have them finished before the end of the period so you won't have any homework." At the secondary level, it is often preferable to reinforce students quietly or privately rather than aloud in front of the entire class. Further, praise delivered publicly by a teacher can be perceived as punishment by some students if it is delivered in the presence of a peer group that does not value academic learning or behavior (Gable et al., 2009).

12.14 How do you react to praise?

Given the documented positive effects of teachers using praise, it is surprising that teachers rarely use praise with general education students (Beauman & Wheldall, 2000), and are even less likely to use praise with students with learning or behavior challenges (Shores, Jack, Gunter, Ellis, DeBriere, & Wehby, 1993). Providing the praise and reinforcement that students need can be a challenge for a busy teacher. Try getting everyone involved in building a positive learning environment by joining you in reinforcing others with praise. See Table 12.1 for ideas on how to do this (based on Gable et al., 2009).

Activity reinforcers are privileges not routinely accorded to everyone. Access to the gym or computer, extra free or recess time, working with a friend, and class responsibilities such as taking messages to the office or helping to decorate a bulletin board are examples of activity reinforcers that many students prefer. The weakness with using such activity reinforcers is that they may not be immediately available. This makes immediate reinforcement impossible and weakens their effectiveness.

Tangible reinforcers are concrete objects that a student needs or wants. Often referred to as *extrinsic rewards*, they include stickers, food, award certificates, and points or tokens redeemable for larger rewards or special events. Bear (2005) suggests that tangible reinforcers be used sparingly and with caution, usually as a last resort when students do not respond to social or activity reinforcers. Verbal

TABLE 12.1 Involving Students in Providing Praise

Individuals Involved	Example of Praise Expression
Teacher provides praise	"Well done, class! Everyone had their science materials put away and their desk cleaned up within five minutes."
Class engages in group praise	"Everyone give yourself a pat on the back for getting cleaned up so quickly."
Peers share praise	"Turn to the person next to you and tell him or her how well he or she did cleaning up and getting ready for the next part of the lesson."
Student self-praises	"Whisper to yourself how well you did cleaning up and getting ready for the lesson."

praise, paired with tangible reinforcement is effective with students with a history of gaining attention by misbehaving (Piazza, Bowman, Contrucci, Delia, Adelinis, & Gold, 1999). However, because these extrinsic reinforcers are seldom related to the desired behavior, they can divert the student's attention away from being a responsible, productive, self-directed learner. Lepper (1983) found, for example, that to motivate students toward more appropriate behavior it is sometimes necessary to initially use rewards but to gradually phase them out as the behavior changes. In contrast, if students are already motivated to behave appropriately, Lepper found that using tangible rewards was harmful because it undermined students' motivation to learn and to behave appropriately.

A less positive but often effective approach to managing behavior is to use **negative reinforcement.** Negative reinforcement is important in helping students to develop self-control in the classroom because the student is in charge of what happens (Hunter, 1990). With negative reinforcement, something unpleasant is removed from the student's life when he or she makes good choices about how to behave. This reinforces the desirable behavior. For example, if a student who has been giggling with a neighbor changes her behavior because of the teacher's glare, the student has removed the negative reinforcer (teacher's glare). Some teachers try to reinforce students by removing homework assignments. What issues do you see with this use of negative reinforcement?

As a teacher, how will you know what kinds of reinforcers will work with your students? One way is to observe the students, especially during free time when they display their interests. Also, especially with older students, you can simply ask them. Many teachers use this information to develop a **reinforcement menu** that lists the various reinforcers available to them as they help students learn to be responsible for their behavior.

Scheduling Reinforcement Teachers who are effective managers are aware of the importance of scheduling reinforcement. **Scheduling** means changing the frequency of reinforcement in response to students' behavior. As students become more comfortable with the classroom rules and routines, teachers should reinforce behavior intermittently rather than regularly. In most situations, teachers can gradually eliminate external rewards as students increasingly experience academic and social success and become intrinsically motivated (Woolfolk, 2010). McCaslin and Good (1992) suggest that unless the reinforcement schedule and rewards are adjusted as students progressively assume more responsibility and self-control, conflict and tension will erupt in the classroom. In other words, although you need to reinforce students for raising their hands in September, you certainly shouldn't still reward that behavior in May!

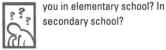

12.15 What reinforcers worked for you in elementary school? In secondary school?

Many times during the school year, life becomes hectic for teachers and students alike. Holidays, report cards, inclement weather, and sports events are a few examples of events that raise stress levels in the classroom. Teachers often resign themselves to the fact that students are going to forget the rules and routines at such times. Instead, you should return to a schedule of regular, frequent reinforcement like that used at the beginning of the year. Returning to a frequent reinforcement schedule and reminding students of their responsibilities enables you to maintain the learning environment during periods of classroom stress.

Responding to Misbehavior

The strategies discussed so far are powerful tools that can prevent problem behaviors and improve the general learning environment in your classroom by creating an orderly and caring haven. Although they are the foundation of a comprehensive classroom management plan, proactive or antecedent strategies can only reduce instances of misbehavior, not eliminate them entirely. Effective managers couple skills in preventing and monitoring inappropriate behavior with skills in quickly stopping misbehavior. Let us now turn our attention to the skills and techniques that effective teachers use in responding to misbehavior that disrupts the learning environment.

 Web Link
National Education
Association

Student misbehavior is any action that the teacher perceives as disruptive to the learning environment. Misbehavior ranges from very subtle actions to physically aggressive behavior. Cangelosi (2007) classifies the most commonly exhibited misbehaviors in elementary and secondary schools as inappropriate talking (that is, excessive talking, talking out of turn, unnecessary talking) and inappropriate movement, such as clowning and out-of-seat behavior. Other common misbehaviors include tardiness, cutting class, not bringing supplies and books, inattentiveness, daydreaming, and mild verbal and aggressive acts. Teachers agree that swearing is getting worse, even among kindergarten students (Kranz, 2006). Teachers also encounter misbehavior such as crying, arguing, fighting, stealing, and cheating. Increasingly, teachers must also react to students' use of narcotics, alcohol, and weapons. Albert (2003) encourages teachers to think of misbehaving students as students with a "choosing disability"—an underdeveloped ability to choose appropriate behavior. Responding to misbehavior, then, is the process of helping students decide to control themselves so that they can function productively in group settings such as the classroom and learn the skills necessary to do this (Bellon et al., 1996). For example, Highlight 12.2 shows how to help students with Attention Deficit Disorder (ADD) organize and control themselves.

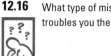 **12.16** What type of misbehavior troubles you the most?

It is important to keep in mind that there is no foolproof method for correcting misbehavior. No single discipline technique will solve the variety of behavior problems exhibited in today's classrooms. To respond to misbehavior in an effective, professional way, teachers must carefully consider the context of the misbehavior and the student's motivation before choosing how to react. That is, they must be good classroom problem solvers (see Chapter 13).

WHY STUDENTS MISBEHAVE

Teachers can respond more appropriately to misbehavior if they understand why students misbehave. Dreikers, Pepper, and Grunwald (1998) propose that, whether they are aware of it or not, students misbehave in order to meet four basic needs. Most misbehavior, at least at the elementary level, and in inclusive classrooms, is due to students *seeking attention* (Albert, 2003; Glasser, 1998; Savage & Savage, 2010). These students need extra attention and want to be center stage. They distract teachers and entertain classmates by making noises, using foul language, and causing interruptions during class. Second, some students misbehave because they

HIGHLIGHT 12.2
Managing ADD Students

His name was Sean and he was diagnosed as having Attention Deficit Disorder (ADD). He had no sense of time and was perpetually late to class, he lost assignments and materials on the way from his locker to the classroom, and his disorganization was legendary. He was endearing and earnest but couldn't focus on class or on assignments. He was a frustrating student for a first-year teacher.

An estimated 5 percent of students in today's classrooms have Attention Deficit Disorder. Students with ADD typically have problems with inattention, impulsiveness, and hyperactivity. They often seem to drift aimlessly from one activity to another without finishing their work. These students are restless, fidgeting in their seats, playing with pencils or other objects, or disturbing other students. Many students with ADD also have trouble following directions or developing friendships with others. By understanding their social and academic needs, you can provide a classroom in which ADD children can build social skills and learn.

Organizational Skills
Many students with ADD have difficulty focusing their attention on tasks and are easily distracted. You can help students like Sean develop organizational and time management skills by providing needed predictability and structure.

- Provide him with an assignment notebook to help organize homework and other seatwork, or provide daily assignment sheets. Give him color-coded folders to help organize assignments and paperwork for various subjects. Have another student help record and organize seatwork and homework in the proper folders and assignment notebook. Check the notebook often and positively reinforce good notebooks.

- Tape a schedule of planned activities for the day or period on the student's desk, and encourage him to check off each activity when it is over. Include a checklist of supplies needed for each activity (e.g., books, pencils, homework assignment sheets).

- Teach him to prepare a workspace free of distractions by clearing away unnecessary books and other materials before beginning assignments. Help him use a wristwatch or timer to manage time when completing assignments and to use a calendar to schedule assignments.

- Ask him to periodically clean out his desk, locker, book bag, and other places where class-related paperwork might get lost.

Behavior Management
Students with ADD often are impulsive and hyperactive. You can help students like Sean learn to control their behavior using techniques that remind them of your expectations for their learning and behavior in the classroom.

- Assign him to a seat near your desk or the front of the room. This enables you to monitor and reinforce his on-task behavior and reduces the number of distractions. Seat a strong student next to the ADD student to serve as a role model and to provide the opportunity for cooperative work or assistance, when needed.

- Use simple, nonintrusive visual cues to help him remain on or return to a task such as holding out your hand or tapping on the student's desk. When talking with him or giving directions, establish eye contact. Give short directions using both visual and oral cues when possible. Stand close to the student to help him focus and pay attention to what you are saying.

- Ignore minor inappropriate, impulsive behaviors. Supervise him during transitions, and give immediate reinforcements or consequences. Use a contract for more impulsive behaviors that need monitoring, such as calling out or interrupting in class, to help him learn self-monitoring techniques.

- If a student is hyperactive, allow him to stand up or even pace in the back of the room when he needs to release energy. Look for ways to channel the extra energy such as by cleaning up or running errands.

Source: Chesapeake Institute & The Widmeyer Group (n.d.).

are *seeking power*. These students want to be in control and want things done their way. To show the teacher and classmates that "you can't push me around," they refuse to comply with rules or requests and are likely to challenge and argue with others. Third, misbehavior may be caused by a student *seeking revenge*. The misbehavior often occurs in response to an earlier power struggle in which the student felt embarrassed, humiliated, or treated with disrespect in front of peers. Students seeking revenge may threaten physical harm or get revenge indirectly by breaking, damaging, or stealing property. A fourth reason students misbehave is that they are *seeking isolation*. These students are trying to avoid failure. They feel inadequate and believe they can't live up to their own, their family's, or the teacher's expectations. They procrastinate, pretend to have disabilities, and turn in incomplete work hoping everyone will leave them alone so they won't have to face the fact they aren't working up to their potential. Unfortunately, being left alone only encourages feelings of inadequacy.

While much misbehavior is due to students' attempts to meet their needs, some misbehavior is actually caused by teachers. Four teacher behaviors cause misbehavior in the classroom. *Inadequate preparation* is perhaps the most common. Failure to plan, structure, and supervise the pace of learning activities causes students to become restless and misbehave. For example, one study found that elementary students working directly with teachers were on task 97 percent of the time. Students working independently were on task only 57 percent of the time (Frick, 1990). Teacher planning and supervision make a difference! And, as discussed earlier, failing to plan how to prevent behaviors such as bullying can destroy the learning and social environment in your classroom (see Highlight 12.3). Second, *differential treatment* of students often causes misbehavior because students think the teacher has certain favorites or enemies. *Verbal abuse*, especially "friendly" sarcasm, also causes student reactions and misbehavior. Finally, if students feel that a teacher *responds unfairly* to misbehavior, further misbehavior often results. The feelings of alienation resulting from this differential treatment characterize many Chicano students, according to Sheets (2002).

In order to manage misbehavior, teachers need to be aware of what motivates students to misbehave and how their own behavior influences the behavior of the students. This suggests that teachers must develop sensitivity and a broad range of skills and techniques to draw upon when reacting to misbehavior in the classroom.

12.17 What caused you to misbehave in school?

DECIDING HOW TO REACT TO MISBEHAVIOR

Teachers who are good classroom managers are also good decision makers (Bellon et al., 1996). When misbehavior erupts, teachers must decide *when* and *how* to intervene. Effective teachers deal with misbehavior as quickly as possible (Albert, 2003; Marzano et al., 2003). But how do they decide how to intervene? At least four concerns should shape the decision: whether intervention will interrupt the lesson, the nature and severity of the misbehavior, the student involved, and the time the misbehavior occurred.

First and foremost, teachers must decide to what extent the intervention will interrupt or interfere with the instructional activity (Bellon et al., 1996). Doyle (1986) warns that interrupting the lesson to deal with misbehavior is "inherently risky" since it distracts from ongoing instruction. For example, the most successful teachers that Kounin (1983) observed kept students on task 98.7 percent of the time. The least successful teachers intervened 986 times a day which meant the students were engaged in learning only 25 percent of the time. Worse yet, Cotton (1990) estimated that only half of all classroom time is used for instruction, and that discipline problems take up most of the rest. How does this compare to the classrooms that you are observing?

Further, decisions on how to intervene should be based on the nature and severity of the misbehavior, the student involved, and the time the misbehavior occurred (Doyle, 1986; Wolfgang & Kelsay, 1995). Beginning teachers are often told they must be consistent in how they deal with misbehavior, or students will become confused and the misbehavior will increase. Many teachers find this expectation confining and frustrating, especially at the secondary level where students may challenge the teachers' fairness. Dreikers and colleagues (1998) suggest that, since the same

12.18 Describe a classroom incident you observed in which the teachers' intervention distracted from the lesson.

"How come when you say we have a problem, I'm always the one who has the problem?"

Students abusing other students is an escalating problem in today's schools. Students are emotionally abusive to each other when they heckle or "put down" others. This behavior often escalates into intimidation and physical aggression. Bullies often operate in secret, such as by writing hurtful graffiti or encouraging classmates to exclude another student. Increasingly, bullies are using technology to circulate gossip and malicious rumors. The prevalence of nasty anonymous e-mails and instant messaging among teenagers reveals the growing intensity and extending reach of teen bullying so that there is no place to escape from the harassment (Oliviero, 2004).

Myths and Misconceptions

Bullying is not simply a phase or a childhood problem. Adults play a major role depending on whether they ignore or work to prevent bullying. The first step for you, as a teacher, to take to prevent bullying is to recognize the misconceptions commonly held about bullying, as described by Cooper and Snell (2003).

Myth 1: Everyone knows what bullying is. Adults need help distinguishing between bullying and "rough-and-tumble" play. Adult supervisors tend to mistake aggression for play about 25 percent of the time (Boulton, 1996).

Myth 2: Boys will be boys. Actually, girls engage in bullying behavior as frequently as boys do. Further, they use the same forms of aggression, although girls more frequently use subtle forms of bullying such as social exclusion and malicious gossip (Craig, Pepler, & Atlas, 2000).

Myth 3: Few students are affected by bullying. At least 10 percent of students are chronic targets of bullying, but most students in a school are affected by bullying and its long-term effects (Perry, Kusel, & Perry, 1988). Bullying creates a school climate of fear and intimidation of which teachers and adult supervisors are often unaware.

Myth 4: Students are just tattling. Too often, adults dismiss students' reports of bullying as tattling. This sends a message to students that adults don't care about bullying. As a teacher, you need to teach students the difference between tattling (trying to get someone in trouble) and reporting bullying (keeping someone safe), and determine to listen attentively to students who report misbehavior.

Taking Action Against Bullying

Research shows that adults can reduce bullying by developing and implementing prevention techniques (Olweus, 1993). A comprehensive plan involving teachers and school staff, parents, and the students themselves is most effective. The following steps can help you develop a plan (Cooper & Snell, 2003).

- Establish guidelines and procedures for student behavior on playgrounds, in hallways, and in other less-structured environments where bullying often occurs.
- Improve supervision by helping adult supervisors recognize bullying and discourage it by being more visible on the playground, in school hallways, in restrooms, etc.
- Stand in the doorway of your classroom during class changes so that you can supervise the hallway and greet students as they arrive.
- Develop specific routines for transitions and out-of-classroom time. Teach rules and routines to new students so that expectations are clear.
- Include social-emotional learning by teaching students to play fairly, show respect for others, and manage their emotions. Intervene and coach students when they do not make good choices about their behavior.

Involving Parents

Parents may come to you for help if they suspect that their child is the target of bullying. Dellasega (2003) offers these suggestions for parents.

- Think prevention. Teach your child relationship skills, how to handle conflict, how to be assertive but not aggressive, and how to find good friends and build relationships.
- Support your child. If your child comes home upset, help the child explore his/her feelings and explore alternative ways to respond. Practice what he/she should do the next time.
- Intervene. If your child has prolonged unhappiness, doesn't want to go to school or other events, experiences frequent headaches or fatigue, or has a serious change in grades, a problem with bullying is likely. Be ready to intervene with your child and the school, adopting a "no blame" approach.

teacher-imposed consequences are not equally effective on all students, it is better to develop a range of intervention strategies. A normally responsible student who neglects to turn in one assignment, for example, should not require the same punishment as a student who repeatedly misses assignments. It is essential, though, that the intervention seems logical and fair to the students and their parents. Ideally, the intervention will educate students about how their actions affect their lives and the lives of those who share the learning environment and experiences with them (Wolfgang & Kelsay, 1995). Further, Curwin, Mendler, and Mendler (2008) encourage teachers to discuss with their students the fact that "fair is not always equal." They should point out that just as students require individualized academic plans to meet their different learning needs, they also have varying social needs that require a range of alternative consequences. This enables teachers to be both consistent and flexible when intervening in students' behavior, especially in diverse, inclusive classrooms.

USING INTERVENTION IN THE CLASSROOM

An **intervention** is any strategy or procedure that, when implemented, reduces the likelihood of challenging or inappropriate behavior in the future. As we have discussed, the most effective interventions for teachers are antecedent or proactive strategies that prevent problems from occurring and shape behavior by reinforcing appropriate choices and actions (Donnellan & LaVigna, 1990). The term **punishment** is often used for interventions that are aversive or coercive; strategies where something undesirable is applied to a student in response to misbehavior (Zirpoli & Melloy, 2001). Effective classroom managers have a repertoire of intervention strategies including verbal reprimands, time-outs, detentions, or more severe verbal or physical reactions. To be effective, intervention strategies must be delivered calmly and firmly, immediately after the misbehavior and must be confined to the offending students (Erickson & Mohatt, 1992). Often, intervention must be coupled with instruction in social or emotional skills that the misbehaving student lacks. Negative responses to misbehavior, such as criticism, shouting, scolding, ridicule, and sarcasm, are not effective (Canter, 1996; Swick, 1987).

How, then, should we react when students misbehave? The following strategies are appropriate for classroom intervention in most school settings. They are arranged from the most subtle, nonintrusive measures to stronger corrective interventions. As you identify intervention strategies that seem appropriate to you, be sure to consult your school and district discipline policies.

Extinction   Effective teachers are aware of but generally choose not to react to minor distractions and instances of inattention. For example, if a student misbehaves to gain the teacher's attention and that attention is withheld, it is likely the behavior will disappear. This "planned ignoring" is a type of **extinction.** It suggests that a teacher should ignore minor attention-seeking misbehavior the first time it happens as long as it is not dangerous or distracting to other students (Hunter, 1990).

It is important to understand that extinction is a nondirective response. That is, while students may cease the distracting behavior, they still don't know how they should behave. Begin by explaining to students that when a misbehavior occurs, such as calling out in class, you will not respond. The key is to ignore the misbehaving student and to praise or give attention to another student near the offender who is behaving appropriately. This reminds students of what they should be doing (Albert, 2003; Hunter, 1990; Martin, 1981).

Let's look at an example. As you begin a lesson, Keyla begins to tap her pencil on the desk in an effort to distract you and gain your attention. In applying extinction, you would ignore Keyla's pencil tapping but turn to Ricardo, who sits nearby, and praise him for listening closely to the directions. This shows to Keyla that in order to gain the teacher's attention, she too must listen closely to the directions.

Although extinction has been used effectively to eliminate disruptive behavior, off-task behavior, tantrums, and aggression (Goetz et al., 1996), it is quite difficult to practice. One reason is that it basically requires you to do something unnatural. You may have been told to be aware of everything going on in your classroom and, upon recognizing misbehavior, to "nip it in the bud." Recall that Kounin's research (1977) shows that effective classroom managers are "withit," or aware of everything that is happening in the classroom, and that they communicate their awareness to students. The principle of extinction suggests that you communicate indirectly with disruptive students by pointing out appropriate behaviors in others. You provide attention or positive reinforcement only when a student chooses to act appropriately.

Another problem with the use of extinction is that it takes time to change behavior. Worse yet, ignoring attention-seeking behavior may, at first, actually increase incidents of misbehavior (Gable et al., 2009). In some cases, ignoring students' behavior leads to aggression, presumably in reaction to increasing frustration. If Sam, for example, gained the teacher's attention in sixth grade by calling out in class, it is likely he will try the same method in your seventh-grade class. If you do not respond the way the sixth-grade teacher did, he may assume that you simply don't hear him and talk even more frequently and loudly. After all, if he gained attention from teachers in the past by behaving in this way, why should he expect a different reaction from you? However, if you consistently ignore the misbehavior and redirect attention toward the appropriate behavior, the misbehavior should eventually disappear. More importantly, you will have prevented interruptions to your lessons.

Mild Desists Effective managers deal with potentially serious disruptions early by using nonverbal intervention and mild desists. Nonverbal strategies, such as establishing eye contact, shaking the head, using facial expressions, moving closer, touching or gesturing, and redirecting attention, are highly effective, yet they do not interrupt the flow of the lesson or distract other students in the class. Indeed, a study of middle school teachers found that nonverbal strategies stopped misbehavior 79 percent of the time. Teachers in the study identified as the "more effective managers" had an even higher success rate, stopping misbehavior with nonverbal strategies 95 percent of the time (Lasley, Lasley, & Ward, 1989)!

Subtle verbal desists are also effective. Slowing your speaking rate, pronouncing things more distinctly, speaking more softly, or (even more powerful) pausing briefly and looking around are all nonobtrusive, more private ways of conveying to students that they need to adjust their behavior. Likewise, using the misbehaving student's name, directing short questions or comments to the disruptive student, calling the name and pausing briefly, or redirecting the student back to the lesson ("Open to page 271 and follow along") are effective yet largely nonintrusive verbal interventions. Brophy (1982, 1983) points out that such subtle but direct public interventions are often more effective than ignoring misbehavior or praising appropriate behavior. This is particularly true for older students who misbehave because they are seeking attention or are bored.

Reprimands Verbal reprimands such as "Stop Talking. Now!" are widely used in classrooms. White (1975) found that teachers in all grades reprimand students once every two minutes. Although experts advise teachers to maintain a ratio of praise-to-reprimands of at least 4:1 (Shores et al., 1993), the number of reprimands far exceeds the amount of praise given in every grade after second grade.

Teachers often reprimand students for not listening, breaking class rules, or making noise. Verbal reprimands usually bring about an immediate change in behavior, but the change is temporary. Although they seem effective, reprimands give the misbehaving student attention and may reinforce the very behavior that you want to eliminate (Alberto & Troutman, 2006). These negative interactions alienate students, undermine the teacher/student relationship, and often further aggravate the situation. Critical teacher comments have been linked to increased student verbal and physical aggression, especially at the secondary level (Van Acker, Grant, & Henry, 1996). In all cases, they interrupt instructional time (see Case 12.1).

12.19 How do you feel when a teacher uses mild desists to correct your behavior?

"Quiet Down, Class!"

Mr. McNamar is frustrated with the level of noise that characterizes his ninth grade English class . . . that "low hum of puberty-driven chatter." Recognizing that some students need a quieter learning environment, he wants a room dominated by silence. He recalls the foolproof method to quiet students that his cooperating teacher used. That teacher assigned sentences ("I will not talk in class"), 25 times for the first offense and 50 for the second.

"I've tried giving detentions, but that is disruptive. 'Johnny, stop talking,' I'll say, to which he responds, 'I'm not talking.' Then we banter back and forth about how when he opens his mouth and words come out, that is considered talking. Then Johnny protests even louder, disrupting the class. Or I'll say, 'Jill, you have a detention for talking,' which is greeted by shouts of 'You're so unfair; those boys were talking, too!'"

At the end of the day, Mr. McNamar is so frustrated that he feels like banging his head against his desk as he wonders, how to get them to shut up?

Source: McNamar (2005).

INVESTIGATING AND SOLVING THE CASE

1. Describe experiences you have had in noisy classrooms.
2. What actions did teachers take to quiet the class, and how successful were they?
3. What level of noise are you comfortable with in a classroom?
4. What advice would you give to Mr. McNamar?

Reynolds (1992) outlines the way effective managers deliver reprimands. They talk with misbehaving students in private rather than in front of the class, thus minimizing power struggles and face-saving gestures. They question the students to determine whether they understood why the way they chose to behave was inappropriate, and they ask for explanations. Also, effective managers make sure that students understand why the behavior is unacceptable; they try to get the students to accept responsibility for the behavior and to make a commitment to change. They instruct or model more acceptable ways for the students to behave. Finally, effective managers warn students about the consequences of continuing the misbehavior, help them understand how the consequences of disruptive behavior are detrimental to them and to the learning community, and ask the students to make a choice about their behavior. They follow through with the consequences if the misbehavior does not change.

Effective teachers also start where the students are. Teacher Jessica Towbin (2010) talks about reprimanding a group of disengaged students in her English class who questioned the value of doing literary analysis. Rather than delivering a coercive reprimand, this effective teacher responded respectfully, pointing out the usefulness of analysis: being able to take something apart, figure out how it works, and then explain what you figured out. "That makes sense," one student replied as he got to work on the assignment. Towbin concluded: "Had I simply reprimanded them for disrupting my instruction and directed them to do the assignment, it is unlikely that anything useful would have resulted. Moreover, it is unlikely that they would have responded positively to this conversation if I had not established credibility with them over the previous four months" (p. 45). As you can see, Ms. Towbin is an effective teacher who set up a positive learning environment and who explores the reasons for disruptive behaviors rather than simply reacting with reprimands.

Time-Out For more serious misbehavior, using a time-out strategy may be effective (Figure 12.6). **Time-out** reduces unwanted behavior by removing the offending student from the situation and, therefore, from the attention and rewards the situation provides. During time-out, the student may be excluded from an activity, asked

FIGURE 12.6 Types of Intervention

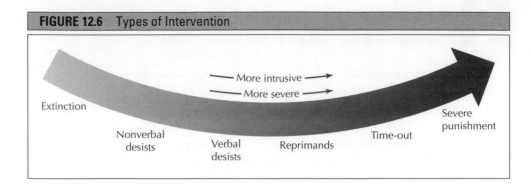

to put her hands or head on her desk, removed to a desk in the back of the room, removed from the classroom, or sent to a time-out room.

Time-out is especially effective for students who misbehave to draw attention from their peers or who are overly active. If, for example, a student kicks the volleyball across the gymnasium during a physical education class to show off to his classmates, the teacher would ask the student to sit on the bleachers for 10 minutes to think about what he has done. If the student enjoys playing volleyball with his teammates, being removed from the situation is punishment. He is likely to consider what he did wrong and resolve to behave appropriately if he wants to reenter the game.

It is important to remember certain guidelines when using time-out. First, the time-out period must be brief, usually from five to 12 minutes, depending on the age of the student. A rule of thumb is that the time-out should be one minute long for each year of the child's age. Longer periods of time do not make the treatment more effective (Kazdin, 2001). An extended time-out period could increase the student's resentment if he or she considers the time-out unfair, or it may cause the student to fall behind in class work.

Second, during time-out, the student must be isolated. It is best to isolate the student in the classroom to retain opportunities for learning (Kazdin, 2001). Asking a disruptive student to leave a math lesson for time-out in the hallway where he gets attention from every passerby may be more of a reward than a punishment, especially if he doesn't like math! However, if the misbehavior is so severe that the student's continued presence is likely to disrupt instruction, the isolation may need to occur outside the classroom. It is important that classmates or other school personnel not talk with the student during isolation. If a student is sent to another classroom or to the office for time-out, school personnel should be asked not to interact with the offending student.

Third, the misbehaving student should be allowed to return to the regular activity after the designated time has elapsed or when she decides to behave appropriately, for example, by cooperating with her small group to complete a project. Some teachers ask students to identify what they did wrong and how they should have acted as a condition for returning to the activity.

12.20 What logical consequences would you use for the common misbehaviors discussed in this chapter?

Finally, students should be held accountable for the work they missed during a time-out. The work should be completed on the students' own time or at home rather than during recess or a special activity which would serve as a second punishment.

Time-out can be an effective way to influence student behavior if you correctly apply and monitor it. Above all, don't forget about the student! Too many teachers remove distracting students from the situation, return to the lesson, and promptly forget about the student in time-out. The extended, unfocused time in isolation negates the impact of the time-out procedure for the misbehaving student.

Severe Punishment   If other interventions are ineffective, some teachers use more severe punishment. **Corporal punishment** is an intervention that involves hitting a student with a hand or object with the intent of causing pain. According to the

National Committee to Prevent Child Abuse (1995), corporal punishment continues to be a common, though unacceptable, intervention for misbehavior. State laws and school policies regarding the use of more coercive verbal and physical interventions vary widely, so it is essential that you work with your principal or an experienced teacher as you develop this aspect of your management plan. Also, remember that while public reprimands, corporal punishment, and other punitive actions may stop misbehavior temporarily, they are ineffective in the long run because they fail to teach constructive substitute behaviors and to emphasize student responsibility and choices (Goldstein, 1989; Wolfgang & Kelsay, 1995). Teachers using these negative and punitive approaches generally find that their students become more aggressive and unsettled and less concerned with learning, which is counterproductive to the learning community (Swick, 1987).

Experts agree that punishment should be reserved for serious misbehavior and generally used as a last resort. You should never punish out of anger or frustration. Don't nag, threaten students, or issue warnings unless you follow-up on those reminders. Finally, be sure that consequences of misbehavior are logically related to the misbehavior. For example, if Preston turns in a poorly prepared paper, the logical consequence is to have him rewrite it, rather than to keep him after school or to assign him additional math problems for homework. Punishments that are not related to the misbehavior may be seen as arbitrary to students, and the teacher may appear dictatorial. This hinders learning. For example, assigning regular schoolwork as punishment is inversely related to gains in students' learning (Brophy & Evertson, 2000).

12.21 What qualities do you have that will help you deal with misbehavior?

Try Activity 12.7

Reestablishing the Learning Environment

No matter how you choose to intervene in a classroom situation, you will need to reestablish a positive learning climate and a positive relationship with the offending student as soon as possible. After all, the message you want to convey is that while the behavior is unacceptable, the student is an acceptable person and an important part of the learning community. You can use the strategies listed earlier in the chapter to reestablish a positive, cooperative relationship among students and with you.

Sometimes the management system established at the beginning of the year just doesn't seem to work, and sometimes the reinforcement and intervention strategies you employ are not effective. Don't panic or resign yourself to putting up with a disorganized or unruly class for the remainder of the year. Evertson (1989) recommends reexamining your management system periodically, discussing it with students, and repairing and restoring the system as needed. These "second beginnings" are best introduced after natural breaks in the school year, such as after a weekend or holiday. They should be implemented using clear communication, student cooperation, careful monitoring, and consistent accountability, just as you would introduce a management plan at the beginning of the school year. There is nothing wrong with making a mistake and starting over, as long as the revised management system contributes to a more effective learning environment.

Some Final Thoughts

Good classroom management is essential to classroom learning. Effective managers plan how to prevent behavior problems, how to monitor student behavior, how to respond when students misbehave, and how to reestablish a positive classroom environment after correcting misbehavior. They know how to review and adjust their management plans. By developing and following proactive management plans, you will help establish an effective learning community for your students and minimize stress in the classroom.

Try Activity 12.8

CHAPTER SUMMARY

- Effective classroom managers are not born, they are made. You can use this chapter to build your management skills.

- Classroom management consists of all the provisions and procedures a teacher uses to create and maintain a classroom environment in which teaching and learning can occur. Traditionally, classroom management focused on reactive management, that is, how teachers reacted to (or disciplined) students who misbehaved. This approach neglected the close relationship between instruction and classroom management. Today's classrooms stress proactive management, or preventing problems from developing in the first place.

- Effective classroom managers prevent classroom management problems by organizing and establishing a classroom environment that is safe and predictable, both physically and psychologically.

- The physical environment consists of those concrete elements that are independent of the people who inhabit the classroom. The psychological environment is intangible and exists only in the minds of teachers and students.

- Seating patterns influence peer interactions, teacher-student interactions, and student attitudes or affect. Students seated at tables interact more than students seated in rows and, consequently, tend to develop better leadership skills. Students seated in a circle speak more to those across from them and less to those seated next to them. An action zone of teacher-student interaction is composed of students seated toward the front and middle of the class. These students enjoy the teacher more and feel more involved in the class. Because no single seating arrangement is ideal, experts recommend a flexible arrangement that the teacher can modify for various learning situations.

- Teachers should ensure that all students have comfortable desks and that materials and equipment are readily available without crowding students or making them wait. Likewise, they should arrange their rooms to produce a safe, stimulating environment for students. This includes arranging furniture to (1) minimize distractions and congestion; (2) establish activity boundaries between incompatible activities; (3) allow the teacher to monitor all parts of the room; and (4) provide open lanes for movement, especially between desks and around supply areas.

- In a classroom with a positive tone, students feel safe, comfortable, respected, and responsible. In such classrooms, (1) students' basic needs are met; (2) color, light, temperature, and displays are used to create softness, stimulation, and emotional safety; (3) mutual respect, cooperation, and student responsibility are present; (4) student and teacher ownership are evident; (5) the environment is busy and task-oriented; and (6) teachers' expectations are clear, and structure is provided.

- Classroom routines that guide and coordinate movement and events help prevent classroom management problems. These routines fall into four categories: management routines, activity routines, instructional routines, and executive planning routines.

- Management problems can be minimized by arranging the classroom environment and establishing routines early in the school year. The task of establishing classroom rules and routines begins on the first day of class. Routines should be clearly communicated, modeled, and taught to students. Teachers should also provide opportunities to practice routines. Finally, teachers should communicate that they are prepared and capable of managing the classroom and should hold students responsible for following the classroom routines.

- Monitoring students' behavior throughout the year by signaling students who are beginning to misbehave and redirecting their attention to the lesson prevents serious misbehavior. Effective monitoring involves the use of withitness, overlapping, smoothness and momentum, and group-alerting techniques.

- Teachers can monitor and maintain students' behavior by using rewards and reinforcement. Behavior that is rewarded is strengthened and likely to be repeated; behavior that is not rewarded is likely to diminish. To be effective, appropriate behaviors must be clearly communicated and must be reinforced immediately after the behavior.

- Since different students respond to different types of reinforcement, teachers should develop a reinforcement menu that meets the needs and wants of individual students. Such a menu should include (1) social reinforcers such as praise, smiles, and physical contact; (2) activity reinforcers such as free time or class responsibilities; (3) tangible reinforcers such as redeemable tokens; and (4) negative reinforcers such as removal from detention.

- As students' behavior improves, teachers must change the reinforcement schedule. Desirable behaviors should be reinforced less frequently following mastery, and more complex behaviors should be reinforced after students have learned simple behaviors.

- Even with a well-planned and monitored management system, misbehavior will occur. Such misbehavior can result from a need for attention, power, revenge, or isolation. Teachers sometimes cause misbehavior by failing to prepare, by treating students differently, by verbally abusing them, or by reacting in ways that students perceive as unfair.

- Teachers must decide when and how to intervene when students misbehave and must respond quickly. When deciding how to intervene, they should consider the extent to which intervention will interrupt instruction, the nature and severity of the misbehavior, the student involved, and when the misbehavior occurred.

- Effective classroom managers have a repertoire of intervention strategies they can use to respond to students' misbehavior. These include extinction, mild desists, reprimands, time-out, and more severe forms of punishment.

- Some educators say that interventions negatively impact student achievement and socialization. Research supports a balanced approach using both reinforcement and intervention, with praise comments outnumbering reprimands.

- After intervening in misbehavior, the teacher often needs to reestablish a positive climate of mutual respect and cooperation. It is a good idea to periodically review the effectiveness of the management plan and to adopt new routines when needed.

KEY TERMS

Discipline, 400	Activity routines, 412	Activity reinforcers, 419
Proactive, 400	Instructional routines, 413	Tangible reinforcers, 419
Antecedent strategies, 401	Executive planning routines, 413	Negative reinforcement, 420
Classroom management, 401	Withitness, 416	Reinforcement menu, 420
Physical environment, 402	Overlapping, 416	Scheduling, 420
Psychological environment, 402	Smoothness, 416	Student misbehavior, 421
Climate, 402	Momentum, 416	Intervention, 425
Action zone, 403	Group alerting, 417	Punishment, 425
Inviting classroom, 405	Proximity, 417	Extinction, 425
Rules, 409	Reinforcement theory, 418	Time-out, 427
Routines, 409	Positive reinforcement, 418	Corporal punishment, 428
Management routines, 410	Social reinforcers, 419	

ISSUES AND PROBLEMS FOR DISCUSSION

ISSUES   Several issues and problems are related to classroom management. Here are a few you might like to discuss in class.

1. What should the goal of classroom management be?
2. Should teachers share their personal lives and interests in the classroom? Why or why not?
3. Do students have rights in the classroom? Do teachers?
4. Is it ethical for teachers to try to influence or control student behavior? Explain your answer.
5. Should teachers be responsible for the behavior of students outside the classroom such as in study hall or on the school bus? Give reasons for your position.
6. Should students' behavior be factored into their grades? Why or why not?
7. Should teachers send misbehaving students to the principal's office? Give examples to support your position.
8. Should principals be expected to support teachers' classroom management practices and decisions? Why or why not? How could you gain a principal's support?
9. Should states outlaw some forms of corporal punishment, such as paddling, even if parents approve of them? Explain.
10. How can teachers respond to the increased bullying and violence in today's schools?

PROBLEMS   Management problems is one of the leading reasons why teachers leave the profession. Anticipating how you would deal with misbehavior is one way of ensuring that you will be a successful manager. How would you address the following situations?

Problem 1:   "The principal assigned Gary, a 'special education' student, to my English class so that he could build relationships with the other ninth-grade students. His reading level is so low that he can't handle *Tom Sawyer* which we're currently reading. Although he seems to like the story, he is easily distracted and bothers students around him."

Problem 2:   "Lab books were due from my three biology classes today, so I have 86 to grade in a week! That's on top of the 29 general science exams, all with an essay question, that I have left over from last week. And the basketball team that I coach has an important game this weekend!"

Problem 3:   "My husband complains when I work on lesson plans during the weekend, and I feel guilty not spending that time with my kids. But I have to get ready for school on Monday!"

Problem 4:   "I was explaining long division this morning, when a snow plow decided to clear the playground which is right outside my windows. The students watched the plow go back and forth, back and forth. Long division was lost."

Problem 5:   "I'm furious! The whole class was gathered around the volcano model, watching the 'eruption' and then, BOOM! A real explosion! We're lucky the sound waves didn't rupture our eardrums! Peter started laughing immediately because he had placed a cherry bomb in the cone of the volcano before it was lit."

ACTIVITY 12.1: Observing Seating Arrangements

1. Ask your cooperating teacher what he or she thinks are the most important things to take into account when deciding how to seat or arrange students in a classroom.

2. Observe several classrooms that have different seating arrangements for students. Draw a diagram of the way the desks are arranged. Then make a sociogram by drawing arrows to indicate the conversational flow among students. Keep track of these student interactions for 10 minutes. When you compare the student interactions across different seating arrangements, what do you notice?

3. Figure 12.7 is a diagram of a music classroom. The 50 students were seated in two rows of folding chairs. The teacher was very frustrated because the students talked and misbehaved so much she could hardly teach. Analyze the seating arrangement and make suggestions about changes that might prevent students from misbehaving. Also suggest instructional behaviors the teacher should adopt to monitor students and hold their attention.

4. Visit a classroom. Observe students and the seats they are assigned to. Do the students seem to "fit" comfortably in their seats? Are left-handed and special-needs students accommodated? Try sitting in a student seat yourself. How does it feel? Could you sit there comfortably for a morning or a day?

ACTIVITY 12.2: Organizing the Physical and Psychological Environments of the Classroom

1. As you enter the classroom, what are your feelings and first impressions? What messages about learning and the teacher does the classroom send? How would you feel about spending many hours each day in this classroom as a student? As a teacher?

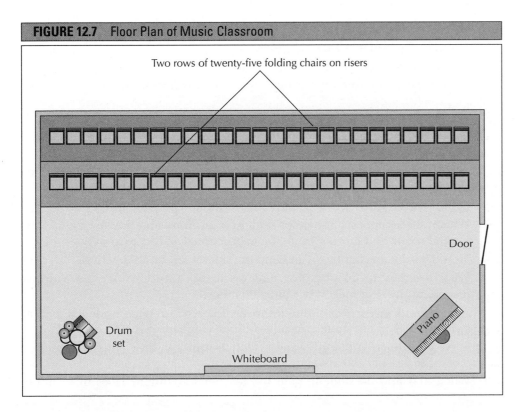

FIGURE 12.7 Floor Plan of Music Classroom

Two rows of twenty-five folding chairs on risers

Door

Drum set

Piano

Whiteboard

2. Draw a floor plan for the classroom. Be sure to include all furniture and work-stations in the classroom on your drawing. Now observe the flow of students around the classroom for 30 minutes. Draw those patterns on your floor plan. Identify areas of heavy traffic flow and bottlenecks that may threaten the students' sense of psychological safety in the classroom.

3. Softness in the room helps students to feel safe and meets aesthetic needs. Look around the room for examples of softness and list them.

4. What do you see that communicates something about the people who occupy this room? How is student ownership of the classroom expressed?

5. Now observe the teacher-student interactions in the room, especially during instruction or discussion. Construct a sociogram showing the patterns of interaction. Try to identify the action zone in the classroom. Does the teacher make any efforts to accommodate students sitting outside the action zone?

6. Does the classroom provide an enriched environment? Identify and describe ways the teacher uses the physical environment to stimulate students' growth and learning.

7. Evaluate the physical and psychological environments you have observed. What are the strengths? From your point of view, how could the classroom setting be changed to make it a more accessible and inviting environment?

ACTIVITY 12.3: Developing Classroom Rules

1. Ask your cooperating teacher about classroom rules.
   a. What are they? Are they posted? Why or why not?
   b. How does the teacher develop the rules?
   c. How does the teacher introduce the rules at the beginning of the year?
   d. Analyze the rules for clarity, simplicity, positive tone, and practicality.

2. Ask a student about classroom rules.
   a. What are they?
   b. How were the rules developed?
   c. How did the students learn the rules?
   d. Are the rules enforced? If so, how and when?
3. Compare responses from the teacher and student with your own observations.

ACTIVITY 12.4: Developing Classroom Routines

1. Ask your cooperating teacher what he or she thinks about routines and which are the most critical.
2. Observe and describe the following management routines in an elementary or secondary classroom or gymnasium.
   a. How does the teacher pass out and distribute student papers and work?
   b. What routines are established for student transitions: entering the room, leaving the room, and moving from one instructional activity to another?
   c. How does the teacher begin and end the school day or class period?
   d. What routines are in place for students to use the restroom, get a drink, dispose of trash, or meet other individual needs?
   e. Are students given responsibilities in the classroom? What evidence do you see of this? How are student responsibilities assigned?
3. Observe and describe the following activity routines in an elementary, middle school, or secondary classroom or gymnasium.
   a. When and how do students gain the teacher's attention? Does this routine

change throughout the day based on the type of activity or other factors?

    b. Identify and describe one activity routine in the classroom.

4. Observe and describe the following instructional routines in an elementary, middle school, or secondary classroom or gymnasium.

    a. What routine or procedure does the teacher use to give directions or assignments?

    b. Listen closely to how the teacher asks questions or leads a discussion. What routines does the teacher follow?

5. Observe or discuss the following executive planning routines your cooperating teacher uses.

    a. When does the teacher plan for instruction?

    b. What executive routines does the teacher have in place for grading papers, photocopying, responding to e-mail, and handling paperwork?

    c. What advice would the teacher give you about balancing your personal and professional lives as a new teacher?

6. From what you have observed and heard, how important do you think routines will be in your classroom? Cite three specific routines you are now aware of that you plan to adopt in your own classroom someday.

ACTIVITY 12.5: Holding Students Accountable

1. Ask your cooperating teacher what he or she does during the first day and week of school.

2. Observe your cooperating teacher. Describe behaviors the teacher uses to communicate to students that he or she is "withit."

3. Describe how your cooperating teacher exhibited the ability to overlap.

4. When observing in your cooperating teacher's classroom, look for things that threaten the smoothness and momentum of the lesson. How does the teacher deal with each of these?

5. Observe as your cooperating teacher monitors students by using nonverbal behaviors. Describe the nonverbal behaviors you observe.

ACTIVITY 12.6: Reinforcement in the Classroom

1. Observe your cooperating teacher for 30 minutes, focusing on teacher-student interactions. List specific examples of social reinforcers the teacher used. How did students respond?

2. What is the teacher reinforcing? Is it behavior or academic performance? (You may need to keep a tally to answer the question accurately.)

3. List specific examples of activity reinforcers you observed. How did students respond to them?

4. List examples of tangible reinforcers or rewards the teacher used. How did students respond?

5. From your observations, which types of reinforcement seemed to be most effective in bringing about desired behavior? How can you explain this?

ACTIVITY 12.7: Types of Intervention

1. Interview three teachers to determine what they think about using extinction or "planned ignoring." Have they tried to ignore inappropriate behavior? Do they think the approach works?

2. Observe a classroom for examples of extinction. How does the misbehaving student respond?

3. Observe a teacher interacting with students for 30 minutes. Keep a tally of the nonverbal and verbal mild desists the teacher uses to intervene in misbehavior. Which approach does the teacher use most frequently? Which approach seems most effective with the students in that classroom?

4. Talk with a variety of teachers and ask them what types of intervention they use. Make a list. Does the type of intervention used vary according to grade level? Years of teacher experience? Other classroom variables?

5. Survey several students, parents, and teachers to see if they agree or disagree with the use of intervention in the classroom. What kinds of interventions do they deem appropriate? What do they think is inappropriate?

6. Use the Internet to find the discipline policy of a local school district. Evaluate it based on what you learned from this chapter and teacher interviews.

ACTIVITY 12.8: Management Websites

1. Use the Internet to develop a list of 10 websites that provide information useful to you as you develop your four-part classroom management plan.

2. Combine your list with those of your classmates and review the content. Do most websites provide information on preventing management problems, monitoring student behavior, reacting when students misbehave, or reestablishing the learning environment?

3. What are the strengths and weaknesses of gathering information about teaching from Internet sources?

REFERENCES

Adams, R. S., & Biddle, B. J. (1970). *Realities of teaching: Exploration with videotape.* New York: Holt, Rinehart, and Winston.

Albert, L. (2003). *Cooperative discipline.* (5th ed.). Circle Pines, MN: American Guidance Service.

Alberto, P. & Troutman, A. (2006). *Applied behavior analysis for teachers.* (6th ed.). Upper Saddle River, NJ: Merrill.

Anderson, L. M., Evertson, C. M., & Brophy, J. (1979). An experimental study of effective teaching in first-grade reading groups. *Elementary School Journal, 79,* 193–223.

Anderson, L. W. (1991). Classroom environment and climate. In *Increasing teacher effectiveness,* 36–53. Paris: UNESCO.

Bartolome, L. (1996). Beyond the methods fetish: Toward a humanizing pedagogy. *Harvard Educational Review, 64,* 173–194.

Bear, G. (2005). *Developing self-discipline and preventing and correcting misbehavior.* Boston: Pearson Allyn & Bacon.

Beauman, R., & Wheldall, K. (2000). Teachers' use of approval and disapproval in the classroom. *Educational Psychology, 20,* 431–446.

Bellon, J. J., Bellon, E. C., & Blank, M. A. (1996). *Teaching from a research knowledge base.* Englewood Cliffs, NJ: Prentice Hall.

Borich, G. D. (2006). *Effective teaching methods.* (6th ed.). Boston: Pearson.

Boulton, M. J. (1996). Lunchtime supervisors' attitudes towards playful fighting, and ability to differentiate between playful and aggressive fighting: An intervention study. *British Journal of Educational Psychology, 66,* 367–381.

Brophy, J. E. (1982). Supplemental group management techniques. In D. Duke (Ed.), *Helping teachers manage classrooms* (pp. 32–51). Alexandria, VA: Association for Supervision and Curriculum Development.

Brophy, J. E. (1983). Classroom organization and management. In D. C. Smith (Ed.), *Essential knowledge for beginning educators* (pp. 23–37). Washington, DC: American Association of Colleges for Teacher Education.

Brophy, J. E., & Evertson, C. M. (2000). *Learning from teaching: A developmental perspective.* Boston: Allyn & Bacon.

Brophy, J. E., & Rohrkemper, M. M. (1981). The influence of problem ownership on teachers' perceptions of and strategies for coping with student problems. *Journal of Educational Psychology, 73,* 295–311.

Cangelosi, J. S. (2007). *Classroom management strategies: Gaining and maintaining students' cooperation.* (6th ed.). Somerset, NJ: John Wiley & Sons.

Canter, L. (1996). First, the rapport—then, the rules. *Learning, 24*(5), 12–14.

Carrol, A., Houghton, S., Durkin, K., & Hattie, J. (2001). Reputation enhancing goals: Integrating reputation enhancement and goal setting theory as an explanation of delinquent involvement. In F. Columbus (Ed.), *Advances in psychology research 4,* 101–129. New York: Nova Science.

Chesapeake Institute & The Widmeyer Group. (n.d.). *Attention deficits: What teachers should know.* Access: www.dbpeds.org/articles/101tips.html.

Cookson, P. W. (2006). Your ideal classroom. *Teaching PreK–8, 36*(5), 14–16.

Cooper, D., & Snell, J. L. (2003). Bullying—Not just a kid thing. *Educational Leadership, 60*(6), 19–21.

Cotton, K. (1990). *School improvement series. Close-up #9: Schoolwide and classroom discipline.* Portland, OR: Northwest Regional Educational Laboratory.

Craig, W. M., Pepler, D. J., & Atlas, R. (2000). Observations of bullying in the playground and in the classroom. *School Psychology International, 21,* 22–36.

Cuban, L. (2001). *Oversold and underused: Computers in the classroom.* Cambridge, MA: Harvard University Press.

Curwin, R. L., Mendler, B. D., & Mendler, A. N. (2008). *Discipline with dignity: New challenges, new solutions.* (3rd ed.). Upper Saddle River, NJ: Merrill.

De Laque, M. F., & Sommers, S. M. (2000). The impact of culture on feedback-seeking behavior: An integrated model and propositions. *Academy of Management Review, 25*(4), 829–849.

Dellasega, C. (2003). *Girl wars: 12 strategies for ending female bullying.* New York: Simon & Schuster.

DiGiulio, R. (2007). *Positive classroom management.* (3rd ed.). Thousand Oaks, CA: Corwin.

Dollard, N. (1996). Constructive classroom management. *Focus on Exceptional Children, 29*(2), 1–12.

Donnellan, A. M., & LaVigna, G. W. (1990). Myths about punishment. In A. C. Repp & N. N. Singh (Eds.). *Perspectives on the use of nonaversive and aversive interventions for persons with developmental disabilities* (pp. 33–57). Sycamore, IL: Sycamore.

Doyle, W. (1983). Academic work. *Review of Educational Research, 53,* 159–199.

Doyle, W. (1986). Classroom organization and management. In M. C. Wittrock (Ed.), *Handbook of research on teaching.* (3rd ed.), (pp. 392–431). New York: Macmillan.

Dreikers, R., Pepper, F., & Grunwald, B. (1998). *Maintaining sanity in the classroom: Classroom management techniques.* (2nd ed.). Florence, KY: Taylor Francis.

Dunn, D. W. (2001). Do seating arrangements and assignments = classroom management? *Education World.* www.educationaworld.com/a_curr/curr330.shtml.

Dykman, B., & Reis, H. (1979). Personality correlates of classroom seating position. *Journal of Educational Psychology, 71,* 346–354.

Eggen, P. D., & Kauchak, D. (2009). *Educational psychology: Windows on classrooms.* (8th ed.). Englewood Cliffs, NJ: Prentice Hall.

Emmer, E. T., Everston, C. M., & Anderson, L. M. (1980). Effective classroom management at the beginning of the school year. *The Elementary School Journal, 80,* 219–231.

Emmer, E. T., Everston, C. M., & Worsham, M. E. (2008). *Classroom management for middle and high school teachers.* (6th ed.). Boston: Allyn & Bacon.

Emmer, E. T., Sanford, J. P., Clements, B. S., & Martin, J. (1982). *Improving classroom management and organization in junior high schools: An experimental investigation.* Austin, TX: Research & Development Center for Teacher Education, University of Texas. (R&D Report No. 6153). (ERIC Document Reproduction Service ED 261 053)

Emmer, E. T., Sanford, J. P., Everston, C. M., Clements, B. S., & Martin, J. (1981). *The classroom management improvement study: An experiment in elementary school classrooms.* Austin, TX: Research & Development Center for Teacher Education, University of Texas. (R&D Report No. 6050). (ERIC Document Reproduction Service ED 226 452)

Englander, M. E. (1986). *Strategies for classroom discipline.* New York: Praeger.

Erickson, F., & Mohatt, G. (1992). Cultural organization of participant structures in two classrooms of Indian students. In G. Spindler (Ed.), *Doing the ethnography of schooling: Educational anthropology in action* (pp. 132–174). New York: Holt, Rinehart, and Winston.

Everston, C. M. (1989). Classroom organization and management. In M. C. Reynolds (Ed.), *Knowledge base for the beginning teacher* (pp. 59–70). New York: Pergamon.

Everston, C. M., Emmer, E. T. (2008). *Classroom management for elementary teachers.* (8th ed.). Boston: Allyn & Bacon.

Everston, C. M., & Harris, A. H. (1992). What we know about managing classrooms. *Educational Leadership 49*(7), 74–78.

Freiberg, H. J. (1996). From tourists to citizens in the classroom. *Educational Leadership, 54*(1), 32–36.

Frick, T. W. (1990). Analysis of patterns in time: A method of recording and quantifying temporal relations in education. *American Educational Research Journal, 27,* 180–204.

Gable, R. A., Hester, P. H., Rock, M. L., & Hughes, K. G. (2009). Back to basics: Rules, praise, ignoring, and reprimands revisited. *Intervention in School and Clinic, 44,* 195–205.

Glasser, W. (1998). *The quality school.* New York: Harper Trade.

Goetz, E., Alexander, P. A., & Ash, M. J. (1996). *Education psychology.* Englewood Cliffs, NJ: Allyn & Bacon.

Goldstein, A. P. (1989). Teaching alternatives to aggression. In D. Biklen, D. Ferguson, & A. Ford (Eds.), *Schooling and disability.* (The Eighty-eighth Yearbook of the National Society for the Study of Education, pt. 1, pp. 168–194). Chicago: University of Chicago Press.

Good, T. L., & Brophy, J. E. (2007). *Looking in classrooms.* (10th ed.). Boston: Allyn & Bacon.

Goodlad, J. (1984). *A place called school: Prospects for the future.* New York: McGraw-Hill.

Granstrom, K. (1996). Private communication between students in the classroom in relation to different classroom features. *Educational Psychology, 16*(4), 349–364.

Grolnick, W. S., Ryan, R. M., & Deci, E. L. (1991). Inner resources for school achievement: Motivational mediators of children's perceptions of their parents. *Journal of Educational Psychology, 83,* 508–517.

Grossman, H. (2004). *Classroom behavior management for diverse and inclusive schools.* (3rd ed.). New York: Rowman & Littlefield.

Gunter, P. L., Shores, R. E., Jack, S. L., Rasmussen, S. K., & Flowers, J. (1995). On the move: Using teacher/student proximity to improve students' behavior. *Teaching Exceptional Children, 28*(1), 12–14.

Hawley, W. D., & Rosenholtz, S. J. (1984). Good schools: What research says about improving student achievement. *Peabody Journal of Education, 61*(4), 15–52.

Hunter, M. (1990). *Discipline that develops self-discipline.* Thousand Oaks, CA: Corwin.

Intrator, S. M. (2004). The engaging classroom. *Educational leadership, 62*(1), 20–24.

Jackson, P. (1990). *Life in classrooms.* New York: Teachers' College Press.

Jones, V. F., & Jones, L. S. (2009). *Comprehensive classroom management: Creating communities of support and solving problems.* (9th ed.). Boston: Allyn & Bacon.

Kazdin, A. E. (2001). *Behavior modification in applied settings.* (6th ed.). Belmont, CA: Wadsworth/Thompson Learning.

Kern, L., & Clemens, N. H. (2007). Antecedent strategies to promote appropriate classroom behavior. *Psychology in the Schools, 44*(1), 65–75.

Kerr, M. M., & Nelson, C. M. (2006). *Strategies for managing behavior problems in the classroom.* (4th ed.). Columbus, OH: Merrill Prentice Hall.

Kounin, J. S. (1977). *Discipline and group management in classrooms.* New York: Krieger Publishing Co.

Kounin, J. S. (1983). *Classrooms: Individuals or behavior settings?* (Monographs in Teaching & Learning, no. 1). Bloomington, IN: Indiana University, School of Education. (Eric Document Reproduction Service ED 240 070).

Kranz, C. (2006, January 8). &*@#! Language on the rise. *The Enquirer.* Retrieved January 10, 2006, from www.news.enquirer.com/apps/pbcs.dll/article?AID=2006601080384

Lasley, T. J., Lasley, J. O., & Ward, S. H. (1989, April). Activities and desists used by more and less effective classroom managers. Paper presented at the annual meeting of the American Educational Research Association. San Francisco, CA.

Leinhardt, G., Weldman, C., & Hammond, K. M. (1987). Introduction and integration of classroom routines by expert teachers. *Curriculum Inquiry, 17,* 135–175.

Lepper, M. (1983). Extrinsic reward and intrinsic motivation: Implications for the classroom. In J. Levine & M. Wang (Eds.), *Teacher and student perceptions: Implications for learning.* Hillsdale, NJ: Erlbaum.

Lewin, K., Lippitt, R., & White, R. (1939). Patterns of aggressive behavior in experimentally created social climates. *Journal of Social Psychology, 10,* 271–299.

Lyman, L., & Foyle, H. C. (1990). *Cooperative grouping for interactive learning: Students, teachers and administrators.* Washington, DC: National Education Association.

Martin, J. R. (1981). A new paradigm for liberal education. In J. F. Soltis (Ed.), *Philosophy and education.* Chicago: University of Chicago Press.

Marzano, R. J., Marzano, J. S., & Pickering, D. J. (2003). *Classroom management that works: Research-based strategies for every teacher.* Alexandria, VA: Association for Supervision & Curriculum Development.

Maslow, A., & Laury, K. (Ed.). (1998). *Toward a psychology of being.* Somerset, NJ: John Wiley & Sons.

McCaslin, M., & Good, T. L. (1992). Compliant cognition: The misalliance of management and instructional goals in current school reform. *Educational Researcher, 21*(3), 4–17.

McGinnis, J. C., Frederick, B. P., & Edwards, R. (1995). Enhancing classroom management through proactive rules and procedures. *Psychology in the Schools, 32,* 220–224.

McNamar, Mr. (2005, September 26). Quiet down, class. *The Daily Grind Blog.* Retrieved October 25, 2005, from www.ahighcall.blogspot.com/

National Committee to Prevent Child Abuse. (1995). *Seven good reasons to stop spanking.* Washington, DC: Author.

Oliviero, H. (2004, August 26). Bully girls. *The Atlanta Journal-Constitution,* pp. B1, B8.

Olweus, D. (1993). *Bullying at school.* Cambridge, MA: Blackwell.

Pace, D., & Price, M. (2005). Instructional techniques to facilitate inclusive education. In D. Schwarz (ed.), *Including Children with Special Needs* (pp. 115–131). Westport, CT: Greenwood Press.

Perry, D. G., Kusel, S. J., & Perry, L. C. (1988). Victims of peer aggression. *Developmental Psychology, 24,* 807–814.

Phi Delta Kappa International. (2006). Classroom management: Dealing with disruptive behavior. *Topics and Trends, 5*(9). Retrieved April 17, 2006 from www.pdkintl.org.9

Piazza, C. C., Bowman, L. G., Contruci, S. A., Delia, M. D., Adelinis, J. D., & Goh, N. L. (1999). An evaluation of the properties of attention and reinforcement of destructive and appropriate behavior. *Journal of Applied Behavior Analysis, 32,* 434–449.

Raviv, A., Raviv, A., & Reisel, E. (1990). Teachers and students: Two different perspectives?! Measuring social climate in the classroom. *American Educational Research Journal, 27,* 141–157.

Reynolds, A. (1992). What is competent beginning teaching? A review of the literature. *Review of Educational Research, 62*(1), 1–35.

Savage, T. W., & Savage, M. K. (2010). Successful classroom management and discipline: Teaching self-control and responsibility (3rd ed.). Thousand Oaks, CA: Sage.

Sheets, R. H. (2002). "You're just a kid that's there"—Chicano perception of disciplinary events. *Journal of Latinos and Education, 1*(2), 105–122.

Sheets, R. H., & Gay, G. (1996, May). Student perceptions of disciplinary conflict in ethnically diverse classrooms. *NASSP Bulletin,* 84–93.

Shores, R. E., Jack, S. L., Gunter, P. L., Ellis, D. N., DeBriere, T. J., & Wehby, J. H (1993). Classroom management strategies: Are they setting events for coercion? *Behavioral Disorders, 18,* 92–102.

Sommer, R., & Olsen, J. (1980). The soft classroom. *Environment & Behavior, 12*(1), 3–16.

Steele, B. F. (1988). *Becoming an effective classroom manager: A resource for* teachers. Albany: State University of New York.

Sterling, D. R. (2009). Classroom management: Setting up the classroom for learning. *Science Scope, 32*(9), 29–33.

Stipek, D. J. (2001). *Motivation to learn: Integrating theory and practice.* (4th ed.). Boston: Allyn & Bacon.

Swick, K. J. (1987). *Disruptive student behavior in the classroom.* (2nd ed.). Washington, DC: National Education Association.

Towbin, J. (2010). When students don't play the game. *Educational Leadership, 67*(5), 42–45.

Van Acker, R., Grant, S. H., & Henry, D. (1996). Teacher and student behavior as a function of risk for aggression. *Education and Treatment of Children, 19,* 316–334.

Walberg, H. J. (1987). Psychological environment. In M. J. Dunkin (Ed.), *The international encyclopedia of teaching and teacher education* (pp. 553–558). New York: Pergamon.

Wang, M. C., Haertel, G. D., & Walberg, H. J. (1993–94). What helps students learn? *Educational Leadership, 51*(4), 74–79.

Wannarka, R., & Ruhl, K. (2008). Seating arrangements that promote positive academic and behavioural outcomes: A review of empirical research. *Support for Learning, 23(2),* 89–93.

Weinstein, C. S. (1987). Seating patterns. In M. J. Dunkin (Ed.), *The international encyclopedia of teaching and teacher education* (pp. 544–548). New York: Pergamon.

Weinstein, C. S., & Mignano, A. J., Jr. (2010). *Elementary classroom management: Lessons from research and practice.* (5th ed.). Boston: McGraw-Hill.

Wheldall, K., & Lam, Y. Y. (1987). Rows versus tables II: the effects of two classroom seating arrangements on classroom disruption rate, on-task behavior and teacher behavior in three special school classes. *Educational Psychology, 7*(4), 151–160.

Wheldall, K., Morris, M., Vaughan, P., & Ng, Y. Y. (1981). Rows vs. tables: An example of the use of behavioral ecology in two classes of eleven-year-old children. *Journal of Educational Psychology, 1,* 171–184.

White, K. A. (1996, October 2). New teaching methods, technology add to space crunch. *Educational Week, 16,* 12.

White, M. A. (1975). Natural rates of teacher approach and disapproval in the classroom. *Journal of Applied Behavior Analysis, 8,* 367–372.

Wolfgang, C. H., & Kelsay, K. L. (1995). Discipline and the social studies classroom, grades K–12. *Social Studies, 86,* 175–182.

Wong, H. K., & Wong, R. T. (2001). *The first days of school.* Mountain View, CA: Harry K. Wong.

Wooden, R. A. (2004, September 9). Needed: A more disciplined approach to learning. *Christian Science Monitor.* Retrieved July 5, 2007, from www.csmonitor .com/2004/0909/p09s02-coop .html.

Woolfolk, A. E. (2010). *Educational psychology.* (11th ed.). Boston: Allyn & Bacon.

Wubbels, T., Brekelmans, M., vanTartwijk, J., & Admiral, W. (1999). Interpersonal relationships between teachers and students in the classroom. In H. C. Waxman & H. J. Walberg (Eds.), *New directions for teacher practice and research* (pp. 151–170). Berkeley, CA: McCutchen.

Wubbels, T., & Levy, J. (1993). *Do you know what you look like? Interpersonal relationships in education.* London: Falmer Press.

Yinger, R. J. (1979). Routines in teacher planning. *Theory Into Practice, 18*(3), 163–169.

Zirpoli, T. J., & Melloy, K. J. (2001). *Behavior management applications for teachers.* (3rd ed.). Columbus, OH: Merrill Prentice Hall.

Problem-Solving Skills of Effective Teachers

CHAPTER 13

What Is a Problem?

Sources of Problems

What Kinds of Classroom-Related Problems Do Teachers Face?
  Affiliation
  Control
  Parent Relationships and Home Conditions
  Student Success
  Time

Preventing and Resolving Classroom Problems
  Preventing Classroom Problems
  Resolving Classroom Problems
  Developing a Problem-Solving Attitude

Some Final Thoughts

Conversation Starters

What do you think causes some teachers to have more classroom problems than others?

Some believe it is because they are just not cut to be teachers. They don't have a knack for it. Others believe that they just haven't learned how to anticipate and resolve classroom challenges. They lack proper, related preparation.

To lessen classroom problems, which do you believe is more important: (a) having a knack for teaching or (b) having good preparation in problem solving?

This chapter intends to help you meet the challenges of teaching. Herein you will be made aware of the most commonly reported problems that challenge teachers. More importantly, you will learn a process that you can use when facing a problem. Armed with knowledge of the problems teachers report and a problem-solving process you can use, you will be better prepared when your turn comes to step up to the plate.

What Is a Problem?

Nearly everyone is challenged or encounters problems. If someone does not, that person is either very lucky or very skillful. Fortunately, you can avoid most problems, and resolve many others. However, before we get into that, let's consider what a problem is.

The simplest definition of a **problem** is goal-response interference. We need or want to achieve or have something, and we cannot (see Figure 13.1). Can you think of something you need or want that is elusive or unattainable? It could be a good job, a particular friend or friends, better living conditions, or the opportunity to participate in a certain activity. You probably need or want to do well in this class to maintain or increase your grade-point average which, in turn, might affect your student teaching assignment and, ultimately, your ability to obtain a teaching position.

You may have noticed we are using the terms *need* and *want*. *Need* designates something that is an absolute necessity to you. You need to breathe. On the other hand, *want* designates something that would be nice to have but is not essential to your well-being. Ice cream is a want. Whether the goal you seek is a need or a want is vitally important, for we must attain a need, whereas we can live without a want. Pursuit of either a need or a want that is elusive or unattainable still designates a problem. The difference is one of kind and degree.

13.1 Are your problems the result of *needs* or *wants*?

Sources of Problems

Our needs can come from virtually any source. However, they all relate to the pursuit of either primary *biological needs* or secondary *learned needs* (see Figure 13.2). Thus, some problems result from the inability to satisfy our inborn biological needs for food, water, and rest. We are driven to meet these primary needs on a regular basis. If you have been deprived of any for any length of time, you know how devastating it can be. The "machine" breaks down.

Unfortunately, you will see students deprived of these basic needs. Teachers working with students of low socioeconomic status (SES) report that such children

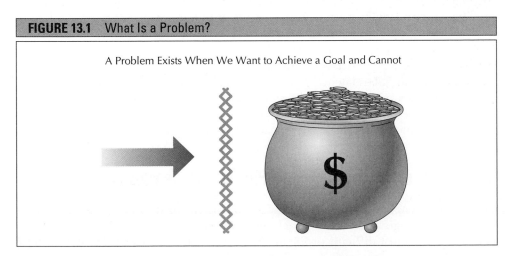

FIGURE 13.1	What Is a Problem?

A Problem Exists When We Want to Achieve a Goal and Cannot

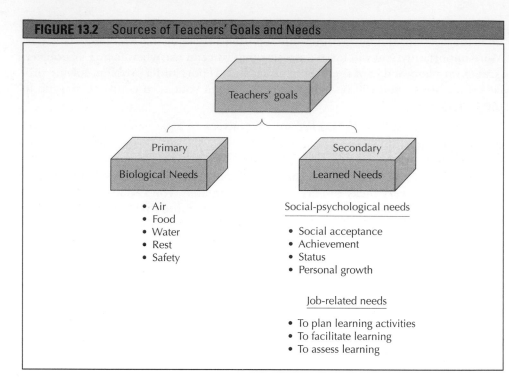

FIGURE 13.2 Sources of Teachers' Goals and Needs

Teachers' goals

Primary
Biological Needs

- Air
- Food
- Water
- Rest
- Safety

Secondary
Learned Needs

Social-psychological needs

- Social acceptance
- Achievement
- Status
- Personal growth

Job-related needs

- To plan learning activities
- To facilitate learning
- To assess learning

Try Incident 1 in Unit 3 of the Practice Teaching Manual

frequently come to school without adequate clothing and are often hungry and sleepy. Teachers also report children arriving cold and wet, stealing lunches, and sleeping in class. Be forewarned: Such problems are not peculiar to low SES children. The primary needs of high SES children also may go unmet.

On the other hand, some of our problems and those of our students are fueled by the inability to meet secondary, or learned needs. In the process of growing up, we learn that we "need" to be friendly, to look good, to be successful, and so on. For the most part, we hope to please others and ourselves. Inability to satisfy our learned needs is likely to make us feel personally unfulfilled and unhappy. All of us have felt disappointed or discouraged when our efforts to achieve secondary needs are thwarted. Students have many problems as a result of their unmet social and psychological needs. They act out, give up, and sometimes break down.

What we do for a living has a direct impact on our ability to meet our primary and secondary needs. Different kinds of work make life easier or more difficult. When our work enables us to satisfy our needs, it hardly seems like work at all. In such cases, we like our job. Conversely, work that is not fulfilling can be killing. Teaching normally is very pleasant work. It enables us to meet our biological needs fairly well, although some teachers in some situations might argue to the contrary. It also has the potential for helping us meet our learned needs. However, that occurs only when we teach well. This brings us to another subcategory of learned needs we will call "job-related." To teach well, we must be good at planning learning activities, facilitating or helping students learn, and assessing learning—activities you have learned about in this book. The end results of teaching well are acceptance, achievement, and personal satisfaction.

What Kinds of Classroom-Related Problems Do Teachers Face?

We have been able to determine what the problems or unmet needs of teachers are as they engage in the act of teaching by asking hundreds of K–12 teachers to describe their most difficult problem each day for up to two weeks. When these thousands of teacher-perceived problems were collected and analyzed, we found that there are sixty *common* problems that fall into five larger categories we call "areas of concern": affiliation, control, parent relationships and home conditions, student success, and time (see Figure 13.3). Let's look at each area.

AFFILIATION

Affiliation is defined as the teacher's need to establish and maintain good relationships with others in the school. This includes students, faculty colleagues, staff, and administrators. Signs of affiliation include staff friendliness, recognition and support of one another's professional work, and working together to achieve common goals (Rhodes, Nevill, & Allan, 2004).

When teachers describe their day-to-day concerns, they report these affiliation related problems: liking some or all of their students, getting students to like them, getting cooperation and support from their colleagues and the administration, being professional in their relationships with others in the school, having confidence in other teachers, and feeling anxious when being supervised.

Having the comforting acceptance, companionship, and support of others is a very real social-psychological need, as Figure 13.2 indicates. Teachers deprived of human support during their workday feel lonely, unappreciated, ineffective, alienated, and perhaps even rejected. Teachers who report frequent affiliation concerns also report they are dissatisfied with teaching and with the school they are in (Myers, 1980).

The need for affiliation is especially strong in persons who elect to teach. According to the late Don Super (2002), when teachers are compared to certified public accountants, engineers, lawyers, and clergy, teachers value four things more highly: (1) having fellow workers they like, (2) working under pleasant conditions, (3) having the respect of others, and (4) enjoying job certainty. Thus, three of the things teachers prize seem directly related to the need for affiliation. Similarly, when Holland (1997) compared teachers with persons in other occupations using an instrument that measures personality types, he found that they rank highest on the "social" scale.

Affiliation probably is of particular importance to us and more difficult to achieve because of the nature of our work. We are constantly in contact with others. Moreover, at certain times we are required to be leaders, while at others we may be equals or followers. Very few occupations regularly require all three interpersonal roles.

Tracey (1980) provides us with affiliation-related problems that teachers report, including:

- I have a problem with a student who swore at me in class. Having had this student in classes for two years, I was disappointed with his lack of respect.

13.3 Have you had teachers who seemed to have problems in one or more of these five areas of teacher concern? What were these teachers like?

13.4 How important to you is getting along with others?

13.5 What kinds of affiliation problems do you think you might have?

13.6 How important to you is getting along with students, colleagues, administrators, and staff?

Try Incidents 12 and 14 in Unit 3 of the Practice Teaching Manual

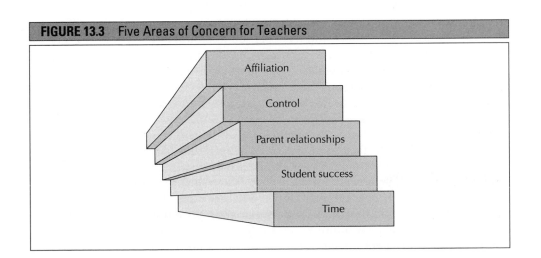

FIGURE 13.3 Five Areas of Concern for Teachers

- The teachers at my grade level had their weekly meeting. Once again, it was them against me. Everything was decided by them. They didn't even know I was there.
- I have heard that my principal thinks I do not work hard enough—that I should have more students and teach more classes. I am already working so hard. I can't believe he thinks so little of me when I work so hard.

As you can see, affiliation concerns seem directly related to our expectations and to those of our students, colleagues, administrators, and staff. Our inability to meet their expectations, and their inability to meet ours, seem to be the root of the problem. Affiliation concerns also come from our inability to interact effectively. Consequently, we need to be aware of what students, colleagues, administrators, and staff expect of us, and we must practice good interpersonal skills such as being sensitive to others and generally trying to assist them in meeting their needs.

Tracey (1980) provides a summary on affiliation:

> Affiliation problems, those which involve relationships with students, fellow teachers, and administrators, are troublesome to many teachers. It is important to seek solutions to these problems because the quality of interactions and the degree of affiliation with others greatly affect personal and professional satisfaction. When dealing with an affiliation problem, examine the expectations held by all the people involved. Not meeting expectations of self or others leads to conflict and frustration. . . . Research about [human] interaction provides helpful information. . . .
>
> Affiliation is a critical and complex [area] for teachers. Valuable [related] information can be learned from work in communication, social psychology, psychology, and sociology. There are no simple explanations for human behavior or simple solutions for establishing better affiliation. (pp. 108–109)

The U.S. Department of Education, recognizing that new teachers have problems affiliating, has published *The Survival Guide for New Teachers*, available on its website. In it veteran teachers offer advice on how to work with other teachers, principals, and parents. (See also Highlights 13.1 and 13.2, which contain ideas for improving relationships with students.)

CONTROL

Control is the teacher need to have students behave well or appropriately. When teachers define *appropriately* they mean students should be reasonably quiet, orderly, courteous, and honest, and they should show respect for others and for property. Case 13.1 (on page 446) presents an illustration of maintaining control.

Teachers report they have several control-related problems: maintaining order, quiet, and control; not knowing how to respond to improper behavior such as swearing and use of obscenities; controlling aggressive behavior; enforcing considerate treatment of property; getting students to use leisure time well; maintaining students' attention; enforcing values such as honesty and respect; removing students who are sources of frustration; and teaching self-discipline.

When students do not behave appropriately, two things can happen. First, animosity can develop between teacher and student, resulting also in an affiliation problem. Second, teachers can feel like and be perceived by students, teachers, administrators, and parents as ineffective classroom managers.

To complicate matters, we suspect that many persons who decide to teach are not strongly control-oriented. Remember, mostly we are *socially oriented*. We want to like and be liked. In fact, many teachers believe that the classroom should be "democratic" and that students should be empowered or given authority to decide things and, essentially, to control themselves. Complicating matters even further, many teachers simply don't have a clue about how to establish and maintain any kind of order. After all, they were conforming and they enjoyed learning and presume that their students will too. When students respond to learning negatively by acting up, many teachers are shocked and stymied.

13.7 In what ways do you hope to change so that you might enhance your affiliation with others?

Web Link
U.S. Department of Education

13.8 How important is control to you?

13.9 What types of control-related problems do you worry about most?

HIGHLIGHT 13.1
Letting Students Know You Care

Your relationships with students can be improved when you

- greet and address them by name when they enter the room.
- show positive emotions such as smiling, humor.
- make sure they understand what has been taught and hold them accountable.

- are firm but fair.
- listen to their concerns.
- complement positive behavior.
- respond to transgressions gently and with explanations rather than sharply and with punishments.
- address their personal needs when possible.

- treat them as individuals and show interest in their out-of-school life.

Source: Stipek (2006).

HIGHLIGHT 13.2
"I Just Don't Like Some Students"

When certain kids get under your skin, which they are bound to do, ask yourself, "Why?" and, "Is part of the problem the way I think about them?"

Here is a four-step remediating process suggested by Corbin (cited in Checkley, 2006):

1. Write a statement about the student. "Larry is a slug. He doesn't do homework, skips out to the bathroom, has parents who don't support me but expect me to bend over helping their son. Mostly, he feels *so* entitled. I can't stand him."

2. Is the statement true? For example, "Do I *absolutely* know that Larry 'feels entitled' or do I just want to believe he does?"

3. Consider how things might differ if you didn't make this judgment about the student. "If I didn't feel Larry felt entitled, I might think that he just has trouble learning and his parents aren't much help. In that case, I might willingly provide the help he needs."

4. Restate the statement. "Larry is entitled to appropriate instruction because he isn't succeeding."

Novak (1980) provides examples of teacher-reported, control-related incidents:

The same boy, DeWayne, who has been causing all the trouble in one of my classes was off and running again today. He had the girl sitting behind him combing his hair. Later in the period, he threw a paper wad across two rows to a boy. And, he was talking to the boys and girls around him. I think that the time has come for the school authorities to be called in. (p. 115)

Try Incidents 2, 4, 10, and 12 in Unit 3 of the Practice Teaching Manual

Chapter 12 contains basic information about organizing, managing, and controlling the classroom that applies to this area of teacher concern. Novak (1980) provides further help. He proposes five principles that can make control less of a problem:

- *Pursue only classroom goals that are truly important and attainable.* Thus, when you teach, modify or scale down overly ambitious intentions. In the case of the above control incident Novak provides, it is very important for DeWayne to

When students have been sent to the [male] principal if they were either unwilling or unable to don a fig leaf to cover their nakedness, we have typically been given one of two responses: "I've seen worse," or "I don't have time to deal with this," which may be a cover for embarrassment or fear. . . . I do believe that . . . [my] mostly young male [colleagues] are potentially asking for a heap of trouble if they confront a young female . . . regarding cleavage and thigh exposure . . .

About once every other day, one of [them] comes scurrying to me pointing out some shocking little piece of eye-candy to ask my intervention. A few days ago it was the young assistant principal who encountered an outfit so provocative he couldn't ignore it, and asked me to corral a young hottie dressed in strategically placed string. . . . [He] stood behind me with his arms crossed, looking like a bull mastiff with a toothache, while I did the actual dirty work:

Me: "Hon, can you c'mere for a second?"

Delilah: "Whut?"

Me: "You are unfortunately in violation of the dress code, and I need to know if you've got something else to change into."

Delilah: "Huh? Whut's wrong with my clothes? I've got two shirts on!"

Me: "Actually, you've got two quarter shirts on, one see-through and one crocheted, and basic math says that that still equals, at best, one-half a shirt. See, when you self-consciously tug the hem of the top layer down, you expose too much cleavage. When the hem immediately snaps back up like a rubber band, we see the bottom of your unmentionables both north and south of your navel. . . . So you need to get a real shirt on, please, so you don't put someone's eye out."

Delilah: "Man, this is WHACK! A'ight, a'ight! Gees!"

AP nods his massive head toward the end of the hallway . . .

Why is this important? I think that a school is for students, not strumpets. We're not asking them to wear uniforms or habits. They can come to school in PJs and slippers. And when we ignore a rule, especially one we've made a big deal out of, we look like jackasses . . .

Source: Cornelius (2005).

INVESTIGATING AND SOLVING THE CASE

1. What is the problem?
2. What do the teachers want to have happen that isn't?
3. What obstacles exist in getting students to "dress properly"? How might the obstacles be removed, overcome, or circumvented?
4. What alternative solution is most likely to achieve the goal?

---

behave appropriately. However, he and the teacher may have to work at it over time. Therefore, the teacher might modify or scale down classroom goals and ask DeWayne to make an effort to behave appropriately in meeting these easier goals. Rather than expect immediate perfection, the teacher should look for progress.

- *Analyze the factors that may be affecting the problem situation.* Novak reminds us that the more you know about the circumstances of a problem, the more likely you will be able to select and employ effective techniques to resolve it. Therefore, he asks that you analyze the learning task and the students' ability to do it, consider the events that occurred before and during the problem's onset (what led up to the incident?), and consider what happened following the control incident (was there peer laughter, ineffective punishment?). By analyzing the situations DeWayne misbehaves in, you may deduce some clues that can explain his actions.

- *Use positive techniques for managing behavior.* Novak believes that when students do not act appropriately, they must learn new behavior patterns. This requires teaching students what is expected of them and recognizing and rewarding subsequent desirable behavior.

Students must have a clear understanding of behavioral expectations and their importance. Some students will misunderstand your expectations unless these expectations are absolutely clear and you are doggedly insistent in their pursuit. Other students will need to learn how to behave somewhat differently to what they are accustomed to in other classrooms or at home. Yet others may have difficulty with you, and you with them, because of some social or emotional shortcoming.

Novak has specific advice as you work with students who have a difficult time behaving appropriately. *First,* he urges that you single them out when they are doing the right thing and applaud their efforts. *Second,* recognize and reward them only when they engage in desirable behaviors. Do not give in to or reward undesirable behaviors. *Third,* ignore inappropriate behavior as often as possible. Do not allow your attention or the other students' attention to be drawn to it. *Fourth,* make sure that recognition and reward for desirable behavior is indeed rewarding. Not all learners will see better grades, teacher praise, or the assignment of more difficult work as positive. *Finally,* engage students themselves in problem solving. They, too, need to know how to go about resolving problems. Chapter 12 contains information you can readily apply in pursuit of Novak's third principle.

- *Use punishment sparingly and appropriately.* Use only punishment that works, use only as much as necessary, and make certain students know what behavior is inappropriate and, conversely, what is acceptable.

- *Teach students to manage their own behavior.* Teach them self-control. Notes Novak, "Self-control means having students behave appropriately in the absence of external control" (p. 149). When students know that inappropriate and appropriate behavior have predictable consequences and when they can recognize and respond to important classroom rules, they can exhibit self-control. Rules can include "When directions are being given, it is especially important to listen" and "When you borrow something, return it." Finally, Novak implores, "Don't be too controlling. Seek reasonable control. It is a lot easier to achieve and less stressful to you and your students" (p. 150).

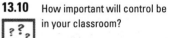

13.10 How important will control be in your classroom?

The You Can Handle Them All website offers suggestions for managing over 100 misbehaviors.

Web Link
You Can Handle Them All

PARENT RELATIONSHIPS AND HOME CONDITIONS

We learned in Chapter 2 that most families and caregivers have great influence on children. Therefore, if you are able to involve parents constructively in their child's education, it is more likely that improved attendance, achievement, and behavior will follow. Teachers recognize the important role parents and significant others play in the lives of students. Beginning teachers report that their biggest challenge is communicating with and involving parents (Metropolitan, 2004–2005). They want to but have difficulty achieving regular, constructive relationships with them. (See Highlight 13.3.)

Teachers are also aware that the conditions in students' homes impact school success. They benefit from knowing what home conditions are like, and most teachers would like to influence those conditions positively. (See Case 13.2 on page 449.)

Many teachers who have participated in our surveys tell us that they find it difficult to have good relationships with parents and to find out about and have a positive effect on home conditions. Specifically, they report problems with the following endeavors: improving life for students by correcting conditions both inside and outside school, keeping students away from people and things that may have a bad influence, improving conditions so that students can study better at home, encouraging parental interest in school matters, holding worthwhile parent conferences, understanding the conditions of home and community, and assisting parents who are having difficulty with their children.

13.11 How important is getting along with parents and other caregivers?

1. Collect e-mail addresses of students and parents. Not everyone has an e-mail address, but many parents and students do and they aren't always the same. [And] don't forget [some] students and parents . . . don't have e-mail access. Always make sure to have an alternative communication mode. . . .

2. Tell parents about the curriculum. You passed out a syllabus at open house, but most parents won't remember it. An e-mailed description of what their child's class is studying or a new unit that's just beginning helps keep parents [informed].

3. Remind students about assignments. Long-term assignments in particular are easy for students to lose track of. A few well-timed e-mails between the start of the project and the due date can help students stay on task, especially those students who are prone to procrastinate.

4. Motivate students to do independent study. For example, if you're teaching art . . . e-mail students [and parents] the URL of the Louvre Museum in Paris and suggest they take a virtual tour.

5. Follow a regular e-mail schedule . . . It helps students and parents get used to reading your messages. But don't overwhelm [them] with too much information or too many e-mails. Consider a weekly Wednesday e-mail to students as a kind of midweek reminder. A Monday "this week ahead" or Friday "weekly wrapup" e-mail can work well for parents.

6. Model good e-mail etiquette. Keep your messages short, professional, and on topic. Use a group "to" name rather than displaying everyone's e-mail address for the whole recipient group to see. Encourage students and parents with questions and issues to phone or visit you for a personal discussion rather than exchanging e-mails on sensitive subjects. And don't neglect the niceties of proper spelling, good grammar, and the like.

Source: Walling (2006).

Try Incidents 11 and 13 in Unit 3 of the Practice Teaching Manual

Mager (1980) suggests that to achieve constructive parent relationships, teachers and parents or guardians must be mutually supportive. For the most part, this means that teachers must accept and support parental values and behaviors and that parents must do likewise for teachers. Easier said than done, particularly when home and school values and behaviors differ. Mager shares a teacher-written illustration: "I was talking to the class about all the fights they had been getting into. The students told me that their parents tell them to hit anyone who does something they don't like. I suddenly realized that it's the school's 'no fighting policy' versus the parents' 'don't be a sissy policy'" (p. 157).

Perceptions of lack of competence also come into play and thus interfere with good relationships. For example, parents may doubt a teacher's decisions. One teacher writes, "I received a phone call from a parent who questioned the worth of an upcoming field trip. I tried to explain why the trip was worthwhile, but I am plagued by the thought that I was not convincing enough" (Mager, p. 156). Conversely, teachers may question the competence of parents. "I understand why Ellen behaves the way she does. These parents just don't care" (Mager, p. 157).

Failure to achieve mutual support may also result simply because barriers prevent teachers and parents from getting together to talk. Teachers may not have the time and energy. They may perceive that parents are too busy, or they may not want parents to "intrude" into their domain. For their part, parents may not wish to visit with teachers because they lack time or energy, they may not want to intrude, or they may perceive teachers as too busy. Additionally, parents may shy away from interactions with teachers because of unhappy childhood memories they have of school, feelings of insecurity, or guilt that their child is having problems. Parents and caregivers may also be reluctant to talk with teachers because they have personal or family difficulties, because they may not be the child's birth parent, or because they cannot converse fluently in English.

"I'm really not feeling well. Can I put my head down?"

"Sure, [Jennifer]. Come and sit here, you can be by yourself." I motioned to a seat next to my desk.

As I sorted through papers, she raised her face from her forearm. A red imprint of her cable sweater was visible on her cheek. Her voice was barely above a whisper, and I moved my chair closer to her as she spoke.

"I was awake all night. My parents were fighting. My stepfather hits my mom when he gets drunk. I'm afraid to go to sleep. She might need me to call 911 or something. I really want to move out of there. Part of me can't wait. I'll be 18 in July. But, I don't want my mom to be left alone. My dad was an alcoholic, too. He's in prison now. I don't know why she puts up with these men. I wonder why we don't just leave."

Source: Matthews (2005).

INVESTIGATING AND SOLVING THE CASE

1. What, if anything, bothers you about this encounter with Jennifer?

2. How and to what purpose might you become involved?

In discussing the teacher's need to know what students' home and community conditions are like and, relatedly, the teacher's desire to influence them in a positive direction, Mager again points out hindrances. First of all, parents and guardians, not teachers, control home conditions. The following anecdote reveals a teacher's frustration on this count. "Today a student came late to my first hour class for the ninth time in four weeks. The main problem is that most of his excuses are legitimate. His lateness can be directly attributed to his parents. Car won't start, alarm doesn't work, mother got breakfast late, he had to babysit until 2 A.M. and so forth" (Mager, p. 161).

Second, home conditions may be beyond the control of parents. Some parents are forced to live in substandard housing in deteriorating, violent communities. Some parents must raise children without adequate financial and human support. Some children must be left to their own devices. Other parents have limited intellect and/or education. Mager shares another teacher anecdote. "I visited the home of a new seventh grader coming from a rural school. He is having difficulty academically and socially. The purpose of the visit was to obtain permission to have him tested. I have come in contact with many deprived families but this one is very sad. Both parents are extremely retarded as is another child, a sixteen-year-old who has never even been to school. Neither parent can read or write" (p. 162). These are realities that neither parents nor teachers alone can overcome.

13.12 Which parent-teacher relationship problems seem most noteworthy to you? Why?

Mager offers suggestions for helping build mutual support with parents and improving home and community conditions. To achieve mutual support, increase the frequency and improve the quality of teacher-parent interactions. Such "interactions" can include sending out a classroom newsletter regularly, perhaps monthly; bringing in parent volunteers; forming a mom and/or dad's club, and so forth. To improve the quality of interactions, you need to learn what parents expect of you, and you need to share what you expect of parents. Usually, unpleasant interactions are the result of unrealistic or failed expectations.

To achieve the goal of optimal home and community conditions, take at least two steps. First, recognize that the relationship between home and community conditions and a student's school experience is complex. Avoid simplistic causal explanations such as "Robert would do better if he could move out of that home and neighborhood." That may or may not be true. Second, remember that the nature of the parents or guardians and the quality of the interactions they have with their children are more important than the material possessions found in the home.

Home and neighborhood trappings do not substitute for quality-of-life relationships. Therefore you should not "judge the book by its cover."

Suggestions for preventing or resolving differences with parents are contained in Highlight 13.4.

STUDENT SUCCESS

Student success is defined as the need teachers have to help learners achieve both academically and socially. It is a very important goal because when you are successful in attaining it, you meet your secondary or learned needs for achievement, status, and acceptance in the teaching profession.

Unfortunately, many teachers struggle with student success. In our studies in which teachers have described everyday problems, a great many fit into this category.

Kinds of Success Problems   Teacher-reported student success problems include those related to insufficient student interest, working with students who have special needs, and a teacher's own instructional shortcomings.

Problems related to teachers' perceptions of insufficient student interest include statements such as "I have a problem having students present and on time; getting students to participate; getting them to work up to their ability; prevailing on them to value grades; and overcoming apathy or even dislike of school and learning."

Problems associated with students who face special challenges include helping children with personal problems; helping those with special physical, social, emotional or intellectual needs; overcoming a student's frustration with self; and getting students to feel they are succeeding.

The third kind of student success problem is related to our personal instructional limitations when planning, teaching, and assessing the learning that has taken place. Specifically, teachers tell us they have trouble planning instruction that adds variety to classroom life, creating student interest, providing for individual differences, using different instructional alternatives, assessing learning, promoting students' self-assessment, and extending learning beyond the classroom.

Obstacles to Student Success   Holton (1980) describes four obstacles to achieving student success. First, "Knowledge about teaching is at best sketchy" (p. 205). Although, as we learned in Chapter 10, knowledge about how to teach is accumulating, we still know less than is needed. If we had what we truly need to know, this text probably would consist of at least five volumes!

A second hindrance to student success is students' individual differences. Chapter 3 was devoted to student diversity. Holton notes that diversity or individual difference is no cliché. According to G. W. Beadle, a Nobel laureate in genetics, if we calculated all possible human characteristics and the resulting permutations, the number of possible different human individuals would be about 2 raised to the 4-billionth power (that is, $2 \times 2 \times 2 \ldots 4$ billion times). So much diversity exists among our students that it is difficult at best to facilitate the learning of everyone.

Third, "schools have many, often vague goals, and not all of them are consistent with student learning" (p. 205). Some people, Holton notes, want schools to teach "the basics," while others are intent on "developing the whole child." The latter would educate them intellectually, morally, socially, emotionally, and physically. Still others want schools to educate children to change or improve society. Each school of thought about educational goals would have teachers doing different things. Teachers have difficulty working toward student learning if the goals are not well-defined and agreed upon and its character is unclear.

Fourth, says Holton, "Teaching is greater than the sum of its parts" (p. 206). There is some "magic" to it. One can carefully construct lessons and still have students fail; there is no guarantee. Holton attributes this to what he calls the unknown and possibly unknowable X factor in teaching. "While we sense the X, it has defied our

13.13   How important to you is getting students to succeed academically and socially?

Try Incidents 3, 7, and 8 in Unit 3 of the Practice Teaching Manual

13.14   Which problems related to student success do you believe may be troublesome for you? Why?

13.15   What do you think the *X* factor is? Do you think you have or can develop it?

Katz and others (1996) suggest ways to establish a climate conducive to open communication with parents and caregivers:

- Let parents and guardians know how and when they can contact you.
- Have an open-door policy.

- Have an open mind.
- In preparation for a meeting, find out what are the parent or caregiver concerns.
- Involve parents in classroom activities.

- Know the school policy for addressing home-school disagreements.
- Use discretion when discussing children and their families.

---

attempts to weigh it, measure it, or catch it. . . . This X factor is what makes the successful classroom greater than the sum of its parts" (p. 206). It is the particular genius of knowing how and when to do something that works.

Teacher Behaviors Linked to Student Success   Holton makes clear that there are a number of teacher attributes and behaviors that are linked to student success. They are clarity, enthusiasm, being businesslike and work oriented, using instructional variety (see, for example, Case 13.3), arousing interest in and adjusting the material to be learned to student ability levels, providing adequate time and opportunity to learn, and helping students get the most out of their school experiences. These teacher attributes and behaviors are very similar to those detailed in Chapters 10 and 11.

13.16   What personal characteristics and professional abilities do you have that will probably serve you well? What related shortcomings would you like to have help with?

TIME

> I would really be able to enjoy teaching, I think, if I had enough time to do it to the best of my ability. But I don't. Teaching feels like a challenge on *Fear Factor*. Not only do you have to do something insanely dangerous or disgusting, but you have to do it in so little time that you can't possibly do it well. (What's Up, 2005)

Lack of time represents a serious problem for teachers. According to the thousands we have surveyed, teachers do not have sufficient time to prepare for classes, complete the planned work, and diagnose and evaluate learning. Furthermore, constraints on time have increased because of (1) large classes, (2) the number of classes teachers are required to teach, (3) increased emphasis on testing, and (4) the assignment of noninstructional tasks such as bus, lunchroom, and playground monitoring. Finally, they tell us they do not have enough time to do personal tasks because of the amount of work they must take home. Lack of time, then, seems to be a major concern (see Spotlight on Research 13.1 on page 453).

13.17   What kind of time-related problems do you think you may have as a teacher?

Unfortunately, there is little likelihood that demands on schools will lessen, and time is not a commodity we can manufacture more of. Rather, for decades, demands have been on the increase—teachers have more rather than less to do. Thus, teacher personal and professional needs seem to be growing inversely in relation to the time available to meet them.

Applegate (1980) suggests that since time is finite, we must learn to use it better, and she offers a number of suggestions. First, *know yourself*. Know your personal and professional needs. Are you spending enough time on the things that are important to you professionally and personally? Know your optimal work times. Are you a morning, afternoon, or evening person? Do you use your "best time" appropriately to get things done? Know your sleep and exercise needs. Are you skimping on or overdoing sleeping or exercising? Have your habits robbed you of vitality?

Second, *know your goals*. Are some in conflict with others, causing you to be counterproductive? For example, do you want both to be a teacher and wealthy?

Try Incidents 5 and 6 in Unit 3 of the Practice Teaching Manual

CHAPTER 13
Problem-Solving Skills
of Effective Teachers

CASE 13.3

If at First You Don't Succeed, Try Something Else

Language arts teacher Steve Simpson worked diligently with a boy who had great difficult writing (he utilized journal free writing, work on sentences, capitalization, word choice, editing, and everything else). Nothing seemed to work. "It didn't seem to bother [the boy] that every assignment he turned in was a mess." However, the boy kept "plugging away, cheerful as could be, working as hard as anyone . . ."

Then one day when Dr. Simpson was teaching a lesson on paragraphs, another idea struck. In his own words, here is what happened.

As . . . [a] change of pace [for the boy], I told him to . . . *type* the assignment using my computer. . . .

As I continued helping other students with their work, I glanced over every once in a while and there he would be, hunting and pecking. . . . I figured I would get something about the same size of a paragraph, easier to read and just as bad [as usual]. But that is not what happened.

He finished his paragraph and printed it. . . . I read it and gave him what had to be the weirdest look of my career. I knew he typed it, one painful letter at a time. I knew it took him all period. But . . . what I was looking at seemed like a miracle. His word choice was good. His sentences were mostly complete. He generally used capital letters correctly and the paragraph, bless his little heart, discussed only one subject.

For who knows what reason, when this student wrote using a keyboard, he processed information in a different way than when he wrote using a pencil. More of the language skills he had learned in his 14 years managed to sneak past the gatekeeper of his mind and made it onto the paper. The whole rhythm of the thing was different . . . Some kind of miracle [had transpired]. . . .

For me it was a pedagogical lesson. I learned that it is important to

try things when working with kids. We don't . . . have to understand everything about what we are trying, but if it makes some kind of sense to us as teachers, test drive it . . . if it does not work, try something else. . . . You never know when something you just make up on the spur of the moment might turn into a real, live education miracle.

Source: Simpson (2005).

> #### INVESTIGATING AND SOLVING THE CASE
> 1. Which of the three kinds of student success problems is this?
> 2. Which of the four obstacles to student success seems to be the case here?
> 3. What teacher behavior(s) made this a success story?

Additionally, are your goals realistic and attainable? Are you willing to invest heavily in order to accomplish something fairly remote? Do you want to be "teacher of the year" so badly that you will sacrifice nearly everything?

Third, *know your work environment.* What aspects of teaching can you control in order to use time better? Can you share instructional and other responsibilities with a colleague? Is it possible to eliminate interruptions that detract from instruction? Can you use uninterrupted time more effectively?

Fourth, *plan.* Do you plan in order to maximize your productivity and leisure? Do your plans support the things you consider most important?

Fifth, *learn to set priorities and to say no.* Having decided what is important, do you say no when other things try to intrude? Applegate notes, "When you say no to such a request, you are saying yes to yourself" (p. 277).

Sixth, *know your support system.* Are you aware of the kind of human and material help that may be available to you? Are you willing to ask for and give assistance?

Seventh, *concentrate.* Do you reserve time and space for uninterrupted concentration? Do you fool yourself by taking work home but then fiddle with it or merely bring it back undone? Is your work space uncluttered and amenable to work?

Eighth, *act. Don't procrastinate.* Do you indulge yourself or socialize to avoid work? Do you put things off because they are not rewarding? Many teachers say they do

13.18 How do you feel about time? Are you in control of your time?

Project STAR (Word and others, 1990) sought to find out if there is a relationship between the size of a K–3 teacher's class and his or her self-reported problems. To do so the researchers asked teachers to respond to 60 problem items on the *Teacher Problems Checklist* (Cruickshank & Associates, 1980).

Two findings resulted. Teachers with larger classes had problems that were no more frequent nor more bothersome than did teachers with fewer students. For K–3 teachers regardless of class size, problems related to "time" both occurred more frequently and were more bothersome. Three of the 60 items were

consistently top-ranked problems both in terms of their frequency of occurrence and their bothersomeness: (35) "Having enough time to teach and to diagnose learning," (20) "Having enough preparation time," and (5) "Having enough free time."

not like to evaluate students' work. That may be one reason some teachers take so long to return tests and homework.

Applegate's last suggestion is, *follow through. Finish.* Do you follow through on things you begin, or do they often end up incomplete and thus represent wasted effort and time?

Gibbon's (2002) study of the kinds and levels of stress experienced by urban teachers reports that time management is the greatest stressor followed by classroom control and student success, specifically lack of student motivation.

Teacher problems also are categorized in Stories of Beginning Teachers (Roehig et al., 2002).

13.19 Which of Applegate's suggestions for using time has the most meaning for you?

Preventing and Resolving Classroom Problems

Try Activity 13.1

At this point we have learned that we have a problem when we need or want something (a goal) but cannot attain it because of obstacles or hindrances. Some of the things we desire we truly need because our biological or social-psychological well-being depends upon our having them. Other goals or objectives, although desirable, are not truly necessary. We merely want them. Additionally, some of our needs are professional, or job-related, such as knowing how to teach well. You are taking this course in large measure because you must learn to teach well in order to get and hold a teaching position. Unfortunately, five categories of problems occur as we engage in teaching. These problems prevent us from teaching as well as we would like. Let's look at how we might prevent these job-related problems.

PREVENTING CLASSROOM PROBLEMS

How can we avoid problems related to affiliation, control, parent relationships, student success, and time? To be relatively immune to these teacher concerns, we must already possess or acquire specific abilities. Some of the abilities we need in order to prevent problems in each of the five categories are shown in Table 13.1.

Perhaps you are blessed with certain of these attributes already. Most likely those attributes you enjoy are related to affiliation and, to some extent, to time management since you have had years of opportunity to acquire both. Gaining as many of the abilities as possible will put you in an enviable position in any classroom. As the saying goes, an ounce of prevention is worth a pound of cure.

RESOLVING CLASSROOM PROBLEMS

It is doubtful that many, if any, of us have or can acquire all the different kinds of abilities noted in Table 13.1. In our studies, we have come across less than a handful of teachers who claim they have no problems. Unless you are very

TABLE 13.1 Abilities That a Teacher Needs to Prevent Problems in the Five Areas of Teachers' Concerns

If You Have Concerns Related to ...	Then You Must ...
• Affiliation	• Be accepting, caring, and supportive of others • Be cooperative • Be professional in relationships • Know of and use interpersonal skills • Know of and be able to meet reasonable expectations others have for you
• Control	• Appear to students to have reasonable expectations for work and behavior • Recognize and reward work and behavior that meet your expectations • Get students to monitor and control their own work and behavior
• Parent relationships	• Have good affiliation skills (see above) • Be able to establish a system of mutual support • Get parents and caregivers involved in the student's education
• Student success	• Be able to create and maintain learners' interest • Be able to meet a wide range of individual differences • Be thoughtful and skillful in planning and facilitating learning and assessment • Have the qualities and abilities of effective teachers
• Time	• Concentrate on doing what is most important • Know when during the day you and your learners work best • Plan • Share mutual work and responsibilities with colleagues • Avoid procrastinating and finish what you start

remarkable or possibly oblivious, you can expect to encounter events that interfere with accomplishing the five major goals teachers share. We can say with assurance that teachers do have problems and that teaching is tough. Obviously, the best way to escape from a problem is to solve it. So let's think about problem resolution.

A problem is solved or resolved only when you are able to either give up the goal (need or want) or get closer to it—while, at the same time, you avoid unpleasant side effects. With the help of extensive literature on problem solving, we have developed a problem-solving approach or regimen that should be advantageous to any teacher in difficulty.

The Problem-Solving Approach (PSA) The PSA consists of five stages and 10 steps:

Stage 1: Problem identification and ownership. At the outset, it is essential that the problem, goal, and the ownership of both be clear. The first three steps are to

1. State the problem. What is it that is bothersome to you?
2. Identify the goal(s). What specifically do you need or want to have happen that is not happening?
3. Identify the problem's owner. Who has the problem? Who needs or wants the goal? Obviously, if it is your goal that is blocked, it is your problem.

Stage 2: Value clarification. Once the problem has been identified and its ownership established, the fourth step is to:

4. Value the goal. Do you really care so much about the goal to continue to pursue it?

Stage 3: Analysis of the problem situation. Assuming that you have found the goal worthy of pursuit, you now enter the problem-analysis stage. The three steps in this stage require that you:

5. Identify the obstacles preventing you from accomplishing your goal. What specifically seems to stand between your goal and its accomplishment?

6. Project strategies for removing, overcoming, or circumventing the obstacle(s).

7. For each of the potential solutions, list possible negative side effects or consequences. Remember that it is one thing to "get your way" and another to get it in a manner that harms you or someone else. You could "win the battle but lose the war."

Stage 4: Rating the potential solutions. In Steps 6 and 7, you projected strategies for reaching your goal and identified possible harmful side effects. Now:

8. Rate each proposed solution to arrive at the best one or ones. Remember, *a good solution is one that gains or puts you closer to your goal without causing unpleasant side effects.*

Stage 5: Implementing and evaluating the best solution. In the last two steps of our PSA, you are asked to:

9. Decide how you would implement the best solution. What precisely would you do?

10. Decide the extent to which the solution has brought you closer to your goal, thus reducing or eliminating your problem.

Even if you do not have all the abilities necessary to prevent the occurrence of classroom problems, you certainly can learn how to be a better problem solver. Table 13.2 provides an outline of the PSA.

Try Activity 13.2

TABLE 13.2   The Problem-Solving Approach (PSA)

Stage 1: Identify the problem and its ownership

1. State the problem. What is it that is bothersome?
2. Identify the goal(s). What do you want to happen that is not?
3. Identify the problem's owner. Who needs or wants the goal?

Stage 2: Determine the value of the goal

4. Value the goal. After thinking about it, decide whether the goal is of

_____unquestionable value.   _____little value.

_____great value.   _____no real consequence.

_____value but negotiable.

Stage 3. Analyze the problem situation

5. Identify the obstacles to goal achievement.
6. Project ways you might achieve the goal by either getting rid of, overcoming, or circumventing obstacles, or thinking of ingenious creative solutions.
7. List some possible consequences each solution might have.

Stage 4: Rate the proposed solutions

8. Rate each potential solution according to the likelihood it would help reach the goal and cause few, if any, unfavorable side effects.

Stage 5: Implement and evaluate the best solution

9. Decide specifically how to put the best solution to work.
10. Decide to what extent the best solution is working.

DEVELOPING A PROBLEM-SOLVING ATTITUDE

No one wants problems, but when faced with one, how do you react and what do you think? Do you consider it a source of irritation and mostly gripe about it? Teachers' lounges are notorious for hosting this activity. Teachers reportedly often stand around and complain to one another. Although this may be a good way to let off steam, it seldom accomplishes much else. Or, do you consider a problem to be a challenge? Do you have a good problem-solving attitude? If so, you may even avoid this use of the teachers' lounge in order to use the time to work toward solving the problem and attaining your goal.

The way you react to problems reveals your problem-solving attitude. As we have talked with teachers, we find those with a positive problem-solving attitude or outlook have certain characteristics. They

13.20 How do you react when you need or want something and cannot readily attain it?

- Have a "let's solve this" approach.
- Refuse to blame others for their inability to gain a goal.
- Accept their problems and respond, "I have a problem. How do I solve it?"
- Focus on the present or future rather than bemoan the past.
- Replace natural emotional, visceral reactions to a problem with goal-oriented, thoughtful ones; they "get the problem out of their stomach and into their head."
- Refrain from jumping to conclusions or solutions.
- Search for new approaches, deviate from old habits, and avoid the obvious.
- Expect disagreements and accept and respect the views of others.
- Ask what they themselves can do to reach their goals rather than depending upon others to act on their behalf.
- Accept approximations to a goal: "Half a loaf is better than none."
- Work toward bettering already satisfactory situations to ensure they remain so.
- Consciously make use of available time for problem solving.

13.21 What characteristics of a good problem-solving attitude do you already possess? Which do you need to work on?

Attitude isn't everything, but it counts a lot in terms of whether we face problems feeling action-oriented or immobilized. Be positive. You can do it. Just do it!

Some Final Thoughts

Teaching indeed is challenging. However, now you know the five areas of challenge. Now you are aware of a reasoned approach to the problems of practice. Should you want even greater awareness or practice we have included problems at the end of many chapters, and Unit 3 of the Practice Teaching Manual is "Room 221: A Simulation: Solving Classroom Problems."

CHAPTER SUMMARY

- A problem exists when we need or want something and cannot readily attain it.
- Problems result from our inability to achieve primary *(biological)* or secondary *(learned)* needs. Biological needs include air, food, water, rest, safety, and security. Learned needs are social-psychological, and some are job-related. Social-psychological needs include social acceptance, achievement, status, and personal growth. Job-related needs include the ability to plan, teach, and assess learning.
- Teacher problems occur mostly in pursuit of social-psychological and job-related needs. Teachers commonly report about 60 problems that fall into five categories: *affiliation, control, parent relationships/home conditions, student success,* and *time.* Studies provide us with theoretical knowledge that helps us understand the problems in each category.

- It is important both to be able to prevent problems and to be able to resolve them. Teachers with certain dispositions and abilities are likely to have fewer problems. Teachers who employ a problem-solving approach are more likely to resolve classroom problems, and teachers with a positive problem-solving attitude also are more likely to meet their needs.

KEY TERMS

Problem, 441	Parent relationships, 447	Time management, 451
Affiliation, 443	Student success, 450	Problem-Solving Approach, 454
Control, 444		

ISSUES AND PROBLEMS FOR DISCUSSION

ISSUES

1. Which of the five teacher goals are most important?
2. Should teachers be expected to resolve most classroom problems on their own?
3. How can teachers become better problem solvers?
4. Where can teachers find specific pedagogical help related to the classroom problems they face?

PROBLEM

Unit 3 of the Practice Teaching Manual contains many examples of classroom problems.

THEORY INTO ACTION: ACTIVITIES FOR PRACTICE AND YOUR PORTFOLIO

ACTIVITY 13.1: Talk with a Teacher about Classroom Problems   If you are involved in a field experience, talk with a teacher about classroom problems. You might ask:

1. What kinds of problems do most teachers in the school seem to have?
2. What might make teaching easier for one teacher and harder for another?
3. What can I do to minimize and resolve the problems I might have?

ACTIVITY 13.2: Record a Teacher's Problem and Analyze It   If you are in a field experience, ask your mentor teacher if you can record a problem and, with the teacher's help, analyze it.

1. With the mentor teacher's assistance, identify a situation where you or the teacher has a goal in mind and there is difficulty achieving it.
2. Write a detailed account of what happened. In other words, what specifically was the problem?
3. With the teacher's assistance, analyze the problem.
   a. What is desirable that isn't happening?
   b. How important is the goal?
   c. What obstacles seem to be in the way of goal achievement?
   d. How might the goal be reached with the fewest negative side effects?

REFERENCES

Applegate, J. (1980). Time. In D. R. Cruickshank & Associates, *Teaching is tough* (pp. 257–302). Englewood Cliffs, NJ: Prentice Hall.

Baker, A., & Soden, L. (1998). *The challenges of parent involvement.* New York, NY: ERIC Clearinghouse on Urban Education. ERIC Digest No. 134.

Checkley, K. (2006 August). Teacher doesn't like me. *Education Update.* Alexander, VA: Association for Supervision and Curriculum Development (pp. 1–2, 6.).

Cornelius, M. (2005, September 12). The naked apes. A Shrewdness of Apes Blog. Access: shrewdnessofapes.blogspot .com/2005/09/naked-ape.html

Gibbons, S. (2002). *Urban elementary and middle school teachers' perceptions of stress associated with standards-based curriculum reforms and mandated statewide testing.* New Brunswick, NJ: Rutgers University. Doctoral dissertation.

Haynes, N. M., Comer, J. P., & Hamilton-Lee, M. (1989). School climate enhancement through parent involvement. *Journal of School Psychology, 27,* 87–90.

Henderson, A. T. (1987). *The evidence continues to grow: Parent involvement improves student achievement.* Columbia, MD: National Committee for Citizens in Education.

Holland, J. (1997). *Making vocational choices: A theory of careers.* Englewood Cliffs, NJ: Prentice Hall.

Holton, J. (1980). Student success. In D.R. Cruickshank & Associates, *Teaching is tough* (pp. 199–256). Englewood Cliffs, NJ: Prentice Hall.

Katz, L., Aidman, A., Reese, D. A., & Clark, A.-M. (1996). Preventing and resolving parent-teacher differences. ERIC Digests. Urbana, IL: ERIC Clearinghouse on Elementary and Early Childhood Education. (ERIC Document Reproduction Services ED 401 048).

Mager, G. (1980). Parent relationships and home and community conditions. In D. R. Cruickshank & Associates, *Teaching is tough* (pp. 153–198). Englewood Cliffs, NJ: Prentice Hall.

Matthews, M. B. (2005, December 1). Close To Home. Access: www .mbmatthews.blogspot.com/

Metropolitan Insurance Company. (2004–2005). *Survey of the American Teacher.* New York: Metropolitan Insurance Company.

Myers, B. (1980). Relationships between classroom problems, personality, and place of work. In D. Cruickshank & Associates, *Teaching is tough* (pp. 303–321). Englewood Cliffs, NJ: Prentice Hall.

Novak, C. (1980). Control. In D. R. Cruickshank & Associates, *Teaching is tough* (pp. 113–151). Englewood Cliffs, NJ: Prentice Hall.

Rhodes, C., Nevill, A., & Allan, J. (2004). Valuing and supporting teachers. *Research in Education, 71,* 67–80.

Roehig, A., Telotta, D., & Pressley, M. (2002). *Stories of beginning teachers.* South Bend, IN: University of Notre Dame Press.

Simpson, S. (2005, March 28). *Take a chance. You might bump into an educational miracle.* Simpson Communications. Box 325, 7829 Center Blvd. Snoqualmie, WA.

Stipek, D. (2006, September). Relationships matter. *Educational Leadership, 64*(1), 46–49.

Super, D. E. (2002). *Work values inventory.* Boston: Houghton Mifflin.

Tracey, K. (1980). Affiliation. In D. R. Cruickshank & Associates, *Teaching is tough* (pp. 75–111). Englewood Cliffs, NJ: Prentice Hall.

Walling, D. (2006, October 3). 6 Tips for teacher-student parent e-mail. *Classroom Tips.* Phi Delta Kappa. Access: www.pdkintl.org

What's Up, Mz Smlph? (2005, October 4). Access: www .thisweekineducation.com/

Word, E., Johnston, J., Fulton, B., Zaharias, J., Lintz, N., Achilles, C., Folger, J., & Breda, C. (1990). *Student/teacher achievement ratio (STAR): Tennessee's K–12 class size study. Final report and final report summary.* Nashville, TN: Tennessee State Department of Education.

Reflective Skills
of Effective Teachers

Conversation Starters

Mind over matter: Can your thoughts and self-reflection affect your teaching ability?

The mind is very powerful. Some assert that it creates "reality" for us because what we think determines what we can and can't see or do.

Do you agree that what you think can change the way you feel and act?

Does this apply to teaching? Specifically, if you think deeply about the way you teach—either before or after the teaching episode—can those thoughts influence your teaching behaviors and effectiveness?

The previous chapters in this book focused on knowledge, characteristics, and skills of effective teachers. Although these are an important part of learning to teach, the ability to manage and succeed in today's unpredictable and complex classrooms requires more than knowledge and skill. It requires a certain disposition: reflection. Knowledge, skills, and the desire to teach are essential for teachers, but reflection enables us to learn from our experience. **Reflection** is the ongoing process of critically examining and refining teaching practice by considering the personal, educational, social, and ethical aspects of teaching and schooling (Han, 1995). Reflection enables teachers to describe and think about what they do, to anticipate and solve classroom problems, and to experience continued professional and personal growth.

Research suggests that reflection is related to effective teaching, especially instructional behavior, classroom organization, and teacher expectations (Giovannelli, 2003). Reflection is especially important for beginning teachers who often hold unrealistic views about the problems they will encounter and believe they already have all the knowledge and skills they will need to be effective teachers (Brookhart & Freeman, 1992). This chapter focuses on the process of reflection. It will help you realize the importance of reflecting on teaching. Further, it will recommend ways to enhance your own reflective abilities.

Try Activity 14.1

Thanksgiving Reconsidered

Student teacher Adrienne worked especially hard to prepare an exciting lesson on the food pyramid that would help the students understand the importance of good nutrition. By tying the lesson in to the approaching Thanksgiving celebration, she could talk about holiday traditions at the same time. She prepared well, using MyPyramid.gov and Kidshealth.org to gather information about nutrition and how to select and plan healthy meals. She developed a PowerPoint presentation with vocabulary words and graphics from nutrition websites. She planned to divide the students into groups of three to plan a healthy Thanksgiving dinner. And, based on a suggestion from her language arts professor, she developed a shape writing activity as her assessment, asking students to write about how they celebrate Thanksgiving inside an outline of a turkey. Adrienne was eager to teach this exciting yet practical lesson.

But the lesson didn't go as well as she had hoped. Although many students shared their Thanksgiving traditions with great excitement, some withdrew from the discussion. She thought they understood the food pyramid after she covered it using the PowerPoint presentation, but when the small groups tried to develop a healthy dinner, many seemed stumped. And the shape writing? Disastrous. True, the sharper students seemed to enjoy the novelty. But other students didn't seem to recognize the shape and significance of the turkey; some clearly were confused about what to write.

Adrienne was disappointed because she had planned a lesson that she, as a student, would have found enjoyable and effective. "Why didn't the lesson work? I really worked hard on this one. I had lots of good information from the websites. I even used a lesson plan that some teachers in Connecticut developed and posted on the web. Go figure!"

At Student Teaching Seminar that night, she shared her disappointment with others in her small group. "It sounds like a good lesson, Adrienne, but let's think about it from a variety of angles," Jason encouraged. As group members posed questions, Adrienne was led to reflect more deeply on the students and her instructional choices. "I knew that I was teaching a diverse class, but since we all live in the same country I thought everyone would celebrate Thanksgiving. I didn't think about how different the cultural background and experiences of the students are from my own and how that would impact their learning." She realized that her well-intended discussion of Thanksgiving traditions prevented students without that cultural background from participating in the discussion. Further, because she was familiar with most of the foods on the food pyramid, she didn't realize that it represented mostly "white" foods. Some students were unable to relate to good nutrition because their ethnic foods weren't on the pyramid.

"I thought it was a great lesson, but now I see that it wasn't even a good lesson for this group of students," Adrienne concluded. "Next time, I won't focus on Thanksgiving. Instead, I'll ask questions about their favorite celebrations and the foods eaten at them. That should draw more students into the discussion because everyone will have some celebration to share. And I guess I'll have to do some extra research to figure out where foods from other cultures fit into the pyramid. I never even heard of some of the foods they were asking about!"

Finally, Adrienne realized that she was so pleased with how some students were motivated by the shape writing that she overlooked students who were struggling with the assignment. "I just thought they were tired or off task. After all, it was the end of the day," Adrienne confessed to her group. "I should have worked with a few of them individually to see if they understood the assignment. Roberto, for example, needs to talk about his ideas first; then he can put them down on paper. He seemed disengaged from the lesson so I assumed he was having a bad day and just left him alone. I guess I misread him. He probably needed my help to get the assignment started."

Adrienne and her fellow student teachers are thoughtful about teaching and learning. They ask themselves difficult questions: "What happened during the lesson? Why did it happen? How did learner characteristics guide me as I developed the lesson? Why did I choose to do things this way? How can I make the lesson more effective?" By asking self-challenging questions, they are reflecting on teaching. They describe and analyze their instructional decisions and assess their personal satisfaction with the lessons. Then, they use these reflections to plan changes in their teaching behavior. As a result, it is likely that they are becoming more and more effective as teachers and that their lessons are getting better and better. These student teachers are becoming reflective practitioners.

Characteristics of Reflective Practitioners

Reflection is a habit in which effective teachers appreciate, apply, and synthesize aspects of good teaching by examining them from different angles (Jay, 1999). Valli (1997) describes reflective teachers as those who have the ability to look back on the teaching and learning in their classrooms, make judgments about them, and change their teaching behavior as a result.

Reflective practitioners, like Adrienne and her friends, share certain other characteristics as well. They are deliberative, open-minded, responsible, and sincere; they have a spirit of inquiry. Let us examine these qualities more closely.

First, reflective practitioners routinely and purposefully *deliberate* or reflect on teaching. You recall that Adrienne reflected about many aspects of her lesson. Reflection helps you make rational decisions about teaching and learning and helps you assume responsibility for the results of those choices in the classroom.

Reflective practitioners are *open-minded* (Dewey, 1997b). They are willing to question their own views of and reactions to their teaching practices and the school culture. Adrienne showed open-mindedness when she questioned her decision to link the nutrition lesson to Thanksgiving celebrations. She openly explored, rather than defended, her decision. Open-minded teachers view situations from multiple perspectives, search for alternative explanations for classroom events, and use evidence to support or evaluate a decision or position.

14.2 Think of a situation when you questioned a classroom event or theory. How did you respond?

Reflective practitioners take *responsibility* (Dewey, 1997b). Adrienne assumed responsibility for her teaching decisions. She decided to use a writing assessment. Some students withdrew and were not engaged in the writing activity. Adrienne accepted responsibility for her decision and realized that she should have intervened with certain students. Thus, reflective practitioners consider and accept the consequences of their decisions and the changes they make in teaching style, in the learning environment, or in the school culture.

Furthermore, reflective teachers are *sincere* as they closely investigate their teaching (Dewey, 1997b). They take reflection seriously. Their reflection is purposeful and exciting because it helps them better understand who they are as teachers and how they can be more effective. We saw this in Adrienne and her friends as they eagerly probed various aspects of the learning experience Adrienne's lesson provided. She did not merely accept the fact that the assessment suggested by her professor works well with some students but not others. She explored why. She thought sincerely about the individual learning that resulted from the lesson. Goodman (1984) points out that this sincerity enables you to work through any fears or insecurities you may have about questioning your teaching, your beliefs, and the educational values you see in the school environment and in society.

Generally, then, we could say that a *spirit of inquiry* characterizes reflective teachers. Reflective teachers are interested in the subtleties of the art and science of teaching. They want to learn all they can about teaching from both theory and practice. They think deeply about their course work and about how it should impact their teaching. Inquiring teachers learn by studying teaching, by observing other teachers, and by analyzing and reflecting on the practice of others (Schön, 1990). They continue to learn when they practice and subsequently analyze their own teaching skills (Cruickshank, 1987).

Because of the individual nature of reflective thinking and the uniqueness of each teacher's reflection, reflective practice has been referred to as **inquiry-oriented teaching** (Wellington, 1991). This process of inquiry leads teachers to become "students of teaching" (Dewey, 1904). Dewey contends that it is more important for you as a future teacher to learn to think about your work than it is to master specific techniques of teaching and classroom management.

What distinguishes teachers who are students of teaching from those who are not? To summarize, they inquire into and analyze their own teaching behavior and the teaching of others. They are sincerely interested in the fine points of the art and science of teaching, and they want to learn all they can about teaching. They are open-minded and willing to consider why they teach as they do. They take responsibility for the consequences of their teaching. They deliberate on their teaching, and, as a result of this reflection, they improve their effectiveness as teachers.

14.3 Are you a student of teaching? Why or why not?

Try Activity 14.2

Benefits of Reflecting on Teaching

Reflection may sound like a lot of work, but preservice teachers like you report that they value and benefit from reflecting on teaching (Richert, 1990). Reflection holds both immediate and long-term benefits for you as a teacher. Even now, reflection can enhance your learning about teaching and increase your ability to analyze classroom events. Later, when you are teaching, reflective thinking can improve your classroom life, enable you to monitor yourself, and stimulate your personal and professional growth.

Perhaps the most important benefit of reflection as you prepare to teach is that it *enhances your learning about teaching.* According to learning psychologists, reflectivity plays a central role in learning from your course work and from your field or school experiences (Han, 1995; Jadallah, 1996). To learn the most from these experiences, you need four things. First, you must have a concrete learning experience, such as grading homework papers for your cooperating teacher. Second, you must have an opportunity to reflect on the experience by recapturing and evaluating it. So, after grading the assignments, you might think back on the distribution of grades, consider the nature of the homework assignment and how students benefited from it, and even challenge why teachers assign homework to students. You might conclude that while good students did well on their homework, less able students did poorly. As a result, you might decide that homework assignments must be individualized to provide a meaningful learning experience for all students.

The third step in the learning process is to integrate your reflections with what you already know and believe about teaching and learning. This leads you to recognize new ways of doing things, resolving problems, or clarifying issues. Finally, you must engage in active experimentation, applying the insights you have gained to make decisions and solve problems (Boud, Keogh, & Walker, 1985). The experience of grading and reflecting on homework assignments may have led you to clarify your beliefs about homework. As a result, you may begin to consider evaluating students' learning using an authentic strategy discussed in Chapter 9, such as portfolios.

This homework scenario suggests that one of the best ways to increase your learning about teaching is to strengthen the link between the learning experience and the reflection that follows; that is, by taking time to reflect on the experiences and ideas you have been exposed to in your teacher preparation program (Boud, Keogh, & Walker, 1985; Emery, 1996).

A second benefit of reflecting on teaching that you can begin to take advantage of now is that reflection *increases your ability to analyze and understand classroom events.* That is, reflection makes you more thoughtful and wise (Cruickshank, 1987; Fien, 1996). Liston and Zeichner (1987) observed that preservice teachers tend to look at classrooms with a wide rather than narrow lens. Perhaps you have experienced this yourself, sitting in the corner of a classroom, observing everything superficially but focusing on nothing closely or critically. The students may appear to be naturally well behaved because you are not concentrating on analyzing and understanding the cues and nonverbal desists the teacher uses to prevent students from drifting off task (see Chapter 12).

Because preservice teachers do not always understand the teaching they observe, Ross (1987) found that most still use whim or emotion as much as logic or evidence in making decisions about how they will teach. Further, most preservice teachers see no logical way to differentiate among conflicting positions or different teaching approaches, such as between direct instruction and discovery learning. They tend to hold tightly to one teaching approach they have observed to be effective, such as discovery learning, rather than to analyze when and how this approach would work best with different groups of students and different instructional tasks.

Reflection enables you to examine and analyze classroom events rather than simply observe them. Reflective teachers like Adrienne are better able to ask themselves basic questions about teaching. They are more analytical and less judgmental when they consider their teaching and that of others. Reflection leads teachers to consider the underlying assumptions about, beliefs about, and implications of the practices they are using and how these practices affect students as they learn (Cruickshank, 1987; Han, 1995). In short, reflective teachers understand what teaching and learning are all about. Preservice teachers who practice analyzing classroom events by reflecting on them are less anxious about student teaching than are their peers who observe classrooms through a wide, unfocused lens (Cruickshank, Kennedy, Williams, Holton, & Fay, 1981).

A third benefit of reflection is that reflecting on teaching will *enhance your classroom life* as a teacher by helping you establish an inviting, predictable, and thoughtful environment. This is because reflective teachers are better able to apply what they have learned from course work to their classroom practice (Cruickshank, 1987). This will benefit both you and your students. Hundreds of teachers and administrators who were asked to consider the personal and professional benefits of higher-level thinking, including reflection, support this. They suggest that teachers with good thinking abilities and habits are usually more sensitive, accepting and empathic, tolerant and open-minded, flexible, wise, reasoning, resourceful, creative, informed, objective, observant, aware, and self-understanding (Cruickshank, 1986). In Chapter 12, we discussed why the attitudes and approaches of such teachers are essential to establishing an inviting, predictable classroom environment in which students feel secure, respected, and free to explore and learn.

Unfortunately, many teachers rely on trial and error rather than reflective thinking when establishing their classroom environments. Dewey (1997a) described trial-and-error activity and reflective activity as two approaches teachers use. With trial and error, he commented,

> We simply do something, and when it fails, we do something else, and keep on trying till we hit upon something which works, and then we adopt that method as a rule-of-thumb measure in subsequent procedure (p. 169).

14.4 Have you seen examples of teachers using trial and error? In what ways, and how did it work?

Using trial and error sets up a random, unpredictable classroom environment that students find upsetting and threatening. In contrast, when teachers consistently use reflective activity to make decisions, their students experience a predictable, inviting classroom environment that makes them eager to learn. Further, when a reflective teacher models thinking and problem-solving skills, students begin to think and to use those skills to resolve their own problems (Martin, 1984). As a teacher, you will indeed enhance your classroom life as students respond to the predictable, thoughtful environment!

A fourth benefit of engaging in reflection is that teachers who use reflective skills become *self-monitoring*. It is impossible for you to be prepared for every situation you will encounter in today's unpredictable, complex classrooms. And, unfortunately, during most of your teaching career you will not receive feedback on your teaching strengths and weaknesses. By analyzing and reflecting on your teaching, however, you can assess your needs and monitor your teaching performance and satisfaction. During reflection, teachers learn by studying themselves, and this helps them grow in self-understanding (Cruickshank, 1987). Reflective thinking helps teachers create and clarify meaning in terms of who they are *per se* and who they are in relation to the world of teaching and education (Schön, 1995). By extracting personal meaning from their teaching and learning experiences, they direct themselves toward their teaching and professional goals (Cruickshank, 1987).

Teachers who are not introspective and self-monitoring tend to be governed by routine, tradition, and authority (Dewey, 1997a). They miss out on *personal and professional transformation*, a fifth benefit of reflective thinking. Smyth (1989) considers the empowerment resulting from reflective practice as its greatest benefit and as a necessity for teachers. As we saw in Chapter 1, a person's preconceptions of teaching, learning, and the purposes of the school greatly influence how he or she interprets teaching experiences. These beliefs and values must be examined through reflection rather than merely accepted.

That is, while reflection helps teachers become more effective in delivering instruction, this is only a beginning. Reflection needs to go beyond that to questioning personal and societal beliefs and values, including issues of social justice (Fendler, 2003). This sort of reflective practice provides teachers with a better way of understanding the role teachers and schools play in addressing or perpetuating social problems. By examining even deeper issues of ethics, morals, and justice in education, reflective thinking engages teachers in the redesign and reconstruction of their world.

14.5 What values and beliefs about teaching and learning will influence your reflective thinking?

14.6 Which benefit of reflection is most important to you?

Try Activity 14.3

Developing Reflective Thinking

To meet the demands of today's complex classrooms, you must be willing and able to reflect on classroom events. Your professional growth and satisfaction as a teacher will, in part, be linked to reflection. Although reflection comes naturally to some teachers, most of us must develop our reflective thinking. Realizing that reflection is a deep thinking *process* rather than an innate *ability* makes the goal of becoming a reflective practitioner more attainable.

THE REFLECTIVE PROCESS

Researchers have identified three levels of thinking in the **reflective process:** descriptive, comparative, and evaluative (Jay, 1999; Jay & Johnson, 2002). Descriptive reflection involves describing significant aspects of a classroom event or a concern. In this first step of the reflective process, you describe what happened. Adrienne, the student teacher presented earlier in the chapter, described the discussion of Thanksgiving traditions when she was debriefing with her peers. It was significant that some students were excitedly engaged in the discussion while others withdrew. She also described how some students were stumped when asked to develop a healthy dinner based on the food pyramid. It was significant because she covered the information and assigned a clear task, yet they were unable to complete the task.

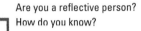

14.7 Are you a reflective person? How do you know?

In comparative reflection, you explore alternative perspectives or interpretations that help you understand why the event described happened that way. In comparative reflection, you ask yourself or others how they interpret or view a situation, or how they would do something differently. Adrienne engaged in comparative reflection when she compared her own culture to that of her students and realized the differences. Comparative reflection suggested that some students didn't participate in the discussion because Thanksgiving was not part of their cultural background. Her reflection on the food pyramid assignment and recognition of its cultural bias also illustrates comparative reflection. Reflecting on the perspective of the students in her diverse classroom enabled Adrienne to see that a lesson that she enjoyed did not "work" for many of her learners.

Evaluative reflection moves beyond describing and understanding an event and seeing it from another point of view to making a judgment about how best to proceed with the next steps or with making changes. Evaluative reflection results in change—change in a lesson plan, in a routine or classroom rule, in teaching behavior, in a way of approaching a parent. For Adrienne, evaluative reflection led to opening up a class discussion to include any celebration, modifying the food pyramid to include ethnic foods, and working with Roberto individually to help him succeed at writing.

Jay (1999) points out that reflection is a personalized process because it is rooted in an individual's own background and experiences, current situation, and approach to life. Yet sometimes it is difficult to get reflection started—to know what to reflect about. Jay (1999) recommends using questions to guide the reflective process and to create more purposeful thinking that can challenge us as teachers and as human beings (see Figure 14.1).

BECOMING A REFLECTIVE TEACHER

How can you engage in the reflective process and become a more reflective teacher? Many methods have been suggested and used; five are presented below. These are even more powerful when technology is included.

Discussions are a way to reflect on and give meaning to your teacher preparation experiences. If your discussion is focused and purposive rather than random, as previously discussed, it will help you engage in higher-level thinking and

FIGURE 14.1 Questions to Guide the Reflective Thinking Process

Type of Reflection Thinking	Purpose	Guiding Questions
Descriptive	Describes the event or issue	*What is happening? Is this working or not working, and for whom? How do I know? What am I pleased about? What am I concerned about? What do I need to understand? What is the goal and is it being accomplished?*
Comparative	Compares alternative views of the event from a variety of sources (students, colleagues, best practices, research, etc.) in order to understand the event or issue from other perspectives	*Why do I think this is happening? What are some different explanations? What are alternative views of what is happening? How would other people involved describe or explain this situation? How would outsiders explain the situation? What else could I do? What does research say about the situation? What are some other ways of accomplishing the goal?*
Evaluative	Uses description and alternatives to make a judgment about the event or issue	*Given these alternatives, their implications, and my own ethics, which is the best way to proceed? Who is served by this decision and who is not served?*

Adapted from Jay (1999).

change your attitudes and teaching practices (Cruickshank, 1986; Jadallah,1996). Researchers have found that talking about experiences is an effective reflection tool because you receive immediate feedback from your peers (Emery, 1996; Pultorak, 1996). That certainly was the case with Adrienne and her fellow student teachers. Electronic discussions, using a secure chat room or bulletin board, are even more powerful because they are more flexible and are free of the social constraints that sometimes limit discussion in a classroom setting. Avoid using e-mail for discussions because your comments can be taken out of context in this nonsecure arena.

Dialogue journals are a powerful tool for promoting reflection. They help you describe, compare, and evaluate your classroom experiences. In a dialogue journal, you recreate significant classroom events and carry on a running conversation that expresses thoughts, questions, and problems related to your roles, responsibilities, and practices as a teacher. A peer, cooperating teacher, or university instructor regularly responds to your entries by sharing thoughts, reactions, and questions that come to mind (see Figure 14.2). In some teacher preparation programs, student teachers video record teaching episodes and upload the films to a server where they can be viewed, analyzed, and discussed with selected others. The running dialogue leads to especially powerful reflection because it is directly linked to the recording. No need to think back and try to remember what happened during the lesson; just hit rewind and play! Imagine how much stronger Adrienne's reflection and analysis would have been if she had the opportunity to view and share a recording of her lesson. Whether electronic or paper, a dialogue journal can help you see alternative ways of dealing with classroom events, recognize the connection between the teachers' actions and student outcomes, and realize links between theory and classroom teaching and learning (Bolin, 1988; Krol, 1996; Lee, 2004).

A *portfolio* provides a structured opportunity for you to document and describe your teaching, to connect this to what you know about teaching and learning, and

 Web Link
Scholastic's Keep a Teaching Journal

Web Link
Teacher Tube

 **Web Link**
Creating a Teaching Portfolio

FIGURE 14.2 Sample Dialogue Journal Entries

Student Teacher Entry

Today's math lesson on sets went well, but a few things bothered me about it. I broke the students down into groups of three and had them sort the blocks with similar characteristics into groups, then count and describe those sets. I'm glad I had them working in groups because they identified a lot of sets . . . more than we would have as a whole class, I think. The thing that bothered me, though, was that some students weren't involved in the group work. About five students seemed to withdraw . . . and how are they supposed to learn if they don't participate? I thought students were supposed to participate more in small groups, not less!

Cooperating Teacher Entry

Your lesson went really well! You had a clear objective and communicated it well to the students so that they knew exactly what they were supposed to do in their small groups.

   I think you are being a little bit hard on yourself about the level of student involvement in the small groups. Because I was observing, I could see perhaps more closely what students in each group were actually doing. Some of the students who seemed to not participate looked to me like they were just participating more sporadically than the more outgoing students in the group. Simon, for example, may have looked uninvolved, but remember that he is a very reflective learner. He just thinks before he acts! If you are concerned about small groups, try to think through how you assigned the students to groups. Are the personalities compatible? Are the ability levels mixed? Are there gender or ethnic considerations? Also, think about what you can do to hold all students accountable for participating in the group in some way. Don't give up . . . small groups are challenging, but also effective!

Student Teacher Entry

I never thought about how complicated it is to assign students to groups, and how that could impact the lesson! I just assigned them randomly for this lesson. They all seem to get along so well together that it never occurred to me that some of them might not work well together in a small-group situation. Can you provide me with any "inside information" you have about potential mismatches so that I can assign the groups more carefully next time?

Cooperating Teacher Entry

I have a committee meeting tomorrow at 3:30, but we could meet for about 15 minutes right after school to discuss my "insights." Also, I have some notes from a cooperative learning workshop that you might be interested in reading. Keep up the good work!

---

to reflect on how and why you teach the way you do (Loughran & Corrigan, 1995; Wolf, Whinery, & Hagerty, 1995; Zubizarreta, 1994). Portfolios require you to collect artifacts that document your teaching approach and experience, to select from among those documents the ones that best illustrate your teaching, and to reflect on the teaching and learning associated with those artifacts. Digital portfolios provide the additional benefits of helping you learn and use technology skills in a relevant context, eliminating storage problems and helping you gain employment (Polonoli, 2000).

   Action research is the process of conducting classroom research to answer questions or solve problems about teaching and learning involving a specific group of students in a particular setting (McKay, 1992). Unlike traditional research that requires you to search books and journals for information and solutions, action research occurs in schools. In action research, a teacher identifies a classroom-related question, plans classroom-based methods of gathering information related to the question, and collects information to better understand the phenomenon under study (Jenkins, 2003). By reflecting on the insights gained, the teacher increases his or her understanding of the event and is able to suggest a course of action. Increasingly, action research is seen as an important activity for professional development for teachers and as being central to school reform (Holly, 1991). You can find examples of teachers using action research as a way to reflect on and change their practice in Spotlight on Research 14.1 and at the website for the journal, *Educational Action Research*.

 Web Link
Preparing Tomorrow's
Teachers to Use Technology

 Web Link
Sample Professional
Teaching Portfolios

 Web Link
Educational Action
Research Journal

 Web Link
Elementary Education Action
Research

 Web Link
What is Action Research?

Web Link
Center for Collaborative
Action Research

Patricia J. Dixon of Tallahassee, Florida, thought she was encouraging her middle-school science students to participate. But they were not reacting as she expected. They were reluctant to ask questions, make assumptions, or join in discussions. She wondered if her nonverbal communication was the reason and decided to use action research to find out.

Using one class with 23 students, Ms. Dixon videotaped the class for five days. She asked the group five questions to get their perception of her nonverbal behavior and recorded their responses. When she analyzed the tapes and student responses, she found out some startling things! This action research helped her become more aware of what she was saying to students and, more importantly, how she was saying it.

- Students most openly and willingly answered questions when she stood with her hands or palms up.
- Participation was discouraged when she placed her hands on her hips, but hands in her pockets or behind her back created a casual atmosphere and encouraged responses.
- Mismatched verbal and nonverbal behaviors confused students.
- Head nodding, especially combined with a smile or laughter, encouraged students to respond.
- Being close to students encouraged them to respond. More important than proximity, however, was showing that she was listening to their response rather than distracted by grading papers, watching the clock, or reading ahead.
- Eye contact showed students that she was listening to them.
- Students preferred an even, uniform tone of voice because it made them feel safe.

Source: Dixon (n.d.) online.

Laboratory experiences are contrived teaching experiences carried out on campus, often with a small group of peers, rather than in an actual classroom setting. Some on-campus laboratory experiences such as microteaching, discussed in Unit 1 of the Practice Teaching Manual, are intended to help you practice and build basic teaching skills. Simulations, discussed in Unit 3, provide you with practice in solving vexing classroom problems.

Reflective Teaching, a program provided in part in Unit 2, was specifically developed to help preservice and in-service teachers become more thoughtful teachers (Cruickshank, 1991). Reflective Teaching provides you with a teaching experience in a supportive environment that serves as the basis for subsequent reflection. In Reflective Teaching, you engage in all aspects of the teaching cycle (planning, implementing, assessing, and reflecting) by presenting a short, content-neutral lesson based on specific objectives to a group of peers. The Reflective Teaching experience is structured to promote analysis and reflection about the teaching and learning processes through small-group and whole-class discussions.

Try Activity 14.5

Research on the effectiveness of Reflective Teaching shows that preservice teachers find it enjoyable and that they benefit greatly from the immediate, nonthreatening feedback (Bainer & Cantrell, 1992; Peters, 1980). More importantly, research suggests that the Reflective Teaching program can make you a more reflective teacher. Preservice teachers who engaged in Reflective Teaching were better able to think and talk critically about teaching (Cruickshank et al., 1981). Troyer (1988) found that if preservice teachers are informed about the nature and importance of reflective thinking, as you have been by reading this chapter, they are even more reflective in analyzing classroom teaching situations.

Some Final Thoughts

Yes, teaching is a complex activity in today's unpredictable classrooms. But in spite of this, you can increase the likelihood that you will be an effective teacher if you develop the ability to reflect on your teaching and the teaching practices of others.

Hopefully, your teacher preparation program and cooperating teachers are helping you to reflect on your own teaching and the teaching you observe. You will surely benefit if, in addition, you take specific steps to develop the types of thinking that characterize the reflective process. You will enhance your learning and teaching as you make reflection a careful, consistent part of your life.

CHAPTER SUMMARY

- Teaching is a complex activity that requires teachers to think about or reflect on what they do.
- Good teachers can become even more effective by reflecting on teaching.
- Reflective practitioners share certain characteristics.
  1. They routinely and purposefully deliberate or reflect on teaching.
  2. They are open-minded, freely questioning their own views and reactions to their teaching practices.
  3. They consider and accept responsibility for the consequences of the decisions they make in the learning environment.
  4. They are enthusiastic and eagerly focus on ways to improve their teaching.
  5. They become "students of teaching" by inquiring into theory and practices related to teaching and learning.
- Reflective thinking offers immediate and future benefits for preservice teachers.
  1. Reflecting on learning experiences enhances learning.
  2. Reflective thinking increases the ability to analyze and understand classroom events.
  3. Reflection enhances the teacher's classroom life by helping him or her establish an inviting, predictable, and thoughtful learning environment.
  4. Reflective teachers are self-monitoring which means they can direct their own personal growth.
  5. Reflection leads to personal and professional growth and empowers teachers to redesign teaching and the school culture.
- Reflection is a deep thinking process involving three levels of learned thinking rather than an innate ability.
  1. Descriptive reflection involves describing significant aspects of a classroom event or a concern.
  2. Comparative reflection explores alternative perspectives or interpretations that help you understand why an event happened the way it did.
  3. Evaluative reflection requires that you make a judgment about how to proceed or make changes.
- Teachers can develop reflective thinking skills in many ways.
  1. Focused and purposeful discussions can build higher-order thinking skills and change teaching behaviors and attitudes.
  2. The interaction provided through a dialogue journal can help you internalize ideas and build flexible, mature thinking about teaching.
  3. Teaching portfolios complement other reflection experiences and help you reflect on teaching more broadly.
  4. Action research, a field-based approach to reflecting on teaching and solving problems related to learning, can contribute to the development of reflective thinking skills.
  5. Laboratory experiences, such as Reflective Teaching, conducted on campus in a supportive environment can enhance reflective thinking skills.

SUPPLEMENTAL RESOURCES
Go to the text's Online Learning Center at www.mhhe.com/cruickshank6e to access the chapter's **study tools** including web links, practice for Praxis™ case studies and video clips.

OLC

ISSUES AND PROBLEMS FOR DISCUSSION

ISSUES   Several issues and problems are related to the process of reflection. Here are a few you might want to discuss in class.

1. Do teachers need to be reflective to be effective at bringing about students' learning and satisfaction? Why or why not?
2. What should teachers reflect about? Should they be compelled to think about some aspects of education more than others?
3. Do you agree with Dewey that it is more important to learn to reflect than to master teaching skills? Why or why not?
4. What prevents teachers from reflecting? What could a building principal do to encourage teachers to become more reflective?

PROBLEMS   Teachers often encounter problems when they try to practice reflection. What would you do in the following situations?

Problem 1:   "I feel like I'm on a treadmill that is in high gear. I know I could be a better teacher, but don't have time during the day to think about my lessons and how I might improve them. And by the end of the day I'm just too tired."

Problem 2:   "Since I'm a new teacher, I really want to do well and help my students learn. Sometimes I try to talk to other teachers if a lesson goes badly or if a student just doesn't get it. It's frustrating, though, because they just tell me 'you'll be fine.' I was hoping we could talk about my teaching and how I could do better."

THEORY INTO ACTION: ACTIVITIES FOR PRACTICE AND YOUR PORTFOLIO

ACTIVITY 14.1:   Ask your cooperating teachers what it means to reflect on teaching. Ask if they reflect on their teaching. If so, when do they reflect? What do they reflect about? What is the result of that reflection?

ACTIVITY 14.2:   Identify and interview a teacher you consider a "student of teaching." Compare the interview results with those your classmates obtain. What commonalities do you find among teachers who are students of teaching?

ACTIVITY 14.3:   Design a weekly schedule for a teacher that would be conducive to reflective thinking. Share it with a teacher or principal for their reaction.

ACTIVITY 14.4:   For two weeks, keep a dialogue journal by carrying on a written or electronic conversation with a friend about your preservice teacher education.

Reflect back on the experience. What did you learn? How did the exchange help you? What problems existed?

ACTIVITY 14.5: With three or four other students, complete one of the Reflective Teaching activities in Unit 2. Discuss the following questions. As a result of this laboratory experience, what did you learn about teaching? What did you learn about learning? What did you learn about yourself as a teacher?

REFERENCES

Bainer, D. L., & Cantrell, D. (1992). Nine dominant reflection themes identified for preservice teachers by a content analysis of essays. *Education, 112*(4), 571–578.

Bainer, D. L., & Cantrell, D. (1993). The relationship between instructional domain and the content of reflection. *Teacher Education Quarterly, 20*(4), 65–76.

Bolin, F. S. (1988). Helping student teachers think about teaching. *Journal of Teacher Education, 39*(2), 48–54.

Borko, H., Michalec, P., Timmons, M., & Siddle, J. (1997). Student teaching portfolios: A tool for promoting reflective practice. *Journal of Teacher Education, 48,* 345–357.

Boud, D., Keogh, R., & Walker, D. (Eds.). (1985). *Reflection: Turning experiences into learning.* New York: Nichols.

Brookhart, S. M., & Freeman, D. J. (1992). Characteristics of entering teacher candidates. *Review of Educational Research, 62,* 26–60.

Cruickshank, D. R. (1986). Critical thinking skills for teachers. *Teacher Education Quarterly, 13*(1), 82–89.

Cruickshank, D. R. (1987). *Reflective teaching: The preparation of students of teaching.* Reston, VA: Association of Teacher Educators.

Cruickshank, D. R. (1991). *Reflective teaching.* Revised Edition. Bloomington, IN: Phi Delta Kappa.

Cruickshank, D. R., Kennedy, J. J., Williams, E. J., Holton, J., & Fay, D. E. (1981). Evaluation of reflective teaching outcomes. *Journal of Educational Research, 75*(1), 26–32.

Dewey, J. (1904). The relation of theory to practice in education.

In C. A. McMurry (Ed.), *The relation of theory to practice in the education of teachers.* Third yearbook of the National Society for the Scientific Study of Education, Part I (pp. 9–30). Chicago: University of Chicago Press.

Dewey, J. (1997a). *Democracy and education: An introduction to the philosophy of education.* New York: Free Press.

Dewey, J. (1997b). *How we think.* Mineola, NY: Dover Publications.

Dixon, P. J. *Encouraging participation in a middle school classroom.* Access: www.enc.org/professional/research/journal/science.

Emery, W. G. (1996). Teachers' critical reflection through expert talk. *Journal of Teacher Education, 47,* 110–119.

Fendler, L. (2003). Teacher reflection in a hall of mirrors: Historical influences and political reverberations. *Educational Researcher, 32*(3), 16–19.

Fien, J. (1996). Reflective practice: A case study of professional development for environmental education. *Journal of Environmental Education, 27,* 11–20.

Giovannelli, M. (2003). Relationship between reflective disposition toward teaching and effective teaching. *Journal of Educational Research, 96,* 293–309.

Goodman, J. (1984). Reflection and teacher education: A case study and theoretical analysis. *Interchange, 15*(3), 9–26.

Han, E. P. (1995). Reflection is essential in teacher education. *Childhood Education, 71,* 228–230.

Holly, P. (1991). Action research: The missing link in the creation

of schools as centers of inquiry. In A. Lieberman & L. Miller (Eds.), *Staff development for education in the '90s: New demands, new realities, new perspectives.* New York: Teachers College Press.

Jadallah, E. (1996). Reflective theory and practice: A constructivist process for curriculum and instructional decisions. *Action in Teacher Education, 18,* 73–85.

Jay, J. K. (1999). *Untying the knots: Examining the complexities of reflective practice.* Paper presented at the American Association of Colleges for Teacher Education conference. Washington, D. C. (ERIC Document Reproduction Service No. 431 732).

Jay, J. K. & Johnson, K. L. (2002). Capturing complexity: A typology of reflective practice for teacher education. *Teaching and Teacher Education, 18*(1), 73–85.

Jenkins, D. B. (2003). Action research with impact. *ENC Focus, 10*(1), 35–37.

Kemmis, S., & McTaggart, R. (1995). *The action research planner.* Victoria, Australia: Deakin University Press.

Krol, C. A. (1996). *Preservice teacher education students' dialogue journals: What characterizes students' reflective writing and a teacher's comments.* Paper presented at the meeting of the Association of Teacher Educators. St. Louis, MO. (ERIC Document Reproduction Services ED 395 911).

Lee, I. (2004). Using dialogue journals as a multi purpose tool for preservice teacher preparation: How effective is it? *Teacher Education Quarterly, 31*(3), 73–97.

Liston, D. P., & Zeichner, K. M. (1987). Reflective teacher education and moral deliberation. *Journal of Teacher Education, 38*(6), 2–8.

Loughran, J., & Corrigan, D. (1995). Teaching portfolios: A strategy for developing learning and teaching in pre-service teacher education. *Teacher and Teacher Education, 1,* 565–577.

Martin, D. (1984). Infusing cognitive strategies into teacher preparation programs. *Educational Leadership, 42*(3), 68–72.

McKay, J. A. (1992). Professional development through action research. *Journal of Staff Development, 13*(1), 18–21.

Peters, J. L. (1980). *The effects of laboratory teaching experience (Microteaching and Reflective Teaching) in an introductory teacher education course on students' views of themselves as teachers and their perceptions of teaching.* Columbus, OH: The Ohio State University. Doctoral dissertation.

Polonoli, K. E. (2000). *Defining the role of the digital portfolio in teacher education.* Paper presented at the West Virginia Network (WVNET) conference. Morgantown, WV. (ERIC Document Reproduction Service No. 447 806).

Pultorak, E. G. (1996). Following the development process of reflection in novice teachers: Three years of investigation. *Journal of Teacher Education, 47,* 283–291.

Richert, A. (1990). Teaching teachers to reflect: A consideration of programme structure. *Journal of Curriculum Studies, 22,* 509–527.

Ross, D. D. (1987). *Reflective teaching: Meaning and implications for preservice teacher educators.* Paper presented at the Reflective Inquiry Conference. Houston, TX.

Schön, D. A. (1990). *Educating the reflective practitioner.* San Francisco: Jossey-Bass.

Schön, D. A. (1995). *The reflective practitioner: How professionals think in action.* San Francisco: Jossey-Bass.

Smyth, J. (1989). Developing and sustaining critical reflection in teacher education. *Journal of Teacher Education, 40*(2), 2–9.

Tremmel, R. (1993). Zen and the art of reflective practice in teacher education. *Harvard Education Review, 63,* 434–458.

Troyer, M. B. (1988). *The effects of reflective teaching and a supplemental theoretical component on preservice teachers' reflectivity in analyzing classroom teaching situations.* Columbus, OH: The Ohio State University. Doctoral dissertation.

Valli, L. (1997). Listening to other voices: A description of teacher reflection in the United States. *Peabody Journal of Education, 72*(1), 67–68.

Wallace, J. (1996). Words, words, words . . . *Science and Children, 33*(5), 16–19.

Wellington, B. (1991). The promise of reflective practice. *Educational Leadership, 48*(6), 4–5.

Wolf, K., Whinery, B., & Hagerty, P. (1995). Teaching portfolios and portfolio conversations for teacher educators and teachers. *Action in Teacher Education, 17*(1), 30–39.

Zubizarreta, J. (1994). Teaching portfolios and the beginning teachers. *Phi Delta Kappan, 76,* 323–326.

Practice Teaching Manual

Practice doesn't always make perfect, but it certainly helps (Scheeler, 2007). This manual provides an opportunity for you to gain much-needed practice in three important areas. In Unit 1, Microteaching: Practicing Critical Teaching Skills, you can try out your ability to demonstrate the personal attributes and professional skills that are vital to teachers, as discussed in Chapters 10 and 11. In Unit 2, Reflective Teaching: Practicing Being a Thoughtful Practitioner, you have a chance to acquire and practice some of the qualities of reflective or thoughtful practitioners; you learned of these in Chapter 14. Finally, in Unit 3, Room 221: A Simulation: Solving Classroom Problems, you can take on the role of a teacher, encounter real-life classroom dramas, and consider how you would respond to each one.

To our knowledge, this is the first book to incorporate practice teaching experiences such as microteaching, Reflective Teaching, and simulation exercises. We are convinced that engaging in these techniques now will better prepare you for life in the classroom.

In Chapters 10 and 11 you learned that effective teachers possess certain distinguishing characteristics and abilities. This unit is designed to help you practice and improve your use of a few of these qualities and skills through microteaching.

Microteaching is scaled-down teaching. By that, we mean that instead of teaching a complete lesson to a complete class, you teach an abbreviated lesson to a small group of your classmates. An additional feature of microteaching is that your lessons are videotaped, thus allowing you to watch your own teaching performance. Using this approach, you can try out important teaching characteristics or abilities to find out how good you may be at them. For example, in Chapter 10 you learned that effective teachers display enthusiasm, and so in this unit you can develop and teach a short lesson in which you try to demonstrate this quality.

Overview of Microteaching

This unit is organized around four microteaching lessons intended to help you apply and refine your professional attributes and abilities. Each lesson is directed at a different aspect of your instructional performance. Microteaching Lesson One focuses on how well you convey the professional attributes of effective teachers. Microteaching Lesson Two helps you develop your ability to establish set. Microteaching Lesson Three helps you hone your questioning skills. And, finally, Microteaching Lesson Four emphasizes refining your ability to expose students to ideas or concepts in ways that are clear to them.

MICROTEACHING FORMAT

Although each of the four activities is directed toward different skills or abilities, each will follow a similar format. You will (1) read about the activity, (2) review information about the specific skills in earlier chapters, (3) plan a short lesson using the guidelines in Chapter 5, (4) teach the lesson to a group of your classmates while being videotaped, (5) view the videotape in order to assess your performance, and (6) when time allows, replan or revise your lesson and reteach it to improve.

Before we begin with Microteaching Lesson One, it may be helpful to discuss guidelines for each phase of the activities.

Reading about the Activity Each microteaching activity is described in this unit. It provides information about the skills to be developed, the length of the lesson, and the way in which the lesson will be evaluated. Reading this information will help you focus your planning and instructional efforts to gain the most from the activity.

Reviewing Relevant Information Remember that these microteaching lessons are intended to help you practice and improve your use of the professional attributes and skills cited in Chapters 10 and 11. Before planning your microteaching lesson, you will be advised to review the sections of these chapters that describe in detail the skills you will be practicing. It will be important that you understand the skill or skills to be developed, the reasons they are important, and the specific instructional behaviors you can use. This information should be used to plan your lesson carefully to help you focus on the specific skills and to remind you to work to incorporate them into your lesson.

Planning the Lesson When planning your microteaching lessons, you are encouraged to follow the principles and guidelines in Chapter 6 for daily lesson planning. For each lesson you should establish objectives and address each of the lesson plan components. Because the microteaching lessons are short (generally ranging from 4 to 12 minutes), your plan will not be terribly long. However, you should be certain to plan thoroughly for each lesson. This will not only improve your lesson performance but also give you an opportunity to practice your planning skills.

A common problem for teachers in microteaching lessons is that they try to teach a great deal more material than the time allows. In fact, at the end of her microteaching lesson a young English teacher whispered to a friend, "Decide what you think you can teach in the time you have, and then try to teach about one-fifth of it!" Although this may be an exaggeration, you should probably attempt to teach only a portion of the concept or topic that first comes to mind. For example, it would be virtually impossible to effectively teach the entire scientific process in a 5-minute lesson. However, you could select one of the four steps in the process, perhaps on developing hypotheses, and teach a thorough and interesting lesson in 5 minutes. Don't try to teach too much.

Teaching the Lesson On the day your instructor establishes, you will teach your lesson to a group of your peers. Depending upon the arrangement the instructor prefers, this may range from a relatively small group (four or five students) to the entire class. The lesson will be videotaped to allow you to view your performance later. Remember to teach to your learners, not to the camera.

To help you learn to manage instructional time, each microteaching lesson will be timed. You will be required to conduct some form of valuable instruction for at least a minimum amount of time, and you will not be allowed to go beyond the established maximum time.

When it is your turn to teach, you will have a short amount of time to prepare the room and your materials. You can move the chairs or desks and use overhead projectors, handouts, or other materials. Then your instructor will make sure the video camera is operating and notify you to begin your lesson. When you have met the minimum length for the lesson, the instructor will give you a signal. Then, when you have reached the maximum allowed time, your instructor will have you stop your lesson. When you receive the signal for the minimum time limit, you might want to determine how much more of your lesson you can teach effectively in the time remaining. (Remember, effective teachers are flexible!) Often it is better to begin at this point to draw the lesson to an end and achieve closure rather than attempt to hurry through the rest of your planned lesson.

Viewing Your Videotaped Lesson After you have finished teaching your lesson, you will have the opportunity to view the videotape of your performance. Your instructor may choose to have you do this alone or with a small group of your peers, or in some instances both. It is wise to watch your lesson at least twice. The first time, simply allow yourself to form a general impression of the quality of your performance and to jot down some notes. Then watch the lesson again, this time using checklists or observation forms that allow you to focus on your use of specific desirable behaviors. Then in each activity, you will identify particular aspects of your performance that you should improve, and you will develop specific suggestions for how you might do so.

Reteaching the Lesson If time allows, your instructor may offer you the opportunity to reteach your lesson to improve your performance. If you are offered this opportunity, you are encouraged to take advantage of it even if your first lesson was satisfactory. Practicing the skills and evaluating how well you use them will help you become even more comfortable and confident.

Microteaching Lesson One: Conveying Positive Personal Attributes

RATIONALE AND OVERVIEW

As previously noted, Microteaching Lesson One gives you the chance to see what you look like as a teacher. Although we all have self-perceptions of what we probably look like when we're teaching, often our actions and words differ from what we imagine. Thus, one of the purposes of this first short lesson is simply to allow you the chance to plan and teach a lesson and then watch yourself on videotape. A more specific purpose is to allow you to compare your teaching "persona" with that of effective teachers. You may remember from Chapter 10 that effective teachers have motivating personalities, are professional, and convey optimism and an orientation toward success. Before you plan your first microteaching lesson, it would be wise to review the personal attributes and characteristics discussed in Chapter 10.

Planning the Lesson Microteaching Lesson One is to be at least 4 and not more than 5 minutes in length. You may teach your lesson on any topic you wish, but you should select a topic or concept that you can genuinely teach to your classmates. In other words, you should not pretend to teach them a concept that most of them are likely to know. As noted earlier, many teachers make the mistake in this first lesson of trying to teach too much in the time allowed. Select a very small concept or subconcept that you can teach thoroughly in 4 to 5 minutes. Develop an objective for your lesson, and follow the format for planning suggested in Chapter 6.

Teaching the Lesson Your instructor will tell you when to begin your lesson, when you have reached the minimum time limit, and when you must stop teaching. You should try to follow your instructional plan—but be flexible. When students don't seem to understand, don't keep pressing on just to "get through the content."

Viewing Your Videotaped Lesson After you have finished teaching your lesson, sit down alone or with some classmates and watch your videotaped lesson. It is probably a good idea to watch the tape twice. Watch it once without stopping, and consider your perceptions of the professional personality you conveyed. After you have watched the lesson, stop the tape and make some notes. If you are watching with classmates, ask them to give you their perceptions. Try to avoid focusing on your hair or clothes, and focus instead on how confident, personable, optimistic, and professional you seem to be. Then rewind the tape and prepare to view your performance

For each behavior listed below, rate the quality of the teacher's performance.

Behavior	Quality Rating			
	Excellent	Good	Fair	Poor
1. The teacher conveyed enthusiasm.	4	3	2	1
2. The teacher used humor effectively and conveyed warmth.	4	3	2	1
3. The teacher seemed credible and worthy of trust.	4	3	2	1
4. The teacher conveyed high expectations for him/herself and for learners.	4	3	2	1
5. The teacher was encouraging and supportive of learners.	4	3	2	1
6. The teacher was professional and businesslike.	4	3	2	1
7. The teacher adapted the lesson when time or learner misunderstanding required it.	4	3	2	1
8. The teacher appeared knowledgeable of the topic, of learners, and of pedagogy.	4	3	2	1

Specific suggestions for improvement:

again using the Observation Form for Microteaching Lesson One to guide your observation (**Table U1.1**).

Reteaching the Lesson   If time permits, your instructor may allow you to teach another 4- to 5-minute lesson to help you become more comfortable teaching in front of the video camera. If you have the opportunity to do so, you will find that future microteaching lessons seem less intimidating, and you can focus your attention on your professional skills rather than on your nervousness.

Microteaching Lesson Two: Establishing Set

RATIONALE AND OVERVIEW

Microteaching Lesson One focused on your professional attributes and characteristics. Lesson Two now emphasizes your use of professional skills. Specifically, Microteaching Lesson Two focuses on your ability to effectively establish set in a short lesson. Remember from Chapter 11 that effective teachers establish three kinds of set to provide a context for the lesson or lessons they are about to teach. In this short lesson, your goal is to identify one of the three types of set you wish to establish and then to do so in a short lesson. Before going on, you should review the suggestions in Chapter 11 regarding establishing set.

Planning the Lesson   Your Microteaching Lesson Two must be at least 8 minutes and not more than 10 minutes in length. As before, you should build your lesson around the guidelines in Chapter 6. However, because Microteaching Lesson Two focuses only on establishing set, you do not need to teach an entire lesson. Consider

the information in Chapter 11, and then determine a topic that you want to introduce as well as which of the three types of set you will use to do so. Since you may select any topic you wish, be creative and attempt to identify a topic that you can introduce in a meaningful, interesting way in the time allowed.

Teaching the Lesson   You will conduct Microteaching Lesson Two in much the same way as your earlier microteaching lesson. You will have some time to organize your materials; then your instructor will notify you to begin, signal you when you have taught at least 8 minutes, and stop you when you reach the 10-minute limit.

Viewing Your Videotaped Lesson   As before, you should view your videotaped lesson at least twice. The first time, make general notes about the way you established set and compare your perceptions with those of your classmates or peer learners. Then, use the Observation Form for Microteaching Lesson Two to evaluate your performance (Table U1.2). Then, based upon your general notes and ratings on the observation instrument, make a few specific suggestions for improving the way you will establish set in future lessons. Be certain to be specific about how and what you will do to improve.

Reteaching the Lesson   The opportunity to reteach your lesson is probably more important in Microteaching Lessons Two, Three, and Four than in Lesson One. These later activities are focused on professional skills that you can improve relatively easily. Thus, the more opportunities you have to practice them, evaluate your performance, and refine your skill, the more effectively you will be able to use them in the future.

TABLE U1.2   Observation Form for Microteaching Lesson Two: Establishing Set

Part I

Circle the number of each of the following behaviors the teacher used in establishing set.

1. The teacher reviewed material from previous lesson(s).
2. The teacher asked a curiosity-provoking question at the beginning of the lesson.
3. The teacher provided an overview of the major points of the lesson.
4. The teacher demonstrated the major concepts or ideas of the lesson.
5. The teacher provided and explained a visual schema depicting the relationships of various aspects or concepts of the lesson.
6. The teacher provided a problem to engage students in processing the concepts to be learned.
7. The teacher pointed out the relevance of the lesson to students' lives and interests.
8. The teacher piqued students' interest or curiosity using a unique or novel question, problem, or scenario.
9. The teacher conveyed interest, enthusiasm, and curiosity about the topic.
10. The teacher informed students of the objectives or goals of the lesson and their responsibilities.

Part II

Rate how well you believe the teacher was able to do each of the following, and use the space below to explain your ratings.

Behavior	Quality Rating			
	Excellent	Good	Fair	Poor
1. The teacher captured students' attention.	4	3	2	1
2. The teacher provided a framework for the lesson.	4	3	2	1
3. The teacher related new information to what students had learned previously.	4	3	2	1
4. The teacher determined students' entry-level knowledge.	4	3	2	1

Specific suggestions for improvement:

Microteaching Lesson Three: Using Questions

RATIONALE AND OVERVIEW

In this activity, you will plan for, use, and evaluate your use of questions in a short lesson. Effective teachers conduct highly interactive lessons and use a variety of questions to keep students engaged, promote higher-order thinking, monitor students' understanding, and introduce variety—among other things. Your ability to use questions effectively is an important but complex skill. Before planning your microteaching lesson, review the discussion of questioning skills in Chapter 11.

Planning the Lesson   Lesson Three is to be between 8 and 10 minutes. In this lesson, you should attempt to include all lesson parts. Thus, address all lesson phases suggested in Chapter 6. Because this lesson is to focus your attention on using questions skillfully, you should not plan a lesson that will require you to present a great deal of information to your learners. Instead, select a topic that allows you to help your learners gain understanding by asking them questions. For example, you might wish to select a controversial issue that you wish

your learners to examine critically. You could build your lesson around questions that would help learners see all sides of the issue, understand various points of view, and appreciate the complexity of the issue. In this type of lesson, you would use questions to guide your learners. Remember as you do your planning to include questions you can use during the lesson closure to help learners draw conclusions about the discussion.

Teaching the Lesson   Microteaching Lesson Three will be conducted just as Lesson Two was. You will have a few minutes to organize the room and your materials, and then your instructor will notify you to begin. When you have taught at least 8 minutes, the instructor will give you a signal and then tell you to stop when you reach 10 minutes.

Viewing Your Videotaped Lesson   As you view your videotaped lesson the first time, focus on how well you used a variety of questions to reach your objective. Did you use many questions? Did the questions seem to guide learners, or did they seem random and unconnected? When you asked questions, did you use silence and effective

TABLE U1.3 Observation Form for Microteaching Lesson Three: Using Questions

For each behavior below, indicate the quality of the teacher's performance.

Behavior	Excellent	Good	Fair	Poor
	Quality Rating			
1. The teacher asked a question early in the lesson to get students involved.	4	3	2	1
2. The teacher phrased questions clearly.	4	3	2	1
3. The teacher avoided repeating questions unless students didn't understand.	4	3	2	1
4. The teacher used adequate wait time after asking questions.	4	3	2	1
5. The teacher frequently asked appropriate questions.	4	3	2	1
6. The teacher called on all students to respond to questions, not just volunteers.	4	3	2	1
7. The teacher included questions at higher cognitive levels.	4	3	2	1
8. The teacher followed up students' responses appropriately.	4	3	2	1
9. The teacher's questions were clearly directed toward helping learners reach the objectives of the lesson.	4	3	2	1
10. Overall, the teacher used questions effectively.	4	3	2	1

Specific suggestions for improvement:

nonverbal behavior to encourage learners to participate? Generally, how do you feel about your use of questioning as you watch the tape? After this first viewing, use the Observation Form for Microteaching Lesson Three to guide your second viewing (Table U1.3). Focus on specific things you did well and on specific aspects of your skill you want to improve; then establish a plan for improving your questioning skills.

Reteaching the Lesson Using questions effectively is a difficult but important professional skill. Beginning teachers generally are uncomfortable using questions and prefer to teach in an expository and less interactive manner. However, we know that interactive teaching is more desirable. Because it is so difficult to become proficient and comfortable using questions, you are encouraged to take advantage of as many opportunities to reteach your lesson as you can. Each time you reteach, work to plan for and implement questions that integrate the suggestions you made for improving your weaknesses.

Microteaching Lesson Four: Providing Clear Instruction

RATIONALE AND OVERVIEW

In Microteaching Lesson One you focused on your professional attributes. In Lesson Two, you taught a lesson in which you attempted to establish set. And in Microteaching Lesson Three you focused on your use of questions. Now, in Microteaching Lesson Four, you will again attempt to teach a lesson that includes set

induction, presentation of content, and closure—a complete lesson. However, in this lesson you will focus on your ability to provide instruction that is clear to learners.

Remember from Chapter 11 that instructional clarity may be one of the most important skills in helping students learn. The specific aspects of clarity can be organized into four categories related to various aspects of the lesson. To make your task more manageable, you will focus on only two of the four areas: (1) introducing and emphasizing content and (2) elaborating on important ideas or concepts. Before going on, return to Chapter 11 and review the discussion of instructional clarity.

Planning the Lesson Microteaching Lesson Four is to be at least 8 minutes and not more than 10 minutes in length. Your primary goal during this exercise is to plan and teach a lesson in which you help learners come to understand clearly the major points of the lesson. The lesson should include all the aspects of a good lesson described in Chapter 6, and you should plan to maximize the reinforcement of major points by repeating them, writing them on the board, reviewing them, and so on. Thus, in planning your lesson, you must identify the two or three major ideas or points you want your learners to understand, organize them logically, develop explanations and examples of each point, determine questions you may use to ensure that students understand, and determine places in the lesson where you will review. You may also wish to highlight particular terms or points by writing them on the board for your learners.

TABLE U1.4 Observation Form for Microteaching Lesson Four: Providing Clear Instruction

Part I

In the space below, enumerate the major points of the teacher's lesson and provide a brief explanation of each.

Part II

Rate the quality of the teacher's performance of each behavior listed below.

Behavior	Quality Rating			
	Excellent	Good	Fair	Poor
1. The teacher organized and conveyed the lesson in a logical manner.	4	3	2	1
2. The teacher identified important points.	4	3	2	1
3. The teacher wrote important points on the board or a chart.	4	3	2	1
4. The teacher repeated important points for emphasis.	4	3	2	1
5. The teacher included summaries and reviews within the lesson.	4	3	2	1
6. The teacher clearly explained important points.	4	3	2	1
7. The teacher presented examples to reinforce each major point.	4	3	2	1
8. The teacher pointed out similarities and differences between things.	4	3	2	1
9. The teacher explained unfamiliar words when necessary.	4	3	2	1
10. The teacher used pauses to reinforce important points or to allow learners to ask questions.	4	3	2	1

Specific suggestions for improvement:

Teaching the Lesson Microteaching Lesson Four will be conducted very much like Lessons Two and Three. Your instructor will give you some time to organize yourself and your materials and then notify you to begin. When you have reached the 8-minute mark in the lesson, the instructor will signal you. At the end of 10 minutes he or she will ask you to stop. Remember that good lessons include a closure to help learners draw conclusions. When you know you are nearing the end of your allotted time, begin to draw the lesson to a close rather than present new content.

Viewing Your Videotaped Lesson Instructional clarity is "in the eye of the beholder." That's why your learners are in the best position to help you determine whether or not you provided clear instruction. If at all possible, you should watch this videotaped lesson at least three times—twice with your learners and once by yourself. During the first viewing, make notes about how clearly you identified and reinforced major points. Did you treat each major point as equally important? Were major points obvious and distinct from their explanations? Can your learners name the major points? Can they explain them? Generally, did the lesson seem to progress logically and clearly?

In the second viewing of the lesson, use the Observation Form for Microteaching Lesson Four with your learners to focus on your use of some of the specific clarity skills (Table U1.4). Then watch your lesson by yourself using your learners' comments and your own impressions to identify the strengths and weaknesses of your instructional clarity. Remember to identify specific aspects of your performance that you believe need to be improved and to suggest specific ways you will attempt to improve them in future lessons.

Reteaching the Lesson Instructional clarity is a complex skill that requires you to consider and implement a variety of behaviors to help learners reach the instructional objectives. As a result, it is not uncommon for teachers to need several videotaped lessons focusing on their instructional clarity skills. If possible, reteach your lesson as many times as necessary to enable you to feel comfortable with your performance. When time allows and you have improved your original lesson, try teaching a new lesson to see if you are able to provide clear instruction with a different set of major ideas or points.

Additional Practice

Although this unit has included four microteaching lessons to help you improve your instructional behavior, good teachers are constantly working to improve their skills. In addition to doing the four microteaching lessons, you are encouraged to continue to practice honing your professional abilities. The following suggestions will help you do so.

EXPANDED MICROLESSONS

One of the things you can do to continue developing your professional skills is to expand the microteaching format to include longer lessons and more or different professional skills. For example, a reasonable next step would be to teach a slightly longer lesson, perhaps 15 to 20 minutes, in which you attempt to establish set, provide clear instruction, and use questions effectively. Or you might try teaching several short videotaped lessons in which you work to provide desirable feedback and reinforcement, monitor students' understanding, or use different instructional alternatives. You could develop your own observation instruments for these lessons using the guidelines for each skill included in Chapter 11.

VIDEOTAPING YOUR CLASSROOM TEACHING

Another way to continue your professional skill development is through constant assessment of your classroom behavior and interactions. Even if you feel quite competent in using the professional skills in short lessons to your peers, you may not be so proficient when faced with a classroom of 30 school-age students. By using guided observation and analysis, you can use your classroom teaching experiences as advanced forms of microteaching. First, you can videotape the lessons you teach during your field experiences. Merely set up the camera in the back of the room, turn it on before you begin your lesson, and turn it off when you are done. Then, carefully view your natural classroom lesson just as you did your microteaching lessons. This type of formal self-analysis will be extremely useful in helping you understand your classroom behavior.

You should also attempt to record some of your actual teaching even after you have finished student teaching and have your own classroom. Even skilled, experienced teachers are surprised at their classroom behavior when they see themselves on videotape. They find that they no longer are as effective in using their professional skills as they once were. Most schools have easy-to-use video cameras that teachers can borrow. Every so often, set up the camera in the back of the room for a couple of lessons and then watch yourself critically. You will be surprised at how some of your professional skills have improved with classroom experience while others have grown less effective. One of the authors videotapes at least one lesson each term—and each time is humbled by the experience. Nevertheless, seeing ourselves on videotape helps us all become more aware of both our strengths and weaknesses.

REFERENCE

Sheeler, M. (2007, September). Generalizing effective teaching skills. *Journal of Behavioral Education, 17,* 145–159.

Teaching is an experience filled with excitement, surprises, frustrations, and delight. By now, you are a step closer to undertaking this challenge.

Think back over your teacher preparation program thus far. Chances are your instructors have used a variety of experiences to ease you into the act of teaching. What were some of those experiences? Perhaps you have read and discussed biographies about the daily lives of teachers, viewed videos and websites about teaching and learning, and observed and analyzed teachers in their classrooms. The next step is to engage you in the act of teaching. Reflective Teaching (Cruickshank, 1991) is a program that allows you to practice the complete act of teaching presented in Part Two. Reflective Teaching requires you to plan a lesson and to implement that plan. Further, it allows you to find out how well your students learned and how satisfied they were with your teaching. Finally, it provides you with an opportunity to reflect on teaching and learning in order to make you a more effective teacher.

As suggested by the title, Reflective Teaching enables you to practice being a thoughtful or reflective practitioner. In Chapter 14 we pointed out that reflective practitioners are more wise and thoughtful about teaching. This is because they routinely and consciously examine their attributes and skills for effectiveness. Their minds are a flurry of questions: What am I doing and why? What are the consequences of my teaching? How could I have done that differently? How can I improve? As a result of this self-analysis, a reflective practitioner is the ultimate student of teaching.

What Is Reflective Teaching?

Reflective Teaching is a contrived teaching experience carried out on campus rather than in an actual school setting. The experience provides you with the opportunity to practice the act of teaching, to evaluate its success, and to gain insights into teaching and learning that should enable you to be even more effective in future teaching episodes.

Although you and a group of friends can independently engage in Reflective Teaching, the program is generally part of a university course or clinical experience. The class is divided into groups of four to six persons. For each Reflective Teaching session, one person from each group is designated as the teacher and provided with the Reflective Teaching Lesson (RTL), which

they will all use during the next session. Each designated teacher prepares the lesson independently, considering the best way to achieve the stated objective and to maximize learners' achievement and satisfaction. After instructing, the designated teachers evaluate their lessons by measuring students' learning and satisfaction. Finally, they analyze and reflect on teaching and learning in their small groups and then in an instructor-led discussion engaging the entire class.

As you can see, Reflective Teaching engages you in all four phases of teaching: planning, implementing that plan, assessing learning, and reflecting on your teaching.

Using Reflective Teaching

Each Reflective Teaching Lesson (RTL) contains a teaching objective, the resources you will need to meet that objective, and a description of ways to measure the learning and satisfaction of your learners. While some RTLs deal with professional education (for example, Good Teacher Task), other RTLs address a variety of topics. The RTLs included in this chapter represent all three instructional domains (cognitive, psychomotor, and affective) and varied levels of learning within those domains. Further, each RTL focuses on a teacher behavior widely used in classroom situations. For example, in the Chisanbop Task, you practice demonstration skills by teaching your students to count using their hands and fingers.

In order to emphasize evaluation and reflection, the lessons are brief—usually 10 to 15 minutes long. Your entire Reflective Teaching session, then, should take about 50 minutes:

- Teaching: 10–15 minutes.
- Evaluation: 5 minutes.
- Small-group discussion: 15 minutes.
- Whole-class discussion: 15 minutes.

Although a total of 41 RTLs are available, six are included in this chapter to help you become a more reflective and effective teacher.

Roles during Reflective Teaching

During a Reflective Teaching session, you will have a variety of responsibilities. These will vary depending on whether you are the designated teacher or a learner.

DESIGNATED TEACHER

When you are the designated teacher, your primary responsibility is to teach an RTL to a small group of your peers. Specifically, you will need to prepare a lesson that will enable your learners to achieve the lesson objectives and to gain satisfaction from your teaching. More importantly, you will prepare for and lead your group in reflecting on the teaching and learning that occurred during the lesson.

Although all designated teachers present the same lesson during a Reflective Teaching session, you may teach the lesson using any method you choose. Use the Learner Satisfaction Forms to assess student satisfaction (see p. 484). Your goal, after all, is to select a teaching strategy that you think will maximize students' learning and satisfaction. You must also ensure that all the materials you need for instruction are on hand when you teach. While you should provide materials related to teaching, your university instructor will provide copies of the test used to evaluate students' learning, scoring boxes, and the Learner Satisfaction Forms used to assess student satisfaction. If you need audiovisual equipment or other resources, communicate those needs to your instructor in advance. After all, planning ahead is part of the teaching process!

On the day of the Reflective Teaching session, arrive early to set up your teaching stations and "classroom." Will you seat your students in rows or a circle? How will you display your visual aids? Will you stand or remain seated while teaching? These are all instructional decisions you will need to make as the designated teacher.

When the learners arrive and all the teachers are ready to begin, the university instructor will signal you to begin teaching. Your RTL will specify how long your lesson should be. While you are teaching, the instructor may observe all or a part of your lesson. When the allocated instructional time has expired, the instructor must promptly stop all lessons and provide you with posttests, scoring boxes, and Learner Satisfaction Forms.

By reviewing these forms, you receive immediate feedback that may help you frame reflection and discussion questions. Then, turn your attention to leading a discussion with your small group of peers. The questions you pose should focus the group's attention on the *processes* of teaching and learning, rather than on the content of the lesson.

To prepare for the 15 minute reflective session, develop discussion questions structured around the three types of reflective thinking presented in Chapter 14: descriptive, comparative, and evaluative. Ask questions such as these:

- What happened during the lesson? Did the lesson go as planned for the designated teacher?
- Did the lesson "work" for the learners? What helped or hindered their learning?

- Do the students' and teacher's perceptions of the lesson's effectiveness match?
- According to posttests and Learner Satisfaction forms, how well did the learners learn? How satisfied were they?
- How did you choose the teaching method used to accomplish the objective? What factors influenced the decision of how to teach the lesson (for example, content of the lesson, availability of materials, the setting, time available, learning style of the designated teacher, nature of the learners, past experiences as a learner)?
- What changes would you make in the lesson to make it more effective for this group of learners?
- What specifically did each participant discover about teaching and learning as a result of this experience?
- What did you learn about yourself as a teacher as a result of this experience?

You may notice that some of these questions address the designated teacher; others are aimed at the learners or addressed to all members of the group. By carefully selecting questions that engage all participants in reflection, you can lead a discussion that will provide you with insights about your teaching.

LEARNER

When you are not assigned to act as a designated teacher, your role will be to receive instruction. It is important for you to be cooperative and available and to be on time. Above all, be yourself; role playing is not usually helpful to the designated teacher or to your learning experience.

When you arrive at class for the Reflective Teaching session, go directly to an assigned teaching station. After the lesson, you will need to complete two evaluations. A posttest will assess how much you learned during the lesson, and the Learner Satisfaction Form will measure how satisfied you were with the lesson. It is most helpful to the designated teacher if you provide honest feedback about how you felt and what contributed to or inhibited your learning and satisfaction.

Following the evaluation, the designated teacher will lead a 15-minute discussion. During the discussion, you should help the designated teacher think openly, honestly, and deeply about the teaching-learning experience. This will provide everyone in your small group with a better understanding of effective teaching.

Following the small group discussion, the entire class will engage in a debriefing led by the university instructor to further inquire into the teaching and learning processes. Your willingness and ability to interact during these reflective sessions will indicate your progress toward becoming a serious student of teaching.

Reflective Teaching Lessons

On the following pages are six sample Reflective Teaching Lessons.* The Block Diagram Task, Redifrication Task, and Good Teacher Task provide learning experiences in the cognitive domain and enable you to practice teaching behaviors such as designating and describing. The Chisanbop Task and Stan Laurel Task provide experiences in the psychomotor domain and focus on demonstration. Finally, in the Tobacco Task, you attempt to get students to "change their minds" about people, habits, and the content learned. This task is in the affective domain.

REFERENCE

Cruickshank, D. R. (1991). *Reflective teaching*. Bloomington, IN: Phi Delta Kappa.

*These six sample lessons are reproduced with permission from Phi Delta Kappa.

THE BLOCK DIAGRAM TASK

Read each section carefully.

Description of Your Reflective Teaching Task

You are one of several participants chosen to teach this brief lesson to a small group of your peers. The exercise is intended to provide an opportunity for you to experience teaching and then to reflect on the shared teaching and learning. Plan to teach the lesson in such a way that you believe both learning and satisfaction will result.

Your lesson will be taught on _____.

INTRODUCTION TO THE LESSON

Teachers describe things—that is they tell about something. The following are examples of teacher describing behavior:

1. A social studies teacher describes the electoral college.
2. A music teacher describes a musical scale.
3. A religion teacher describes doctrines of the church.
4. The Girl Scout leader describes how to survive in the wilderness.

Below is an objective that requires you to describe something to a small group of your peers. The task was selected because your success in accomplishing it probably will not be dependent on your knowledge of some academic subject or previous experience you might have had.

YOUR OBJECTIVE

Your goal is to get as many of your listeners as possible to produce an exact replica of the blocks as shown on the attached diagram. You will have ten minutes in which to accomplish your goal.

MATERIALS

1. Resources: A Block Diagram (attached)
2. One piece of paper for each listener (provided by you)

3. Learner Satisfaction Forms (provided by college instructor)
4. Scoring box (attached)

SPECIAL CONDITIONS AND LIMITATIONS

1. You may use only words when you teach the lesson. You may not show the learners a picture of the blocks.
2. Seat your learners in a circle but facing outward so that they will not be influenced by each other's work.
3. You may not use any special devices such as rulers.

ENDING THE LESSON

Notify the college instructor as soon as you have completed the task. (You may finish early.) Obtain copies of the Learner Satisfaction Form.

Show your learners the correct arrangement of the blocks so they can correct their diagrams.

Next, pass out the Learner Satisfaction Forms, and while they are being completed, collect the diagrams and record the scores in the scoring box. Return the diagrams and collect the learner satisfaction forms.

Begin to work through the questions for small group discussion with your learners.

The idea for this RTL was contributed by Betty Myers, Shepherd College, West Virginia.

A BLOCK DIAGRAM

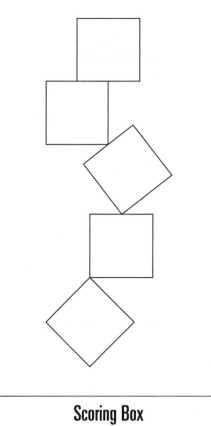

Scoring Box

Directions   Place 1 in the scoring box if the learner succeeds, a zero if not.

	Learner's Name	Performance Score (0 or 1)
1		
2		
3		
4		
5		
6		
	TOTAL (add down)	

Read each section carefully.

Description of Your Reflective Teaching Task

You are one of several participants chosen to teach this brief lesson to a small group of your peers. The exercise is intended to provide an opportunity for you to experience teaching and then to reflect on the shared teaching and learning. Plan to teach the lesson in such a way that you believe both learning and satisfaction will result.

Your lesson will be taught on _____.

INTRODUCTION TO THE LESSON

Teachers demonstrate—that is they show learners how to do something. The following are examples of teacher demonstrating behavior:

1. A physical education teacher demonstrates how to guard a basketball player.
2. A dance teacher demonstrates how to execute a dance step.
3. A business education teacher demonstrates how to sit at a typewriter.
4. A French teacher demonstrates how to form lips to say a word.
5. An English teacher demonstrates how to read expressively.

Below is an objective that requires you to demonstrate something to a small group of peers. The task was selected because your success in accomplishing it probably will not be dependent on your knowledge of some academic subject or previous experience you might have had.

YOUR OBJECTIVE

Your goal is to teach your learners how to press all numbers from 1 to 99 using chisanbop. You will have 15 minutes to accomplish your goal.

MATERIALS

1. Resources: Using Hands and Fingers to Compute (attached)
2. Test (provided by college instructor)
3. Scoring box (attached)
4. Learner Satisfaction Forms (provided by college instructor)

SPECIAL CONDITIONS AND LIMITATIONS

You will not be given a copy of the test until after you have taught your lesson. Test each learner only once.

ENDING THE LESSON

Notify the college instructor when your learners are ready to take the test. (You may finish early.) Obtain copies of the test, scoring box, and learner satisfaction form.

Test your learners one at a time and record their scores in the scoring box using the criteria given with the scoring box.

Next, pass out the Learner Satisfaction Forms. After these are completed, return the tests and collect the Learner Satisfaction Forms.

Begin to work through the questions for small group discussion with your learners.

The idea for this RTL was contributed by Richard Wolfson, Montclair State College, New Jersey.

Using Hands and Fingers to Compute

Chisanbop is a Korean method of computation that uses your hands and fingers as a calculator. Literally translated chisanbop means "finger calculation method." Before using chisanbop for calculating, you must first learn how to count using the chisanbop method.

COUNTING FROM 1 THROUGH 99 USING THE CHISANBOP METHOD

The "tools" used in chisanbop are your fingers and the numerical values they represent.

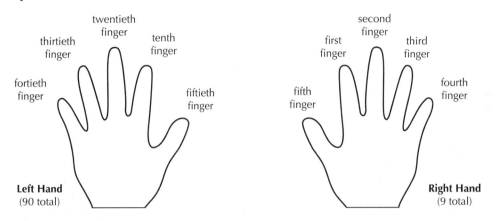

Using your fingers for counting is much like playing the piano, except that a desk or table is used instead of a keyboard. Imagine your fingers placed over the keys. Just as you would strike one or more keys, so you will strike or press the surface with one or more fingers, as required by the number you wish to represent.

The symbol "Y" will be used to show which particular finger will make contact with the table surface. Lifting of a finger, or clearing, will be represented by the symbol "Λ". A finger represented as being in a pressed position will be darkened.

Start counting from 1 through 10 by . . .

Pressing 1 . . . first finger
(keep other fingers suspended)

Then 2 . . . first and second fingers
(other fingers suspended)

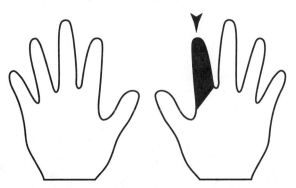

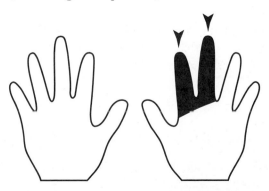

Then 3... first, second, and third finger

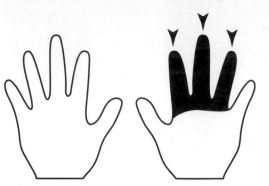

Then 4... first, second, third, and fourth finger

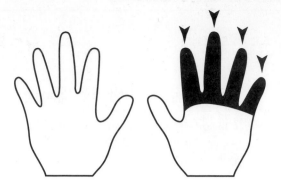

5 ... proceed from 4 to 5 by pressing fifth finger and simultaneously clearing the first, second, third, and fourth fingers

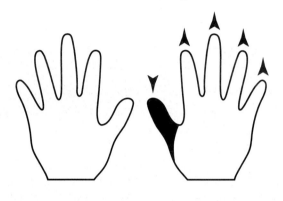

6 ... fifth and first fingers

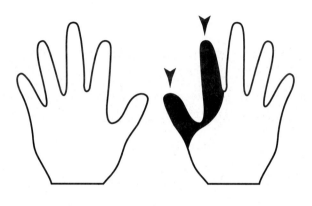

7 ... (fifth, first, and second fingers)

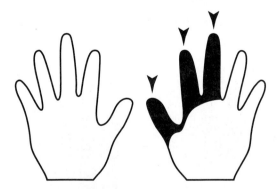

8 ... (fifth, first, second, and third fingers)

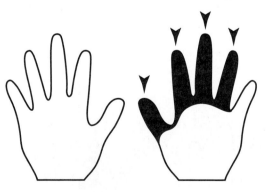

9... fifth, first, second, third, and fourth fingers

10... proceed from 9 to 10 by simultaneously clearing first, second, third, fourth, and fifth fingers, and pressing tenth finger

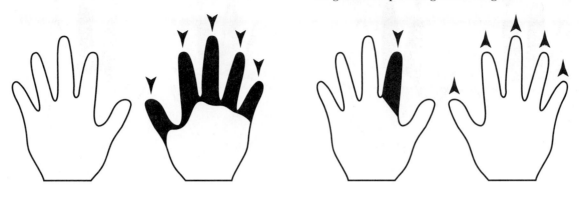

Continue counting from 11 through 99 in the same manner. Use the following diagrams as a guide.

11

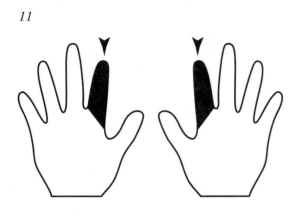

12

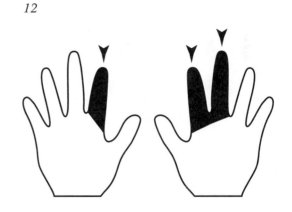

17

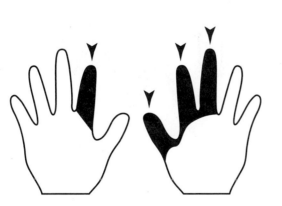

23... notice that both the tenth and twentieth finger are pressed

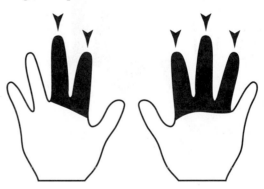

37

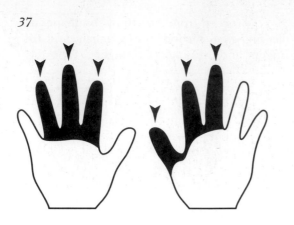

42

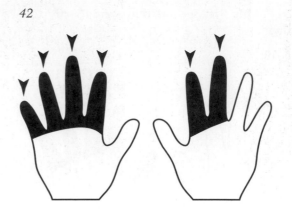

49

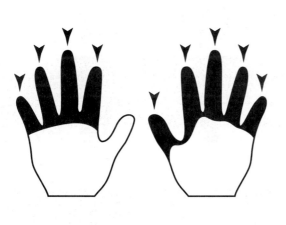

50 . . . proceed from 49 to 50 by simultaneously clearing right hand and fortieth finger, and pressing fiftieth finger

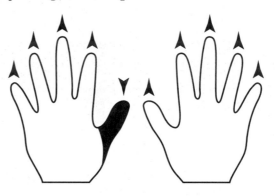

58

75

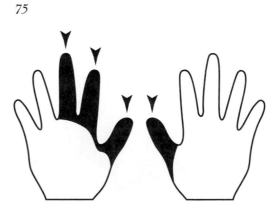

90

97

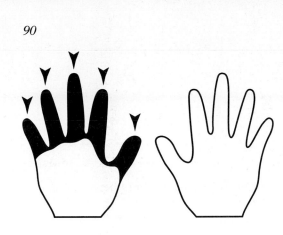

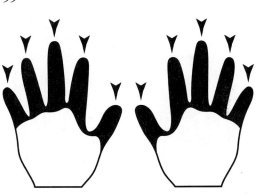

98

99

Name _____

The following five numbers were selected at random from all numbers between 0 and 100.

Assemble your learners in a line facing away from you. Ask them to press each number in turn. Look over their shoulders and judge the correctness of the pressed numbers. Use the diagrams below as a guide.

Do not inform your learners of any error until the test is complete.

On the chart provided, give each learner a score of 1 if he/she pressed each number without error. Give a 0 if an error is made. After the learners have been tested, total the number of 1s and 0s.

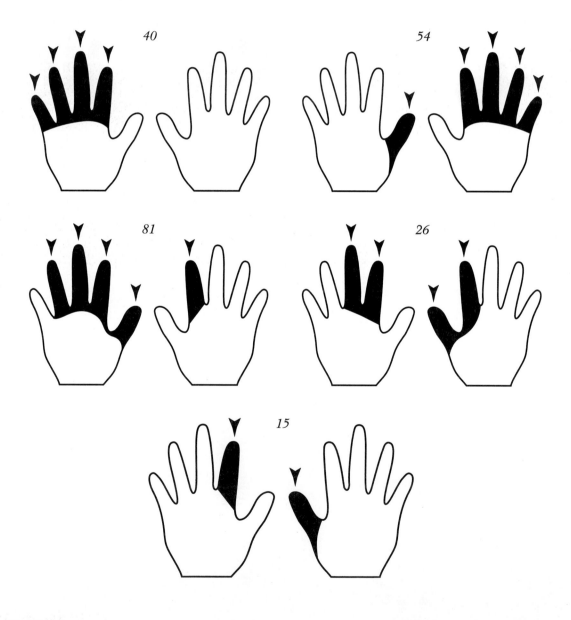

THE CHISANBOP TASK: Scoring Box

Directions   Give each learner:

1 point for each number pressed correctly,
0 points for an incorrect number.

	Learner's Name	Performance Score (0–5)
1		
2		
3		
4		
5		
6		
	TOTAL (add down)	

THE GOOD TEACHER TASK

Read each section carefully.

Description of Your Reflective Teaching Task

You are one of several participants chosen to teach this brief lesson to a small group of your peers. The exercise is intended to provide an opportunity for you to experience teaching and then to reflect on the shared teaching and learning. Plan to teach the lesson in such a way that you believe both learning and satisfaction will result.

Your lesson will be taught on _____.

INTRODUCTION TO THE LESSON

Teachers designate things—that is they denote things directly and specifically for learners. The following are examples of teacher designating behavior:

1. A foreign language teacher tells students the names of the German prepositions which always take indirect objects.
2. A chemistry teacher tells students the names of all the elements of the periodic table which are inert gases.
3. A health education teacher tells students the names of the classes of foods.
4. A geography teacher tells students the names of the world's five highest mountains.
5. A math teacher tells students the names of all the prime numbers between one and twenty.

Below is an objective that requires you to designate something to a group of your peers. The task was selected because your success in accomplishing it probably will not be dependent on your knowledge of some academic subject or previous experience you might have had.

YOUR OBJECTIVE

Your goal is to get as many of your learners as possible to name and correctly order 11 teacher behaviors identified as showing the greatest relationship to student achievement. You will have 15 minutes in which to accomplish your goal.

MATERIALS

1. Resources: Teacher Behaviors Related to Student Achievement (attached)
2. Test (attached)
3. Learner Satisfaction Forms (provided by college instructor)
4. Scoring Box (attached)

SPECIAL CONDITIONS AND LIMITATIONS

None

ENDING THE LESSON

Notify your college instructor when your learners are ready to take the test. (You may finish early.) Obtain copies of the learner satisfaction form.

Give your learners the test and when they have finished (no more than three minutes), read them the correct answer so that they can correct their own tests. Use the criteria given with the scoring box for scoring.

Next, pass out the Learner Satisfaction Forms, and while they are being completed, collect the tests and record the scores in the scoring box. Return the tests and collect the Learner Satisfaction Forms.

Begin to work through the questions for small group discussion with your learners.

The idea for this RTL was contributed by Betty Myers, Shepherd College, West Virginia.

Teacher Behaviors Related to Student Achievement

From a review of more than 50 research studies that had investigated teacher behaviors that appeared to have the strongest relationship to student achievement, Rosenshine and Furst* identified 11 behaviors. These are listed in order from the strongest relationship to the weakest relationship.

1. *Clarity*—being clear means, among other things, giving explanations that pupils understand, being able to answer their questions intelligently, and giving a clear presentation.

2. *Variability*—using a variety of teaching styles, instructional materials (films, charts, etc.), types of tests, and student activities. Variability can also mean the teacher's flexibility in procedure.

3. *Enthusiasm*—the enthusiastic teacher is one who shows involvement, excitement, and interest regarding his/her subject matter.

4. *Task-oriented and/or businesslike behavior*—being task-oriented and/or businesslike means, among other things, encouraging students to work hard and do independent work, and being concerned that students learn something rather than enjoy themselves.

5. *Learner opportunity to learn criterion material*—making students aware of what is to be learned and providing an opportunity for the students to learn the material on which they will be tested.

6. *Use of learner and general indirectness*—this means, among other things, acknowledging a student's idea by repeating or modifying it, accepting students' feelings, or giving praise and encouragement.

7. *Criticism (negative relationship)*—the stronger the criticism the less likely students are to achieve. There is no evidence to support a claim that teachers should avoid telling a student that he/she was wrong or should avoid giving academic directions.

8. *Use of structuring comments*—use of structuring comments by teachers include giving signals to indicate the beginning and end of a lesson, providing an overview of what is about to happen, or telling a student that "this is important."

9. *Types of questions*—research has been done on using divergent/convergent and higher order cognitive/lower order cognitive questions. The results of using one over the other are not conclusive.

10. *Probing*—this generally refers to teacher responses to a student's answers which encourage the student (or another student) to elaborate upon his/her answer.

11. *Level of difficulty of instruction*—the student's perception of the level of difficulty of instruction is related to student achievement.

* Barak Rosenshine and Norma Furst, "Research on Teacher Performance Criteria," in B. O. Smith, ed., *Research in Teacher Education: A Symposium.* Englewood Cliffs, N.J.: Prentice-Hall, Inc., 1971.

Name _____

Name and correctly order the 11 teacher behaviors identified by Rosenshine and Furst as showing the strongest relationship to student achievement. (One point for each named. Three points for correct order.)

1.

2.

3.

4.

5.

6.

7.

8.

9.

10.

11.

THE GOOD TEACHER TASK: Scoring Box

Directions   Give each learner:

> 1 point for each of the 11 behaviors named, and
> 3 additional points if all 11 are in the correct order.
> Maximum score is 14 points.

	Learner's Name	Performance Score (0–14)
1		
2		
3		
4		
5		
6		
	TOTAL (add down)	

THE REDIFRICATION TASK

Read each section carefully.

Description of Your Reflective Teaching Task

You are one of several participants chosen to teach this brief lesson to a small group of your peers. The exercise is intended to provide an opportunity for you to experience teaching and then to reflect on the shared teaching and learning. Plan to teach the lesson in such a way that you believe both learning and satisfaction will result.

Your lesson will be taught on_____.

INTRODUCTION TO THE LESSON

Teachers describe things—that is they tell about something. The following are examples of teacher describing behavior:

1. A social studies teacher describes the Equal Rights Amendment to the Constitution.
2. An English teacher describes symbolism.
3. A health teacher describes shock.
4. A science teacher describes saturation.

Below is an objective that requires you to describe something to a small group of your peers. The task was selected because your success in accomplishing it probably will not be dependent on your knowledge of some academic subject or previous experience you might have had.

YOUR OBJECTIVE

Your goal is to get as many of your learners as possible to answer correctly questions about redifrication. More specifically, your learners should be able to apply both Fitzwell's Rule and Rule Two. You will have 10 minutes in which to accomplish your goal.

MATERIALS

1. Resources: Medifers in Condrins (attached)
2. Test (provided by college instructor)

3. Answer sheet and scoring box (provided by college instructor)
4. Learner Satisfaction Forms (provided by college instructor)

SPECIAL CONDITIONS AND LIMITATIONS

You will not be given a copy of the test until after you have taught your lesson.

ENDING THE LESSON

Notify the college instructor when your learners are ready to take the test. (You may finish early.) Obtain copies of the test, answer sheet and scoring box, and learner satisfaction form.

Give your learners the test, and when they are finished (no more than five minutes), read them the correct answers so that they can correct their own tests. Use the criteria on the answer sheet for scoring.

Next, pass out the Learner Satisfaction Forms, and while they are being completed, collect the tests and record the scores in the scoring box. Return the tests and collect the Learner Satisfaction Forms.

Begin to work through the questions for small group discussion with your learners.

The idea for this RTL was contributed by Jerry Mager, Syracuse University, New York.

Medifers in Condrins

Redifrication is the process by which medifers are arranged by some preset rule, in a limited space called a condrin. The rule by which redifrication is governed must be consistently applied in each process in order that any medifer may be located quickly, regardless of which condrin it has been placed in. The rules, of course, may vary between sets of condrins depending on who has organized the redifrication procedure.

For some redifrication, the medifers are arranged according to their weight, from heaviest to lightest. This fairly standard rule is known as Fitzwell's Rule, after the inventor Joseph Fitzwell. The obvious advantage of this arrangement is that each of several condrins will contain medifers which are about equal in weight. A general rule of thumb is that condrins will hold three of the heaviest medifers or as many as eight of the lightest medifers. For example, these medifers are arranged according to Fitzwell's Rule:

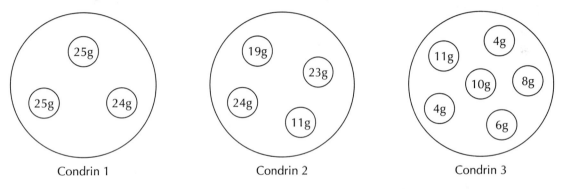

Condrin 1   Condrin 2   Condrin 3

The second, fairly standard rule, has yet to be named, but may be called Rule Two. According to this rule, medifers are arranged so that each condrin has a range of weights from light to heavy. In the following example, the same medifers as shown above are rearranged according to Rule Two:

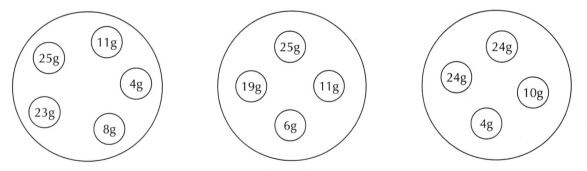

Of course, no matter which rule is used in redifricating, it must be remembered that all condrins are of the same size and shape. Thus any redifrication is limited in its flexibility by this fact.

Note: *The medifers in these diagrams are drawn the same size only because it is easier to do so. Actually, larger medifers should be larger in size than smaller ones.*

Name_____

1. Redifricate these medifers according to Fitzwell's Rule.

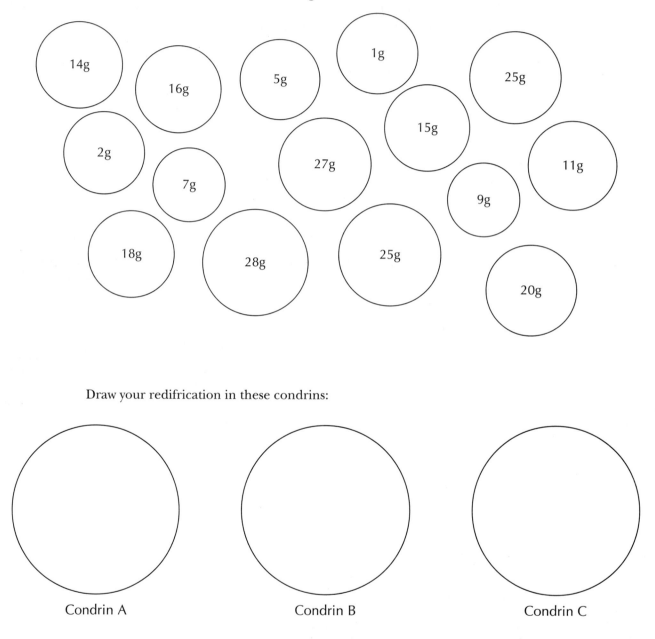

Draw your redifrication in these condrins:

Condrin A   Condrin B   Condrin C

2. If the above redifrication were to proceed according to Rule Two, what would be the greatest possible range of medifers in any one of the condrins?

from _____ to _____

3. Which of the two rules for redifrication discussed in the presentation would be probably most helpful to someone studying only light medifers?

_____

4. In this institution, Rule Two is most widely employed. It might therefore be implied that each condrin contains about:

a) 3 medifers.
b) 5 medifers.
c) 7 medifers.

5. Anyone establishing his/her own redifrication must:

a) limit the number of medifers used.
b) average the number of medifers per condrin.
c) be sure the preset rule is used consistently.

THE REDIFRICATION TASK: Answer Sheet

(15 points)   1. Subtract one point for each misplaced medifer.

Condrin A should contain 28g   27g   25g

Condrin B should contain 25g   20g   18g   16g and maybe   15g

Condrin C should contain 15g (if not placed in condrin B)

14g   11g   9g   7g   5g   2g   1g

(2 points)   2. from 28g to 1g

(1 point)   3. Fitzwell's Rule

(1 point)   4. b) 5 medifers

(1 point)   5. c) be sure the preset rule is used consistently

THE REDIFRICATION TASK: Scoring Box

Learner's Name	Place the number of points for each question in the correct box					Total Points (add across)
	1	2	3	4	5	
1						
2						
3						
4						
5						
6						
TOTAL (add down)						

THE STAN LAUREL TASK

Read each section carefully.

Description of Your Reflective Teaching Task

You are one of several participants chosen to teach this brief lesson to a small group of your peers. The exercise is intended to provide an opportunity for you to experience teaching and then to reflect on the shared teaching and learning. Plan to teach the lesson in such a way that you believe both learning and satisfaction will result.

Your lesson will be taught on_____.

INTRODUCTION TO THE LESSON

Teachers describe things—that is they tell about something. The following are examples of teacher describing behavior:

1. A typing teacher describes the correct placement of the fingers on the keyboard of the typewriter.
2. A physical education teacher describes how to execute a forward roll.
3. A science teacher describes the correct way to pour acid.
4. A driver education teacher describes how to start a car.

Below is an objective that requires you to describe something to a small group of your peers. The task was selected because your success in accomplishing it probably will not be dependent on your knowledge of some academic subject or previous experience you might have had.

YOUR OBJECTIVE

Your goal is to get as many of your learners as possible to execute correctly and smoothly the Stan Laurel behavior of knee slapping, ear covering, and mouth covering. You will have 15 minutes in which to accomplish your goal.

MATERIALS

1. Resources: A Psychomotor Task (attached)
2. Scoring box (attached)
3. Learner Satisfaction Forms (provided by college instructor).

SPECIAL CONDITIONS AND LIMITATIONS

You may *not* demonstrate the objective.

ENDING THE LESSON

Notify the college instructor when your learners are ready to take the test. (You may finish early.) Obtain copies of the Learner Satisfaction Form.

Test each of your learners one at a time and record their scores in the scoring box. Allow no more than five minutes for testing.

Next, pass out the Learner Satisfaction Forms and collect them when they are completed.

Begin to work through the questions for small group discussion with your learners.

The idea for this RTL was contributed by Randy L. Hoover, Youngstown State University, Ohio.

A Psychomotor Task

You are to teach the following psychomotor task to your learners in such a way that they will perform the task without hesitation during the testing period.

DESCRIPTION OF THE TASK

The task consists of a series of hand and arm movements such that the left ear and right ear are covered alternately with the hand of the opposite side of the body. In addition, the hand not covering an ear must cover the mouth simultaneously whenever an ear is covered. Each covering of an ear and the mouth begins with slapping the top of both knees with both hands at the same time.

Note: *You may not demonstrate the task.*

PROCEDURE

1. Person is seated with right hand on top of right knee and left hand on top of left knee.
2. Slap the knees simultaneously and bring the right hand to cover the mouth as the left hand covers the right ear.

3. Immediately upon touching the ear and the mouth, the hands return and slap the knees.
4. Immediately upon slapping the knees, the right hand is brought to cover the left ear as the left hand covers the mouth.

This represents one complete cycle of the Stan Laurel task. The object is to repeat the cycle over and over with no hesitation so that a rhythm is established.

Directions Give each learner:

1 point for a correct 30-second demonstration,
1 additional point for smoothness, and
1 additional point for speed.

Learner's Name	Performance Score (0–3)
1	
2	
3	
4	
5	
6	
TOTAL (add down)	

THE TOBACCO TASK

Read each section carefully.

Description of Your Reflective Teaching Task

You are one of several participants chosen to teach this brief lesson to a small group of your peers. The exercise is intended to provide an opportunity for you to experience teaching and then to reflect on the shared teaching and learning. Plan to teach the lesson in such a way that you believe both learning and satisfaction will result.

Your lesson will be taught on _____.

INTRODUCTION TO THE LESSON

Teachers foster attitude change—that is they attempt to get students to change their minds about people, events, content to be learned, and so forth. The following are examples of teachers fostering attitude change:

1. An English teacher attempts to get students to recognize the value of literature.
2. A classroom teacher attempts to get students to be more understanding of handicapped people.
3. A civic teacher attempts to get students to be more tolerant of people of different racial groups.

Below is an objective that requires you to foster attitude change with a small group of your peers. The task was selected because your success in accomplishing it probably will not be dependent on your knowledge of some academic subject or previous experience you might have had.

YOUR OBJECTIVE

Your goal is to get as many of your learners as possible to change their attitude toward a more favorable position about smoking and smokers. Specifically you should try to get your learners to disagree with as many of the following statements as possible:

- Smoking is obnoxious.
- Smokers are obnoxious.
- Smokers should never smoke around nonsmokers.
- Smoking should be illegal.
- There is no excuse for anyone to smoke.

The idea for this RTL was contributed by Randy L. Hoover, Youngstown State University, Ohio.

You will have 15 minutes in which to accomplish your goal.

MATERIALS

1. Resources: Smokers Deserve Consideration (attached)
2. Pretest (attached)
3. Posttest (attached)
4. Learner Satisfaction Forms (provided by college instructor)
5. Scoring box (attached)

SPECIAL CONDITIONS AND LIMITATIONS

Before you begin teaching, obtain copies of enough pretests for each learner. Distribute the pretest and have learners respond to it. Collect the pretests before you start to teach.

ENDING THE LESSON

Notify the college instructor when your learners are ready to take the posttest. (You may finish early.) Obtain copies of the posttest and learner satisfaction form.

Give your learners the posttest, and when they are finished (no more than two minutes), return their pretests and ask them to indicate any changes which they may have made from pre- to posttest.

Next, pass out the Learner Satisfaction Forms, and while they are being completed, record the changes in the scoring box. Return the pre- and posttests and collect the Learner Satisfaction Forms.

Begin to work through the questions for small group discussion with your learners.

Smokers Deserve Consideration

Let us resolve once and for all that people who smoke tobacco are no less human than anyone else. In fact, let us argue that the smokers of this nation deserve all the consideration and understanding that society can muster. Let us try to recognize the belief that certain highly intense individuals suffer from stress and self-imposed frustration to such a degree that smoking is the only reasonable manner of coping with demands of life as they feel them.

One must grant that antismoking research is based only upon longevity as a criterion, rather than upon the quality of the smokers' lives in the determination of its evilness. Is it not possible that for certain people the opportunity to smoke may represent a viable outlet for frustration and nervousness? Is there not a possibility that for some people the likelihood of suffering from stress-related disease may be lessened because of the outlet that smoking provides?

Certainly, nobody would deny the soldier in the foxhole a cigarette. Likewise, should we attempt to deny the diplomat, the priest, or the hard-working classroom teacher a chance to relax and unwind from stress and worry? There is no substitute that can aid the addicted in relieving the tensions that are lessened by the nicotine. Our society has gone to great lengths and expense to help the people addicted to alcohol or hard drugs. Is it too much to ask that understanding or a least tolerance be shown to those who maintain their composure and social ability by smoking?

THE TOBACCO TASK:Pretest

Name _____

Following are statements about tobacco and smoking. Rate each on the basis of whether you agree or disagree with it by placing a checkmark (✓) in one column after each statement. The checkmark must be in a box and not on a line.

STATEMENTS	Strongly Agree	Agree	Disagree	Strongly Disagree
1 Smoking is obnoxious.				
2 Smokers are obnoxious.				
3 Smokers should never smoke around nonsmokers.				
4 Smoking should be illegal.				
5 There is no excuse for anyone to smoke.				

Give yourself:

0 points for each item checked in the Strongly Agree column,

1 point for each item checked in the Agree column,

2 points for each item checked in the Disagree column, and

3 points for each item checked in the Strongly Disagree column.

Total individual pretest score = _____

Name _____

Part A

Following are statements about tobacco and smoking. Rate each on the basis of whether you agree or disagree with it by placing a checkmark (✓) in one column after each statement. The checkmark must be in a box and not on a line.

STATEMENTS	Strongly Agree	Agree	Disagree	Strongly Disagree
1 Smoking is obnoxious.				
2 Smokers are obnoxious.				
3 Smokers should never smoke around nonsmokers.				
4 Smoking should be illegal.				
5 There is no excuse for anyone to smoke.				

PART B

Do you think that your attitude toward tobacco and smoking has been modified somewhat by this Reflective Teaching experience? (*check one box*)

☐ YES   ☐ NO

PART C

Give yourself:

    0 points for each item checked in the Strongly Agree column,

    1 point for each item checked in the Agree column,

    2 points for each item checked in the Disagree column,

    3 points for each item checked in the Strongly Disagree column.

Total individual posttest score = _____

Part D

Total individual posttest score minus total individual pretest score = _____

This represents the amount of individual change. (You may have a negative number.)

When learners have completed the posttest, total the change scores (Part D, posttest) and record below.

Total learner's change	
Number of students with no change (zero change score)	
Number of students with change toward goal (positive change score)	
Number of students with change opposite goal (negative change score)	

From Part B

How many of your learners felt their attitudes were moderated toward tobacco and smoking from this experience? _____

LEARNER SATISFACTION FORM

Name of Designated Teacher _____

Name of Reflective Teaching Lesson _____

1. During the lesson, how satisfied were you as a learner? In arriving at a rating, consider the teaching methods used and how well they met your needs.

4	3	2	1
Very Satisfied	Mostly Satisfied	Somewhat Dissatisfied	Very Dissatisfied

2. What did your teacher do that contributed to your satisfaction?

3. What could your teacher have done to increase your satisfaction?

One thing is certain, teaching is never dull! That is because each day you face different intellectually and emotionally challenging situations. We thought you might both enjoy and benefit from encountering a few of the more bothersome and frequently occurring situations that teachers report. That's why we have created Room 221: A Simulation: Solving Classroom Problems. This unit contains 14 incidents that happen to you as a new teacher at Lincoln Park Middle School. Similar incidents occur in elementary and high schools.

The simulation begins as you visit your new school and chat with Pat Taylor, the principal. It continues as you work through all or a selection of the incidents that follow. These incidents, by the way, relate directly to various chapters in this book that deal with student diversity, learning, teaching, assessment, and so forth. They also represent the five major areas of teachers' concerns you learned about in Chapter 13: affiliation, control, parent relationships, student success, and time. The simulation provides a good opportunity to see how well you can apply what you have learned. Have fun—and good luck!

Meet the Principal

My name is Pat Taylor, and I'm principal of Lincoln Park Middle School. I'm so glad you could come in a few days before school starts. This way, you'll have a chance to become familiar with the school and the cumulative record information available for your students.

Let me tell you a few things about our community and school. As you know, we are a suburb of Capital City. Really, the city just grew to us. At one time, we were separated by farms and orchards. We're not what you would call an affluent suburb. Our income level is about average for the state, but it is a little bit lower than most nearby communities. Most of our families have blue-collar jobs, although a number own small businesses, and a few fathers and mothers are professionals.

Seventy percent of our students live with both biological parents, 15 percent live with their mothers, and 4 percent with their fathers. The others live with one parent and a stepparent, with other relatives, or in foster homes. A very few live in a residential care facility for court-referred children. Most people think of this as a community of hard-working people who have high aspirations for their children. They tend to expect more than we are able to deliver. But that's all right. It's good to be challenged!

The 750 students in our grade-five-through-eight school score near average on most of the national standardized achievement tests, although they do better in reading than in mathematics: Average daily attendance is high, between 96 and 98 percent, so we must be doing something right. We think it's instruction. Our goal is to make classes so exciting that kids want to be here. Of course, attendance and tardiness are things we work at constantly. We also work at making kids proud of the school, keeping it neat and clean. I would describe Lincoln Park as orderly without being rigid, quiet without being permissive, and focused on the business of learning. In my mind we are the best school not only in the district but in the county. The kids know what is expected of them. And they do the best they can. They do their work, and they treat the school right. Generally, they're cooperative, happy, and proud they go to Lincoln Park.

You probably would like to know a little about your colleagues. There are 39 teachers in Lincoln Park. Thirty are female, nine are male; four are black, or, if you prefer, African American, one is Hispanic, and another, Korean. The majority have been prepared as elementary teachers. Not many middle school teachers are prepared as such, but in our experience, these teachers do really well. In addition, we have an assistant principal, Dale Seymour; a guidance counselor, Merriam Roget; four teachers for exceptional children; a librarian; a home-school coordinator; and a nurse.

Our program reflects newer ideas in middle-level education, including such concepts as team teaching, detracking, and cooperative work. By team teaching, we mean that some teachers from different subject areas plan and sometimes teach together. For example, last year the social studies, English, music, and art teachers planned and jointly taught a unit on Colonial America. By detracking, we are moving toward more cooperative working teams, each consisting of diverse students. We also believe in invitational learning. Perhaps you've read about it in one of your textbooks. I don't want you to think that these are the answers to all education problems, but right now our faculty believes we are moving in the right direction.

One thing the teachers don't particularly like is that Lincoln Park is separated into four separate "houses."

Because of the separation, some of them feel isolated from others they know and like to be with. We have several different "house" teaching arrangements. In the Orange House, which you are in, the classes all are self-contained; that is, one teacher is pretty much in charge of a group of students for the whole day. Most of our new teachers like to start this way and then move into something more challenging. Other "houses" feature team teaching, multiage grading, and block scheduling. That's when, instead of having about eight 50-minute class periods, you have three 2-hour classes every day.

Our parents are pretty satisfied with Lincoln Park School. We did a survey last year, and 87 percent said that we are meeting the children's educational needs well or extremely well. Ninety percent agree that the teachers expect the students to do their best and behave well. We understand that students are vulnerable and sensitive and that they should not be embarrassed. They should be respected.

We collect food and clothing for the needy and occasionally raise money for a worthy community cause. The teachers want students to have a strong sense of community involvement and charity toward others.

The Lincoln Park parents like the idea of having a middle school that is a mixture of both elementary and secondary grades. They see it as starting secondary school earlier but in a warm, protected environment. The students here like to think of themselves as young adults, too old for elementary school.

That's enough for now. I'll let you get on with the things you came in here to do. Dale and I will be around. Give us a nod if you need help.*

Fourteen Classroom Incidents

INCIDENT 1: SLEEPLESS IN ROOM 221

For the past hour, your students have been working in small groups on a project they seem to enjoy. However, as you monitor the activity, you notice that Ashley Smith has been somewhat lackadaisical. She has said nothing, and her head is down, resting on her arms. You make a mental note to talk with her later.

At the end of the group activity, you ask the students to return to their seats. As they move about the room, you hear loud laughter in one area. Sharon is repeating, "Wake up, Ashley—Ashley, wake up! You're in my seat." As you approach, Ashley has a dazed look and she rubs her eyes.

*The description of Lincoln Park School and community was partly suggested by J. Lipsitz. (1984). *Successful schools for young adolescents* (pp. 27–58). New Brunswick, NJ, and London: Transaction Books.

Later you talk to Ashley about sleeping in class. She tells you that both her parents work a second shift and that she takes care of her younger siblings until they go to bed. Then she watches late-night television because she doesn't like to go to sleep until her parents are home.

You know Ashley can ill afford to miss any class work. She has barely passing grades and has been absent and tardy a number of times. How can you help?

Cumulative Record Information Ashley Smith lives with her mother, stepfather, and four younger school-age siblings in a blended family. Her parents work the afternoon-evening shift in a manufacturing plant. Except for weekends, the children are on their own, with Ashley as their primary supervisor. All the children have absence and tardiness problems. Ashley seems to have average academic ability, although her school achievement has been marginal. She has a slight hearing loss in both ears and has difficulty maintaining personal hygiene. Generally, her peers have little to do with her. She does not seem to have any close friends.

INCIDENT 2: ANGELO FIGHTS BACK

Angelo is a beautiful boy with dark, wavy hair, large brown eyes, and an olive complexion. The girls in class and throughout the school are very attracted to him—probably for his good looks, charm, and talent. He is also an accomplished guitarist, singer, and dancer. Angelo's appeal to the girls annoys the boys. To worsen matters, Angelo is disinterested in sports and other "masculine" activities.

This year Angelo has been the subject of considerable taunting. Occasionally, he has been pushed around. Today, when school began, a group of girls related that Angelo was beaten up on the way to school. Within 15 minutes, Angelo and his older brother enter the classroom, and the older brother shouts at one of the students, "Leave Angelo alone or else." What should you do?

Cumulative Record Information Angelo Carpanian lives with both parents and an older brother and sister. His family is part of an extended family living on the edge of the school community. The Carpanians own a used-car business and also operate games and rides at county fairs. They speak their own language and, in public, speak that language with their children. The Carpanians appear happy and reasonably prosperous. Angelo and his siblings have not had an easy time in school. They normally are not permitted to mix freely with the other children, and after school they help their parents.

The girls like Angelo. He is a very handsome, thoughtful boy. He also is quite fun-loving when in their company. He plays guitar and dances.

Angelo's achievement throughout the grades has been very marginal. Mostly, he seems to have been eased upward through the grades. All his teachers agree that he is fun-loving but find him trying as a learner.

INCIDENT 3: SCHOOL IS BORING, BORING!

You really like Tom. He is good natured, laid back, has lots of friends, and never causes a problem. A perfect child? No! Tom doesn't like to learn. You find this strange for a boy who is on time and in school every day.

In school, he putters along, almost keeping up with the task at hand, but when it comes to homework or studying for exams, Tom is almost never ready. You have met with his mother on many occasions. She wants desperately to work with you and has taken all your suggestions including monitoring his efforts and withholding television until work is completed. This proves difficult because she isn't always certain what Tom must actually do; he is unclear, and she is not able to sit with Tom by the hour.

After months of this, you finally get Tom to do more than shrug his shoulders and smile when you ask what's wrong. Today he told you, "School is just plain boring." How do you react?

Cumulative Record Information Thomas Lindgren lives with his mother, stepfather, and two younger sisters from his mother's second marriage. Tom's natural father left when he was an infant, and Tom has not seen or heard from him. Mrs. Lindgren has tried to find Tom's father in order to obtain child support. Tom has above-average ability according to standardized test results. However, his school achievement is marginal, with grades fluctuating in all subjects. Teachers describe him as an outwardly happy, friendly youngster who needs constant prodding to stay on task both with schoolwork and other responsibilities.

INCIDENT 4: MARNA, MARNA!

You had always dreaded having a student in the class who is regularly disruptive. Unfortunately, she has arrived. Marna is an attention grabber. You name it, she does it: won't stay put, calls out in class, talks constantly with those nearby, pokes others with her pen, takes things without permission, drops books, hums, won't take turns, and so on. You thought it was cruel when other teachers told you they wished one of their students—Marna—would move out of the district! Now you are embarrassed to realize that you are beginning to feel this way, too. The students are alternately annoyed and pleased by Marna: When her actions disrupt *them*, they get angry. When her antics disrupt *you*, they laugh. You think you are becoming paranoid, but

you know that your relationship with the class is generally very good. What do you do?

Cumulative Record Information Marna Wright lives with her parents. She is an attractive girl with above-average academic ability. Throughout school, she has been cited as exhibiting immature social behavior; as early as grade 1, she has been referred to the school psychologist. The psychological reports are more descriptive than useful. They describe Marna as an only child born after her parents had been married 17 years. Both parents are very strict, and Marna presents no problem at home. When the school has contacted Marna's parents, they are chagrined to learn of her school behavior and vow to talk to her. At the same time, they have made clear that this seems to be a school problem and, to that extent, is beyond their control. On one occasion, they raised questions about the competency of Marna's teacher. Pat Taylor, your principal, has had lots of talks with Marna and feels she will eventually grow up.

INCIDENT 5: TEACHERS ARE SUPPOSED TO TEACH!

The class is working quietly on independent study assignments, and you are moving among the students monitoring their efforts, when one of Mrs. Armstrong's students enters the room announcing "Mrs. Armstrong ran out of paper. Can she borrow some?" This interruption is the second already today and was sufficient to get the students off-task and buzzing.

A few minutes later another student appears at the door and hands you a note from Pat Taylor, the principal. "Please have all students take a recess between 10:00 and 10:30. We have a plumbing problem, and the water will be shut off after, 10:30. Thanks."

At noon, you peruse the office bulletin board announcements and are reminded that student health screening will begin tomorrow, student progress cards are to have written comments this marking period, quarterly attendance forms are due, and your assignment for helping with the School Fair is to run the popcorn booth with one of the parents.

You stand there in almost a catatonic state thinking, when will I have time to plan and teach?

INCIDENT 6: HOW CAN I DO THAT?

You have been led to believe that to be a good teacher you must do three things: plan, teach, and assess students' learning. At least that's what you were taught in professional education courses. However, each of these activities takes lots of time. Where does it come from?

Of course, you must teach, and to be very good at it, you must plan. So, understandably, you devote almost all of your time and energy to these tasks. At the same time, you are feeling unprofessional because your assessment activities seem limited to making up and scoring tests. What you don't do very much is "informal assessment" such as systematic observation, use of checklists and rating scales, and collecting and evaluating the everyday work students do. You ask yourself—where will I get the time to do that?

INCIDENT 7: AM I GOOD ENOUGH?

You love teaching. Even before you decided to become a teacher, you thought a lot about the future and about the different ways you could help other people. Teaching seemed a pretty clear choice since you always liked school and enjoyed learning. However, it is becoming increasingly clear to you that some students do not share your attraction to school and learning. Some, like Tom Lindgren, find it boring and say so publicly, which doesn't help. Others are more passive and just doodle their time away, doing only what is required and giving one another sour looks—if they do anything at all. You are reminded of some popular movies and books about teachers who were great. How could you be more like them? Maybe that would make students enjoy learning more.

INCIDENT 8: TEACHING EVERYONE

If all the students in the class were alike, it would be so much easier to teach. Unfortunately (or fortunately), they are not. The students of most concern to you are those who can't keep up. Andre Harrison is one. Today he sheepishly hands you the following note.

Dear Teacher:

Please excuse Andre from completing his homework. He worked very hard from the time he had supper until he went to bed. He even missed his favorite TV show. As you know, Andre is not a good reader, but he does try very hard. I know the homework wasn't too difficult, so in no way are we blaming you. We would appreciate any kind of help you can give our son.

Yours truly,

Mrs. Alberta Harrison

How can you individualize instruction in order to help more students learn?

INCIDENT 9: CRIME AND PUNISHMENT

One thing you hate to do is to punish students. To you, it is an admission that you haven't done something right—that you may have failed. Nevertheless, sometimes punishment is required. Pat Taylor, the principal of Lincoln Park Middle School, feels it is time to review the school's policy on discipline and punishment. All teachers have been asked to begin by writing a one-page response to the following questions:

1. Under what circumstances are discipline and punishment warranted?
2. What kinds of discipline and punishment should be allowed in our school?

What will you write?

INCIDENT 10: ATTENTION!

You are convinced that movies, MTV, computer software, and the like so dazzle students that it is difficult for teachers to compete for their attention. Certainly, from a student's point of view, school must look pretty bland and colorless—the same thing in the same way day after day. You have decided to make a list of ways to better capture and hold students' interest. What will you put on your list?

INCIDENT 11: PARENTS TO THE RESCUE

The older, more experienced teachers at Lincoln Park Middle School talk constantly of the "good old days." Frankly, you get a little tired of it, but there is probably truth in some of what they say. In fact, the entire staff is bothered by the seeming lack of parental support for school. On many occasions you have heard stories of parents who blame teachers for students' misbehavior, low grades, dislike of school, and so forth. When a child gets in trouble, more than likely the parents will find fault with the school and the teacher. Some teachers excuse this, pointing out that more parents are working longer hours, experiencing rough economic conditions, and having difficulty maintaining satisfying marriages. Accordingly, it is very difficult to get parents to help out when needed.

As a novice teacher, you want to withhold judgment. However, you do want to gain parent support. What can you do to get it?

INCIDENT 12: GETTING TO THE BOTTOM OF THINGS

Assessing students is anything but fun. It takes lots of time to do it well: hundreds of hours evaluating papers and tests, and then more time to figure out the grades for report cards. This marking period was no different, so you felt pretty good when you entered the last mark on the last report card yesterday before leaving school. Looking over your shoulder on the way out the door, you regarded the stack of cards on your desk as a major accomplishment.

Today, the day the report cards were to be distributed, they were nowhere to be found. Later, Don Parsons, a school custodian, entered the room with the cards in his rubber-gloved hand. "I found these in the urinal," he noted in a quiet voice. Several nearby students tittered. Looking back on the incident, you ask yourself—how could anyone do such a thing? What should you do?

INCIDENT 13: CATCH-22

Several of your students work pretty hard, but to little avail. They just don't get it. Although they listen and attend to each assignment, their work is often minimal or incorrect. Your heart goes out to these kids, and you are caught in a catch-22. If you give them passing grades, you are deceiving both them and yourself. If you fail them, they will likely give up. You say to yourself, there must be a solution. You decide to send home midterm failure notices. The next morning one child's mother confronts you in the hall and demands, "Are you prejudiced against my son?" How would you react?

INCIDENT 14: SO MUCH FOR PROFESSIONALISM

You believe that teachers are professionals. It has been disheartening for you to hear and see teachers criticizing one another, making personal remarks about their students, gossiping, complaining about the principal, joking about parents, and taking sick days when they aren't sick. You vow never to go into the faculty lounge again. But you can't do that. What can you do?

ONE MORE INCIDENT: WHAT TO DO?

Recall a teacher dilemma you have witnessed. Write it down and share it with your peers.

Glossary

The following terms include selected boldfaced words and concepts defined in the text as well as some words and concepts used but not defined in the text.

abused children Those treated in ways deemed to cause physical, emotional, or other kinds of harm.

academic games Learners compete with each other, one-to-one or team-to-team, to determine which individual or group is superior at a given academic task (including spelldowns, anagrams, and so forth).

academic instruction time Time when the teacher is conducting instruction.

academic learning time (ALT) Amount of academic instruction time during which students are actively and successfully engaged in learning.

academic optimism Characteristic of teachers who believe all students can learn and that teachers make a difference.

accommodations Adaptations made to an assessment or assessment context to enable a student with particular special needs to demonstrate mastery of assigned objectives or standards. Accommodations do not change the nature or level of the objectives the student is to meet; these are often specified in a child's IEP or 504 plan. (See also **modifications.**)

accountability The idea that teachers should be held responsible for what and how much students learn.

achievement gap Persistent differences in achievement between minority and majority students (particularly white, black, and Hispanic) as indicated by scores on standardized tests, teacher grades, and other data.

achievement tests Tests that measure what a student knows or is able to do in a subject area (for example, mathematics) compared to what other, like students know.

action research Process of conducting school or classroom research to improve teaching and learning.

action zone The triangular area, defined by imaginary lines across the front and down the middle of the classroom, where most student-teacher interaction occurs.

active listening When a teacher permits or encourages a learner to provide information or express some feeling and then repeats, paraphrases what the learner has said.

active teaching Instructional method containing five parts: the opening, development, independent work, homework, and review.

activity reinforcers Privileges given to students when they behave appropriately in order to increase the likelihood that they will repeat the behavior.

activity routines Classroom routines established to minimize problems related to such things as the location of materials and acceptable behaviors.

advance organizers Procedures teachers use to prepare learners to attend to and understand new information. For example, a teacher can connect new information with information students already possess.

affective domain The area of learning that focuses on students' feelings, interests, attitudes, appreciation; focuses on the attitudinal, emotional, and valuing goals for learners. Five subdivisions of this domain are receiving or attending, responding, valuing, organization, and characterization.

affiliation need Teacher's need to get along with students, parents, and other teachers.

alignment The extent to which what is taught and tested coincides with state curriculum standards.

allocated time Amount of mandated time intended or scheduled for academic activities.

alternative responses Portion of a series of multiple-choice questions that offer possible solutions to the stem.

analysis The process of breaking down material into component parts so it can be understood.

anecdotal comments Brief, teacher-written descriptions about students, usually found in school records.

antecedent strategies Actions taken prior to a behavior or event that changes the environment with the intent of preventing inappropriate behavior.

anticipatory set An introductory activity that captures students' attention, helps them see the purpose and value of what they are to learn, and relates what they are to learn to what they already know.

applied behavioral analysis (ABA) Teachers reward or reinforce learners when they do the right thing. Based on principles of operant conditioning.

aptitude tests Tests that measure a student's general potential to learn.

artifact Any object produced by the student or teacher related to the schooling experience.

assessment Process of collecting, synthesizing, and interpreting information to aid in decision making.

assessment system A coordinated set of assessments that are intentionally selected and used by a teacher to make complete and accurate judgments about student learning and the effectiveness of teaching over a specific period of time.

at-risk students Students most likely to experience school failure.

attention A necessary condition in order for formal learning to occur.

attention deficit disorder (ADD) and attention deficit hyperactivity disorder (ADHD) Children with ADD have problems staying on task and focusing. They may be impulsive, fidgety and restless—full of unfocused energy—and easily distracted. Some children with ADD are also hyperactive (ADHD). Hyperactivity, a disorder of the central nervous system, makes it difficult for affected children to control their motor activities.

authentic learning Learning that occurs when students engage in real experiences, for example learning library skills in the library rather than reading about them.

baseline Information about how often a specified student presently performs a desired behavior.

basic practice Teaching method emphasizing supervised student practice and teacher provision of corrective feedback.

behavior disorders Conduct disorder, anxiety-withdrawal disorder, and immaturity.

behavior modification Systematic attempt to change behavior by using rewards or punishments.

behavioral learning theory School of thought that attempts to explain why we behave as we do.

benchmarks Accomplishments along the way toward reaching a particular goal. For example, knowing the sounds of letters in order to read.

brainstorming Learners are asked to withhold judgment or criticism while they produce a large number of ideas for something such as how to resolve a problem.

case approach Learning by studying and analyzing real situations. We can learn about and analyze many school events and phenomena by looking at cases such as those contained throughout the text.

case study Written document that pieces together all kinds of student information to obtain a more complete and articulated picture of the student.

centers of interest Classroom displays used to interest learners in themes or topics.

charter schools Publicly funded schools that are somewhat autonomous, given freedom to innovate and improve student learning.

child abuse See **abused children.**

Children's Defense Fund Organization that advocates on behalf of America's children.

clarity See **instructional clarity.**

classical conditioning Learning that occurs when we already have an established connection (contiguity) between a stimulus and a response, and then a new stimulus is paired with the original stimulus long enough to evoke the same response when the original stimulus is absent.

classroom and class-size effects How classroom physical size and class size affect the learning environment.

classroom management Using the provisions and procedures needed to create and maintain an environment in which teaching and learning can occur.

climate Sociopsychological dimensions of the classroom including the emotional tone and the comfort level students feel with the teacher, with learning tasks, and with one another as a social group.

cognitive development Intellectual development that evolves through four stages: sensorimotor, preoperational, concrete operational, and formal operational.

cognitive domain Area of educational objectives that contains objectives related to intellectual tasks such as recalling, comprehending, applying, analyzing, synthesizing, and evaluating information.

cognitive learning theory School of thought that attempts to explain what goes on in the brain when we are learning; focuses on information processing (how we take in, store, and retrieve information) and meaningful learning (how to organize, structure, and teach information so that it might be best used).

cognitive style The consistent ways an individual responds to a wide range of perceptual learning tasks.

colloquium A guest or guests are invited to class to be interviewed about their interests or activities.

completion item Type of test item that requires students to supply missing words in a statement or a short phrase.

computer-assisted instruction (CAI) The use of computers to present programmed instruction or to assist learners with specific learning tasks.

conceptual tempo Style of learning based on usage of time; tempo falls between "impulsive" and "reflective."

concrete operational stage Piaget's third stage of intellectual development (approximately 7 to 11 years of age). Children become capable of logical thought and learn to solve specific problems and think logically about concrete experiences.

conflict resolution A method used in Teacher Effectiveness Training to encourage teachers to establish open and honest communication in the classroom in order to resolve problems.

constructivism An approach to learning that asserts that for students to gain deep understanding, they must actively come to know (construct) knowledge for themselves.

contiguity Simple stimulus-response pairing or connection. When one stimulus is regularly associated with another, a response (S-R connection) is established. If two events occur together repeatedly they will eventually become associated, so that even if only one of the events occurs, the response will occur with it.

contracts Written agreements students and teachers enter into that describe the academic work the student is to accomplish at a particular level in a particular period of time.

control need Teacher's need to have students behave well or appropriately.

convergent thinking Style that predisposes people to think in conventional, typical ways by encouraging them to look for a single answer or solution to a problem. Contrasts with divergent thinking.

cooperative learning Learners work together in small groups and are usually rewarded for their collective accomplishments.

corporal punishment A coersive intervention that involves hitting an individual with a hand or object with the intent of causing pain.

created response items Test questions that require students to develop or create a response in their own words.

criterion-referenced scores Scores that are compared to a specific, preestablished standard or criterion.

cumulative record A personal record kept for each school enrollee that contains personal information, home and family data, record of school attendance, school grades, standardized test scores, and teacher anecdotal comments.

curriculum alignment See **alignment.**

curriculum guides Describe what is to be learned at each grade level and provide related instructional suggestions.

debates Formal discussions in which a few students present and contest varying points of view with regard to an issue.

demonstrations Form of presentation whereby the teacher or learners show how something works or operates or how to do a particular task.

development Orderly changes that occur in a person over time from conception to death. Includes physical, emotional, or cognitive changes across time.

developmental stages Erikson's comprehensive theory of emotional and social development suggests that there are eight critical stages, each leading to a positive or negative outcome—trust vs. mistrust, autonomy vs. shame and doubt, initiative vs. guilt, industry vs. inferiority, identity vs. role confusion, intimacy vs. isolation, generativity vs. stagnation, and integrity vs. despair.

dialogue journal A journal recording a running conversation that expresses thoughts, questions, and problems related to the roles, responsibilities, and practices of teaching.

differentiated instruction See **individualized instruction.**

direct teaching or instruction (expository teaching) Teachers control instruction by presenting information, giving directions to the class, and using criticism; associated with teacher-centered, teacher-controlled classrooms; an instructional procedure for teaching content in an efficient, straightforward way.

disabled or challenged children Students with special needs. May be mentally or physically challenged, emotionally disturbed, learning disabled, or have communication or behavior problems.

discipline Specific actions teachers take in response to students who ignore a school procedure or rule.

discovery learning Learning that occurs when students derive their own meaning from experiences they have and/or from experiments.

discussion Occurs when students, or students and a teacher, converse back and forth to share information, ideas, or opinions, or to resolve a problem.

disengaged children Those who are inattentive, disinterested in school. Also called reluctant learners.

distance education When instruction is provided for persons off-campus through the use of computers, telephone, printed materials, and so forth.

divergent thinking Style that predisposes a person to think in independent, flexible, and imaginative ways; often equated with creativity. Contrasts with convergent thinking.

domains of learning Cognitive, affective, and psychomotor kinds of learning that parallel the cognitive, humanistic, and behavioral schools of thought about learning.

dyslexia Reading impairment; often the result of genetic defect or brain injury.

economically disadvantaged children Children whose parents fall below a governmentally determined poverty line.

educational challenges Challenges to teachers to: foster equity, help students achieve world-class academic success, support families, celebrate diversity, and to utilize technology.

educationally disadvantaged children Children who: do not perform well academically, or lesson often identified as "challenged", drop out of school at a higher rate, and are more likely to enter school with experiential deficits.

efficacy Having a sense of control over one's circumstances.

emotional intelligence (EQ) The ability to get along with others.

established structure The class rules and routines that effective teachers establish and enforce.

establishing set See **set induction.**

evaluation Process of making a qualitative judgment based on collected data.

evaluative set When teachers establish what students already know about a topic.

exceptionality The special physical, social, emotional, or mental needs or gifts certain children have. Exceptional children may be either disabled or gifted.

executive planning routines Classroom routines that help a teacher to manage personal time and to fulfill the many roles of teaching, such as completing paperwork and clerical chores, grading papers, and planning.

explanation Attempt to make something clear and understood.

explicit instruction Teachers review and check homework, present new content/skill, guide students' practice, provide feedback and correctives, move to independent practice, and conduct regular reviews.

expository teaching or expository lesson (direct instruction) Occurs when teachers present information and direction to students. Teacher-centered, goal-oriented, structured approach to teaching.

extended response items Type of created response item that does not place any restrictions on student responses, thus allowing greater creativity and flexibility of response.

extinction The elimination of minor misbehavior by ignoring it (as long as it is not dangerous or distracting to other students).

family culture The unique ways a family chooses to live.

family trends How the family is changing and the impact on teachers and schools.

feedback Information teachers provide to inform students of their progress and to help them learn to monitor themselves and improve their own learning.

field observation Observations made or work carried on in a natural setting. Also referred to as fieldwork or field trips.

field-dependent Cognitive style of a person who sees the larger picture but not its specifics or details. Field-dependent learners "see the forest" rather than the individual trees.

field-independent Cognitive style of a person who sees the specifics or details of something but not the larger picture. Field-independent learners "see the individual trees" rather than the forest.

field-sensitive See **field-dependent.**

follow-up Phase of the questioning process where the teacher reacts to the student's response to a question.

formal curriculum What the state and school district expect will be taught and learned.

formal interview A structured, face-to-face meeting with the explicit purpose of obtaining specific information about the interviewee's experiences, views, likes, and so forth.

formal observation Carefully planned observational efforts to obtain specific information about a target student or students.

formal operational stage Piaget's fourth stage of intellectual development, beginning at about age 11. At this level, children are more able to deal in abstractions or perform activities mentally.

formative assessment Ongoing student assessment conducted during the course of instruction and used to make adjustments in instruction.

gender roles Male/female roles learned early in life.

generativity The ability to have and nurture children and/or be involved with future generations. Productivity and creativity are essential features.

Gifted and Talented Act (Public Law 95-561) Provides federal funding for gifted education.

gifted and talented learners Children who possess outstanding abilities or potential in the areas of general intellectual capacity, specific academic aptitude, creative or productive thinking, leadership ability, visual or performing arts, and psychomotor ability.

grade equivalent scores Scores that describe the pupil's level of performance in comparison to pupils in a particular grade.

group alerting The process of keeping the students' attention and of holding them accountable for their behavior and learning.

Head Start program Preschool program intended to counteract lack of advantages of economically disadvantaged 3- and 4-year-old children.

higher-level cognitive skills The intellectual ability to analyze, synthesize, and evaluate information.

high-stakes tests Assessments that are used to make critical decisions about the performance of students, teachers, or schools.

humanistic learning theory School of thought emphasizing the development of the learner as a psychologically healthy person.

hurried children Children whose caregivers hurry or pressure them to excel and/or to grow up.

hyperactivity Behavior disorder characterized by abnormal amounts of movement, inattentiveness, and restlessness.

identity The organization of the individual's drives, abilities, beliefs, and history into a consistent self-image.

impulsive learning/thinking style Cognitive style of responding quickly but often inaccurately. Contrasts with reflective learning style.

independent study Any school-related assignment done more or less alone by students.

indirect teaching or instruction (learner-centered instruction) Teachers provide students with experiences or information and then ask students for their observations and conclusions. Contrasts with direct instruction or expository teaching.

Individualized Educational Plan (IEP) A learning program that teachers, parents, a qualified school official, and perhaps the student develop for a student with special learning needs. It sets forth goals, services, and teaching strategies for that student.

individualized or personalized instruction Instruction that attempts to tailor teaching and learning to a learner's unique strengths and needs.

Individuals with Disabilities Education Act (Public Law 105–17) Law requiring that students with disabilities be placed in the least restrictive, or most normal, school environment they can succeed in.

informal interview A face-to-face meeting that is more like casual conversation, allowing talk to flow naturally and spontaneously in more or less any direction.

informal observation Casual, unplanned observation of a student(s).

information processing Efforts to understand how we take in and store new information and how we retrieve it when it is needed.

inquiry learning See **discovery learning**.

inquiry-oriented teaching Highly individual process of reflecting on one's teaching in order to make rational, deliberate decisions about teaching and learning.

instructional alternative Any of a number of ways of teaching that can be used to facilitate student learning and satisfaction.

instructional clarity A quality of effective instruction that helps students come to a thorough and accurate understanding of the material.

instructional objective Statement of concepts, attitudes, or skills that students are expected to achieve by the end of some period of instruction.

instructional planning Process by which someone (usually a teacher) decides how best to select and organize a learning experience to maximize both teacher and student achievement and satisfaction.

instructional routines Routines or procedures teachers regularly follow when they teach such as the formats for giving directions, monitoring student work, and questioning students.

intervention Any strategy or procedure that reduces the likelihood of a challenging or inappropriate behavior occuring in the future.

inviting classroom An appealing, positive place that provides a sense of physical and emotional safety for both students and the teacher.

Inviting School Success A program developed to get teachers to communicate to learners that they are "responsible, able, and valuable" people.

laboratory experiences Scaled-down teaching experiences carried out on campus, often with a small group of peers, rather than in an actual classroom setting. See the Practice Teaching Manual.

latchkey children Children between about 6 and 13 years of age who do not have adult supervision for some part of the day.

latchkey programs Before- and after-school programs for children who otherwise would be without adult supervision.

learning abilities Classified by Sternberg as memory, analysis, creativity, and application.

learning module A self-contained package of individualized learning activities that guides students to know or to be able to do something.

learning style A consistent pattern of behavior and performance an individual uses to approach learning experiences. Includes how a person learns best; the person's learning personality; and the learner's tendency to use different sensory modes to understand experiences and to learn (visual, auditory, kinesthetic).

learning theory-based direct instruction The sequence of instructional events followed by teachers who are guided by what is known about learning.

least restrictive environment A school setting that is as normal as possible given a child's special problems and needs. Often involves placing a child with disabilities into a regular classroom for all or part of the day.

lesson objectives Define the outcomes of a lesson and greatly influence how it may be taught. May be in the cognitive, affective, or psychomotor domain of learning.

lesson plan A guide to teaching a lesson that includes lesson objectives, how the lesson will be taught, and how student learning and satisfaction will be assessed.

long-term memory Seemingly limitless and permanent storage system where we keep information for a long time.

magnet schools Schools that specialize in a particular subject (e.g., the arts) to attract students.

mainstreaming Placing a challenged child in a regular classroom for as much of the day as possible.

management routines Classroom routines used to organize the classroom and direct student behavior; nonacademic routines.

mandated time Formal time scheduled for school or academic activities.

mastery learning Causes students to study academic material at their own pace until they learn it.

matching items Test questions that ask students to match items in one column with related items in another.

meaningful learning Occurs when information is effectively organized, structured, and taught so as to maximize its understanding and usefulness.

measurement Process of gathering objective, quantitative, information or data about student performance.

modifications Modifications refer to adaptations made to an assessment that change the nature or level of the objectives a student is expected to meet. In contrast to accommodations, modifications result in assessment that measures something different than is measured for other students. Modifications, like accommodations, are generally specified in a child's IEP or 504 plan. (See also **accommodations**.)

momentum The flow of activities and the pace of teaching and learning maintained in a classroom.

moral development A progressive increase in the capability for moral reasoning. Piaget suggests that moral development/reasoning evolves through two levels: morality of constraint and morality of cooperation.

moral education Akin to character education, values education, and citizenship education. Intended to help learners develop more responsible behavior both in school and out.

morality of constraint The first of two levels in Piaget's stages of moral reasoning. At this stage, children regard rules as sacred and unchangeable, and punishment as inflexible.

morality of cooperation Piaget's second stage of moral reasoning. At this stage, individuals regard rules

as flexible, believe there can be exceptions to them, and believe that punishment must take into account the circumstances surrounding the misbehavior.

motivation to learn Interest, willingness to learn.

multiethnic education Educational practices that encourage learners to revere their roots and culture, as well as the cultures of others.

multiple-choice items Test questions that consist of a stem, which presents a problem or asks a question, followed by several alternative responses. Students are expected to select the alternative that offers the best solution to the problem or best answers the question presented in the stem.

multiple intelligences The belief that we are possessed of many "intelligences" (abilities and talents) including: linguistic, logical–mathematical, musical, spatial, body–kinesthetic, interpersonal, intrapersonal, naturalistic, spiritual, and existential.

negative reinforcement Encouraging desirable behaviors by removing or omitting an undesirable or aversive stimulus.

non-graded (ungraded) school One in which students complete a grade level's work at their own pace. Some may do so in less than the standard year's time and accordingly are moved to the next level of work.

nonnegative affect A manner teachers have that makes learners feel psychologically safe and secure.

norm-referenced scores Scores that are compared to those of others who took the test.

normal curve Bell-shaped graph depicting the frequency with which particular scores are expected.

norming group The class-, school-, district-, statewide, or national group of students to which scores are compared.

observational learning Also called social learning. Occurs when learners learn by watching; in order for observational learning to be effective, learners must attend to someone's behavior, retain what they observed the "model" do, imitate or reproduce the behavior they saw, and experience reinforcement or satisfaction as a consequence.

online schools Also called electronic, virtual, or cyber schools. They provide online learning both for homeschooled students and students in attendance at neighborhood schools.

operant conditioning Learning facilitated through reinforcement. Behaviors are strengthened or weakened depending upon the reinforcement or punishment received.

orientation set An instructional activity that engages students' attention.

overcorrection The compulsory practice of appropriate behavior as a result of undesirable behavior.

overlapping Teacher's ability to attend to more than one classroom activity or episode at a time.

parent relationships and home conditions need Teachers' need to maintain constructive relationships with parents and to be aware of the impact of home conditions on school success.

pedagogy The art and science of teaching; instruction in teaching methods.

peer assisted learning A form of tutoring whereby students help each other.

percentile rank (PR) score Indicates what percentage of people taking the test scored at or below a given score.

perceptual modality preferences Learner's tendency to prefer different sensory modes to understand experiences and to learn (visual, auditory, kinesthetic). (See **learning style**.)

performance differences The way students vary with regard to school performance. Some students do well at most things, others do poorly at most things, but most students demonstrate an unevenness within a range of school activity.

personality The totality of one's traits of character and behavior that make him unique.

physical environment Those aspects of the classroom that are concrete, easily identifiable, and exist independent of the people who inhabit the classroom.

physically challenged or impaired Having orthopedic handicaps, epilepsy, cerebral palsy, or other physical challenges.

portfolio Artifacts selected to represent a student's performance. See **artifacts**.

portfolio assessment Using a collection of student artifacts to make judgments about the quality of a student's performance or growth over time.

positive expectations Expecting all children to be successful.

positive reinforcement Giving students praise, rewards, or a positive reaction when they behave appropriately.

precision teaching Overlearning content through continued practice.

preoperational, prelogical stage Piaget's second stage of intellectual development, lasting from approximately 2 to 7 years of age. Young learners at this stage develop knowledge from personal experience, explore and manipulate concrete objects, and learn the three Rs and other basic knowledge and skills.

presentation Informative talk a more knowledgeable person makes to less knowledgeable persons.

proactive management Classroom management that focuses on preventing problems from arising in the classroom by eliciting student cooperation and involving students in educationally relevant activities.

probing Asking additional questions of a responding student to help expand or raise the level of the student's response.

problem Goal-response interference.

problem solving Requires learners to consider how they would attain a goal. Different types of problems include well-structured problems (subject matter–related) and ill-structured problems (life-related).

proficiency tests Usually refer to state tests that students must pass in order to gain promotion. A type of "high-stakes" test.

project method Allows learners to choose and work on projects and activities.

protocols Original records of some important event that learners study to try to understand the event or its consequences.

proximity Amount of space between teacher and students. Proximity can influence students' behavior and keep them alert.

psychological androgyny Having the best traits of both genders.

psychological environment The social and emotional climate of the classroom. How students feel about the teacher, learning tasks, and one another as a social group.

psychomotor domain The area of learning that deals with students' physical abilities and skills. It includes behaviors such as handwriting, typing or keyboarding, swimming, sculpting, and so forth. There are seven divisions of this domain: perception, set, guided response, mechanism, complex or overt response, adaptation, and origination.

psychosocial development Theory of development that describes the relationship between the individual's needs and the social environment. Suggests that adult personal and social characteristics are a result of the life stages in which individuals resolve various dichotomies (for example, trust vs. mistrust, autonomy vs. shame, industry vs. inferiority).

Public Law 93-247 A law defining abuse and neglect as "physical or mental injury, sexual abuse, negligent treatment, or maltreatment of a child under 18 by a person who is responsible for the child's welfare under circumstances which indicate that the child's health or welfare is harmed or threatened thereby."

Public Law 94-142 (Education of All Handicapped Children Act) Law requiring that students with handicaps be placed in the least restrictive (most normal) environment.

Public Law 95-561 (Gifted and Talented Act) Provides federal funding for gifted education.

punishment Something undesirable, painful, or discomforting that is applied to a student as a result of misbehavior.

raw score The number of test items or points that a learner obtains on a test. For example 8 of a possible 10.

reactive management Classroom management that focuses on reacting to students' misbehavior.

reception learning When teachers present students with carefully organized and structured new information.

reciprocal teaching When the teaching function is slowly and systematically given over to students.

recitation Students are given information to study independently and then recite what they have learned when the teacher questions them.

redirecting When teachers ask another student to answer the same question.

reflection Learning from experience through the process of critically examining and refining teaching practice and/or other aspects of education practice.

reflective learning style Cognitive style of responding slowly, carefully, and accurately. Contrasts with impulsive learning style.

reflective process Deep thinking about a situation or event that involves descriptive, comparative, and evaluative thought.

reflective teaching A laboratory teaching experience in a supportive environment that allows one to teach a lesson that serves as a basis for subsequent analysis and introspection. See Practice Teaching Manual, Unit 2.

reinforcement A principle of learning that recognizes that learners are more likely to do things when they feel good about doing them, usually by receiving some reward or recognition.

reinforcement menu A list of rewards that are effective with a particular student or group of students.

reinforcement theory The idea that a teacher can influence student behavior by rewarding desirable behaviors and ignoring or discouraging undesirable behaviors.

reliability The quality of providing consistent measurement results over time; a measure of how well a test evaluates what it is meant to evaluate from one situation to the next.

reliability coefficients Numeric indicators of test consistency ranging from 0.00 to 1.00.

remediation Help for students who did not master a learning task the first time.

rephrasing Restating the same question in different terms to help a student understand it.

research-based direct teaching or instruction The sequence of events followed by teachers more effective in bringing about student learning.

resilient children Children who are able to overcome negative life circumstances and achieve successes.

resource unit A plan for teaching something in the curriculum available from a source such as the state education department.

restricted response items Created response test questions that set explicit parameters within which students are to respond.

role confusion Having an inconsistent image of self with respect to one's drives, abilities, beliefs, and history.

role playing An activity in which learners take on the role of another person to see what it would be like to be that person.

routines Established procedures whose main function is to control and coordinate movement and events in the classroom.

rubric A matrix or list of indicators characteristic of particular levels of student performance; used to evaluate student work, usually projects or performances.

scaffolding Teachers providing extra support and help to make sure that students can complete a task successfully.

scheduling Changing the frequency of reinforcement based on students' behavior.

score band Range of scores that includes the student's actual score (usually at the middle of the band) and indicates how far above or below that score the student might have performed on a different day.

selected-response items Test questions that require students to select or choose a correct response from a list of possible answers.

self-directed learning When students are permitted to set their own learning goals and means of attaining them.

self-esteem Feelings of personal worth.

self-fulfilling prophecy When a person gets what he or she expects or achieves at the level he or she expects to reach.

self-referenced grading system When grades are determined by comparing a student's current performance with past performances. The grade is based upon improvement or growth.

sensorimotor stage The first of Piaget's four stages of intellectual development, lasting from approximately 0 to 2 years of age. During this stage, the intellect develops primarily through the use of senses and motor activity.

set induction An introductory activity that captures students' attention, helps them see the purpose and value of what is to be learned, and relates what they are to learn to that which they already know.

short-term memory Severely limited human storage system that holds only a small amount of information for merely seconds. Also referred to as working memory.

simulation games Competitive games that mirror some aspect of life, e.g., getting a job.

simulations Experiences intended to give the appearance or have the effect of some situation in order to provide "firsthand experience" with how that situation works, e.g., solving a classroom problem. See Practice Teaching Manual, Unit 3.

smoothness Moving students through a lesson with few interruptions.

social learning See **observational learning.**

social reinforcers Positive messages, either verbal or nonverbal, given to a student who behaves appropriately so as to increase the likelihood that the behavior will be repeated.

socioeconomic status (SES) A person or family's social and economic position, i.e., prestige and wealth.

sociogram Diagrammatic representation of the social relationships that exist within a group at a particular point in time.

sociometry Technique used to obtain information about the social acceptability of individuals within a group.

special needs children Those who require additional attention due to any disadvantage, gift, or talent.

speech impairment The inability to produce effective speech because of difficulties in articulation, stuttering, or voicing.

standard scores Norm-referenced scores that report a student's performance in relation to the mean and standard deviation of the norming group.

standardized test score Score that shows how one student's performance compares to others.

standardized tests Tests that have controlled, consistent administration, scoring, and interpretation procedures. These tests allow a given student's score on a specific test to be compared with scores made by a very large number of similar students who have taken the same test.

stanine scores A nine-value scale that reports standardized test results; 5 is the midpoint or mean and each standard deviation is 2. Stanine scores are more easily interpreted than z scores and T scores because stanine scores are less precise.

state standards Standards set at the state department of education level that indicate what students must know and be able to do.

stem The part of the multiple-choice question that presents a problem or asks a question.

student cooperation and accountability In direct instruction, holding students accountable for their academic work and for assisting each other and sharing materials.

student interview Procedure used to learn about students by informally talking with them or by way of a preplanned formal interview.

student observation Procedure used to learn about a student by formally or informally observing his behavior.

student questionnaires Carefully developed paper and pencil device used to obtain student information.

student stressors Factors and events considered worrisome by students, e.g., grades, peer relationships.

student success The need of teachers to help learners succeed both academically and socially.

subject matter knowledge How well teachers understand the academic subjects they teach.

summative assessment Assessment conducted after instruction is completed; used to make final judgments about a student's learning and to summarize a student's achievement or progress.

sustained expectations Teacher-held expectations that do not accurately reflect changes in the student's ability.

synthesis The ability to put component parts together in a new and different way.

tangible reinforcers Concrete objects (rewards) given to a student who behaves appropriately to increase the likelihood that the behavior will be repeated.

task orientation Characteristic of direct instruction that places the primary emphasis on academic learning.

taught curriculum What is actually taught by teachers. Includes the formal curriculum and whatever is done to supplement or complement it.

teachable moment Taking advantage of something that happens unexpectedly and learning about it: e.g., a thunderstorm.

teacher centrality Characteristic of direct instruction whereby teachers exert strong instructional direction and control.

teacher sense of efficacy The extent to which a teacher believes that he/she is competent and in control of the classroom.

team teaching Teachers collaborate to teach a group of students.

temperament The thinking, behaving, and reacting characteristics of a person. Often thought of on a continuum from good to ill-tempered.

test blueprint Matrix that depicts the relationship between instructional objectives or topics covered, cognitive levels, and items on an assessment; used as a guide to developing teacher-made tests.

test sophistication The degree to which a student is comfortable and knowledgeable about how to complete tests efficiently.

time need The need to have sufficient time to do what needs to be done.

time on task Time when students are actively engaged in academic tasks.

time-out Removing the student from a disruptive situation and from attention and rewards in order to reduce unwanted behavior.

transition set Information that helps students understand how new material relates to what they learned previously.

transitions Points in an instructional interaction when the context changes in some way, for example, when moving from one activity to another.

triangulation The use of two or more assessments or measures to obtain information on students' performance.

true-false items A type of selected response questions in which students indicate whether a statement is true or false.

unit plan A plan for learning a major section or topic within a course. Usually learned over a period of weeks and limited to one topical area.

valence and challenge arousal Ability to engender students with curiosity and enthusiasm and get them involved in independent work.

validity The degree to which an assessment and conclusions match what was intended.

values clarification Methods whereby learners (1) identify how they feel or

what they believe about something; (2) value that feeling or belief; and (3) if valued, act on it.

variety and challenge The ability to identify and assign independent study assignments that are different enough to be interesting and challenging enough to maintain attention.

virtual, online, or e-schools See **online schools.**

wait time The pause between a teacher question and student response and the pause between student response and teacher reaction.

Wheel of Instructional Choice Depiction of a number of ways to teach. See Chapter 7.

withitness The ability of a teacher to communicate to students that he or she is aware of student behavior throughout the classroom at all times, even when the teacher is not nearby or looking directly at the students.

Credits

VISUAL CREDITS

p. 6 Ford Button, *Recess Time: The Best Cartoons from the Kappan*, Kristin Herzog (ed.), Phi Delta Kappa, Bloomington, IN, 1983, p. 79.

p. 10 Martha Campbell (January 2001). Phi Delta Kappan, Vol. 82, No. 5, p. 383.

p. 25 Chuck Morman, *The Student Body: Great Cartoons from the Kappan*, Carol Bucheri, Terri Hampton, and Victoria Voelker (eds.), Phi Delta Kappa, Bloomington, IN, 1991, p. 81.

p. 44 James Estes (January 1999). Phi Delta Kappan, Vol. 80, No. 5, p. 363.

p. 76 Robert Hageman (March 1994). Phi Delta Kappan, Vol. 75, No. 7, p. 511.

p. 96 Martha Campbell, *Scholarship: More Great Cartoons from the Kappan*, Kristin Herzog and Mary Miller (eds.), Phi Delta Kappa, Bloomington, IN, 1985, p. 90.

p. 97 Martha Campbell, *Recess Time: The Best Cartoons from the Kappan*, Kristin Herzog (ed.), Phi Delta Kappa, Bloomington, IN, 1983, p. 29.

p. 98 Martha Campbell, *Recess Time: The Best Cartoons from the Kappan*, Kristin Herzog (ed.), Phi Delta Kappa, Bloomington, IN, 1983, p. 18.

p. 105 Ford Button, *Recess Time: The Best Cartoons from the Kappan*, Kristin Herzog (ed.), Phi Delta Kappa, Bloomington, IN, 1983, p. 74.

p. 118 Randy Glasbergen, *The Student Body: Great Cartoons from the Kappan*, Carol Bucheri, Terri Hampton, and Victoria Voelker (eds.), Phi Delta Kappa, Bloomington, IN, 1991, p. 57.

p. 126 Dave Carpenter, *The Student Body: Great Cartoons from the Kappan*, Carol Bucheri, Terri Hampton, and Victoria Voelker (eds.), Phi Delta Kappa, Bloomington, IN, 1991, p. 78.

p. 168 Frank Cotham, *Recess Time: The Best Cartoons from the Kappan*, Kristin Herzog (ed.), Phi Delta Kappa, Bloomington, IN, 1983, p. 68.

p. 169 Glen Dines, *Recess Time: The Best Cartoons from the Kappan*, Kristin Herzog (ed.), Phi Delta Kappa, Bloomington, IN, 1983, p. 69.

p. 205 Matthew Henry Hall.

p. 223 Glen Dines, *Recess Time: The Best Cartoons from the Kappan*, Kristin Herzog (ed.), Phi Delta Kappa, Bloomington, IN, 1983, p. 58.

p. 229 Martha Campbell (March 1989). Phi Delta Kappan, Vol. 70, No. 7, p. 511.

p. 244 Fred Thomas, *The Student Body: Great Cartoons from the Kappan*, Carol Bucheri, Terri Hampton, and Victoria Voelker (eds.), Phi Delta Kappa, Bloomington, IN, 1991, p. 105.

p. 244 Frank Cotham, *Recess Time: The Best Cartoons from the Kappan*, Kristin Herzog (ed.), Phi Delta Kappa, Bloomington, IN, 1983, p. 55.

p. 274 Fred Thomas (1995, December). Phi Delta Kappan, Vol. 4, No. 1, p. 315.

p. 284 Bo Brown, *The Student Body: Great Cartoons from the Kappan*, Carol Bucheri, Terri Hampton, and Victoria Voelker (eds.), Phi Delta Kappa, Bloomington, IN, 1991, p. 36.

p. 306 Fred Thomas, *The Student Body: Great Cartoons from the Kappan*, Carol Bucheri, Terri Hampton, and Victoria Voelker (eds.), Phi Delta Kappa, Bloomington, IN, 1991, p. 55.

p. 312 Dave Carpenter, *The Student Body: Great Cartoons from the Kappan*, Carol Bucheri, Terri Hampton, and Victoria Voelker (eds.), Phi Delta Kappa, Bloomington, IN, 1991, p. 64.

p. 318 Bo Brown, *The Student Body: Great Cartoons from the Kappan*, Carol Bucheri, Terri Hampton, and Victoria Voelker (eds.), Phi Delta Kappa, Bloomington, IN, 1991, p. 36.

p. 327 Randy Glasbergen, *The Student Body: Great Cartoons from the Kappan*, Carol Bucheri, Terri Hampton, and Victoria Voelker (eds.), Phi Delta Kappa, Bloomington, IN, 1991, p. 22.

p. 333 Art Bouthillier, *The Student Body: Great Cartoons from the Kappan*, Carol Bucheri, Terri Hampton, and Victoria Voelker (eds.), Phi Delta Kappa, Bloomington, IN, 1991, p. 53.

p. 352 Francis H. Brummer, *The Student Body: Great Cartoons from the Kappan*, Carol Bucheri, Terri Hampton, and Victoria Voelker (eds.), Phi Delta Kappa, Bloomington, IN, 1991, p. 104.

p. 356 Art Bouthillier, *The Student Body: Great Cartoons from the Kappan*, Carol Bucheri, Terri Hampton, and Victoria Voelker (eds.), Phi Delta Kappa, Bloomington, IN, 1991, p. 115.

p. 362 Art Bouthillier, *The Student Body: Great Cartoons from the Kappan*, Carol Bucheri, Terri Hampton, and Victoria Voelker (eds.), Phi Delta Kappa, Bloomington, IN, 1991, p. 85.

p. 372 James Estes, *The Student Body: Great Cartoons from the Kappan*, Carol Bucheri, Terri Hampton, and Victoria Voelker (eds.), Phi Delta Kappa, Bloomington, IN, 1991, p. 12.

p. 374 Martha Campbell, *The Student Body: Great Cartoons from the Kappan*, Carol Bucheri, Terri Hampton, and Victoria Voelker (eds.), Phi Delta Kappa, Bloomington, IN, 1991, p. 9.

p. 382 Frank Cotham, *The Student Body: Great Cartoons from the Kappan*, Carol Bucheri, Terri Hampton, and Victoria Voelker (eds.), Phi Delta Kappa, Bloomington, IN, 1991, p. 68.

p. 423 George Abbot, *The Kappan*, Vol. 74, No. 2, October 1992, p. 171.

All other illustrations by Kathy Grossert.

PHOTO CREDITS

Part Opener 1, Purestock/Getty Images; **CO-1,** Ariel Skelley/Blend Images/Corbis; **CO-2,** © Creatas/PunchStock; **CO-3,** Blend Images/Alamy; **CO-4,** © Creatas; **CO-5,** BananaStock/PictureQuest;

Part Opener 2, Photodisc/Getty Images; **CO-6,** © Mary Kate Denny/PhotoEdit; **CO-7,** BananaStock/PictureQuest; **CO-8,** Purestock/Getty Images; **CO-9,** Photodisc/Getty Images;

Part Opener 3, © Punchstock; **CO-10,** Image Source/Getty Images; **CO-11,** © Thinkstock/PunchStock; **CO-12,** BananaStock/AGE Fotostock; **CO-13,** © Skjold Photographs/PhotoEdit; **CO-14,** © Spencer Grant/PhotoEdit

Name Index

Subject Index

teacher attitude toward parent involvement, 29
teacher behaviors
    affecting classroom misbehavior, 423
    affecting student success, 451
    related to student development, 495
teacher centrality, 282
teacher education, influence of, 17
teacher experience and preparation in education, 3
teacher knowledge and student learning, 362
teacher personality, 6, 7
teacher planning, Chinese, 197
teacher presentations, 211–212
Teacher Problems Checklist (Cruickshank & Associates), 453
teacher-centered strategy, 204
teacher-made assessments, 316–326
teacher-pupil planning, 195
teachers
    beliefs of, 6–8
    factors affecting specific, 16
    perception and expectations of students, 131
    personal attributes of, 350
    planning instructions for new, 167–169
    relationship with students, 445
    role in purpose and characteristics of discussion, 216
    role in purpose and characteristics of independent study, 224
    and supervisors, other, 14
teacher-team planning, 195
teaching
    as giving and guiding homework assignments, 222–230

high quality, 379
in most efficient way, 282–293
to multiple intelligences, 76
received by teacher, 8–9
simple best approach, 108–110
as telling and showing, 204–213
teaching experience, 5
teaching learners to like and care for one another, 260–296
teaching methods, 294
teaching preparation, 10–11
teaching skills, practicing, 474–480
teaching units, 186
team planning, 195–196
team teaching, 205
team-assisted individual and team-accelerated instruction (TAI), 262
teams, games, tournaments (TGT), 261–262
technological know how, influence of, 5
technology
    on assessment and grading, 338
    use of, 50
technology in teaching
    digital age preparation, 248–249
    digital content use, 247–248
    software and website selection, 247
television, 44
temperament, 70
temperamental differences, 70–71
tests. *see also* pencil-and-paper tests; standardized tests/testing
    achievement tests, 119
    administration of, 325–326
    aptitude tests, 118–119
    blueprint for, 324
    construction of, 326
    guidelines for administering, 326
    as measurement instrument, 338
    or projects, 305–306
    packaging, 324–325

proficiency tests, 172
sophistication of, 312
textbook influence on planning and curriculum, 168
time, 232–233, 456
    academic instruction time, 374
    academic learning time, 374
    allocated time, 374
    available time, 15
    class time, 453
    classroom-related problems, 451–453
    instruction time available vs. curriculum content, 173
    instructional time efficiency, 373–377
    mandated time, 373
Time (magazine), 64
time on task, 373
time optimization, 373–377
    maximizing momentum, 376
    smooth transitions, 376–377
timeline, 185
time-out, 427–428
Tobacco Task lesson, 507–511
tone, 405–408
topical outline, 186
transformation, personal and professional, 464
transition set, 369
triangulation, 305
true-false items, 322
tutoring, 235–236, 245

understanding, 280–281
unexpected underachievement, 82
unfair response, 423
unit plan preparation, 185–187
unit planning, 183
unit plans, 189
unstructured problems, 101
U.S. Department of Education, 241, 346, 349, 400, 444
Using Questions lesson, 477–478

valence and challenge arousal,
validity, 307, 339
values clarification, 103, 454–455
variety, use of, 370, 372–373
    instructional activities and materials, 370, 372
    interaction with students, 372–373
variety and challenge, 225
verbal abuse, 423
verbal information, 179
virtual schools, 236
visual aids, 207
visual learners, 76

warmth and humor, 352–354
Web tools, 247
weighted number of performances, 337
well-structured problems, 101
whole child approach to learning, 48–49
withitness, 225, 416
working poor, 34
workplace, context of
    available time, 15
    class and classroom size, 12–14
    influence factors on teaching, 11–15
    lesson objectives, nature of, 15
    material and equipment availability, 14–15
    national imperatives, 15
    other teachers and supervisors, 14
    student differences, 11–12
world-class academic standards, 50
writing
    rubrics for evaluating, 330
    state standards, types of, 172

The Yearling (Rawlings), 177
yearly and semester planning, 183–185
youth employment, 30